MILLENNIUM

Also by Tom Holland

Rubicon:
The Triumph and Tragedy of the Roman Republic

Persian Fire:
The First World Empire and the Battle for the West

MILLENNIUM

*The End of the World and the
Forging of Christendom*

Tom Holland

Little, Brown

LITTLE, BROWN

First published in Great Britain in 2008 by Little, Brown

A CIP catalogue record for this book
is available from the British Library.

ISBN HB 978-0-316-73245-1
ISBN CF 978-1-4087-0086-0

Typeset in Spectrum by M Rules
Printed and bound in Great Britain by
Clays Ltd, St Ives plc

Papers used by Little, Brown are natural, renewable and recyclable
products made from wood grown in sustainable forests and certified
in accordance with the rules of the Forest Stewardship Council.

Mixed Sources
Product group from well-managed
forests and other controlled sources
www.fsc.org Cert no. SGS-COC-004081
© 1996 Forest Stewardship Council

FSC

Little, Brown
An imprint of
Little, Brown Book Group
100 Victoria Embankment
London EC4Y 0DY

An Hachette Livre UK Company
www.hachettelivre.co.uk

www.littlebrown.co.uk

For Patrick.
Wine!

Contents

Acknowledgements

Since pilgrimage is one of the major themes of this book, perhaps it is only fitting that the writing of it should often have seemed a long and winding road. I owe an immense debt of gratitude to everyone who helped me finally to arrive at my journey's end. To Richard Beswick and Iain Hunt, my editors, and miracle-workers both. To Susan de Soissons, Roger Cazalet, and everyone else at Little, Brown, for all their unswerving support. To Jake Smith-Bosanquet, for his doughty batting as well as for his suave negotiating technique, and to Patrick Walsh, the best of agents, and the dedicatee of this book. To Gerry Howard, for his encouragement at a key moment of despondency, and to Frits van der Meij, for all his trained medievalist's guidance. To James Palmer and Magnus Ryan, for giving the manuscript an exactingly – indeed, intimidatingly – close reading, and for being so incredibly generous with their time, scholarship and advice. To Robert Irwin, the *non-pareil* of contemporary orientalists, for reading the chapters on Christendom's engagement with Islam. To Ben Yates, who bodes well to be the future of Norse studies in this country, for reading the final draft through despite all the other demands on his time – and to invaluable effect. To David Crouch, for opening my eyes fully to the challenges that lay ahead. To Michael Wood, for confirming me in my opinion that there is no period more fascinating and under-studied than the tenth century. To Andrea Wulf and Maike Bohn, who more than made up for my deplorable lack of German – and yes, Andrea, Holy Lances *are* more interesting than plants. To Jamie Muir, for reading the chapters through as they were written with all his customary acuity and good humour, and for accompanying me around the housing estate that now occupies the site where Harald Hardrada fell. To Caroline Muir, for running round and round the local park with me whenever I felt the need to escape the first Millennium – or, indeed, to reflect upon it away from my desk. To Father Dunstan Adams OSB, for enabling me to share, if only briefly, in the daily rhythms that once animated Cluny. To Marianna Albini, for accompanying me to Canossa. To my brother, James Holland, for buying me a Norman helmet. To my parents, Jans and Martin Holland, for bringing me up in the very heartlands of Wessex. Above all, to my beloved family, Sadie, Katy and Eliza, for putting up with my lengthy bouts of hermit-like seclusion, for accompanying me uncomplainingly around Danish tumuli and Auvergnat churches alike, and for allowing me to name our cats Harold and Edith. *Beatus vir qui implevit faretram suam.*

List of Maps

Preface

Just the worst time of the year for a journey – and the worst of years as well. Everyone was talking, that late December, about how there had never been a winter like it. Snow had been falling for weeks, and in the mountains, across the Alps, the drifts lay especially thick. No surprise, then, that as a small party of some fifty travellers toiled and switchbacked their way up the steep slopes of Mount Cenis, they should have been urged by locals to turn round, to delay their mission, to await the coming of spring. 'For so covered with snow and ice were the gradients ahead,' they were warned, 'that neither hoof nor foot could safely take step on them.'[1]

Even the guides, men seasoned by years of Alpine storms, confessed themselves alarmed by the savage conditions. Dangerous though the ascent was, they muttered, yet the descent would prove even worse. And sure enough, so it did. Blizzards and freezing temperatures had transformed the road that led down towards Italy into one lethal flume of tightly packed ice. As the women of the party gingerly took their places on sledges fashioned out of ox hides, so the men were left to slip and slither onwards on foot, sometimes clutching the shoulders of their guides, sometimes scrabbling about on all fours. An undignified way for anyone to travel – but especially so for a Caesar and his entourage.

One thousand and seventy-six years had passed since the birth of Christ. Much had changed over the course of that time: strange peoples had risen to greatness, famous kingdoms had crumbled away, and even Rome herself, that most celebrated of cities, the one-time mistress of the world, had been left a wilderness of toppled monuments and weeds. Yet she had never been forgotten. Although the dominion of the ancient Caesars might be long vanished, the lustre of its fame still illumined the imaginings of its inheritors. Even to peoples who had never submitted to its rule, and in realms that had lain far beyond the reach of its legions, the person of an emperor, his cloak adorned with suns and stars, appeared an awesome but natural complement to the one celestial emperor who ruled in heaven. This was why, unlike his pagan forebears, a Christian Caesar did not require taxes and bureaucrats and standing armies to uphold the mystique of his power. Nor did he need a capital – nor even to be a Roman. His true authority derived from a higher source. 'Next after Christ he rules across the earth.'[2]

What, then, and in the very dead of winter too, was God's deputy up to, collecting bruises on a mountainside? Such a prince, at Christmas time, should properly have been seated upon his throne within a fire-lit hall, presiding over a laden table, entertaining dukes and bishops. Henry, the fourth king of that name to have ascended to the rule of the German people, was lord of the greatest of all the realms of Christendom. Both his father and his grandfather before him had been crowned emperor. Henry himself, though he was yet to be graced formally with the imperial title, had always taken for granted that it was his by right.

Recently, however, this presumption had been dealt a series of crushing blows. For years, Henry's enemies among the German princes had been manoeuvring to bring him down. Nothing particularly exceptional there: for it was the nature of German princes, by and large, to manoeuvre against their king. Utterly exceptional, however, was the sudden emergence of an adversary who held no great network of castles, commanded no great train of warriors, nor even wore a sword. An adversary who nevertheless, in the course of only a few months, and in alliance with the German princes, had succeeded in bringing Christendom's mightiest king to his knees.

Gregory, this formidable opponent called himself: a name suited not to a warlord but to the guardian of a '*grex*', a flock of sheep. Bishops, following the example of their Saviour, were much given to casting themselves as shepherds – and Gregory, by virtue of his office, was owner of the most imposing crook of all. Bishop of Rome, he was also very much more than that: for just as Henry liked to pose as the heir of the Caesars, so did Gregory, from his throne in Christendom's capital, lay claim to being the 'Father', the 'Pope', of the universal Church. A sure-fire recipe for conflict? Not necessarily. For centuries now, a long succession of emperors and popes had been rubbing along together well enough, not in competition, but in partnership. 'There are two principles which chiefly serve to order this world: the hallowed authority of pontiffs and the power of kings.' So it had been put by one pope, Gelasius, way back in AD 494.

Admittedly, the temptation to blow his own trumpet had then led Gelasius to the grand assertion that it was he, and not the emperor, who bore the graver responsibility: 'for it is priests, at the hour of judgement, who have to render an account for the souls of kings'.[3] But that had been just so much theory. The reality had been very different. The world was a cruel and violent place, after all, and a pope might easily find himself hemmed in around by any number of menacing neighbours. A shepherd's crook, no matter how serviceable, was hardly proof against a mail-clad predator. As a result, over the centuries, while no emperor had ever clung for protection to a pope, many a pope had clung to an emperor. Partners they might have been – but there had never been any question, in brute practice, of who was the junior.

And everyone knew it. No matter the fine arguments of a Gelasius, it had long been taken for granted by the Christian people that kings – and emperors especially – were men quite as implicated in the mysterious dimensions of the heavenly as any priest. They were regarded as having not merely a right to intrude upon the business of the Church, but a positive duty. On occasion, indeed, at a moment of particular crisis, an emperor might go so far as to take the ultimate sanction, and force the abdication of an unworthy pope. This was precisely what

Henry IV, convinced that Gregory was a standing menace to Christendom, had sought to bring about in the early weeks of 1076: a regrettable necessity, to be sure, but nothing that his own father had not successfully done before him.

Gregory, however, far from submitting to the imperial displeasure, and tamely stepping down, had taken an utterly unprecedented step: he had responded in ferocious kind. Henry's subjects, the Pope had pronounced, were absolved from all their loyalty and obedience to their earthly lord – even as Henry himself, that very image of God on earth, was 'bound with the chain of anathema',[4] and excommunicated from the Church. A gambit that had revealed itself, after only a few months, to be an utterly devastating one. Henry's enemies had been lethally emboldened. His friends had all melted away. By the end of the year, his entire realm had been rendered, quite simply, ungovernable. And so it was that, braving the winter gales, the by now desperate king had set himself to cross the Alps. He was resolved to meet with the Pope, to show due penitence, to beg forgiveness. Caesar though he might be, he had been left with no alternative.

A race against time, then – and one made all the more pressing by Henry's awareness of an uncomfortable detail. Reports had it that Gregory, despite his venerable age of fifty-five, was out and about on the roads that winter as well. Indeed, that he was planning to make his own journey across the snow-bound Alps, and hold Henry to account that very February within the borders of the German kingdom itself. Naturally, as the weary royal party debouched into Lombardy, and 1076 turned to 1077, there was a frantic effort to pinpoint the papal whereabouts. Fortunately for Henry, fine though he had cut it, so too, it turned out, had his quarry. Gregory, despite having made it so far north that he could see the foothills of the Alps ahead of him, had no sooner been brought the news of the king's approach than he was turning tail in high alarm, and beating a retreat to the stronghold of a local supporter.

Henry, dispatching a blizzard of letters ahead of him to assure the Pope of his peaceable intentions, duly set off in pursuit. Late that

January, and accompanied by only a few companions, he began the ascent of yet another upland road. Ahead of him, jagged like the spume of great waves frozen to ice by the cold of that terrible winter, there stretched the frontier of the Apennines. A bare six miles from the plain he had left behind him, but many hours' twisting and turning, Henry arrived at last before a valley, gouged out, it seemed, from the wild mountainscape, and spanned by a single ridge. Beyond it, surmounting a crag so sheer and desolate that it appeared utterly impregnable, the king could see the ramparts of the bolt hole where the Pope had taken refuge. The name of the fortress: Canossa.

On Henry pressed, into the castle's shadow. As he did so, the outer gates swung open to admit him, and then, halfway up the rock, the gates of a second wall. It would have been evident enough, even to the suspicious sentries, that their visitor intended no harm, nor presented any conceivable threat. 'Barefoot, and clad in wool, he had cast aside all the splendour proper to a king.' Although Henry was proud and combustible by nature, his head on this occasion was bowed. Tears streamed down his face. Humbly, joining a crowd of other penitents, he took up position before the gates of the castle's innermost wall. There the Caesar waited, the deputy of Christ, shivering in the snow. Nor, in all that time, did he neglect to continue with his lamentations – 'until', as the watching Gregory put it, 'he had provoked all who were there or who had been brought news of what was happening to such great mercy, and such pitying compassion, that they began to intercede for him with prayers and tears of their own'.[5] A truly awesome show. Ultimately, not even the stern and indomitable Pope himself was proof against it.

By the morning of Saturday 28 January, the third day of the royal penance, Gregory had seen enough. He ordered the inner set of gates unbarred at last. Negotiations were opened and soon concluded. Pope and king, for the first time, perhaps, since Henry had been a small child, met each other face to face.[6] The pinch-faced penitent was absolved with a papal kiss. And so was set the seal on an episode as fateful as any in Europe's history.

Like the crossing of the Rubicon, like the storming of the Bastille, the events at Canossa had served to crystallise a truly epochal crisis. Far more had been at stake than merely the egos of two domineering men. The Pope, locked into a desperate power struggle though he certainly was, had ambitions as well that were breathtakingly global in their scope. His goal? Nothing less than to establish the 'right order in the world'.[7] What had once, back in the time of Gelasius, appeared merely a pipedream was now, during Gregory's papacy, transformed into a manifesto. By its terms, the whole of Christendom, from its summit to its meanest village, was to be divided into two. One realm for the spiritual, one for the secular. No longer were kings to be permitted to poke their noses into the business of the Church. It was a plan of action as incendiary as it was sweeping: for it required a full-out assault upon presumptions that were ultimately millennia old.

However, even had Gregory appreciated the full scale of his task, he would surely not have shrunk from it. What lay at stake, so he believed, was the very future of mankind: for unless the Church were kept sacrosanct, what hope for a sinful world? No wonder, then, presented with the opportunity, that the Pope had dared to make an example of his most formidable opponent. 'The King of Rome, rather than being honoured as a universal monarch, had been treated instead as merely a human being – a creature moulded out of clay.'[8]

Contemporaries, struggling to make sense of the whole extraordinary business, perfectly appreciated that they were living through a convulsion in the affairs of the Christian people that had no precedent, nor even any parallel. 'Our whole Roman world was shaken.'[9] What, then, could this earthquake betoken, many wondered, if not the end of days? That the affairs of men were drawing to a close, and the earth itself growing decrepit, had long been a widespread presumption. As the years slipped by, however, and the world did not end, so people found themselves obliged to grope about for different explanations. A formidable task indeed. The three decades that preceded the showdown at Canossa, and the four that followed it, were, in the judgement of one celebrated medievalist, a period when the ideals of Christendom, its forms of government and even its very social and economic fabric 'changed in almost every respect'. Here, argued Sir Richard Southern, was the true making of the West. 'The expansion of Europe had begun in earnest. That all this should have happened in so short a time is the most remarkable fact in medieval history.'[10]

And, if remarkable to us, then how much more so to those who actually lived through it. We in the twenty-first century are habituated to the notion of progress: the faith that human society, rather than inevitably decaying, can be improved. The men and women of the eleventh century were not. Gregory, by presuming to challenge Henry IV, and the fabulously ancient nimbus of tradition that hedged emperors and empires about, was the harbinger of something awesome. He and his supporters might not have realised it – but they were introducing to the modern West its first experience of revolution.

It was a claim that many of those who subsequently set Europe to shake would no doubt have viewed as preposterous. To Martin Luther, the one-time monk who saw it as his lifetime's mission to reverse everything that Gregory had stood for, the great Pope appeared a literally infernal figure: '*Höllenbrand*', or 'Hellfire'. In the wake of the Enlightenment too, as dreams of building a new Jerusalem took on an ever more secular hue, and world revolution was consciously enshrined as an ideal, so it appeared to many enthusiasts for change that there existed no greater roadblock to their progress than the Roman Catholic Church.

Not that one necessarily had to be a radical, or even a liberal, to believe the same. 'We shall not go to Canossa!'[11] So fulminated that iron chancellor of a reborn German Empire, Prince Bismarck, in 1872, as he gave a pledge to the Reichstag that he would never permit the papacy to stand in the way of Germany's forward march to modernity. This was to cast Gregory as the very archetype of reaction: a characterisation that many Catholic scholars, albeit from a diametrically opposed perspective, would not have disputed. They too, like the Church's enemies, had a stake in downplaying the magnitude of what Canossa had represented. After all, if the papacy were to be regarded as the guardian of unchanging verities and traditions, then how could it possibly have presided over a rupture in the affairs of Europe no less momentous than the Reformation or the French Revolution?

Gregory, according to the conventional Catholic perspective, was a man who had brought nothing new into the world, but rather had laboured to restore the Church to its primal and pristine state. Since this was precisely what Gregory himself had always claimed to be doing, evidence for this thesis was not hard to find. But it was misleading, even so. In truth, there existed no precedent for the upheaval exemplified by Canossa – neither in the history of the Roman Church, nor in that of any other culture. The consequences could hardly have been more fateful. Western Europe, which for so long had languished in the shadow of vastly more sophisticated civilisations, and of its own ancient and vanished past, was set at last upon a course that was to prove irrevocably its own.

It was Gregory, at Canossa, who stood as godfather to the future.

Ever since the West first rose to a position of global dominance, the origins of its exceptionalism have been fiercely debated. Conventionally, they have been located in the Renaissance, or the Reformation, or the Enlightenment: moments in history that all consciously defined themselves in opposition to the backwardness and barbarism of the so-called 'Middle Age'. The phrase, however, can be a treacherous one. Use it too instinctively, and something fundamental – and distinctive – about the arc of European history risks being obscured. Far from there having been two decisive breaks in the evolution of the West, as talk of 'the Middle Ages' implies, there was in reality only one – and that a cataclysm without parallel in the annals of Eurasia's other major cultures. Over the course of a millennium, the civilisation of classical antiquity had succeeded in evolving to a pinnacle of extraordinary sophistication; and yet its collapse in western Europe, when it came, was almost total. The social and economic fabric of the Roman Empire unravelled so completely that its harbours were stilled, its foundries silenced, its great cities emptied, and a thousand years of history revealed to have led only to a dead end. Not all the pretensions of a Henry IV could truly serve to alter that. Time could not be set in reverse. There had never been any real prospect of reconstituting what had imploded – of restoring what had been lost.

Yet still, long after the fall of Rome, a conviction that the only alternative to barbarism was the rule of a global emperor kept a tenacious hold on the imaginings of the Christian people. And not on those of the Christian people alone. From China to the Mediterranean, the citizens of great empires continued to do precisely as the ancient Romans had done, and see in the rule of an emperor the only conceivable image of the perfection of heaven. What other order, after all, could there possibly be? Only in the far western promontory of Eurasia, where there was nothing of an empire left but ghosts and spatchcocked imitations, was this question asked with any seriousness – and even then only after the passage of many centuries. Hence the full world-shaking impact of the events associated with Canossa. Changes had been set in train that would ultimately reach far beyond the bounds of western Europe: changes that are with us still.

To be sure, Gregory today may not enjoy the fame of a Luther, a Lenin, a Mao – but that reflects not his failure but rather the sheer scale of his achievement. It is the incomplete revolutions which are remembered; the fate of those that succeed is to end up being taken for granted. Gregory himself did not live to witness his ultimate victory – but the cause for which he fought was destined to establish itself as perhaps the defining characteristic of Western civilisation. That the world can divided into church and state, and that these twin realms should exist distinct from each other: here are presumptions that the eleventh century made 'fundamental to European society and culture, for the first time and permanently'. What had previously been merely an ideal would end up a given.

No wonder, then, as an eminent historian of this 'first European revolution' has pointed out, that 'it is not easy for Europe's children to remember that it might have been otherwise'.[12] Even the recent influx into Western countries of sizeable populations from non-Christian cultures has barely served to jog the memory. Of Islam, for instance, it is often said that it has never had a Reformation – but more to the point might be to say that it has never had a Canossa. Certainly, to a pious Muslim, the notion that the political and religious spheres can be separated is a shocking one – as it was to many of Gregory's opponents.

Not that it had ever remotely been Gregory's own intention to banish God from an entire dimension of human affairs; but revolutions will invariably have unintended consequences. Even as the Church, from the second half of the eleventh century onwards, set about asserting its independence from outside interference by establishing its own laws, bureaucracy and income, so kings, in response, were prompted to do the same. 'The heavens are the Lord's heavens – but the earth He has given to the sons of men.'[13] So Henry IV's son pronounced, answering a priest who had urged him not to hang a count under the walls of his own castle, for fear of provoking God's wrath. It was in a similar spirit that the foundations of the modern Western state were laid, foundations largely bled of any religious dimension. A piquant irony: that the very concept of a secular society should ultimately have been due to the papacy. Voltaire and the First Amendment, multiculturalism and gay weddings: all have served as waymarks on the road from Canossa.

Yet to look forward from what has aptly been dubbed 'the Papal Revolution', and to insist upon its far-reaching consequences, is to beg an obvious question: whatever could have prompted so convulsive and fateful a transformation? Its origins, as specialists candidly acknowledge, 'are still hotly debated'.[14] When Gregory met with Henry at Canossa, the papacy had already been serving as a vehicle for radical change for almost three decades – and pressure to reform it had been building for a decade or so before that. What could possibly have been astir, then, during the early 1030s, capable of inspiring such a movement? The question is rendered all the more intriguing by a most suggestive coincidence: that the very years which witnessed the first stirrings of what would go on to become the Papal

Revolution have been identified by many medievalists as the end-point of an earlier, and no less fateful, period of crisis. A crisis that was centred, however, not in the courts and basilicas of the mighty, but out in the interminable expanses of the countryside – and not in Germany or Italy, but in France. Here, from around 980 onwards, it has been argued, a violent 'mutation' took place, one that served to give birth, over the span of only a few decades, to almost everything that is today most popularly associated with the Middle Ages: castles, knights and all.

Admittedly, the precise scope and character of this upheaval is intensely controversial, with some scholars disputing that it even so much as happened, and others claiming that it was a decisive turning point for Western Europe as a whole.[15] Indeed, in a period of history that hardly lacks for treacherous bogs, the question of what precisely happened in France during the final decades of the tenth century and the opening decades of the eleventh has ended up as perhaps the most treacherous of all. French historians, for whom the entire debate has become a somewhat wearisome fixture, tend to sum it up with a single phrase: '*L'an mil*', they call it – 'the year 1000'.

A most arresting title. Scholarly shorthand it may be – and yet the date sounds no less hauntingly for that. Or does it only seem so to us – we who have passed from the second Christian millennium into the third? Historians, ever concerned not to foist contemporary presumptions on to the past, have conventionally argued as much. Indeed, until a couple of decades ago, even those who made the case most exuberantly for a wholesale transformation of western Europe around the time of the Millennium were content to regard the year 1000 itself as having been one with no more inherent significance than, say, 1789 or 1914. That it lay slap bang in the middle of a period identified by many historians as the birth-pangs of a radically new order – this, sober scholars insisted, was a mere coincidence, and nothing more. Certainly, any notion that the date might have generated the kind of apocalyptic anxieties that we, in the approach to the year 2000, projected on to the prophecies of Nostradamus and the Millennium

Bug was regarded as utterly ludicrous: a fantasy to be slapped down quite as mercilessly as *outré* theories about the pyramids or the Templars. 'For the moment that one stops combating an entrenched historical error,' as one eminent medievalist sighed with weary hauteur, 'back it immediately springs to life.'[16]

No doubt – and yet lay into a hydra too indiscriminately and there is always the risk that truths as well as errors may end up being put to the sword. A neck may twist, and coil and snake – and yet, for all that, not merit being severed. 'The false terrors of the year one thousand',[17] as one recent book termed them, have tended to be dismissed as a febrile and flamboyant concoction of the nineteenth-century Romantics – and yet that was not wholly fair. Often – surprisingly often, indeed – the myths about the first Millennium that twentieth-century historians set themselves to combat were of their own devising. A universal conviction that the world would end upon the very striking of the millennial hour; princes and peasants alike flocking to churches in panic as the fearful moment approached; an entire Christendom 'frozen in utter paralysis'[18] – here were 'false terrors' indeed, grotesque and implausible straw men set up largely by the sceptics themselves. Not only were they distortions, in many cases, of what nineteenth-century historians had actually claimed; they were also, and infinitely more damagingly, distortions of the evidence that survived from the time of the Millennium itself.[19]

To talk of 'terrors' alone, for instance, is to ignore the profound degree to which, for the wretched, for the poor, for the oppressed, the expectation of the world's imminent end was bred not of fear but rather of hope. 'It comes, it comes, the Day of the Lord, like a thief in the night!'[20] A warning, certainly, but also a message of joy – and significant not only for its tone but for its timing. The man who delivered it, a monk from the Low Countries who in 1012 had been granted a spectacular vision of the world's end by an archangel, no less, had not the slightest doubt that the Second Coming was at hand. That more than a decade had passed since the Millennium itself bothered him not a jot: for just as the 'terrors of the year 1000' were not simply terrors, so also were they far from being confined to the year 1000 itself.

To be sure, the millennial anniversary of Christ's birth was an obvious focus for apocalyptic expectations – but it was not the only, nor even the principal, one. Far from abating in the wake of its passing, anticipation of the Day of Judgement seems, if anything, only to have grown over the course of the succeeding thirty-three years – as why, indeed, should it not have done? For to the Christian people of that fateful era had been granted a privilege that appeared to them as awesome as it was terrible: 'to pass the span of their earthly lives in the very decades marking the thousand-year anniversary of their divine Lord's intervention into human history'.[21] No wonder, then, 'at the approach of the millennium of the Passion',[22] that anticipation of the Second Coming seems to have reached a fever pitch: for what was there, after all, in the entire span of human history, that could possibly compare for cosmic significance with Christ's death, resurrection and ascension into heaven? Nothing – not even His birth. The true Millennium, then, was not the year 1000. Rather, it was the anniversary of Christ's departure from the earth He had so fleetingly trodden. An anniversary that fell in or around the year 1033.

Such arguments – that people were indeed gripped by an anticipation of the end days in the build-up to the Millennium, that it inspired in them a convulsive mixture of dread and hope, and that it reached a climax in the one-thousandth anniversary of the Resurrection – have ceased, over the past couple of decades, to rank as quite the heresies they previously were. Medievalists, like everyone else, have their fashions – and debate on the apocalyptic character of the year 1000 has recently been all the rage. No doubt, as critics have pointed out, the controversy owes much to timing: it can hardly be coincidence that it should have picked up such sudden pace over the years that immediately preceded and followed the year 2000. Yet this does not serve to debunk it. Historians will inevitably garner insights from the times in which they work. To live through the turning of a millennium is a chance that does not come along every day. What, then, could be more self-defeating than to close one's eyes to the perspectives that such a once-in-a-thousand-years experience might provide?

Certainly, it would be vain of me to deny that this study of the first Christian Millennium has not been inspired, to a certain degree, by reflections upon the second. In particular, it has been informed by a dawning realisation that the move into a self-consciously new era is not at all how I had imagined it would be. Nervous as I was, in my more superstitious or dystopian moments, as to what the passage from 1999 to 2000 might bring, I had vaguely assumed that the world of the third millennium would feel brighter, more optimistic – younger even. But it does not.

I can remember, back when I was in my teens, and living in the shadow of the Cold War, praying that I would live to see the twenty-first century, and all of the world with me; but now, having crossed that particular threshold, and looking ahead to the future, I find that I am far more conscious than I ever was before of how infinitely and terrifyingly time stretches, and of how small, by comparison, the span of humanity's existence is likely to prove. 'Earth itself may endure, but it will not be humans who cope with the scorching of our planet by the dying sun; nor even, perhaps, with the exhaustion of Earth's resources.'[23] So wrote Martin Rees, Britain's Astronomer Royal, in a jeremiad cheerily titled *Our Final Century: Will Civilisation Survive the Twenty-First Century?*

Far from having been inspired by any mood of *fin de siècle* angst, that book was in fact written in the immediate wake of the new millennium; nor, since its publication in 2003, does the mood of pessimism among leading scientists appear to have grown any lighter. When James Lovelock, the celebrated environmentalist, first read Rees's book, he took it 'as no more than a speculation among friends and nothing to lose sleep over'; a bare three years on, and he was gloomily confessing in his own book, *The Revenge of Gaia*, 'I was so wrong.'[24] The current state of alarm about global warming being what it is, even people unfamiliar with Lovelock's blood-curdling thesis that the world is on the verge of becoming effectively uninhabitable should be able to guess readily enough what prompted his volte-face. 'Our future', he has written memorably, if chillingly, 'is like that of the passengers on a small pleasure boat sailing quietly above the Niagara Falls, not knowing that the engines are about to fail.'[25] And Lovelock's best estimate as to precisely when climate change will send us all over the edge? Within twenty to thirty years: some time around, say, 2033.

More than a thousand years ago, a saintly abbot drew upon a very similar metaphor. The vessel that bore sinful humanity, he warned, was beset all around by a gathering storm surge: 'perilous times are menacing us, and the world is threatened with its end'.[26] That the abbot proved to be wrong does not offer us any reassurance that James Lovelock and his fellow prophets of calamitous climate change are necessarily wrong as well: for science, no doubt, can offer a more reliable guide to the future than the Bible has tended to do over the years. Though the fretful Christians of the tenth and eleventh centuries may appear remote to us, and remote all their presumptions and expectations, we in the West are never more recognisably their descendants than when we ponder whether our sins will end up the ruin of us. The sheer range of opinions on global warming, from those, like Lovelock, who fear the worst to those who dismiss it altogether; the spectacle of anxious and responsible people, perfectly convinced that the planet is indeed warming, nevertheless filling up their cars, heating their houses and taking cheap flights; the widespread popular presumption, often inchoate but no less genuine for that, that something, somehow, *ought to be done*: here are reflections, perhaps, that do indeed flicker and twist in a distant mirror. Certainly, the sensation of standing on the threshold of a new epoch (though the reader may laugh) has not been useless to the historian of the first Millennium.

The feeling that a new age has dawned will always serve to concentrate the mind. To leave a momentous anniversary behind is invariably to be made more sensitive to the very process of change. So it was, it seems to me, that concerns about global warming, despite the evidence for it having been in place for years, only really picked up pace with the new millennium. The same could be said of anxieties about other deep-rooted trends: the growth in tensions between Islam and the West, for instance, or the rise of China. So too, back in the 1030s, this book argues, men and women who felt themselves to have emerged from one order of time into another could not help but suddenly be aware of how strangely and disconcertingly the future now seemed to stretch ahead of them. For a long while, the notion that the world would be brought to an end, that Christ would come again, that a new Jerusalem would descend from the heavens, had been a kind of answer. With the disappointment of that expectation, the Christian people of western Europe found themselves with no choice but to arrive at solutions bred of their own restlessness and ingenuity: to set to the heroic task of building a heavenly Jerusalem on earth themselves.

The story of how they set about this, and of how a new society, and a new Christendom, came to be raised amid all the turmoil of the age is as remarkable and momentous as any in history – and one that must inevitably possess a certain epic sweep. A revolution such as the eleventh century witnessed, after all, can only truly be understood in the context of the order that it superseded. So it is that the narrative of this book reaches far back in time: to the very origins of the ideal of a Christian empire. The reader will be taken on a journey that embraces both the ruin of the *pax Romana* and the attempts, lasting many centuries, to exhume it; will read of a continent ravaged by invasion, social collapse, and the ethos of the protection racket; will trace the invention of knighthood, the birth of heresy and the raising of the earliest castles; will follow the deeds of caliphs, Viking sea kings and abbots.

Above all, however, this is a book about how an anticipation of the end of days led to a new beginning: for seen from our own perspective, the road to modernity stretches clearly from the first Millennium onwards, marked by abrupt shifts and turns, to be sure, but unriven by any total catastrophe such as separates the year 1000 from antiquity. Though it might sometimes appear an unsettling reflection, the monks, warriors and serfs of the eleventh century can be reckoned our direct ancestors in a way that the peoples of earlier ages never were. *Millennium*, in short, is about the most significant departure point in Western history: the start of a journey that perhaps, in the final reckoning, only a true apocalypse will serve to cut short.

Europe in the year 1000

Novgorod

RUSSIANS

R U S

ND

Kiev

RY

PECHENEGS

BULGARIANS

Constantinople

Z A N T I N E   E M P I R E

Jerusalem

FATIMID CALIPHATE

Cairo

'But do not ignore this fact, beloved, that with the Lord one day is like a thousand years, and a thousand years are like one day.'

2 Peter 3.8

'The Faith is Europe. And Europe is the Faith.'

Hilaire Belloc

1

THE RETURN OF THE KING

The Whore of Babylon

'All these will I give you,' said Satan, showing Jesus the kingdoms of the world, 'if you will fall down and worship me.'[1] But Jesus, scorning empire, refused the temptation. And Satan, confounded, retired in great confusion; and angels came and ministered to the Son of Man. Or so, at any rate, his followers reported.

The kingdoms shown to Jesus already had a single master: Caesar. Monarch of a city which had devoured the whole earth, and trampled it down, and broken it to pieces, 'exceedingly terrible',[2] he swayed the fate of millions from his palace upon the hill of the Palatine in Rome. Jesus had been born, and lived, as merely one of his myriad subjects. The rule proclaimed by the 'Anointed One', the 'Christ', however, was not of this world. Emperors and their legions had no power to seize it. The Kingdom of Heaven was promised instead to the merciful, the meek, the poor. 'Blessed are the peacemakers, for they shall be called sons of God.'[3] And Jesus – even facing death – practised what he had preached. When guards were sent to arrest him, his chief disciple, Peter, 'the rock' upon whom it had been prophesied that the Church itself would be built, sought to defend his master; but Jesus, healing the man wounded in the ensuing scuffle, ordered Peter to put up his weapon. 'For all who take the sword,' he warned, 'will perish by the sword.'[4] Dragged before a Roman governor, Jesus raised no voice of complaint as he was condemned to death as an enemy of Caesar. Roman soldiers guarded him as he hauled his cross through the streets of Jerusalem and out on to the execution ground, Golgotha, the Place of the Skull. Roman nails were hammered through his hands and feet. The point of a Roman spear was jabbed into his side.

In the years and decades that followed, Christ's disciples, insisting to the world that their master had risen from His tomb in defiance of Satan and all the bonds of death, not surprisingly regarded the empire of the Caesars as a monstrosity. Peter, who chose to preach the gospel in the very maw of the beast, named Rome 'Babylon';[5] and it was there that he, like his master, ultimately suffered death by crucifixion. Other Christians arrested in the capital were dressed in animal skins and torn to pieces by dogs, or else set on fire to serve the imperial gardens as torches. Some sixty years after Christ had departed from the sight of His disciples, a revelation of His return was granted to a disciple named John, a vision of the end of days, in which Rome appeared as a whore 'drunk with the blood of the saints and the blood of the martyrs', mounted upon a scarlet beast, and adorned with purple and gold – 'and on her forehead was written a name of mystery: "Babylon the great, mother of harlots and of earth's abominations."'[6] Great though she was, however, the doom of the whore was certain. Rome would fall, and deadly portents afflict mankind, and Satan, 'the dragon, that ancient serpent',[7] escape his prison, until at last, in the final hour of reckoning, Christ would come again, and all the world be judged, and Satan and his followers be condemned to a pit of fire. And an angel, the same one who had shown John the revelation, warned him not to seal up the words of the prophecy vouchsafed to him, 'For the hour is near.'

But the years slipped by, and Christ did not return. Time closed the eyes of the last man to have seen Him alive. His followers, denied a Second Coming, were obliged to adapt to a present still ruled by Caesar. Whore or not, Rome gave to them, as to all her subjects, the fruits of her world-spanning order. Across the empire, communities of Christians spread and flourished. Gradually, step by tentative step, a hierarchy was established capable of administering these infant churches. Just as Jesus had given to Peter the charge to be shepherd of His sheep, so congregations entrusted themselves to 'overseers': 'bishops'. '*Pappas*', such men were called: affectionate Greek for 'father'. Immersed as they were in the day-to-day running of their bishoprics, such men could hardly afford to stake all their trust in extravagant visions of apocalypse. Though they remained passionate in their hope of beholding Christ's return in glory, they also had a responsibility to care for their flocks in the present. Quite as much as any pagan, many came to realise, they had good cause to appreciate the *pax Romana*.

Nor was justification for this perspective entirely lacking in Holy Scripture. St Paul – although martyred, as St Peter had been, in Rome – had advised the Church there, before his execution, that the structures of governance, even those of the very pagan empire itself, had been 'instituted by God'.[8] Indeed, it struck many students of the apostle that the Caesars had a more than incidental role to play in his vision of the end of days. Whereas St John had portrayed Rome as complicit with the Beast, that demon in human form who was destined, just before Christ's return, to establish a tyranny of universal evil, seducing men and women everywhere by means of spectacular miracles, chilling their souls and dimming the Church beneath a tide of blood, Paul, it seemed, had cast the empire as precisely the opposite: the one bulwark capable of 'restraining' Antichrist.[9] Yet such an interpretation did not entirely clear up the ambivalence with which most Christians still regarded Rome, and the prospect of her fall: for if the reign of Antichrist was self-evidently to be dreaded, then so also might it be welcomed, as heralding Christ's return. 'But of that or that hour,' as Jesus Himself had admonished His disciples, 'no one knows, not even the angels in heaven, nor the Son, but only the Father.'[10] That being so, many Church fathers concluded, it could hardly be reckoned a sin to hold Rome's empire in their prayers.

3

For redeemed though they hoped to be, even the devoutest Christians were sinners still, fallen and fashioned out of dust. Until a new heaven and a new earth had been established upon the ruins of the old, and a new Jerusalem descended 'out of heaven from God',[11] the Church had no choice but to accommodate itself to the rule of a worldly power. Laws still had to be administered, cities governed, order preserved. Enemies of that order, lurking in dank and distant forests, or amid the sands of pitiless deserts, still had to be kept at bay. As the fourth century of the Christian era dawned, followers of the Prince of Peace were to be found even among the ranks of Caesar's soldiers.[12] Later ages would preserve the memory of Maurice, an Egyptian general stationed at the small town of Agaunum, in the Alps, who had commanded a legion entirely comprising of the faithful. Ordered to put to the sword a village of innocent fellow Christians, he had refused. And yet, as Maurice himself had made perfectly clear to the infuriated emperor, he would have found in an order to attack pagan enemies no cause for mutiny. 'We are your soldiers, yes,' he was said to have explained, 'but we are also the soldiers of God. To you, we owe the dues of military service – but to Him the purity of our souls.'[13]

The emperor, however, had remained toweringly unimpressed. He had ordered the mutineers' execution. And so it was that Maurice and the entire legion under his command had won their martyrs' crowns.

Ultimately, it seemed, obedience to both Christ and Caesar could not be reconciled.

A New Rome

But what if Caesar himself were a servant of Christ? Barely a decade after Maurice's martyrdom, and even as persecution of the Church rose to fresh heights of ferocity, the hand of God was preparing to manifest itself in a wholly unexpected way. In AD 312 a pretender to the imperial title by the name of Constantine marched from Gaul – what

4

is now France – across the Alps, and on towards Rome. The odds seemed stacked against him. Not only was he heavily outnumbered, but his enemies had already taken possession of the capital. One noon, however, looking to the heavens for inspiration, Constantine saw there the blazing of a cross, visible to his whole army, and inscribed with the words, 'By this sign, conquer.' That night, in his tent, he was visited by Christ Himself. Again came the instruction: 'By this sign, conquer.' Constantine, waking at dawn, obeyed. He gave orders for the 'heavenly sign of God' to be inscribed upon his soldiers' shields.[14] When battle was finally joined outside Rome, Constantine was victorious. Entering the capital, he did not forget to whom he had owed his triumph. Turning his back on a whole millennium of tradition, he offered up no sacrifices to those demons whom the Caesars, in their folly and their blindness, had always worshipped as gods. Instead, the dominion of the Roman people was set upon a radically new path, one which God had clearly long been planning for it, to serve Him as the tool and agent of His grace, as an *imperium christianum* – a Christian empire.

'And because Constantine made no supplications to evil spirits, but worshipped only the one true God, he enjoyed a life more favoured by marks of worldly prosperity than anyone would have dared imagine was possible.'[15] Certainly, it was hard for anyone to dispute that his reign had indeed been divinely blessed. In all, Constantine ruled for thirty-one years: only a decade less than the man who had first established his fiat over Rome and her empire, Caesar Augustus. It was during the reign of Augustus that Jesus had been born into the world; and now, under Constantine, so it seemed to his Christian subjects, the times were renewing themselves again. In Jerusalem, earth and rubbish were cleared from the tomb in which Christ had been laid. A Church of the Holy Sepulchre, 'surpassing all the churches of the world in beauty', was raised above it, and over Golgotha, the hill of the crucifixion.[16] Simultaneously, on the shores of the Bosphorus, what had formerly been the pagan city of Byzantium was redeveloped to serve the empire as a Christian capital. Constantine himself, it was said,

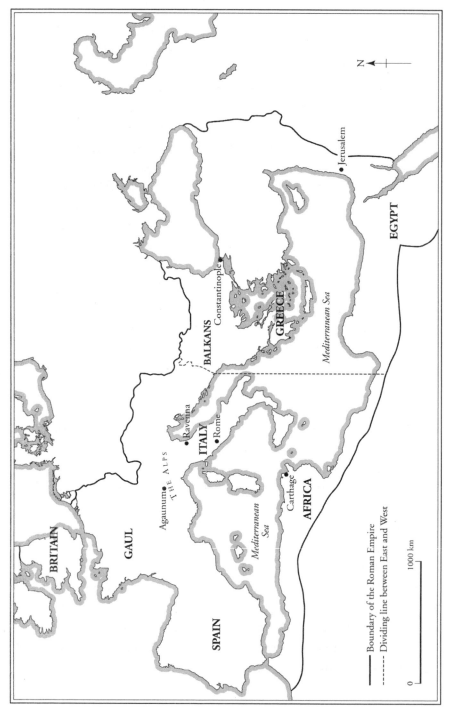

The Roman Empire in AD 395

BRITAIN

GAUL

SPAIN

THE ALPS
Agaunum

ITALY
Ravenna
Rome

Mediterranean Sea

Carthage
AFRICA

BALKANS

Constantinople

GREECE

Mediterranean Sea

Jerusalem

EGYPT

N

—— Boundary of the Roman Empire
---- Dividing line between East and West

0   1000 km

marking out the street plan of his foundation with a spear, had been guided by the figure of Christ walking before him. Never again would pagan temples be built on Byzantine soil. No palls of smoke greasy with sacrifice would ever drift above the spreading streets. Graced with the splendid title of 'the New Rome', the capital would provide the first Christian emperor with the most enduring of all his memorials. Ever after, the Romans would know it as 'the City of Constantine' – Constantinople.

A seat of empire, to be sure – but hardly a monument to Christian humility. The leaders of the Church were unperturbed. Scarcely able as they were to credit the miracle that had transformed them so unexpectedly from a persecuted minority into an imperial elite, they raised few eyebrows at the spectacle of their emperor's magnificence. Since, as St John had seen in his vision, the New Jerusalem would not be descending to earth until the very end of days, it struck most of them as a waste of time to preach revolution. Far more meritorious, the world's fallen state being what it was, to labour at the task of redeeming it from chaos. It was order, not egalitarianism, that the mirror of heaven showed back to earth.

What were the saints, the angels and the archangels if not the very model of a court, ranked in an exquisite hierarchy amid the pomp of the World Beyond, with Christ Himself, victorious in His great battle over death and darkness, presiding over them, and over the monarchy of the universe, in a blaze of celestial light? A Christian emperor, ruling as the sponsor and protector of the Church, could serve not merely as Christ's ally in the great war against evil, but as His representative on earth, 'directing, in imitation of God Himself, the administration of this world's affairs'.[17] In the bejewelled and perfumed splendours of Constantinople might be glimpsed a reflection of the beauties of paradise; in the armies that marched to war against the foes of the Christian order an image of the angelic hosts. What had once been the very proofs of the empire's depravity – its wealth, its splendour, its terrifying military might – now seemed to mark it out as a replica of heaven.

7

Naturally, the Christ to whom Constantine and his successors compared themselves bore little resemblance to the Jesus who had died in excruciating and blood-streaked agony upon a rough-hewn cross. Indeed, whether in the meditations of theologians or in the mosaics of artisans, He began to resemble nothing so much as a Roman emperor. Whereas the faithful had once looked to their Messiah to sit in awful judgement over Rome, now bishops publicly implored Him to turn His 'heavenly weapons' against the enemies of the empire, 'so that the peace of the Church might be untroubled by storms of war'.[18] By the fifth Christian century, prayers such as these were turning shrill and desperate – for increasingly, the storms of war appeared to be darkening all the world. Savages from the barbarous wilds beyond the Christian order, no longer content to respect the frontiers that had for so long been circumscribed by Roman might, were starting to sweep across the empire, threatening to despoil it of its fairest territories, and to dismember a dominion only lately consecrated to the service of God. Was this the end of days come at last? Christians might have been forgiven for thinking so. In AD 410, Rome herself was sacked, and men cried out, just as St John had foreseen that they would, '"Alas, alas for the great city!"'[19] Still waves of migrants continued to flood through the breached frontiers, into Gaul and Britain, Spain and Africa, the Balkans and Italy; and this too, it struck many, St John had prophesied. For the end time, he had written, would see Satan gather to himself nations from the far ends of the world; and their numbers would be like 'the sand of the sea'.[20] And their names, St John had written, would be Gog and Magog.

To emperors struggling to hold together their disintegrating patrimony, such talk was pure sedition. To their servants in the Church as well, desperate to see the imperial centre hold, the strident anti-Roman sentiments of St John's Revelation had long been an embarrassment. In 338, a council of bishops had sought to drop it altogether from the canon of Holy Scripture. In the East, where the more prosperous half of Rome's empire was at length, and with colossal effort, shored up against collapse, the Book of Revelation would not be restored to the Bible for centuries. Even as the western half of the empire crumbled away into ruin, an emperor remained sufficiently secure behind the massive battlements of Constantinople to proclaim that God had granted him authority over the affairs of all humankind – and to believe it. Whatever the barbarians might be who had overwhelmed the provinces of the West, they were self-evidently not Gog and Magog – for the end of days was yet to come, and the Roman Empire still endured.

This conviction, simultaneously vaunting and defiant, would remain constant throughout the succeeding centuries, even in the face of renewed calamities, and the dawning recognition, hard for any people calling themselves Romans to accept, that the empire was no longer the world's greatest power. Smoke rising from the passage of barbarian war bands might repeatedly be glimpsed from the walls of the very capital; enemy fleets might churn the waters of the Bosphorus; frontiers and horizons might progressively contract, as Syria too, and Egypt, and Cyprus, were lost to the New Rome: and yet the citizens of Constantinople, no matter what the tides of disaster lapping at them, still trusted to their destiny. Like the Jews, they presented themselves as God's elect, both afflicted and favoured on that account – and, like the Jews, they looked to the future for their ultimate deliverance.

So it was, some time in the seventh century, and amid an unprecedented series of defeats, that startling prophecies began to circulate. Written, it was claimed, by Methodius, a saint who had been martyred some three hundred years previously, these appeared to lift the veil, just as St John's vision had done, from the end days of the world. No matter that Methodius himself had been executed on the orders of a Caesar, the writings attributed to him endowed the Roman Empire with an altogether more glorious role than it had been granted in Revelation. Teeming although its pagan enemies already were, Methodius warned, its greatest test was still to come. The hour of Gog and Magog, long dreaded, would come at last. Imprisoned for aeons on the edge of the world behind great walls of brass, these were barbarians of unspeakable savagery, devourers of 'the vermin of the earth, mice and dogs and kittens, and of aborted foetuses, which they eat as though gorging on the rarest delicacies'.[21] Against the eruption of such monstrous foes, only the emperor in Constantinople – the last Roman emperor of them all – would stand firm; and in the end he would bring Gog and Magog to defeat. That great victory achieved, he would then travel to Jerusalem; and in Jerusalem, the Son of Perdition, Antichrist himself, would be revealed.

And then the last emperor, Methodius prophesied, would 'go up and stand on the hill of Golgotha, and he would find there the Holy Cross, set up just as it had been when it carried Christ'. He would place his diadem on the top of the Cross and then raise up his hands in prayer, delivering his monarchy into the hands of God. 'And the Holy Cross on which Christ was crucified will be raised to heaven, and the crown of kingship with it'[22] – leaving the last emperor dead on Golgotha, and all the kingdoms of the earth subject to Antichrist, steeped in that profoundest darkness that would precede the dawn of Christ's return.

So it was to come: the last great battle of the world. Small wonder that Methodius's prognostications should have attracted attention even in imperial circles. They may have been lurid and intemperate, yet they could offer a hard-pressed emperor precisely what St John, in Revelation, had so signally withheld: reassurance that the Roman Empire would continue in heaven's favour until the very end of days. More flatteringly, indeed – that the death of its last emperor would serve to precipitate the end of days. Had not St Paul, when he spoke of Rome 'restraining' Antichrist, implied as much? No matter how shrunken the dominion ruled from Constantinople, its rulers needed desperately to believe that it remained the fulcrum of God's plans for the universe. What in more prosperous times had been taken for granted was now clung to with a grim resolution: the conviction that to be Christian was synonymous with being Roman.

Posterity, as though in mockery of Constantine's pretensions, has christened the empire ruled from his foundation 'Byzantium', but this

was not a name that the 'Byzantines' ever applied to it themselves.*
Even as Latin, the ancient language of the Caesars, gradually faded
from the imperial chanceries, then from the law courts, and finally
from the coinage, the citizens of Constantinople continued to call
themselves Roman – albeit in their native Greek. Here was no faddish
antiquarianism. Rather, the prickliness with which the Byzantines, the
'*Romaioi*', guarded their name went to the very heart of their self-
image. It offered them reassurance that they had a future as well as a
past. A jealous concern with tradition was precisely what marked
them out as a Chosen People. It served, in short, to define their
covenant with God.

The City of God

It is true that the identification of Christendom with empire was not
entirely without its problems. A certain degree of awkwardness arose
whenever the *Romaioi* were obliged to have dealings with Christians
beyond their frontiers. Imperial lawyers had initially spun the optimistic formulation that all of Rome's former provinces, from Britain
to the furthest reaches of Spain, remained subject to the emperor. In
the earliest days of their foundation, some of the barbarian kingdoms
established in the West had been perfectly content to play along with
this fiction – and even those that did not had on occasion been flat-
tered into accepting certain tokens of subordination. After all, trinkets
and titles from a Roman emperor were never readily to be sniffed at.

In AD 507, for instance, a confederation of Germanic tribes known
collectively as the Franks, axe-throwing pagans who had seized control of much of northern Gaul, had won a great victory that extended
their sway southwards as far as the Mediterranean – and Byzantine
agents, hurrying to congratulate them, had awarded Clovis, their
king, the sonorous if wholly empty title of consul. A year later, and

---

* The name was reserved by the native citizens of Constantinople for themselves.

Clovis had shown himself even more an enthusiast for things imperial by accepting baptism.* What precise role the ambassadors from Constantinople might have played in this decision we do not know; but it must surely have struck them as a development rich in promise. For, by their own lights, to be a Christian was to be a Roman.

Not by the lights of the Franks, however. Although Clovis's people had plunged after their king into the waters of baptism, and although, a century later, missionaries dispatched from Rome would begin persuading the pagan English too to bow their necks before Christ, no submission to a mortal power was implied by these conversions. Just the opposite, in fact. Kings who accepted baptism did so primarily to win for their own purposes the backing of an intimidatingly powerful god: so it was, for instance, that Clovis, as a symbol of his newly Christian status, had taken to sporting 'a salvation-giving warhelmet'.[23] The very notion of tolerating an earthly overlord was anathema to such a man. Neither Clovis nor his successors had any wish to see a global empire re-established.

And already, by the seventh century, memories of Rome in the West were fading into oblivion. Massive still, beyond fields returned to scrub or marsh or forest, or above the huddled huts of peasants long since freed of imperial exactions, or framing perhaps even the high-gabled hall of a chieftain and his carousing warriors, Roman buildings continued to loom against the sky – but as the wardens now of an order gone for ever, slowly crumbling before the passage of suns and rains. All the complex apparatus of bureaucracy, the same that in Constantinople still served to feed the emperor, his armies and his taxes, had collapsed utterly into ruin, leaving, amid the rubble, only a single structure standing. The Church in the West, had it followed the course of its eastern counterpart and insisted that Christendom was indeed synonymous with the rule of Rome, would surely have shared

---

* Although France officially celebrated the 1500th anniversary of Clovis's conversion in 1996, a consensus has increasingly formed among historians that 508 is a much likelier date for his baptism than 496.

in the general ruin. As it was, it endured; and by enduring, preserved something of the imperious spirit of what had otherwise been left a corpse.

'To rejoice in the vast extent of an earthly kingdom is behaviour that no Christians should ever indulge in.'[24] So had pronounced Augustine, a bishop from north Africa, during the calamitous final century of the Western Empire's existence. But what of God's kingdom? That was quite a different matter. Bishops in the West, no longer able to rely upon a universal empire to shield their flocks from danger, could find in the writings of Augustine a theology infinitely better suited to their tattered circumstances than anything originating from the palmier days of the *pax Romana*. The great division in the affairs of the world, Augustine had argued, lay not between civilised and savage, Roman and barbarian, but between those earthly dominions of which Rome had been merely the most prominent example and a dominion incalculably greater and more glorious: the City of God. Within the infinite walls of the heavenly Jerusalem, all might hope to dwell, no matter what their origin; and the entrance way to this city, its portal, was the Church.

A glorious role indeed. Great empires, borne upon the surging flood tides of human sinfulness, might rise and conquer and fall; 'but the Heavenly City, journeying on pilgrimage throughout our fallen world, summons people from every nation, speakers of every language, taking no account of how they may differ in their institutions, their customs, or their laws'.[25] Here, for all Christians in the West, whether in the old imperial provinces of southern Gaul, where bishops descended from senators still sat proudly amid the carcasses of Roman towns, or upon the mist-swept fringes of the world, where Irish hermits raised prayers to the Almighty above the ocean's roar, was a message of mission and hope. Everywhere, across the whole, wide span of the fragmented, tormented world, was the City of God.

And as evidence for this, Augustine had turned, as had so many questers after divine secrets before him, to the vision of St John. Specifically, he had turned to a passage controversial even by the vertiginous standards of Revelation. 'Then I saw an angel coming down from heaven,' St John had written, 'holding in his hand the key of the bottomless pit and a great chain. And he seized the dragon, that ancient serpent, who is the Devil and Satan, and bound him for a thousand years, and threw him into the pit, and shut it and sealed it over him, that he should deceive the nations no more, till the thousand years were ended.'[26] And for the thousand years of Satan's imprisonment, until he should again 'be loosed for a little while', to fight the last battle that would see evil defeated once and for all, there would be a rule of saints. But when? Theories as to that, over the centuries, had come thick and fast. Most, feverish with mingled dread and hope, had proclaimed the start of the Millennium imminent. Augustine, however, in a typically innovative manoeuvre, had looked, not to the future, but to the past for the true solution. The rule of saints, he had argued, was already begun. It had been inaugurated by Christ Himself, after His death upon the Cross, when He had descended into the depths of hell and there bound up Satan, in witness of His victory over sin. Within the City of God, where Christ had ascended to reign in splendour, the saints and the martyrs already sat about Him upon their thrones. The Church too, earthly though it was, and therefore unavoidably tainted, was shot through with the radiance of their glory.

St John's vision, Augustine had argued, contained no road map of what was to come. Rather, it offered guidance on what it meant to be a Christian in the here and now. To speculate when the world would end on the basis of Revelation was pointless. Why, not even St John's allusions to a millennium were to be taken literally. 'For he intended his mention of "a thousand years" to stand for the whole span of our world's history. How else, after all, is one to convey an immensity of time save by deploying a perfectly round number?'[27]

The centuries passed. Kingdoms rose and fell. Christians who marked the times felt themselves to be living in an age of shadow. 'Cities are destroyed, proud strongholds stormed, fair provinces emptied of people, and the whole earth become a solitude.'[28] Yet though they mourned, those content to submit themselves to the inscrutable will of God did not despair: for still, proof against the breaking of the world, and illumined, however flickeringly, by the splendour of Christ in His undimmed glory, the Church continued to prosper. And so it seemed increasingly to its leaders that Augustine had been right: that the Millennium spoken of by St John had indeed begun. Those who disagreed, turning to Revelation in the hunt for their own answers, were deluding themselves – or worse. Wild talk of saints ruling upon earth could not help but undermine those already charged with the task of 'governing souls – which is the art to end all arts'.[29] What bishops in Constantinople claimed for their embattled empire, a role as the vehicle for divine providence, even to the very end of days, when Christ would at last return to rule the living and the dead, bishops in the West claimed for themselves. A sense of urgency gnawed at them. 'Once the world held us by its delights,' wrote one, gazing mournfully about him at the desolation of an emptied and crumbling Rome. 'Now it is so full of disasters that the world itself seems to be summoning us to God.'[30] Yet precisely for that reason – precisely because the end of times did indeed appear close at hand – so was it all the more essential that the Church not speculate as to the date. Those entrusted with the shepherding of fallen humanity could not risk infecting their flocks with extravagant terrors and enthusiasms. The sheep who in nervous anticipation of the Second Coming broke free of the fold might prove sheep forever lost. Only through the Church could the New Jerusalem be attained. Only through the Church could there be found a path to the rapture of Christ's return.

No wonder, then, that its leaders should have felt, often to a dizzying degree, a sense of their own elevation above the common run of things. Some bishops, man's sinful nature being what it was, duly succumbed to the temptations of pride and greed; others, burdened by the cares of office, found themselves gazing anxiously into their souls and yearning for solitude; but not one ever doubted that he was possessed of a sacred charge. Those same blessed hands that Roman soldiers had centuries earlier nailed to the Cross had once touched the heads of the apostles; and the apostles in turn had laid their hands upon the heads of their successors; and so it had continued, without break, down to the present. A bishop at his consecration, in witness of the awful trust being placed upon him, would be anointed with an unguent of prodigious holiness, blended of oil and a fabulously sweet-smelling, fabulously expensive resin, balsam. Chrism, this concoction was called: a mixture of such remarkable power that it needed only to be sprinkled on a sea to purge its depths of demons, and on a field to bless its soil with fertility. Upon flesh and blood too, its effects were transformative: for as it passed through a man's pores, penetrating his body, seeping deep into his soul, so did it serve to suffuse him with an eerie and numinous potency. A bishop adorned upon his head and hands with holy oil could know himself fitted to handle the very profoundest mysteries of his faith: to officiate at a Mass, transforming bread and wine into the body and blood of Christ; to confront and banish demons; to intercede with God. Anointed of the Lord, he was touched by the divine.

And even the humblest priest, consecrated in his own turn by a bishop, could be brought to share in the magic. Once, before the Church had begun its great labour of erecting a boundary between the sacred and the profane, the two had seemed interfused. Streams and trees had been celebrated as holy; laymen had laid claim to visions; prophets had read the future in ox dung; mourners had brought offerings of food and drink to tombs. Increasingly, however, the clergy had succeeded in identifying the dimensions of the supernatural as exclusively their own. By the eighth century, Christians uninitiated into the priesthood were losing confidence in their ability to communicate with the invisible. It was not only over the splendours of the City of God, after all, that the Church claimed to stand guard. Just as awesomely, its clergy patrolled the gateway that opened up to the realm of the dead, where angels or demons, heaven or hell, awaited the soul. No longer did people trust themselves to aid their departed kin as they embarked on this last dread journey. Only through the celebration of the Holy Mass, the Church had pronounced, could there be any hope of helping souls in the other world – and only a priest could conduct a Holy Mass.

Why, even the words he spoke while performing this miraculous ritual served to elevate him as a man apart; for in the West, unlike the East, whose missionaries thought nothing of translating their holy texts into any number of barbarous tongues, there was but a single sacred language. This was Latin; and its use was no less incumbent upon the clergy in Ireland or in the lands beyond the Rhine, where Roman rule had never penetrated, than it was upon their brethren in the former heartlands of the empire. For all the babel of jabberings spoken on the outer limits of forest or ocean, yet even Northumbrians or Thuringians or Frisians, if they had been properly consecrated to the service of Christ, could share in the common language that marked them out as priests.

Indeed, scholars from England who crossed the Channel were shocked to discover that the Latin spoken in Gaul appeared vulgar and decayed compared with the exquisitely frozen language that they had imbibed with such care from their school books. Even to those who had always fancied themselves native speakers of the 'Roman tongue', the antique Latin penned by Church fathers such as Augustine was becoming something dead. This, among priests who had the opportunity to learn it, only added to its appeal. A tongue unmangled by laymen could be reckoned all the more satisfyingly holy. As a result, even as the use of Latin as a spoken language declined in Italy, in Gaul, in Spain, to be replaced by bastard dialects, so the study of it by churchmen continued to flourish and spread. For the first time since the fall of Rome, an elite deployed across a vast extent of Europe could share in a common vocabulary of power. The Church in the West was becoming a Latin Church.

But not by any means a Roman one. True, Christian lands were formed of an immense patchwork of dioceses – and the boundaries of these dioceses, in the old imperial heartlands at any rate, dated all the way back to the time of the Caesars. It was true as well that when bishoprics were established in newly converted territories, beyond the borders of the ancient empire, it had become the custom to look to Rome for permission to establish supremos – 'arch-bishops' – capable of co-ordinating them. Yet the Bishop of Rome himself, although widely acknowledged as the most senior churchman in the West, was no Constantine. He might command the respect of kings, but not their obedience; he might send them letters of guidance or advice or solace, but not instruction. Even had he aspired to impose his authority on Christendom, he lacked the means. 'When all things are good,' Augustine had once written, 'the question of order does not arise.'[31] But shadow lay everywhere across the fallen world, even across dominions ruled by Christian kings – and so the question of order was one that the Church could hardly avoid. Chaos in a soul and chaos in a kingdom both sprang from the same self-evident cause: human evil. Robbery and oppression of the weak were bred of anarchy; and anarchy was bred of Satan, whose other name was Belial, a word which meant, learned doctors taught, 'without a yoke'.[32] Only at sword point, in a society collapsing into violence, could Satan be restrained, and the yoke of the law be restored.

Beyond all doubt, then, the trampling down of malefactors was to be reckoned a Christian duty – and yet it was still, even so, one hardly befitting a man of God. A bishop presided over his diocese as its father, not its constable. That role had to be shouldered instead by another, one better qualified to handle sword and spear – as indeed had been the case since the very earliest days of the Church. That Rome's empire had splintered into nothingness did not diminish this regrettable truth. If anything, indeed, it made it more pressing. For centuries, the Church had been obliged to accommodate itself to a bewildering array of warlords. The more rulers it had converted, the more it had mutated in response to their various styles of rule. Though it claimed to be universal, it was the very opposite of a monolith. Like the West itself, it constituted instead a kaleidoscope of differing peoples, traditions and beliefs.

Even in Rome herself, the very mother of the Church, the

pressures of worldly circumstance never ceased to weigh upon the city's bishop. Back in the sixth century, armies dispatched from Constantinople had invaded Italy and restored to the empire its ancestral heartland. 'The ancient and lesser Rome' had been incorporated into the dominion of 'the later, more powerful city',[33] and her bishop had humbly acknowledged himself the subject of the far-off emperor. A Byzantine governor had moved into the city of Ravenna, on the Adriatic coast, administering as a province the emperor's conquests in northern Italy, the Eternal City included; Byzantine titles and gewgaws had been lavished upon the Roman aristocracy; Byzantine fashions had become all the rage. The bishop himself, every time he celebrated a Mass, would pray for his absent master in Constantinople. Every time he wrote a letter, he would date it by an emperor's regnal year.

And yet a sense of his own dignity never left him. Although excessive uppitiness might on occasion be punished by exile or threats of execution, the pre-eminence of Rome's bishop as 'the head of all Churches' was something that had been long and ringingly proclaimed by Byzantine law.[34] Despite his best efforts, not even the Patriarch of Constantinople, leader of the Church in the empire's very capital, had been able convincingly to rival it. Small wonder, then, that this authority should increasingly have tempted ambitious bishops in Rome to set themselves up as masters in their own city. They were, after all, at a gratifyingly distant remove from the emperor's actual person – and the same crisis that in the seventh century had inspired Methodius's prophecies of a last Roman emperor had served only to widen that remove. Greece had been infiltrated by savage barbarians from the North; the sea lanes preyed upon by corsairs; communications between Italy and Constantinople rendered perilous in the extreme. Byzantine officials in Rome, turning ever more native by the year, had fallen into the habit of obeying their bishop rather than the governor in Ravenna – and the bishop himself into the habit of issuing them with commands.

Perhaps a measure of imperiousness would have come naturally to any man who dwelt in a palace, the Lateran, that had originally been a grant from the Emperor Constantine, and who ruled as the effective master of the former mistress of the world. Early in the eighth century, indeed, plans were being drawn up – although never completed – to build him a second residence on the Palatine Hill: a site so associated with the age of the emperors that the very word 'palace' echoed it. Yet the bishops of Rome did not derive their authority merely from the legacy of the imperial past. Their patrimony was something infinitely more awesome – indeed, so they proudly asserted, the most awesome of all time. Christ Himself, in naming Peter as His rock, had given to him the keys of heaven, with the power of binding and loosing souls everywhere on earth – and Peter, before his martyrdom, had ruled as the very first bishop of Rome.[35] A trust more mystical and dreadful could hardly have been imagined. Peter's successors, proclaiming themselves the apostle's 'vicarii', or 'deputies', had long since laid claim to it as their own. In Constantinople, where it was the emperor who believed himself entrusted by God with the leadership of the Church, this cut predictably little ice: by the early eighth century, doctrines were being laid down by imperial fiat in the teeth of howls of protest from Rome.

In the kingdoms of the West, however, lacking as they did the dazzling pretensions of an ancient Christian empire, men were far more inclined to be impressed by the spectacle of a bishop on the throne of the chief apostle. Indeed, to see him as the very essence of a bishop. 'Pappas' – that ancient Greek word for 'father' – was still, in the eighth century, being claimed as a title by bishops everywhere in the East; but in the West, Latinised to 'Papa', by the Bishop of Rome alone. So far as the Latin Church was concerned, it had only the one Holy Father. It acknowledged just a single Pope.[36]

And the Bishops of Rome, bruised as they were by snubs from their imperial masters, were duly appreciative. 'How regrettable it is', a papal letter of 729 dared to sneer, 'that we see savages and barbarians become civilised, while the Emperor, supposedly civilised, debases himself to the level of the barbarians.'[37] Two decades later, and relations between Rome and Constantinople had turned frostier than ever. Divisions over subtle issues of theology continued to yawn. Trade links as well as diplomatic contacts had atrophied, leaving the papacy effectively broke. Most alarming of all, however, from the Pope's point of view, was the failure of the emperor to fulfil his most sacred duty, and offer to God's Church the protection of his sword and shield. Rome, long a frontier city, was starting to feel ever more abandoned. With the imperial armies locked into a series of desperate campaigns in the East, Byzantine efforts to maintain a presence in Italy had focused almost exclusively on Sicily and the south. The north, as a result, had been left fatally exposed. In 751, it was invaded by the Lombards, a warrior people of Germanic origin who for almost two centuries had sat ominously beyond the frontier of Byzantine Italy, waiting for their chance to expand at the empire's expense. Ravenna, rich with palaces, splendid churches and the mosaics of saints and emperors, had fallen immediately. Rome herself, it seemed inevitable, would be next.

But hope still flickered, despite the negligence of Constantinople. The Pope was not utterly without protection. One year previously, a fateful embassy had arrived in Rome. It had borne an enquiry from a Frank by the name of Pepin, chief minister in the royal household and, to all intents and purposes, the leader of the Frankish people. Their legitimate king, Childeric III, although a descendant of Clovis, was but a feeble shadow of his glorious predecessor, and Pepin, eager to adorn his authority with the robes of monarchy, had resolved to thrust his master from the throne. Not wishing to offend against Almighty God, however, he had been anxious first to secure the Church's blessing for his coup – and who better to turn to for that than the Vicar of St Peter? Was it right, Pepin had duly written to the Pope, that a king without any power should continue to be a king? Back had come the answer: no, it was not right at all. A momentous judgement – and one, unsurprisingly, that had secured for Rome the pretender's undying gratitude. The Pope's ruling, it would soon be revealed, had set in train dramatic events. These would affect not only the papacy, not only the Franks, but all of Christendom.

God's plans for the world had taken a startling and far-reaching turn.

Haircuts and Coronations

In 751, the same year that saw the fall of Ravenna to the Lombards, Pepin struck against the hapless Frankish king. Childeric's spectral authority was terminated, not by death, but with a haircut. The Franks had long held a king to possess a mysterious communion with the supernatural, one that could provide victory in battle to their men, fertility to their women and fruitful harvests to their fields: a magical power dependent upon his having a luxuriant head of hair. It was hardly a belief calculated to delight scrupulous churchmen – but such considerations, back in the turbulent times of Clovis, had not weighed heavily. Two and a half centuries on, however, and the Franks had become a far more dutifully Christian people. The pagan affectations of their kings now struck many of them as an embarrassment. Few protests were raised when Pepin, having first snipped off Childeric's resplendent locks, immured him and his son in a monastery. The usurper, however, wishing to affirm his legitimacy as well as his brute power, moved quickly to cover his back. A great assembly of his peers was summoned. The letter from the Pope was brandished in their faces. Pepin was elected king.

And yet election alone was insufficient to assure him of the authentic charisma of royalty. Although the Franks were Christian, they had never entirely abandoned their ancestral notion that kings were somehow more than mortal. Childeric's dynasty, which claimed descent from a sea monster, had flaunted its bloodline as something literally holy: a blatant foolishness, bred of an age of barbarism, which only the gullible and ignorant had continued to swallow. Yet Pepin too, in laying claim to the kingship of the Frankish people, needed to demonstrate that his rule had been transfigured by the divine. The solution – naturally enough, for God had imprinted the pattern of the future as well as the past upon its pages – lay in the Bible. The ancient Israelites, oppressed by the depredations of their enemies, had called upon the Almighty for a king, and the Almighty, duly obliging, had given them a succession of mighty rulers: Saul, and David, and Solomon. As the mark of his elevation, each one had been anointed with holy oil; and Pepin, faithful son of the Church, now laid claim to a similar consecration. He would rule not by virtue of descent from some ridiculous merman, as Childeric had done, but *'gratia Dei'* – 'by the grace of God'. The very same unction that served to impregnate a bishop with its awful and ineffable mystery would now imbue with its power the King of the Franks. Pepin, feeling the chrism sticky upon his skin, would know himself born again and become the mirror of Christ Himself on earth.

A momentous step indeed – and one that brought immediate benefits to all involved. If Pepin was clearly a winner, then so too was the Church that had sanctioned it – and especially that oppressed and twitchy cleric, the Bishop of Rome. In the late autumn of 754, a pope travelled for the first time into the wilds of Gaul. Ascending the Alps amid gusts of snow, Stephen II toiled up an ancient road left cracked and overgrown by centuries of disrepair, travelling through a wilderness of thickening mists and ice, until finally, reaching the summit of the pass, he found himself at the gateway of the Kingdom of the Franks. Below the road, beside a frozen lake, there stood the ruins of a long-abandoned pagan temple: a scene of bleak and menacing desolation. Yet Stephen, no matter what emotions of apprehension may temporarily have darkened his resolve, would soon have found his spirits reviving as he began his descent: for the way-stop ahead of him, his very first in Francia, offered spectacular reassurance that he was indeed entering a Christian land. Agaunum, where four and a half centuries previously the Theban Legion had been executed for their faith, was now the Abbey of St Maurice: a reliquary raised in stone above the sanctified remains of Maurice himself. No people in the world, the Franks

liked to boast, were more devoted to the memory of those who had
died for Christ than them: for 'the bodies of the holy martyrs, which
the Romans had buried with fire, and mutilated by the sword, and torn
apart by throwing them to wild beasts, these bodies they had found,
and enclosed in gold and precious stones'.[38] The Pope, arriving in the
splendid abbey, breathing in its incense, listening to the chanting of its
monks, would have known himself among a people ideally suited to
serve as the protectors of St Peter, that most blessed martyr of them all.

Nor was Stephen to be disappointed in his expectations. Six weeks
after heading onwards from the Abbey of St Maurice, he finally met
with the Frankish king. Bursting into floods of ostentatious tears, the
Pope begged Pepin to march to the protection of St Peter, and then,
just for good measure, reapplied the chrism. The Franks he ringingly
endorsed as latter-day Israelites: 'a chosen generation, a royal priesthood, a holy nation, a peculiar people'.[39] Nor did Pepin, self-assured in
a way that came naturally to a warlord anointed of God, stint in fulfilling his own side of the bargain. In 755, Lombardy was invaded, and
its king briskly routed. Two years later, when the Lombards made the
mistake of menacing Rome a second time, Pepin inflicted on them an
even more crushing defeat. The territories that the Lombards had
conquered from Byzantium were donated in perpetuity to St Peter.
Arriving in Rome, Pepin personally and with a great show of senten-
tiousness laid the keys of the cities he had conquered upon the
apostle's tomb. And as caretaker of this portfolio of states, he
appointed – who else? – St Peter's vicar: the Bishop of Rome.

This was, for the papacy itself, a spectacular redemption from the
jaws of catastrophe. That God in His infinite wisdom had ordained it
appeared irrefutable. It was true, most regrettably, that there were a
few too blinkered to recognise this, with officials from what remained
of Byzantine territory in southern Italy voluble among them – but a
succession of popes, confident in Pepin's backing, blithely dismissed
every demand for restoration of the emperor's property. What were
the arid pettifoggeries of diplomats when set against the evident will of
the Almighty? The shocking manner in which the savage Lombards

had presumed to menace the heir of St Peter was an outrage committed not merely against the papacy itself, but against the whole of Christendom. No wonder that God had moved the heart of the Frankish king to such transcendent and gratifying effect. The surprise, it could be argued, was not that the papacy had been granted its own state to govern, but rather the very opposite – that no ruler had ever thought to grant it one before.

Or had the Pope's archivists perhaps been overlooking something? Long centuries had passed since Constantine first established the Bishop of Rome in the Lateran – and who was to say what documents might not have been mislaid in all that time? Papal officials, keen to justify their master's claim to his new possessions, appear to have spent the decade that followed Pepin's victory over the Lombards ransacking the musty libraries of Rome. Certainly, it was at some point during the second half of the eighth century, even as the papacy was battling to keep hold of the grant of territories it had received from the Frankish king, that a remarkable and hitherto wholly unsuspected document was produced.* Its contents, from the papal point of view, could hardly have been more welcome. The foundations of the state donated to St Peter, it appeared from the document, were far more venerable than anyone in the Lateran had dared to imagine. They had been laid, not by Pepin, but by the most glorious Christian ruler who had ever lived: Constantine himself. The content of the document added sensational details to the biography of the great emperor. A sufferer, it was revealed, from 'the squalor of leprosy',[40] he had been miraculously cured by the then Bishop of Rome, a sage of towering holiness by the name of Sylvester. Constantine, submitting humbly to the will of Christ, had then headed off to install himself in Constantinople – but not before he had first adorned Sylvester in all

---

* The first certain use of the document by a pope occurred as late as 1054, but its origin in the events of the second half of the eighth century is almost universally accepted by scholars, with a majority agreeing that it must first have appeared in the 750s or 760s.

the splendid regalia of empire, and surrendered to him and to the heirs of St Peter for ever the rule of Rome, together with what were vaguely termed 'the regions of the West'.[41] The implication could hardly have been more pointed: the papacy, far from depriving the emperor of his property, had merely been reclaiming its due.

Its case was helped, admittedly, by the fact that even the most learned had only the haziest notion of who Constantine had actually been. Just as the great monuments of the emperors now stood as disfigured ruins, obscured beneath the spread of weeds and grass, so memories of the ancient past had long since faded into myth. In the West, unlike the East, there survived no contemporary account of the life of Constantine. Nothing to demonstrate that he had not, in fact, been a leper; that Pope Sylvester, far from presiding over the Church, had in truth been an ineffectual nonentity, much given to bleatings about his old age and poor health; that Constantine could certainly not have departed the Lateran for Constantinople, since he was yet to found the city at the time. Scholars in the West, far from uncovering these inconvenient details, never even imagined that they might exist to be exposed. Why should they have done? Great convulsions, the wise knew, only rarely ushered in novelty – for it was seen as the likeliest consequence of change that what had vanished would be repeated, repaired or restored. No dispensation of God stood revealed in the affairs of the world that had not, at some stage, been portended or foretold. It beggared belief, therefore, that a development as momentous as Pepin's donation of a state to the Pope should not have been foreshadowed by a similar gesture back in ancient times. Had the 'Donation of Constantine' not existed, papal officials might well have argued, it would have been necessary to invent it.

And in this they would have been very much in the spirit of their age. As the eighth century drew to a close, so men far beyond the purlieus of Rome felt themselves possessed of a new and stirring sense of mission. '*Correctio*', they called it: the ordering of the disordered, the burnishing of the besmeared. Here was a programme to whet the ambitions of warlords as well as scholars, and to send men into battle beneath the fluttering of banners, the hiss of arrows and the shadow of carrion crows quite as much as into the mildewed quiet of libraries. Even as a succession of popes struggled to establish their supremacy in Italy, so from the North, beyond the Alps, momentous achievements were being bruited of the Franks.

In 768, King Pepin had died after a glorious reign, leaving behind him two sons, Charles and Carloman. These, as was the Frankish custom, had divided up their father's lands, and ruled alongside each other for three uneasy years. Then, in 771, after an illness, Carloman had followed his father into the grave. Charles had immediately laid claim to his dead brother's kingdom. He was not the man to squander the opportunity that God had so evidently granted him. Considerable though his dominions now were, he wanted more. A bare few months after Carloman's death, and he was passing the Rhine, scouring the windswept heathlands of Saxony, embarking upon a ferocious campaign of pacification against 'the brutish peoples' who lurked there 'without religion, without kings'.[42] The following year he invaded Italy, and five years after that he crossed the Pyrenees into Catalonia. By the 790s, he ruled an empire that stretched from Barcelona to the Danube, and from Lombardy to the Baltic Sea. Of all the lands of western Christendom, only the British Isles and a few small kingdoms in Spain still remained beyond the writ of the Frankish king. No wonder that monkish chroniclers, astounded by Charles's continent-shaking exploits, would commemorate him as '*le magne*', bastard Latin for 'the great': as 'Charlemagne'.

Warfare had long been the activity of choice among the Franks. Back in the days of Childeric, it had served to win them Gaul, after all. Leaders who failed to provide their followers with the spoils of pillage rarely endured for long. No sooner had winter thawed into spring than the Frankish people, dusting down their spears, would prepare to follow their king out on campaign. Charlemagne, whose hunger for booty was insatiable, had inherited to the full the appetites of a primordial line of warrior-chiefs. Yet though he ruled as a Frank, and gloried in the name, Charlemagne was heir as well to traditions more awesome and sanctified still. Like his father, he had been anointed with the dreadful power of the chrism, nor ever doubted that he was a new David, that mighty King of Israel, whose enemies the Almighty had broken 'like a bursting flood'.[43] It was in the perfect consciousness of this that Charlemagne made the wastes of Saxony to flow with pagan blood; that he spread even among the barbarous Slavs who swarmed on the outer reaches of the world awful rumours of the wrath and terror of his name; that he returned every autumn from his campaigns with lumbering wagon trains of booty, spoils with which to strengthen the Christian order throughout his vast domains. Just as he had taken it upon himself to push back the frontiers of Christendom, so also, within its boundaries, did he aim for its reform and purification – its '*correctio*'.

Charlemagne himself had little doubt how this was best to be attained. God's will obliged Christian men to show obedience to their earthly lords – and, above all, to their anointed king. There were few Franks disposed to contest this. Resentment of Charlemagne's supremacy, although it never entirely faded away among the greatest of the Frankish lords, was strongly tempered by self-interest. Decades of lucrative warfare had brought Charlemagne unprecedented resources of patronage. The aristocracy, restraining a naturally rumbustious sense of independence, duly knuckled down to playing the part of loyal dependants.

The Frankish bishops too, eager to profit from the great labour of Christian reform, had no hesitation in proffering Charlemagne their submission. In 794, a council of Church leaders drawn from across the Latin West hailed him, in fateful terms, as 'king and priest'. Such a formula was not original: it had long been applied to the emperor in Constantinople. Charlemagne, however, as master of Europe, and the Lord's anointed to boot, felt no obligation to truckle to the exclusiveness of the distant Byzantines. Whereas they had merely preserved a Christian empire, he could argue, he was labouring to bring one back to life. After interminable centuries of chaos, it was the Franks who had restored to the West the benefits of order, and after darkness returned it to the light. 'Once, the whole of Europe was stripped bare by the flames and swords of barbarians.' So wrote Alcuin, a scholar originally from Northumbria, in the north of England, a kingdom far removed from the limits of the Frankish Empire, but who had nevertheless been attracted to Charlemagne's side much like a moth drawn to a lamp. 'Now, thanks to God's mercy,' he exulted, 'Europe burns as brightly with churches as does the sky with stars.'[44]

Even the Pope himself, St Peter's own heir, had little choice but to acknowledge the Frankish king as head of 'the Christian people'. Fifty years previously, the papacy had negotiated with Pepin almost as an equal – but its bargaining position, as the eighth century drew to a close, had been sorely eroded. Charlemagne, who instinctively regarded bishops as he did everyone else, as his servants, to be exploited and patronised as he saw fit, certainly made no exception for the Bishop of Rome. Back in 774, following his invasion of Italy, he had seized the heavy iron crown of the Lombards for himself, and, from that moment on, the ramshackle state entrusted by Pepin to St Peter had been repeatedly trimmed back in the interests of Lombardy's new master.

So too, and perhaps even more hurtfully, had the papacy's claims to responsibility for the Church. In 796, when news of the election of a new pope, Leo III, was brought to him, Charlemagne was blunt in spelling out how the balance of responsibilities between the two of them stood. His own role, he wrote to Leo, was to defend the Church against pagans, to protect it from heretics, and to consolidate it across the whole span of Christendom by everywhere promoting the Catholic faith. The Pope's role was to lead prayers for the Frankish king's success. 'And in this way,' Charlemagne concluded with gracious condescension, 'Christians everywhere, Holy Father, will be sure to gain the victory over the enemies of God's sacred name.'[45]

The Holy Father himself, perusing this manifesto, may well have felt less than thrilled by it. Nevertheless, whatever his private disappointment at the attenuated role granted the papacy in Charlemagne's scheme of things, Leo made sure to conceal it. No less than his brother bishops of the Frankish Church, he appreciated that obsequiousness might bring its due reward. Accompanying Charlemagne's letter, for instance, there had rumbled into Rome wagons piled high with treasure, gold looted from the pagans, which Leo had immediately set about lavishing on Rome's churches, and on his own palace of the Lateran. Three years later, in 799, and he had even more cause to bank on Charlemagne. Even though his election had been unanimous, Leo had enemies: for the papal office, which until recently had brought its holder only bills and overdrafts, was now capable of exciting the envious cupidity of the Roman aristocracy. On 25 April, as the heir of St Peter rode in splendid procession to Mass, he was set upon by a gang of heavies. Bundled off into a monastery, Leo succeeded in escaping before his enemies, as had been their intention, could blind him and cut out his tongue. Lacking any other recourse, he resolved upon the desperate expedient of fleeing to the King of the Franks. The journey was a long and perilous one – for Charlemagne, that summer, was in Saxony, on the very outer reaches of Christendom. Wild rumours preceded the Pope, grisly reports that he had indeed been mutilated. When he finally arrived in the presence of Charlemagne, and it was discovered, to general disappointment, that he still had his eyes and tongue, Leo solemnly asserted that they had been restored to him by St Peter, sure evidence of the apostle's outrage at the affront to his vicar. And then, embracing 'the King, the father of Europe', Leo summoned Charlemagne to his duty: to stir himself in defence of the Pope, 'chief pastor of the world', and to march on Rome.[46]

And to Rome the king duly came. Not in any hurry, however; and certainly not so as to suggest that he was doing his suppliant's bidding. Indeed, for the fugitive Pope, humiliation had followed upon humiliation. His enemies, arriving in Charlemagne's presence only days after Leo, had publicly accused him of a series of extravagant sexual abuses. Commissioners, sent by Charlemagne to escort the Pope back to Rome and investigate the charges against him, drew up a report so damning that Alcuin preferred to burn it rather than be sullied by keeping it in his possession. When Charlemagne himself, in the early winter of 800, more than a year after Leo's arrival in Saxony, finally approached the gates of Rome, the Pope humbly rode out to greet him twelve miles from the city. Even the ancient emperors had only required their servants to ride out six.

But Leo, a born fighter, was still resolved to salvage something from the wreckage. Blackened though his name had certainly been, he remained the Pope, St Peter's heir, the holder of an office that had been instituted of Christ Himself. It was not lightly given to any mortal, not even Charlemagne, to sit in judgement on Rome's bishop. In token of this, when the proceedings against Leo formally opened on 1 December, they did so, not within the ancient limits of the city, but in the Vatican, on the far side of the Tiber, in implicit acknowledgement of the rights of the Pope, and the Pope alone, to rule in Rome. Papal officials, displaying their accustomed talent for uncovering ancient documents just when they were most needed, presented to Charlemagne papers which appeared conclusively to prove that their master could in fact only be judged by God. Charlemagne, accepting this submission, duly pronounced the Pope acquitted. Leo, placing his hand on a copy of the New Testament, then swore a flamboyant oath that he had been innocent all along.

And now, having triumphed over his enemies in Rome, he prepared to snatch an even more dramatic victory from the jaws of all his travails. Two days after the Pope's acquittal, Charlemagne attended Christmas Mass in the shrine of St Peter in the Vatican. He did so humbly, without any insignia of royalty, praying on his knees. As he rose, however, Leo stepped forward into the golden light cast by the altar candles, and placed a crown on his bare head. Simultaneously, the whole cathedral echoed to the ecstatic cries of the congregation, who hailed the Frankish king as 'Augustus' – the honorific of the ancient Caesars. Leo, never knowingly less than dramatic, then prostrated himself before Charlemagne's feet, head down, arms outstretched. By venerable tradition, such obeisance had properly been performed only for one man: the emperor in Constantinople.

But now, following the events of that momentous Christmas Day, the West once again had an emperor of its own.

And it was the Pope, and no one else, who had granted him his crown.

The Decline and Fall of the Roman Empire

So it was that Charlemagne came to rule as a second Constantine. The emperor's joy was not entirely unconfined. Though he was content to acknowledge the hand of God in his elevation, he was reluctant, as was only natural, to admit that he might owe anything to the Bishop of Rome. The whole coronation, Charlemagne would later declare, had come as a surprise to him, a bolt from the blue. Indeed, 'he made it clear that he would not have entered the cathedral that day at all, although it was the very greatest of the festivals of the Church, if he had known in advance what the Pope was planning to do'.[47] Here he spoke, not as an emperor, but as a proudly Frankish king: disdainful of the customs of other peoples; reluctant even to set aside his native dress; pointedly unwilling, when in Rome, to do as the Romans did. While his new title was glamorous, Charlemagne refused to be dizzied by it. He never forgot where his power base lay. He certainly had no intention of alienating his own people by appearing to be in hock to a foreign bishop.

Cause enough, then, for the new emperor to deny all foreknowledge of his coronation. Yet still an aura of mystery lingered around the ceremony. Had Charlemagne truly been as ignorant of Leo's plans as he subsequently claimed to be, then it was all the more eerie a coincidence that he should have been in Rome, and in St Peter's, on the very morning that he was. Eight hundred years had passed to the day since the birth of the Son of Man: an anniversary of which Charlemagne and his advisers would have been perfectly aware. Over the preceding decades, the great programme of *correctio* had begun to embrace even the dimensions of time itself. Traditionally, just as popes had employed the regnal year of the emperor in Constantinople on their documents,

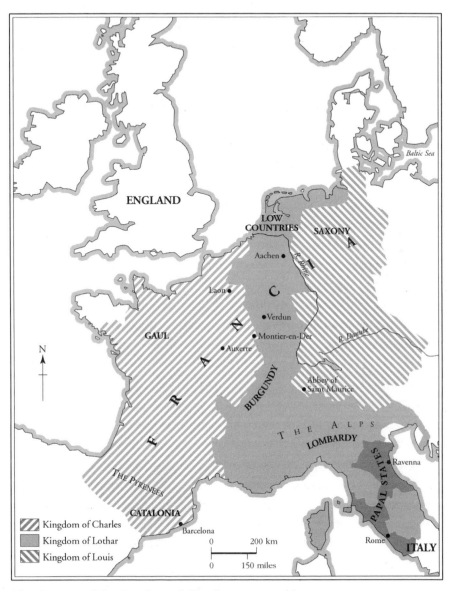

The Empire of the Franks and Charlemagne and his successors

so other churchmen had derived dates from a bewildering array of starting points: the accession of their local ruler, perhaps, or an ancient persecution, or, most extravagantly, the creation of the world. Such confusion, however, to scholars sponsored by the Frankish king, was intolerable. A universal Christian order, such as Charlemagne was labouring to raise, required a universal chronology. How fortunate it was, then, that the perfect solution had lain conveniently ready to hand. The years preceding Charlemagne's accession to the Frankish throne had witnessed a momentous intellectual revolution. Monks both in Francia itself and in the British Isles, looking to calibrate the mysterious complexities of time, had found themselves arriving at a framework that was as practical as it was profound. From whose accession date, if not that of some earthly emperor or king, were years to be numbered? The answer, once given, was obvious. Christ alone was the ruler of all mankind – and His reign had begun when He had first been born into the world. It was the Incarnation – that cosmos-shaking moment when the Divine had become flesh – that served as the pivot around which all of history turned. Where were the Christians who could possibly argue with that? Not at the Frankish court, to be sure. Clerics in Charlemagne's service had accordingly begun to measure dates from 'the year of our Lord' – '*anno Domini*'.

Here was a sense of time, Christian time, that far transcended the local: perfectly suited to a monarchy that extended to the outermost limits of Christendom. Charlemagne, crowned upon the exact turning point of a century, could hardly have done more to identify himself with it. Yet there was, perhaps, a further reason why he might have determined upon a coronation in AD 800 – nor was it one that he would have cared to publicise. Although shadow, on that fateful day in St Peter's, would have lain heavy beyond the flickering wash of the candlelight, yet it was not so heavy, perhaps, as the shadow of foreboding that lay across many people's souls. If the moment of Charlemagne's coronation had significance as the dawning of a new Christian century, then so also, according to a very different dating system, did it herald the ultimate in cosmic convulsions. Christ's birth was not the only potential starting point for a universal calendar. It was possible as well, many had long believed, to measure the centuries from the very moment of the earth's creation. Theologians back in Augustine's day had taught that six long millennia would pass, and that then, upon the six-thousandth year of the world's existence, the time of Antichrist would dawn, and the world be brought to an end. Not all Augustine's own magnificent scorn had been able entirely to demolish men's trust in these abstruse calculations. Over and again, preachers had emerged, willing to defy the disapproval of the leaders of the Church, and to remind people of the date long set for the coming of Antichrist. In the decades before Charlemagne's corona- tion, it seems, such prophets had begun to teem in growing numbers. In 789, a royal decree had been issued, ordering that their letters, if seized, be ceremonially burned. The authorities had good cause to be jumpy. The supposed date of the end of the world, which back in Augustine's day had been many centuries off, was now alarmingly imminent. Few who gathered in St Peter's to see Charlemagne crowned emperor would have been ignorant of it. Measured by the timescale that Charlemagne himself had done so much to promote, the appearance of Antichrist could be expected at any moment. To be precise – *anno Domini* 801.[48]

The year passed. Antichrist did not appear. It may be that the lead- ers of Christendom had never believed that he would. Yet still there remains the mystery of Charlemagne's coronation, and why, astute statesman though he was, astute and fiercely proud, he should have been content to accept the crown from the hands of the Bishop of Rome. Perhaps not all his calculations had been political, after all. Charlemagne held no light sense of his mission. He and the learned scholars in his train, although they did not broadcast the fact, certainly shared in the widespread fear that the world was growing old – and that Europe's master had a duty, 'at this last dangerous period of history, to rule and protect the Christian people'.[49] A fearsome responsibility, to be sure. Against the coming of Antichrist, what pos- sible defences could there be? Holy Scripture provided just the single hint. 'You know what is restraining him now so that he may be revealed in his time.' By this, theologians were still agreed, St Paul had been referring to the Roman Empire. And now, in the very year anciently foretold as the date of Antichrist's appearance, a Roman Empire had been refounded in the West. If truly a coincidence, then a blessed one indeed.

Not that Charlemagne, once crowned, had any intention of staying in Rome, to rule from there as a Caesar. The city remained an alien and perhaps unsettling place to him. A few months of imperious weight-throwing, and then he was off again, heading back north of the Alps. Just as he had come, so he left: as King of the Franks. Yet there were few in his train who would have doubted that something haunting had occurred to their master in the ancient capital of the Christian faith. Shadowy still it may have been, insubstantial as befitted a dead thing summoned from its grave, and yet the spectre of Rome's vanished empire, battening on to Charlemagne's greatness, had been supplied, after long and stony centuries, with a sudden wealth of nourishment. Only angle the mirror that the Frankish kingdom held up to its own pretensions, and the form of the revenant, seemingly undead, might there be glimpsed. In the wide-flung dominions won by the swords of the victorious Franks, but now newly christened a 'Roman' empire; in the palace complex that Charlemagne, returned from Italy, had begun to raise at Aachen, far distant from Rome, it was true, but beautified with columns redeemed from the city's marmoreal wreckage; in the image of the great emperor himself, that same haughty chauvinist who in real life had accepted only twice to wear the dress of a Roman, but who was portrayed on his coinage adorned with an antique robe and a laurel wreath. Though Charlemagne had always shown himself to be brutally practical in the cause of conquest, he was also a visionary – and his vision was of the distant past. Inevitably so, perhaps. Where else, save backwards, to that of Rome, could Europe's master have looked for the ultimate pattern of a Christian empire? Its ghost shimmered always before him. Even on his very seal, its renewal was inscribed as his mission statement. To the

Frankish monarchy, this was what building Christendom's future had come to mean.

It was an authentically imperial presumption. So much so, indeed, as to seem a virtual spoil of war. 'Ever since the time of Constantine the Great, the Roman Empire was held by the Emperors of the Greeks; but now, thanks to Charlemagne, it has been transferred to the Kings of the Franks.'[50] So the propaganda ran: as flattering to everyone in the West as it was, of course, news to the outraged 'Greeks'. Yet even they, who had greeted reports of Charlemagne's coronation with a predictable mixture of fury and derision, were steeling themselves to conciliate the Frankish king. Constantinople was teetering on the edge of ruin. While the Franks had busied themselves subduing peoples 'whose names not even the ancient Romans had learned',[51] the armies of the New Rome had been suffering a run of dismal defeats. Then, in 811, an emperor suffered the ultimate humiliation of being killed in battle by the Bulgars, a people so irredeemably savage that they swore their oaths over slaughtered dogs and mounted the skulls of their fallen enemies in silver cups. One year later, and Byzantine envoys made their grudging way to Aachen. Arriving there, they granted Charlemagne the ultimate in earthly approbation. Holding their noses as they did so, no doubt, and through firmly gritted teeth, the envoys from the New Rome hailed, for the first time, a barbarian king as '*Basileus*': 'emperor'.

But not, however, as a Roman. That, for the Byzantines – the *Romaioi* – was still a step too far. Ushered into Charlemagne's presence, the envoys had found themselves in a throne room blatantly copied from that of their own master: a display of gauche vulgarity that would have served only to emphasise to them how profound, how unbridgeably profound, remained the chasm between the western upstarts and themselves. Diplomats from Constantinople had long experience of fathoming the murk of the savage mind. For centuries, they had been flattering and befuddling their neighbours with the appurtenances of civilisation. Now, in their dealings with Charlemagne, they found themselves with little choice but to push this strategy to the limit. Hailing him as 'emperor', distasteful though it was, could best be justified as a holding operation. After all, no matter how sedulously the Frankish king sought to ape the dignity of the Romans, a barbarian he remained – and the character of a barbarian was proof against any number of splendid titles. The Franks, lacking the awful and ancient traditions of governance to which the New Rome was heir, were bound to succumb sooner or later to their own base nature, and start brawling among themselves. Inevitably, the rickety dominion they had presumed to term an 'empire' would then totter and collapse; the new highways they had built return to mud; all their fantasies of shaping Christendom melt and dissolve like mist. And once again, as was only proper, the *Basileus* would be obliged to acknowledge no equal save for himself.

And so it all came to pass. In 813, the aged Charlemagne crowned Louis, his son, as joint emperor: a pointed snub to the Pope, who was not even invited to the ceremony, and a seemingly ringing declaration that the future was to be as imperial as it was Frankish. Yet Charlemagne, despite passing on his dominions undivided, in the authentic manner of a Roman emperor, would rather not have done so. His original plans for the succession had been darkened bitterly by bereavement. Two sons, one after the other, had died only months previously. Had they lived, then Charlemagne, obedient to the primordial customs of his people, would certainly have divided his dominions into three. As it was, when he too, one year later, was summoned to meet his maker, he left behind him just the single heir. Louis ascended to the rule of the Frankish world unopposed. The empire of the West continued to acknowledge but a single master. Circumstance, for the while, had preserved it whole.

Yet still the potential for crisis festered. Despite the new king's own best efforts, tensions between the fantasy of a Roman Empire and the very different realities of Frankish custom and society were not easily squared. Louis, like his father, was a prolific breeder; and his sons, unlike Charlemagne's, tended to survive. Already, even before his death in 840, they had begun scrapping over their inheritance. After his death, they tore the West to pieces. In 843, Louis' three surviving sons, Charles, Louis and Lothar, met in the town of Verdun, where this dismemberment was solemnly formalised. Charles received the western portion of Francia, while Louis received the German-speaking lands that stretched eastwards of the Rhine: a division that, in the long run, would prove an enduring and fateful one.

Lothar, meanwhile, the eldest son, had to be content with a peculiarly rackety inheritance: a tranche of disparate territories running from the Low Countries down through Burgundy and across the Alps into Italy. It was to Lothar as well that the imperial title had been awarded: a dignity already spectral, but soon to plum yet profounder depths of devaluation. Like father, like son: it was becoming the habit for Frankish kings to leave behind them heirs in threes, and Lothar, before he died in 855, had carved up his own patrimony into thirds to meet the needs of his own progeny. This had left Louis, his eldest son and successor as emperor, with only the kingdom of Italy as his inheritance, a perilously attenuated base from which to claim the sway of the Christian world. Already, in a desperate attempt to shore up his prestige, Louis II had submitted to being crowned and anointed by the Pope, as both his father and grandfather, in similar moods of beleaguerment, had already done: for Charlemagne's successors, lacking the brutal self-confidence of the first Frankish emperor, had increasingly craved the validation that it was felt only St Peter's heir could provide. As a result, papal involvement in imperial coronations had become ever more a given, and all Charlemagne's efforts to eliminate it lost to memory. A bare half-century on from the momentous Christmas Day of 800, and Leo's shade could be well pleased. Only a pope, it was now accepted, had the power to bestow an imperial crown.

Yet a coronation, even one staged in Rome, was hardly sufficient in itself to make an emperor. In 871, a gloating missive from Constantinople arrived at Louis' court, pointing this out in the most undiplomatic terms. No longer did the *Basileus* feel any call to kowtow to the Franks. The *Romaioi*, long pressed and harried by their enemies, were now everywhere back on the offensive. As their fortunes were resurrected from the nadir of the previous century, so also was their ancient birthright of regarding foreigners with contempt, which Charlemagne's pre-eminence had briefly threatened, restored to them in all its traditional vigour. They naturally dismissed the shrunken figure of Louis II, a barbarian adorned in Roman robes, with a particular relish. No longer were they prepared to tolerate the right of anyone save their own master to the imperial title. The *Basileus* himself, in his letter to Louis, spelled this out in acerbic terms. There was, as there had always been, only the single empire – and the Franks had no claim to it.

Three decades on, and few even among the Franks themselves could deny that their imperial pretensions were in a state of chronic disrepair. The dominion raised to such heights of greatness only a century previously was everywhere collapsing. Kings and emperors ruled with all the authority of ghosts. The ancient wellsprings of prestige, drawn on to such effect by Charlemagne, appeared increasingly drained. In 901, the grandson of Louis II, determined to revive the fortunes of his house, had himself crowned emperor; four years later, and he had been captured by a rival warlord, blinded and banished to Burgundy, there to wither for the rest of his life. Never again would the family of Charlemagne lay claim to the dignity of an imperial title: a shrivelling of its fortunes rendered all the more terminal by the near-simultaneous extinction, in 911, of the royal line of East Francia. It was true that the great nobles of Germany, keen to perpetuate a sense of continuity with the glorious past, promptly looked for a replacement to Franconia, a princedom in the very heartlands of the kingdom – and whose duke was, as his title suggested, authentically and reassuringly a Frank.

This advantage aside, however, the newly elected king, Conrad I, brought few qualifications to the job: overshadowed by his peers, and increasingly, despite all his shrill protestations, ignored by them as well, he found his authority remorselessly bleeding away. Meanwhile, in the lands beyond his duchy, rival magnates sparred for advantage, warring with one another when not with their anointed king, all of them looking to profit from the confusion of the times. The kingdom itself, prey to such manoeuvrings, naturally enough continued to splinter. It appeared that half of the Frankish Empire was on the verge of a total disintegration.

And even in the western half, where a descendant of the line of Charlemagne still sat upon a throne, supposedly illuming his realm with the radiance of his prestige, a charisma granted of God Himself, the age was no less tempest-racked. The King of the Franks in the West, twin pillar of Christendom though he may have been, was quite as troubled by the ambitions of mighty princes as was his counterpart across the Rhine. Unsurprisingly so: for his kingdom had no settled borders, no shared institutions, not even a name. In many of the fairest principalities of the West – in Catalonia and Flanders, in Provence and Aquitaine – only the dimmest loyalty was still professed to the house of Charlemagne. Indeed, there were many among the leaders of the Franks, dukes with holdings quite as widespread as those of any king, and with treasure chests often deeper, who aspired to the royal dignity themselves. In a world without fixed frontiers, and an ever-weakening centre, there was much that seemed up for grabs. Wars duly blazed. In West Francia, as in the East, the shifting borders of great duchies were invariably traced with blood. Rare, however, was the struggle that proved more than local. Amid all the chaos and violence, a balance of power somehow held. 'That this was so reflected not any lack of Frankish princes with the requisite nobility, courage and wisdom required to rule, but rather their very dignity and power, which rendered them all so evenly matched. None was able to put the others in his shadow. None was able to command the ungrudging submission of his fellows.'[52] On such an inglorious basis, then, were the descendants of the house of Charlemagne, the 'Carolingians', enabled to keep their crown: the want of an alternative.

That a Christian land, if it were to flourish, did indeed require a king to rule over it was never for a moment doubted. Without one, so the wise had long taught, there could be no justice, no order, no peace. It was a king who served the Lord of the Heavens as His deputy, and whose duty it was, a most fearsome and burdensome one, to uphold for Him the world. Even in his very travails, if these were endured for the good of a suffering people, there might be glimpsed an imitation of the Passion of Christ Himself. And yet there was, for this reason, in the steady collapse of the royal authority established by Charlemagne, much more at stake than the future of the Frankish crown alone. To many Christians, the troubled condition of kingship in Francia appeared to speak of a sickness that might sap the order of the very universe, and menace God's people wherever they lived. Only human sinfulness, poisoning the world so that 'men behave like monsters of the deep, blindly devouring all those weaker than themselves',[53] could explain the evident scale of heaven's anger. The landscape of Christendom, which under Charlemagne had been compared to a tapestry of blazing stars, appeared increasingly to be returning to blackness. As the tenth century since the Incarnation continued to darken, so men looked at the world about them, and dreaded the portents that they read there.

In the sky, for instance, phantom hordes might sometimes be seen, their ranks formed of swirling fire; and yet, since the turning of the century, there had been deadlier signs, and more terrifying hordes, unleashed upon the groaning earth itself. Back in 899, wild squadrons of horsemen, so strange and savage as to seem a sudden eruption from the nightmares of every civilised Christian, had descended upon the plain of Lombardy, and stripped it bare. 'Of disgusting aspect, with deep-set eyes and short stature',[54] the invaders were rumoured even to have drained their victims of their blood. One year later, and the hoof beats of the mysterious barbarians had made all Bavaria shake. Soon, they were being heard as far west as Provence. Every year, somewhere in the decaying Frankish Empire, new fields, new villages, new monasteries were scoured and plundered utterly.

Against foes such as these, clouds of monstrous hornets, possessed of such speed as to seem barely human and the devilish ability to fire arrows even while on the gallop, resistance seemed futile. Not until the earth split open, the invaders were reported to have boasted, would they ever be brought to defeat. Their wretched victims were inclined to agree. Certainly, there were few among the local princes who seemed capable of making a stand. Even when the raiders were at their most vulnerable, withdrawing to their lairs on the Danube along rutted and muddy trails, their wagons piled high with loot, their trains encumbered by tethered and stumbling captives, they were rarely confronted. To survivors of their razzias, the scenes of devastation that were their inevitable aftermath – the countryside blackened, the churches still smoking, the corpses of those not fit to be enslaved left fly-blown amid the ashes – appeared visions conjured up from hell. That the invaders were in truth not demons but rather tribesmen from the outer limits of the world, a people known as the Hungarians, was widely acknowledged. Yet so too, among the overwhelming majority of those who bore the brunt of their attacks, was the notion that such a plague was in itself the symptom of an evil more than human. 'For they say that this is the last time of the age, and the end of the world is near, and therefore the Hungarians are Gog and Magog. Never were they heard of before – but now, behold, it is the end of time, and they have materialised!'[55]

The monk who recorded these opinions did so in order to refute them. He wrote with a self-assurance that came naturally, perhaps, to a man ensconced at a safe distance from the devastation, in Auxerre, in northern Burgundy. Those more directly in the Hungarians' path tended to be less sanguine. It was not only 'the frivolous', wild-tongued prophets from beyond the ranks of the priesthood, who dreaded that 'the last time of the world has dawned'.[56] The Burgundian monk, attempting to calm such fears, did so in response to a letter from a bishop, no less, the Primate of Verdun, whose flock had repeatedly suffered from the depredations of the Hungarians. Surely, the bishop had asked in a tone of high panic, the end of the world was drawing near? The brethren of the monastery in Auxerre, famed as they were for their learning in the study of Revelation, were growing used to such anxious enquiries. Patiently, although with more than a hint of the long-suffering schoolmaster, they would admonish those who presumed to imagine that the mysteries of God's plans for the future could ever be fathomed. 'For to grieve over the end of the world', as the Bishop of Verdun was reminded pointedly, 'is the business only of Him who plants the roots of His heart in the love of the world.'[57] The orthodoxy of the Church, as it had been formulated many centuries previously by Augustine, still held. The terrors of the age were a summons, not to panic, but to repentance. They should be met, not with wild prophecies, but with prayer, and contrition, and penance, and good works. To imagine otherwise was the very height of sacrilege.

So it was that there was set up in the souls of dutiful Christians everywhere an excruciating tension. On the one hand, it was all too clear to them that 'great calamities, the fruits of divine judgement, are everywhere increasing, heralding the end of the age of men'.[58] Not since the very earliest days of the Church, when the return of Christ had been hourly expected, had a sense of the imminence of the end of days so utterly possessed the ranks of the faithful. That the world was hurtling towards the fiery ruin so long prophesied for it appeared to most Christians, amid all the violent tribulations of the century, self-evident.

For even if it were granted that the Hungarians might not be Gog and Magog, then what could the more general savagery of the times possibly portend if not the imminence of Antichrist? There were certain signs, after all, that not even the most sceptical could dispute. The empire of the Romans, refounded by Charlemagne to serve Christendom as its watchtower and its bulwark, was everywhere dissolving back into chaos. No other barrier to the coming of Antichrist existed. Whether the Son of Perdition would be born to the union of Satan and a virgin, as most presumed, or of a Jew and his daughter, as other learned men argued, the time of his triumph was certainly approaching fast. But *when* precisely? The yearning to pose this question was all the more terrible for the fact that the fate of all humanity so clearly hung upon the answer. Yet it could not be asked. The veil drawn by God across the future was not to be parted by mortal sinners. Even the angels were forbidden to know. The more palpable the proofs that a universal conflagration was at hand, the more strenuously it behoved good Christians to refrain from adducing the hour.

True, there were some who found the temptation too great to resist. One seeming clue, more than any other, haunted the calculations of these imprudent souls. St John it was, in his vision of the binding of Satan, who had reported how the angel responsible for throwing the Evil One into a pit had 'shut it and sealed it over him, that he should deceive the nations no more, till the thousand years were ended'. 'The thousand years': how was this figure best to be interpreted? Abstractly, as Augustine had so forcefully argued, and the Church continued to affirm? Or, was it possible, some dared to wonder, that St John had meant the number literally, after all? To Christians grown increasingly comfortable with dating years from *anno Domini*, this question was far more pressing than it might otherwise have been. Nine hundred years and more had passed since the blessed feet of Christ had walked the earth; and now the thousandth was drawing near.

No wonder, then, that there were those even in the ranks of the priesthood who looked at the approaching Millennium with a mingled dread and anticipation – and were prepared to admit as much. In one cathedral, for instance, in Paris, a thriving market town, there was a preacher who stood up in the presence of the entire congregation, and bluntly warned all present that Antichrist would be upon them 'the moment that one thousand years are completed'.[59] A second priest, startled by this dramatic lurch into unorthodoxy, moved quickly to demolish his colleague's claim with multiple and learned references to Holy Scripture; but still the prophecies came, 'and rumour filled almost all the world'.[60]

And rumour bred rumour in turn. Certainly, there existed no firm consensus as to the likeliest date of Antichrist's birth. Whether as nervous whisperings, or as claims made in public letters, or as enquiries posted to learned monks, new hypotheses were regularly being floated. Ambiguity had haunted even the seemingly ringing pronouncement of the preacher in Paris: for was the Millennium to be measured from Christ's coming into the world, or from His ascension into heaven? A perilous question to put to public debate – and an irrelevant one too, perhaps. For if the coming of Antichrist were truly at hand, then it little mattered whether it would occur on the anniversary of Christ's birth or of His Resurrection. What did matter, and awesomely so, was the widespread sense that the rhythms of human life, and of the seasons, and of the very earth itself, which had continued unchangingly since the Creation, lay under a sentence of imminent termination: that at some point, either on or shortly after *anno Domini* 1000, all things would be brought to a fiery end. 'The sons of mankind come and go in sequence, the old die, and the young who take their place wax older in their turn – and this is what it is to be human in this world, this Middle Earth.'[61] But not, perhaps, for very much longer. Whether as a leaden anxiety, or as a tormenting apprehension, or as a passionate expectation, this conviction abided, and would not go away.

To many, indeed, in an age afflicted by seemingly insoluble crises, it promised a resolution. History, by the mid-tenth century, had become a nightmare from which the Christians of Francia were struggling to awake. Confidence in their ability to shape their own future had been largely abandoned. This was true not only of the poor, the hungry, the oppressed, but even of those in power. At the court of the King of the Western Franks, concerns about the imminence of Antichrist went right to the very top. By the late 940s, it seemed as though his arrival could not be long postponed. Signs of the ruin of West Francia appeared everywhere lit up by fire. Not only had the Hungarians, sweeping well beyond their customary haunts, penetrated almost to the far north-east of the kingdom, where the royal capital of Laon stood, but aristocratic feuding, savage as ever, had attained fresh peaks of sacrilege.

Laon itself, at one point, had been captured and plundered, and the king, Louis IV, briefly held a prisoner. No wonder, then, that his wife, the Saxon queen Gerberga, should have turned for advice, not to a great warlord, but rather to a churchman who was famed above all for his knowledge of Antichrist: Adso, the Abbot of Montier-en-Der. The celebrated scholar, in his reply to Gerberga, did not succumb to the temptation of giving a precise date for the end of days; but he did feel able to confirm that it was imminent. 'In fact,' he informed the terrified queen, 'the times we live in being what they are, there is no topic of more pressing urgency.'[62] And for those of the royal house of the Franks more than for anyone: for it was they, and they alone, who stood between the world and Antichrist.

It was a sensational assertion – but one arrived at on the back of flawless logic, nevertheless. After all, if it was the Roman Empire that had served as the bulwark against Antichrist's coming, and the Franks who were the heirs of the Roman Empire, then what could the collapse of their kingdom possibly spell if not the end of the world? Morale-boosting though Adso might have imagined this conclusion to be, it hardly served to ease the burden of responsibility on the shoulders of the Frankish king. Nor was the abbot done yet with piling on the pressure. 'What I say is not a product of my own thoughts or fancy,' he insisted, 'but due to my diligent research'[63] – and Adso, in his library, had been studying St Methodius. The vision of the ancient martyr, with its prophecy of a Roman emperor who would conquer the world before travelling to Jerusalem, laying down his crown upon the hill of Golgotha, and setting in train the Second Coming, had originally been translated into Latin in the eighth century; but it was only in Adso's time that its implications had been fully grasped by scholars in the West. How arrogant the Greeks had been, how arrogant and grotesquely wrong, to have imagined that it was one of their emperors who would lay claim to Jerusalem! Rather, a Frank was destined [to] 'in the last of days, be the greatest and last of all kings'. So Adso, with all the weight of his great scholarship, pronounced. 'And this will be the end and the consummation of the Roman Empire – which is to say, the Empire of the Christians.'[64]

Almost five hundred years had passed now since the collapse of Rome's dominion in the West. Ghoul-like, though, its spectre continued to haunt the dreamings of all those who sought to interpret God's plans for the future of mankind. As in the age of Charlemagne, so in the infinitely more troubled age of Adso: no solution to the problems confronting Christendom could be conceived of saving a return to the long-vanished past. No climax to human history either. The ship-wreck of things might be dreaded, yet it was simultaneously conceived of as a harbour: as the escape from innumerable tempests and violent waves. In the end would come a new heaven and a new earth, and the return of the Son of Man; but first, 'although everywhere we look we see it lying in almost total ruin', there would have to be the return to a Roman Empire.

It is hard to imagine a programme more expressive of paralysis and despair. Beyond the walls of Adso's monastery, great princes feuded with one another, and fields were trampled by rival armies, and the borders of Christendom were lit by flames and dyed with blood. Still, as their only solution to this crisis of desolation, the subtlest and most learned minds in Francia whispered decrepit fantasies of global empire. Yet these same fantasies, even amid the general chaos of the times, had not entirely lost their ability to transfix kings as well as scholars. Adso, writing to Gerberga, had presumed that any future emperor was bound to be a Frank. The times, though, were changing – as Gerberga herself, a Saxon princess, might well have chosen to remind the abbot. For the Franks, even as Adso penned his letter, were no longer the only people to have been charged with the rule of a great dominion. To the east of their heartlands, on the very margins of Christendom, a new power was rising. A power capable, as time would prove, of securing the West against its most fearsome enemies, and of forging a new Roman Empire, even as all the while the Millennium drew ever nearer.

2

THE OLD ORDER CHANGETH ...

The Thousandth-Year Reich

Though Christendom was embattled, not all its frontiers were col-lapsing. In the marches of Saxony, along the banks of the Elbe, the broad-flowing river which served East Francia as its flank, Christian warriors stood on watchful sentinel, and dreaded no one. The Saxons, as they contemplated the heroic struggle to uphold God's order, knew themselves in its vanguard. Beyond the Elbe to the east, in sinister groves adorned with idols and animal horns, Slav tribes, known col-lectively by the Saxons as the 'Wends', still worshipped demons and indulged in their 'vain superstitions';[1] but westwards, the very land-scape bore witness to the protecting hand of Christ. Wherever the soil was fertile, and the wilderness capable of being tamed, there the marks of His favour thrived: farms, and homesteads, and raw stone churches. Even on the Elbe itself, the border forts were prospering – and this despite the continued enthusiasm of Wendish war bands for crossing it in search of plunder.

The linchpin of the defences raised against such raids was the fortress of Magdeburg: originally founded by Charlemagne as a frontier station, where the bags of merchants travelling out of Christendom could be inspected for contraband armour and weapons,

The Saxon *Reich*

it already ranked, by the early tenth century, as the capital of the eastern marches.[2] Flush with the profits of trade, and a booming hinterland, it could boast churches, markets and even a '*Hof*' – a court for the entertainment of Saxony's duke. Meanwhile, beyond its haughty gatehouses, and the road which led eastwards over the Elbe, the pagans 'lived in such brutish poverty that what in Francia would seem an insupportable burden is counted by them almost as a pleasure'.[3] As it had been back in the earliest days of the Magdeburg customs post, even a mail shirt was held a wonder by many tribes. Indeed, such was the awe with which helmets and hauberks were regarded by the Wends that armour was likeliest to adorn, not their warriors, but their gods. Deep immured in forest shrines, their idols stood, blank-eyed and menacing, 'fearsomely girt in mail'.[4]

To the Saxons, the folly of this demon-worship was all the more minatory for the fact that they had once shared in it themselves. A people who had learned to rejoice in the felling of trees and the raising of churches on root-cleared plains could not forget that they too, barely a century and a half before, had staged their most sacred rituals in the darkness of oaken glades. The dreadful rumours of what had been practised there still darkened the nightmares of Christian homilists. Prisoners, it was whispered, hung from the boughs of sacred trees, having been pierced through with spears: for the spear had been sacred to Woden, most far-seeing of the gods. To the initiates of this sacrifice, awful privileges had been owed: to those who harvested the blood of the still-writhing victims, and traced it over runes, the wisdom of Woden himself; and to those who consumed their beating hearts, a power over the dead. Charlemagne, storming the strongholds of this monstrous evil, had felt himself obliged to purge it thoroughly with axe and sword. Trees holy to Woden had been hacked down and the branches consigned to fire.

The Saxons themselves, as obdurate in their paganism as in their reluctance to accept the Frankish king, Christ's own anointed, as their new master, had been treated with a matching ferocity. After one particularly savage rebellion, thousands of prisoners had been beheaded in a single dispatch; the populations of entire areas forcibly relocated; death introduced as the penalty for refusing baptism, for clinging to the ancient rites, even for eating meat during Lent. Not since the age of the Caesars had atrocities been committed on quite so imperious a scale – and never before with the goal of imposing the love of Christ.

There were many in Charlemagne's train who had paled at the knowledge. To wage a war of aggression and conquest, even against heathens steeped in the most idolatrous savagery, appeared to them the very opposite of the Christian ideal. 'Faith', as Alcuin had put it anguishedly, 'arises from the will, not from compulsion. You can persuade a man to believe, but you cannot force him. You can haul him to the waters of baptism, but not to faith itself.'[5] Time, however, had proved this warning wrong. The Saxons, exhausted by their struggle against Charlemagne, had in due course been brought to acknowledge the full scale of their defeat. Woden had failed them. The Christ of the victorious Franks had proved Himself invincible. It could be held no shame to submit to such a god. And so the Saxons had duly submitted. Woden, toppled from his throne, had been banished from Middle Earth. On occasion, it was reported, at nightfall, he and his followers, she-wolves, carrion crows and the spirits of the dead, surrounded by black clouds, would return to intrude upon their ancient dominion, crashing through the woods, riding the icy winds; but there was nothing in such a superstition to impress the Saxon elite. Those on the margins of the retreating wilderness, peasants and pioneers, might sometimes bow their heads before the passage of the demon hunt; but never the aristocracy. They knew perfectly well what they owed to the favour of Christ. No longer wallowing as the Wends still did, in a brutish poverty, they were now the peers of anyone in Christendom – even their former conquerors. 'For moulded by the Christian faith into brothers, they had become almost an identical people with the Franks.'[6]

So much so, indeed, that by the early tenth century, and with the realm of East Francia on the brink of seeming collapse, men could even speak of the Duke of Saxony as a possible future king. Henry, head of the Liudolfing clan, fully merited such excited approbation. Since inheriting his title in 912, he had shown himself 'a lord rich in wisdom, abounding in severity, and of righteous judgement'.[7] To the pagans beyond his borders, he had proved a predictably stern and tireless foe. To the ambitions of the clans within them, he had been a more subtle, but no less effective, opponent. The great warlords of Saxony, whose instinct had always been to indulge themselves in murderous rivalries, had been systematically broken to his will: variously menaced, bought off and cajoled. Talents such as Henry could deploy, in a failed state such as East Francia was fast becoming, were not lightly to be ignored. Even Conrad, its prickly but increasingly hapless king, was finally brought to acknowledge as much. In 915, abandoning all his earlier efforts to check the ambitions of his unsettlingly able neighbour, he signed a truce that effectively appointed the Saxon duke his deputy. Three years later, as Conrad lay dying, he told his brother, Eberhard, to propose Henry as his successor. The following spring, in May 919, Eberhard dutifully followed up this deathbed advice. The Frankish nobility joined with their Saxon peers in acclaiming Henry as king. For the first time, the rule of East Francia was entrusted to a man who was not even a Frank.

No wonder that the fateful moment would later be enshrined in legend. Messengers sent to inform the new king of his elevation, it was said, had been unable to find him at first, and only after several days had he finally been tracked down to a wild marshland, where Henry, an avid huntsman, had been painstakingly setting traps for ducks. It was an apt reflection, certainly, of the predatory cool and patience that 'the Fowler' now brought to the task of redeeming East Francia. Careful not to aggravate the great dukes of his tottering realm, men who still regarded themselves, at the very least, as his peers, Henry forwent the self-indulgence of being anointed. Yet even as he colluded in the dimming of the royal aura, and promoted himself, not as the heir of Charlemagne, but rather as something altogether more modest, as merely a first among equals, he was stalking his opponents. Over the next few years, a succession of potential rivals were methodically humbled, or else seduced with high-sounding titles and offers of marriage into the Liudolfing house. Soon enough, the princes of East Francia found themselves hopelessly entangled in a delicate mesh of dependency and obligation. By 935, when Henry met at a summit with his brother kings of Burgundy and West Francia, he did so not merely as their equal, but as the dominant figure in Christendom. There was certainly no one now to dispute the right of a Saxon to rule as 'King of the Franks': as the lord of what his subjects, in their own language, termed their 'Reich'.*

It was a startling achievement – and yet Henry, even while breaking in the fractious dukes of East Francia, had simultaneously been keeping his eye on more threatening game. It was not sufficient to haul the Reich back from the brink of internal collapse; it also had to be preserved from the onslaughts of those who would bleed it to death from without. The Hungarians, whether the outriders of Antichrist or not, had somehow to be confronted – and Henry the Fowler, as ever playing a long game, was patiently preparing his traps. In 926, trading temporary humiliation for future advantage, he agreed to pay tribute in return for a truce. Warriors, like hawks or hunting dogs, needed to be trained for the kill. Those among his followers who could afford the costs of a warhorse were encouraged to invest as well in the even more crippling expense of a mail coat, to transform themselves into 'loricati': men of iron. Poorer levies, meanwhile, were set to work raising fortresses along the Reich's eastern frontier, bases suited not merely to defence, but also to the launch of counter-offensives. Even criminals were summoned to the cause. At Merseburg, a stronghold some seventy miles south of Magdeburg, a legion of thieves and bandits was installed, and instructed to train itself for battle by launching expeditions against those perennial objects of Saxon prowess, the Wends. In 929, when a Wendish army, stung by such aggravation, presumed to

---

* The Latin term used by the chroniclers of Henry I's reign is 'imperium'. The German word – despite its unfortunate connotations – conveys a much better sense of its meaning than any alternative word in English.

launch a counter-raid across the Elbe, it was met in open battle, and annihilated. Warriors on horseback, newly coated in their expensive shirts of iron, provided the shock force. Three years later, feeling sufficiently confident at last to bait his snare, the Fowler cancelled his tribute payments to the Hungarians, sending them, instead of gold, a tailless and crop-eared dog. The Hungarians, responding to provocation just as the Wends had done, dispatched a raiding party to pillage Saxony: it too was cornered, confronted and wiped out. Once again, it was the heavy cavalry, singing to the Almighty as they rode, who led the slaughter.

The victory, it was true, had hardly been decisive. Already, Henry had to assume, beyond the frontiers of the *Reich*, in the great plain of the Danube, that teeming womb of pagans, a dreadful vengeance was being planned. The supreme test, one that would witness either the Hungarians destroyed as a threat for ever, or else the ruination of East Francia, was still to come. Yet now at least there seemed hope for Christendom. In 936, as Henry, succumbing at last to age and weariness, prepared to meet his maker, he set the seal on a lifetime's labours by refusing to sanction the carve up of his legacy. Instead, in a pointed reversal of Frankish custom, he bequeathed it entire to Otto, his eldest son: 'a great and far-spreading dominion – not one that had been handed down to him by his forefathers, but won instead by his own exertions, bestowed upon him by God alone'.[8]

And that the Almighty had indeed blessed the Saxons, and granted to them a role of fateful moment in His plans for Christendom, could be witnessed by virtue of a heavenly proof. Back in 926, the same year that had seen the truce signed with the Hungarians, Henry's attentions had been devoted to browbeating his brother king of Burgundy. By the terms of a treaty signed that year, Henry had agreed to hand over a chunk of the province of Swabia – what is now Switzerland and Alsace – in exchange for a treasure 'infinitely precious': a spear of terrible power. No one doubted that it was the Saxon king who had secured the bargain by this arrangement. Men claimed that the weapon had long ago belonged to Constantine – and that it had won for him the empire of the world. As well it might have done: for upon the head of the spear were crosses fashioned out of nails, those very same spikes of iron that had once pierced the hands and feet of Christ, 'joining the realm of the mortal to that of heaven'. The Saxons, whose ancestors, in their vulgar credulity, had imagined Woden swaying the world with a spear, could now contemplate with wonder an authentically earth-shaking relic. For such a weapon, in the hands of a great king, would surely render him as invincible as Constantine had been: 'certain of victory against all his enemies, visible and invisible, assured of perpetual triumph'.[9] And so for Henry it had proved.

But now he was dead; and the peoples of the *Reich* waited with bated breath to gauge the measure of their new king. Certainly, Otto could have had no illusions as to the full weight of the burden that was being laid upon his youthful shoulders: for at his coronation, it was made manifest to all Christendom. 'Drive away the enemies of Christ,' the Archbishop of Mainz instructed him in dreadful tones, handing him a sword. 'Establish an enduring peace for Christians everywhere.'[10] Yet if the trust being placed in the new king was awesome, then so too were the rituals that pronounced him worthy of it. Unlike his father, Otto had no compunction about being anointed with holy oil; nor in laying claim, very obviously, to the mantle of Charlemagne. Not only was the ceremony staged at the great emperor's capital of Aachen, but the Saxon king even made sure, in a pointed one-off, to dress for the occasion in the distinctive torso-hugging tunic of a Frank. To the dukes and great lords who stood assembled before the royal chapel, gazing up at Otto as he sat in splendour upon the throne of Charlemagne, the point could hardly have been driven home any more forcibly: the traditional notion of kingship as something uniquely elevated, sacred even, was back.

Delight at this among the battle-hardened magnates who had grown accustomed to Henry's more collegiate manner was, unsurprisingly, less than universal. Even as Otto, looking to celebrate his coronation in the by now traditional Saxon manner, headed eastwards across the Elbe to extort tribute and submission from the

Wends, so resentment was already festering among the great princes of the *Reich*. Particularly threatening was the mood in Franconia, where the aged Duke Eberhard had good cause to take umbrage at Otto's high-handedness: for he it was, after all, back in 919, who had done much to secure the throne for the Liudolfings. Yet even Eberhard's sense of disenfranchisement was as nothing compared with that of Otto's bitterest enemy, and most malignant rival of all: Henry, his younger brother. The two had been jockeying for position since childhood; and Henry, denied all royal status by the terms of his father's will, had responded to his exclusion with predictable fury. Indeed, so abusive had he become that Otto, rather than risk any disruption of his coronation, had ordered his brother to be imprisoned for the duration of the ceremony.

In general, however, naked though Henry's indignation was, the new king showed himself strikingly reluctant to punish it. Instead – as though out of a guilty sense that it might even be justified – he worked hard to appease it. Only a few months after his coronation, Otto arranged for Henry to marry the most eligible heiress in the realm: Judith, the daughter of the Duke of Bavaria. This was to grant his troublesome sibling a rare dignity – for Bavaria, despite the depredations inflicted upon it by the Hungarians, was a duchy endowed with resources of an almost regal scope. Indeed, of all the princedoms of the East, only Saxony itself offered more to an ambitious ruler. Otto's gamble in granting his brother the opportunity to put down roots there was, therefore, a considerable one – and doomed, it appeared, to failure. Henry, resolutely unmollified, continued to breathe sedition. His new in-laws, with reasons of their own to resent Otto's imperious style of lordship, were more than happy to back the young pretender in his plotting. From the Alps to the North Sea, the whole of East Francia began to seethe with rebellion.

Yet Otto himself, for all the scruples that inhibited him in his handling of his brother, remained, in his dealings with the other magnates of the realm, magnificently self-assured. Rather than attempt to appease insubordination, he preferred to slap it down: not

57

by inflicting savage tortures or brutal executions on those who presumed to defy him, but by the no less effective expedient of mocking
them. When Duke Eberhard, pursuing a feud with one of his vassals,
presumed to destroy a fortress sited on Saxon territory, Otto's
response was prompt. Having first whipped the Franks on the field of
battle, he next summoned the venerable duke and his retainers to
Magdeburg, where they were obliged to star in a great ritual of disgrace. To the raucous jeers of the whole town, a procession of
warhorses was led up to the *Hof*, and presented with splendid ceremony to the king: a fitting – and hugely expensive – expression of
ducal penitence. Yet mortifying though the sound of hoofs clopping
through Magdeburg must have been to the duke, even worse was to
follow: the yapping of hounds. The sight of the beasts, borne squirming and slavering in the arms of his red-faced henchmen, would have
been the final rubbing of Eberhard's nose in his own humiliation.
There was, for a Frankish nobleman, no greater shame than to be witnessed in public carrying a dog.

To be sure, the deliberate humbling of a duke, on the eve of a possible *Reich*-wide rebellion, might have been thought not the most
sensible of policies. Otto, however, had known what he was doing. To
be seen as a man of honour, of strength, of magnanimity; to be the
cynosure of watching, gawping crowds; to be enshrined in admiring
talk as a hero truly worthy of his rank; this, in East Francia, was the
very essence of lordship. Although the duties of governance were burdensome, even they were not so pressing as the need always to be on
display. So it was that Otto, conscious of the need to look as well as
behave like a king, had perfected an intimidating trick of throwing
glances that were said to flash like lightning. He also worked at accen-
tuating his prime physical asset: for he was, even by Saxon standards,
quite magnificently hairy. Not only did he grow his beard out, but he
made sure to display the 'the shaggy lion's mane'[11] which adorned his
chest at every opportunity. Restlessly, from day to day, from stopover
to stopover, Otto would grace his subjects with the roadshow of his
majesty. The spectacle he had staged in Magdeburg, of a king

enthroned in splendour, dispensing justice, in the full assurance of his power and physical strength, was one that he never tired of reprising. A great king, such as Otto aspired to be, had little choice but to promote himself as great.

True, there were some, Eberhard and his own brother Henry prominent among them, who aimed to call his bluff. In 938, they and their supporters finally rose in open revolt. Once again, however, Otto proved more than capable of turning a crisis to his own account. In 939, after a year of desperate struggle, he brought his enemies to crushing defeat on the banks of the Rhine, at Andernach. Two of the rebel dukes were left as corpses on the battlefield – and one of them was Eberhard. Otto, obliged to appoint his successor, coolly nominated himself. Franconia, from that moment on, was to serve him like Saxony, as a personal power base. His vaunting claims to greatness, so crucial to his authority as king, could now be raised on an impregnable bedrock of lands and wealth. Those who had presumed to question his prestige had served only to burnish it to an even more brilliant sheen. As in his peacetime migrations, so amid the carnage and chaos of war, Otto never neglected an opportunity to enhance the glory of his name. Indeed, such was his talent for grandstanding that not even being caught out in a palpable blunder could throw him off balance for long. Trapped in the course of one campaign on the opposite side of the Rhine to his vastly outnumbered men, he had barely broken a sweat. Instead, ordering the Holy Lance to be planted on the river bank, he had fallen to his knees, and begun to pray before it with a flamboyant and ostentatious fervour. His troops, inspired by this edifying spectacle, had duly pulled off a startling victory. Warrior king and talisman washed in Christ's holy blood: the two had proved themselves invincible together.

Henry, meanwhile, that fractious rebel against his brother's authority, had been left to nurse not only his injured pride but an arm that had been almost severed clean off in the fighting. Only his heavy armour – now more than ever the surest mark of rank in East Francia – had served to keep him from permanent disfigurement.

59

Bruised in both body and mind, he proved sufficiently chastened by the final collapse of the rebellion to seek an accommodation with his brother – and Otto, with his customary imperious magnanimity, was content to grant it. 'Be a lion in battle, but like a lamb when taking vengeance!'[12] So the wise advised – and besides, Henry's days of fratricidal ambition appeared brought to a close at last. In 947, he was installed by royal decree as the new Duke of Bavaria – and this time, Otto's gamble proved a sound one. Henry, although as restless and combative as ever, now had new opponents, and new horizons, in his sights.

For no sooner had he taken possession of his dukedom than he was leading his followers into the scorched and perilous no man's land that marked Bavaria's eastern frontier, and beyond which lay that breeding ground of pagan blood-drinkers, the plain of Hungary. An enterprise such as this was of an order to keep even Henry's hands full: for no one had ever before presumed to beard the Hungarians in their own lair. Yet though the fighting was of a predictably relentless ferocity, it was not, as events would prove, an altogether reckless initiative that the new Duke of Bavaria had launched: for in 950, he succeeded in inflicting an unheard-of humiliation upon the Hungarian warlords. Just as they had always dealt with the *Reich*, so now he dealt with them: breaking through into their heartlands, abducting their women and children, despoiling them of their gold. Such a triumph could not be hailed by the Bavarians with a wholly unqualified enthusiasm, for they knew that what their duke had done was, in effect, to fling a stone at a hornets' nest. The Hungarians, accustomed as they were to preying on their victims with impunity, were hardly the people now to turn the cheek themselves. A full-scale assault on the realm of the Eastern Franks would not be long postponed. The hour of reckoning was drawing near at last.

And it would be for Otto, as Christendom's greatest king, to pass the fearsome test. Almost two centuries had passed now since the Saxons, the objects of Charlemagne's mingled frustration and self-righteousness, had been brought to Christ at the point of his smoking sword; and still, by the Saxon aristocracy, it was taken for granted that warfare might be a Christian's ultimate duty. It was true that numerous churchmen, in the years following the conversion of Saxony, had sought tirelessly to combat this presumption – not only foreign missionaries, but native scholars too, those who had actually studied the Gospels and pondered their unsettling, pacific teachings. These could not help but appear bizarre to most Saxons, yet there had been heroic attempts made to propagate them, even so. A monkish poet, back in the very earliest days of Saxon Christianity, had gone so far as to put words directly into the Saviour's mouth: 'If I wished to fight, then I would make the great and mighty God aware of it, so that He would send me so many angels wise in warfare that no human beings could stand up to the force of their weapons.' So Christ had been imagined as telling Peter, at the moment of His arrest. 'We are to bear whatever bitter things our enemies do to us.'[13] A message not unsuited, it might have been thought, to its earliest listeners, still bleeding as they were from the wounds of the Frankish conquest. But to a people such as the Saxons, blessed by Providence, had subsequently become? That was a quite different matter. Once, it was true, they had been compelled to swallow the gall of defeat, and to humble themselves, and to bow their necks before their conquerors – but they had not been left forever prostrated in the dust. God's hand, manifesting itself through the irrefutable proof of all the great victories granted them, had restored to the Saxons their vanished glories – and multiplied them a hundredfold. And now a lord of Saxon blood sat on the Frankish throne, guarded about by his warriors, like 'angels wise in warfare' – and opposed to them were the hordes of a ravening paganism. Who was it, after all, who had entrusted the defence of East Francia to Otto, and endowed him with a martial splendour, and brought into his hands the Holy Lance, if not the Almighty Himself? A cloistered virtue, at such a moment, could hardly be relied upon for the saving of Christendom.

Anno Domini 954, and the storm broke at last. The Hungarians had chosen their moment well. Feuding among members of the Liudolfing clan, kept in check since the defeat of Henry's revolt, had recently erupted into flames once again. The principal agitator against Otto this time, however, was not his brother, but Liudolf, his eldest son – and the rebellion was directed as much against the Duke of Bavaria as against the king. Liudolf, resentful of his elders, and quite as impatient as his uncle had ever been for power, had secured allies for himself as far afield as Italy, and with these had succeeded in capturing Regensburg, the site of Henry's palace and treasury, and convulsing all of Bavaria. Henry himself, humiliated and fast sickening, had found himself impotent to retrieve the situation.

Simultaneously, on the borders of Saxony itself, where Otto's iron rule had brought his subjects there a measure of peace, the Wends were displaying an alarming upsurge of enthusiasm for their traditional pastimes: the slaughter of garrisons, the abduction of women, the lighting up of the Elbe by fire. Depredations such as these, which Otto had trusted stamped out for ever, spoke to a beleaguered East Francia of a peril even more menacing than the seemingly bottomless capacity of barbarism to renew itself; for the Wendish leader, a warlord of bloody reputation by the name of Stoinef, had recruited as his lieutenants two Saxon renegades. Wichmann and Ekbert were brothers: prominent noblemen, offshoots of the royal line, men who should properly have been fighting at the side of their lord. Darkness, it appeared, might shadow the souls of Christians as well as pagans. Evil might rise from within as well as without the realm of an anointed king.

Yet Otto did not despair. Rather, as was ever his habit in moments of crisis, he laid on a spectacular masterclass in the art of turning weakness into strength. Neglecting for the moment the Wendish threat to his own duchy, he marched instead for Bavaria, where he loudly accused his son of being in league with the Hungarians. The charge, true or not, had an immediate and devastating effect on Liudolf's fortunes. As the Hungarians withdrew from the *Reich* with their customary trains of looted treasure and stumbling captives, the revolt against Otto imploded. With summer fading into autumn,

Liudolf himself was brought to surrender. With winter melting into spring, the last outposts of the revolt followed him in submitting to their lawful duke. In April, Regensburg was finally restored to a now grievously ill Henry, and Bavaria could stand united once again.

And not a moment too soon. That summer of 955, even as eastern Saxony burned, grim news was brought to Otto from his dying brother. The Hungarians, swarming across the frontier, had returned to the *Reich* – and in numbers never seen before. The unprecedented scale of the invasion force, not to mention the presence in its train of siege engines, suggested a chilling possibility: that the Hungarians, after decades of contenting themselves with hit-and-run raids against Bavaria, had resolved at last upon its outright conquest. And yet, as Otto's entire reign had demonstrated, in peril might lie opportunity – and in the very ambitions of his enemies their potential ruin. Always, for as long as the Hungarians had been preying upon Christendom, they had delighted in outpacing the cumbersome armies of the Germans; but now at last, it seemed, they might be tempted into open battle. News that warfare on Saxony's frontier with the Wends was reaching an unprecedented pitch of ferocity would certainly have been brought to their leaders; and they had clearly calculated that Otto, if he did dare to confront them, would be able to summon only a fraction of the potential manpower of East Francia to his banner. And so it proved.

No more than a small bodyguard of Saxon horsemen could be spared for the desperate expedition to Bavaria. There were other duchies that sent no contingents at all. Of those princes who did answer Otto's summons, there were many who had been in open revolt against him only the previous summer. And yet still, with per-haps some three thousand warriors in his train, Swabians, Franconians and Bavarians as well as Saxons, and the Holy Lance borne proudly aloft, Otto did ride to war; and on 9 August, as he advanced southwards along the bank of the River Lech, a tributary of the Danube, he saw on the horizon ahead of him black smoke, and caught on the breeze a smell of death.

A few miles distant lay the city of Augsburg. There, in the fields before its eastern gate, the cathedral garrison had been desperately attempting to stave off the Hungarians' assault, while behind them men laboured to repair the crumbling ramparts, and women walked in procession, raising up tearful prayers. That the Almighty had heard these, and in the very nick of time too, even as the siege engines of the Hungarians were crawling towards the walls, was confirmed for the Augsburgers when the great pagan host, pausing in its assault, broke up abruptly and started streaming northwards. News that the King of East Francia had come against them did not, as it would once have done, prompt the Hungarians to turn tail and seek to elude him; instead, reassured that Otto was indeed grievously outnumbered, they prepared themselves to wipe him out. Twilight was already darkening over the Lech as they closed in on the tiny royal army. Halting for the night by the side of the river, they fed their horses, made sure of their bow strings and waited with a fierce expectancy for the dawn.

Otto's warriors, meanwhile, having spent the day in prayer and fasting, were looking forward to the morning with no less confidence. At sunrise, they swore solemn oaths of fellowship to one another, and then began their advance along the western bank, their heavy mail shirts glinting, their banners fluttering, their warhorses trampling down the dew-wet grass. It was Otto's intention to take the Hungarians by surprise; and yet, as had happened to him many years previously, in the war against his brother, it was he and his men who were ambushed first. The enemy, as lethally mobile as ever, emerged seemingly from nowhere, and fell upon their rearguard; three of the seven divisions under Otto's command were routed; only desperate resistance by a fourth, the Franconian, prevented the fighting from being over almost before it had begun. The king, granted a crucial breathing space by the valour of the Franks, frantically marshalled what remained of his host into the semblance of a battle line; and then, above the hissing of arrows, the screaming of the wounded and the keening '*hiu-hiu*' of the Hungarians, he cried out to his men, calling on them in the name of God to unsheathe their 'invincible swords'. 'For

64

who are we, to submit to such an enemy? We, who should blush at the very idea! We, who are the lords of almost all of Europe!'[14]

So it was, at the great tipping point of his reign, that Otto spoke not as a Saxon, not even as King of East Francia, but as the defender of all Christendom; and it was as a Christian that he now urged his followers into battle. Wheeling his horse round to face the enemy, he reached for the Holy Lance; and then, answering the harsh ululations of the Hungarians with a proud war cry of his own, he led the charge. Behind and all around him, the hoofs of their great warhorses making the field of the Lech to shake, there galloped his cavalry, the *loricati*, the men of iron: a strike force of killers long forged for such a moment. Although their numbers were sorely diminished even from the host that had left camp at dawn, there was to be no withstanding Otto's warriors that day. With a surging crash, the steel-armoured tide flooded over the hordes of the enemy, hacking and spearing and trampling them down; for against the *loricati*, trapped at close quarters, the unarmoured Hungarians found themselves defenceless.

The slaughter was prodigious; and of those who attempted to flee, many were drowned in the waters of the Lech, others cornered in villages where they had sought refuge and burned to death, while others still were hunted down like wild beasts. It was this harrying of the defeated, even more than the Battle of the Lech itself, that proved the true calamity for the Hungarians; and Otto, as harsh towards his pagan enemies as he was magnanimous towards Christian rebels, set the seal on his triumph with an act of calculated savagery. Against every usage and custom of war, he chose not to ransom the Hungarian princes who had fallen into his hands. Instead – one last gift to his brother as he lay on his deathbed – Otto ordered them sent to Regensburg. There, strung up from the public gallows, the warlords who had thought to subdue all Bavaria and far beyond were left to twist and rot.

Otto, even as the corpses of his deadliest enemies were being picked clean by carrion birds, was already heading north, to confront Stoinef, the Wendish warlord, and a second great host of pagans. It was late in the campaigning season by the time he arrived back in Saxony, amid 'wild dancing and celebration';[15] and not until 16 October did he at last bring Stoinef to battle. No less than it had been at the Lech, however, Otto's ultimate triumph was as brutal as it was complete. The paganism that for so long had menaced the borders of the *Reich* suffered a second decapitation. Otto, as if to demonstrate this in the most literal manner possible, ordered the beheading of all his Wendish prisoners of war, while the head of Stoinef himself, who had fallen in the battle, was sawn off and mounted on a pole. Only towards Wichmann and Ekbert, the two Saxon brothers who had so grievously betrayed him, did Otto display his more habitual magnanimity, permitting them to return from the exile into which they had fled after Stoinef's defeat, and restoring to them their lands; but they were his countrymen – and Christians.

Mercy, that virtue proper to any lord, was not to be wasted on the barren soil of pagans' hearts. East Francia had suffered too long and too bloodily at the hands of the Hungarians for her king to countenance any notion of toleration or compromise now. With barbarians so insensate in their savagery that they dared to trample upon the laws of the Almighty, there could be no accommodation: so Otto devoutly believed. Cutting the pagans down, he had done so as God's champion. That this was no arrogant self-deception on his part appeared, after the *annus mirabilis* of 955, beyond dispute. For the first time in almost a century, the eastern ramparts of Christendom stood secure. A new march, constituted on Otto's direct orders, would henceforward serve to keep the *Reich* from all further Hungarian incursions: 'the Eastern Command', as it was known, or '*Ostarrichi*' – 'Austria'. Not since the conquest of Saxony had there been such a victory won for Christ. Not since Charlemagne had there been so puissant a Christian king.

No wonder that the men who had followed Otto to the Lech should have hailed him, in the aftermath of the great battle, as '*imperator*': a Latin title of portentous ambiguity. Once, in the fabulously distant past of Rome, the word had been used to acclaim a victorious general; but it had also, over the centuries, come to possess a far more fateful meaning – 'emperor'. In the West, the holders of that title had long been withering away in dignity – until, by 924, there had been no one to lay claim to it at all. Such a vacancy, to a man such as Otto, could hardly help but present a glittering opportunity. Already, back in 951, he had ventured over the Alps in an attempt to secure an imperial coronation for himself, until the crisis back in Bavaria had obliged him to abandon the effort. Even four years later, when there was no one who could justly dispute the merit of his claims, the rivalries of Rome's fractious princelings, as limited in their achievements as Otto was famed for his, threatened to render any expedition to the city quixotic. Like hungry dogs tossed shreds of meat, the various factions scrapping it out in Italy served to diminish the value of the very prizes over which they fought – and it was the papacy, that supreme prize, which had come to seem the most diminished of all.

In 955, five months after the Battle of the Lech, open scandal made explicit what had long been evident: the subordination of the Holy See to the ambitions of a single clan. For decades, the Theophylacts, Rome's most powerful family, had been securing the election of assorted supine puppets to the Lateran; now they went one better, and elevated one of their own. Octavian, who had succeeded to the leadership of the Theophylacts only the year previously, was hardly a man cut out for a papal career. Notorious, even by the standards of the Roman aristocracy, for his promiscuity and partying, he made little effort to disguise his boredom with anything that smacked of the spiritual. He was also barely sixteen. Not even a change of name to the more satisfyingly apostolic 'John' could dampen the gossip that was soon swirling around the teenage Holy Father.* It was claimed that he had converted an entire wing of the Lateran into a brothel; that when

---

* Only one man had previously changed his name on being elevated to the Papacy: John II, back in 533. Following Octavian's initiative, however, the practice became increasingly common, until, by the beginning of the eleventh century, it was the norm.

he was not blinding or castrating priests, he was ordaining them in his hunting stables; that he was in the habit of offering up drunken toasts to Satan. A pope capable of such blasphemies was hardly likely to prove accommodating to a mere earthly king. Saviour of Christendom or no, Otto and his imperial ambitions cut little ice with John XII.

It did not take long, however, for the papal tearaway to be tripped up by his own ambitions. Otto, well practised in the art of leaving his adversaries to fall flat on their faces, watched patiently from beyond the Alps as John, proving himself as ill-disciplined in the field of diplomacy as in every other sphere, steadily affronted his neighbours. By 960, he found himself menaced on all sides by predatory princes. After an abortive attempt to meet them in battle – yet another scandal to set alongside all the others – he found himself with little option but to do as Stephen II and Leo III had done before him: look north for a protector. Late that year, a frantic embassy was dispatched to East Francia; and Otto, needing no further encouragement, swung immediately into action. By the following year, he had secured both Lombardy for himself and the papal patrimony for John; and in February 962, having arrived in Rome at last, he exacted his price. The Pope, lowering the imperial diadem on to Otto's head, confirmed him in the title that his warriors had first bestowed upon him seven years previously, beside the Lech. All was now official. There ruled, once again, an emperor in the West.

But what precisely, in an age far removed from that of Charlemagne, let alone that of the ancient Caesars, did being an emperor mean? John, and Rome's other clan leaders too, had cheerfully presumed that the title would prove an empty one: an optimistic notion, and one of which Otto was quick to disabuse them. When John, attempting to pull rank, sought to make his customary trouble, the new emperor briskly convened a synod amid the awful splendour of St Peter's, and had the Pope arraigned on multiple charges of moral turpitude. It did not take long for the accused, palpably guilty as he was, to be convicted, deposed and replaced with a candidate more amenable to Otto's wishes; but John, citing the ancient principle that no earthly power could judge the Bishop of Rome, refused to accept the verdict. The result was an outrage: two competing popes. Not even John's death a year later from a stroke, the result of overly strenuous grapplings with a married woman, served to ease the tribulations of the Holy See.* Otto, leaving no one in any doubt as to what he judged his prerogatives to be, continued with his policy of crushing all hints of papal independence. One pope, Benedict V, merely for the sin of having been elected without imperial approval, had his staff ceremonially broken over his head, before being exiled for life to Hamburg; his successor, John XIII, installed and maintained in office at the point of Otto's sword, scrabbled with unsurprising servility to do his master's every bidding. A humiliation for the papacy, naturally – but resounded splendidly to the emperor's already refulgent prestige.

Sure and just indeed, the Saxons might have reflected, were the workings of Providence. Less than two centuries it had taken the Almighty to raise them from their condition of utter ruin to one in which they stood as the very shapers of Christendom. Few had seen it coming – not even among the ranks of the Saxon royal family itself. Gerberga, the Queen of West Francia, writing in her despair to Adso of Montier-en-Der, had done so barely a decade before the Battle of the Lech: a victory won by a man who was not merely her compatriot, but her elder brother. That the heirs to the dignity of the Roman Empire might prove to be her own family had simply never crossed Gerberga's mind. Now, however, with Otto enthroned as emperor, the master of Rome herself, who was there left to doubt it? Who left to doubt that he and his empire stood as the surest bulwark against those encroaching shadows that had so oppressed Gerberga's dreams: the shadows of chaos, of evil, of Antichrist?

All his reign, Otto had known it his duty as a Christian king to combat God's enemies on the fields of battle. His subjects – despite the earnest attempts of missionaries and scholars to persuade them

---

* An alternative version of his death claims that John XII was murdered by the outraged husband.

otherwise – had known it too. Deep in their souls, the Saxons had understood, as only a people brought to Christ through conquest could possibly have understood, that the God they worshipped was indeed a god of war. This was a presumption that Otto, with the Bishop of Rome directly under his thumb, was now in a position to propagate in the very capital of Christendom. No matter that it ran directly contrary to the traditional teaching of the Church. The days when Christians from the more ancient heartlands of the faith had condescended to the Saxons as ignorant barbarians were long gone. Who was John XIII to lecture the emperor, his patron and guardian? Indeed, far from Otto being rendered more Roman by his sojourn in the ancient capital, it was the papacy, huddled in his far-spreading shadow, humiliated by its blatant dependency and diminished by ceaseless scandal, that appeared to be adopting the perspective of the Saxons. In 967, John XIII confirmed this impression by formally establishing Magdeburg, that stern and bristling stronghold on the frontier of Christendom, as an archbishopric. Just as the city had long served Saxony as its foremost bulwark against the malice of the pagan Wends, so now was it to serve the Church. By papal fiat, all the Slavs who dwelt beyond the Elbe were pronounced subject to Magdeburg's new archbishop: 'both those converted, and those to be converted still'.[16]

So was constituted a fortress of the Christian faith as strong in its proofs of God's favour as were the eastern marches in their ramparts and their armoured horsemen. This was a destiny for which Otto had long been preparing Magdeburg. As far back as 937, only a year into his reign, he had founded a great monastery there, and, from that moment on, had never ceased to lavish splendid gifts upon it: 'precious marble, gold and gems';[17] estates both in Saxony and on the far bank of the Elbe; dues of silver raised as tribute from the Wends. Here, it might have been thought, was a standing provocation: the endowment of such a treasure house in the full view of the malignant heathen. Fortunate, then, and ample evidence of Otto's careful planning, that the saint to whom it had been dedicated was well qualified to guard his own.

Maurice, the captain of the Theban Legion, had long been a favourite of the Saxons. Typically, they admired him not as the passive martyr who had preferred death to the drawing of his sword in an unjust cause, but rather as 'Christ's own soldier';[18] and in 961, looking to imbue his favoured monastery with a truly celestial impregnability, Otto had ordered the saint's relics translated there from their former resting place, 'to the salvation of Saxony'.[19] Just as the emperor himself, long the shield of his kingdom, could now bend his frown upon the East and know that everyone would shrink from it, so had it been charged to St Maurice, that warrior of God, to stand sentinel over the Elbe, dauntless and unflinching, the heavenly warden of the *Reich*. No wonder that in time, even the Holy Lance should have come to be regarded as his, and its association with Constantine quite forgotten. To the Saxons, Maurice appeared infinitely less distant than did a long-dead Roman emperor. It was only two centuries previously, after all, that their ancestors had been putting their faith in a similarly supernatural being and his spear.

The vision of warfare that the Saxons still clung to, as an undertaking that might indeed be blessed by the heavens, remained from that past; but the pagan kings of old had never been brought to such prosperity by Woden as Otto had attained by the grace of Christ. By the time he died, on 7 May 973, he was famed across the whole of Christendom as a king 'who had ruled his subjects with a fatherly beneficence, freed them from their enemies, conquered the arrogant foe by force of arms, subjugated Italy, destroyed the sanctuaries of pagan gods among neighbouring peoples, and established churches and orders of clergy everywhere'.[20] Even beyond the frontiers of the *Reich*, in lands still steeped in heathenism, Otto and his fearsome god, the celestial emperor who had so palpably brought the Saxons all their greatness, were spoken of with awe.

With envy too. It was true that the Wends, with the sullen obduracy of the brutalised, still spurned the faith of their conquerors; but they were coming to seem a mere island of paganism, one lapped by an ever-rising tide of conversions. East of them, for instance, Miesco, the duke of a barbarous people known as the Poles, had been formally baptised in 966. His first church, a chapel built inside the stronghold of Gniezno, had been begun shortly after that. In due course, so enthused was he by his new religion that he would take a Saxon, a former nun, no less, to be his bride. Meanwhile, in the same year as Otto's death, a bishopric was established south of the Wendish marches, in the young dukedom of Bohemia, led by priests trained at Magdeburg. Even in Hungary, where the war bands shattered at the Lech had for years been licking their wounds and questioning the gods who had so comprehensively failed them, missionaries from Bavaria were reaping a prodigious harvest of souls. It was an age of miracles indeed.

No longer, in short, was it Christendom that lay under siege. No longer was it East Francia that had to fear for its borders. No longer, after the reign of Otto the Great, who had redeemed both his own kingdom and the Roman Empire from the very brink of destruction, did the world's end appear quite so sure and imminent.

Everybody Wants to Rule the World

In Constantinople, however, they had their doubts. There, like autumn leaves borne on the chill winds of the Bosporus, anxieties swirled and gusted through the streets of the great city. Innumerable proofs of a looming convulsion in human affairs had begun to afflict the venerable empire. Earthquakes and thunderbolts, torrential rains and fearsome signs lighting up the sky; all, to those who tracked them, appeared to foretell 'that the expected Second Coming of the Saviour and God is near, at the very gates'.[21]

More unsettling than any of these wonders, however, were reports of what in East Francia had prompted only relief and rejoicing: the rout of pagan armies. For so long had the citizens of Constantinople been habituated to defeat, and to the dull slog of staving off their empire's total ruin, that they had quite forgotten their ancient habits

72

of victory. The reign of their city's founder, who had been the master of Christendom in fact as well as name, now seemed incalculably remote from them. They had come to regard the monuments of Constantine and his successors, all the haughty statues and triumphal arches that still adorned the New Rome, as the repositories of eerie portents, profoundly alien to themselves. In the weathered frieze-work of such trophies, in the scenes of battle, and fettered captives, and emperors riding in glory, they identified messages bequeathed to them by ancient necromancers: prophecies set in stone, foretelling how the world would end.[22] Now, with prisoners and treasures once again being paraded through Constantinople, 'in so great a quantity as to resemble an abundantly flowing river',[23] the gawping citizens felt a sense of dread as well as pride. Surely, with the frontiers of their empire everywhere expanding, the days of the fabled last Roman emperor, who was destined to rule the whole world, were near at hand? Learned scholars, performing abstruse calculations, confirmed that his coming was indeed only decades away.[24] And after him, and his death upon Golgotha, the reign of Antichrist.

Small wonder, then, that the citizens of Constantinople should have regarded with some ambivalence a programme of imperial expansion that threatened such a climax. Nor did it help that they were being bled white to fund it. The larger the army, and the length-ier the campaigning on distant frontiers, the higher their taxes. It was no coincidence that the most proficient of their warrior emperors, the aptly named Nicephorus, or 'Victory Bearer', should also have been the most widely hated. A battle-hardened ascetic from the empire's eastern front, capable of drilling a pike through the front of an armoured enemy and out the other side, and with the appearance, so it was reported,[25] of a wildly bristling pig, he had paraded a hair-shirted distaste for the sensibilities of the metropolis. The same man who, on the frontiers of the empire, had busied himself with the capture of 'more than a hundred towns and fortresses',[26] had also, back in Constantinople, transformed his palace into an army camp, throwing up imposing battlements to screen himself from his subjects, and hunkering down behind them. A fruitless precaution, however – for his enemies had lurked everywhere.

In 969, his own nephew, an ambitious young officer by the name of John Tzimiskes, had put himself at the head of a plot to usurp the throne. Shortly before Christmas, he and an assassination squad had rowed across the Bosphorus to where the walls of the palace met the sea. There, dangling from an upper balcony, they had found a basket, lowered in anticipation of their arrival. Men would later say that it was the empress herself, enraptured by Tzimiskes's inexhaustible aptitude for sexual gymnastics, who had betrayed her husband with this fatal act of treachery; for she was known to have been as vicious as she was insatiable. Whatever the truth of the rumour, however, it is certain that Tzimiskes and his accomplices, stealing into the emperor's private chapel, had there found their victim wrapped in a bearskin, snoring gently on the floor. A hail of knives had done their work. Nicephorus's head, severed to provide a token of Tzimiskes's accession, had been brandished from a palace window. The people of Constantinople, revelling in the excitement of regime change, had cheered the murderers, and the dispatch of the greatest conqueror to have graced their empire's throne for three long centuries and more.

In the West too, at the Saxon court, news of the coup had been greeted with delight. No surprise, perhaps, that Otto and Nicephorus, both of them peerless warriors, both of them claimants to the title of emperor, should have regarded the pretensions of the other with resentment. In 968, hostilities between Christendom's two greatest monarchs had come to a head: Otto, attempting to annex southern Italy, had invaded the territories there still ruled from Constantinople; shortly afterwards, finding his campaign bogged down, and resolved to redeem the situation through a display of quite breathtaking nerve, he had sent an ambassador to the imperial capital and demanded a princess for his younger son and namesake, Prince Otto. This was a gambit that Nicephorus, unsurprisingly, had dismissed with furious snorts of scorn; but Tzimiskes, a well-honed athlete much given to vaulting over horses, had shown himself more willing to take a leap into the dark. The youthful Otto may have been barbarian – yet he was not a wholly worthless catch. Liudolf, the rebellious crown prince, had died back in 957 – leaving Otto as his father's only heir. Whoever married him, so Tzimiskes had calculated, was likely to end up Empress of the West. A tempting prospect – even by the standards of Constantinople. So it was that in 972 a young girl of perhaps twelve or thirteen, adorned in the heavy robes of an authentic Byzantine princess, weighed down with gold and precious stones, and accompanied by an intimidating train of flunkeys, treasure chests and changes of wardrobe, had been dispatched to Rome. Her name was Theophanu; and both the elder and the younger Otto had been dazzled by the show of her arrival. The marriage contract, inscribed on parchment painted to look like purple silk, had licensed the most splendid wedding in Saxon history. St Peter's had provided the venue; the Pope himself had officiated; the very union of East and West had seemed achieved as the squat and ginger-haired groom was joined to his willowy bride.

Only in the complaints of a few curmudgeons, muttered behind the emperor's back, had the awkward truth been whispered: Theophanu was not, as everyone at the Saxon court had initially been led to believe, Tzimiskes's daughter at all, but his niece. Some had even suggested that she be returned to Constantinople as damaged goods. Otto I had refused. It had not taken him long to appreciate the pearl he had obtained in his new daughter-in-law. By the time of his death, barely a year after his son's wedding, Theophanu was already casting the spell of her star quality over East Francia. Indeed, so protean were her abilities that the Saxons could not even agree as to what they were. Some praised their empress for her modesty, 'which is, of course, a rare thing in a Greek';[27] others for the very opposite, an eloquence which they felt might easily shade into 'insolent prattling'.[28] All, however, were agreed on her talent for forging the kind of political friendships that were so essential in the *Reich*, fractured as it was, and fractious too. On her own, Theophanu could hardly hope to mitigate the more turbid characteristics of her husband's court, and yet her very presence at the side of Otto II, elegant, silken and bejewelled, served as a constant reminder of a very different style of monarchy: a touch, in the heart of Saxony, of the ineffable glamour of the New Rome.

For Theophanu herself, the experience of life in the West, where displays of riotous merriment were held to impair the kingly dignity not a jot, would certainly have provided a most striking contrast with the decorousness she had left behind. The court of the *Basileus*, its conceit burnished by its antiquity, persisted in its sublime ambition to hold a mirror up to heaven. The emperor himself, elevated and aloof, presided over his table as the image of Christ; the empress by his side as the Virgin Mary; even the eunuchs, sexless go-betweens, flitted around in the manner of angels. Back in the West, where one of the distinctive marks of royal table manners was held to be the ferocious cracking open of animal bones for their marrow, such role playing would have been regarded as so stiff and chill as to be grotesque; and yet Otto II, under Theophanu's influence, showed himself not immune to its appeal. So it was, for instance, in the years following his accession, that he and his wife paraded their devotion to the Virgin with a quite exceptional show of piety – even as the Virgin herself, not previously famed in the West for having dripped with priceless jewellery, began to be portrayed across the *Reich* in the manner of a Byzantine empress. The glory of this, even as it dignified Theophanu, naturally redounded upon Otto as well – and hinted at the aspirations that were starting to gnaw at him.

For less than a decade into his reign, and East Francia was already coming to seem altogether too cabined a stage for his dreams. Whether it was the whisperings of his empress that had seduced him or the impetuosity of his own desires, Otto, bold and wilful, appeared no longer content with the sway of his native land. In the winter of 980, he and Theophanu left Saxony for Italy. By the spring, they were in Rome. Here, in the months that followed, Otto drew up plans to subdue the whole peninsula. A primordial fantasy, one that had haunted many generations of princes, was once again stirring from its troubled sleep. The dream of an empire without limits, of a universal dominion – of a Rome reborn.

Yet it remained the nature of this phantasm to mock all who sought to embrace it. Beyond the southernmost limit of Otto's Italian kingdom, as tantalising as any mirage, there stretched regions that in ancient times had been both the playground and the breadbasket of the Caesars. Ruins from this fabulous past – palaces and temples, theatres and baths – still dominated the landscape, their hulking stonework defying the passage of the centuries, whether looming up from the curve of the Bay of Naples or frowning down upon the winding, inland roads. All their massy grandeur, however, served only to emphasise their abandonment – and the desolation of the badlands in which they now stood. It was barely a decade previously, after all, that southern Italy had been a war zone, fought over by the rival empires of East and West; and now, in the summer of 981, Otto II was minded to make it so again. The bonds of alliance woven by his marriage to Theophanu had already snapped: for in Constantinople John Tzimiskes was dead – poisoned by a eunuch, it was claimed – and Theophanu herself, implacably hostile to the dynasty that had replaced her uncle's, clearly believed the rumour true. In September, when the Saxon emperor, riding at the head of a great force of iron-sheathed *loricati*, advanced southwards out of Rome, his queen was by his side. That it was Otto's intention to lay claim to the entire inheritance of the ancient empire, in defiance of the new regime in Constantinople, Theophanu knew and surely approved. Empress of the West, perhaps she dared to imagine herself raised to rule the East as well.

Not that the new regime in Constantinople was the only enemy facing her husband in his ambition to lay claim to Italy – let alone the world beyond. As Otto and his horsemen clattered southwards that autumn, they knew that there lurked ahead of them a danger far deadlier and more immediate than the garrisons of the New Rome. Marks of it were everywhere. By the roadside, ancient towns stood abandoned and crumbling, while in the distance new settlements

Italy in the reign of Otto II

clung nervously to hilltops, hunched against the horizon, and ringed about by walls. Alongside the coast, and especially the banks of estuaries, the desolation grew even more menacing. There, as the Saxons watered their horses, they found no vineyards, or villages, or fields, but only desolation – and over it all a stillness like that of a rifled grave. Terror, in southern Italy, came surest by the sea.

Indeed, what the tattoo of thundering hoofs had once sounded out to those in the path of the Hungarians, the glimpse of triangular sails on the Mediterranean signalled to those who lived anywhere south of the Alps. The pirates, although they had originally spread from Africa, were certainly not confined to the lower reaches of Christendom. Some, sailing into the waters off Marseille, had secured a base for themselves on Frankish soil, at a village named Garde-Freinet, securely situated on a cliff top, and surrounded by bristling cacti, 'so that if any man stumbled against one of them it would cut clean through him like a sword'.[29] Others took to the Alps, where they infested the mountain passes. Others, in the most shocking and impious predation of all, had established their vipers' nest beside the mouth of the River Garigliano – less than a hundred miles south of Rome itself. The Holy City, its surrounds laid to waste by decades of plundering, had found itself being throttled. Even the horses in the papal stables had begun to starve. A succession of popes had begged, cajoled and exhorted their neighbours to flush out the corsairs. Finally, in 915, after decades of papal hectoring, and an unprecedented alliance of assorted Italian powers, the lair had been swept clean at last. The Holy Father himself, in his excitement at having helped to forge such a victory, had charged the enemy twice. Heaven's forgiveness of this offence, witnessed by the startling but widely attested appearance of Saints Peter and Paul in the battle line, had provided a fitting measure of the crisis.

Now, however, the corsairs were returning to their former haunts. The shadow of peril was deepening and lengthening northwards once again. Otto's determination to confront it even through the rigours of a winter campaign was a reflection less of bravado than alarm.

Pledged as he was to the defence of Rome, he knew that the Holy City was the prize of which the pirates had been dreaming for more than a century. Why, back in 846, they had even dared to sail up the Tiber, and sack St Peter's itself. Stripping the shrine bare of all its treasures, they had ritually desecrated its altar, to the scandal of the faithful everywhere, and flung a spear at an icon of Christ. Blood, it was said, had immediately begun to flow from the wound; but the pirates had only jeered, and boasted that they had made the god of the Christians bleed.

It was a terrifying prospect, then, that the descendants of such men might sweep into Rome again. Who precisely were they, these blasphemers, who had dared to scoff at Christ Himself? Pagans, self-evidently; but there were few, even among their victims, who cared to know anything more than that. It was not the superstitions of the corsairs that made them hated, but rather their cruelty, their savagery, their greed. Why should any Christian care what such monsters might believe? True, the odd dark rumour had arisen: that the origins of the corsairs lay in the aptly merciless sands of Arabia; that they prostrated themselves in prayer before idols; that the greatest of their gods was named 'Mahound'. Also dimly recalled was the manner in which their ancestors had once ranged far beyond the bounds of the Mediterranean, burning and looting deep into Francia, indeed, as far north as Poitiers; and that only their defeat there in a great battle, at the hands of Charlemagne's grandfather, had served to roll them back.

All that, however, had long since faded from the memories of most Christians; and if those in the eye of the storm generally responded to their tormentors with an indomitable lack of curiosity, then those far away in Francia enjoyed an even profounder ignorance. Certainly, to those riding in Otto's train, the enemy ahead of them would hardly have appeared an exceptional one. A relish for violence and plunder was, in the opinion of the Saxons, the mark of pagans everywhere. Both the Wends and the Hungarians had preyed on the fold of Christendom; and both of them had been mightily repulsed. Why, then, should the emperor's current enemies not be crushed in a similar manner? Indeed, there seemed little to suggest that they and their kinsmen, the race of pagans known by the learned as 'Saracens', might be an enemy of Christendom like no other.

Theophanu, however, riding by her husband's side, would have offered Otto an altogether more chilling perspective. In Constantinople, even young girls in their nurseries had heard of the Saracens, and learned to shiver at their name. During all her long reign as the Queen of Cities, the New Rome had faced many terrible enemies; but none so terrible as those which, like lightning from a clear blue sky, had blazed out of the Arabian desert more than three centuries previously, and in the course of a bare few decades conquered for themselves the fairest portion of the Christian world. From Carthage in the West, where St Augustine had once studied, to Jerusalem in the East, with its incomparably holy shrines, all had been lost to the empire of the New Rome. Twice the Saracens had sought to capture Constantinople herself, their armies massed jackal-like on the shore of Europe, their ships crowding the Bosphorus. Twice, by the grace of the Virgin, protectress of the Holy City, they had been repulsed. The empire had been held together.

Still, though, the flood tides had continued to lap at its ramparts. In southern Anatolia, along the margins of a dominion much shrunken from its former greatness, raiding parties of infidel fighters – '*mujahidin*', as they termed themselves – had yearly stained the mountain passes with blood, until Nicephorus, 'the pale death of the Saracens',[30] had at last, and with a mighty effort, succeeded in pushing back the frontier. Even now, with the empire at its largest extent in centuries, the soldiers of the New Rome could not afford to relax their guard. Just as they knew Constantinople to be the bulwark of Christendom, so too did their enemies. The West, which imagined the Saracens pagans like any other pagans, was deluding itself. These were no pagans. These were something infinitely more menacing. That Constantinople remained, as she had always been, the prize most hungered after by the Saracens reflected a sense of mission on their part that no pagan would ever have understood: the belief that all the universe would one day submit to their faith.

Where had it come from, this presumptuous and terrifying heresy? 'Many false prophets will arise,' Christ had warned his disciples, 'and lead many astray'[31] – and so it had proved. 'Mahound', whom scholars in the West took for an idol, had in truth, their Byzantine counterparts knew, been something quite different: the founder of the Saracens' pestiferous superstition, and a veritable 'forerunner of Antichrist'.[32] Through his life and teachings, he had provided his followers with their surest model of behaviour, a model that all in Constantinople found so abhorrent as to seem diabolical. Christ, seized by His enemies, had ordered Peter to put away his sword; but Mahound – or Mohammed, as the Saracens called their prophet – had gloried in war and conquest.

Startling evidence of this bellicosity had been obtained by Nicephorus, in the course of his victorious campaigns, when he had captured a fortress containing a truly fearsome relic: a sword that the Saracens claimed had belonged to their prophet himself. '*Zulfiqar*', they called it; 'the Cleaver of Vertebrae'. Fitting weapon for a man who had, if the Saracens' own boasts were to be believed, fought in battles, staged mass executions and even commissioned murder squads.[33] 'Do prophets come with sword and chariot?' So the Byzantines, from the very onset of the Saracens' assaults upon them, had asked in revulsion. That Mohammed had indeed been 'an impostor', and his heresy an affliction sent by God as punishment for their sins, appeared to them beyond all doubt. 'There is no truth to be found in the so-called prophet. There is only the shedding of blood.'[34]

It was true that the Saracens were not alone in believing that instruments of war might be cherished of God. Otto, as he advanced into enemy territory, had the Holy Lance go before him. The more barbarian he, the Byzantines might well have retorted. No matter that they had been obliged for centuries to fight against enemies pledged to the capture of their holy city and the utter prostration of their faith, they had still, throughout it all, clung with a heroic obstinacy to the conviction that war was evil – indeed, 'the worst of all evils'.[35] That this sat awkwardly with the venerable claims of the New Rome to universal rule was something that most in Constantinople were content, by and large, to overlook. Gazing into the murky depths of human nature, and drawing on the teachings of the Fathers of their Church, they had judged that a lust for conquest could not help but corrupt the soul. What surer proof of this was there than the Saracens themselves, in whom violence and sanctimony appeared blended to such deadly effect? 'Fight those who believe not in God,'[36] Mohammed had commanded his followers: an injunction that, to the Byzantines who had for so long borne its brunt, appeared nothing but the most vicious hypocrisy, merely 'a licence to loot in religion's name'.[37] Especially repugnant to them was the claim, which for centuries had inspired the Saracen faithful on their larcenous raids, that any warrior who fell far from his own country, in the struggle to spread the dominion of his faith, might be reckoned a martyr, his sins forgiven, his soul translated to paradise. When Nicephorus, who had lived altogether too long 'in the shadows of swords',* had made the shocking demand of his bishops that they sanction a matching doctrine, one that would grant to any soldier who died in defence of the Christian empire a martyr's crown, they had recoiled in the utmost horror. The Church's ruling on the matter, they had pointed out with icy finality, was clear. Any soldier who shed blood, even in defence of his fellow Christians, existed in a state of sin: only three years of the strictest penance could serve to purge him of the offence. Trust to Providence, the Church advised, rather than to the swords of sinful men. God's hand would achieve all. In due course – and perhaps sooner rather than later, if the forecasts of the world's imminent end were to be believed – global dominion would be restored to Constantinople. In the meantime, however, it was the duty of the empire's leaders to man the ramparts,

---

* Mohammed, in a celebrated hadith (*The Book on Government*, 4681), declared that 'the gates of Paradise are under the shadows of the swords': a sentiment profoundly shocking to Byzantine sensibilities.

to patrol the frontiers and always 'to prefer peace above all else, and refrain from war'.[38]

Small wonder, then, that the instincts of the Byzantine military, to a quite striking degree, should have inclined to the defensive. Better the negotiations of diplomats, the payment of bribes and tributes, even the exercise of treachery, than open combat. Battle and the loss of life were to be avoided at all costs. So it was, for instance, in southern Italy, where the garrisons were perilously undermanned, that the high command had made little attempt to combat the Saracen incursions, preferring instead to sit them out. To a man such as Otto, and a people such as the Saxons, it was a policy that could not help but appear pusillanimous.

In January 982, when the mailed horsemen of East Francia first crossed into Byzantine territory, they too were met by bolted gates, just as the corsairs had been. Infuriated by the refusal of his fellow Christians to join him in the campaign against the Saracens, their common foe, Otto nevertheless bided his time, giving them every opportunity to submit; but by April his patience was exhausted. News had reached him that in Sicily, long a stronghold of the corsairs, a Saracen prince was mustering a massive expeditionary force against him; and Otto, resolved as he was to confront this menace head on, knew that he would need a secure base in his rear. Accordingly, 'after a brief but forceful attack',[39] he seized the port of Taranto from its Byzantine garrison, and formally proclaimed himself, in portentous terms, sole Emperor of Rome. With the city echoing to the sound of warhorses being shod, hauberks being prepared and over two thousand reinforcements clattering through the streets, Otto's self-justification for this step could hardly have been more ringing. Constantinople, through her own cowardice and feebleness, had forfeited all rights to the name of Roman. No longer did she deserve to be ranked as the shield of Christendom. The title was now Otto's alone.

In July, its standards proudly fluttering, the massive task force assembled for the conquest of southern Italy duly advanced against the Saracens, cornered them south of Cotrone by the sea, engaged them in a great and terrible battle – and was annihilated. Most of Otto's heavy cavalry, the shock force of the *Reich*, perished amid the carnage. The cream of the nobility too. Otto himself, obliged to borrow a horse from a passing Jew and ride it out into the sea, barely escaped with his life. To compound his humiliation, the ship that rescued him, 'a galley of marvellous length and speed',[40] had been dispatched to Italian waters from Constantinople. 'Let us hope', the mortified Otto found himself muttering to its captain, 'that your emperor, my brother, will be a loyal friend to me in my time of need.'[41] Not that he had any intention of hanging around to find out. Arriving off the coast where Theophanu was waiting for him, he plunged into the sea and swam frantically ashore, there to be reunited with his wife and his few surviving troops: chastened, mightily relieved still to be alive, and dripping wet.

So ended Otto's attempts to sweep the Saracens into the sea. Rumour would subsequently have it that Theophanu, furious at her husband for his incompetence, had insisted, with a tactless flare-up of patriotism, that her countrymen would never have blundered into such a catastrophe. If true – and Saxon gossip about the empress was often malicious – then she had only put into words what most people in southern Italy were thinking. Not that Byzantine *schadenfreude* could reign wholly undiluted. Even though the captain of the Saracens, the 'Emir', as he was termed, had fallen in the very hour of his great victory, everyone knew that the corsairs would be back, and more bloodily than ever. And so it would prove. Far distant from the beleaguered Italian front, however, in the chanceries of Constantinople, news of Otto's defeat had confirmed the imperial elite powerfully in their vision of the world. It was a vision in which, unchangingly, there could be room only for two great powers, locked, as they had always been, in a globe-spanning embrace of rivalry, arch-antagonists doomed to their mutual hatred until the very end of time: themselves, of course, and the Saracens. A vision, certainly, which left no room for barbarian emperors from the North.

Otto, doubting the courage and the resolve of Constantinople, had been grievously mistaken. Dutiful son of the Church a *Basileus* might be, and yet still boast that his spear 'had never been seen at rest', that all his life he had 'kept vigilant, guarding the children of the New Rome'.[42] Nicephorus, so ascetic in the private practice of his faith that he had dreamed of retiring to a monastery, was far from being the only emperor to have stained his weapons with blood. Even as Otto was limping northwards from the toe of Italy, great deeds were being plotted in Constantinople. Against the empire's enemies in the Balkans, where the frontier remained menacingly unstable, a full-scale strategy of invasion and annexation was being planned, with the goal of permanently securing the northern approaches to the capital, just as Nicephorus had secured the South. Yet imperial policy, even when setting its sights, as ultimately it would, upon the limits of the Danube, never ceased in its essence to be defensive – and fixated on the threat from its deadliest foe of all. Turbulent and dangerous though the northern barbarians – the Bulgars, the Croats and, yes, the Saxons too – were, they appeared, compared with the Saracens, the merest clods, brutish thugs bred of forest, and rock, and mud. Men understood, in Constantinople, a truth as unsettling as it verged on the scandalous: the Saracens, their eternal opposite, were their mirror image too.

Mon semblable, mon frère. Infinitely more than any Christian power, it was the kingdoms of those who most yearned to conquer her, the followers of Mohammed, that offered up to the New Rome the surest reflection of her own splendour and sophistication. Courts bejewelled and silken with luxuries, immense and teeming cities, baths and gushing fountains, bureaucracies and standing armies: the Saracens had them all. The people whom the wretched peasants of Italy knew only as pirates were in truth the possessors of a stupefyingly vast and flourishing dominion, stretching in a mighty crescent from the western ocean to the rising of the sun. 'There are two empires,' a Patriarch of Constantinople had written early in the tenth century, 'that of the Saracens and of the Romans, which hold between them the entirety of

86

power in this world, shining like twin torches in the celestial firma-
ment.'[43] The observation had been made in a letter sent to the fabulous
city of Baghdad, where there had sat enthroned in fearful splendour a
prince whose claim to the rule of every nation under the sun was
made manifest in his very title: that of the 'Caliph', or 'Successor', to
Mohammed. Yet ambitions of global conquest, the Patriarch had
argued, if permitted to blaze with an equal ferocity in both
Constantinople and Baghdad, would surely expose both to the risk of
annihilation. Rather than compete to rule the world, might not the
truest course of wisdom be to accept its division into two? The Caliph,
committed as he was by his rank to work for the propagation of
Mohammed's faith to the outermost limits of the universe, had given
this proposal predictably short shrift; but opinion formers in
Constantinople, unperturbed by this rebuff, had continued to push for
a policy of *détente*.

Which they had been able to do, as the decades passed, from a position of gathering strength. Increasingly, with the single exception of
the Italian front, the Saracen frontier appeared stable, even pacified.
Beyond it, meanwhile, in the heartlands of the Caliphate, all was disintegration. True, a caliph still reigned in Baghdad, but he did so only
as the cipher of a Persian warlord, one of numerous adventurers who
had begun systematically to carve up the Saracen world between
them. Nor was he any longer the only ruler who claimed the rank of
Mohammed's successor. In Egypt, which had been lost to Baghdad
back in 969, the master of that most ancient and wealthy of kingdoms
also wore the title of 'Caliph', claiming as his justification a supposed
descent from Mohammed's daughter, Fatima. Diplomats in
Constantinople, well versed in the art of stirring up trouble among
their adversaries, had naturally tracked all these developments with
relish. To the 'Fatimid' Caliph, as an encouragement to him in his
ambitions, they had duly sent *Zulfiqar*, Mohammed's sword: a splendid gift, to be sure, but a treacherous one as well. After all, with a rival
caliph still enthroned in Baghdad, and a host of squabbling emirs
beyond their frontiers, it appeared likeliest to be Saracen vertebrae

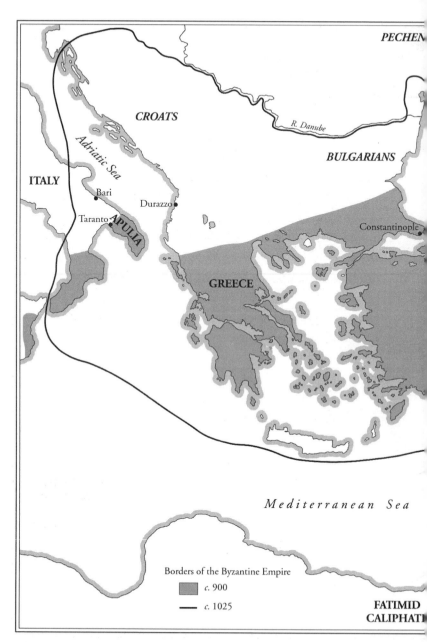

The Byzantine Empire

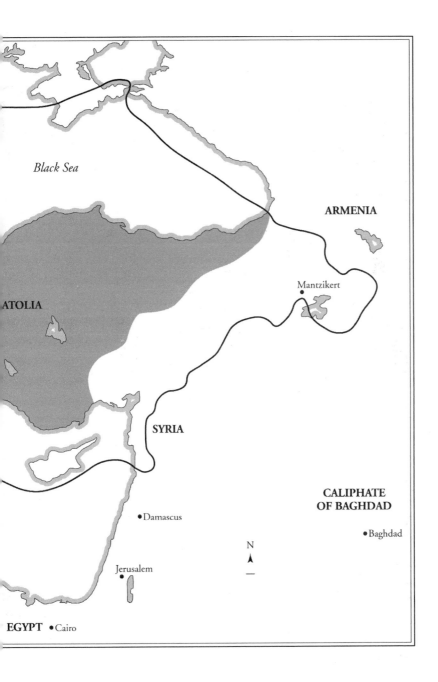

Black Sea

ARMENIA

Mantzikert

ATOLIA

SYRIA

CALIPHATE
OF BAGHDAD

• Damascus

• Baghdad

N

Jerusalem
•

EGYPT • Cairo

that would end up cleaved by the Fatimids, not the spines of the *Romaioi*.

Otto might have doubted the backbone of Constantinople, but the Saracens no longer did. 'The field is left open to her,' acknowledged a commentator at the Fatimid court as he mournfully surveyed the spectacle of the splintered Caliphate. 'She has been able to seize what was previously closed to her, and to nurture ambitions that until recently would have been unthinkable.'[44] No wonder, then, when set against such a drama, the tectonic grinding of two such ancient and mighty powers, each one the opposite and the semblance of the other, that the pretensions of upstarts such as Otto should have appeared a boorish irrelevance. If indeed, as all the signs seemed to indicate, the end of the world was nearing, then it was the rivalry of Caliph and *Basileus* that would surely pattern it, just as it had patterned the centuries past. 'Twin torches': so the Patriarch had described the Caliphate and the empire of the New Rome. Set against such a blaze, what could Francia be accounted, save a twilit backwater, a doltish wilderness of ignorance and bloodstained shadows?

Eurabia

As Otto stumbled back to Rome with his shattered retinue, he would have found himself passing by ruins familiar to him from his outward journey: looming reminders of the vanished empire whose heir he claimed to be. The menace of these silent temples and amphitheatres would have borne down ominously upon the imperial party. It was not only ghosts that were rumoured to haunt their mouldering stonework. Saracen raiders, always on the lookout for secure strongholds, had long been in the habit of setting up camp within the shells of outsize classical buildings. Well might Italians have come to regard the memorials of their Roman past as things baleful and accursed. Many, abandoning them altogether, had decamped to walled towns up in the hills. Others, rather than endure the dread that the ancient structures inspired, had been known to pull them down. In Naples, for instance, at the start of the tenth century, panic had inspired a veritable frenzy of demolition. Fearful that a Saracen emir of notorious rapacity and sadism might be descending upon their city, the Neapolitans had sought to leave nothing standing for the marauders to occupy. Far along the seafront, celebrated monuments had been sent crashing into the shallows. Most spectacular of all the casualties had been the palace in which the last Roman emperor of the West, some five hundred years previously, had passed his days.

Here, in the pile of rubble left where such a haughty villa had once stood, was dramatic illustration of how profoundly Italy had slumped from her one-time greatness into impotence and poverty. That Saracen war bands preferred to occupy ancient ruins rather than monuments raised in more recent times was sombre evidence of how shrunken the resources available to most Italians had become. It was certainly not in the hope of plundering any great treasure that the corsairs kept returning to their old haunts. For a long while now, across vast swaths of the Italian countryside, the bones had been picked almost clean. Yet what did remain was self-evidently more than lure enough. 'Behold,' a pope had mourned, back in the ninth century, 'the towns, castles and estates perish – stripped of inhabitants'.[45] An exaggeration? Not if stunned reports of the near-industrial scale of the slave trade were true: one traveller, witnessing a great flotilla of ships in Taranto, then in Saracen hands, claimed to have seen some twelve thousand captives being loaded ready for transport to the markets of Africa.[46]

System as much as savagery was what underpinned this trafficking. The duties of slavers were carefully divided up. Some would guard the ships, others prepare the irons, others bring in the captives. Some even specialised in the rounding up of children. The natives too – those with the determination to profit from the slavers rather than to end up as their victims – had their roles to play. Italians at every level of society were profoundly implicated in the hunting down of their fellow Christians. Even a pope, it was rumoured, feeling the pinch, had

91

once dabbled in it on the quiet. There were others who positively flaunted their collaboration. Amalfi, a city perched on the edge of a rocky peninsula south of Naples, was particularly notorious for her partisanship of the Saracens. So too, indeed – the occasional panic notwithstanding – was Naples herself. These two cities, by offering support and supplies to the slave trade, and by systematically frustrating all attempts to combat it, had begun gradually to pull themselves free of the general impoverishment of the times. Only the cost to their souls, perhaps, had to be put on the debit side. Already, in the ninth century, the markets of Naples had grown so bustling that visitors commented on how they appeared almost African in their prosperity. The Amalfitans, meanwhile, defying the barrenness of their native rock, had profited even more shrewdly from their links to the slavers, and transformed their cliff-top city, somewhat implausibly, into a hub of international trade. While other Italians huddled together for refuge on bleak hilltops, the merchants of Amalfi were to be found in harbours across the entire Mediterranean, from Tunisia to Egypt to Constantinople, flush with Saracen gold.

And all the while, the attentions of the Saracens themselves had been growing ever more predacious. No longer, by the late tenth century, were most slavers operating as freebooters: instead, they had begun to receive official backing in their activities from the rulers of Sicily. The brother of one emir, indeed, had been known to lead slaving expeditions in person. This was an ominous development indeed. No wonder that some Christian leaders, marking the sweep of corsairs across entire provinces of Italy, the winnowing of cities for human booty and the sustained harrowing of the countryside, had begun to wonder whether the depredations might not be motivated by something more sinister than simply greed. Christendom, it appeared to them, was being systematically drained of her lifeblood: her reservoir of human souls. Worse – the more she was emptied, the more those who fed on her were sustained. 'For it is the fate of prisoners of our own race,' as one despairing monk observed, 'both male and female, to end up adding to the resources of the lands beyond the sea.'[47]

Such paranoia was not unjustified. True, the main concern of the slavers remained, as it had always been, the harvesting of profit; and their ignorance of their own faith – to say nothing of their appalling Arabic and their fondness for raw onions – were things of scandal across the Saracen world. Nevertheless, state sponsorship of the corsairs had increasingly, throughout the tenth century, served to grace their marauding with a sheen of religiosity: for it was the practice of the rulers of Sicily, even as they creamed off their own percentage, to cast their subjects' brigandage as a spiritual discipline. '*Jihad*', they termed it: a word of rare and suggestive potency, signifying as it did the eternal struggle, incumbent upon all followers of Mohammed, to spread his faith to the utmost limits of the world. Corsairs, even as they glided in through the gates of an unsuspecting Italian town, could do so in the certainty that they were following in the footsteps of the divine. 'How many cities have We destroyed?' So God Himself, according to Mohammed, had demanded. 'Our punishment took them on a sudden by night or while they slept for their afternoon rest.'[48]

Well might jurists in the Caliphate have termed the world beyond their frontiers 'the House of War'. Its strife-torn poverty and backwardness appeared to those who preyed upon it merely the natural state of things: irrefutable proof that God had indeed abandoned the 'infidel', and transferred dominion into their own hands. Mohammed himself, the very first of his faith to have assaulted and despoiled a foe, had been graced with a firm assurance of this by the archangel Gabriel, no less. So, at any rate, it was recorded in the Qur'an: the holy book of his revelations. To the Prophet, and to all who followed him, had been granted the 'spoils of war'[49] – and a constituent part of this plunder, divinely gifted, had been human livestock.* All loot, if diverted to the proper charitable causes – 'to near relatives, orphans, the needy, and the wayfarer'[50] – might be reckoned to serve God's purpose; but

---

* Or, as Gabriel put it, 'those whom thy right hand possesses out of the prisoners of war whom God has assigned to thee': Qur'an 33.50.

prisoners, perhaps, most of all. Slavery did not have to be for life. Mohammed, who had prescribed that only infidels be sold as chattels, had also declared the freeing of converts a blessed act. Even a priest abducted from his church, as he toiled in a foreign field, or a nun, stolen to serve in a master's bed, might find food for thought in that.

To be sure, there were many Christian slaves, putting their trust in the life to come, who did stay true to their native faith; but there were many more who did not. Conversion to their masters' religion, for such renegades, brought not only the prospect of freedom, but a measure of dignity. All men, Mohammed had taught, were equal before God – for all men, even the very greatest, were His slaves. So it was that the Prophet's followers referred to themselves not as 'Saracens', a word that meant nothing to them, but as 'Muslims': 'those who submit'. In the prayer halls of their places of worship, the '*masajid*', as they were termed, or 'mosques', it was not merely the slaves who abased themselves before their divine master, kneeling, bowing, pressing their foreheads to the dust, but the entire community of believers. Expressed through this surging and mighty wave of prostrations was the great paradox of Mohammed's faith: that servitude, to the slaves of God, was the wellspring of their greatness. In their facelessness lay their identity; in their surrender, their victory. As one body, free and unfree, in lands that embraced the limits of the horizon, across all the vast and peerless extent of the Caliphate, that incomparable empire won by the dauntless swords of the faithful, they acknowledged their submission – what they called, in Arabic, '*islam*'.

One day, when all the world was Muslim, there would be no more wars, and no more slavery. In the meantime, however, the merchant who shipped his human cargo to Tunis or Alexandria could be regarded as performing a deed that was meritorious as well as lucrative; just as the captives transported in all their stupefying numbers from Europe to Africa were something more than merely the tribute of flesh and blood that the weak had timelessly paid the strong. God was great. Not a fragment of masonry shaken loose from the House of War but it

In the Book of Revelation, Saint John described his vision of how the world was set to end. Two scenes from it are represented here. In the top illustration, Satan is shown being bound by an angel within a bottomless pit; below it, 'the dragon, that ancient serpent, who is the Devil and Satan,' is shown breaking free after an imprisonment of a thousand years. From the so-called 'Bamberg Apocalypse': commissioned for imperial use in or just before the year 1000, the manuscript bears telling witness to the fascination with millennial themes at the very apex of Christendom.

The conversion of the Roman emperor Constantine to Christianity was a defining moment in European history. In its wake, Christians would increasingly take for granted that a Caesar might rule on earth as the deputy of Christ. Nevertheless, by the time this representation of Constantine's baptism was painted in the mid-twelfth century, people in the West had only the haziest notion as to who the first Christian emperor had actually been.
(Morgan Library)

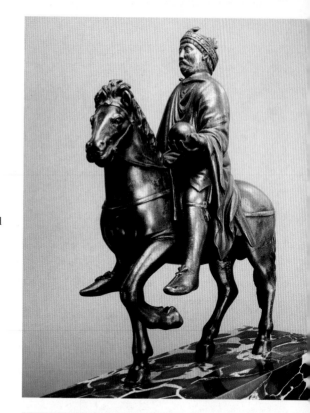

Charlemagne: Frankish warlord, and restorer of the Roman Empire in the West. Two hundred years and more after his death, when this statue was sculpted, he remained the very model of a Christian king. (Réunion des Musées Nationaux)

By the early tenth century, the empire forged by Charlemagne was splintering and crumbling away. Christendom itself appeared on the verge of ruin. Unsurprisingly, there were many, caught up in the savagery and violence of the times, who openly dreaded that 'the last time of the world had dawned'. This biblical battle scene, drawn by a monk in the Low Countries, held up a fitting mirror to the anarchy of the age.

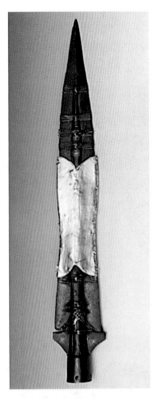

The Holy Lance: a weapon of reputedly awesome power. Believed to have been owned by Constantine, and to be adorned by the very nails that had once pierced the hands and feet of Christ, it was said to guarantee its owner 'perpetual triumph'. Its purchase in 926 by Henry the Fowler, the first Saxon king of the German *Reich*, served as a potent symbol of his status as the dominant figure in Christendom. (Kunsthorisches Museum)

he marble coronation throne at Aachen cathedral. Dating back to the time of Charlemagne, it was where tto I, in 936, sat to be crowned. 'Drive away the enemies of Christ,' he was solemnly instructed by the ficiating archbishop. 'Establish an enduring peace for Christians everywhere.' Words that Otto would ver forget. (Author photo)

In 962, Otto I travelled to Rome for a second coronation: this time as emperor. Once again, after a vacancy of almost sixty years, the throne of the Roman Empire in the West had an occupant. From that moment on, whenever Otto documents needed to be stamped, it would be done with an authentically imperial seal.

Otto II and Theophanu: Saxon Caesar and Byzantine princess. Their marriage in St Peter's was the most glamorous that Rome had staged for many centuries. As sophisticated as she was imperious, Theophanu would illumine her husband's reign with a rare star quality. (Author photo)

There was no one in the France of the Millennium more proficient in the revolutionary new art of castle building than Fulk Nerra, 'the Black', Count of Anjou. His princedom was studded with fortifications – with some, like this keep at Loches, so cutting-edge as to be constructed entirely out of stone. By 1035, it reached thirty-six metres high.
(Author photo)

forests were places to be feared as the haunts of wolves and demons, then so also could they provide asants with ready storehouses: ones that did not depend on the ploughing and harvesting of fields. Here, an English work calendar from the early eleventh century, hogs are shown sniffing the September air for e scent of acorns. (British Library)

Of all a peasant's possessions, the most precious were his oxen. Keep them, and he would preserve his freedom. Lose them, and he was almost guaranteed to lose his freedom as well. (British Library)

If castles were one mark of the gathering tide of social upheaval that afflicted many regions in France in t approach to the Millennium, then so too were the gangs of mail-clad thugs employed to garrison them. 'Cnichts', they were called in English, or 'knights': a novel and menacing order.

could be put to use in the walls of the House of Islam. Cannibalisation, indeed, had long been the fate ordained for Christendom. Slaves garnered from frontier wars had only ever been conceived of as a beginning. Conquest, outright conquest, promised the richest opportunities. Mohammed, as shrewd and innovative an empire-builder as there had ever been, had carefully prescribed for his followers how best to make their victories pay. Christians, once brought to acknowledge their own subjugation, were not to be slaughtered or obliged to convert, but carefully husbanded, as befitted a valuable resource. It was more profitable in the long run to fleece a flock of sheep than to put them all to the sword. 'Otherwise,' as one of the Prophet's earliest followers had put it, 'what would be left for the Muslims who will come after us?'[51] Jesus, eyes fixed on the Kingdom of Heaven, might have disdained to elaborate a fiscal policy – but not Mohammed. Tolerance had been set carefully at a price. The extortion of protection money from both Christians and Jews had been laid down by the Prophet as a most solemn duty of the faithful. All those who paid it – '*dhimmis*', as they were termed by their Muslim conquerors – were to be made to 'feel themselves subdued'.[52] Travelling to pay their tax, they were forbidden to ride a horse, a privilege reserved for the faithful; if on a mule, they had to sit side-saddle, like women; as they handed over their money, they were obliged to keep their hands below those of the official collecting it. In the House of Islam, it was the ledger book no less than the sword that imposed subordination.

Indeed, without *dhimmi* taxes, it might prove hard to pay for an army at all. This was why, in a seeming paradox, it was those states with the largest number of Christians that could most readily afford *jihad*. In Sicily, for instance, which had finally been secured for Islam only in 902, the emirs regarded their vast population of infidel subjects with a cagey ambivalence. Devout Muslims that they were, and naturally mistrustful of those who did not share their faith, they were regular sponsors of new mosques and mass circumcisions across the Christian heartlands; but they also had to reckon with the need to husband their tax base. By the time of the expedition against Otto II, the Muslim population of Sicily was nudging perhaps a third of the island's total, and it appeared that the perfect balance of manpower and revenue had been attained. Bureaucracy had fused with banditry to forge a state that was lethally primed for war. The corpses left on the beach by Cotrone had borne sufficient witness to that.

Yet the notion that tax collectors might present quite as grave a threat to Christendom as corsairs was profoundly alien to the Saxons. Otto, master of a far-spreading dominion though he was, had no great reservoir of bureaucrats on which to call, no elaborate system for keeping track of his subjects, not even a capital. Indeed, to those Muslim leaders who deigned so much as to note its existence, the *Reich* appeared barely to qualify as a functioning state at all. One of them, addressing an envoy sent to his court by Otto I, had been open in his scorn. 'Why does your king not concentrate power in his own hands?' the ambassador had been asked in withering tones. 'Why does he allow his subjects to have such a share of it? He doles out the various regions of his empire among them, expecting in that way to win their loyalty and submission, but he is deluding himself. For all he fosters is rebellion and pride!'[53]

Here had spoken a man whose own sense of what was due to him had never needed the slightest boosting. Abd al-Rahman bin Mohammed bin Abd Allah, not content with the rank of emir that he had inherited from his grandfather, had even laid claim to that very ultimate in honorifics, the title of Caliph. No less than his peers in Baghdad and Egypt, Abd al-Rahman had made sure to justify his pretensions to global dominion with a truly spectacular display of wealth and power. Otto's ambassador, an abbot from the Rhineland by the name of John, had certainly never seen anything to compare. The Caliph's palace, he reported years later in still breathless tones, stretched for miles. Everywhere he had looked, there were soldiers standing to menacing attention, or riding on horseback, staging intimidating manoeuvres, 'filling our party with consternation, such was their arrogance and swagger'. Even the dustiest gatehouse had been adorned 'with carpets and precious fabrics'.[54]

It was all in startling contrast with the décor of a monastery; but even those visitors who were not Frankish abbots might well be stupefied. Abd al-Rahman had regarded it as below his dignity to deal in anything but the most extravagant superlatives. Twelve thousand loaves of bread, it was claimed, were required to feed his fish alone. Indoors, away from the draped courtyards, the flower-scented lawns and the moated zoo, silks blended with stucco, precious metals with patterned tiles. At the very heart of the fabulous complex, in the great reception hall, there stood a pool of mercury, capable, when stirred, of sending shivers of reflected sunlight dancing across the marble walls; while above it, suspended from the gold and silver roof, there hung a giant pearl.

All this splendour, however, had provided merely the setting for the palace's truest jewel. Alone on a cushion-laden dais, 'like a god accessible to none or very few',[55] there had reclined the Caliph, Abd al-Rahman himself. Dumpy he may have been, and prone to melancholy, confiding to his diary that in all the forty-nine years of his reign, he had known only fourteen days of happiness – and yet he and his family, the Umayyads, provided a living link to Islam's most heroic age. Like the Fatimids, they could trace their bloodline back to the time of the Prophet. Unlike the Fatimids, they could also lay claim to an even more exclusive status: that of Islam's first-ever dynasty of caliphs. From their capital of Damascus, in Syria, they had witnessed Muslim armies besiege Constantinople, cross the Indus and raid deep into Francia. For almost a century, from 661 to 750, they had been the most powerful family on earth. Abd al-Rahman, in short, had pedigree.

Yet though the Umayyads' blood undoubtedly was blue, so also, by the tenth century, were their eyes. Their skin was pale; Abd al-Rahman himself, concerned to appear properly a son of the desert, had been obliged to dye his beard black. Much had befallen the Umayyads over the previous two centuries. Toppled from power in 750 by the dynasty that would subsequently transfer the capital of the Caliphate to Baghdad, most had been systematically eliminated, often amid grotesque brutalities: the tongue of the ruling Caliph, for instance, had been hacked out and fed to a cat. Indeed, of all the Umayyad princes, only one had succeeded in escaping the blood-bath – and he had done so by fleeing to the far ends of the earth. Never again would the Umayyads return to their beloved capital.

Over the centuries, to be sure, they had done their best to assuage their abiding sense of homesickness. Abd al-Rahman's entire palace, so commanding, so sumptuous, so exquisite, appeared to visitors from Damascus like a fantasy conjured up from their city's golden age. Raised as it had been upon tiers carved out of the gently sloping foothill of a mountain, it was possible to look out from one of its many levels and see, in the valley below, a landscape that likewise appeared transplanted from the Umayyads' much-missed homeland: a vision of almond blossom, date palms and pomegranate trees. Travel beyond the palace and scenes even more evocative of Syria might be found, plains adorned with glittering fretworks of irrigation, fed by the groaning of immense hydraulic wheels, and nourishing fields of fantastical plants: figs and oranges, rice and sugar cane. Yet these were not Syrian fields. Damascus was more than two thousand miles away. Abd al-Rahman's palace stood not in the Near East but in that abode of exile that was the furthest west, on the very edge of the world – in Spain.

The Ornament of the World

Muslim armies had first crossed from Africa into Europe long previously, back in 711. Beyond the straits of what would ultimately, after the general who had led the invasion, be known as 'Tariq's Mountain', or '*Jabal Tariq*' – 'Gibraltar' – there had lain the kingdom of a people named the Visigoths. These, like the Franks, had originally been invaders from beyond the frontiers of the Roman Empire: fiercely, even violently Christian, their kings had ruled from the craggy heights of Toledo, in the very heart of the peninsula, which they had adorned with splendid churches, and termed with soaring pride a 'new Jerusalem'. Indeed, believing themselves, to a degree exceptional even by the standards of the times, a chosen people, and aiming to overawe their native subjects, it was the Visigoths, long before Pepin, who had first presumed to anoint their kings with holy oil. All to no avail. For reasons that would later be much debated – an epidemic of sodomy being the favoured explanation – the Visigoths had been abandoned by God. Their armies had been shattered upon the Muslim advance. Their kingdom had been delivered up into the hands of the invaders. Only in the bleakest wilds of the peninsula, in the poverty-stricken mountains of Galicia, in the farthest north-west, had there been left so much as the rump of a Christian state. Secure in their remote fast-nesses, the men of this tiny kingdom had succeeded not only in keeping the Muslims at bay, but even, with a painful effort, at clawing back lost territory. Two and a half centuries after it had seemed as though the whole of the peninsula might fall to the invaders, upwards of a third of it had been redeemed for Christendom. The nerve centre of Christian resistance was no longer to be found in the mountains, but further south, on an open plain, within the walls of the ancient Roman fortress of León. Toledo, its crags now as adorned with minarets as they had once been with bell-towers, stood almost on the front line.

Yet the Caliph and his advisers, though hardly complacent in the face of this Christian resurgence, felt no great cause for alarm. The men of León, long confined to mountains and desolate plains as they had been, appeared to the Muslims like wolves: dangerous certainly, but only if permitted to intrude from the wilderness that was properly their home. So it was that everywhere along the frontier, raised to stand bristling proof against Christian predators, there loomed bat-tlements and mighty watchtowers: fortifications that the Muslims termed '*husun*'. North of these, drear and savage, the House of War; south of them, as blooming a garden as any in the House of Islam, rich with crops, studded with great cities, and adorned with the arts of peace, a 'paradise' hailed even by her Christian enemies as 'the ornament of the world',[56] the land known to its inhabitants as 'al-Andalus'.*

Indeed, such was the flourishing condition of Spain's Muslims that they had long since ceased to depend for their prosperity upon the exploitation of infidels. This was just as well; for increasingly, under the lengthy rule of Abd al-Rahman and of his able and sophisticated son al-Hakam, al-Andalus had come to lose its character as a frontier society. Conversions to Islam, once a trickle, had become a flood. At the start of the tenth century, it has been estimated, the population of al-Andalus was only one-fifth Muslim; by the time al-Hakam died, in 976, that percentage had been reversed.[57] The status of Christians in Islamic Spain had always been a second-class one; and certainly, burdened as they were by extra taxes, banned from employment in the state bureaucracy, and saddle-sore, no doubt, from perpetually riding mules, they had hardly lacked for incentives to abandon their ancestral faith. Yet while to be a *dhimmi* in the House of Islam had always been both expensive and a source of petty humiliations, so also, by the tenth century, had it become something even more debilitating: unfashionable. The Church in al-Andalus had long been thundering against the passion of its flock for Saracen chic; but increasingly, whether translating the scriptures into Arabic, or adopting Muslim names for themselves, or dancing attendance on the Caliph at his court, even bishops were succumbing to its allure.

Only in the countryside, far removed from the wealth and glamour of city life, did sizeable numbers of Christians still endure; and they, in the opinion of Muslim sophisticates, were little better than wild beasts. 'For when they cast off the yoke of obedience,' so one complained, 'it is hard to make them return to it, unless they are exterminated – and

---

* The origins of the name are notoriously problematic. Some derive it from the Vandals, invaders of the Roman Empire who passed through Spain on their way to North Africa; others from Atlantis, the legendary island written about by Plato, and which was supposed to have been located in the furthest west. The uncertainty persists.

that is a difficult, prolonged process.'[58] In al-Andalus, the days of living off the fruits of extortion, whether plunder or taxes, were gone for good.

There were many Muslims, nostalgic for the time when their ancestors 'were admirable and excellent, determined in *jihad* and eager for God's rewards, throwing themselves on the Christians in warfare and siege',[59] who regretted this; but the majority were too busy making money in less strenuous ways to care. The Caliphate may have been politically fractured, but it still offered, to the ambitious merchant, a free-trade area like no other in the world. Far eastwards of al-Andalus it extended, to Persia and beyond, while in the markets of the great cities of Islam were to be found wonders from even further afield: sandalwood from India, paper from China, camphor from Borneo. What was Christian Spain, with her flea-bitten little villages, to compare? Why, unlike their equivalents in Italy, they were not even good for slaves! The Andalusis, whose ancestors, back in the valiant first flush of conquest, had once dispatched thirty thousand prisoners to Damascus in a single train, had long since lost their taste for grubbing around after human prey. Now it was they who were the importers; and a swarm of Christian suppliers, with little else to offer which might serve to tickle Andalusi palates, had competed to corner the market no less eagerly than their Muslim competitors. The fair hair of the Umayyad caliphs, bred of concubines from the distant North, was only one proof of their success. A second was the palace guards who had so alarmed Abbot John; for these were not native Andalusis, but '*Saqaliba*' – Slavs. In Arabic, as in most European languages, the word was becoming, by the tenth century, increasingly synonymous with human cattle: a reflection of how widely, when demand required it, the tendrils of trade might extend beyond the House of Islam, even to the limits of the House of War.

Nothing, indeed, in the fractured Europe of the time, was more authentically multicultural than the business of enslaving Slavs. Wends captured in the wars of the Saxon emperors would be sold by Frankish merchants to Jewish middlemen, who then, under the shocked gaze of Christian bishops, would drive their shackled stock along the high roads of Provence and Catalonia, and across the frontier into the Caliphate. A cosmopolitan perspective was no little help when it came to gauging the likely demands of a sophisticated foreign market such as al-Andalus. Few opportunities were neglected in the struggle to obtain a competitive edge. In the Frankish town of Verdun, for instance, the Jewish merchants who had their headquarters there were renowned for their facility with the gelding knife. A particular specialisation was the supply of '*carzimasia*': eunuchs who had been deprived of their penises as well as their testicles. Even for the most practised surgeon, the medical risks attendant on performing a penectomy were considerable – and yet the wastage served only to increase the survivors' value. Exclusivity, then as now, was the mark of a luxury brand.

And luxury, in al-Andalus, could make for truly 'fabulous profit'.[60] The productivity of the land; the teeming industry of the cities; the influx of precious metals from mines in Africa: all had helped to establish the realm of the Umayyads as Europe's premier showcase for conspicuous consumption. While it was the Caliph himself, naturally enough, who stood at the apex of the pyramid, and skimmed off most of the taxes, he was certainly not alone in profiting from the orderly conditions of his empire. Five miles west of the great caliphal palace, for instance, there sprawled a city that in its size and sophistication was no less a wonder of the age – and no less dependent for its prosperity on stable governance. Córdoba, like León, had originally been a Roman foundation – but the capital of al-Andalus, as befitted a city so fattened on the fruits of peace, had long since burst its ancient walls. Indeed, so utter had been the transformation of the original Christian town that even its street plan had been obliterated: for Muslims, who had never quite got the hang of carts, had no need of wide streets or squares. Instead, all was labyrinthine, a stupendous agglomeration of winding alleyways and crowded markets, of palaces and gardens, of a hundred mosques and a thousand baths. Just as Otto, emperor though he was, lacked a residence that could rival so much as the gatehouse of the palace of the Caliph, so was there nowhere else in western Europe a settlement that remotely approached the scale and splendour of Córdoba. Indeed, in the whole of Christendom, there was only a single city that could boast of being a more magnificent seat of empire – and that was Constantinople, the Queen of Cities herself.

As the caliphs of Córdoba were well aware. Back in the palmiest days of their family's greatness, when their ancestors had reigned in Damascus, emulation of the New Rome had been as much an Umayyad tradition as attempts to breach her walls; so much so, indeed, that their habit of '*Qysariyya*' – of 'behaving like a Caesar' – had come to shock and perturb the faithful. The Umayyads themselves, befittingly imperious, had scorned all the bleats of the pious. 'None would believe in his power,' as the dynasty's founder had put it, 'if he did not behave and look like an emperor.'[61] Three centuries on, and the *Basileus* remained the standard by which the Umayyads measured themselves. Byzantine diplomats, skilled as they were in the art of setting their enemies at one another's throats, had not failed to recognise opportunity in this. Numerous embassies had been dispatched to al-Andalus. Sedulously, these had fortified the Umayyad Caliphate in its inveterate rivalry with the Fatimids – and had presented, as seasoning to their encouragements, a whole array of splendid gifts. So it was that the Caliph's palace outside Córdoba had been beautified with treasures from the workshops of Constantinople: here a row of marble columns, there an onyx fountain adorned with sculpted beasts. So it was too that in the very holiest place in al-Andalus, the Great Mosque of Córdoba, the golden mosaics which covered the Caliph's private prayer room glittered with the unmistakable stamp of the Byzantine; courtesy of a master craftsman sent by Nicephorus, that notorious bane of the Saracens.

And yet, to the Caliph himself, the intrusion of Christian fingers upon the most sacred recesses of the mosque had implied no sacrilege. The very opposite, in fact. Turn from the aureate shimmer of the Byzantine mosaics, and fragments of other empires, of other traditions, all of them blended into a regular and awe-inspiring symmetry, could be seen receding towards the daylight that blazed in through the prayer hall's nineteen doorways. Tent-like in its spareness, the ceiling of the Great Mosque was supported upon a mighty forest of pillars, some salvaged from the ruins of pagan temples, others from the demolished cathedral that had once stood on the site. The arches, which alternated brick with stone, white with red, had been constructed according to Roman methods; the horseshoe style of their curves had originally been Visigothic. No unease was felt by the architects at this wholesale appropriation of infidel traditions. Why should there have been? Just as slaves, uprooted from the House of War, could soon be brought to forget their origins, and learn to think of themselves as Muslims, nothing more, so similarly might the glories of a defeated civilisation, once they had been absorbed and transmuted into something holy, something authentically Islamic, serve to contribute to the greater glory of God. As evidence of this, no more haunting proof existed, and none more majestic, than Córdoba's mosque.

'God desires that if you do something you perfect it.'[62] So Mohammed had instructed his followers; and they, raising upon the ruins of toppled empires the dominion of his faith, had fashioned out of the rubble the greatest empire of them all. The centuries had passed, and the House of Islam had fractured; yet still, the devout believed, there could be seen in its architecture a glimpse of that even more profound order, the eternal order of God. Muslim scholarship, in its attempt to fathom creation's mysteries, had drawn quite as profitably on the learning of infidels as the bureaucracy of the Caliphate had drawn on their wealth. Both, after all, were legitimate spoils of war. If God, in His mysterious wisdom, had granted insights to pagans, then so also had He granted to Muslims the opportunity to appropriate those insights, to assimilate them and to render them their own. Mathematicians who explored the nature of infinity did so using numerals derived from the idol worshippers of far-off India; mystics who pronounced that salvation might be attained through a mastery of the sciences depended for their philosophy upon the teachings of Pythagoras and Plato, long-dead Greek idolaters who had never heard of Mohammed. Even in al-Andalus, where overexcited scholars and their speculations had traditionally been regarded with frowns of disapproval, a sublime fantasy had begun to flourish: that the wisdom of the entire world might be comprehended. Enthusiasm for this heroic ambition had reached to the very top. Caliph Al-Hakam, in particular, had been celebrated for his obsession with books. Remarkable stories were told of the fruits of his mania. The library in the caliphal palace, it was rumoured, had ended up numbering more than four hundred thousand volumes – of which forty-four 'were employed in the mere catalogue'.[63]

Meanwhile, in what had once been the very wellspring of pagan wisdom, the lands of the Romans, or *Rum*, all appeared decay and ignorance. In Constantinople, to be sure, there were still certain texts from antiquity preserved, the writings of ancient philosophers and savants; and some of these, on occasion, might even be dusted down and sent to the various capitals of the Caliphate as gifts. Yet the *Rum*, to Muslim eyes, appeared unworthy of their peerless heritage. Deep in the countryside beyond Constantinople, one ambassador reported, there stood a temple where the ancient pagans were said to have worshipped the stars, piled so high with manuscripts that it would have taken a thousand camels to carry them away; and all the manuscripts were crumbling into dust. Compared with the rest of Christendom, however, Constantinople appeared a veritable treasure house of learning. No books could be expected of the Saxon king, for instance. Abd al-Rahman, wishing to congratulate Otto I on his victory at the Lech, had sent him, not a rare manuscript, but gifts more calculated to impress a barbarian: 'lions and camels, ostriches and apes'.[64] Indeed, in the whole of western Christendom there were few libraries more than a thousandth of the size of the Caliph's in Córdoba. So rare were books that the going rate for one on the black market might be a warhorse. Al-Hakam, had this been brought to his attention, would hardly have been surprised. Rather, it would have confirmed him in all his certitudes: that God had turned His back on the Christians; and that the

House of Islam would inherit the world for sure. Without learning, after all, what hope for order – and without order, what hope for any empire?

Such questions haunted many in Christendom itself. Just as Queen Gerberga, in her desperation to find some pattern in the anarchy of the times, had looked to a famous scholar for answers, so were there famous scholars, oppressed by similar anxieties, who had turned to the books of pagans. The most celebrated of them all was a peasant, as upwardly mobile as he was precocious, by the name of Gerbert; and it was whispered by his detractors that he had actually studied in Córdoba. Whether indeed he had visited the Saracens in their very lair, it was certain that he was familiar with their learning; for Gerbert, despite being a native of the town of Aurillac, in the remotest Auvergne, had completed his education in a monastery in Spain. Here, on the outermost frontier of Christendom, he had mastered branches of knowledge so exotic that later generations would brand him a necromancer: from the strange Indian numerals used by the Saracens to the operation of an abacus. Yet Gerbert was no sorcerer. His passion – one which 'boiled within him'[65] – was for the tracing of God's order amid seeming chaos. So it was, as a teacher in Reims, that he had constructed out of delicate bronze and iron wires a series of fantastical instruments, designed to demonstrate to his pupils the orderly circling of the planets about the earth, and the turning of the universe on its poles. So it was too, in Rome, amid all the festivities for Otto's wedding to Theophanu, that Gerbert had distinguished, as though they formed their own 'ingenious mechanism',[66] the filigrees spun by God to encircle and order time itself. Once there had been a Christian empire that embraced all the world, and brought to humanity the inestimable fruits of order and peace; and so there would be again. This conviction was hardly original to Gerbert; but rarely had it been held by a man of such erudition and brilliance. Born a peasant he may have been; but Gerbert's genius had served to win him the attention of emperors and kings. Back in 971, in Rome, he had tutored the young Otto II. A decade later, shortly before Otto left on his disastrous invasion of southern Italy, Gerbert had appeared before the imperial court again, this time in a formal debate with the *Reich*'s most formidable scholar, the head of the cathedral school in Magdeburg – and wiped the floor with him. In 983, with Otto licking his wounds back in Rome, Gerbert was formally appointed to the imperial service. At such a time of crisis for the *Reich*, the conviction of Christendom's most famous scholar that a Roman Empire might still be restored was an asset not lightly to be overlooked.

Further calamities, however, would soon enough test even Gerbert's optimism to the limit. In an empire laid claim to by a single ruler, an earthquake in southern Italy might reverberate as far as the forests of the distant North; and sure enough, in the summer of 983, the Wends rose suddenly in revolt, burning the cathedrals raised over their lands by their occupiers, pursuing the Saxons 'as though they were deer',[67] and ravaging as far as Hamburg. Although Magdeburg itself stood firm amid the firestorm, and the line of the Elbe was eventually stabilised, all that lay beyond it, won with such effort by Otto's father, was permanently lost. Otto himself, brought the news in Rome, was obliged to abandon his plans for further campaigns against the Saracens, and prepare wearily to head back north: a prospect rendered all the more agonising by the swollen state of his haemorrhoids. Before he could so much as mount his saddle, however, he fell ill with violent diarrhoea; and on 7 December Otto II Augustus, 'Emperor of the Romans', died.

Otto's sudden end left the *Reich* rudderless. His son and heir, the third Otto in succession, was only three years old. Taken to Aachen, the little boy was consecrated king, just as Charlemagne had been crowned emperor, on Christmas Day, but was then almost immediately abducted. The kidnapper, proving himself very much a chip off the old block, was none other than the son and namesake of Henry, Duke of Bavaria, whose endless machinations had caused so much trouble for Otto I. The second Henry, whose nickname of 'the Quarreller' was a fitting measure of the man, had already proved himself inveterately rebellious – but now, sniffing opportunity as a wolf scents blood, he surpassed himself. In 984, on Easter Day, he formally laid claim to the throne. The nobility, torn between their loyalty to Otto III and their dread of being ruled by a child, havered. It appeared that the *Reich* itself was on the verge of civil war.

'Ruined, ruined,' Gerbert wailed. 'What hope can there possibly be?'[68] But he did not despair for long. As Theophanu, having buried her husband in St Peter's, hurried northwards to beard the usurper in East Francia, Gerbert was already hard at work, writing to the princes and bishops of the *Reich*, stiffening them in their loyalty to their rightful king. So effective was his campaign that by the time Theophanu crossed the Alps, in May, Henry the Quarreller found that all his supporters had melted away. A month later, sulkily, he surrendered the infant Otto to his mother, and retired in high dudgeon to Bavaria.

Theophanu, 'that ever august empress, always to be loved, always to be cherished',[69] was appointed regent on behalf of her son. In this role, she proved formidably effective. 'Preserving her son's rulership with a manly watchfulness, she was always benevolent to the just, but terrified and conquered rebels.'[70] Three years after the crisis of 984, she even obliged a fuming Henry, along with three other German dukes, to serve as waiters at Otto's table, in full view of the *Reich*'s nobility, who had all gathered at court for the feast of Easter. Although she died in 991, while her son was still legally a minor, Theophanu had successfully secured the empire for Otto III. In September 994, he was presented with the arms of a warrior, and officially came of age.[71] One year later, and he was leading his men in that traditional rite of passage for a Saxon king, a campaign against the Wends. By 996, the year of his sixteenth birthday, all that remained was to be crowned emperor – and so it was, that very spring, that Otto III announced his departure for Rome.

And all this Gerbert had followed with the keenest interest. Although Theophanu, with the ingratitude that was an empress's proper prerogative, had failed to reward his services with commensurate patronage, the great scholar had not stinted in his loyalty to her or to her son. Mathematician, astronomer and historian, Gerbert could hardly have been oblivious to the date that was approaching. 'It seems', he had pronounced sensationally back in 991, 'that Antichrist is at hand.'[72] He knew as well – for he was a friend of Adso, and owned a copy of the famous letter to Gerberga – that the end of days would be presaged by a great convulsion in the affairs of the Roman Empire. And now, four years before the one-thousandth anniversary of the birth of Christ, a prince with the blood of both West and East in his veins, of the twin halves of the ancient empire, so long divided, to the scandal of Christians everywhere and to the profit of its foes, was travelling to Rome.

Well might Gerbert have dreamed of meeting him: for he appreciated better than anyone that it was Otto's destiny to rule in interesting times.

The Last Roman Emperor

Pilgrims heading southwards to worship at the tomb of St Peter knew that what awaited them was a cityscape like no other in the Latin West. 'O Rome,' went the song, 'noble Rome, mistress of the globe, there is nowhere that can rival you, most excellent of cities!'[73] Even visitors from the great capitals of Islam might find themselves stupefied: one Muslim merchant, approaching Rome and seeing in the distance the city's churches, mistook the green-grey lead of their roofs for the waves of a sea. On Christians from the North the impact was overpowering. Nothing in their own muddy homelands could have prepared them for the spectacle of the ancient capital of their faith. That a city might boast a population numbering some twenty-five thousand souls; that her walls might stretch for twelve miles; that these walls might contain a seemingly infinite number of shrines: all this had to be seen to be believed. Otto, as he arrived in Rome, would have felt himself entering a dreamlike realm of wonders.

And into his destiny as well. 'Rome, head of the world, and mistress of cities, alone makes emperors of kings.' So the peoples of the North had long acknowledged. 'Cherishing as she does in her heart the prince of saints, it is she who has the right, if she so wishes it, to enthrone a prince over all the lands of the earth.'[74] The irony of this – that it was the very blood spilled by the pagan Romans that had preserved their city's title to the rule of the world – never ceased to delight the devout. The victory of St Peter over those who had martyred him was manifest wherever one looked in Rome. Monuments that had once proclaimed her Babylon the Great, 'the devil's own city',[75] were leprous with decay. Squalid hovels crowded the squares of forgotten emperors; around the Colosseum, which in ancient days had been 'stained purple with saintly blood',[76] there now hung the haze of malarial swamps and the fumes of corpse-pits; on the Palatine Hill, nothing remained but rubble of the palace of the Caesars. Debris, as though the breath of an angel had swept the scene, lay everywhere; and where the debris ended open fields began.

Yet Rome endured, and more than endured: for though she was capital of the dead, yet it was not the shades of pagan emperors, howling to see cattle wander where once their chariots had rolled, whose presence animated the spectacle of her desolation, but rather the martyrs, whose holy bones were the city's most priceless treasures. Everywhere, repositories of an awesome supernatural power, churches stood guard over them, their stonework suffused with the charisma of the departed saints themselves. Many shrines, like St Peter's itself, were of a venerable antiquity; but from others there came hammering or the smell of drying plaster. Even amid her decay, Rome was forever renewing herself. 'Daily, rising up out of the ruins of shattered walls and decayed temples, we see the fresh stonework of churches and monasteries.'[77] Here, then, perhaps, in the Holy City, lay a vision of how the world itself might be renewed.

Otto, certainly, was of a mind to think so. Still only fifteen when he first arrived in Rome, the emperor was as precocious as he was visionary, a young man of already luminous ambition. He was well schooled in all the attributes expected of a Saxon king, and his mother had sought to stamp him with something of Constantinople too. As his tutor – and godfather – she had duly appointed a Greek from southern Italy, one John Philagathos, an abbot who combined formidable learning with a ferocious self-assurance. Byzantine education was famously stern: its goal was to instil in children nothing less than the demeanour of saints. Theophanu, in her choice of teacher, had shown her customary eye for scholarly talent. The young emperor, though celebrated for his charm, had grown to manhood distinguished as well by a profound solemnity; a sense of the great and terrible charge which had been laid upon him since his earliest years. No less than any *Basileus*, Otto believed in the Roman Empire as the chosen agent of God's will. It was a Roman emperor, after all, at the end of days, who was destined to obtain for Christ and His Church all the limits of the world – and who was to say, the times being what they were, that the end of days was not at hand?

Well might Otto have fixed his gaze beyond the horizons of Saxony. Already, looking to seal his rank as a prince of East as well as West, he had dispatched his old tutor, John Philagathos, to Constantinople, with instructions to arrange a marriage for him with the daughter of the *Basileus*. Meanwhile, in Rome itself, the papacy was being broken to his will. To a degree that even his father or his grandfather would have found startling, Otto regarded the Pope as his subordinate, to be nominated as he saw fit. Not even the customary fig leaf of an election was to be permitted the papal see. When news had reached Otto, as he was heading to Rome, that the reigning Pope was dead of a sudden fever, he had recognised in this accident the certain hand of God. At once, he had moved to foist his own candidate on the Holy City: not a Roman, not even an Italian, but a twenty-four-year-old Saxon, his cousin Bruno.

Early in May 996, the first German ever to sit on the throne of St Peter was duly consecrated as Pope Gregory V. Rome's traditional power brokers, stunned by the sheer audacity of Otto's manoeuvre, had found themselves impotent to counter it. The most feared of their number, a hardened strongman by the name of John Crescentius, was reduced to begging the young emperor not to send him into exile. Imperiously, and before the full gaze of Rome, Otto graced him with his mercy. No one was to be left in any doubt that the city – and indeed all of Christendom – now had an emperor who was Roman in more than name. On 21 May, Ascension Day, Otto was formally crowned in St Peter's, 'to the plaudits of all Europe'.[78] His cousin, having first anointed him, then delivered a sword into his hand. On to the new emperor's finger was slipped a ring: symbol of his union with the Christian people. From his shoulders there hung a cloak, and on it, 'marked out in gold',[79] were scenes from the Book of Revelation: St John's vision of the end of the world.

None, perhaps, should have been surprised at the speed and daring that had brought Otto to this spectacular coronation. Young he might have been – but he had already been well instructed in the demands of power upon a king. He had seen the villages of his own people burned and corpse-strewn, and he had torched the villages of the Wends in turn; he had ridden across blood-soaked fields, and trampled his slaughtered foes underfoot. Such was the doom of sinful man, on Middle Earth: to suffer and wither and die. Yet Otto, crashing through the Wendish forests with his *loricati*, had also stared into a profounder darkness. Trees were already reclaiming the churches planted there by the Saxons. Walls were crumbling away which had once sheltered the body and blood of Christ. The Wends, unlike the Saxons themselves, had refused to accept the Prince of Peace at the point of a conqueror's sword. What, then, confronted by such obduracy, was Otto to do? He knew that above the fallen world, invisible but effulgent, its radiance brighter than even the most interminable pagan forest was steeped in darkness, there soared the City of God – and that it was his duty, as a Roman emperor, to bring the heathen to acknowledge its glory. Yet he could never forget either, even as he looked to shape Christendom and the realms beyond it to God's purpose, what Christ Himself had taught His followers: to love their enemies, to turn their cheeks, to sheathe their swords. Otto, as sensitive to his own moral failings as he was insistent upon his godlike dignity as a Caesar, never ceased to be tormented by the resulting tension. 'Outwardly he assumed a cheerful expression; but within his conscience groaned under the weight of many misdeeds from which, in the silence of night, he continually sought to cleanse himself through vigils, earnest prayers, and rivers of tears.'[80]

Perhaps it was hardly surprising, then, that Otto should have found himself peculiarly obsessed by Rome. In the fabulous juxtaposition that it presented of the vaunting and the humble, the martial and the pacific, the mortal and the eternal, the city must have appeared to him like a mirror held up to his soul. Lingering there after his coronation, he could admire details on antique columns which portrayed the slaughter of barbarians by stern-faced emperors; just as he could attend, 'day and night', to a very different lesson, one taught him by a monk who was famous, notorious even, for his scorning of worldly titles, an admonishment that Otto should 'regard himself not as one of the great, not as a Caesar, but as a mortal man, and therefore destined, all his great beauty notwithstanding, to end up as ashes, rottenness, and food for worms'.[81]

The name of this spiritual pundit was Adalbert. Though he was cloistered in a Roman monastery, across the valley from the ruins on the Palatine, far distant from the marches of the *Reich*, he was nevertheless profoundly sensitive to the pressures weighing on Otto's shoulders. This was because, to a degree, he had shared in them himself – and buckled beneath them too. Born in Bohemia of aristocratic parents, educated in Magdeburg, appointed by Otto II to the bishopric of Prague, Adalbert properly ranked as one of the great men of the *Reich*. Far from revelling in his high office, however, he had grown so troubled by the compromises required of him that it was said he had forgotten, such was his unhappiness, how to laugh. Run out of town after his attempts to halt the slave trade had threatened the income of the local duke, Adalbert 'had laid the dignity of his bishop's office aside, and become a humble brother'. Yet even as 'merely one among many',[82] he had continued to stand out from the crowd. Take off dirty shoes at his monastery, for instance, and Adalbert would immediately swoop to clean them: a display of humility striking enough in any monk, let alone one who still ranked officially as a prince of the Church. Other bishops, needless to say, were appalled by such eccentricities; but Otto, who had been brought up to admire holy men, and actively to seek them out, preferred to regard it as the mark of saintliness. Adalbert, who had only to pray and the croaking of frogs in the Roman marshes would mysteriously be silenced, was evidently a man with a formidable talent for instilling serenity in the troubled – and Otto was certainly troubled. With news reaching him in the summer of 996 that the banks of the Elbe were once again ablaze, Adalbert seemed to offer him what he most craved: a way through the darkness ahead. Otto was not the only man, amid the stifling summer heat of Rome, to have his thoughts fixed on the wilds of the East. Adalbert too was planning to leave for there. He would travel, though, not in the pomp of his ecclesiastical vestments, but in his tattered habit; not as a prince, but as a humble missionary. Yes, he insisted, it was indeed possible for the pagans to be brought to see the City of God – and it did not have to be done at the point of a sword.

The following spring, by the side of an icy lake, a bare day's journey beyond the borders of Poland and the protection of Boleslav, its Christian duke, Adalbert was hacked to death. His killers were Prussians, a heathen and turbulent people, much given to tattooing themselves and downing pints of blood, who had scorned the missionary's preaching as the sinister work of a 'German god'.[83] Otto, brought the news in Aachen, was predictably distraught. Yet even as he mourned his loss, miraculous things were already being reported of Adalbert's death. An angel, it was said, sweeping down from heaven, had caught the martyr's head as it was sent flying through the air by a Prussian axe, and later, reuniting it with the decapitated trunk, had left the corpse to be found on the far side of the lake. From there, it had been tenderly transported by two of Adalbert's disciples back across the border, to safety, and the awestruck reverence of the Poles. Boleslav, delighted to find himself with such a potent relic in his possession, had promptly sealed his ownership of the martyr's body by entombing it at Gniezno, the capital that he had inherited from his father, Duke Miesco. To his subjects, a people who only four decades previously had been quite as heathen as the Prussians, the shrine raised over Adalbert appeared an awesome and a wondrous thing, a beacon of blazing holiness, a joining of earth to heaven. It had needed no burning of villages to ensure this, no mass gibbets, no planting of Saxon garrisons. In death, if not in life, Adalbert had fulfilled his dearest wish. He had indeed helped to purge heathenism from the eastern wilds – and the only blood shed had been his own. A new people had been confirmed in their membership of Christendom. The Poles had been secured for Christ.

And for Otto as well? So he certainly trusted. Despite the loss of Adalbert, and despite the continued violence along the frontier with the Wends, the emperor's sense of mission and self-confidence remained undimmed. Indeed, if anything, it was coming to shine more radiantly still. Adalbert was not the only inspirational figure to have entered Otto's orbit the previous year. Gerbert too had been in Rome in the wake of the coronation. Struggling, as he had been doing ever since his brush-off by Theophanu, to secure an office worthy of his talents, he had travelled there originally to petition the Pope; but soon enough, having turned the full glare of his charisma on to Otto, had found himself being employed as the emperor's secretary. Although this role had lasted only a few weeks, until Otto's departure from Italy, Gerbert had had no intention of letting his opportunity slip. By October, he had successfully insinuated himself back into the emperor's company.[84] That autumn, both he and Adalbert had spent over a month closeted with Otto, 'day and night', as Gerbert later proudly boasted.[85] It was never divulged which topic had proved so fascinating as to keep Christendom's greatest ruler distracted from affairs of state for such an unusual length of time with two clerics; but events would soon serve to offer a hint.

In the summer of 997, Otto formally issued Gerbert with what the great scholar had long craved: a command to serve him as his mentor. 'Demonstrate your distaste', went the order, 'for Saxon parochialism'[86] – and Gerbert obliged with relish. Even as Otto laboured late into the campaigning season to secure the frontier of his homeland, his new counsellor was steeling him in a sense of the global role that it was his to play. 'For you are Caesar Augustus,' Gerbert reminded him exuberantly: 'Emperor of the Romans, sprung from the noblest blood of the Greeks', the master of Italy, of Germany, and, yes, of 'the brave lands of the Slavs' as well. 'The Roman Empire – it is ours, ours!'[87]

So it was that Christendom's most enduring spectre was summoned from its grave once again, and saluted as though it might be flesh and blood. Gerbert, as practical-minded as he was polymathic, could not have been oblivious to the tension between all his exultant sloganeering and the chaos that was the true state of the world. Neither – for he had spent the entire year of 997 bludgeoning the Wends out of Saxony – could Otto. Yet the bleeding state of things, far from tempering the bold talk of restoring a universal order, seems only to have made it more grandiloquent. In 998, the ambition would appear inscribed on Otto's seal, pledging him, every time that he stamped a document, to the '*renovatio*' – the renewal – of the Roman Empire. A quixotic fantasy? So it might have seemed. No hint was offered, either by Gerbert or by Otto himself, as to what a programme of *renovatio* might actually mean – still less how it was to be achieved. Yet this silence, far from expressing any lack of purpose, almost certainly veiled the very opposite: a consciousness of mysteries too earth-shaking and arcane to be spoken of publicly, of a mission literally cosmic in its implications, and of a duty shaped by the patterns of the revolving centuries.

At Magdeburg, when first summoned there by Otto, Gerbert had dazzled the assembled courtiers by demonstrating to them that it was possible, with the proper learning, and a fantastical instrument named the astrolabe, to track and measure the stars. Ancient sages had known this, and Saracen astronomers too; but never before had it been demonstrated with such brilliance by a Christian philosopher. God's creation, it appeared, might indeed be apprehended through a grasp of mathematics: 'for numbers both encode the origins of the universe', as Gerbert had put it, 'and serve to explain its functioning'.[88] What significance, then, in the lengthening shadow of the Millennium, that year which 'surpasses and transcends all other years',[89] did he identify in the magical number 1000? Infuriatingly, intriguingly, we have no certain answer. Not a single mention of it appears in all the surviving writings of Christendom's greatest and most enquiring mathematician: a silence so profound, in the circumstances, as to be deafening. Formidable scholar that he was, and devout Christian, Gerbert would have been well aware of Augustine's teachings on the end days. He would have known how sternly it had been forbidden to speculate as to their possible timing. Did he, as a consequence, scorn to pay any attention to the imminence of the Millennium? Or did he, encouraged by his imperial patron, secretly dare to follow the more dangerous course, and consider that perhaps Augustine had been wrong, and that the one thousand years spoken of by St John, after which evil was to triumph across the world, might, just might, have been meant literally? After all, if anyone had the sanction to engage in such perilous enquiries, then surely it was Otto III, the Roman emperor whose dominion was the single bulwark capable of being raised against the coming of Antichrist, and whose fate it was to be ruling with the one-thousandth anniversary of the Incarnation just a couple of years away?

Certainly, the nearer the Millennium drew, the more Otto seems to have felt oppressed by a sense of urgency – as though the passing of days itself were a flood stream to be breasted. If it were true that time was indeed running out, then the challenge of securing the Roman Empire was evidently not to be a simple one – not in the face of all that a transcendent and gathering malice appeared to be hurling against him. No matter that the Wends, by the end of 997, had been pacified at last. A fresh and more insidious threat to Otto's ambitions was already looming. Alarming news had arrived from the very heart of the great project of *renovatio*: Rome herself. The city's erstwhile tyrant, John Crescentius, unappeased by the pardon granted him following Otto's coronation, had made a sudden power grab. Pope Gregory, who had originally pleaded with his cousin to grant Crescentius mercy, had himself been served with exile. As his replacement upon the throne of St Peter, and the willing stooge of his Roman sponsors, there had emerged blinking into the limelight a most unexpected figure: Otto's own godfather, one-time tutor and ambassador to Constantinople, John Philagathos. No matter that his attempt to secure a princess from the *Basileus* had ended in failure – the embassy had evidently done nothing to diminish his conceit. Indeed, if anything, it appeared to have boosted it; for Byzantine diplomats, despite their private scorning of Philagathos as 'slime, the son of perdition, worthy of every curse, a pile of steaming excrement, obese, a man whose true god protrudes just below his wobbling paunch',[90] had cheerfully puffed him up in his ambitions, keen as they were to see a Greek as the Bishop of Rome. Crescentius too, whose family had long had close affiliations with Constantinople, was widely suspected of being an agent of the *Basileus*. Meanwhile, Philagathos himself, as the countryman of one Roman emperor and the godfather of a second, was sublimely confident of securing the support of both men for his papacy. This was a reasonable enough calculation, perhaps; except that neither he nor any of the conspirators had quite grasped what Otto believed to be at stake.

In February 998, the Holy Lance was planted before the walls of Rome. Behind it there spread the massed ranks of the imperial army, the hardened veterans of a thousand bloody skirmishes in the forests and bogs of the North, a sight fit to strike terror into the heart of any southerner. Philagathos, discovering too late the full, horrendous scale of his misjudgement, had already fled the city. Crescentius, equally appalled by what he had drawn down upon himself, was holed up in his private fortress, in the shadow of St Peter's, waiting for the storm to pass. But it did not pass. The emperor and his army remained implacable. In desperation, after several weeks of the siege, Crescentius disguised himself in a monk's cowl and slipped out from his strong-hold, to throw himself on Otto's mercy. Coldly, Otto sent him back to his doom. Shortly afterwards, once Easter was past, the deployment of immense siege engines enabled the citadel to be stormed. Crescentius himself, taken prisoner, was briskly decapitated. His headless corpse, so as to warn others against being 'deceived by the devil's wiles', was first flung into a ditch, and then 'hung by the feet from a gibbet, on the highest precipice of the fortress'.[91]

Yet even his fate was not so salutary as that of the wretched Anti-pope. Philagathos had been quickly hunted down. Although his life was spared, such were the mutilations inflicted on him that he might well have yearned for execution: for first his eyes were removed, then his nose, and then his lips and tongue. When the hideously disfigured prisoner was finally hauled into the imperial presence, the spectacle of what had been done to his old tutor reduced Otto to appalled silence; but not to clemency. The captors were given rich rewards; while Philagathos himself was handed over to the tender mercies of the man whom he had thought to replace. Pope Gregory, keen to brand his rival an apostate before the public gaze of the entire city, ordered him fitted with a cap of animal skins, and then had him 'placed on the back of a donkey, facing towards the tail, as a public crier led him through the various parts of Rome'.[92] Finally, to set the seal on his degradation, Philagathos was ceremonially expelled from the priesthood, stripped of his pontifical robes and led away to a monastery, there to count the long days until his death. By such decisive measures, Otto could reflect with grim satisfaction, had the Holy City been preserved against the tide of darkness that had seemed almost ready to swallow it.

Except that there were men of God, even peers of Adalbert, who were not so certain that it had been preserved. While the Roman crowds had cheerfully entertained themselves by kicking the corpse of Crescentius as it was dragged past them, or pelting Philagathos with dung, those whose approval Otto most desperately craved, his spiritual advisers, were horrified. One of them, a hermit of legendary saintliness by the name of Nilus, had even dared to confront the emperor directly. Despite being in his nineties, and weak from his Lenten fast, he had tottered along to the trial of Philagathos and begged for mercy on behalf of the fallen Anti-pope. When this plea was rejected, he had cursed Otto and Gregory both. 'For if you do not forgive him whom God has delivered up into your hands,' Nilus had warned the two cousins, 'neither will the heavenly Father forgive you your own sins.'[93] Then, ignoring all Otto's appeals to stay with him and grant him absolution, the aged hermit had turned on his heels and headed away southwards, back to the lonely valley that sheltered his cell.

Otto did not pursue him. After all, a retreat from the world was hardly an option open to a man pledged to the fateful mission of preserving Christendom from Antichrist. If the Roman Empire were indeed to be restored to its vanished potency, then the securing of Rome itself could rank only as a beginning. Though it was bejewelled with churches, the ancient city had to be fitted once more to serve as the capital of an empire. Orders were duly given that the ruins on the Palatine, 'that seat and head of all the world',[94] should be cleared of their rubble and rendered habitable again.[95] Ceremonial too was upgraded, to match the prestigious new imperial address. No more cracking open of animal bones for Otto; instead, in an echo of the gilded rituals of his mother's native city, he began to sit at feasts aloof from his henchmen, at a semicircular table, and to be saluted as 'the Emperor of Emperors'. Even the titles with which he graced his courtiers in turn – 'senator', 'consul', 'prefect of the fleet' – had all been fastidiously pilfered from the lumber box of antiquity. In short, it was a display of pageantry like nothing seen in Rome for many centuries – and those who witnessed it were accordingly dazzled. To the excitable, it seemed almost as though Otto's work were already done; as though, through the sheer force of his will, he had indeed brought the Roman Empire back to life and restored its greatness to its ancient limits. Both Baghdad, 'the empire of iron', and Constantinople, 'the empire of gold', were imagined by admirers as bowing in stupefaction before 'great Otto'.[96] 'Rejoice, O Pope,' as one of them put it, 'rejoice, O Caesar! Let the Church exult in a fervour of joy, and let joy be great in Rome, let the imperial palace rejoice! With this pope, under this Caesar, the age itself is renewed!'[97]

But the young Caesar himself was racked by doubts. Visionary he may have been – but he was not naïve. He had patrolled the frontiers of Saxony. He knew perfectly well that Rome, although the heart of Christendom, was not the world. He knew too – for the words of Nilus still sounded in his memory – that all his labours to fortify his empire, all the blood he had spilled and all the brutalities he had committed, might have served only to put his fitness as God's anointed into doubt. For a year, he continued to ignore the promptings of his conscience. Then, in February 999, and with the anniversary of the Lenten atrocities fast approaching, Pope Gregory fell suddenly sick and died. The cause was malaria – but how was Otto to attribute it to anything save the effect of Nilus's curse? Abruptly after his cousin's death, he left Rome and headed southwards. Although he did not neglect the due business of an emperor on the way – taking hostages here, dispensing favours there, exploiting the rivalries of his Italian subjects with his customary dextrousness – he also made sure to perform acts of very public penance. Wherever there was a shrine, he would walk to it barefooted. By the time he found himself approaching Nilus's cell, it was evident that his contrition had been accepted as truly heartfelt: for the old man, leaving his cave, walked to the side of the road, from where he saluted the emperor fondly. Otto, slipping down from his saddle, knelt in tears before the hermit; and then removed his crown. A portentous gesture: for so it had been prophesied that the last Roman emperor would do, as he knelt upon Golgotha, and thereby usher in the end of days. Nilus paused – and then, demonstrating that he regarded the man before him as guiltless of any presumption, gave him his blessing. Finally, with due reverence, he handed the emperor back his crown.

Otto, returning to Rome, could do so with his sense of mission powerfully fortified. Even the death of his cousin, which only a few weeks earlier had struck in him a knell of icy foreboding, now appeared the working of Providence. At a fateful moment for him and for all mankind, with the one-thousandth anniversary of the Incarnation only months away, and the great labour of *renovatio* weighing down implacably upon his shoulders, he had been graced with the opportunity to promote to St Peter's throne the man best qualified to help him. On 2 April 999, Gerbert of Aurillac, the peasant from the Auvergne, was crowned Pope. The name he took – Sylvester II – signalled unmistakably to all the world how he saw his own role and that of his master. Just as the first Sylvester was supposed to have served Constantine, so would he serve Otto: Pope and emperor together, they would shepherd the Christian people.

And swell their numbers too. Ancient prophecies long current in Italy foretold how at the end of times the last Roman emperor would summon all the pagans in the world to baptism; and now, as the fateful year of the Millennium dawned, a Roman emperor was preparing to do just that. Not at sword point – the example of Adalbert would hardly have licensed forced conversions – but rather in a manner as pacific as it was mystical. So it was, for instance, that the chieftain of the Hungarians, those one-time predator horsemen, was sent a replica of the Holy Lance by Otto, and a diadem by Pope Sylvester, and publicly welcomed, as King Stephen, into the order of Christian royalty. So it was too, in the spring of the millennial year, that the Roman emperor himself, travelling eastwards to where the ancient Caesars had never reached, crossed the border into Poland and processed to Gniezno. Columns of brightly dressed warriors stood massed to greet him as he walked, barefoot once more, to the shrine of St Adalbert. Then, having prayed beside the tomb, Otto rose and set out to complete what his murdered friend had begun. The Polish duke, like the Hungarian prince, was presented with a crown and a copy of the Holy Lance; the fur-clad Boleslav, not to be outdone, reciprocated by giving the emperor one of St Adalbert's arms. Otto, profoundly moved, burst into tears. 'And that day the two men were joined together with such bonds of affection that the Emperor called Boleslav his brother, and proclaimed him a friend of the Roman people.'[98]

Among the Byzantines, distaste for the spilling of blood on battlefields was paralleled by a no less fervent conviction that Constantinople should rule the world. Despite widespread unease back in the capital, a succession of tenth-century emperors threw themselves with gusto into the task of pushing back the imperial frontiers. As the Millennium approached, the empire of the New Rome appeared more formidable than it had done for centuries. (Vatican Museum)

With its Roman brickwork, its Visigothic arches, and its pillars plundered from a demolished cathedral, the Great Mosque of Córdoba was no less triumphantly Islamic for its wholesale cannibalisation of infidel traditions. As Mohammed himself had put it: 'God desires that if you do something you perfect it.' (Commons.wikimedia.org)

Otto III: the robes of a Caesar, the posture of Christ in heaven. Four women, representing Rome, France, Germany and the lands of the Slavs, bring the Emperor gifts, while his attendants watch on, each with the hint of a smile. But no smile lightens the expression of Otto. Enthroned in majesty he may be, yet he has the look of a man burdened by the fearful conviction that he is ruling at the end of time.
(Bayerische Staatsbibliothek/SuperStock)

Astounding as Gerbert's achievements appeared to his contemporaries, they appeared something altogether more sinister to subsequent generations. Surely, it was presumed, only the blackest magic could have brought a peasant to sit on Saint Peter's throne? Here, in a fifteenth-century illustration, Gerbert sports a sinister 5 o'clock shadow while beaming complacently at the Devil.
(Wikipedia)

True, there was in all this a steely measure of calculation. The Poles were valuable allies in the struggle against the Wends. That Otto retained his hard-edged streak of pragmatism was evident from the presence in his train, even as he prayed by Adalbert's tomb, of hostages from Italy. Yet pragmatism, in the shadow of the end time, could go only so far. Dimensions infinitely beyond that of the earthly present were also in play: the threads of history, woven according to God's plan throughout the centuries, were on the verge of being gathered up and placed into Otto's hands. Or so Otto himself appears devoutly to have believed. It is certainly hard to explain otherwise why, after an absence from his homeland of many months, with his nobility fractious and his countrymen resentful of all their emperor's foreign adventuring, his principal concern should have been to consult, not with the living, but with the dead.

By late April, barely a month after leaving Gniezno, and having toured Saxony at a blistering speed, Otto was in Aachen: site of the tomb of Charlemagne. On Pentecost – the day when the Holy Spirit, descending upon the earliest disciples, had imbued them with the fire of an unearthly wisdom – he and three companions passed down into the opened crypt. There, within its tenebrous depths, they supposedly found Charlemagne sitting as though asleep, a golden crown on his head, a sceptre in his gloved hands; 'and the fingernails had penetrated through the gloves, and were sticking out'.[99] Otto, having first knelt in homage before his great predecessor, next ordered the corpse to be clothed in white robes, those very garments which, at the end of time, in the great battle with Antichrist and all his cohorts, would be worn by 'the armies of heaven'.[100] Then, re-emerging from the darkness of the underworld into the light of day, he prepared to move on again: not to Saxony, but back to Italy. Well might his countrymen have felt themselves snubbed and undervalued. As one chronicler phrased it with diplomatic understatement: 'the Emperor's doings received a somewhat mixed reaction'.[101]

Otto himself was not oblivious to the mutterings. He knew that many of his actions were bound to strike his subjects as bizarre, or even unsettling. That, however, could not be helped. The mission with which he believed himself charged by God was hardly one that he could parade. Already, however, to those in the know, the proofs of its success must have appeared manifest. Day by day, month by month, 'the one thousandth year since the Incarnation was being completed happily'[102] – and Antichrist had not appeared. That did not mean, however, that Otto could afford to let slip his guard. Just the opposite. Christ's life had contained many significant moments – and who was to say from which of them the one thousand years, after which Satan was to be loosed from his prison, were properly to be measured? Already, as the new year of 1001 dawned, there came a sobering reminder that the forces of darkness were very far from spent. The Romans, whom their emperor had 'loved and cherished above all',[103] were reported to have risen in revolt. Otto immediately hurried to the ancient city. Only a full-scale onslaught by his soldiers, and the unveiling of the Holy Lance, 'glinting terribly'[104] in the hands of the bishop who wielded it, served to quell the insurrection. Despite being stunned by the Romans' ingratitude, and besieged by their repentant tears, Otto did not permit his devotion to the city to override his strategic judgement: a full-scale withdrawal was ordered to Ravenna. From here, now menacing his foes, now mollifying them, he continued to display his customary political acuity. Although Rome herself remained too unsettled to serve him as his capital, he knew that she would not defy him for long. In the autumn of 1001, he dispatched orders to East Francia, summoning fresh troops. They were to be with him by late January. Passing the winter in Lombardy, the emperor could rest confident that not only Rome but all of Italy would soon be his.

And perhaps even more as well. Otto's efforts in the millennial year to buttress the Roman Empire had self-evidently been sufficient to keep Antichrist at bay; but there was much still left to be done. All his labours notwithstanding, Christendom remained divided. Accordingly, in the summer of 1001, Otto had dispatched a second embassy to Constantinople, led by a bishop more trustworthy than Philagathos – and this time his demand for a princess had been met.

Indeed, it was reported that she was already on her way, and could be expected, like Otto's reinforcements, come the spring: the two halves of the Roman Empire seemed on the verge of being joined at last. Even that prospect, however, giddy though it was, seems barely to have satisfied the young emperor. For what if there were a still greater and yet more terrible destiny awaiting him, one prophesied for many centuries and fated to convulse all the universe? Confirmation of his suspicions, in that year of 1001, seemed to lie right on his doorstep.

Beyond the great palaces and churches of Ravenna, those monuments to long-dead Christian emperors, there stretched a pestiferous wasteland of salt marshes and mudflats, all stagnancy and whining insects, unutterably desolate. Not wholly so, however: for occasionally, amid the bleakness, there might be glimpsed a makeshift shack. In each one of these, barefoot and unkempt, there lived a hermit; and among them, on a remote and boggy island, was their leader, the most renowned saint in all Italy. The name of Romuald was one to put even Nilus's in the shade. Holiness was manifest in the very appearance of his skin, which had turned hairless and bright green, 'like a newt's', following an extended immersion in a swamp.[105] On those rare occasions when the saint did deign to clean himself, his dirty bathwater, it was reported, could heal the sick. One group of villagers, on discovering that he was planning to move on from their neighbourhood, had even plotted to murder him and saw his body up into relics, such was his reputation as a miracle-worker. Spared dismemberment by pretending to be mad, Romuald had survived and flourished, to become a living model of sanctity. No wonder, then, that Otto should often have made the journey out into the marshes beyond Ravenna. These trips, however, were not mere spiritual tourism. The emperor, as he pondered the future, had a particular reason to consult with the saint. Both men, despite all the immeasurable differences in their station, were embarked upon a matching quest. Both shared the passionate conviction that the Second Coming was imminent; and both had resolved to meet it by leaving as little as possible for the returning Christ to condemn.

'For who is not terrified,' as one of Romuald's disciples would later put it, 'who is not shaken to his very roots, by that statement of the Lord Himself in the Gospel: "Like lightning flashes from the east as far as the west, so will the coming of the Son of Man be."'[106] The way of life established by Romuald at Ravenna was a consciously heroic effort to keep this dread of judgement at bay. An existence of implacable and excruciating deprivation, whether lived in a swamp, or in the depths of a forest, or bricked up in a cell, with nothing for company save for birds and the vermin that swarm and feed on rags: such, argued the saint, was the only serviceable preparation for the end of days. Here was a conviction with which his imperial visitor had evidently expressed great sympathy: for one of Romuald's companions, after Otto had left them for the last time, turned and asked his master in perplexity, 'What has happened to the King's noble resolution, the promise he confided secretly to Christ, to become like one of us?'[107] But it is evident too that Otto's vow, however he may precisely have phrased it, had been misunderstood. Not for the emperor a shack in a swamp. Instead, he had revealed to Romuald, it was his intention to travel to Jerusalem, and there to lay down 'the badge' of his royalty: his earthly crown.[108] 'For after three years, during which I will set right all that is wrong in my empire, I will abdicate my kingship. And I will offer it instead to one who is better than me.'[109] Romuald's followers may have failed to grasp whom their visitor had meant by this – but Romuald surely knew.

The king to whom Otto intended to hand his crown was Christ. The world once readied for the hour of judgement, the emperor would climb the hill of Golgotha, and kneel, and commit his soul to God; and thereby usher in the end of days. Romuald, by granting Otto his blessing, had shown that he, like Nilus, approved of this intention. He had shown that he believed himself in the presence of the last Roman emperor.

But all his hopes, and those of Otto himself, were to be dashed. When the emperor, early in 1002, began his advance on Rome, the venerable hermit was by his side. As the expedition headed southwards, however, a giant dragon was spotted overhead, glittering brightly in the winter sky. Everyone who saw it knew it for a certain portent of doom. Sure enough, soon afterwards, Otto fell sick of malaria – and by late January he was dead. Many plans, many dreams perished with him. The reinforcements summoned from East Francia had been only a single day's march away as their emperor breathed his last. The princess sent from Constantinople to serve as Otto's bride had no sooner landed than she was being sent back home again. The new King of Saxony had no time for fantasies of global rule. For Henry, Duke of Bavaria, son of 'the Quarreller' and grandson of the Henry who had schemed so tirelessly to steal the crown from Otto I, it was sufficient that one of his line had the rule of the *Reich* at last. Not until 1014 would he finally succeed in battling his way south to Rome, and his coronation as emperor; and when he did so, there would be no Pope Sylvester waiting for him there with brilliant talk of *renovatio*.

Gerbert, who had loyally followed Otto to Ravenna, had returned to the Lateran following his patron's death; and there, in May 1003, after a miserable year of being bullied by the resurgent Crescentius family, he too had died. It had not taken long for his extraordinary story to be transmuted into myth. That a peasant – still more a non-Italian peasant – should have risen to hold the office of pope appeared to most too remarkable to credit to mere human agency. So it was that Gerbert of Aurillac, 'the philosophical pope',[110] who had devoted the last years of his life to buttressing the Roman Empire, would be remembered, not for all his labours in the cause of learning and of Christendom, but as a thing of Antichrist, a beast, 'risen up from the abyss shortly after the completion of a thousand years'.[111]

'Caesar is gone. And with him gone, all future ages are thrown into confusion.'[112] This epitaph, composed in the confused months that followed Otto's death, was not, perhaps, a wholly exaggerated one. A tipping point had indeed been reached: the dream of universal empire as a solution to the world's problems, for all that it might still animate the chanceries of Baghdad and Constantinople, would never again, as a practical policy, serve to motivate a monarch of Latin Christendom.

'Like one of the pagan kings of ancient times, he struggled to resurrect the glories of Rome, that city with its deep-buried foundations – but in vain.'[113] So it would be remembered of Otto. None of his successors would follow his example. His dreams had been too dazzling – and his failure too total as well. Although he never did make it to Jerusalem, and although he never did surrender his crown into the hands of Christ, Otto would prove to have died as what he had long imagined himself to be: the last Roman emperor.

3

... YIELDING PLACE TO NEW

The Beginning of the Birth-pangs

Eight years before the one-thousandth anniversary of the Incarnation, in 992, an old man robed in black tottered up the gangplank of a ship bound for Jerusalem. Adso, who had long since stepped down from the abbacy of Montier-en-Der, was by now in his eighties, and perilously frail to be making such a voyage. The rigours of life at sea were notorious – and sure enough, no sooner had the voyage begun than the aged monk was sickening. Five days later, and he was dead. Father Adso would never tread the Holy Land.

But why, at such a venerable age, had the great scholar been travelling there in the first place? 'He will come to Jerusalem': so Adso had written long previously, in his celebrated discourse on the career of Antichrist. For it was there, on the Mount of Olives, 'in the place opposite to where the Lord ascended to heaven', that the climactic battle against the Son of Perdition would be fought; 'and the Lord Jesus will slay him with the breath of his mouth'.[1] No mortal could know for certain when this cosmos-changing event was to take place; and Adso, in his concern to emphasise this point, had famously reassured the Queen of the Western Franks that Antichrist would not appear for so long as her husband's family – the Carolingians, the dynasty of

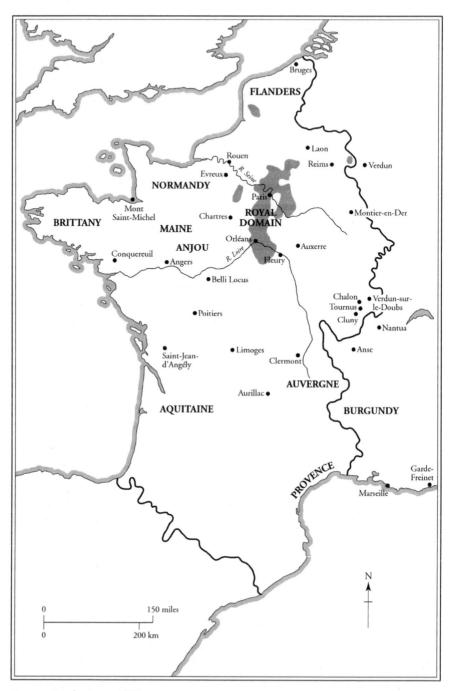

France in the year 1000

Charlemagne – remained in power. But times had changed. No sooner had Adso completed his letter than fearsome portents of doom had begun to overtake the royal line. In 954, Louis IV, Gerberga's husband, had clattered out through the gates of Laon, down the hill on which the royal capital stood hunched, and galloped off into the wilds that stretched beyond. There, deep in the woods, he had caught sight of a wolf and set off in hot pursuit – but alas, the creature had proved to be a demon, and the king, thrown from his horse, had suffered crippling injuries. Stretchered to a sickbed, he had soon succumbed to a loathsome disease, which had set his body to rot: '*elephantiasis pestis*'.[2] Death had followed shortly afterwards.

A baneful and portentous end. 'Cruel and savage, fit only for wild beasts'[3]: so it was said of the forest in which Louis IV had met with the demonic wolf. The same might well have been said of his violence-ravaged kingdom. The only realm still to be ruled by a descendant of Charlemagne was subsiding inexorably into gangsterism. As the authority of the Carolingians faded ever more into shadow, so did the realm they ruled appear ever more threatened with collapse. Of Louis himself it was said that he had owned nothing 'but the title of royalty';[4] and yet the succeeding decades had proved his heirs more wraithlike still. 'Justice slept in the hearts of kings and princes';[5] and increasingly, across all the assorted territories that still professed a shadowy loyalty to the King of the Western Franks, the mystique of Charlemagne's bloodline had come to seem a phantom thing. So much so, indeed, that in 987, upon the death of Louis V, a feckless fashion obsessive nicknamed by his despairing subjects 'the Sluggard', the great men of West Francia had taken a fateful step. Louis, irresponsible to the last, had died childless; and so it was, at a specially convened council, that the Frankish princes had felt themselves justified in electing one of their own number to the throne.

Hugh Capet, the new king, was a man not altogether lacking the stamp of royalty: descended from a long line of war heroes, he was also, on his mother's side, the grandson of Henry the Fowler. Nevertheless, he was no Carolingian; and the Frankish lords, by

131

electing him, had very pointedly ignored the claims of a rival who was. Louis V's uncle, an embittered and slippery schemer by the name of Charles, was widely loathed by his peers; but when, in 988, he had pressed his claim to the throne by going to war with Hugh, he had been able to make considerable headway, and even to seize back the royal capital. For three years, a bloody stalemate had prevailed; until, hoist by his own petard, Charles had been betrayed by a schemer even more devious and underhand than himself. Adalbero, the Bishop of Laon, was a man of ineffable hauteur, snake-like intelligence, and 'a reputation for virtue', as one of his fellow bishops phrased it diplomatically, 'that was not all it might have been'.[6] Outsmarted for once, Charles had been duly handed over to his enemies, and immured within the Capetian stronghold of Orléans. By the end of 991, he was dead. The Carolingian dynasty was now effectively extinct. A few weeks later, and Adso was taking ship for Jerusalem.

Meanwhile, proofs that the great scholar might have been correct in his calculations, and that the moment was indeed a perilous one, had not been lacking upon the broad stage of the world. In 988, in that same city of Orléans where the last Carolingian was soon to meet his end, an icon of the crucified Christ had wept 'a river of tears',[7] and a wolf, appearing in the cathedral, had pulled on the bell rope with its teeth, making the bell toll. Then, one year later, a fearsome comet had blazed over Christendom.* What precisely this might have portended – whether 'famine or pestilence or war or the destruction of the earth'[8] – no one could tell for sure. There were many, however, who found themselves gripped by foreboding. Even those who had most prospered from the deposition of the Carolingians were not immune to a certain twitchiness.

Hugh Capet's eldest son, Robert, who would succeed his father in 996, was notoriously sensitive to any hint that the world might be nearing its end. 'What does it mean?' he would demand urgently of scholars whenever news was brought to him of some particularly

---

* Halley's Comet. It would be seen next in 1066.

menacing wonder. 'Send me back your answer at once. Send it back by the same messenger I sent you!'[9] His agitation – bred, perhaps, of a not entirely easy conscience – was hardly surprising; so too the circumspection with which most scholars chose to reply. Naturally, they knew their Augustine; but they knew as well what Adso had written about the coming of Antichrist, and all that it might imply for the new dynasty. One who wrote to Robert duly advised him to summon a council, to stamp out 'divergent opininons',[10] and affirm once and for all that the date of the Judgement Day could not be known; but there were others who replied in more sombre terms. Unsurprisingly, it was inexplicable manifestations of blood, whether falling from the sky as rain or bubbling up from springs, which tended to elicit particularly dire warnings. Whether the imminent fracturing of things which they appeared to foretell was in turn to be interpreted as heralding Antichrist, there was no scholar bold enough to say; but there were some, in their answers, who did presume to offer hints. One, in a letter to King Robert, went so far as to echo the words of Christ Himself, when He had sat on the Mount of Olives and been asked about the ending of the world. 'Nation will rise against nation,' the Lord had answered, 'and kingdom against kingdom, and there will be famines and earthquakes in various places. All this is but the beginning of the birth-pangs.'[11]

Food for thought indeed. Not that the scholars who wrote to the king were calling on him to despair. Blood-curdling though their jeremiads might be, they were practical men, and they trusted Robert, as God's anointed, to respond with practical measures. That, after all, in a fallen world, was what kings were for: to tame disorder, no matter where and how it threatened. The king himself was quite agreed. Just as solemnly as the Carolingians had done, Robert interpreted lawlessness among his subjects as a menace to the harmony of the very universe. Devotedly, he had been raised by his father to yield to no one in the grandiose quality of his self-esteem. In 981, seven years before his election to the throne, Hugh Capet had been granted an audience with Otto II in Rome; and the trauma of that experience, a mingling of awe and humiliation, had steeled in him a resolve never again to be upstaged by anyone. Because Otto, perfectly aware that his guest did not speak Latin, had insisted on speaking exclusively in that language, Hugh had provided for his son the finest teacher in all Christendom: Gerbert himself. Then, only five months after his own coronation, he had insisted that Robert be crowned joint king – like Charlemagne, on Christmas Day. As a daughter-in-law he had even sought – in vain – to procure a Byzantine princess. Had Hugh's ambitions for his son been the sole determinant of power, then Robert would have been a very great king indeed.

But image, although important to be sure, could take the new regime only so far. For all the exuberance with which Hugh and Robert laid claim to the awesome traditions descended from Charlemagne, the unsettling truth was that the inheritance they had come into was one of impotence and crisis too. No less than the Carolingians, the Capetian kings were obliged to operate from a power base cruelly inadequate to their ambitions. Great and intimidating had Hugh seemed as a prince among other princes: the '*Dux Francorum*', the 'Duke of the Franks'. Seated upon the throne, however, he had soon begun to appear much shrunken. Royal weight-throwing did not come cheap – and Hugh had only marginally more resources available to him than his hapless predecessors had done. His estates, which had appeared so extensive when he ruled them as a duke, appeared a good deal less so now that they were required to bankroll him as a king. Running as they did only from Paris to Orléans, the leverage that they brought him over the great principalities of the south was precisely zero, with the result that he was first ignored there, and then, as the years passed, increasingly forgotten. Even in the more northerly dominions, where he inevitably loomed much larger, Hugh's former peers could not quite shake off the habit of regarding him as a player not so very different from themselves. Indeed, all his regal pretensions, far from instilling in his subjects a due sense of deference, tended instead to provoke only hilarity and taunts. 'Who made you a count?' Hugh once sniffily demanded of a magnate from Aquitaine. Back, swift and cutting, came the inevitable reply: 'Who made you a king?'[12]

Still, then, unstaunched by the enthronement of the upstart Capetians, authority continued to ebb away from the crown. It was not only the kings themselves who found this disorienting. Fractious or predatory a Frankish nobleman might be – but he was still likely to cherish memories of the gilded days of Charlemagne, when the counts and bishops of the kingdom, having travelled amid magnificent pomp to attend upon the king, would share with him in the great feasts of Easter or Christmas or Pentecost, and deliberate over the affairs of the world. Indeed, for generations of noblemen, the royal court had been the only stage of choice. There were few who would have relished being confined to a merely local power base. To moulder far from the king had traditionally been regarded as the very mark of cloddish failure. Even under the Capetians, the presence of great lords and prelates at the royal court was not unknown. Watching the Count of Flanders, say, or the Archbishop of Reims, or the Bishop of Laon, taking council with the king a spectator might have been tempted to imagine that nothing much had changed. Yet remorselessly, over the course of the calamitous tenth century, things had changed; and with consequences for Frankish society that would prove, in the long run, momentous indeed.

It was the Capetians themselves – ironically enough – who had most potently blazed a trail.* Long before Hugh's elevation to the throne, his predecessors had set about forging themselves into a novel kind of dynasty, and their many holdings into a novel kind of inheritance. Gradually, painfully, but in the end decisively, they had ended up reconfiguring their very notion of what a family might be. No longer, as the Franks had done since time immemorial, did they take

---

* The family name 'Capetian' actually derived from Hugh Capet himself, but in the interests of clarity, I have chosen to apply it retrospectively to his forefathers as well. Properly, these should be termed 'Robertians', 'Robert' being a name that looms large in the early pages of the family's history.

for granted the benefits of belonging to a vast and teeming clan: for these, amid the convulsions of the age, no longer appeared quite so certain as anciently they had done. Weight of numbers, after all, had not done much for the heirs of Charlemagne. Quick-fire breeding, far from preserving their imperial patrimony intact, had served in the end only to reduce it to ribbons. The great dynasties of the kingdom, long since denied the opportunity to pillage pagan enemies, had turned instead upon themselves. The resulting factionalism, which even the feuding warlords might on occasion find wearying, had begun to inspire, by the mid-tenth century, an inevitable revulsion. It was the Capetians, as befitted the most powerful Frankish dynasty of all, who had taken the lead. To a great lord such as Hugh Capet's father, a man publicly acknowledged by Louis IV himself as 'second only to the king throughout the kingdom',[13] the advantages accruing from a vast array of second cousins had appeared far from self-evident. Remorselessly, the definition of what constituted a Capetian had begun to narrow. The more distant the relations, the more ruthless the pruning. Those family members who did remain were reduced ever more to a state of inequality and dependence. By 956, when Hugh Capet succeeded his father as Duke of the Franks and inherited all the core holdings of the dynasty intact, even his younger brothers had found themselves effectively sidelined. By 996, when Hugh passed away in turn, no one was remotely surprised that Robert should have scooped up everything, lands as well as crown. As with the royal family of East Francia, so now with that of the Frankish Empire's western half: the eldest son took all.

Bad news for the siblings of a crown prince; but good news, by and large, for the prospects of the dynasty itself. Such, at any rate – if imitation is to be judged the sincerest form of approbation – was the opinion of the Capetians' former peers. Ferocious and unrelenting were the demands of power among the Franks; and no prince, if he wished to maintain himself in the front rank of greatness, could afford to overlook a potential competitive advantage. The Capetian drive to forge a coherent domain, one that could be handed down from father to son intact, generation after generation, had not gone unremarked by other lords. There were some, indeed, who had already trumped it. Beyond the royal heartlands that extended around Paris, for instance, bordering the northern seas, there stretched a principality already so compact and unitary that it made the Capetian domain look positively moth-eaten in comparison. Proudly, the counts of Flanders boasted of their origins as lieutenants of the Carolingians; but that was hardly telling all the story. Indeed, as their many enemies saw it, their posing as upholders of the *status quo* was risible: for to their neighbours they were nothing but predators, slippery and ever-ravening, 'replete with the venom of viperish guile'.[14] As far back as 862, the first Count of Flanders had begun a long family tradition of brutal opportunism by abducting a princess from under the nose of her royal father; and from that moment on, as count succeeded count, the dynasty had ruthlessly expanded and consolidated its holdings. Indeed, bearing in mind what was evidently a hereditary aptitude for illegality and violence, there was nothing, perhaps, that better illustrated the consistent effectiveness of those who ruled the principality than their ability to box in the ambitions of their own kindred. Only once, in 962, had a count been compelled to hive off some of his holdings to a separate branch of the family – and only then because he was old and his son had just unexpectedly died. The mood of crisis notwithstanding, he had still insisted on appointing as his own successor his grandson – who at the time was merely a child. Time had proved this decision the correct one: the dynasty had endured. Indeed, by the time of the Millennium, it was as entrenched and formidable as it had ever been. Potent testimony to what might be won, amid the troubles of the age, by the simple expedient of passing down an inheritance intact to a single heir. Not all the fustian of tradition in which the princes of Flanders continued to adorn themselves could serve entirely to obscure just how startling had been their achievement in building up, from virtually nothing, a power base quite without precedent in the previous century.

Indeed, as the year 1000 drew nearer, so the entire political frame-work of the West Frankish kingdom appeared to be splintering and foundering upon the ambitions of rapacious princes. Unlike the counts of Flanders, most of these, as they manoeuvred for advan-tage, saw not the faintest advantage in claiming legitimacy from the failed institutions of the past. Along the valley of the Loire, for instance, west of the royal stronghold of Orléans, right on the doorstep of the Capetian domain, the very contours of ancient ter-ritories had begun to fade from memory, like fields abandoned to scrubland. In their place, patched together out of the plundered rubble of toppled lordships, the foundations of wholly new princi-palities were being laid: states that would ultimately owe little either to tradition or to mouldering property deeds. Those labouring at such a work of creation, rather than feeling any sense of embarrass-ment at their parvenu status, preferred instead to exult in it. As why should they not have done? They were proving themselves in the snake-pit to end all snake-pits, after all. What more certain badge of quality than to have pieced together, out of the shards of a ruined order, a state sufficient to prosper and endure? How telling it was that in the decade before the Millennium, and the decades that fol-lowed it, the prince who would most triumphantly put the Loire in his shadow bore the title of a county that seemed, in 987, when he ascended to its rule, a mere thing of shreds and patches. Such a prin-cipality – rootless, fragmented, lacking any natural boundaries – appeared to the region's scavengers, as they sniffed at it, easy prey. But they were wrong. Time would more than demonstrate the for-midable potential of Anjou.

Its new count, Fulk 'Nerra' – 'the Black' – claimed descent from a forester. No matter that his immediate predecessors had made a sequence of brilliant and profitable marriages, and that his own mother was a cousin of Hugh Capet, Fulk preferred not to boast of his connections with the international aristocracy, but rather to emphasise how his family had sprung like a flourishing oak from the rich, deep soil of his beloved Anjou. Generation after generation, the county had been pieced together by a succession of martial counts, each one of them characterised by a ferocious aptitude for self-aggrandisement and a memorable epithet: Fulk the Red, Fulk the Good, Geoffrey Greycloak. What inspired Fulk Nerra's own nickname – whether the bristling colour of his beard or the notoriously savage quality of his rages – we do not know; but it is certain that he exemplified to the full every attribute of his terrifying family. Although, at seventeen, he was still young when he became count, all his childhood had been preparation for such a moment: for his father, whether amid the business of the court, or the hunt, or the mud and carnage of the battlefield, had been assiduous in steeling him for power. This was just as well: 'for new wars', as one Angevin chronicler observed pithily, 'will always break out quickly against new rulers'.[15] Indeed, during the early years of his reign, Fulk Nerra found himself locked in a struggle for survival so desperate that the very existence of Anjou appeared at stake, and only bold measures served ultimately to redeem it. In 991, at Conquereuil, a plain just beyond the north-western limits of his lands, the young count dared to stake everything upon a single throw: a pitched battle against the most menacing of all his enemies, the Duke of Brittany. The Bretons, 'an uncivilised and quick-tempered people, lacking any manners',[16] and with an authentically barbarous taste for milk, were most dangerous opponents; and yet Fulk it was, amid great slaughter, who ultimately secured the victory. Among the dead left on the battlefield was the Duke of Brittany himself. Fulk Nerra, still only twenty-three, had secured a name for himself as one of the great captains of Christendom.

Evidence for that, ironically enough, lay in the fact that he would hardly ever again have to prove his generalship in open combat. Nothing was regarded by experienced commanders as more jejune than a taste for pitched battles when they were not strictly necessary: for in warfare, as in the habits of daily life, it was self-restraint that was seen as the truest mark of a man. Renowned for his ferocity Fulk Nerra may have been, but he was even more feared for his guile. Certainly, he was not afraid to be underhand when the situation required it. Kidnappings were a favoured stratagem; poisonings and assassinations too. On one notable occasion, in 1008, Fulk's agents even dared to ambush a royal hunting party, and strike down the palace chamberlain, a notorious anti-Angevin, in full view of the startled king. Crimes such as this were very much a family tradition: so it was, for instance, that Fulk's grandfather and namesake, a man who had owed his epithet of 'the Good' to his widespread reputation for piety, had not hesitated to rub out his own ward and stepson when the young boy had stood in the way of his interests. Yet Fulk Nerra, even judged by these elevated standards of ruthlessness, brought something new to the arts required of an ambitious prince: brutal and cunning he may have been, but he was also something more. In an era of ceaseless and bewildering change, he knew instinctively how best to turn all the many dramatic upheavals of the age to his own ends. Unlike so many of his contemporaries, Fulk had no dread of what were termed by the suspicious '*novae res*': 'new things'. On the contrary – he embraced them.

The proofs of this, raised first in wood and then increasingly, as his reign progressed, in forbidding stone, were to be found every-where across Anjou. Otto II, riding with his men through the badlands south of Rome, had witnessed the marks of something very similar: an all-consuming drive to throw up fortifications wherever possible that had been termed by the Italians, in their bastard Latin, '*incastellamento*'. This mania had reflected something more than simply a dread of the Saracens: for it had also served to stamp southern Italy very clearly as a land without a king – to Otto's disgust. Battlements, it had always been taken for granted in Francia, were properly the business of royalty, and royalty alone. How else was the public order of a kingdom to be maintained? An alarming ques-tion – and one becoming, even in the lands beyond the Alps, ever less theoretical by the year. As with the silks and jewellery and exotic cook-ing ingredients imported by the Amalfitans, so with their fortifications: the Italians knew how to set a trend. *Incastellamento* was spreading northwards.

In West Francia especially, borne upon the general ebbing of royal power, the taboo against private fortresses was increasingly in full retreat. The Capetians, as they struggled to assert their authority over even the patchwork of territories that constituted the royal domain, were hardly in any position to forbid distant princes from raising fortifications of their own. The consequence, sprouting up suddenly across region after region of West Francia, like toadstools from rotten wood, was a great host of strange and unsettling structures, as menacing as they were crude: what would come to be termed in English 'castles'. Here, bred of the throes of the Millennium, was yet another far-reaching convulsion – and right at its forefront, testing its limits, was the Count of Anjou.

Fulk's enthusiasm for castles reflected a typically cold-eyed insight: that their defences might be deployed as tools of aggression. The fortifications raised in Anjou, unlike the much larger '*castella*' which Otto II had ridden past in southern Italy, were designed to intimidate, not protect, the local population. Planted as a forward base in hostile territory, planned as merely one of a whole ring of similar structures, investing an obdurate target and gradually throttling it into submission, a castle founded by Fulk was built to provide shelter for its garrisons, and no one else. The great discovery, one exploited ruthlessly along the whole length of the Angevin marches, was that a fortification might be no less effective for being basic. Castles, in the first revolutionary flush of their existence, provided immediate payback for an often minimal outlay of effort. It did not take much to construct one. The ideal was to locate a rock, or a spur, or a lonely hillock – a feature, in short, of the kind that only a few years previously would have been regarded as quite valueless – and plant on it some rudimentary wooden battlements. Even where the Loire valley was at its flattest, artificial mounds – or 'mottes', as they were termed – could be thrown up in a matter of months. Then, with the site secured, the castle could be progressively upgraded. Fulk, as befitted a wealthy prince with a taste for the cutting edge, often ended up constructing battlements on an awesomely imposing scale. By the end of his reign, Anjou was shielded all along its frontiers by great donjons of solid stone. Castles and county alike: both had been built to last.

Yet if the new technology could be made to buttress a prince's ambitions, so also might it menace them. In the millennial year itself, for instance, the citadel in Angers, Fulk's capital, was seized and held against him. As a stab in the back, this revolt was especially shocking: for its captain was Fulk's own wife, Elizabeth, who had been caught out in an affair. The cuckolded husband, never known for his good temper at the best of times, duly swept into town upon a great firestorm of rage. The citadel was stormed; much of Angers laid to waste; Elizabeth herself captured and burned at the stake. A brutal reprisal, to be sure – but bred, as was so often the case with Fulk, of measured calculation. Even had he wished to, he could not possibly have shown mercy to his wife. Treachery from those who most owed him their love imperilled everything. If rebellion could flare up in his household, in his marriage bed, then where else might its embers lie, waiting to burst into flames? In every castle there was a castellan, appointed to serve as its captain; and in every castellan a taste for violence and ambition. 'No house is weak that has many friends.' So Geoffrey Greycloak, Fulk's father, had advised his son. 'Therefore I admonish you to hold dear those of your followers who have been faithful to you.'[17] A wise prescription, and one that Fulk adhered to throughout his life; yet never once did he presume to take those followers for granted. Humbly, in exchange for gifts of property, whether lands or strongholds or both, they were obliged to acknowledge their submission. Genuflecting before their lord, placing their clasped hands in his, humbly offering his foot or leg a kiss, they proclaimed themselves to all the world his 'vassi': his 'vassals'. This, an ancient Gaulish word, had once referred only to the very lowest of the low, the most desperate, the unfree; and even though, by the time of the Millennium, it had proved itself a term so upwardly mobile that it was held no shame even for a count or a duke to acknowledge himself the *vassus* of a king, the submission that it implied was no less solemn for that. Every vassal of Fulk knew of the penalties that would be exacted for any hint of treachery: the wasting of all he owned, and the desecration of his body. A lord prepared to burn his own wife, after all, could hardly have made the consequences of rebellion any clearer. No wonder, then, that Fulk's castellans generally opted to keep their heads down. His vassals, by and large, proved themselves true to their oaths. Anjou cohered.

Nevertheless, even on a man as hard as the Black Count, the pressures of lordship were immense. Much more was at stake than his own fortunes. 'Fearful of the day of judgement':[18] so Fulk described himself. The same blood that had soaked the fields of Anjou, and served to fertilise his greatness, could not help but remind him too of the terrifying vanity of all mortal wishes. 'For the fragility of the human race being what it is,' as he acknowledged bleakly, 'the last moment may arrive at any time, suddenly and unforeseen.'[19] Always, amid the harrying of his adversaries, and the trampling of their ambitions, and the shattering of their swords, he dreaded ambush by the deadliest foe of all. Strategies to blunt the meat-hook of the Devil, and to fend off his assaults, were never far from Fulk's mind. So it was, for instance, haunted by the thought of the Christian blood he had spilled at Conquereuil, that he founded 'a church, a most beautiful one',[20] in a field named *Belli Locus*, the Place of Battle. The count's many enemies, scornful of what they saw as his crocodile tears, were naturally exultant when on the very day of its consecration a violent wind blew down its roof and a part of its wall: 'for no one doubted that by his insolent presumption he had rendered his offering void'.[21] Perhaps – and yet to damn Fulk as a hypocrite was to misrepresent just how profoundly he feared for his soul, and for the troubled times in which he lived. 'The end of the world being at hand, men are driven by a shorter life, and a more atrocious cupidity consumes them':[22] so had written a monk living in Poitiers, on the southern flank of Anjou, even as Fulk's horsemen were raiding the fields beyond his monastery. Yet Fulk himself, had this judgement been brought to his attention, would not have disputed it. All his crimes and ravins, and all that he had won by them as well, he presumed to dedicate to a cause far nobler than his own.

How precisely Fulk saw his role was evident from his church at the Place of Battle, which he dedicated first to the Holy Trinity and then, and with great emphasis, to 'the holy Archangels and the Cherubim and Seraphim'.[23] These were the warriors of heaven: serried in glittering ranks before the Almighty's throne, they served Him watchful and unsleeping, ready, whenever called upon, to descend upon His enemies and restore order to the cosmos, howsoever it might be threatened. In this, then, what did the Cherubim and Seraphim resemble, if not the followers of an earthly count – and what were the holy archangels, if not the counterparts of Fulk himself?

A most flattering conceit, of course – and inoperable without an anointed king to play the part of God. Fulk himself, shrewd and calculating, understood this perfectly. True, Robert Capet's ministers might occasionally have to be eliminated, and his manoeuvrings blunted, and his armies put to flight; but never once, not even when tensions were at their height, did Fulk forget the courtesies that were due the king as his overlord. Robert himself reciprocated. 'Most faithful':[24] so the Count of Anjou was named in royal documents. An example of near-delusional wish-fulfilment, it might have been thought – except that Fulk did indeed see himself as solemnly bound by the ties of vassalage. Even a fantasy, then, if repeated with sufficient conviction, can come to then, own ghostly truth. Adversaries on numerous occasions they may have been – and yet king and count had need of each other. Mighty though Fulk and the lords of other counties were, they could not afford to cut themselves entirely loose from the seeming corpse that was the crown. For any of them to have done so – to have repudiated the authority of the Capetians, to have declared a unilateral independence, to have pronounced themselves kings – would have been to shatter irrevocably the whole basis of their own legitimacy. The threads of loyalty that bound their own vassals to them would at once have been snapped. The entire social fabric would have begun to unravel, from top to bottom, leaving behind only ruin. Every pattern of authority would have been lost. Nothing would have been left, save anarchy.

And so it was – just – that the centre held. Splintered into rival principalities the kingdom may have been, yet a sense of shared identity persisted all the same. Even among the great lords of the south, where initial hostility towards the Capetians had soon dulled into indifference, no one ever doubted that there had to be a king. In truth, if anything, they needed the idea of him even more urgently than did a powerful count such as Fulk. In their territories too, the spectacle of rough-hewn castles was becoming a familiar and ominous one; but, unlike in Anjou, it was rarely the princes who were responsible for building them. 'For their land is very different from our own,' as one traveller from the north explained. 'The strongholds I saw there were built on foundations of solid rock, and raised to such a height that they seemed to be floating in the sky.'[25] Perhaps even Fulk would have found such fortresses a challenge to subdue.

His brother lords of the south certainly did. No iron grip on their castellans for them. As a result, if the authority of the king lived on in the region as little more than a memory, then so too, increasingly, did the authority of the princes themselves. Like fish, the southern principalities appeared to be rotting downwards from their heads. But how far, and how completely, would the rottenness serve to spread? And how incurably? On the answer to these questions much would hang. Perhaps, as Adso appeared to have died believing, the very future of all humanity: for that a multiplying of wickedness was to herald the end days had been asserted a thousand years previously by Christ Himself.[26] Certainly, the future of millions would prove to be at stake: men and women caught up in a terrifying escalation of lawlessness, one that would result in an unprecedented reordering of society, and leave their lives, indeed their whole world, transformed utterly. A storm was brewing, one that would ultimately come to affect all the lands that acknowledged a Capetian as their king: lands that it is perhaps not too anachronistic to refer to henceforward as France.*

Knightmare

No matter that they had been a Christian people for many centuries, the Franks were still more than capable of a red-blooded love of violence. So much so that Saracen commentators, with the insight that often comes most naturally to outsiders, ranked it as one of their defining characteristics – together with a ferocious sense of honour and a distaste for taking baths. Even though it was true that Frankish warriors themselves were trained to value self-restraint as the cardinal virtue of a warlord, this was in large part because, like gold, it was so precious for being rare. The black fury which descended upon Fulk Nerra at Angers, and resulted in the burning of much of the town, was

---

* And yet anachronistic it remains. Tracing the evolution of the phrase '*Regnum Francorum*', 'the Kingdom of the Franks', into the modern French word 'France' is a notoriously complex business. It was not until the thirteenth century that the formula '*Roi de France*', 'King of France', was first used in royal documents, with its implication that there was a territory, rather than simply a people, of which to be the king. Nevertheless, even though the phrase that I have been using, 'West Francia', is nothing but a historian's convenience, people did have, from the mid-tenth century on, a sense of a West Frankish kingdom that was distinct and independent from what had become the empire to the east. The old sense of Frankish commonality was gone, and in its place were the two distinct entities that would ultimately become France and Germany. Chroniclers at the time of the Millennium may still have employed the phrase '*Regnum Francorum*', but what they meant by that was clearly what would later be known as France. It is that, most historians feel, which justifies the use of the word to describe the lands which acknowledged the early Capetians as kings.

regarded by his contemporaries as nothing greatly out of the ordinary. Flames invariably spread in the wake of war bands, no matter who their leader. A horseman preparing for an expedition would sling a fire-starter from his belt as instinctively as he would draw his sword. The farms and fields of an adversary were always held to be fair game. His dependants too. No less a lord than Hugh Capet, a man famed for his coolness and sagacity, thought nothing of reducing an enemy's lands to a wilderness of blackened stubble, and littering it with corpses. 'In such a wild fury was he,' men reported, 'that he scorned to spare a single hut, even if there were no one more threatening in it than a mad old crone.'[27]

Not that a practised village-waster such as Hugh would have made much distinction between a mad old crone and any other class of peasant. From the vantage point of an armed man in a saddle, they were all of them indistinguishable, mere bleating sheep, who milled and cowered and never fought back: '*pauperes*'. This word, which in ancient times had been used to describe the poor, had gradually, by the tenth century, come to possess a somewhat different meaning: 'the powerless'. This was a revealing shift, for it reflected how arms, once held to be the very mark of a free man, of a '*francus*', a Frank, had become the preserve of the wealthiest alone. No peasant could afford to dress himself in chain mail, still less maintain a warhorse. Even an arrowhead might prove beyond his means. No wonder that the finding of a horseshoe was held the supreme mark of good luck. A great lord, knowing that there were men willing to grub in the dirt after iron that had once served to shoe his mount, could hardly help but feel confirmed in all his lofty scorn for them. Filth and mud and shit: such were seen as the natural elements of the peasantry. They were 'lazy, misshapen and ugly in every way'.[28] Indeed, so it struck the '*potentes*', the 'powerful', there was something almost paradoxical about their ugliness: for while cropped hair, the traditional mark of inferiority, might serve as one means of distinguishing peasants from their betters, then so too did the opposite, a matted and loathsome unkemptness, befitting men who were presumed to eat, and sweat, and rut like beasts. Men, it might be argued, who fully merited being rounded up like beasts as well.

For give them half a chance, and peasants, just like pigs in a wood, or sheep on a mountainside, might all too easily stray. Once, back amid the upheavals that had followed the collapse of the Roman Empire, there were those who had slipped entirely free of their landlords, liberating themselves so successfully from an enfeebled regime of extortion that they had ended up almost forgetting what it meant to be screwed for taxes. A scandalous state of affairs – and not one that could be permitted, in the long run, to carry on. Charlemagne, labouring to rebuild the order of Rome's vanished empire, had made certain as well to renew its venerable tradition of exploiting the *pauperes*. The aristocracy, their wealth and authority increasingly fortified by the expansion of Frankish power, had needed no encouragement to sign up to such a mission. Briskly, and sometimes brutally, they had set about reining in the errant peasantry. Stern rights of jurisdiction and constraint, known collectively as the 'ban', had been granted them by the king. Armed with these fearsome legal powers, the counts and their agents had been able to sting their tenants for a good deal more than rent – for now there were fines and tolls to be imposed, and any number of inventive dues exacted. The natural order of things, which for so long had been in a tottering state of dilapidation, had once again been set on firm foundations. All was as it should be. The peasantry toiled in the fields; their betters skimmed off the surplus. It was a simple enough formula, and yet upon it depended the dominance of even the greatest lord.

On that much, at any rate, all the *potentes* could agree. The disintegration of Charlemagne's empire, unlike that of Rome's, did not noticeably serve to weaken their capacity for extortion. Even as peasants learned to beware the feuding of rival warlords, and to dread the trampling of their crops, the looting of their storehouses and the torching of their homes, so were they still obliged to cough up rents, and to endure the grinding exactions of the 'ban'. There were those, as season followed season and year followed year, who found it ever more impossible to meet the demands being piled upon them. Divine as well as human intervention might serve at any moment to waste a peasant's meagre fortune. Blessed indeed was the year when he did not find himself hag-ridden by a dread of famine. Every spring, when the supplies of winter were exhausted, and the fruits of summer yet to bloom, the pangs of hunger would invariably grip; but worse, infinitely worse, were those years when the crops failed, and the pangs of hunger followed on directly from harvest time.

No wonder, then, that peasants learned to look to the heavens with foreboding: for even a single hailstorm, if it fell with sufficient ferocity, might prove sufficient to destroy the fruit of a whole year's labours. Whether such a calamity was to be blamed upon divine wrath, or the malevolence of the Devil, or perhaps even the hellish skills of a necromancer, there would be time enough to debate as the icy nights drew in and people began to starve. Then 'men's very voices, reduced to extreme thinness, would pipe like those of dying birds';[29] women, desperate to feed their children, would grub about despairingly, even after 'the unclean flesh of reptiles';[30] wolves, their eyes burning amid the winter darkness, would haunt the margins of human settlements, waiting to chew on the withered corpses of the dead. In such desperate circumstances, who could blame the man prepared to countenance a fateful step, and barter away the few genuine assets that might still be left to him? An ox, for instance, which in good times could go for a whole hectare of land, was far too valuable, even during a famine, simply to be butchered for meat. Nevertheless, so ruinous a step was it for a peasant to sell his cattle that there were certain bishops, in times of particularly terrible hunger, who would grant money to the most impoverished, or dispense grain to them free of charge, so as to steel them against the temptation. These were acts of true charity: for once a peasant had struck a deal, and seen his precious oxen driven away, he would be left, come the spring, without the means to drive his plough. Nor would he have anything much further to sell: only his plot of land and then, last of all, himself. No longer a *francus*, he would, from that moment on, rank as merely a '*servus*': a serf.*

A bitter and beggarly fate. And yet would the neighbours of an unfortunate prostrated so utterly have discerned in his ruin anything more ominous than an individual tragedy? Most likely not. Man was fallen, after all, and suffering was his lot. There were worse calamities, perhaps, in a world blighted by sickness, and deformity, and pain, than servitude. More universal ones too. In the decades leading up to the Millennium, a peasant did not need to have a startling amount of flesh upon his bones, nor of supplies stored away for the winter, nor of oxen in his barn, still to feel conscious of his liberty. Darkly though the storm clouds of famine and war had massed over France during the previous century, there remained a majority of peasants, perhaps a large majority, who persisted in defining themselves as something more than serfs – as men who were free.

This was a delusory consolation, it might have been thought, bearing in mind all the harsh exactions imposed upon them. Yet it was not wholly so. The peasantry still had some muscle. Community leaders – '*boni homines*' – continued to be elected. Assemblies, at which the free peasants of a neighbourhood would gather in an open field, continued to be held. Rights still existed which might be cruelly missed once they were gone. How grim an irony it was, for instance, for any peasant who did lose his livestock and his land to find himself, from that moment on, bound to both far more implacably than he had ever been while free. 'I work hard,' the typical serf was imagined as eternally sighing. 'I go out at first light, driving the oxen to the field, yoking them to the plough. No matter how bleak the winter, I dare not linger at home, out of fear of my lord; instead, having yoked my oxen, and fastened their harness, every day I must plough a full acre or more.'[31] To the

---

* '*Servus*', even more than '*pauper*', is a word with a complex history. Originally, it meant 'slave'; and the course of evolution by which it came to mean 'serf' remains intensely controversial. At the time of the Millennium, it could still be used with both meanings.

free neighbours of such a wretch, watching him hunched against the dawn cold, toiling to break up the frozen ground, bone-weary even amid snow or the iciest sleet, the spectacle would have served as a fearsome admonition. They too, of course, had to toil; but not so hard as did a serf. The crops harvested by a free man were not his only source of nutrition. Beyond the spreading fields redeemed with such labour from the great murk of the wilderness, dark and tangled forests still stretched across much of France, forbidding, to be sure, and perilous, the haunt of wolves, and angry boars, and bandits, and banished demons; but mighty storehouses rich in food and resources too. Any peasant prepared to venture out of the daylight into the primordial shade of the trees could set his pigs to eat there, or hunt game, or burn wood for charcoal, or collect wax and honey, or gather up mushrooms and herbs and berries. If there was a river flowing near by, then funnel-shaped baskets could be rigged up in its waters, to serve as makeshift fishing weirs. Even out on open fields, there were always birds to be hunted. With so much to forage, there was certainly no need to depend for sustenance on corn.

But that, in the view of great landowners, was hardly the point. Reduced harvests meant reduced surpluses; and reduced surpluses meant less for the ambitious lord to extort. Seen from this perspective, peasants who insisted on sloping off from their fields to go rabbit hunting or blackberrying or fiddling around in rivers with wickerwork were wastrels, plain and simple, letting down their betters. What other purpose did the poor have, if not to deliver the full potential of their capacity for sweat and aching muscles? Far-sighted landlords, during the final decades of the millennium, found themselves reflecting on this question with a mounting sense of frustration – for the very earth, like a woman no longer content to cloak her own fertility, had begun to reveal to those with the necessary ingenuity and resolve to test it a hitherto unsuspected degree of fruitfulness. Startlingly, even against a background of often terrible famines, and a widespread sense that God's creation was winding down, the scope for improving harvests appeared to be on the upsurge. Heavier makes of plough, better styles of animal harnesses and more productive methods of rotating crops – none of them novel technologies, by any means – were starting to be adopted across northern Europe on a hugely expanded scale. The finger of the Almighty too, tracing patterns across the face of the earth, appeared to be bearing witness to a swelling fecundity. Those who farmed the foothills of the Alps, for instance, could mark how the glaciers were retreating, and the tree line rising. Those who lived by coastal marshes could trace a steady shrinking of their waters. The climate was changing, with temperatures rising everywhere. To many, it was true, the resulting extremes of heat and rainfall appeared simply a further portent of doom; and yet for all that, over the long term, the warmer seasons were indisputably boosting crop yields. Or rather, they were boosting crop yields for a certain kind of lord: one whose tenants were willing without complaint to bend their backs, to reap and plough and sow, not just in fits and starts, but relentlessly, season in and season out. No easy task, to condition men and women to such a life. Whole communities first had to be bound to the soil, bound utterly, and broken to all the rhythms of the agricultural year, without any prospect of exemption or release. And yet, if that could be achieved, how great might be the rewards! How flourishing the profits from the gathering revolution in the fields! How irresistible the incentive to bury the freedoms of the peasantry once and for all!

And this not least because there was now one more nail at hand, delivered with a fatal timing to the strong and ruthless everywhere, to the final doom of the independent poor – and already, by the Millennium, being hammered with great violence into their coffin. France's first great social upheaval was heralded, not by the storming of a single brooding fortress, as a later one would be, but by the very opposite, the raising across the whole country of a great multitude of battlements. Brilliantly although a warlord such as Fulk Nerra might learn to deploy castles to serve his strategic interests, their most seismic impact was to be experienced not in the realm of military affairs at all, but across the countryside, in the forests, the farms and the fields. Even the most prosperous of free peasants would soon learn to dread the sight of makeshift walls and towers being erected on a nearby hill. No more ominous silhouette could possibly have been imagined than that of a castle on its rock. Tiny it might be, and inaccessible, and crudely built – and yet the shadow cast by such a stronghold would invariably extend for miles. Never before had an entire generation of landlords come so suddenly into the possession of so lethal a coercive tool. Entire communities could now be dominated, cabined in and patrolled.

It was no coincidence, then, that those same decades which witnessed the sudden spread of castles over France should also have been distinguished by the systematic degradation of the peasantry's right to roam. Woods and rivers, those primordial sources of sustenance, began to be ringed around with tolls, or else placed off-limits altogether. Inexorably, the easier it became for a lord to enforce restrictions, and to privatise what had once been common land, the faster it occurred. The poor man out with his bow and arrow in the woods, tracking some game for his cooking pot, just as his forefathers had always done, suddenly found himself branded a poacher, a criminal. No more hunting, shooting or fishing for the peasantry. Those who wanted food would now have to work for it in the fields the whole year round.

All change, it went without saying, was wicked; but change so violent and disruptive seemed especially so. Nevertheless, as even the most despairing peasant had to acknowledge, the cruelty of new laws could hardly serve to invalidate them – not if the lord responsible was a mighty prince, a duke or a count possessed of the 'ban'. To campaign against such an awesome figure was immediately to be guilty of rebellion. In 997, for instance, at Evreaux, in northern France, where the peasantry had responded with naked fury to having the forests and streams closed off to them, the local count answered the supplications of their elected emissaries by having their hands and feet cut off. A perfectly pitched atrocity: for the agitators, witnessing the mutilated state of the *boni homines*, duly bowed their heads and melted away back to their ploughs. Naturally, terror of the count's armoured horsemen was what

153

had most immediately served to chill their spirits – but there had been something more as well. No less than princes, peasants lived in dread of anarchy. They might find the iron demands of an unjust law fearsome, yet there was one thing that they tended to fear even more: a world in which no laws existed. For then the weak would find themselves the prey of the strong indeed. The horror of this had been most eerily articulated back in 940, by a peasant girl named Flothilde: for she had reported to a listening monk a terrible dream, one which had returned to her every night, in which armed men pursued her, seeking to capture her and throw her down a well. Countless other peasants too, mute witnesses to the times, must have been haunted by similar nightmares. They knew the darkness which might lurk within the human soul. Better order, then, most appear to have reckoned, any order, even the harshest, than the lack of it. And so it was, in counties ruled by iron-willed princes, where the new laws, though brutal, could nevertheless be regarded as legitimate, and despite all the suffering and the misery and the restlessness which accompanied their introduction, that the poor did not revolt. The prerogatives of lordship, linking top to bottom, were maintained. Society did not crumble.

Yet princedoms as steel-girt as Flanders or Anjou were aberrations. In southern France especially, it was not long before the assaults upon the *pauperes* were attaining such a pitch of relentlessness and illegitimacy that it did indeed appear to many, witnessing the collapse of entire regions into savagery, as though everything were falling apart. Here, when a castellan laid claim to the powers of the 'ban', it was most likely to be a fraud. Rarely would he have had permission to build his castle from some higher authority. The opportunities were simply too spectacular, and the competition too ferocious, for any man of ambition to hang around waiting for that. Indeed, the would-be castellan had little choice but to move as urgently as he could, rushing with a desperate sense of greed to secure a suitable rock or hill for himself, before anyone else could beat him to the site. 'For then he could do what he liked without fear, in full confidence that his castle would protect him – whereas others, if they tried to oppose him, could now be overcome easily, since they would have nowhere to hide.'[32] A wildcat lord such as this, smelling the fresh timber of his battlements, feeling solid rock beneath his feet, knowing himself the master of all he surveyed, could afford to thumb his nose at the world. He owed no duty to a count, nor to anyone, except himself.

And certainly not to the *pauperes*. Indeed, bleeding the locals white was not merely an option for the ambitious castellan, but an absolute necessity. Banditry and intimidation had to sanction what legitimacy could not. Castles – and men to garrison them – had to be paid for. Warriors, if they were to supply their lord with effective muscle, did not come cheap: their arms, their armour and their horses all had to be purchased, to say nothing of their loyalty. To contemporaries, the gangs of mail-clad thugs increasingly being employed by castellans appeared a caste as novel as they were alarming; and chroniclers, thumbing through dusty tomes, struggled at first to find suitable terms to describe them. In English, they would end up being known as '*cnichts*': a word customarily applied to household servants, and strongly suggestive of servility and baseness. Who these 'knights' truly were appears to have varied from region to region; and yet it is evident that many must indeed have been of less than noble origin. Where else, after all, was an upstart lord to find recruits, if not from among the ranks of the local peasantry? And where better could an ambitious peasant, especially one with a taste for violence and a lack of scruples, look for gainful employment, than to a castellan? Food, accommodation and the chance to kick people around: all came as perks of the job. It was an attractive package – and especially amid the carnivorous nature of the times. Out on patrol with his lord, marking from his saddle how a one-time equal might flinch at the sight of him, or cringe, perhaps, in the dirt, or beg in his misery for the return of a missing daughter, or a bag of grain, or a cow, a knight would have no doubt what he was glimpsing: a fate that might easily have been his own.

And perhaps it was precisely for this reason, a terror of the abyss that still awaited them if all their menaces failed, and all their

scavenging left them empty-handed, that the knights and their masters were so merciless. Month by month, season by season, year by
year, their exactions grew ever worse. How gruesomely apt it was that
their favoured mode of torture should have been a garrotting-chain,
the '*maura*', notorious for inflicting upon its victim 'not one but a
thousand deaths'[33]: a literal tightening of the screws. Robberies too, and
rapes, and kidnappings: all were deployed with a brutal gusto by
hit squads determined to trample underfoot every last vestige of
independence in the countryside, and to reduce even the most prosperous of peasants to servitude.

So far reaching in its implications was this programme, and so convulsive in its effects, that any lord with half an aptitude for driving it
through could track its progress simply by gazing out from his castle,
and marking its imprint upon the fields and settlements spread out
below. Landscapes fundamentally unchanged for a millennium were
in the process of being utterly transformed. Rather than being left to
live as they had done since Roman times, on scattered farms, or clus-
tered around villas, or migrating year by year from hut to hut and field
to field, peasants increasingly found themselves being herded together
into what was in effect a human sheep pen: a 'village'. Here, in this
novel style of community, was the ultimate refinement of what had
for so long been a lordly dream: to round up the peasantry for good.
As raw and sinister as a newly founded prison, a village might bear
witness to the servitude imposed not just upon the odd luckless
individual, but upon an entire community. Battered down and bloodied, those peasants adjusting to the novel experience of having to live
cheek by jowl with their neighbours would labour henceforward as
serfs: for the subtle and various shades of freedom that might once
have served to define them had been smeared and blotted out. They
were all of them unfree now: living trophies, the spoils of violence and
crime.

Not that the castellans were always blatant in their illegalities.
Upstart lords, by virtue of the various prerogatives that they had
usurped from the aristocracy, did often attempt to cloak their

depredations behind a semblance of legitimacy – but few of their victims were fooled by that. Peasants, looking back to more prosperous times, knew perfectly well that their fathers and grandfathers had not been obliged to put up braggardly knights in their hovels; nor to walk up to the gates of a nearby castle, there to hand over all the riches of their harvest; nor to toil as unpaid porters, sweating and stumbling as they served in the train of some upstart castellan. That all these outrages could claim some vague precedent in the obligations of the 'ban' did not make them any less shameless or grotesque. Justice, which had once been administered to them by their own elected leaders in open fields, beneath the sight of heaven, had been stolen from them. And so the peasantry spoke of the new customs that the Millennium was serving to bring them as 'evil'; and even as they cursed, they cried out for release from their wretchedness.

But who was there to heed their prayers? Christ and His saints in heaven, of course; and sure enough, on occasion, a saint might indeed blaze out a reply. Terrifying prodigies capable of bringing a wicked lord to his senses, and dousing 'the torches of his avarice', were naturally much prized by the poor: for increasingly, interventions by the supernatural appeared the only sure way 'to stop their meagre possessions from being despoiled'.[34] Saints who did not protect their devotees were much resented: one woman, for instance, outraged that St Benedict had failed to protect her from an evil lord, physically assaulted the altar in his shrine, beating it with her fists, and roundly abusing her heavenly patron. It was a truth as evident as it was regrettable, however, that even miracles performed by a living saint such as Romuald were hardly to be relied upon: for while the celebrated hermit was more than content, on occasion, to punish robber lords by having them choke to death on the meat of stolen cows, or be struck down by invisible arrows, he could hardly punish every thieving castellan, as ultimately it was his very isolation from the turbulent currents of human sinfulness that marked him out as holy. Yet even amid the swamps, Romuald and hermits like him might serve as an inspiration to the oppressed and groaning peasantry because they bore witness to the power of a lord greater and infinitely more powerful than even the most brutal castellan. The poor did not despair of the protection of Christ; nor did they doubt that He heard their groans, and pitied them. Perhaps they knew as well what had been foretold in the Holy Scriptures, that He was to come again at the end of days, to judge the living and the dead, and that the oppressed would be bade welcome, and sat at His right side, to take their place in the New Jerusalem, while the wicked were delivered over to eternal fire.

But when? When? Always the question: when? Whether there were those among the peasantry who were aware of the Millennium we do not know – for the silence of the poor is almost total. Yet such was the scale of the horrors that had overwhelmed them, and such their yearning for redemption from all their miseries, that it seems implausible that they could have been wholly ignorant of so portentous and fearsome a date. That they were living through the one-thousandth anniversary of their Saviour's life, even as the shadows that had engulfed them were thickening into an ever more hellish darkness, would surely have struck many as a coincidence too far. Certainly, there were those among the learned who had no doubts. 'For it is revealed as an evident fact by the Holy Gospel that as the last days go by, so love will be chilled, and iniquity will blossom amongst men. And they will face dangerous times for their souls . . . Here, then, is the cause of the evils which, on an unprecedented scale, have afflicted every portion of the world, on and around the thousandth anniversary of the birth of our Saviour and Lord.'[35]

Such was the judgement of one observer of his times, a monk named Rudolf Glaber; and it could hardly be dismissed as an eccentric one. The monastery in Burgundy to which he belonged was no backwater, no nest of cranks or heretics. Indeed, in all Christendom, there were few assemblages of stone and mortar that could boast a greater charge of holiness than the monastery of Cluny. The voice of prophecy to which Rudolf laid claim was nothing less than his prerogative as one of its brothers. 'Truly, our life lasts one thousand years.' So had warned Odo, the second of Cluny's abbots, decades before the anarchy that would mark the passage of the Millennium. 'And now here we are, arrived at the last day of the very span of time itself.'[36] These were words that no Christian could readily ignore: for they had issued from the place that seemed to its admirers, more than any other, the nearest there was to heaven on earth.

Knocking on Heaven's Door

Evil times made for perilous journeys. Even before the spread of castles across the kingdom had helped to make lords out of bandits, and bandits out of lords, the roads were not lightly trodden. Hugh Capet himself, returning from Rome and his mortifying audience with Otto II, had been able to escape the attentions of kidnappers only by submitting to a yet greater humiliation, and travelling in the disguise of a groom. The decades that followed his accession had seen the dangers grow ever worse. The poor were far from alone in being the prey of predatory knights. Merchants too, as they travelled to markets, would increasingly find themselves being stopped and obliged to pay extortionate tolls, or else 'be whipped for their possessions'. Pilgrims, huntsmen out with their dogs, even 'noble women journeying in the absence of their husbands': all might end up as targets.[37] '*Omnia permixta sunt*': 'chaos reigns everywhere'. It was hard for the nervous traveller, hurrying to find shelter as the light thickened, glancing anxiously over his shoulder, ever fearful of the sound of distant hoof beats, to doubt that this was so. Man had indeed become predacious, it appeared, as predacious as the wolf, that sniffer after carrion, and no less cruel, no less savage in his appetites. Where, then, as the twilight gathered, was shelter to be found?

Perhaps – God's mysterious hand being what it was – amid the very worst of the disorder. Just as there were whole regions of France that had been spared dramatic upheaval, so were there others that had been convulsed by a particular violence. In Burgundy, for instance, on the easternmost frontier of the kingdom, royal authority had collapsed no less totally than elsewhere in the south. Here, however, exceptionally, King Robert had sought to make a stand. For decades, he and his armies would persist in trampling the fields of the duchy, while the local castellans, profiting from the conditions of ceaseless warfare, grew fat on the carnage like flies on gouts of blood. A traveller did not have to venture far across Burgundy to witness marks of agony. It was no wonder to find the bodies even of children lying by the roadside. Men driven lunatic by what they had witnessed – or perpetrated, perhaps – haunted the region's woods, spectral figures wasted by despair.

Yet Burgundy was not all horror. Very far from it. Though the duchy was violent, it was also the seat of something miraculous: a refuge from the evils of the times that even the papacy, in naked awe, acclaimed as Christendom's most impregnable sanctuary, a veritable 'haven of piety and salvation'.[38] So it was, for instance, that after a particularly maddened soldier was found wandering naked in the woods outside Nantua, a town just to the south of Burgundy, the monks caring for him had no hesitation in sending him northwards to be cured, back on the very road that led to the duchy's killing fields. An unsettling journey, no doubt, and a dangerous one – but with the promise, at its end, of true asylum.

It was the Almighty Himself, it appeared, who had fitted Cluny for such a role. All around the wide valley on which the abbey stood there stretched wooded hills, sheltering and enclosing it against the outside world – very much like the cloisters of a monastery. It was only a century previously, however, that this resemblance had first been noted: for until then the valley had been a hunting ground, and inordinately prized as such by its original owner, the Duke of Aquitaine. But in 910, William, the holder of that title, had been old and childless – and with murder on his conscience. Accordingly, for the sake of his soul, he had resolved to found an abbey; and the monks to whom he had confided this ambition had immediately pointed out, with a certain grim relish, that the ideal spot for it would be none other than his favourite hunting ground. Any reluctance that William might have felt at the prospect of forfeiting such a prize had been sternly overridden. 'For you know which will serve you better before God: the baying of hounds or the prayers of monks.' To that, there had been no possible comeback; and so it was, on 11 September 910, that William had signed away the valley.

One century on, and it was evident to everyone who drew near to Cluny that the Almighty had looked favourably indeed upon the Duke of Aquitaine's gift. Or to almost everyone, perhaps. A deserter such as the wild man of Nantua, traumatised as he was, and fearful of battlements, would no doubt have found the spectacle of the abbey's ramparts a most alarming one at first: for flourishing monasteries, it was true, did often wear a menacing aspect. So it was, for instance, at Fleury, a celebrated foundation on the Loire, and Cluny's only real rival as the pre-eminent monastery in France, that there towered a donjon 'of squared blocks'[39] no less imposing than anything raised by Fulk Nerra; while at Cluny itself, its abbot, Father Odilo, was a great enthusiast for replacing wood with stone. Yet no matter how intimidatingly the gateway of the abbey might loom above them, there was nothing beyond it for the poor to fear: no stronghold of robber knights. 'For I was hungry and you gave me food.' So Christ Himself had spoken. 'I was thirsty and you gave me drink, I was a stranger and you welcomed me, I was naked and you clothed me.'[40] Daily, therefore, when the starving poor gathered before the gates of Cluny, up to thirty-six pounds of bread would be handed out to them by the brothers of the monastery; and the monks, as they performed their work of charity, would prostrate themselves before each and every recipient of their alms, as though before the Saviour.

Even the abbot himself, one of the greatest men of Christendom, if he were obliged to ride out into the world, would make certain never to turn away anyone 'from the bosom of his mercy'.[41] The sainted Odo, for instance, had not shrunk from carrying a foul-smelling sack filled with garlic and onions for one weary old man, to the horror of his companion; while Odilo, elected to his post only six years before the Millennium, would pause whenever he saw a corpse by the roadside and have a grave dug for it, then kneel to wrap it with great tenderness in his cloak. For come the Day of Judgement, he knew, his every account would have to be rendered.

And from what lay waiting beyond the Day of Judgement, that moment of supreme and joyous mystery, when the old earth would pass away and the new Jerusalem descend from God 'as a bride adorned for her husband',[42] it was the glory of Cluny, more than any other shrine raised by the hands of man, to part the veil. Always the gaze of its brethren was fixed, not on the fallen world, but on the splendours of the next. Indeed, it was their aspiration, a truly awesome one, to transcend their own mortal nature. 'For if monks are perfect,' Odo had argued, 'then they are rendered similar to the blessed angels.'[43] The wild man of Nantua, led cringing to the gates of Cluny, would surely soon have found his terrors set at ease. Noble though the accents of the monks would have proclaimed them, nobler, often, than many a castellan, in almost every way they would have appeared to the deserter not as *potentes* at all but as *pauperes*, just like himself. At Cluny, every brother lived by an ancient and unbending rule, one that had described the practice of humility as a ladder ascending to God; and its most solemn command, 'the twelfth degree', was that a monk's humility should be made manifest to all the world. So it was that, shamingly, he would wear his hair even shorter than a peasant's, shaved to form a tonsure, in appearance like a crown of thorns; he would dress in a black cowl, drab and unadorned, no better than a workman's; and at all times he would 'keep his head bowed, and his eyes fixed upon the ground'.[44] Inviting the wretched deserter from Nantua to sit down by the monastery gateway, the monks charged with his reception would have bowed before him, and then brought water, and washed and dried his feet. Only incidentally, however, was this done as a personal service to a filth-encrusted lunatic: for the truest benefit was to the souls of the humbled monks themselves.

Yet even that was not the highest purpose of the ritual. Back in the early years of the abbey's existence, St Odo had laid down a potent marker of all his hopes for the infant monastery, by insisting that visitors' shoes as well as their feet should be washed. Excessive? There were some monks at the time who had grumbled that it was. And yet how muddied by a lack of ambition, to say nothing of worldly pride, all such moaning had been – for Cluny, as Odo had trusted, was fated to be no ordinary monastery. Unprotected by the swords and spears of mortal warriors it may have been – and yet impressions of the abbey as a mighty citadel, girt around by fearsome ramparts, were not so wide of the mark.

Of the delicate and aristocratic Odilo it was said that he had the look, not of a duke, but of a prince of the archangels – which was to cast the monastery he headed as a radiant bridgehead of heaven. No wonder, then, that demons were widely believed to lie encamped all around its outer walls, placing it under a perpetual siege, driven by 'the malice that the Devil has always harboured against Cluny';[45] but fated, so long as the abbey's sanctity held firm, never to make a breach. No wonder either that the brethren who served as its gatekeepers should have required all who entered it to be cleansed – yes, and to have their shoes washed too. Filth was precisely what enabled demons to flourish. At Fleury, for instance, in a typically fiendish display of cunning, devils had made an attempt to steal through the sewers that led up to the brothers' lavatories; and only the monastery's patron saint, standing invisible guard over the urinals, had served to foil their plot. At Cluny likewise, the watch kept by the monks had to be tireless and unblinking. No hint of pollution could be permitted to infect the sacred space. The infernal and the earthly: both had to be kept at bay. To pass into Cluny was indeed to pass into a realm of angels.

But what was the abbey's secret, what the source of its fearsome sanctity? Even a visitor as lunatic as the wild man of Nantua, taking his first tremulous steps inside the monastery, would surely have found himself conscious within seconds of something strange. To any refugee from chaos, Cluny could offer that rarest and most precious of all balms: order. It was to be found in the regular spacing of rich tapestries along the walls and of sumptuous carpets along the floors, as dazzling as they were beautiful, serving to soften every footfall, and to proclaim the praises of God. Even to a visiting dignitary, fittings such as these would have appeared rare luxuries – but to a beggarman such as the deserter from Nantua they would have appeared a glimpse of paradise. Which, in a sense, they were: for the monks of Cluny, in their own estimation at any rate, were the nearest to heaven of mortals any-where. To the great bishops of the kingdom, long accustomed to look down upon abbots such as Odilo, this was a display of arrogance that verged almost on the blasphemous; but Odilo himself and the brethren he commanded were unperturbed. They knew that the end days were drawing near. At such a moment of excruciating peril, with the future of all humanity hanging in the balance, what else should they be doing but securing on earth an impregnable outpost of the City of God?

Earlier generations of monks, following the prescriptions of their rule, had devoted themselves to manual labour, so as to display humil-ity, and to scholarship, so as to train their souls; but the monks of Cluny had little time for either activity. Instead, hour after hour, day after day, year after year, they sang the praises of the Lord: for this, in heaven, was what the choirs of angels did. Indeed, on one occasion, it was claimed, a monk had ended up so lost in his devotions that he had actually begun to levitate. Prayers and hymns, anthems and responses: the chanting never stopped. Odo had required his brethren to recite one hundred and thirty-eight psalms a day: more than three times what had traditionally been expected of a monk. Barely a minute of a Cluniac's life went by, in short, but it was governed by ritual, as unwearying as it was implacable. Hence, for its admirers, the monastery's unprecedented nimbus of holiness: 'for so reverently are the masses performed there,' as Rudolf Glaber put it, 'so piously and worthily, that you would think them the work, not of men, but of angels indeed'.[46]

Here, then, was the well-spring of Cluny's power: mysterious, tute-lary, literally supernatural. Among those who reverenced it, of course, were the monks of Nantua, who had dutifully sent the deserter found wandering in the woods to be healed at the more celebrated monastery; nor was their faith betrayed. Brought before Odilo, the wild man was first permitted to listen to the brethren of the abbey as they chanted their psalms, and then sprinkled with holy water. His sanity was restored. Wonders such as this were widely reported – and the cause of much admiration. Even a living saint such as Romuald – no slouch himself when it came to performing miracles – was impressed by Cluny's reputation. It was, the hermit pronounced, the 'flower' of monasteries: a pattern for all the world.[47] If such was the view from as far afield as Italy, then the perspective of those who lived directly in Cluny's shadow was, unsurprisingly, touched even more directly by awe.

Which was just as well – for the legions of Satan were not the only adversaries hemming in the monastery. The local castellans, if not precisely demons, were menacing neighbours, nevertheless. To men whose fortunes derived from the morality of the protection racket, the monastery could not help but seem tempting prey – and all the more so because Cluny, unlike most other foundations, had no earthly lord to whom it could turn for protection. Instead, by the terms of Duke William's charter, the abbey had been declared 'free from the rule of any king, bishop, count, or relative of its founder',[48] and placed under the wing of a heavenly patron: none other than St Peter himself. Naturally – with the Prince of Apostles absent on pressing celestial duties, and his earthly vicar, the Pope, far away in Rome – this had meant, in effect, that the abbot was on his own. An alarming prospect, certainly, with 'the waves of evil breaking ever higher';[49] but it was also, amid all the gathering blackness, precisely what enabled Cluny to blaze with such effulgence as a beacon of sanctity. Independence presented Odilo with opportunity as well as danger: for it ensured that his monastery could be seen as neutral – as an honest broker. This, in an age of murderous rivalries, was no negligible qualification; and all the more so because Cluny's aura of holiness appeared to demonstrate that it was indeed guarded over by St Peter. Such a reflection was sufficient to give even the most brutal knight pause – for who, with the end time nearing, wished to give needless offence to the keeper of the keys of heaven?

No surprise, then, that the presence in their midst of an abbey belonging to the mightiest of all the saints should have served to inspire in the local castellans a quite unaccustomed measure of unease. There were many, it was true, who sought to vent this in the surest way they knew how. Cattle-rustling, horse-stealing, the wasting of crops in fields: Cluny endured the full range of knightly crimes. A particular explosion of violence greeted Odilo when he was elected abbot in 994. The monastery's servants were nakedly assaulted; some were even killed. Murders such as these served to highlight the grievance that had aggravated the castellans more than anything: a trend for impoverished peasants, desperate to escape the mercies of the local knights, to opt for the lesser of two evils, and bind themselves over to the monastery as serfs. Better to be the dependants of St Peter, such wretches had evidently calculated, than the things of a violent warlord. The monks of Cluny agreed. Certainly, they had no qualms about putting peasants to work for them in their fields, their barns, their mills. What else was a mortal's duty, after all, if not to labour to the greater glory of God and His Church? There were some men who were called to sing psalms all day; and there were others who were called to dig. Even castellans, according to this formulation, might not always have to prowl beyond the pale: for what if they too had their part to play? 'A layman who serves as a warrior', St Odo himself had argued, 'is perfectly entitled to carry a sword if it is in order to defend those who have no swords themselves, like an innocent flock of sheep from the wolves that appear at twilight.'[50] As a demonstration that this was not merely wishful thinking, Odo had cited the example of one particular aristocrat, Gerald, the lord of Aurillac, Gerbert's birthplace, who all his life had refrained from stealing the land of the poor, who had only ever fought in battle using the flat of his sword, and who, in short, had been such a paragon that he had ended up a saint. 'And every second year,' Odo had added, in a hopeful postscript, 'he would go to the tomb of St Peter with ten shillings hung around his neck, as though he were a serf, paying his due to his lord.'[51]

To expect castellans as well as peasants to become the dependants of St Peter was, perhaps, pushing things – and yet the hope that the local lords might be persuaded, not merely to tolerate Cluny, but actively to contribute to its greater glory, and to that of its patron saint, the Prince of Apostles, was not a wholly ludicrous one, even so. The more grievous a sinner's crimes, the more terrible his dread of hell was likely to be. Assaults on Cluny's estates may indeed have been escalating – but so too, simultaneously, were donations of property to the monastery. Odilo, shrewd tactician that he was, had moved quickly to take advantage of this seemingly bizarre paradox. No sooner had he been elected abbot than he was brokering an emergency council at the nearby town of Anse. Presided over by two archbishops, no less, a formidable array of local dignitaries sought to back him up as thunderously as it could. The abbey and all its swelling portfolio of estates were declared sacrosanct. Fearsome curses were pronounced against all who encroached upon them. The knights and their masters were called upon to swear a solemn oath of peace. Yet even as the shimmering inviolability of Cluny was proclaimed anew, and in terms that brooked no possible misunderstanding, Odilo was careful to extend an olive branch to the castellans.

The anarchy of the times, brutally though it menaced the abbey, menaced its assailants too. Even the most lawless of warlords, once installed in a castle, had a stake in preserving what he had seized. No longer was it possible for the distant king to bestow legitimacy upon a usurper – but St Peter could. Odilo, by inviting all the local castellans to swear the oath of peace together as equals, was laying before them a fearsome choice. Either they could persist in their savagery, cause and symptom alike of the cracking of the age, portents, no less than plague or famine, of the imminent end of days; or else they too, like Odilo's monks, could take up their place in the line of battle, to serve as the warriors, not of Antichrist, but of God Himself.

Much would depend upon the castellans' answer; and not only in the neighbourhood of Cluny. To the west, in the uplands of the Auvergne and across the great duchy of Aquitaine, where order had collapsed no less grievously than in Burgundy, attempts were being made to set the world back upon its feet that were, if anything, even bolder and more radical than Odilo's. As early as 972, more than two decades before the Council of Anse, clergy from the Auvergne had gathered at Aurillac, site of the tomb of St Gerald, that splendid model of how a warrior should behave, to demand that the local castellans cease their oppression of the poor; by 989, the trend for peace councils had spread to Aquitaine; and over the following decade, more than half a dozen would be staged across southern France. The instigators, by and large, were not abbots like Odilo, but bishops: men of impeccably aristocratic lineage, whose ancestors, ever since the unimaginably distant days of Roman Gaul, had believed themselves charged by Christ Himself with the maintenance of a Christian society. Now, fed up as they were with the collapse of law and order, and despairing of the ability of dukes or counts, still less of the distant king, to do anything about it, they were resolved to try to succeed where the princes themselves had failed. In this ambition, ironically enough, they were actively encouraged by the most prominent of all the region's great aristocrats, William, the Duke of Aquitaine: for he, far from feeling that his toes were being trodden on, was desperate to shore up his crumbling authority in any way that he could. Yet it was a sign of how strange the times had become that even his backing was of less value to the bishops, those magnificent princes of the Church, than was that of the despised and bleeding poor. Desperate for assistance against the castellans, and resolved to make one final defence of their vanishing freedoms, peasants of every class, 'from the most prosperous, through the middling ranks, to the lowest of all', flocked to the peace councils – and in such numbers that it seemed to startled observers as though they must have heard 'a voice speaking to men on earth from heaven'.[52] Febrile and ecstatic was the mood; and the bishops, resolved to bring all the pressure that they could upon the castellans, 'those wicked men who like thornbushes and briars ravage the vineyard of the Lord',[53] did not shrink from harnessing it.

So it was that the councils were summoned, not to the cloistered security of great churches, but rather to the open fields: those same fields where the peasantry, by ancient tradition, had always held their assemblies, meeting as men who were free. 'And great were the passions that were stirred. High in the air the bishops lifted their crosiers, in the direction of heaven; and all around them, their hands upraised, their voices become a single voice, the people called out to God, crying, "Peace, peace, peace!"'[54]

And the foes of peace, the castellans – what was their response to be? As in Burgundy, so in Aquitaine: hesitation, initially, and some alarm. The bishops were far too sacrosanct, and the peasants far too numerous, merely to be ridden down. Nor, the truth be told, were either the most intimidating presence at the councils anyhow. To ride into a field where the Peace of God had been proclaimed was, for a castellan and his followers, to enter an arena that appeared suffused by the very breath of heaven, numinous and terrifying, where swords and spears, if unsheathed, might prove worse than useless. Beyond the seething mass of the peasantry, beyond the gorgeously arrayed ecclesiastics with their crosses, 'embellished all over with enamels and gold, and studded with a great variety of gemstones flashing like stars',[55] and beyond the stern-faced princes, the true enforcers of the Peace of God stood arrayed in silence. From their crypts all across southern France the saints had been escorted, led in candlelit procession amid the chanting of psalms, the clashing of cymbals and the blowing of ivory trumpets: an awesome sight. In the south it was the habit, 'a venerable and antique custom',[56] to enclose the remains of the sainted dead within statues of gold or silver, so that they looked, brought together, like a phalanx formed out of metal. There was none there, it was true, who rivalled St Peter in rank; and yet who could dispute the terrifying power of those saints that had been assembled? Awaiting the castellans at the peace councils were relics known to have halted terrible

169

epidemics, to have freed innocent prisoners from their chains, to have restored eyeballs to the blind, to have brought mules back to life. Why, in the very fields consecrated to the Peace of God, the holy remains had been giving certain proofs of their potency: for 'many a bent arm, and many a bent leg' had been straightened, 'and in such a manner that the miracles could not be doubted'.[57] Well, then, might the knights in attendance at the councils have bowed their heads, slipped down from their saddles and fallen to their knees, there to swear a solemn oath before the glittering army of reliquaries that they would indeed keep God's peace.

This was a step not to be taken lightly. Fearsome were the sanctions proclaimed against any horseman who might subsequently go back upon his word. A lighted candle, extinguished by the fingers of a bishop himself and dropped into the dust, would serve to symbolise the terrible snuffing out of all his hopes of heaven. 'May he render up his bowels into the latrine'[58] such was the venerable curse. Filth, indeed, was the natural condition of all oath-breakers: for it was well known that, at the very moment of his death, an excommunicant's flesh would start to reek terribly of excrement, so that consecrated ground would refuse to receive his corpse, but would instead vomit it up in a furious spasm, to serve as food for wild beasts. What greater contrast with the relics of the saints, fragrant still within their bejewelled reliquaries, could possibly have been imagined?

It would have been no wonder, then, as the horsemen swore their oaths, if all their hopes of redemption had been shadowed by a certain sense of foreboding. Most castellans were not oblivious to the terrible yearning of their victims for a new age, one in which 'the spear would rejoice to become a scythe, and the sword become a ploughshare'.[59] Standing as they were in the shadow of the Millennium, they could not even discount the possibility that Christ Himself, ablaze with fearsome glory, might soon be returning to usher in a reign of peace and justice, and to consign the wicked to eternal fire. Who, after all, looking around the fields in which the Peace of God had been proclaimed, where glittering reliquaries stood massed in an impregnable battle line, could doubt that the reign of saints was indeed at hand? Which, in turn, served to prompt one obvious question: on whose side, that of the demons or of the warriors of heaven, did the castellans and their knights wish to range themselves?

In 1016, outside the Burgundian town of Verdun-sur-le-Doubs, a great cavalcade of horsemen clattered along the local roads and lanes on the way to swear a fresh oath of peace.[60] They had been summoned by the local bishop; but the true inspiration, just as he had been at Anse, was Odilo of Cluny. It might have seemed, in the intervening two decades, that nothing much had changed in France. Violence was still general across the south. So too were the anguish and the misery of the poor. No less than in the decades before the Millennium, it appeared that the moment of which St Odo had warned his successors, when time itself would be fulfilled, and 'the King of Evil enter in triumph into the world',[61] might be imminent. No matter that the anniversary of the Incarnation had passed – the yet more fateful anniversary of Christ's ascension into heaven was still to come. Hugh of Châlons, the bishop who had summoned the knights to Verdun, would certainly not have been oblivious to the swirl of apocalyptic speculations. The seat of his bishopric was Auxerre: still, as it had been back in the time of the Hungarian invasions, a famous centre for the study of the end of days. It was at Auxerre, for instance, some ten years previously, that one scholar had publicly identified the monks of Cluny with the 144,000 harpists who were destined, according to the Book of Revelation, to 'sing a new song' at the hour of judgement, and to 'follow the Lamb wherever he goes'.[62] Now, by summoning his council at Verdun, Bishop Hugh was hoping to follow the example of Odilo. As well he might have done – for Cluny, at any rate, had gone from strength to strength. Popes and kings alike had ringingly affirmed its independence. Monasteries across France – including in Auxerre – had formally submitted to the authority of its abbot.

Yet the most remarkable of all the displays of Odilo's leadership – and the most suggestive too – had been over men who were not even

tonsured. Since the Millennium, the violence that had for so long tormented the neighbourhood of his monastery had begun finally to be
tamed. The local knights, inspired to share in something at least of the
heroic disciplines of Cluny, had been recruited by Odilo to take their
place beside the monks, to range themselves on an invisible battlefield
thronged by angels and warrior saints. Such, at any rate, was the ideal.
Another way of putting it was to say that Odilo, looking to rein in the
criminal gangs massed against him, had succeeded in persuading them
to abandon their careers of violence in exchange for his blessing and
a degree of legitimacy. Certainly, however his achievements were
spun, they were palpable in the valley where the famous monastery
stood. A brutal convulsion in society had been successfully negotiated.
Peace had been brought to the fields – and respectability to the neighbouring castles. The tide of violence, at last, had begun to recede from
Cluny.

Demonstration of a potent truth indeed: that the very measures
taken to buttress humanity against the looming onslaught of
Antichrist, and to prepare the world for its fiery end, might serve as
well to secure a new beginning, and a new model of society. Odilo was
not the only leader of the peace movement to flirt with this paradox.
So it was, for instance, at Verdun, that Bishop Hugh cast the horsemen
assembled there both as 'knights of Christ', sworn upon the relics of
saints to serve as shock troops of the heavenly, and as the agents of an
ambitious programme to restore the rule of law. Where the harm,
after all, in hedging a bet? Perhaps the world would end; perhaps it
would not. Either way, the duty of the Church to labour in the cause
of peace was hardly lessened.

Not that mixed motives were confined to abbots or bishops.
The knights also had calculations to make. The pledges that they
were obliged to give at Verdun were indisputably stern ones. All their
favourite pastimes appeared to have been proscribed. No longer were
they to amuse themselves by assaulting the defenceless; by rounding
up livestock; by attacking churches; by setting fire to harvests and
barns. Yet forbearance might bring its own rewards – and not in

heaven alone. Upstarts as many of the horsemen were, they knew that it was no small matter to be blessed in public by a bishop. Knighthood, once it had been sanctified by oaths sworn upon holy relics, could hardly be dismissed as a criminal calling. Even the most unreasoning and thuggish henchman of a castellan, as he stood at Verdun alongside the other horsemen of the region, and knelt before the glittering reliquaries, would surely have felt, with a surge of pride, that he was being inducted into an elite. A shared code, a shared ethos, a shared commitment to the use of arms: all were being granted him. His horse, his spear, his mail shirt: these, in the eyes of God, were what would henceforward serve to define his role in the Christian order. The division between knight and serf, between a person who carried a sword and a person who carried a mattock, was being rendered absolute. If indeed the end days were imminent, then this would hardly matter: for all the different orders of society would naturally be dissolved upon the melting of heaven and earth. If, however, Christ did not return, and if the New Jerusalem did not descend from the sky, and if the seasons continued to revolve as they had always done, year after year after year, then the organisers of the Peace of God would effectively have set their seal upon the enserfment of their very allies: the poor. Such might not have been their intention – and yet they would have served as the midwives of a new order, all the same. Peace, it appeared, might indeed be redeemed from anarchy – but the price to be paid for it was the last vestige of freedom of the peasantry.

And this, as a bargain, was one that even the peasants themselves were increasingly too punch-drunk to resist. Better a master bound by the strictures of the Peace of God, perhaps, and a storehouse well stocked for the winter, than liberty and a pile of smoking rubble. Not that the master necessarily had to be a castellan. The men and women who toiled in the fields around Cluny as the serfs of St Peter were far from the only peasants to have ended up the dependants of a great monastery. The concern of churchmen for the poor – though it might be heartfelt – was likely as well, at least in part, to reflect a concern for

173

their own finances. No less than the castellans, great abbots and bishops stood to profit handsomely from the wholesale enserfment of the peasantry – as long as order and the rule of law could be upheld. Once, of course, the peace campaigners would have looked to the king to provide them with their security; but it was a mark of how utterly everything changed, how it had been utterly turned upside down, that the king was now looking to them. By 1016, Robert Capet had finally crushed his enemies in Burgundy. Concerned to see order established in his new domain, he toured it that same summer amid a great show of magnificence – and among the towns that he visited was Verdun-sur-le-Doubs. Over the succeeding years, he would repeatedly demonstrate his approval of what the peace campaigners were attempting to achieve – even to the extent of hosting his own councils, and affecting an ostentatious religiosity. So it was that the king, just as though he were a saint, would feed the poor at his own table; hand out his robes to them; even have it whispered that he could cure them of leprosy. That he was in truth a warlord just as rapacious for land as any castellan, and had even managed to end up excommunicated by the Pope for marrying his cousin, mattered not a jot. 'Robert the Pious' he came to be called. The King of France, in short, had taken to aping the Abbot of Cluny.

There were many among the Frankish elite who were duly appalled. Bishops, in particular, haughty grandees from the ancient royal heartlands, the very cockpit of the traditional order, loathed Odilo and everything that he stood for. The Peace of God they dismissed as dangerous rabble-rousing; the claims of Cluny's monks to be heaven's shock troops as a grotesque blasphemy; and Odilo himself as a puffed-up castellan, 'the lord of a warlike order',[63] shamelessly usurping the prerogatives of his betters. King Robert himself was serenely unperturbed. Amid all the continuing agonies of his kingdom, he had no doubt that he possessed in Cluny a truly priceless attribute, a spiritual powerhouse to illumine the present, and light the way to the future. What that future might be – whether the destruction of the world or its renewal – only time would tell. But that change was inevitable – indeed, was already irreversible – even Odilo's bitterest critics had little choice but to acknowledge. 'The laws of the land melt away, and the reign of peace is no more.' So mourned Adalbero, the aged Bishop of Laon, whose scheming, decades earlier, had helped to secure the throne for Hugh Capet. Yet even as he sought to roll back the years, to warn King Robert against the blandishments of Cluny and to resurrect the Carolingian order that he himself had helped consign to its grave, he knew that his cause was doomed. The past was gone for ever. Well might Adalbero lament: 'Changed are all the orders of society! Changed utterly are the ways of men!'[64]

4

GO WEST

Normandy Landings

Robert Capet was not the only Christian ruler to have identified in Cluny the radiance of an awesome and potent mystery. In 1014, messengers arrived at the abbey from Rome, bringing with them a remarkable gift. The man who had sent it was Henry II: 'King of the Germans, Emperor of the Romans, Augustus'.[1] It had taken Otto III's successor more than a decade to be daubed with the imperial chrism, and the Pope, to mark the occasion of the delayed coronation, had presented to Henry a dazzling reminder of what still officially remained his global mission: an orb shaped like an apple, divided into four by precious jewels and surmounted by a golden cross. Dispatched to Cluny, along with the emperor's coronation robes, his sceptre and his crown, the presence within the abbey walls of this spectacular array of imperial regalia suggested just how far the monastery's horizons were widening. It certainly required no great penetration to fathom the prophecy encoded within the emperor's gift. Just as the apple was divided into four quarters, so too, according to the learned, was the globe; and just as a cross surmounted the apple, so had it been foretold that the Cross of Christ was to redeem all the world. Peoples everywhere would be brought to follow it.

None, no matter how savage or remote, was to be left behind. Odilo, taking possession of the orb, was so delighted by its message that he ordered it put on display whenever a major festival was celebrated: a reassurance, etched in gold and jewels, that the conversion of the heathen was at hand.

Cluny might have been far removed from the wastelands of paganism, yet such were the reservoirs of spiritual power that it had generated, and such the efficacy of all the psalms and anthems sung within its walls, that even those demons skulking beyond the frontiers of Christendom, haunting the foul sump of their own darkness, had been dazzled by the blaze of its holiness. This, at any rate, was what Henry himself was evidently banking on. As a Roman emperor, stationed at the very edge of time, he naturally needed all the supernatural assistance that he could obtain. Like his predecessor, he had no doubt that he had been charged directly by God with the bringing of barbarians to Christ. So it was that he had married his own sister to Stephen, the King of the Hungarians. So it was too that he had lavished endowments upon the Church, with the stated goal of 'destroying the paganism of the Slavs'.[2] Nevertheless, the trampling down of demons was not Henry's only responsibility. As a Caesar, it was his duty as well to keep the Roman Empire together. Sometimes, regrettably, this might require him to dirty his hands. One problem, festering beyond the eastern frontiers of the *Reich*, was a particular irritant. Boleslav, the same Duke of Poland who had been awarded the title of 'friend of the Roman people' by Otto III, had recently begun to prove himself a good deal less than amiable. Henry, resolved to slap down the high-aiming Pole, had been obliged to scout around for allies. In due course, and to the horror of Christians everywhere, he had settled upon the most monstrous choice imaginable.

In 1003, on Easter Day, the holiest festival of the year, Christendom's greatest king had signed a formal treaty of friendship with the Wends: a people who still unashamedly worshipped idols, offered up human sacrifices, and decided policy by putting questions to a horse. Even with the backing of his new allies, however, Henry had been unable to land a killer blow on Boleslav. The hostilities had continued to smoulder. In 1015, one year after Henry's coronation in Rome, they burst into flames again. As the newly anointed emperor rode to war against the Duke of Christian Poland, the Holy Lance borne ahead of him, and anthems sounding in his ears, so were the Wends, marching beneath the banners of their goddess, still massed in all their unregenerate paganism at his side.

A scandal, certainly. And yet, for all Henry's undoubted equivocations, the dream of St Adalbert – that the wilds of the heathen East might be tamed and transformed into a garden of the City of God – still endured. Even in lands far removed from the front line of the *Reich*, Christians were moved and haunted by its implications. 'The gospel must be proclaimed throughout the whole world,' demanded one English bishop in urgent tones, 'and it must be done before the world's end. So books tell us – and afterward the end will be as soon as God wishes.'[3] Missionaries, risking death no less boldly than Adalbert himself had done, duly continued to follow in the martyr's footsteps, tramping over dusty plains, through dripping forests, along the banks of ice-locked rivers. The most brilliant of them all, a Saxon monk by the name of Bruno, even managed to end up murdered precisely as his master had done, beheaded beside a lake by a war band of angry Prussians; but only after he had spent years preaching to other tribes, from the Balkans to the Baltic, no less menacing than his killers. Indeed, following several months of sermons, he had even succeeded in converting thirty Pechenegs: nomads who haunted the steppes above the Black Sea, and who were notoriously the most savage people in the world.

Certainly, to Bruno's countrymen, secure behind the ramparts of the *Reich*, the names of the various barbarians whom he had laboured to win for Christ – the Pechenegs and Prussians, the Lithuanians and Swedes – appeared suggestive of a truly abhorrent savagery. Sinister temples 'entirely decked out in gold';[4] altars splashed with blood; groves hung with the rotting corpses of humans, horses and dogs: such were the nightmare visions that haunted the Saxons, whenever they sought to imagine what horrors might be lurking on the margins of the world. Yet the exploits of men such as Bruno suggested that the optimism of St Adalbert remained well founded: that there was nowhere so steeped in darkness that it might not be penetrated by the light of Christ, nor any soul so fierce that it might not ultimately be won for Christendom.

Indeed, there were some Saxons who went so far as to ponder whether the heathen, once safely converted, might not actually have some lessons to pass on to them in turn. The savagery that came naturally to barbarians did certainly appear to lend itself to 'the strict enforcement of the law of God'. So reflected Thietmar, a friend of Bruno from childhood, and bishop of that same frontier town of Merseburg which Henry the Fowler, almost a century before, had garrisoned with bandits. Though Thietmar was proudly chauvinist, and had a contempt for the Poles, in particular, that knew few bounds, even he could not help but admire the robust manner in which their leaders 'keep the populace in line, much as one would a stubborn ass'. Wistfully, he reflected on how a Polish bishop might encourage his flock to keep a fast by the simple expedient of punching out the teeth of anyone who broke it. Other moral standards were upheld in an even more no-nonsense way. A convicted prostitute, so Thietmar reported approvingly, was liable to have her genitals sliced off and hung from her doorpost; while a rapist, nailed by his scrotum to a bridge, would then, 'after a sharp knife has been placed next to him', be confronted with the unpleasant options of self-castration or suicide. Food for thought indeed. 'For though such customs are undoubtedly harsh,' pronounced Thietmar sternly, 'yet they are not without their positive side.'[5]

Times, then, had clearly changed, when the cruelties of an alien people could be regarded, not as a menace, but as a potential buttress of Christendom. Within living memory, after all, there were those who had dreaded that the entire world of Christian order was doomed to collapse, shaken to fragments by the thunderous hoof beats of paganism, and consigned to its sacrilegious flames. Yet Christendom

179

had not succumbed. Its laws, its rituals, its mysteries had endured. Rather, like a phantom dissolved upon the splashing of holy water or the singing of a psalm, it was the heathen assailants of Christendom who had found themselves, in the final reckoning, confounded, disarmed, transfigured. In Hungary, such a paragon of godliness was Caesar's brother-in-law, King Stephen, that he would end up officially proclaimed a saint; in Gniezno, at the tomb of the blessed Adalbert, stupendous miracles continued to be performed, to the awe and wonder of all; even further east, on the very margin of the world, where Gog and Magog had once been believed to wait, there now sat a Christian prince within a Christian city, the fabulous stronghold of Kiev. Perhaps, then, in the cross-surmounted apple sent by the emperor to Odilo, there was to be found a symbol, not merely of hope, but of celebration. Already, it appeared, such was the golden brilliancy of the heartlands of Christendom that its glow was spilling outwards to the ends of the earth.

Yet in truth, it was not along the limits of the Christian world, among distant barbarians, in lands with grotesque and unpronounceable names, that the most startling evidence of all was to be found of how a savage nation might be redeemed. Instead, it lay directly on the doorstep of the King of France himself. North-westwards out of Paris, that nerve centre of Capetian power, there wound a mighty river, the Seine; and as its currents flowed onwards to the sea, so they passed by 'woods teeming with wild animals, fields ideal for growing corn and other crops, and meadows lush with cattle-fattening grass'.[6] A province, in short, not to be surrendered idly; and sure enough, for many centuries, ever since the first coming of Clovis into Gaul, it had served as a prized adornment of the empire of the Franks. And yet, under the heirs of Charlemagne, the empire of the Franks had let it slip. So terminally, indeed, that with the dawning of the second millennium a new word was starting to be used to describe the region, a word that branded it the property, not of the Franks at all, but of barbarians who had long seemed, even more than the Hungarians or Saracens, a horror risen up from the most anguished depths of

Christian nightmares. 'Normandy', people were coming to call it: the land of the '*Nordmanni*' – the 'Northmen'.

It was a name fit to inspire terror. That the frozen rim of the world might make for danger had been appreciated since ancient times. 'A hive of nations':[7] so one historian, writing in the early years of Constantinople, had termed the furthermost North. Centuries on, and a more detailed knowledge of the intimidating expanses of Scandinavia had done nothing to impair this judgement. Given their interminable winters, what else was there for the inhabitants to do, save to copulate and breed? It had certainly come as little surprise to venturesome missionaries to discover that many of the demons worshipped by the Northmen should have been prodigious fornicators: one of them, for instance, a giant-slaughtering hammer-wielder by the name of Thor, was a compulsively enthusiastic rapist; while a second, Frey, boasted a 'phallus of truly enormous dimensions'.[8] Alarming revelations, to be sure: for people capable of worshipping gods such as these, violent in their ambitions, insatiable in their lusts, could hardly help but prove a menace to Christendom, rather as lascivious promptings might beset a virtuous soul. The Northmen, certainly, were notorious for setting few limits on their ravening. To harvest women, 'leading them down to a bright ship, fetters biting greedily into their soft flesh';[9] to deny their bodies to rivals; then to father on them a teeming plenitude of sons: these were held the surest proofs of manliness. 'And so it is that these people soon grow too numerous for their native land to support them – and the consequence is that a war band of young men has to be selected by lot, according to an ancient custom, and these are then sent out into the world, to seize new lands for themselves at the point of a sword.'[10]

Such, at any rate, among Christian moralists, was the favoured explanation for the deadly waves of pirates from Scandinavia who, surging and withdrawing and then surging yet again, upon a seemingly endless tide, had been bloodying the shores of Christendom for more than two centuries, ever since the time of Charlemagne. Whether the theory was true or not, there was certainly a grim satisfaction to be had in believing it.* Although the depredations of the Northmen were demoralising, the notion that it was mere bestial appetite which had propelled them across the sea did at least serve to reassure their victims that, inviolable amid all the rapine, the values of Christendom remained those of virtue and order. Women might be abducted, monasteries plundered, even whole cities burned – and yet the memory of such atrocities, growing ever more lurid with the retelling, only helped to confirm in most Christians an impregnable sense of their own superiority. Just as the monk murdered by a Northman could draw his last breath confident in the knowledge that he was bound for a throne in heaven, so could the warrior who unsheathed his sword against the pirates and stood to block their path know with an iron-forged certitude that he was performing the work of God.

So it was that even by the time of the Millennium, a century after the worst of the firestorm had passed from France, great princes were still in the habit of flaunting battle honours won by their forefathers against the Northmen. A dynasty which lacked them, indeed, was felt to verge on the illegitimate. Nothing, for instance, had been more fatal to the martial reputation of the Carolingians than their failure, back in 886, to finish off an army of pirates who had presumed to lay siege to Paris; just as the Capetians, one of whose ancestors had performed prodigies of valour during the great assault on the city, never let anyone forget their own family's heroic record as Northmen-fighters. 'Swords and spears slippery with bright blood';[11] 'skewered bodies sprawled as though asleep in town gate-ways';[12] 'gobbets of carrion stuck to the claws and beaks of crows':[13] such were the scenes of carnage that had first served to fertilise Capetian greatness.

And the greatness of many other Frankish dynasties too. It was no coincidence that many of the most formidable princedoms of the

---

* The current consensus among historians is that the theory was not true. Studies of rural settlements in Scandinavia do not, in fact, appear to indicate excessive population growth.

kingdom, from Flanders to Anjou, stood guard over broad-flowing estuaries: those fatal confluences where waters from the heart of France met and mingled with the sea. Just as it was the Seine which had enabled the Northmen, 'oars thrashing, weapons crashing, shields striking shields',[14] to penetrate to the bridges of Paris, so too had other fleets thrust their way up the Loire, snaking deep into the very innards of the kingdom, so that even Orléans, back in 856, had been captured and brutally despoiled. On the lower reaches of the river, not surprisingly, the devastation had been more protracted: the county of Anjou, which by the year 1000 would stand so thriving, so puissant, so fair, had been, not much more than a century earlier, so infested with Northmen as to appear almost lost to Christendom. Angers, the proud city that would serve Fulk Nerra as his capital, had been repeatedly occupied by pirates, and transformed into their lair. Other towns, one jittery contemporary had wailed, 'are emptied so utterly, alas, that they are become the habitation of wild beasts!'[15]

But this had been to overdo the pessimism. In truth, even at the height of the Northmen's assault, outposts of Frankish rule had endured along the entire reach of the Loire; nor had the structures of governance there ever wholly collapsed. Proficient at carting off loot the pirates may have been – but they had signally failed to lay their hands on any effective levers of power. It had not taken long for the new masters of Angers, planted in the city after its final liberation in 886, to demonstrate the full scale of this error. By 929, the Vicomte of Angers had cheerfully promoted himself to the rank of 'the Count of Anjou'; a few decades on, and even the greatest in the land had accepted his right to be reckoned their peer. Francia being what it was, an ancient and Christian realm, loot pilfered from its monasteries could never hope to compare as a long-term investment with lands and a glamorous title. Fulk Nerra's ancestors, because they had instinctively appreciated this, had been able to raise a princedom that, by 1000, could stand comparison with any in France. The Northmen, because they had not, had long since been swept from the Loire back into the sea.

And yet, to a menacing degree, they had always been fast learners. As pirates, living by their wits, they had needed to be. Whether it was raiding a monastery on the occasion of its saint's day, or sweeping into a market place just as the stalls were going up, or mastering, perhaps, the unfamiliar Frankish arts of horsemanship, the Northmen had long shown themselves adept at profiting from an attentive study of their prey. They were certainly not oblivious to the underlying strengths possessed by a Christian state – nor to the threat that these presented to themselves. Along the lower reaches of the Seine, for instance, where the Northmen had settled to far more formidable effect than they ever had along the Loire, the props of Frankish power truly had been obliterated, and its foundations systematically smashed to pieces. By the early years of the tenth century, not only had the local nobility been destroyed, and all traces of native officialdom wiped out, but even the Church itself, as a functioning organisation, had begun to disintegrate.

It was true that in Rouen, on the very mouth of the Seine, the local archbishop had somehow, against the odds, managed to cling to office; but all around him and his beleaguered flock, as palpable as a gathering twilight, there had been the sense of a deadly wasteland closing in. '*Invia*', such a wilderness was properly termed by the learned: a dimension of trackless forests and bogs and scrubland, where no decent Christian would ever think to venture, but which had long been the haunts of the heathen, the theatre of their loathsome rituals and the womb of their ambushes. 'Out in the field no man should move one foot beyond his weapons,' the Northmen sang. 'For a man never knows, travelling abroad, when he may need his spear.'[16] By 900, all the region of the Seine estuary had become *invia*: a wasted, rubble-strewn no man's land, where it was indeed the spear alone which ruled, while fugitives from slavery and sacrifice and war watched over their shoulders, and slunk fearfully through weed-grown fields.

And yet by the early years of the tenth century, the sheer scale of the ruin had come to threaten the outlanders no less than the wretched natives. Increasingly, with all the region of the Seine scavenged bare, the Northmen had been obliged to look ever further afield for pickings. In 911, leaving their coastal bases far behind them, they had plunged deep into enemy territory, as far as Chartres, some sixty miles south-west of Paris. Here, confronted by a Frankish army led by Hugh Capet's grandfather, they had been brought to defeat – but not to destruction. The aftermath had left both sides in a mood for compromise. Even as the defeated war bands were retreating to lick their wounds on the banks of the Seine, messengers from the Frankish king had been following in their wake. Brought into the presence of the most fearsome and formidable of all the Northmen, a celebrated warlord by the name of Rollo, the ambassadors had proposed a bargain. The pirate chieftain was to abandon his heathen ways; he was to become the vassal of the Frankish king; he was to stand sentry against other pirates on the upper reaches of the Seine. In exchange, he was to be acknowledged as the rightful overlord of Rouen and all the lands around it: the peer, in short, of any native-born count. Rollo, no less shrewd than he was brutal, had immediately grasped what was being offered. Rouen was certainly worth a mass. The terms had been accepted. In 912, the new lord of the city, bowing his head, had duly received baptism at the hands of its no doubt highly relieved archbishop.[17]

Few, on either side, had expected the bargain to stick for long. Enthusiasts for the new regime would later make much play of Rollo's born-again piety – but more disturbing rumours had never ceased to swirl around his name. Once, at least, he had returned to his old ways, leading raids across his borders with an authentically piratical abandon; while on his deathbed, it was darkly whispered, he had cast all inhibitions aside, 'and ordered a hundred Christian captives beheaded before him in honour of his native gods'.[18] Calumny or not, neighbouring lords had long persisted in regarding the upstart county as a nest of heathenish vipers. In 942, when Rollo's son, William Longsword, had travelled to a parley with the Count of Flanders, he had done so unarmed, as befitted a Christian lord meeting with a fellow prince; and the Count of Flanders, as befitted a Christian lord meeting with a dangerous pirate, had ordered him hacked to death. Twenty years on, and Richard, the murdered Longsword's son, had found himself so menaced by a coalition of his Frankish neighbours that he had been reduced, in his desperation, to calling in assistance from across the seas. His appeal had been answered with a ferocious enthusiasm; squadrons of dragon-headed ships had come gliding into the Seine; 'foaming streams had blushed with blood, warm gore had smoked above the grass';[19] and the Franks had been repulsed. Yet the Count of Rouen himself, even with his frontiers stabilised, had remained on his guard. The Frankish world beyond him had still appeared hostile and menacing, one vast and yawning mouth, waiting to swallow him and all his princedom; and so Richard, in his concern to preserve the distinctive character of his lands, had continued to encourage immigration from across the realms of the North.

The result, over the succeeding decades, had been such an influx of settlers that by 996, when Richard, after a long and triumphant reign, finally died, the mongrel character of his subjects could be hailed as their defining glory. For Rollo, it would be claimed, long before ever landing on the banks of the Seine, had been granted a dream of a mighty flock of birds, 'each one of a different breed and colour',[20] but all of them distinguished by having a left wing the colour of blood: the mark of warriors, of peerless warlords, brought together to share in a common purpose, and a common destiny. 'One nation fashioned out of a mixture of different ones':[21] such was the boast of those who had already come to see themselves as a unique and glorious people – the Normans.

Perhaps it was not surprising, then, that their neighbours, almost a century after Rollo's baptism, should have persisted in regarding the county ruled by his grandson as somehow sinister and alien: a lair of pirates still. Despite the fact that only Flanders among the great princedoms of the kingdom could boast a more venerable pedigree, the Norman state had never entirely lost its aura of the alien. In Rouen, for instance, the harbour remained as thronged with shipping from across the northern seas as it had ever been; flush with 'profits from the trade borne on the surging tides',[22] the port was precisely the kind of stronghold that had always been most treasured by the Northmen. Even away from the Seine, the county remained a place where sea-wanderers might feel at home: in the west of Normandy especially, there were many who still spoke their language; while at Richard's court, a praise-singer from Scandinavia would always be assured of a welcome. Violence, and slaughter, and gloating, and bragging: these were the invariable themes of a poem composed by a Northman.

Elsewhere too, escaped from the limits of song, hints of a primordial heathenism were rumoured to linger. The winter gales which screamed across the woods and fields of Normandy were notorious for being ridden by demonic huntsmen; and leading the hunt, men whispered, was none other than the ancient king of the gods himself. The same demon whose sacred groves in Saxony had long since been torched by Charlemagne was still worshipped by the Northmen under the name of 'Odin': a cloaked and one-eyed figure, the master of magic, a pacer of the realms of the night. Perhaps, in the final years of Richard's rule, it was a certain resemblance to the fabled 'All-father' that helped to explain the awe with which the aged count had come to be regarded: for just like Odin, he was bright-eyed and long-bearded, and it was said that after dark he would wander the streets of Rouen, cloaked and alone, and fight with the shades of the dead. Certainly, when he died at last, the grave in which he was buried appeared almost a spectre itself, conjured up from the mists of his forefathers' past: an earthen mound, looking out to sea.

Yet if Richard had always kept one eye firmly fixed on the world of the North, then so too, with great skill and patience, had he sought to demonstrate to his fellow princes that he was one of their own number: that he and all his dynasty had forever cleansed themselves of the ordure of barbarism, and become the epitome of Christian lords. No matter the sophistries deployed by the Count of Flanders to justify his brutal assassination of William Longsword – Richard and all the Normans had been righteously appalled. 'For he was a defender of peace, and a lover and consoler of the poor, and a defender of orphans, and a protector of widows – shed tears, then, for William, who died innocently.'[23] That a monk had felt able to compose this eulogy with a straight face had reflected, almost certainly, something more than simple time-serving. William it was, even as he had dyed the frontiers of his county with Frankish blood, who had first demonstrated that taste for founding – or refounding – monasteries, and then for lavishing spectacular donations on them, that would become, under his successors, a positive obsession. By 1000, the holy places desecrated by the fury of the Northmen had long since been lovingly restored; the relics put into safe keeping brought out of hiding; the men of God restored from exile. When the chaplain to the new count, Richard's son and namesake, hailed his master as 'magnanimous, pious and moderate, an extraordinary, God-fearing man!',[24] his hero worship came naturally: Richard II was indeed a patron of churches fit to stand comparison with any prince in France. Yet nothing, perhaps, better illustrated the full astounding completeness of the Normans' assimilation into the heart of Christendom than the fact that they too, by the time of the Millennium, had ended up no less prone than their Frankish neighbours to dismiss anyone who lived on the edge of the world as a savage. This, it might be thought, coming from the descendants of pirates who were widely believed to have been forced into exile from their native lands due to their own incontinent taste for rutting, was a truly heroic display of hypocrisy. Of the Irish, for instance, a people who had been Christian for half a millennium, one Norman poet could assert with a cheerful dismissiveness: 'They couple like animals, not even wearing trousers, because they are forever having sex.'[25] The wheels of snobbery had turned full circle.

Not that the Normans' new ruler was done with his own social climbing quite yet. Unlike many other princes, Richard II was assiduous in cultivating the King of France. It helped that relations between his family and the Capetians had always been excellent: Hugh Capet's grandfather, it was claimed, had been godfather to Rollo, while one of his sisters had certainly been married to Count Richard I. King Robert, hemmed in all about as he was by enemies, was naturally grateful for support wherever he could find it: Norman horsemen had a formidable reputation, and warriors dispatched by Richard II regularly took starring roles in the royal campaigns. And the *quid pro quo*? Well, for Richard himself, there was always the satisfaction of being regarded as a loyal vassal. That, however, was far from the limit of his ambitions. The Count of Rouen had his gimlet eye fixed on a source of even greater prestige. In 1006, a charter was issued in which he was for the first time termed, not a count at all, but a '*dux*' – a duke.[26] A truly vaunting self-promotion: for to be a duke was to rank as the superior of everyone save a king. In the whole of France, there were only two other lords who could convincingly lay claim to the title: the princes of Burgundy and Aquitaine. Exclusivity was precisely what gave it such cachet. If Richard's right to the title were widely accepted by his fellow princes, then it would rank, for a descendant of pagan warlords, as a truly remarkable prize.

Yet the uncomfortable truth was that many of his neighbours remained deeply suspicious of him precisely because they could not forget his origins. Years before Richard laid claim to his grandiose title, hostile Frankish chroniclers had already named his father a duke – 'the Duke of Pirates'.[27] Now, with the Millennium, there was a renewed bitterness in the perennial charge of Norman wolfishness. Out on the seas, the Northmen were back on the move. Dragon-ships were docking again in the harbours of Normandy. Her markets were filling up once more with the plunder looted from an ancient Christian people. True, it was not the Franks this time who found themselves the objects of the Northmen's rapacity. But they had only to raise their eyes and look northwards to the realm of another anointed king, a wealthy and famous one, to be reminded of their own agony at the hands of the pirates, and to shudder.

For the kingdom of the English was burning.

The British Isles in the year 1000

Bound in with the Triumphant Sea

'Middle Earth's doom is at hand.'[28] This conviction, which gnawed at many in the lands of what had once been the Frankish Empire, was no less a cause of anxiety on the opposite side of the Channel. That the seas would dry up; that the earth would be consumed by fire; that the heavens themselves would be folded up like a book: here were the staples of many an English sermon. Naturally, those who delivered them tended to hedge their prophecies with anxious qualifications: for they were the heirs to Alcuin and numerous other learned scholars, and knew perfectly well that it was forbidden for even an angel to calculate the timing of the end of the world. Nevertheless, like a child with a scab, they found it hard to let alone. Typical was a sermon which can be dated with great precision to the year 971.[29] Scrupulously, despite having taken the Day of Judgement as his theme, its author forbore to make any mention of the looming Millennium. 'For so veiled by secrecy is the end of days,' he warned his flock sternly, 'that no one in the entire world, no matter how holy, nor even anyone in heaven, except the Lord alone, has ever known when it will come.' So far, so orthodox; but the preacher's self-restraint was not to last for long. Indeed, with his very next breath, he was off, soaring away into giddy speculation. 'The end cannot be long delayed,' he proclaimed all of a sudden. 'Only the coming of the accursed stranger, Antichrist, who is yet to appear on the face of the earth, is still awaited. Otherwise, all the signs and forewarnings that our Lord told us would herald Doomsday have come to pass.'[30]

Except that, to the preacher's audience, it would not have been at all clear that they had. England, in 971, was in a notably well-ordered state. Symptoms of the end of the world appeared safely confined to overseas. The Channel stretched wide indeed. Even as the empire of the Franks was fragmenting amid all the various convulsions of war and social upheaval, the English had found themselves being melded into a single nation; even as the line of Charlemagne was withering away into spectral impotence, a monarchy of unprecedented wealth and power was being entrenched in England. The dynasty called itself '*Cerdicingas*', 'the house of Cerdic': a title gilded with all the prestige that only a really stupefying antiquity could provide. For Cerdic, back in the far-off days when the ancestors of the English had first arrived in Britain, had been at their head, a Saxon adventurer with a mere five ships at his back, but who had nevertheless succeeded in winning himself a kingdom.

To be sure, there were many other warlords who had done the same; but it was Wessex, the land of the West Saxons, a realm ruled without break by Cerdic's heirs over all the long succeeding centuries, that had ended up paramount.[31] As the first millennium drew to a close, it dominated not only southern England, where its own heartlands lay, but all the lands where the English had settled, so that even the Northumbrians, who back in the time of Charlemagne had been a proud and independent people, 'were in mourning for their lost liberty'.[32] In England, running decisively against the grain of what had been happening elsewhere in Christendom, ancient princedoms had been brought, not to splinter, but to cohere and coalesce. The King of Wessex had ended up the King of the English too. The lands he ruled had become a united kingdom.

This was a bold and brilliant achievement. What had served to render it truly remarkable, however, was that its foundations had been laid in the most unpropitious circumstances imaginable, amid the fire and slaughter and calamity of defeat. Realms such as Northumbria had first lost their independence more than a hundred years previously – and it had not been to the West Saxons. Other foes, far more agile, far more predatory, had been abroad. Set as the English were upon an island, in kingdoms studded with rich and defenceless monasteries, it was hardly to be wondered at that they should have found themselves the targets of the Northmen. They had termed the invaders '*Wicingas*': 'robbers'. As well they might have done; for the *Wicingas*, the 'Vikings', had sought to strip their kingdoms bare. Realm after realm had been plundered, dismembered and brought crashing down.

192

Even Wessex itself, for a few terrible months, had seemed on the verge of collapse: for in the winter of 878, its king, Alfred, had been ambushed, and sent fleeing into a marsh. This, as a moment when the entire future of a Christian people had hung in the balance, suspended between the twin poles of ruin and redemption, had been a test more perilous than anything ever faced by a king of Francia. Alfred had passed it: he had not buckled, and by refusing to buckle, he had saved his people for Christendom. Emerging from the marshes, he had suc-ceeded in scouring his kingdom free of the invaders; he had planted towns, ringed about with fortifications and endowed with marke places for the generation of war taxes, at regular intervals all over Wessex; he had steeled his people for continued struggle. The harvest of these labours, reaped by his heirs over the succeeding decades, had been a truly spectacular one. The Viking overlords who had clung on to power beyond the borders of Wessex had been systematically sub-dued; so too, in the Celtic fastnesses, where the English had never settled, had the Cornish, the Welsh and the Scots. In 937, in a bloody and titanic battle that would long be celebrated as the greatest victory ever won by an English king, Athelstan, the grandson of Alfred, had confronted an assemblage of foes drawn from across the British Isles, and routed them all.[33] On his coins and in his charters, he had laid claim to a title even more resonant than 'King of the English': 'King of all Britain'. Across the sea too, in Ireland, admirers had been brought to acknowledge him as 'the very roof-tree of the dignity of the west-ern world'.[34]

But it was not only on the margins of Christendom that men had marvelled. From beyond the Channel, in France, none other than Hugh Capet's father, the mighty 'Duke of the Franks', had sent mes-sengers seeking the hand of one of Athelstan's four sisters in marriage. As a dowry, the duke had dispatched to England a rich collection of relics – including, most priceless of all, the very spear that had pierced the side of Christ. Once owned by Charlemagne, and wielded by him in his wars against the Saracens, this had been a weapon of self-evidently miraculous power.[35] All the more fitting, then, that it should have passed into the hands of the *Cerdicingas*: for so triumphant had been their fightback against the Northmen that their achievement had seemed almost a miracle in itself. Other Christian kings, certainly, had been able to draw from it a most potent and inspiring lesson: not merely that the heathen could be repulsed, but that their defeat might provide a stepping stone to empire.

Naturally enough, perhaps, it was in Saxony, the primordial homeland of Cerdic, that the victories of the House of Wessex had been tracked most appreciatively of all. In 929, the Lady Edith, another of Athelstan's sisters, had duly travelled there to marry a teenage prince, the future Otto the Great: a man with an imperial destiny indeed. Just like the House of Wessex, the Saxon royal family had already come into possession of a supernaturally charged spear, a Holy Lance of their own; but the presence at Otto's side of a saintly and much-loved English queen had undoubtedly served his people as a yet further reassurance of the glories ordained for them by God. It was at Edith's urging, for instance, that her husband had embarked on the building of his great monastery at Magdeburg; and years later, with Edith long dead and Otto himself crowned Caesar, it was to the selfsame monastery that he had moved the relics of St Maurice and – when it was not required out on campaign – the Holy Lance itself.

Meanwhile, back in England, the *Cerdicingas* had begun to look a trifle provincial in comparison. Athelstan, concerned to secure his subjection of the Cornish, had set about refurbishing the frontier town of Exeter; and it was here, in an abbey church founded by the king himself, that he had enshrined his own holy lance. Priceless relic or not, however, it had soon begun to gather dust: for whereas Magdeburg stood sentinel over vast expanses of heathendom, beyond Cornwall there extended only the sea. No matter that it was the kings of Wessex who had originally blazed the imperial trail; they could never hope to compete in the glamour stakes with an emperor anointed by a pope in Rome. In 973, when Athelstan's dwarfish but formidable nephew, Edgar, who had already been crowned once, decided that he wished to emulate Otto's coronation, the best venue

that he could come up with for the ceremony was Bath: a place lit-
tered with relics of the Roman past, to be sure, but hardly the Eternal
City. Even his next stunt – summoning assorted Celtic princelings to
row him down a river – was in truth not quite as impressive as it must
have appeared to the gawping spectators watching him glide by: for
already, since Athelstan's day, the lordship claimed by the English king
over his turbulent neighbours had declined to little more than show.
The rule of 'all Britain' had shown itself a will-o'-the-wisp, melting
through Edgar's outstretched fingers. The sober truth was that all his
attempts to promote himself as imperial served only to emphasise
how small scale, in comparison with the *Reich*, the kingdom of the
English actually was.

Small-scale – but compact as well. This, as developments were to
show, was no disadvantage: for it had enabled an experiment in state-
building that was to prove as enduring as it was innovative. While the
lands ruled by the House of Wessex may have lacked diversity, they
made up for it in cohesiveness. The seas that bounded in Edgar's ambitions had helped to foster in the lands that he did rule a precocious
sense of unity. Even in the most northerly and bloodstained reaches
of the kingdom, through which a West Saxon king would only ever
travel with a bristling military escort, and where a dynasty of Viking
warlords, in the wake of Athelstan's death, had blazed a spectacular
if fleeting comeback, the people of Northumbria could still recognise
themselves as English. Though they might be distant from the royal
heartlands of the south, they nevertheless spoke the same language
as the West Saxons, venerated the same saints and gloried in belonging
to the same national Church. Above all – and here, perhaps, was the
most startling of all the feats of statecraft achieved by the House of
Wessex – they acknowledged the right of the same central authority
to administer them, and to poke its nose into their affairs. In England,
there were no equivalents of the Count of Flanders or Anjou. A figure
of menacing and even ferocious power a Northumbrian earl might
be – and yet he swayed the north, not by virtue of heredity, but as
an appointed agent of the king. Further south, and royal control was

even more inescapable. The *Cerdicingas* owned lands everywhere. There was no question of Edgar permitting his nobles to run amok, whether by building castles, or recruiting private armies, or usurping control of the public courts. Whereas in Francia the sight of a mutilated corpse abandoned by the side of a road for birds to peck at was a cause for alarm among travellers, a mark of lawlessness, in England it was likelier to speak of the opposite: of the long reach of the state. Blindings, scalpings, hangings: all were sponsored with a grim efficiency. Violence was met with violence; savagery with savagery. Even whole counties, if they presumed to oppose the royal will, might be systematically ravaged. Justice and order were what Edgar, in his coronation oath, had sworn to give the English; and justice and order, by his own stern lights, were precisely what he delivered. That such an iron-fisted man could end up being known as 'the Peaceable' suggested that his subjects did not disagree.

Were preachers merely deluded, then, when they warned the English that the signs of Doomsday were all around? There were many who feared not. When Edgar died in 975, only two years after his jamboree in Bath, the united kingdom of England that he left behind him was still very much a work in progress: none could be certain that it would hold together. As the *Witan*, the assembly of the greatest men of the realm, met to elect a new king, so a comet began to scorch across the heavens, leading many to dread what it portended. As well they might have done – for the throne was claimed by rival half-brothers. The first, Edward, was vicious, unstable, possibly illegitimate – and in his teens. The second, Ethelred, was the son of the Lady Aelfrida, the most powerful and ambitious woman in the kingdom, and Edgar's anointed queen – but he was only seven. The vote duly went to Edward. Aelfrida withdrew into an embittered retirement.

Civil war was avoided; but beneath the surface the rival factions continued to manoeuvre. In 978, three years after ascending the throne, Edward dropped his guard sufficiently to go hunting near Corfe, a stronghold on the Wessex coast where his stepmother just happened to be staying. As he rode through the forest, a group of armed men suddenly confronted and surrounded him; his right arm was seized and broken, and a dagger plunged into his side; the dying king, his foot caught in his stirrup, was then dragged away through brambles and over trackways by his bolting horse.* The corpse, when it was finally recovered, was flung into a bog.[36] 'No worse deed for the English race was done than this,' it would subsequently be judged, 'since they first sought out the land of Britain.'[37] The murder of an anointed king, and the failure of his kinsmen to avenge him, could hardly help but appear an ominous sign of the times. A column of fire, it was reported, flickering over the wasteland to which Edward had been consigned, marked the awful spot where his dishonoured body lay; still more frighteningly, even as the ten-year-old Ethelred was being consecrated king, 'a bloody cloud was seen, many times in the likeness of flames; and it appeared most of all at midnight; and it was formed of various beams; and then, when it became day, it glided away'.[38] Well might his subjects have shuddered; for there were some among them, no doubt, who would have recalled that the appearance of 'a great bloody cloud arising in the North, and covering all the heavens',[39] was to be reckoned a certain proof that the Last Day had come at last.

Yet still it did not arrive. No matter that Ethelred was only a child; no matter that his mother – whether justly or not – stood under suspicion of murder; no matter that he was only the second king, after his half-brother, to inherit the rule of a united England, rather than to have to fight for it: the kingdom did not fall to pieces. Indeed, that Edward's murder was seen as peculiarly shocking was evidence of just how habituated his contemporaries had become to the rule of law; for the young king, it has credibly been suggested, was 'the first man of high blood to have perished as a result of civil strife among the English for more than fifty years'.[40] Ethelred's advisers did all they could to

---

* The evidence for this depends on an autopsy conducted on Edward's bones in 1963. It is possible, of course, that the pathologist's conclusions were mistaken – or indeed that the bones were not those of Edward at all.

ensure that he would also be the last. Rivalries were consciously dampened. The Lady Aelfrida, who had returned to court purring with triumph, was sufficiently gracious in her victory to ensure that prominent partisans of the murdered king were granted their fair share of the available public offices. Nor even, a year into Ethelred's reign, did she object to the dredging up of her stepson's corpse, and its reinterment with full royal honours. In no time at all, visitors to the tomb were reporting spectacular miracles and hailing Edward a martyr: potent testimony to the hold that a king from the House of Cerdic, even one who in life had certainly been no saint, could exert on the English. Hardly surprising, then, that Ethelred should have survived the years of his childhood unchallenged, for he had been left the very last of his famous line.

Yet ultimately, as was evident from the wretched end of the Carolingians, the pretensions of even the most glorious dynasty were nothing if not raised on solid foundations. Prestige had to be earned as well as inherited, a maxim that the West Saxon kings had always adhered to with a hard-headed literalness. The most precious legacy that Edgar had bequeathed to his successors was not the aura of sanctity with which he had sought to endow himself at Bath, but rather a measure enacted in the same year of 973, one so ambitious that it had provided him with a licence, literally, to coin in his kingdom's cash. A single currency for a single people: such had been the philosophy of Edgar. Foreign coins, obsolete coins, coins lacking the requisite purity of silver: all had been pronounced illegal tender. Here, at a time when anything up to twenty different currencies might be in circulation within a single county of France, was a truly imperious reform. A lucrative one as well: for not only was the kingdom transformed into a single market, but it was made easier to soak. No wonder that Ethelred should have persisted with the reform. Regularly, from the year of his coronation onwards, he would order all the silver pennies in the kingdom to be recalled, restamped and then – after he had taken a cut – reissued. The penalty for forgery was ratcheted up from mutilation to death. Estates were obsessively quantified, audited and assessed for tax. Here was intrusiveness of a degree fit to be admired in Constantinople or Córdoba. Certainly, nothing remotely comparable to it existed anywhere else in the Christian West. England might not have been a far-spreading empire, nor the seat of an anointed Caesar; but its rulers certainly had cash to burn.

Yet just as the merchant who travelled from market to market with silver in his saddlebags was taking a risk, so too was Ethelred. Even as the towns founded by Alfred grew and prospered, even as the aristocracy lavished gold and incense and silks on great churches and on themselves, and even as the treasure chests of the king continued to fill to overflowing, still there lurked a nagging question in the back of many people's minds: what if the *Wicingas*, the 'sea-robbers', were to return? Of Northmen in England, certainly, there was no lack. The terrible assaults of the previous century, which had seen entire kingdoms appropriated by Viking warlords and parcelled out among their followers, had left the eastern counties densely planted with settlers. Several generations on, and the descendants of these immigrants might still affect a distinctive look: the men, for instance, had a taste for eye-liner, and for shaving the backs of their heads. Most scandalous, to pious English eyes, was their habit of taking a bath every Saturday: a mark of effeminacy held all the more surprising in a people so notorious for their bestial savagery. Nevertheless, there were many natives, jealous of the success with women for which the Northmen had become famed, who were not above adopting some of their more dandyish habits themselves; and integration, with Englishmen and Scandinavians pooling make-up and hair-styling tips, had long been gathering pace. It helped that the immigrants, as a consequence of the treaties forced on their forefathers by Alfred and his successors, were Christian; it helped as well that their language, their laws and their customs were similar to those of the English. Not, to be sure, that Ethelred could afford entirely to lower his guard: for in Northumbria especially, where much of the aristocracy was Scandinavian, treachery was a constant rumour. Yet in general, the West Saxon authorities could rest content in the presumption that the king's peace benefited immigrants no less than natives. So long as it held firm, the Scandinavians in England appeared unlikely to prove an enemy within.

It was true, of course, that the sway of the House of Wessex did not extend to all the Northmen who had emigrated to the British Isles. In Ireland, following their favoured policy of putting down roots beside an estuary, Viking pirates had founded a particularly flourishing stronghold by the 'Dubh Linn', or 'Black Pool', near the mouth of the River Liffey: so flourishing, indeed, that the settlement had ended up boasting the largest slave market of anywhere in western Europe. Unsurprisingly, it was the Irish themselves who provided the Dubliners with their richest source of exports; even so, all those who took to the ocean or lived by its shores had to reckon themselves potential targets. On one notorious occasion, the wife of a Frankish viscount, no less, had been kidnapped and held captive for three years; only the intervention of the Count of Rouen himself had served finally to set her free.

By the 980s, the English too, particularly in the west of the country, were suffering a steep rise in the number of raids being launched against their coastline. The experience of being bundled on to a slaver's longboat was a predictably unpleasant one: indeed, an ordeal to be wished only on one's very worst enemy. 'He was subjected to insults and urinated upon, and then, stripped naked, forced by the Vikings to perform the sexual service of a wife':[41] so gloated one Norman poet, contemplating the fate of a rival, an Irishman, who had been abducted by pirates. Gang-rape – 'the practice of foul sin upon a single woman, one after another, like dogs that care not about filth'[42] – was common. No wonder that churchmen in England should regularly have compared the Devil himself to a slaver, one 'who leads his prisoners as captives to the hellish city, in devilish thralldom'.[43] Yet even as they raised their voices in pious protest, and even as Ethelred dispatched ships on patrol into the Irish Sea, the truth was that the slave trade could provide profit as well as loss. The supply chain that linked the Vikings to the fabulous wealth of al-Andalus had opened up opportunity for English merchants too. Just like the Dubliners, they even had a ready supply of Celts on their doorstep – the '*Weallas*', or Welsh, whose very name had long been synonymous with 'slaves' – and a booming port, ideally located for the export of human cattle. 'You could see and sigh over rows of wretches bound together with ropes,' it was said of Bristol, 'young people of both sexes whose beautiful appearance and youthful innocence might move barbarians to pity, daily exposed to prostitution, daily offered for sale.'[44] An exaggeration, of course: for barbarians tended not to be moved to pity by the spectacle, nor the merchants of Bristol either. Indeed, by the Millennium, the port was coming to rival Dublin itself as the entrepôt of the western seas, with a record of trading slaves to the Caliphate and beyond, to Africa, that betokened a brilliant commercial future.

Nevertheless, as the new millennium drew ever nearer, it would have taken a perversely cheery sense of optimism to see in the gathering upsurge of Viking raids a boost to the prospects of anywhere in England. An alarming realisation was dawning over Ethelred: that there were simply too many pirates infesting English waters for them all to have originated in Ireland. So immense was the treasure piled up in his kingdom, it appeared, that its glint was showing even beyond the grey expanse of the mist-filled northern seas, in Scandinavia. How telling it was, for instance, that the most feared of all the Viking captains should have been a man 'skilled in divination',[45] whose talent for throwing the bones of birds and reading in them the pattern of what might otherwise have remained hidden had won for him the sinister nickname of '*Craccaben*' – 'Crowbone'. Olaf Trygvasson was a Norwegian, a man of the 'North Way', a realm so far distant from all that made for Christian order that even its women, it was said, grew beards, 'and sorcerers and enchanters and other satellites of Antichrist' swarmed everywhere.[46] Whether as a consequence of necromantic skills or not, Trygvasson certainly had a nose for loot; and sure enough, like a raven tracking the perfume of carrion, he had ended up haunting the English sea lanes.

By 991, such was the glamour and prestige of Trygvasson's name that there were no fewer than ninety-two other ships sailing alongside his own, ravaging the coasts of Kent and Essex, plundering and burning almost unopposed. Then, in August, while camped near Maldon, north of the Thames estuary, Trygvasson and his fellow freebooters were finally pinned down by the English; challenged to cross from the island where their ships were moored, the Vikings did so, only to find themselves in danger of being wiped out.[47] Savagely, they fought their corner until at last, with a bloody and desperate effort, they succeeded in putting the Essex men to flight. Left behind as a corpse on the field of battle was the English commander, Britnoth, a white-haired and valiant earl, who had stood with all his bodyguards together unyielding amid the slaughter, arrow-feathered, axe-hewn, refusing to bow.

His was a heroic end, to be sure; but although Britnoth himself had scorned to 'buy off the onslaught of spears with tribute-money',[48] his defeat had left Ethelred with little alternative, if Kent and Essex were to be spared further ruin. Ten thousand pounds' worth of taxes were duly levied, 'Dane-geld', as it came to be known; and yet even as this prodigious sum was handed over, everyone knew that it would serve only as a palliative. Trygvasson's appetites had been fed, not satiated; and sure enough, in 994, he was back for more. First he led an assault on London; then, after that had been beaten back, he stole horses for his men, and cut a deep swath across the Wessex heartlands. An open challenge to Ethelred, in short, and a calculated insult too. All drew their breath, and waited to see what the King of England would do.

The counter-move, when it did come, proved a good deal less than glorious. No attempt was made to confront Trygvasson. Instead, Ethelred opted to put the screws on his hapless subjects once again. The sum raised this time was £16,000. The English, already the most heavily taxed people in Christendom, were predictably driven to much cursing by this initiative; and while the king himself, as the Lord's anointed, remained immune to direct criticism, the same was not true of his advisers. Whispered under people's breath, a punning title began to be applied to Ethelred: '*unræd*', 'the ill-advised'.[49] Yet this was uncharitable. A measure of bafflement in the royal counsels was only to be expected. Ethelred was adrift in uncharted waters. There was not another ruler anywhere in the Christian West, after all, who could boast of administering a more efficient government, or of governing a more prosperous people, or of raking in more cash for himself; and yet, bizarrely, rather than strengthening the kingdom, these same achievements appeared to be setting it only to totter. The more Ethelred found England's wealth a source of vulnerability, the more, in his perplexity and desperation, he sought to turn it back to his advantage. So it was, groping his way to a possible solution, that he settled upon a two-pronged response: he would keep as firm a grip upon the royal mints as he possibly could, fortifying them, even transferring them, wherever feasible, to remote and primordially ancient hill-forts; simultaneously, he would try to spend his way out of trouble.

Derided it might have been; but as a policy, this was in fact very much in the grand tradition of measures adopted by harassed kings. The payment made to Trygvasson had come with a number of familiar strings attached. Like Rollo, he had been obliged to become a Christian; to cease his plundering; to ally himself with the very lord whom he had previously been assailing. Not, however, that it was any part of Ethelred's intentions to see a new Normandy established on English soil. Far from it. The presence of Viking ships in Norman ports, and of English slaves and loot in Norman markets, had not gone unremarked across the Channel. Indeed, such was the bad blood between the lords of England and Normandy that the Pope himself had been obliged to intervene, and remind the Count of Rouen of his Christian duty not to fraternise with pirates. Richard had duly apologised, signed a treaty – and continued precisely as before. Menacing evidence, it must have struck Ethelred, that even a baptised Northman could never wholly be de-fanged. Plunder, it appeared, would always be his truest god. No matter that Olaf Trygvasson, at his baptism, had become Ethelred's godson; clearly, it was out of the question for him to be permitted to put down roots in England.

Fortunately, Trygvasson himself agreed. His ambitions were set higher than Rollo's. Already the toast of excitable poets across the entire Viking world, and rolling in English silver, he had become fired with the zeal of a true convert as well: convinced that Providence had personally chosen him to become King of the North Way, and bring his countrymen to the faith of Christ. It was an intoxicating notion – and one that had first come to him, it would later be claimed, as the result of a fortuitous encounter with a prophetic hermit. Far likelier, however, it was Ethelred, enthroned amid the wealth and magnificence proper to his exalted rank, who had first whispered in Trygvasson's ear that he too might aspire to wear the crown of a Christian king. Certainly, as the Norwegian captain headed off for his homeland, stopping occasionally along the way to loot and murder in the name of the Prince of Peace, he did so with his godfather's fervent blessing. Well might Ethelred have breathed a sigh of relief. His triumph had been a considerable one. Compared with Trygvasson and his war bands, the Vikings left behind in English waters were a nuisance, little more. Fields might still be burned, manors plundered and captives stolen; but Ethelred, in the approach to the Millennium, was starting to throw his own weight around on a far more swaggering scale. In the year 1000, he led one expedition in person, northwards into Scotland, ravaging with the best of them, while a second was dispatched to Normandy, there to launch a raid on the Vikings and give the pirates a taste of their own medicine. Two years later, and Ethelred appeared a sufficiently intimidating figure to persuade the Count of Rouen himself to come to heel, and patch up a second treaty. 'And then in the spring the Lady, Richard's daughter, came to this land.'[50] So an Englishman reported the arrival in Wessex of Emma, Richard II's sister, a woman of formidable intelligence, talent and ambition, and fully worthy of a king. Sent by her brother to set the seal on his new alliance, she was married to Ethelred that very spring. Seated beside her royal husband, Emma appeared to the English a living reassurance that the worst was over: that the wheat field of Ethelred's kingdom had been secured at last against the trampling of foreign feet, and bloody flames, and blight, and storms, and ruin.

Yet for Ethelred himself there remained one final step to be taken. Charged as he was by God with the defence of the English people, and aware, as he surely must have been, of the awful signif-icance of the dawning of the new millennium, how could he not have dreaded what else, aside from wheat, might be flourishing in the rich soil of his kingdom? 'He who sows the good seed is the Son of Man.' So Christ had explained to His disciples. 'The field is the world, and the good seed means the sons of the kingdom; the weeds are the sons of the evil one, and the enemy who sowed them is the devil; the harvest is the close of the age, and the reapers are angels. Just as the weeds are gathered and burned with fire, so will it be at the close of the age.'[51] And now, it seemed, the close of the age was at hand; so it was time to gather the weeds and consign them all to the flames. Though Trygvasson and his men were gone, there were other Northmen, Danes, living openly in the towns of England, merchants drawn there in huge numbers by the peerless wealth of the kingdom, and living peaceably enough, it was true – but Northmen nevertheless. Who, then, could tell what atrocities they might be plotting? Who tell what succour they might provide a Viking invader? And so it was, as Ethelred's self-justification put it, 'that a decree was sent out by me with the counsel of my leading men and magnates, to the effect that all the Danes who had sprung up in the island, sprouting like weeds among the wheat, were to be destroyed by a most just extermination – and this decree was to be put into effect even as far as death'.[52]

The massacre took place on 13 November: St Brice's Day. It was, if the bald descriptions of contemporaries are to be trusted, awesomely comprehensive. Ethelred was evidently as efficient at organising a pogrom as he was at stinging his subjects for taxes. Considerations of Christian charity appear not to have moderated the ruthlessness with which the operation was carried out. In one particularly chilling episode, in Oxford, the Danes were incinerated as they huddled together for protection inside a church. Far from serving as a reassurance to the English that their kingdom was being secured against the coming of Antichrist, such an act of desecration led many to dread the opposite. 'But of that day and hour no one knows.'[53] These were the familiar words deployed by Wulfstan, London's bishop, and Ethelred's most brilliant counsellor, as he sought to reassure his flock that the end time was still to arrive; yet even he could not conceal from his listeners what the surest portent of Antichrist was to be. The casting down of God's temple, of God's house: such was to be the sign.

And now the stones of a church lay smoking in the heart of England, greasy with human ashes, a veritable charnel-house. If truly a sign, then it was a threatening one indeed.

Ragnarok

Strange tales were told of Olav Trygvasson's return to Norway. One day, it was claimed, after he had successfully toppled the local strongman and driven him to a squalid end in a pigsty, decapitated by his own thrall, the new king was in a fit mood to be entertained. At his side there suddenly appeared an old man, cloaked and white-haired, with only a single eye. Entering into conversation with the stranger, Trygvasson found that there was nothing the old man did not seem to know, nor any question to which he could not give an answer. All evening the two of them talked; and even though the king was eventually persuaded to retire to bed by a twitchy English bishop who had grown suspicious of the one-eyed stranger, Trygvasson could still not bear to end the conversation, continuing it even as he lay on his furs, late into the night. At last, the old man left him, and the king fell asleep; but his dreams were strange and feverish. Waking up abruptly, he cried out for the stranger again. Even though his servants searched high and low, however, the old man could not be found; and Trygvasson, brought to his senses by daylight, shuddered at his close escape. When it was reported to him that two sides of beef, a gift from the stranger, had been used in a stew, he ordered the entire cooking pot flung out. A godly and responsible act: for clearly, it was out of the question for him, as a follower of Christ, to feast on meat supplied by Odin.

Quite what his own followers thought of their king's scruples as they watched their supper turn fly-blown out on the dungheap, we are not told. Some, no doubt, would have felt roundly puzzled. A lord with any instinct for self-preservation denied nothing to his retinue. The supply of good things to the men who fought for him, whether beef, or golden armlets, or red cloaks, or coats of mail, was the only sure duty that a leader of Northmen had. Fail in that, and his doom would be swift. Trygvasson, who had never travelled anywhere but wolves and ravens attended on him, who had become the hero of myriad gore-bespattered songs, who had made all the West bleed so that he could bestow its treasures upon his warriors, was certainly not the man to have forgotten this basic truth. The beef he had been obliged to throw out would surely have been replaced with meat stolen or extorted from some other source. His tables would never have been permitted to stand empty. That same evening, no doubt, as his followers feasted in his hall, Trygvasson, the peerless ring-giver, would have scattered gold among them, or else ornamented helmets, or perhaps sword-belts clad in silver, wondrous treasures set to glitter by the blazing fire.

No wonder that the king of the ancient gods had paid him a call. The scene of a great lord sharing plunder with his followers was one well known to delight Odin; and perhaps, as the story of Trygvasson's late-night conversation implies, it did indeed require an effort of will for any Northman, even a baptised one, to send the 'All-father' on his way. Yet Trygvasson himself, whose entire career had been an exercise in worshipping force, had ultimately not hesitated in his loyalty to Christ – and for much the same reason that his own retinue continued to follow him. Far from cramping his style as a warlord, the Christian God appeared to offer him and all his predatory appetites, all his lust for power and gold, all his relish for combat, devastation and scenes of bloodshed, gratification on a truly awesome scale. As

befitted a man so ambidextrous that he could hurl a spear simultaneously from both hands, Trygvasson certainly felt no call to choose
between his new religion and his career as a marauder – for the one
served to fuel the other. With the same buccaneering enthusiasm that
he had previously brought to pillaging the English, he now swaggered
up and down the North Way, smashing idols, menacing local pagan
leaders and forcing conversions at the point of his sword. No matter
the resentful mutterings he left behind him in his wake, Trygvasson
was not the man for qualms: everything that he did was calculated to
redound to his own glory. He had seen enough of Christendom, and
of the dignity, the splendour and the wealth of her kings, to know that
heathendom offered nothing to compare. Just as Christ reigned
supreme over other gods, so would he, as the image of Christ, reign
supreme over his countrymen.

His countrymen, not surprisingly, responded with varying degrees
of resentment and alarm to this. The arrogance of braggart warlords
was nothing new in Scandinavia. Loot pilfered from Christendom had
long served to strengthen the mighty, great chiefs as well as kings, at
the expense of lesser men. Here, perhaps, rather than in the consequences of excessive rutting, as Christian moralists liked to claim, lay
the true reason for the waves of emigration that had sent so many
Northmen over the years sailing for Normandy, Britain and Ireland.
Some, indeed, had sailed even further west. Beyond the setting of the
sun, dotted across 'the northern region of the earth from where all
waters pass down',[54] adventurers from Scandinavia had discovered a
succession of darksome islands, sundered realms formed of glaciers,
and mountains, and the occasional expanse of grass. 'Iceland', the first-
found of these had been named – fittingly enough, it appeared, if the
claims of travellers were to be believed, for it was reported that any
Icelander who ventured out into the open during wintertime, and
then so far forgot himself as to wipe his nose, would find it snapping
off, 'frozen mucus and all',[55] and be obliged to discard it in the
snow. Other inconveniences persisted all the year round, even into the
nightless summers: from the troublemaking spirits who had lived in

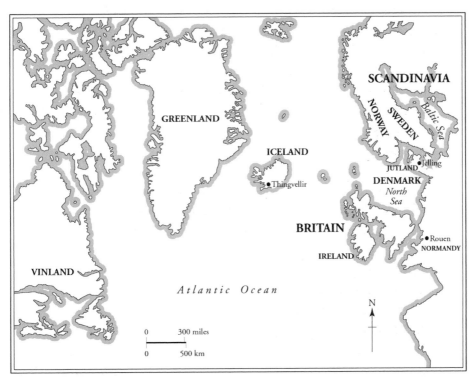

The world of the Northmen

Iceland since the beginning of time, and would lure the distracted to their ruin amid lava fields or into pools of hissing mud, to the island's notoriously indigestible food, its seaweed, suet and buttered porridge, which played such hell with the settlers' stomachs that the glaciers were said to echo to the thundering of their farts.

Such drawbacks notwithstanding, however, Iceland had filled up rapidly in the decades that followed the arrival of the first colonisers, back in the 870s – so much so that by the 930s all the prime farmland had been taken. Men had duly begun to scan around for fresh horizons. In 986, during a time of terrible famine in Iceland, an expedition of some twenty-five ships had set sail for a vast and empty land that lay even further west: 'Greenland' as it had been named by an early prospector, somewhat disingenuously, for all its eastern flank stood barricaded by colossal walls of gleaming ice. On the western coast, however, along the margins of jagged fjords, there were indeed patches of grass, and even meadows, to be found; and it was on these, at an unimaginable distance from the fjords of their ancestral homeland, that the settlers from Iceland, some 450 of them in all, had sought to put down their roots.

'A house of your own, however mean, is good.'[56] Nothing better illustrated the passionate intensity with which the Northmen clung to this conviction than their scattered presence, by the side of the bleak immensity of the western ocean, on the windswept shores of Greenland. Their new home may have been teeming with wildlife, but it was in almost all other ways barren of resources; and so it was not surprising that some of the colonists, in their quest for timber, above all, should have continued to strike out west. Over the succeeding years, such expeditions would bring back reports of yet further islands, including one, named 'Vinland' by those who claimed to have discovered it, on which grapes were said to grow wild, 'producing excellent wine':[57] a fabulous story. Perhaps, as the tall tales told by the Greenlanders suggested, there did indeed lie strange lands along the westernmost limits of the world; but if so, then they might just as well not have existed at all, for it was clearly out of the question to settle such fearsomely distant isles. Some few of the more lunatic among the explorers, it would subsequently be claimed, had made the attempt – but their enterprises had failed. Vinland – if it truly existed – was a stepping stone too far, that much was evident. The settlers' lines of communication, drawn out as they had been over many thousands of miles, across savage and storm-swept seas, a whole world away from Scandinavia, had been stretched to breaking point.

For even the Icelanders, clinging to the habitable margins of their harsh and smouldering isle, were dependent for their ultimate survival on links with the lands they had left behind. Like the Greenlanders, they had to look abroad for timber, let alone the gold and silver that were the essential marks of status for any self-respecting chieftain. As a result, captains from Iceland were regular visitors to the harbours of the North Way – where their presence did not go unnoted by Olaf Trygvasson. Neither – a standing provocation to the self-appointed warrior of Christ – did the fact that many of them remained ruggedly, even defiantly pagan. Trygvasson, who was hardly the man to find his fingers around a windpipe and not apply a little squeeze, duly announced his kingdom closed to all heathen traders. Those already present in the North Way were arrested and taken as hostages. The news, brought back to Iceland, caused its inhabitants predictable dismay and consternation. Even at a distance of 750 miles, it appeared, the shadow of a warlord such as Trygvasson could reach out across the ocean to menace them. Perhaps there really was no escaping kings.

Yet rather than admit this, and submit to all they had sought to escape, the Icelanders were prepared to countenance any expedient; even to embrace the faith of Christ, if that was what it would take. Not on Trygvasson's terms, however. Rather, they would do it as free men, gathered together from all across the island, meeting in the *Thingvellir*, the rough-grassed plain that was the site of their assembly, and the cockpit of their self-governance. Ever since 985, the task of presiding there as the Icelanders' 'law-speaker', the arbitrator of all their disputes, had belonged to a chieftain famed for his powers of foresight by the name of Thorgeir Thorkelsson: a pagan, to be sure, but respected even by those who had already begun to worship Christ. All the Icelanders assembled on the *Thingvellir*, Christian as well as pagan, duly agreed to accept his judgement on what the faith of Iceland should be; and Thorgeir accepted the fateful charge. 'He lay down and spread his cloak over himself, and lay all that day and the next night, nor did he speak a word.'[58] Then abruptly, on the following morning, he sat up and ordered the Icelanders to accompany him to the great Law Rock – and from there he delivered them his verdict. Some customs, Thorgeir pronounced, were to continue unchanged. Men were still to be permitted to eat horseflesh; to expose unwanted children; to offer sacrifices, provided that it was done in private. In every other respect, however, they were to submit themselves to the laws of the new religion. Whether in cold water or warm, all were to be baptised. The inhabitants of Iceland were to become a Christian people.

Such a judgement, for Thorgeir himself, must have been a painful one to deliver. What had he glimpsed, lying curled up beneath his cloak, not eating or drinking or stirring, that had led him to arrive at it? We can never know for certain; but it is evident enough, Iceland being what it was, a haunted and uncanny land, where mortals tended to regard themselves as mere interlopers, that Thorgeir's aim had been to pass into the dimensions of the otherworldly and to look for guidance there. Not all the spirits that populated the island were malign. If Thorgeir's own visions remain unknown to us, then there are hints, nevertheless, in an eerie story told of a black-hearted king and of his fiendish attempt to subdue the free men of Iceland, of what the law-speaker might conceivably have seen during his dreams. This tyrant, it was reported, had commissioned a necromancer to swim ahead of his fleet in the form of a whale; but the spirits of Iceland, adopting various forms, whether of dragons, or of bulls, or of venomous toads, had stood sentry over the fjords, until at last a huge cliff-giant armed with an iron flail had chased away the whale . 'And the king, brought the news, had turned his fleet around, and sailed back for home.'[59] Evidently, the dread of overambitious warlords might serve to chill even the realm of the supernatural.

And who might have been the tyrant capable of inspiring such fantastical tales? Not Olaf Trygvasson, but rather an earlier Christian king, one who had become, among the Northmen, an even blacker and more flame-lit legend, a rumour of wrath and terror. Beyond the southern reaches of the North Way, across the icy and reef-strewn waters known as the *Jotlandshaf*, lay the heath-clad flatlands of Jutland, seat of the kings of Denmark. The realm was an ancient one: indeed, back in the time of Charlemagne, the Danes had treated with the Franks as their equals, and although, over the following century, the ruling dynasty had torn itself quite spectacularly to shreds, their erstwhile subjects had never wholly lost a sense of shared identity. By the middle of the tenth century, a new line of kings had risen to power in Denmark: one with sufficient ruthlessness and resolve not to let slip its hold upon the kingdom. Show-place of the dynasty's power was Jelling, a stronghold in the heart of Jutland, a place of ancient graves, and rows of monoliths, and gold-ringed warriors set on guard outside mighty-gabled halls. Two huge mounds of earth dominated the scene: the work of Gorm, the dynasty's first great ruler, and of Thyri, his queen, pagans both. Yet between the two barrows, the traveller to Jelling would have found, not a temple, not a shrine to Odin or Thor, but a church; and beside the church, a great block of granite carved with a crucified, serpent-entangled Christ. 'King Harald had this memorial made,' it was inscribed on the stone, 'for Gorm his father and Thyri his mother: that same Harald who won for himself all Denmark and Norway, and made the Danes to be Christian.'

This was a boast that veiled as much as it revealed. The truth was that 'Bluetooth',* as Harald was known, had only ever exercised the

---

* An equally plausible translation is 'Blacktooth' – 'Bluetooth', however, has been immortalised as a sobriquet by its use as a name for wireless technology, uniting different technologies just as Harald was supposed to have united Denmark and Norway. The contemporary enthusiasm for recasting tenth-century warlords as peaceable multiculturalists is a peculiar one – and one from which the Caliphs of Córdoba have regularly benefited as well.

most threadbare hegemony over the North Way; that his conversion to Christianity had been prompted, in part at least, by a panicky desire to forestall invasion by Otto the Great; and that for many years he had cringed before the Saxon emperor, paying him both homage and tribute. Nevertheless, within the limits of his own kingdom, his sway had been fierce and iron-fisted, a potent demonstration to later warlords, Olaf Trygvasson notable among them, that the Christian faith might comfortably be squared with the traditional enthusiasms of a Viking: indeed, that it might help to make the practice of robbery and intimidation even more effective. Whether it was by building massive fortresses all over Denmark, or by extorting tribute from his weaker neighbours, just as Otto had extorted tribute from him, Bluetooth had aimed to throw his weight around in the authentic manner of a Christian king. If the sponsorship of talking whales was not in truth a noted feature of his preparations, then the ability to outfit menacing amphibious expeditions, and to unleash them upon his enemies, most certainly was. The assaults launched to such devastating effect against England in the final decade of the millennium were a demonstration of just how potent a role model Bluetooth had been.

And not only to Trygvasson. Cruising alongside him in the raids of 991 and 994, and standing next to him amid the dust of Maldon, had been a Viking lord no less feared and widely sung: Sweyn, known as 'Forkbeard', Harald Bluetooth's son.[60] Chill and calculating where Trygvasson was headstrong, Forkbeard had learned much from his father – so much so that in the previous decade he had paid the example set by Bluetooth its ultimate compliment by knifing the old wolf in the back. In 982, the year of Otto II's defeat by the Saracens at Cotrone, and the Wendish invasion of Saxony, the Danish king too, dispatching his own war bands across the frontier, had sought to scavenge pickings for himself; but it was Forkbeard who had secured all the glory of the venture, and then exploited it to topple his father. Various tales were told of Bluetooth's end: the grisliest had him wandering off after a parley with his son, and then, 'as he squatted down behind a bush for the purpose of emptying his bowels',[61] being hit square between the buttocks by an arrow. A spectacular death, if true – and one that had certainly left Forkbeard secure in his inheritance.

'Not a ruler, but a destroyer':[62] such was the judgement of his near neighbour, Thietmar, the ever-sniffy Bishop of Merseburg. This, however, was to mistake Forkbeard's talent for wreaking destruction – which was indeed prodigious – as having no goals other than itself. In truth, it was precisely by destroying that he ruled: a coldly calculating approach to the demands of lordship that would ultimately enable him to put even Trygvasson in the shade. The two kings might once have been brothers-in-arms, but a man responsible for having his father shot in the rectum was hardly likely to feel inhibited by any sense of fraternal loyalty. Sure enough, in the years that followed the parting of their ways, and Trygvasson's arrival right on Forkbeard's doorstep, beyond the *Jotlandshaf*, the rivalry between the two had grown increasingly deadly. Coolly, patiently, and in the end to lethal effect, the Danish king had prepared his trap. In the year 1000, a great host of ships manned by allies recruited from across Scandinavia, the North Way included, joined with Forkbeard's fleet, looking to deprive Trygvasson of what every Viking warlord needed in order to survive: command of the sea lanes. Trygvasson himself, flamboyant as ever, responded by sailing into Danish waters in the longest and most glamorous dragon-ship ever built, at the head of sixty ships only marginally less dazzling, hoping that the brilliance of the armada, and of his own fearsome reputation, would serve to put his foes to flight. But they did not: Forkbeard's ambush was sprung, and after a day of desperate fighting even the *Long Serpent*, Trygvasson's flagship, ended up riven, boarded and cleared of her men. Trygvasson himself, adorned in golden armour and a bright-red cloak, leapt from the clawing fingers of his enemies into the sea; and when they made an attempt to rescue him, 'he threw his shield over his head, and vanished beneath the waves'.[63] His triumph was to have died as he had lived, the very model of a Viking hero; but Forkbeard's was to have secured for himself power beyond the dreams of all his forebears.

And this was the man whom Ethelred, by giving orders for the massacre of St Brice's Day, had thought to intimidate. Perhaps, against a foe of a different order, his murderous calculation might have paid off; but the Danish king was not just any foe. Among the victims of the pogrom, it was said, had been one of Forkbeard's own sisters, the Lady Gunnhild, but the murder of even the least of his subjects would have been sufficient to sanction a blood feud. The onslaught unleashed against Ethelred the following year duly aimed to pile humiliation upon humiliation. Symbols of the authority of the House of Wessex were ruthlessly targeted. At Exeter, where King Athelstan had enshrined his dynasty's spear of power, only the courage of a quick-thinking monk enabled the priceless relic to be rescued from the Danish firestorm. At Wilton, site of the richest and most splendid nunnery in Wessex, where numerous members of the royal family lay buried – pre-eminent among them Ethelred's own half-sister, Edith, recently proclaimed a saint – all the lands around the holy enclosure were systematically torched.

For the Danish captains, no doubt, it must have been a gloriously satisfying experience to burn and loot, and menace an enemy's women, just as their ancestors had always done: a reassurance that the old ways still endured. Forkbeard, however, even as he dispatched his war bands to plunder England, had his eyes fixed on a more novel order of things. No less than his father and Trygvasson had been, he was keenly alert to the many advantages that might be reaped by a Christian king. Concerned to show that he took the role seriously, he had duly founded the odd town, installed the odd bishop, even struck the odd coin. When it came to more gruelling responsibilities, however, such as forging a state capable of fleecing his subjects efficiently and of providing him with regular taxes, his enthusiasm had tended to flag. As well it might have done. It was easier by far to menace England, and outsource the whole tedious business to Ethelred. Which is precisely what Forkbeard did.

And with such merciless and brutal efficiency that the English king found his own strategy, that of using his wealth to sow discord among his foes, turned back fatally against him. As year followed year, and still the Danes returned, each time with forces bigger, better equipped and more devastating than before, so the bonds of loyalty to Ethelred within England began at last to fray. All the formidable powers of the West Saxon monarchy, built up by generations of the *Cerdicingas* before him, appeared increasingly to the English to be serving, not their own interests, but those of their oppressors. It was as though Ethelred him- self – the heir of Alfred, of Athelstan, of Edgar – had become merely a thrall-like servant of the interests of the Danish king. As royal agents continued with remorseless efficiency their business of levying taxes to fund their master's strategy, and the mints continued to churn, so it struck many among the English that what they were being obliged to pay for was nothing less than their own ruin.

Then at last, in 1012, there was a seeming success. Just as Olaf Trygvasson, almost twenty years before, had been won over to Ethelred's side, so now was another celebrated Viking captain, Thorkell, together with forty-five of his ships, persuaded to enter the service of the English king: a hint, perhaps, of dawn. Yet this brief moment of hope was in truth to prove a portent of the very opposite, an onset of the blackest night – for the news, when it was brought to Forkbeard in Denmark, stirred him into preparing something more than merely another raid. As with Trygvasson, so with Ethelred: the Danish king had been playing a lengthy game. England, drained as she was of her lifeblood, now appeared ripe for decapitation. In 1013, Forkbeard landed south of York, where Danish settlement had always been at its densest, and received the immediate submission of the region's immigrant communities. Nor did it take long for the exhausted and battle-scarred English aristocracy to bow to the inevitable as well. Across England, terms duly began to be arranged; hostages handed over; homage offered up to Forkbeard. By the end of the year, even Ethelred was buckling. Boxed up in London, his last stronghold, he ordered the Lady Emma and their children to board a ship and embark across the wintry seas for exile, while he himself set sail to spend a miserable Christmas skulking off the Wessex coast. Then, disdaining to play the part of a Viking any longer, he too crossed the

Channel. His destination: the court of his brother-in-law, the Duke of Normandy. This final humiliation set the seal on all the others.

Peace – if of a brutal kind – had been brought to England at last. But it was not to endure. In February 1014, at the very height of his triumph, Forkbeard died. The English earls and bishops, already repenting of their submission to a barbarian, at once invited Ethelred to return; 'for they said that no sovereign was dearer to them than their natural lord – if only he would govern them better than he had previously done'.[64] Evidently, the line of Cerdic still retained something of its mystique; but it was too late now for Ethelred to burnish it. Prostrated by illness, his only consistent policy upon his return was to haunt his sickbed; in 1016, at last, he slipped into the grave. His subjects barely noticed. Already, the battle for the rule of England had moved on to a younger generation. Even before Ethelred's death, his eldest surviving son, Edmund, a warrior of such charismatic fortitude that he would come to be hailed as 'Ironside', had laid claim to the throne. But he was not alone in his ambition: for Forkbeard too had left a son.

'Only a boy, you ship-batterer, when you launched your boat, no king was younger than you,'[65] wrote one praise-singer of the precociously terrifying Canute. Already, even before landing in England to press his right to the kingdom, the young prince had shown himself practised in the grimmer arts of Viking lordship, mutilating the hostages left in his care by Forkbeard and then sending them back to their relatives, the great lords in their high-beamed halls, to serve as a gruesome warning of the folly of resistance. Sure enough, in the stumps where once the hostages' hands had been, and in their noseless faces, and in the cropped remains of their ears, the English had indeed been granted fair warning of the horrors soon to come. Ironsided Edmund may have been – but Canute was forged of ice. All the summer of 1016, the two men fought each other; until ultimately, with the pair of them brought to a bloody standstill, there seemed no possible resolution to the conflict, save to divide the kingdom in two. A month after the treaty had been signed, however, Edmund died: the last king of purely English stock ever to sit on the country's throne. Naturally, men suspected murder – as well they might have done.

Canute had gambled much on his attempt to win his prize – and now it was payback time. Many warriors had followed him across the northern seas, 'men of metal, menacing with golden face'[66] – and their captain, just like any other, needed to be a scatterer of treasure, or nothing at all. In Canute, the larcenous instincts that had long propelled generations of Northmen across the seas were set to attain their apotheosis – for he had his sword at the throat of an entire kingdom. Already, over the course of the unfortunate Ethelred's reign, ton upon ton of silver had been delivered into the hands of the Danes. Now, with all the honed apparatus of English governance directly in his own hands, there was nothing to stop Canute from imposing a truly swingeing tax. Which was what he duly did: at a rate, in effect, of 100 per cent. It took his agents months to screw out; but by the end of 1018, the kingdom's entire income for that year had vanished into his treasure chests.

Perhaps, then, many among the English must have wondered, this was how the world was to end: with a tax demand. Even the man who was now Archbishop of York, the brilliant and devoutly orthodox Wulfstan, openly warned that the Danes might prove the shock troops of Antichrist. Already, summoning the English to prepare themselves for the Day of Judgement, he had advocated barefoot displays of penance, the singing of psalms and public prayer; and in 1014, during the dark days that followed Forkbeard's conquest of the kingdom, he had flatly declared the end time imminent. 'For nothing has prospered now for a long while either at home or abroad, but there has been military devastation and hunger, burning and bloodshed.'[67] Even pagans, however, as they observed the state of the world, might on occasion fall to pondering what its fracturing portended. One did not have to be a Christian to be conscious of Christian dates. Was it merely coincidence, for instance, that Thorgeir, summoning the Icelanders to decide whether they should abandon their ancient gods, had chosen to do so in the year 1000? What prospect, if the end were indeed approaching, that any of the heathen gods, even Odin himself, could hope to keep it at bay? Despite the triumph of the Danes in the killing fields of England, many Northmen, suspended between their new faith and their ancient beliefs, were not immune to the anxieties of Wulfstan. 'Kin', wrote one of them, in dread of the end days, 'will break the bonds of kin':

> A harsh world it will be, whoredom rampant,
> An axe-age, a sword-age, shields shattered,
> A wind-age, a wolf-age before man's age tumbles down.[68]

The very sentiments of the archbishop – and composed, it may well be, by a man who had heard him utter them.[69] Yet the end of the world sung by the poet was one illumined not by the light of Christ, but by the fiery extinction of the ancient gods, 'fire flaring up against fire'.[70] No immortality, according to such a vision, awaited those who followed Odin: for he, like the sun itself, was fated to be devoured by a monstrous wolf, while all around him 'the brilliant stars are dashed down from the skies'. His death, like the death of all those whom the pagans had foolishly worshipped as deathless, was a certainty. Such was '*Ragnarok*' – the Doom of the Gods.

And Canute, certainly, wanted no part of it: for it was hardly his ambition to play the part of either Odin or Antichrist. Though he might be avaricious and brutal, he was not unthinkingly so. For all the ruthlessness with which he had extorted treasure from the English to pay off his followers, he had no wish for his reign to continue as a wolf-age. So it was that in 1018, even as his tax collectors were bleeding England white, he allowed himself to be persuaded by Wulfstan into swearing that he would uphold all the laws of Edgar and Ethelred: that he would rule, in short, as the heir of the *Cerdicingas*. Living evidence of this, crowned and no less imperious than she had ever been, could already be found at his side: none other than the still-nubile Emma, Ethelred's widow, and now once again England's queen. The taking to bed of a rival's woman was very much in the finest tradition of Viking manhood; and yet Emma was far too significant a prize to rank as merely a sexual trophy. Canute's marriage to her had been no show of scorn – indeed, just the opposite. Norman Emma may have been, with a Dane for a mother, and most likely fluent in Danish herself – but it was as a living embodiment of the West Saxon monarchy, of all its traditions and pedigree, that she had her truest value. Better than anyone, she offered an imprimatur of class.

And it was class, in the final equation, not rings of gold, nor dragon-prowed ships, nor the florid praises of poets, that Canute most hankered after. If it was as a Viking warlord that he had conquered England, and transformed all the northern seas into his private lake, then it was as the model of a Christian king that he aimed to rule. So it was, even as he persisted in his empire-building, that he began to pose, in a familiar process of metamorphosis, as a prince of peace. A terrorist who had waded through blood, he permitted Archbishop Wulfstan to write laws in his name that proclaimed the virtues of humility and self-restraint: 'For the mightier or of higher rank a man is, so the deeper must he atone for wrong-doing, both to God and to men.'[71] A disinheritor of the oldest royal line in Christendom, he became a regular visitor to the nunnery at Wilton, riding there with Emma, dismounting respectfully outside the precincts, praying among the tombs of the women of the House of Wessex. A Northman from the margins of the civilised world, he took time from all his labours and his wars to go on pilgrimage to the capital of the Christian faith, and there, amid the ancient and fabulous splendours of Rome, to kneel before the tomb of St Peter, and 'diligently to seek his special favour before God'.

For to be sure, as Canute himself publicly acknowledged, there was much that needed forgiving – 'whether through the intemperance of my youth or through negligence'.[72] But he was not in Rome merely to pray. The streets, when Canute arrived there in March 1027, were teeming with the elite of imperial society. Three years earlier, the Emperor Henry II had died, the last of the line of Saxon kings; and now, desperate for the legitimacy that only a pope could grant, his elected heir, Conrad II, a Frankish lord from the Rhineland, was camped out in the city. Here was an unbeatable opportunity for Canute to play the international statesman – and he seized it with relish. Whether hob-nobbing with Conrad himself, or taking Mass with Abbot Odilo of Cluny, or negotiating with the Holy Father, he revelled with an unabashed glee in his presence on such a stage.

The starriest role of all was granted him on Easter Day, when the new emperor, to the acclamation of princes and bishops drawn from across Christendom, was crowned in St Peter's – and Canute was by his side. The occasion was, so it appears, a thoroughly overwrought one. Two archbishops, disputing which of them should lead Conrad into the cathedral, almost fell to blows, while Conrad himself, it is reported, overcome by the significance of the moment, burst suddenly into tears. Yet if there was anyone present in St Peter's that day justified in feeling emotional, then surely it was Canute. The glory, after all, was not merely his own, but God's as well. It was barely a decade previously that Henry II had dispatched his imperial regalia to Cluny, as an expression of his hope that the faith of Christ would expand to the limits of the earth; and now, stood by the side of his successor, in the city of the Caesars, was the great-grandson of a pagan warlord.

Meanwhile, far away across the northern ocean, in lands unknown to Constantine or Charlemagne, below the lava fields of Iceland and besides the fjords of Greenland, the children of pagans were raising churches and calling themselves Christian. Much had changed in the world, and doubtless much would continue to change – for the one-thousandth anniversary of Christ's Resurrection was only a few years off. And yet, despite the widespread mood of trepidation, and despite all the convulsions, and the bloodshed, and the suffering of the previous decades, perhaps it was becoming legitimate, even in the shadow of the Millennium, to look to the future, not with foreboding, but with hope. To believe that the clouds were lifting. To believe that anything might be possible.

mid the darkness of the times, the abbey of Cluny radiated a special brilliance. What Christ had said to his ostles, popes would say to Cluny: 'You are the light of the world.' (Author photo)

'To thee, O Lord, I lift up my soul.' This phrase from the Psalms, inscribed on the open book held by the priest in this ninth-century ivory, might well have served as the manifesto of the monks of Cluny. The singing of praises to God filled their days to an unprecedented degree: for their ambition was nothing less than to emulate the angelic choirs of heaven. (Fitzwilliam Museum/Bridgeman Art Library)

It was the practice in southern France for churches and monasteries to house the relics of their patron saints within statues made of precious metals and adorned with jewels. Most were seized and melted down during the French Revolution; but this one, from a safely remote pilgrimage centre in the Auvergne, survived. The bones of Saint Faith, a young girl martyred by the Romans, were stored inside the statue's glittering cranium. (Church of St Foy, Conques, Lauros/Giraudon/Bridgeman Art Library)

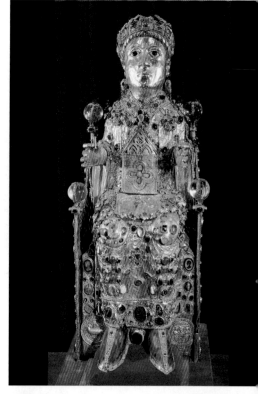

A bristling phalanx of Northmen, seaborne and ready for battle. By the time of the Millennium, the piratical spirit of earlier Scandinavian warriors had mutated into something altogether more disciplined, ambitious and menacing. (Bibliothèque Nationale, Paris/Bridgeman Art Library)

A longship takes to the seas, while in the scene above it a horseman is mounted on an eight-legged stallion. The rider is almost certainly Odin, the Scandinavian king of the gods. Not all the labours of Christian missionaries could serve to banish the 'All-father' entirely from the imaginings of the Northmen. In Normandy, for instance, tales of a ghostly hunt, led by a huntsman very like Odin, would endure well into modern times. (Werner Forman Archive)

Across the Channel from France, the tenth century had been characterised, not by a collapse in royal authority, but by its spectacular consolidation. Edgar, shown here piously offering up the foundation charter of a new cathedral to Christ, was the unchallenged ruler of a newly united kingdom: England. (British Library)

A gold coin issued by Edgar's son, Ethelred. England was easily the richest kingdom in western Europe, and the ability of its rulers to manage a single currency reflected a precocious degree of centralisation. Wealth, however, as Ethelred himself would find out, was not always a guarantee of security. (British Museum)

The Jelling stones in Denmark. The larger, on the left, was deliberately placed between the twin tumuli of his pagan parents by Harald Bluetooth, a king notorious for his opportunism and taste for bragging. Carved on to the runestone, Harald described himself as the man 'who won all Denmark and Norway, and made the Danes to be Christian'. The boast, while not entirely accurate, has come to be commemorated as 'the baptism of Denmark'. (Author photo)

Canute, despite having waded through blood to seize the rich prize of England from its native dynasty, was eager to change his public image from that of terrorist to Christian king. Here he is shown posing as the heir of Edgar, while Christ looks on approvingly from above. Facing Canute is Aelfigu, the English wife he refused to divorce even when he married Emma, widow of the deposed Ethelred. (British Library)

Christ is shown returning in glory at the end of time. To men and women living through the three decades that constituted the millennial anniversary of their Saviour's life, marks of the imminent end of the world appeared everywhere. That it was sternly forbidden to speculate as to the precise hour of Christ's return did little to dampen the mingled anxiety and hope felt by many of the Christian people at the prospect of witnessing the hour of judgement. (British Library)

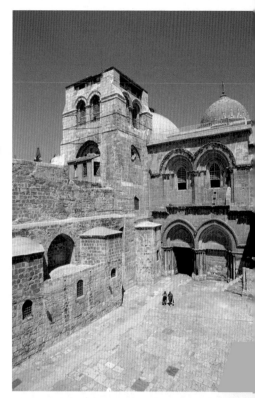

The Church of the Holy Sepulchre in Jerusalem marked the precise spot where Christ was believed to have been crucified and buried. Its destruction in 1009 by the Caliph al-Hakim provoked horror across Christendom. Only the speed with which it was rebuilt under the sponsorship of Constantinople served to ease the mood of shock. (Corbis)

A crypt looking like a public lavatory, set amid the concrete bleakness of a 1960s municipal square, is all that remains of the one-time jewel of Limoges: the abbey of St Martial. It was here, in 1010, that the young Adémar saw a vision of the crucified Christ weeping tears of blood over the city; and here too, nineteen years later, that he was publicly branded a fraudster, and forced to flee in disgrace. (Author photo)

Christ as a pilgrim, carved in a cloister in a monastery in Spain. The first decades of the new millennium witnessed a startling upturn in the number of pilgrims taking to the roads. In 1033, in particular, the flood of people who descended upon Jerusalem appeared to one chronicler 'an innumerable multitude, gathered from across the whole world, greater than any man before could have hoped to see'. (AISA)

The notion of 'fastening to Christ's Cross the picture of a dying man' had traditionally struck Christians as a repulsive one. Nevertheless, the decades either side of the Millennium witnessed a startling and enduring innovation: the portrayal of Christ in all his human suffering. The so-called 'Gero Crucifix', which hangs in Cologne Cathedral, dates from the late tenth century, and shows Jesus not merely dying, but actually dead. (Author photo)

Bruno of Toul, who in 1048 was crowned in Rome as Pope Leo IX. The illustration shows him (on the left) consecrating a single monastery church; but it was Leo's ultimate ambition to see the whole Church re-consecrated. The energy, ability and hard-headedness that he brought to this task ensured that his reign would subsequently be commemorated as the starting point of the papal revolution. (Burgerbibliothek, Bern)

At the end of time, it was the Archangel Michael who was destined to slay Antichrist, and to trample down the Devil. This illustration of the saint was drawn in Normandy, at Mont-Saint-Michel: a shrine that encouraged many Normans to regard the Archangel as their particular patron. Tellingly, it was at a second shrine sacred to Saint Michael, on Mount Gargano in Apulia, that Norman pilgrims were first recruited to serve as mercenaries in southern Italy: a fateful development for all concerned. (Bridgeman Art Library)

5

APOCALYPSE POSTPONED

The Mahdi Blues

At the end of time, so St Paul had taught, Antichrist was destined to appear in Jerusalem, seated upon the mount where Solomon in ancient times had built his temple, 'proclaiming himself to be God'.[1] Yet it was the sublime character of Scripture that its meaning, even when to the unlearned it appeared precise, could be interpreted by the wise on many levels. Much had happened since the apostle had delivered his prophecy. The Temple of the Jews had long since been overthrown and destroyed utterly – even as churches had spread across the world. How, then, was the 'temple' in which Antichrist would take his seat best to be understood? 'Does it mean the ruins of the Temple built by King Solomon, or might it actually mean a Christian place of worship?'[2] It was this question, put by St Augustine many centuries before the Millennium, that had haunted Wulfstan in the wake of the St Brice's Day massacre, and led him to see, in the rubble of a desecrated church, a possible proof of Antichrist's imminence. Certainly, whether it was to be on the Temple Mount or within the shell of a Christian shrine, ruins seemed the only fitting backdrop to the throne of the Son of Perdition.

Over time, Wulfstan's anxieties had begun to fade. The sufferings of the English had not proved fatal; and Canute, far from pillaging churches, as his ancestors had done, grew famous instead for refurbishing them. Travelling to Rome, he had ostentatiously deposited whole cloakloads of silver on the altars of abbeys; 'and indeed whatever altar he passed, be it ever so small, he would give it gifts, and bestow sweet kisses upon it'.[3] Nor was the mania for sponsoring churches by any means confined to kings. In France and Italy especially, wherever a pilgrim such as Canute travelled, he was likely to pass carts weighed down with timber and columns plundered from ancient ruins, and to discover, in village after village, walls of white stone rising up above the shacks. A new church, almost as much as a castle brooding on its hill, was an emphatic marker of the grasping new order of things: for a wealthy castellan, by funding a place of worship, and privatising what had previously been held in common, was effectively branding the worshippers that it served as his property.

Yet the peasants too, robbed of their freedoms and coerced into villages as they invariably had been, had their own stake in seeing a church established in their midst. No demand was more vigorously pressed by enthusiasts for the Peace of God than that the upstart lords and their swaggering, bullying knights accept the inviolability of consecrated ground. To cross into the *cimiterium*, the area surrounding a church where the dead were buried and the living gathered in peace, whether to hold a market, or to hear a law suit, or to celebrate a wedding, was thunderously forbidden to any man bearing arms. Invisible the ramparts of a churchyard might be – and yet every knight who swore an oath of peace was obliged to accept that they rose no less impregnably than those of a donjon. Seen as such, the village church was not the complement of the castle, but rather its mirror image: twin citadels both, one serving to guard the powerful, and the other to shelter the weak; one the lair of warlords and the other a stronghold of God. No wonder, then, that there were many who found in the unprecedented surge of building activity a mark, not of oppression, but of renewal, of promise, of hope. 'For it was as if the whole world were shaking itself free, shrugging off the burden of the past, and cladding itself everywhere in a white mantle of churches.'[4] Such was the judgement of Rudolf Glaber, seated in that mightiest of all bastions of holiness, the abbey of Cluny. As a man who had no doubt that demons stalked the earth – and indeed had seen one, blubbery-lipped and hunchbacked, menacing him in his bed – his exultancy came as no surprise. For to behold Christendom clad in a mantle of churches was to know it transformed into one immense *cimiterium* – to know it fortified against Antichrist.

Yet always, no matter how widely the mantle was cast, there remained the leaden possibility that it might not prove enough: that the dark lord might still manifest himself, lit by flaring shadows, and enthroned in awful splendour, amid the wreckage of a Christian shrine. 'You see all these, do you not?' Christ Himself had asked His disciples, pointing to the buildings of the Temple. 'Truly, I say to you, there will not be left here one stone upon another, that will not be thrown down.'[5] And so it had happened; and so, no doubt, before the Day of Judgement, it was fated that the ruin of the Temple would be mirrored by no less monstrous desecrations. In 991, for instance – a perilously close thing – fire had threatened the shrine of St Peter in Rome; and all the Romans and assembled pilgrims 'as one man had given out a terrible scream and turned to rush to confess the Prince of the Apostles, for a long while crying that if he did not watchfully protect his church at this time then many men would fall away from the faith'.[6] Sure enough, the flames had at once miraculously retreated and vanished; but the whole scare had nevertheless served as a salutary reminder to the faithful everywhere of the potential vulnerability of even their holiest shrines. Indeed, to an alarming degree, the holier the shrine, the more vulnerable it tended to be. Fire was not the only threat to Christendom's capital. In 1004, for instance, a fleet of pirates had sailed up the River Arno, sacking Pisa, and temporarily cutting off Rome from the north. The Saracens, unlike the Vikings, still held fast to their defiance of the Christian faith – and to their habit of tracing the frontiers of Christendom with blood.

Nor was St Peter the only apostle they were able to menace. In the

north-west corner of Spain, set amid the mountain-ringed realm of
Galicia, there stood the tomb of a second: St James. Here was a fabulous claim, it might have been thought: for Santiago, as the Christians
of Spain called him, had been executed, on the certain authority of
Scripture itself, in the Holy Land. Yet the story that his disciples had
sailed with his corpse to the rocky Galician coast, that they had buried
him forty miles inland, and that his final resting place had lain forgotten for some 800 years, until at last it had been discovered by an
enterprising bishop, appeared proved beyond all shadow of a doubt by
the spectacular miracles performed upon his relics.[7] The kings of León
certainly presumed so: delighted to find themselves with a genuine
apostle on their hands, they had duly begun to promote his cult for
all they were worth, hailing him as their celestial patron, and raising
a splendid basilica over his tomb. Already, by the middle of the tenth
century, its fame had spread far beyond the limits of Spain, so that
pilgrims from the furthest reaches of Francia, including even counts
and bishops, were to be found making the gruelling journey to the distant shrine, 'to beg mercy and help from God and Santiago'.[8] Increasingly,
of all those holy places in Christendom where the earth was held to be
touched by heaven, only Rome was illumined by a greater renown.

And then, catastrophe. On 10 August 997, amid the fearsome
cacophony of trumpets and pipes that invariably heralded an assault
by Saracens, a great army had descended upon the shrine. For a week,
the invaders pillaged and burned everything that they could. The
cathedral itself they razed to the ground. Its bells, brought crashing
down, were loaded on to the shoulders of Christian captives. When
the Saracens, content with their work of destruction, withdrew at last,
their human pack-animals were compelled to accompany them,
sweating and stumbling, all the way to Córdoba. Christian chroniclers,
in horror at the humiliation visited upon Santiago, would subsequently claim that the invaders had been struck down by diarrhoea, a
godly punishment indeed, and had perished amid the effluvia of their
own bowels – but this was mere wishful thinking. Entering Córdoba,
the warriors of the Caliphate did so unperturbed by stomach upsets.

Proofs of their triumph were indisputable and manifold. Unloaded into the Great Mosque, the bells from the despoiled cathedral were suspended from the ceiling, to serve the Muslim faithful as lamps, lighting their way to prayers. Of the prisoners of war, some were kept in their chains, and set to labouring on a great extension to the mosque. Others, led to the esplanade that ran beside the River Guadalquivir, were publicly decapitated, and their severed heads paraded through the market place, before being hung from the main gates of the citadel.[9]

Grisly trophies such as these had long adorned Córdoba. No duty was more incumbent upon a commander of the faithful than that of waging *jihad*, and Abd al-Rahman, by laying claim to the title of Caliph, had pledged himself and his successors to at least the occasional expedition against the infidel. The heads of slaughtered Christians, dispatched from the front line, could serve not only as proof to an admiring people of their master's victories but as stirring evidence of his piety. 'Give firmness to the Believers,' God had instructed His Prophet. 'I will instil terror into the hearts of the Unbelievers: smite ye above their necks.'[10] Just as Mohammed himself, in the wake of his first great victory on the battlefield, had been presented by a servant with the severed head of his deadliest enemy, so had the caliphs harvested the heads of Christians – and by doing so proclaimed to the world their fitness to serve as the heirs of the Prophet.

Yet the commander who had led the raid on Santiago was not a caliph. For all that an Umayyad still ruled as the nominal lord of al-Andalus, true power had slipped the dynasty's grasp. Hisham II, son of the shrewd and cultivated al-Hakam, had shown himself pitifully unworthy of his famous lineage. Succeeding to the throne in 976, at the tender age of fourteen, he had passed the entire span of his reign within the gilded cage of Córdoba's citadel, the anonymous and indolent victim of his own general uselessness. Effective mastery of the Caliphate had been seized instead by his regent, a celebrated warrior and religious scholar by the name of Ibn Abi Amir, a man as stern and masterful as Hisham was dissipated, and who had adopted, in 981, the richly merited title of '*al-Mansur*' – 'the Victorious One'. Indeed, not since the time of the first coming of the Muslims to Spain had the Christians faced such a dangerous foe. Whereas in the time of Abd al-Rahman they had found it no great challenge to rebuff most of the assaults launched against them, and had even, on one noted occasion, succeeded in capturing the Caliph's personal Qur'an, it seemed, by the time of the Millennium, that there was no resisting the Saracen firestorm. Santiago was far from the only target of al-Mansur's fury. Barcelona too had been burned, and the lands of Christian lordships everywhere laid to waste. Even the kingdom of León, the most flour-ishing and formidable of them all, had been set to totter. As year followed year, and victory for the Saracens followed victory, so many Christians had come to dread whether their faith had a future in Spain at all.

Al-Mansur himself was certainly committed to its overthrow. *Jihad* was in his blood. Granted, his campaigns were not wholly lacking in expediency: for as an effective usurper, the pressure on him to legit-imise his regime was greater even than it had been on the caliphs. Nevertheless, although he undoubtedly was a ruthless and calculating political operator, al-Mansur was also something much more: a man who devoutly believed himself the sword and shield of God. The infi-dels to the north were not the only objects of his righteous scorn. Indeed, even though he claimed descent from an Arab who had par-ticipated in the original conquest of Spain, he appears to have viewed the entire character of al-Andalus with a disdain that bordered on con-tempt. No less than the worthless Caliph immured in his palace, his compatriots struck him as dissipated and lacking in due piety. A man who felt himself called to scour the infidel from Spain could hardly remain oblivious to the canker of moral laxity among his co-religionists. Even in what should have been the great bastions of right thinking in al-Andalus, in the schools where the Qur'an was taught, and in the famous libraries that were the glory of Córdoba, the austere verities of Islam appeared, to him, under constant and insidious threat. So it was that al-Mansur had scholars suspected of heresy publicly crucified; and so it was too that he did not hesitate to winnow even the celebrated library of al-Hakam of offending volumes, and consign the chaff to a bonfire. By 1002, when he died in the midst of his fifty-second campaign of *jihad*, it appeared that his life's mission to impose God's order upon the world had reaped a truly spectacular harvest – in the House of Islam itself no less than in the bloodied House of War.

And so it had – but not in the way that al-Mansur himself had intended. Appearances could be deceptive. In truth, it was not the kingdom of León, nor any of the other Christian lordships left mangled by the long decades of *jihad*, that faced implosion. Rather, it was the Caliphate itself, which had seemed, under the leadership of al-Mansur, raised to such intimidating heights of glory as to put even the furthest reaches of infidel Spain in its shadow, that was teetering on the edge of ruin. Few, in the immediate wake of the great warlord's death, would have suspected as much; but there were some, even back in the glory days of the Umayyads, who had sensed a rottenness in al-Andalus, and feared where it might end. One of them, ironically enough, had been al-Mansur himself. As a youthful and talented player in the often deadly game of harem politics, he had been granted plentiful opportunities to study at close hand the functioning of al-Hakam's regime – and to mark just how dependent it had become for its muscle on foreigners. As in the days of Abbot John's visit to Córdoba, most of these were slaves, transported to al-Andalus from the far-off lands of the Slavs – but some were mercenaries, Muslim Berbers from Morocco. Al-Mansur had come to know the quality of these men well: for early in his career he had served among them in North Africa. Stern in the practice of their religion, and 'famed for their exploits, qualities and valour in the face of the Christians',[11] the Berbers had seemed to the young officer everything that his compatriots were not: warriors ideally suited to keeping an ambitious *jihadi* in power. And so it had proved. Al-Mansur's reign had witnessed a prodigious influx of Berber war bands into al-Andalus. By the time of his death, they were to be found billeted across the Caliphate, loathed and feared in equal measure by the natives. Naturally enough, as the tax rate spiralled ever upwards, so the resentment of the Andalusis at being obliged to fund the promotion of immigrants – of savages! – over their own heads had grown increasingly sulphurous. In Córdoba especially, the great maze of streets had begun to seethe with ethnic hatreds. The capital had been transformed into a kindling box.

This was an alarming inheritance, certainly, for any ruler to come into. For six years, however, al-Mansur's eldest son, a *jihad*-seasoned alcoholic by the name of Abd al-Malik, succeeded, despite his most un-Islamic enthusiasm for the bottle, in maintaining his dynasty's grip on both Córdoba and al-Andalus. Rather than flaunt his power, he did as his father had done, and paid dutiful lip service to Hisham II; rather than parade his dependence on the Berbers, he sought to veil it. When he too died, however, and was succeeded by his brother, the son of a Christian concubine known to the Córdobans by the derisive nickname of 'Sanchuelo', both policies were flung out of the window. Subtlety was not the new regent's forte. First, he leaned on the wretched Hisham to appoint him the formal heir to the throne of the Caliphate; then, just for good measure, he ordered everyone at court to start wearing a Berber style of turban. As Sanchuelo set off northwards on the obligatory campaign of *jihad*, he left behind him a capital that was smouldering. At the news that he had crossed the frontier, it exploded into flames.

The spark that lit the conflagration had been struck by an Umayyad fugitive, Muhammed bin Hisham. Sneaking back into Córdoba, he had succeeded in rallying the disinherited members of his clan to his cause – and now, with Sanchuelo far distant in the lands of the infidel, he deposed the feeble Hisham II and took his place upon the throne. News of the coup was greeted ecstatically by the Córdobans, who set about celebrating it with a delirious orgy of theft and violence. The slums emptied as the palaces built by al-Mansur and his two sons were systematically trashed. 'Such was the sacking,' one historian recorded, 'that even the doors and beams disappeared.'[12] The new Caliph, far from attempting to restrain the rioters, encouraged them all he could. This was the measure of his authority: it depended on a lynch mob. As did his justice. Staking out Sanchuelo's harem, the new Commander of the Faithful cherry-picked the most beautiful women, raped some of the others and shared out the remainder among his henchmen. Learning that Sanchuelo himself had been abandoned by his army and assassinated, he ordered the corpse brought back to Córdoba and stuck up on a gibbet. Seeking to raze the principal buttress of the toppled regime, and ingratiate himself with the anti-immigrant Córdobans, he placed a bounty on the head of every Berber.

'And slay them wherever ye catch them, and turn them out from where they have turned you out; for tumult and oppression are worse than slaughter.'[13] The Córdobans, who had long felt that the 'tumult and oppression' of the hated Berbers more than qualified them to be slaughtered, now set to obeying the Prophet's injunction with a sanguinary literalness. As black smoke rose above the immense city, so mobs began to gather once again, pillaging Berber barracks and homes, and hunting down their inhabitants. The men were slaughtered; the women raped, then tethered together to be sold as whores. Those found to be pregnant had their babies sliced out of their bellies.

Yet the Berbers were not so easily excised from the guts of al-Andalus. By 1010, the vengeful comrades of those who had been massacred the year before were camped around the walls of Córdoba, and for three years they remained there, slowly starving the city to death. The Córdobans, flaunting their refusal to surrender, went so far as to sanction cannibalism rather than submit to the hated foreigners. Most, however, were civilians – and such gestures were the effective limit of their defiance. The ruin of Córdoba, when it came at last, was total. The Berbers, taking possession of the city in the spring of 1013, mercilessly beslathered the 'Ornament of the World' with gore. All its gilded splendours, all its fabulous pretensions, were trampled underfoot. Among the corpses left piled in the smoking streets, almost certainly, was that of Hisham II, the heir of the Umayyads, his pale and perfumed body sharing in his capital's desecration, his caliphal blood serving to feed the ruined city's flies.

And yet his death went unremarked. Set against the titanic scale of the ethnic hatreds that had torn the Caliphate to pieces, the doings of its rulers had come to seem a matter almost of insignificance. The Córdobans, during the course of the terrible siege, had thought nothing of executing Mohammed for the horrors he had brought down upon them, and restoring Hisham to his throne; and after Hisham's disappearance, there were other factions who adopted candidates of their own. Yet few paid these spectral caliphs any attention. The unity of al-Andalus was gone for ever, and across the lands that had once been ruled from Córdoba local warlords were already looking to their own. The Muslims would call these upstarts '*Taifa*' kings: 'faction' kings. The ambition of al-Mansur, that a revived and triumphant Islam would complete the business begun three centuries previously and subdue the whole of Spain, was dead. The goal of the *Taifa* kings was less aggrandisement than survival. Nothing remained of the Caliphate save a corpse to be scavenged over.

And nothing of its capital save a shell. For those who had known Córdoba in the full radiance of her glory, the agony of what she had become was unbearable. 'Prosperity has been changed into a sterile desert, society into frightful loneliness, beauty into rubble-strewn plains. Where peace once reigned, great chasms now yawn: the haunt of wolves, of ghosts, of demons.'[14] So wrote Ibn Hazm, a high-born intellectual and Umayyad loyalist, whose fruitless nostalgia for the decaying Caliphate had led him to endure years of imprisonment and exile. Specifically, he was describing the anguish of a lover parted from the object of his passions: an anguish that he himself had known well. In 1013, amid the horrors of Córdoba's fall, Ibn Hazm had been forced to flee the city and leave behind him the first great love of his life: a young and exquisitely lovely slave girl, modest, refined and with a voice 'that could pluck at heart-strings'.[15] Six years on, however, when he met her again, he found her so lined and withered as to be unrecognisable. Feeling that wherever he looked there was nothing

but decay, Ibn Hazm had traced in the preternaturally wrinkled face
of a slave woman the lineaments of a more universal decay. The rooms
of the country estate in which he had grown up, and Córdoba herself,
and the once-flourishing lands of al-Andalus – all were ruined too.
'Those halls inscribed with beauteous scripts, those adorned boudoirs
that used to shine like the sun, possessed of a loveliness that had the
power to banish all misery from the soul; now they are overwhelmed
by desolation, standing like the open jaws of savage beasts. And by
doing so, they proclaim the doom that awaits the world.'[16]

A sentiment worthy almost of Cluny. Certainly, Christians were
not alone in dreading that the end days might be at hand. During the
reign of al-Hakam, indeed, a Muslim philosopher who had thought to
deny the coming of the Day of Judgement had been put to death for
heresy. Just as the Great Mosque of Córdoba incorporated within its
architecture the columns and brickwork and mosaics of superseded
empires, so had the infinitely grander edifice of Islam not disdained to
cannibalise the revelations of the Christians. Jesus, Muslims were
taught, had been a mighty prophet of God, and at the end of time, he
would descend from the skies, just as St John had written, and would
fight and conquer the hordes of the '*Dajjal*' – Antichrist. Not alone, however: for at his side would appear an even greater warrior, 'a descendant
of Fatima',[17] the Prophet Mohammed's daughter, whose fateful task
it would be 'to fill the earth with justice and equity, just as now it
is filled with oppression and tyranny'.[18] This greatest of all caliphs would
be termed '*al-Mahdi*': 'the Rightly Guided One'. And his rule would serve
to put an end to suffering and injustice for ever.

But when? A familiar question. Muslims, tipped off by the Prophet,
believed that the moment would come upon the turning of a century.
The passage of a hundred years was what haunted their imaginings,
not a thousand. Four centuries had gone by since Mohammed, fleeing his native city, had set about establishing the first Muslim state –
and the precise anniversary of this epochal event was, according
to the Christian calendar, 1009. Small wonder, then, in the troubled
decades falling either side of this date, that Muslims too should have

anticipated the ending of the world. It was no coincidence, for example, that Muhammed bin Hisham, the Umayyad pretender who had
laid claim to the caliphal dignity in the very year 1009, should have
presumed to adopt the title of Mahdi. A pathetic and vain expedient – and yet powerfully suggestive of a mood of anxiety that had
come to grip not merely al-Andalus, but the whole of the House of
Islam.

For Córdoba, after all, was not the only capital of a caliphate – to
the east, in Cairo, there ruled a family that had never ceased to
imagine itself the gatekeeper of the end days. The Fatimids – the
descendants of Fatima – had always sought to draw deep from the
wellsprings of the mysterious. The founder of the dynasty, back in 909,
had actually believed that he was the Mahdi himself, and although
time – and his death – had proved him mistaken, his successors had
shrugged aside any resultant sense of let-down. Instead, with a vaunting and unabashed conceit, they had continued to insist that they were
supremely touched by the supernatural. The Caliph who swayed
Egypt at the dawning of the fifth Muslim century was no exception.
Indeed, to an unprecedented degree, al-Hakim bin-Amr Allah claimed
directly to be an incarnation of God. His subjects, far from laughing
this pretension to scorn, were almost universally awestruck by it. Tall,
broad-shouldered and with a stare that was reported to glitter like
fiery gold, al-Hakim had only to look at his subjects as he toured the
streets of Cairo to send them grovelling in the dust. When he shouted,
it was claimed, men had been known to drop dead of terror on the
spot. Sober in his tastes, puritanical in his instincts and unstintingly
imperious in all his moods, al-Hakim was not a man readily crossed.
When he claimed to have penetrated the veiled secrets of God, there
were few who openly disputed it; and when he sought to shoulder the
responsibilities of the Mahdi, there were even fewer who cared to
obstruct him.

So it was that while the Caliphate of the Umayyads, far distant
in the West, collapsed into terminal anarchy, the reign of al-Hakim
was marked by titanic efforts to reorder the world and prepare it for

the end days. True, some of the Caliph's strategies, even to the most committed of his followers, could not help but appear a trifle eccentric.
The selling of watercress, for instance, was solemnly banned; so too
the playing of chess. Other policies, however, were more readily expli-
cable. What objection, for instance, could a pious Muslim raise against
al-Hakim's command that all the dogs in Cairo be put to the sword
and their corpses dumped out in the desert, when everyone knew the
creatures to be unclean? Or indeed against his campaign to check the
potentially even filthier appetites of women? A conviction that these
merited regular chastisement had often been a caliphal trait: of Abd al-
Rahman, for instance, it was said that he had never visited his harem
without a sword and an executioner's leather mat. Even when set
against such precedents, however, al-Hakim's terrors of where female
promiscuity might lead the faithful were extreme. So too his plans to
counter them. First he ordered women everywhere to be veiled when
out in public; then he banned them from leaving their homes; finally
he forbade them even so much as to peer out of windows or doors.
Cobblers were instructed to stop making them shoes. Those whose
voices disturbed the Caliph as he walked through the streets might
expect to be walled up and left to starve.

These were robust measures, certainly – and yet justified, al-Hakim
would no doubt have insisted, by the troubled character of the times.
If it were true, as the Caliph himself appears devoutly to have believed,
that a mighty convulsion in the affairs of the world was looming, then
clearly there could be no excuse for delaying the purification of the
House of Islam. Dogs and women, however, were the least of the Caliph's
problems. Other menaces festered infinitely more worrisome. Egypt,
even in comparison with al-Andalus, still teemed with Christians
and Jews. The Fatimids, not content with extorting taxes from them,
as the Prophet had prescribed, had also, over the years, profited handsomely from the tribute of their expertise. *Dhimmis*, as a result, had come
to throng the caliphal ministries – and the caliphal bedrooms. Even
al-Hakim's own mother was a Christian. What could this appear, to
the pious Muslims of Egypt, but a scandal and a blasphemy? Indeed,

only a year before al-Hakim's accession, in 995, a bloody marker of their resentments had been served to the future Caliph when a mob had gone on the rampage and massacred over a hundred Christians in a single pogrom. A marker that al-Hakim, as time would prove, had noted well.

He may have been a son of a Christian, but even as a young boy of eleven, inheriting the throne while out on campaign against the infidels of Constantinople, he had believed himself implacably fated to prove the doom of his mother's faith. As his reign progressed, *dhimmis* who had once basked in the radiance of caliphal favour found themselves increasingly subjected to humiliations and harassments. Christians and Jews alike were forbidden to appear in public unless wearing distinctive turbans of black. As a further refinement, Christians were obliged to hang crosses around their necks, and Jews heavy blocks of wood. They were also banned from employing Muslims – a measure which immediately served to plunge most *dhimmi* businesses into bankruptcy. There were some, however, who lost more than their income. In 1009, the dawning of the fifth Islamic century, numerous non-Muslim officials in the imperial bureaucracy were scourged to death and their corpses fed to Cairo's few remaining dogs. Others, under threat of torture, were obliged to convert to Islam. Yet even these outrages, in the view of the Caliph's horrified Christians, were not the most shocking of their master's crimes. Worse then murder or oppression, after all, was sacrilege – and al-Hakim just happened to have within his power the very holiest of their shrines.

Jerusalem, where Jesus had died and been buried, remained, under the Fatimids, a predominantly *dhimmi* town. True, back in the first century of the Islamic Empire, when the Umayyads had ruled as the masters of a unified Caliphate, a mosque and a mighty dome had both been built on the site of the obliterated Jewish Temple: imperious symbols of Muslim dominance. Nevertheless, as a native of the city who frequented them grumbled, 'Everywhere the Jews and Christians have the upper hand, and the mosques are void of either congregation or assembly of learned men.'[19] One unhappy consequence of this, so

Muslims liked to believe, was the appalling standard of hygiene in the public baths: 'Nowhere will you find any filthier.'[20] Another, even more distressing, was the sheer ostentation in Jerusalem of *dhimmi* rituals. The Jews, for instance, deprived of their ancient sanctuary on the Temple Mount, had relocated their place of public prayer to the Mount of Olives, directly across the valley from the city's most famous mosque; but even the Jews were less offensively in Muslim faces than were the Christians. Almost seven centuries had passed since the Emperor Constantine, arriving in Jerusalem, had ordered the building of a great basilica over the site of Christ's tomb; and still it stood there, the Church of the Holy Sepulchre, a place of such awesome and refulgent sacredness that there was nowhere in all Christendom, not even in Rome, that could possibly rival it. To Christians 'from across the entire face of the world',[21] in the West as well as the East, it was, quite simply, beyond compare: 'the heart of the earth'.[22]

But to al-Hakim, it was a standing provocation. Plans for its destruction were first drawn up at the end of 1007[23] – one year after a star of exceptional brightness, blazing suddenly in the constellation of Scorpio, had served to reassure the Caliph that he was indeed touched by the divine. Nevertheless, even with his workmen primed, al-Hakim had no intention of hurrying. Naturally, as befitted a would-be guardian of the end days, he knew that timing was everything. Not until 1009 itself – the Muslim year 400 – were the demolition teams finally set to work. 'The Church of the Dungheap',* as Muslims derisively termed Constantine's great basilica, was first stripped of all its treasures and furnishings, and then, right the way down to the bedrock, dismantled brick by brick. The very tomb of Christ was hacked about and 'assaulted by a prodigious fire'.[24] All the church's magnificence was methodically demolished and left as dust.

In mosques everywhere, it is said, lengthy prayers of joy were raised, and the praises of the Caliph were of an unparalleled extravagance.[25]

---

* '*Kanisat al-Qumana*' – a pun on the Arabic for Church of the Resurrection, '*Kanisat al-Qiyama*'.

Meanwhile, as reports of what had been done spread beyond the frontiers of the Caliphate, and into the heartlands of Christendom, so the rumours that swept the appalled Christians of the West grew ever more confused and terrifying. Some claimed, rather far-fetchedly, that the entire outrage had been plotted by the Jews of Orléans, who had sent letters to al-Hakim, encouraging him in his act of desecration. Others named the Caliph the King of Babylon, who in ancient times had destroyed King Solomon's Temple. Others noted how the heavens had broadcast their revulsion at the sacrilege, frowning upon the world, and inflicting upon mankind 'severe dry spells, very much rain, many plagues, severe famines and numerous failures of the sun and moon'[26] – and drew their own conclusions.

And as they looked to the skies they hugged their souls and wondered what, in an age marked by such prodigies, sinful humanity should do.

Jesus Wept

By 1010, reports of the destruction of the Holy Sepulchre had reached as far as Aquitaine. As southern France was racked by widespread violence and upheaval, the shock wave broke across the duchy with an especial force. In one town in particular, the news served to induce an almost personal sense of horror: for Limoges, an ancient and flourishing settlement in the heart of France, was the proud possessor of a holy sepulchre all of its own. St Martial, while hardly on a par with apostles such as Peter and James, was nevertheless much cherished by the locals: for, back in the third Christian century, he had first brought the Gospel to Aquitaine. His tomb, deep in the crypt of a monastery that bore his name, was widely reverenced as the reservoir of an awful power. Back in 994, on the occasion of a trail-blazing peace council, the mere process of transporting the saint's earthly remains to a nearby hill had been sufficient to prompt an earthquake. As an immense crowd moaned and shuddered at the sight of the relics, a terrible pestilence of 'invisible fire' had been lifted from Limoges, and the duke and all his lords had together sworn 'a pact of peace and justice'.[27] Over the succeeding years, miracles had continued to be performed upon St Martial's tomb. Pilgrims had flocked to it in prodigious numbers. As the new millennium dawned, and the weather turned increasingly freakish, afflicting the region with heatwaves, and violent rainstorms, and strange wonders written in the sky, so the inhabitants of Limoges had begun to imagine themselves a chosen people, appointed by God to serve as witnesses to the fracturing of the times. Indeed – in an excitable display of immodesty – the town had dared to conceive of itself almost as a new Jerusalem. And then had come the baleful tidings from the Holy Land.

Nightmarish news, to be sure – and there must have been many in Limoges, during the course of that strange and menacing summer, who suffered sleepless nights as a consequence. We know for certain, however, of only one: a monk by the name of Adémar, a twenty-year-old of good family who had recently journeyed from his own monastery to study at St Martial. Proud and sensitive, the young scholar appears to have been a natural loner, one who combined a restless intellect with emotional depths so turbulent that he sought, by and large, to conceal their existence. We do not know the extent of his nightmares in 1010; but Adémar did record how one night, unable to sleep and looking out at the sky, he was granted a vision infinitely more disturbing than any dream. Indeed, so shattering was the spectacle of what he found confronting him that night, rising over Limoges and framed against a blaze of brilliant stars, that he would end up keeping it to himself for almost twenty years. High against the southern sky, planted as if in the heavens, he saw a giant crucifix – and nailed to it was Christ Himself. 'And the figure of the Lord, hanging on the cross, was weeping forth a great river of tears.' Adémar, struck dumb with fear, could do nothing as he gazed at this harrowing apparition but fall to weeping himself. 'In all, he saw this cross and the image of the Crucified One, the colour of fire and deep blood,

239

for half a full night hour, until the sky closed itself. And what he saw he sealed in his heart.'²⁸

As well he might have done. The implications of the Saviour's tears, shed in rivers over Limoges, could hardly but have appeared overwhelming to the shaken monk. Almost a thousand years had passed since Christ wept over Jerusalem; and now, with His own tomb desecrated, He had appeared in the heavens to weep again. What, then, could this portend, if not the fatal moment of which St Paul had warned, when Antichrist would emerge upon his throne and lay claim to the rule of the world? Indeed, who was to say that he had not already done so? Was it not by trampling down the Temple in Jerusalem, and putting the faithful to the sword, and proclaiming his own divinity, that Antichrist was destined to announce himself? Had not the Prince of the Saracens fulfilled every last term of the prophecy?

No wonder, then, with strange eclipses shimmering above Limoges, and her streets broiling in murderous heat, and her rivers drying up as though scorched by celestial fire, that a sense of terror began to sweep through the town. It needed no vision of a weeping Christ to panic the citizens – nor to set them looking for scapegoats. The same gusts of rumour that had brought the news from the Holy Land had also served to broadcast to them the shocking charges against the Jews of Orléans. The Christians of Limoges – fearful, it appears, that the reign of Antichrist was come indeed, and that his cohorts might be lurking in their very midst – had begun to fix their suspicions upon the Jews of their own town. The local bishop, sensitive to the mood of rising paranoia, duly summoned a council. Adémar, writing some fifteen years later, described what happened next. For a month, the wretched Jews of Limoges were bullied and hectored in what was laughably termed a 'debate'.²⁹ At the end of the proceedings, they were ordered to convert to the Christian faith. Only three or four could bring themselves to do so. The remainder, so Adémar recorded, were then driven from the town.

This, as a breakdown in community relations, was certainly

240

ground-breaking – indeed, a bolt from the blue. Bishops in the West were not in the habit of harassing Jews, still less of deporting them. Better by far to affect a lofty blend of contempt and indifference: such had been the judgement of St Augustine, an authority not readily brooked. For the Jews, the great doctor of the Church had ruled, despite undoubtedly having the blood of Christ on their hands, had not known, when they dispatched Him to crucifixion, that they were killing the Son of God; an extenuation that Christian kings and bishops had been more than content to accept. As in the lands of the Saracens, so in Christendom: tolerance was firmly rooted in self-interest. Jews would be offered protection, and even special privileges, so that their talents might then all the more readily be exploited. And sure enough, whether as court officials, or as physicians, or as linch-pins of the slave trade, they had long provided their sponsors with an excellent return. No wonder, then, over the years, that the Jewish communities of Francia had grown increasingly prosperous – and increasingly well integrated too.[30] Not only did they live cheek by jowl with their gentile neighbours, but they tended to wear the same clothes, speak the same language and even give their children the same names. There was nothing, in short, in centuries of peaceful co-existence with the Franks, that could have prepared them for the sudden ethnic cleansing of Limoges.

And it is possible – indeed probable – that the persecutions of 1010 were even more brutal than Adémar could bring himself readily to acknowledge.[31] Later in his career, when he came to emend his account of the treatment of the Jews of Limoges, he let slip a telling indiscretion. 'And some', he wrote, 'preferred slitting their own throats to avoid baptism.'[32] This, it appears, had been the true climax of the 'debate' staged in the town by the bishop. Nor, necessarily, had the atrocities been confined to Limoges. Rudolf Glaber, recording the paroxysms of that feverish year in the more heated terms that came naturally to him, described the whole of Christendom as gripped by a blood lust. 'For once it had become quite clear that it was the wicked-ness of the Jews which had brought about the Temple's destruction,' he explained, 'they became the objects of universal hatred: they were driven from the cities, some were put to the sword, others were drowned in rivers, and many found other deaths; some even took their own lives in diverse ways.' A grotesque exaggeration, it might be thought – and not least because Glaber concluded with a palpable falsehood, a smug assertion that 'after this very proper vengeance had been taken, very few Jews were to be found left in the Roman world'.

In truth, whatever the precise details of the persecution that was launched against the Jews in 1010, it could hardly have been on the scale of the pogroms that were simultaneously tearing al-Andalus apart – for 'the fury of the Christian people', as even Glaber admitted, in a tone of some disappointment, 'did not take long to cool'.[33] The sudden eruption of Jew-killing, as unprecedented as it had been savage, subsided quickly. As well it might have done – for it carried a penalty, according to a papal mandate that had been issued only two years previously, of excommunication. With the mobs laying down their weapons, so the dust began to settle. Communities everywhere set to picking up the pieces. Across France, the Christian authorities resumed gracing the Jews with their customary disdainful tolerance. On both sides, it appears, there was a determination to regard the violence as an aberration – or indeed as something that had never happened in the first place.

This attitude was dictated for the persecuted by simple common sense – and for the persecutors by something like embarrassment. All well and good, no doubt, to turn on the enemies of Christ during the reign of Antichrist, that time of terrible and cosmic danger when, as Adso had pointed out, 'the Jews will flock to him, in the belief that they are receiving God – but rather they will be receiving the Evil One'. As it proved, however, the desecration of the Holy Sepulchre had not served to usher in the end days – just as al-Hakim had not turned out to be Antichrist. Indeed, far from persisting in his persecution of the Christians, strange rumours began to spread in the West that he had become a Christian himself. By 1021 he was dead, lost in the Egyptian desert, and in such mysterious circumstances that there were some, both Muslim and Christian, who claimed he had been taken up to heaven by an angel.* Meanwhile, in Jerusalem, work had soon begun on rebuilding the Church of the Holy Sepulchre, so that within two decades of its destruction services were once again being celebrated before its altar, and pilgrims, entering the shrine, could gawp at all its beauties, at 'its coloured marbles, its ornamentation and sculptures, its Byzantine brocade with pictures spun in gold'.[34] No wonder, then, back in the lands of the West, that the hysteria that had followed its original destruction was a source of some mortification, and one that most people preferred to forget.

Yet this was not always easily done. There were those for whom the terrors of 1010 had been so overwhelming as to shake them to their very core. How, for instance, as Limoges returned to normal, and the years gradually slipped by, and even the banished Jews began to limp their way back to the town, was Adémar to make sense of his vision of the weeping Christ? Tellingly, when he finally came to write down what he had seen, he still could not bring himself to confess the precise context of his revelation. Instead, with a finicky display of deceit that only a true scholar could possibly have attempted, he set out to muddy it. History, in Adémar's chronicle, was painstakingly rewritten. The destruction of the Holy Sepulchre was dated, not to 1009, but to the succeeding summer. The likelihood that it had been the alarming news from Jerusalem which inspired the persecution of the Jews – not to mention Adémar's own vision – was discreetly buried. In all his account of the harrowing events of 1010 not a hint remained that they had been prompted, as a later and more scrupulous historian would put it, 'by a rumour spread in many places across the globe, one that frightened and saddened many hearts, that the end of the world was at hand'.[35]

---

* A theory that is accepted to this day by the Druze of Lebanon, Syria and Israel, who worship al-Hakim as what the Caliph had claimed to be: an incarnation of God.

Yet still, in Adémar's own soul, at any rate, the question must have abided: why had his saviour appeared to him, nailed to a cross, and weeping? There was nothing in his monastery that would have prepared him for such a spectacle. Just as the ancient Romans, shrinking from imagining their god as a victim of torture, had preferred to think of Him instead as a celestial emperor, ablaze with the glory of His triumph over death, so too had their successors, in the Latin West no less than in Constantinople, persisted in representing Christ as a *Basileus*, serene and remote, enthroned in heaven. His cross, when it was portrayed at all, was conceived of less as an instrument of execution than as a victory standard, dyed by His blood an aptly imperial purple. That Jesus, who had once trod the earth as a human being, had experienced suffering no less excruciating than that endured by the most wretched of peasants, that He had hungered, and thirsted, and even wept: all these were details that scarcely registered with most Christians. Well might Adémar, then, have found himself perturbed by his vision.

And all the more so because he would have suspected that what he had been shown that fateful night was something that might prove perilous to acknowledge. There were many, since the Millennium, who had laid claim to strange revelations. Most of these, in the view of anxious clerics such as Adémar himself, derived not from any parting of the veil of heaven, but rather from shadows and phantasms risen up from the fumes of hell. In the fateful year 1000, for instance, a French peasant by the name of Leutard had dreamed that a great swarm of bees entered his body through his anus, and spoke to him, 'ordering him to do things impossible for human kind';[36] simultaneously, Vilgard, a grammarian at Ravenna, imagined himself in the company of assorted ancient pagans;[37] and in 1022, most alarmingly of all, it was reported that twelve clerics in Orléans, one of whom had been high in the favour of King Robert himself, were in the habit of being visited regularly by the Devil, 'who would appear to them sometimes in the guise of an Ethiopian, and sometimes in the form of an angel of light'.[38]

Bewilderingly diverse in their origins and their social backgrounds the men who experienced these visions may have been – and yet all had been inspired by a similar shocking notion: 'They did not believe that there was such a thing as the Church,'[39] it was said of the clerics of Orléans. So it was likewise reported of Leutard, who had set himself to vandalising shrines, and of Vilgard, who had claimed that poets were the only source of wisdom. All of them, inspired by their super-natural interlocutors, had come to scorn the rituals and the doctrines of the Church, its ancient hierarchy, its sumptuous adornments, its aids to prayer, its tithes: everything, in short, of its massy order which had been constructed with such labour over the long millennium since the life of Christ.

Where had they sprung from, these heretics?[40] Just as bishops had never thought to harry the Jews until the dawning of the new mil-lennium, so similarly had it never before crossed their minds to root around for heresy.[41] Only during the end days, after all, so Christ had admonished, were the weeds to be sorted out from the wheat, 'and burned with fire'. Yet now the Millennium was here – and suddenly, it appeared to jumpy churchmen, there were weeds sprouting up everywhere. Adémar, for instance, nervously marking the times from the watchtower of his monastery, described the fields and forests of Aquitaine as teeming with heretics; and the more he sought to keep track of them, the more obsessed by them he became. Like the 'wicked-ness and pride' that he dreaded were coming to infect the souls of the faithful everywhere, 'the endless warfare, and the famine, and the pestilence, the terrors seen in the heavens, and all the other signs', they were self-evidently a fateful portent: 'messengers of Antichrist'.[42] And yet in truth, to a man such as Adémar, the heresy being preached on his very doorstep must have appeared a uniquely devilish menace. Unlike the Jews, who were at least open in their hostility to the Christian faith, it was the perverse and subtle cunning of heretics that they scorned the Church for not being Christian enough. Their ideal was an existence of rough-hewn simplicity, such as the original disciples had known. In their beginning was to be their end: for the heretics, by attempting to found the primitive Church anew in Aquitaine, aimed at nothing less than the hastening of the return of

Christ. 'They affect to lead their lives as the apostles did,'[43] it was reported of communities in the Périgord, a bare fifty miles south of Limoges. An accusation fit to chill the soul of Adémar, certainly – for how could it not have served to awaken a dark and unnerving suspicion in him? The rolling back of the Millennium to its starting point, the annihilation of time: was this not precisely what his own revelation had accomplished, by showing him Christ nailed and bloody upon the Cross?

These were treacherous waters indeed. No wonder that Adémar hesitated for years to confess his vision. No wonder either that he should have noted with a particular alarm how the heretics, even as they preached their pestilential doctrines in the woods and villages beyond the walls of his monastery, sought to set themselves apart from the common run of sinful humanity – 'precisely as though they were monks'.[44] One eccentricity in particular stood out: their vegetarianism. Indeed, a repugnance for eating meat appeared a characteristic of heretics wherever they were found. In Saxony, for instance, suspicions would immediately be aroused if a peasant showed himself reluctant to kill a chicken – for squeamishness had come to be regarded as a certain symptom of heresy. So too, in France, had 'a pale complexion':[45] the inevitable consequence of only ever nibbling on turnips. In Milan, the archbishop himself stepped in to try to persuade a group of heretics, a countess among them, that it was no sin to be a carnivore – but in vain. Back came the defiant reply: 'We do not eat meat.'[46]

Here, in this bold statement, was something more than merely the articulation of a dietary fad. For if it were true, as all the signs suggested, that the end time was fast approaching, and the New Jerusalem about to descend, then how better could humanity prepare itself, so the heretics appear to have concluded, than by aspiring to a literally fleshless state? To fast – and if not to fast, then to subsist on vegetables – was the closest that a mortal could hope to come to the incorporeal condition of an angel. Well might this serve to make a bishop nervous – for what role did it leave to him? Yet if there was any order of the Church likely to feel threatened by the sudden mushrooming of heretics, and by their ambitions to live like angels, then it was – just as Adémar had noted – the monks. And specifically, the monks of Cluny. For they too conceived of themselves as beings set apart from the polluted world of flesh and dirt and sin; and they too, as befitted soldiers of God, did not eat meat. Any monk who presumed to break this prohibition, so Abbot Odo had warned, would find himself choking on the offending morsel to death. Even the use of lard, on those regrettable occasions when oil ran short, required a special dispensation. Not for warrior monks the more robust appetites of a bishop such as Henry of Lund, the keeper of Canute's treasure in Denmark, who 'revelled and stuffed his belly so full that at last he suffocated and burst';[47] nor of a king such as Sancho of León, who ended up so stupefyingly fat that he could barely walk, let alone climb on to a horse, and had to be put on a crash diet by a Jewish physician summoned all the way from Córdoba specifically to slim him down.

Notorious prodigies of gluttony such as these served merely to showcase what was anyway self-evident enough: that gourmandising, in a world racked by hunger, was above all a marker of rank. The monks of Cluny, who certainly had no wish to see the world turned upside down, appreciated this perfectly well; nor did they ever think to begrudge an eminent visitor the meat that they denied themselves. Indeed, on occasion, when the monastery found its larder understocked, the odd miracle might help them to make up the shortfall: as on the evening when a bishop and his entire retinue dropped by unexpectedly, and a huge boar was discovered shortly afterwards sitting on the porch, drooling over the stonework and 'offering itself up willingly to be slaughtered'.[48] That even the pork served at Cluny's tables might be touched by the supernatural was certainly dazzling evidence of the monastery's holiness – and that the monks themselves still stuck to the fish course even more so.

Which was just as well – for the Church, if it were to meet the challenge of heresy, desperately needed its own exemplars of otherworldliness and purity. The challenge of those who in their longing for Christ's return imagined that the gates of the celestial could be forced open, and the Second Coming hastened, had to be met and sternly rebuffed. Not all of them could be brought to the satisfying end of Leutard, who in his despair at finding himself abandoned by his followers had committed suicide by jumping down a well. Nor could they all be burned: the fate of the Orléans dozen. To be sure, the fact that the convicted clerics had spontaneously dissolved into ash at the merest touch of the fires had clearly signalled divine approval of their sentence; nor was their execution, the first ever for heresy in the West, by any means to be the last. Yet the Church itself, in the main, shrank from the prospect of harrying heretics to their death – so that when, for instance, in Milan, the city fathers condemned the vegetarian countess and her associates to the flames, the sentence was vigorously opposed by the very archbishop who had interrogated them in the first place. 'Error coupled with cruelty,'[49] said one bishop of the policy of executing heretics. In part, this reflected practical considerations: the Church simply lacked the apparatus of state control that the Umayyads or al-Mansur had been able to draw upon in their own, far bloodier, campaigns against heresy. Yet it also reflected something profounder: a determination to confront the heretics on their chosen ground, directly on the battlefield of the supernatural, before the gates of the City of God. That the Christian people, sensing the world to be entering the end time, and buffeted as they were by portents and wonders and upheavals, should yearn to journey on the path of righteousness, in the expectation that it would lead them to behold the coming of Christ Himself – this, perhaps, was only to be expected. What mattered, however, was not to cede control of the journey to the heretics: to remind the faithful that it had only ever been through the Church that sinful humanity had been brought to approach the City of God.

So it was that the heretics and the monks, even as the millennium of Christ's Resurrection drew ever closer, went head to head. Against the rugged simplicities of those who sought, beneath trees or out on dusty roads, to lead their lives as the apostles had done, without splendour or ritual, there was arrayed a very different model of sanctity.

Foremost in the line of battle, as was only to be expected, was that princely captain, Abbot Odilo of Cluny. The piety of the brethren under his authority, the literally superhuman continence of their habits and the angelic beauty of their singing combined to suggest that paradise might indeed be created on earth. As the years passed, so Cluny's fame and influence continued to spread. Ever more monasteries came to submit themselves to Odilo's rule. All were rigorously purified by a programme of reform. Once cleansed of every taint of corruption, they stood qualified to serve the Christian people as outposts of heaven. Or so, at any rate, the enthusiasts for reform proclaimed.

These, by the 1020s, extended far and wide. The model of Cluny was coming to have a truly international appeal. The prayers and anthems which were raised there, no matter how scorned they might be by heretics, were increasingly regarded by most Christians as the surest defence that existed against the Devil. Nor, adding sensationally to their appeal, did their potency cease with death. Anxious sinners, fretting about their prospects of salvation, could rest assured that there was nothing more certain to cut short their sufferings amid the flames of the afterlife, and to secure their entry into paradise, than to be remembered amid the cloisters of Cluny. Not that this necessarily came cheap. A mention in the chantings of the monks was a passport to heaven so precious that the greatest in the land would pay prodigiously for it. Yet Odilo, even as Cluny benefited handsomely from the endowments of the wealthy, did not forget the souls of the poor. So it was that he made sure to introduce a new festival to the monastery's calendar, to be celebrated every 2 November, a commemoration of the dead that could serve to profit all the Christian faithful. On All Souls' Day, the prayers of the monks were raised in the cause of the departed everywhere: obsequies of such awesome power that they were believed to help swing open the gates of heaven.

And sure enough, the knowledge of this, and the conviction that the monks of Cluny and its associated houses were indeed worthy to guard the celestial, did much to blunt heresy's sting. Yet still, beyond the walls of the monasteries, the great mass of the Christian people remained nervous and uneasy – and still they yearned for more. The peace councils, at which the parading of relics was a particular attraction, had served to instil in them a taste for mystery and spectacle; nor, for all that they admired the secluded sanctity of the monks, were they content to have everything holy locked away. Ground down as most people were by the harshness and sheer monotony of their existence, the chance to set out on a journey to a famous shrine, to look upon the remains of a saint, and perhaps to witness a miracle, had become a precious one indeed.

So it was, in the first decades of the new millennium, that the roads came increasingly to swell with pilgrims – and many of these, exceptionally, were peasants. This, in a world where most people never thought to raise their gaze beyond the brow of the nearest hill, was yet another prodigy – and not the least unsettling. Women, in particular, finding themselves and their families suddenly abandoned, were liable to accuse their husbands of setting off on pilgrimage out of 'vain curiosity rather than any devotion to religion'. Yet they needed to watch their tongues. The saints did not take kindly to shrews. A woman in Normandy, for instance, who had presumed to nag her husband to stay at home and put food on his family's table, rather than visit a local shrine, found 'her blasphemous mouth, the organ through which she had shamelessly uttered outrageous language against God and her husband, elongated rigidly in a distorted and deformed way, so that it became fixed to both her ears'.[50] A fitting punishment, no doubt; and yet, the truth be told, there were plenty of monks who would not have disagreed with her criticisms. The increasingly vulgar character of the pilgrims at their shrines had not gone unmarked. Particularly resented was the tendency of peasants to camp out in churches and stay up all night telling rude jokes. Some monks, driven to distraction by their 'abominable shouting and unruly singing',[51] would go so far as to lock them out.

Yet invariably, whenever this occurred, the saints themselves would show their disapproval by miraculously unfastening the doors. This was a lesson that most monasteries, not surprisingly, were quick to absorb. Uncouth the peasants might be, but a shrine that could harness their undoubted fervour, and their yearning for wonders, was a shrine with a future. Increasingly, then, far from discouraging the masses, monasteries sought to attract them in ever vaster numbers. Whereas once it had been forbidden to disturb the bones of the saints, now, in the wake of the peace councils, monks began to send their relics out on tour, to the accompaniment of clanging cymbals, soaring anthems and flickering torches. Sometimes, if the holdings of a neighbouring house made it worthwhile, they might arrange a swap. Sometimes, if they felt their own to be inadequate, they might attempt an upgrade. The most audacious example of this took place in Aquitaine, when the monks of the hitherto obscure monastery of St-Jean-d'Angély suddenly announced a truly sensational discovery: the head of John the Baptist. Quite how it had ended up there, buried within a mysterious pyramid of stone, was never fully explained. The enthusiasm of the pilgrims who soon descended upon the monastery, crowding the narrow stairways in their excitement, pushing and shoving their way down into the shrine, ensured that it did not have to be. Even King Robert himself, on a rare trip south, and in dread of the Day of Judgement, came to reverence it. Not surprisingly, then, monks in other monasteries too, keen for a share of the action, began to rifle around in their own crypts. Yet more spectacular finds were duly made. Such discoveries, coming as they did only years before the millennial anniversary of Christ's Passion, powerfully intensified the mood of febrile expectation. 'For it was as though the relics had been waiting for a brilliant resurrection and were now at last, by God's permission, revealed to the gaze of the faithful. Certainly, they brought much comfort to many people.'[52]

But not, however, to all. Sometimes, above the excited hubbub of the pilgrims, dark mutterings about idol worship might be overheard. Heretics, scornful of what they saw as the Church's mummery, flatly refused to respect 'the honour of God's saints'.[53] As a result, monks who wished to boost the profile of their relic holdings had to tread

251

carefully. They could not afford to push their luck too shamelessly. Crowds who felt that they were being taken for a ride might very well turn ugly. Nothing better illustrated this than a particularly over-ambitious attempt at self-promotion by the monastery in Limoges. The monks there, rather than grubbing up some new relics, had opted instead to promote the saint whose bones they already owned. St Martial, it was grandly announced in the autumn of 1028, rather than the obscure missionary that everyone had previously assumed him to be, had in fact been one of the original apostles: the nephew of St Peter, no less. Though this claim was wildly implausible, it had nevertheless secured a heavyweight supporter: Aquitaine's leading historian, Adémar himself. For eight months, displaying yet again his inimitable talent for blending erudition with wilful distortion, the famous scholar cobbled together an impressive number of works designed to prove that St Martial had indeed been an apostle. Finally, on 3 August 1029, the fateful day arrived when the whole campaign was officially to be blessed, at a special service in the cathedral of Limoges.

Adémar, basking in the glow of his achievement, had even invited his parents to come and witness his hour of glory. Unfortunately, however, he had reckoned without the scepticism of an unexpected visitor: a rival scholar, an Italian from Lombardy by the name of Benedict. Ferociously, even as the service was about to begin, the Lombard denounced the whole farrago as an outrage – and Adémar himself as a fraudster. The people of Limoges, far from backing the campaign to proclaim their patron saint an apostle, promptly swung against it. When a panicky Adémar, hurrying out from the service to confront Benedict in public, attempted to press his case, they howled him down. Later that evening, in the monastery itself, the two schol-ars clashed again – and once again it was Adémar who was routed. The following morning, humiliated beyond all hope of recovery, he duly ceded the field to his conqueror and slunk away from Limoges, burn-ing with shame, his reputation in ruins.[54]

But still, despite it all, he could not bear to confess his defeat. Instead, over the next three years, Adémar persisted in arguing his ruined case. Hoax was piled upon hoax; forgery upon forgery. Everything he wrote, in the gathering frenzy of his bitterness, had only the single aim: to prove that St Martial had indeed been a companion of Christ. Adémar, the same monk who in his youth had stood transfixed before a vision of his crucified Lord, now sought, with a phenomenal but twisted display of learning, to imagine himself back into the world in which the human Jesus had lived. A form of madness, no doubt; and yet, if so, it was one that he shared with multitudes beyond the bounds of his monastery, as the 1030s finally dawned. The one-thousandth anniversary of Christ's Passion was now a mere three years away – and upon its approach 'many wonders were made manifest'.[55] And the greatest of them all, a wonder that appeared to 'portend nothing other than the advent of the accursed Antichrist, who, according to divine testimony, is expected to appear at the end of the world',[56] was the resolve of people in unparalleled numbers to set out on a great pilgrimage, not to their local shrine, not to Santiago, not even to Rome, but to the very city which the blessed feet of their Saviour had trodden, and where He had been nailed to a cross, and risen from the dead: Jerusalem.

The swell of this great wave had been building for some decades. Although originally there had been few travellers from the West prepared to make the long and arduous journey to the Holy Land, the years around the Millennium had seen a startling upsurge of pilgrims setting out for Jerusalem. Most, such as that venerable expert on the end days, Adso of Montier-en-Der, were eminent and wealthy: travellers well able to afford a berth on a ship. Indeed, even celebrated princes had been known to make the trip. Fulk Nerra, for instance, taking time off from terrorising his neighbours, had ended up travelling to Jerusalem no fewer than four times. His second journey, made in 1009, had been his most heroic of all: for no sooner had he arrived outside the Church of the Holy Sepulchre than he had found himself caught up in the horrors of its desecration. Braving the dangers with his customary swagger, he had even succeeded in breaking off a fragment of Christ's tomb, and bearing it back in triumphant

piety to Anjou. This formidable achievemen had confirmed his reputation as a near-legendary figure. Yet even Fulk was put in the shade
by the sheer scale of the human tide inspired by the millennium of
the Passion of Christ, a great flood of men and women who were not
necessarily noblemen, or abbots, or bishops, but people of infinitely
humbler stock: 'an innumerable multitude, gathered from across the
whole world, greater than any man before could have hoped to
see'.[57]

And among them was Adémar. Defeated, embittered, and no doubt
conscience-stricken as he was, there was nothing to keep him in
Aquitaine. Leaving his own monastery late in 1032, he travelled first to
Limoges, where he deposited his forgeries in the library of St Martial:
a dossier so detailed and convincing that within a few decades it would
serve to convince everyone of his case, and win for him a posthumous
victory over all his critics. That done, Adémar then went back on to
the open road, joining the throngs of other penitents who were similarly heading east. Most of these did not, as had for so long been the
custom, take a ship for the Holy Land; for since the Millennium, and
the conversion of the Hungarians, it had become possible to make the
entire journey overland. True, Hungary itself was still not without its
dangers: one monk from Regensburg, travelling across its plains in the
early 1030s, was startled to see a dragon swooping menacingly overhead, 'its plumed head the height of a mountain, its body covered with
scales like shields of iron'.[58] Nor were such monsters the limit of the
perils that a pilgrim might be obliged to face: for beyond Hungary
there awaited cheating Greeks, and officious Saracens, and thieving
Bedouins. Yet it was in the very rigours of a pilgrimage that its truest
value lay – and Adémar, arriving at length before the gates of the Holy
City in the fateful year 1033, could only trust that he had proved himself worthy to witness whatever wonders might soon unfold.

The heavens, however, remained resolutely empty. Antichrist did
not appear. The end of the world stood postponed, and all those pilgrims who had assembled in such huge numbers on the Mount of
Olives found themselves waiting in vain for their Saviour's return.

Soon enough, as 1033 became 1034, most of them set off back for home. But not all. There were some, whether through a surfeit of 'indescribable joy',[59] as the pious proclaimed, or perhaps through despair, who would never leave Jerusalem – except for heaven. And Adémar was one of them. He died in 1034. 'Come, eternal King,' he had implored, in a prayer that was probably the last thing he ever wrote, 'come and watch over your kingdom, our sacrifice, our priesthood. Come, Lord ruler; come snatch away the nations from error. Come Lord, Saviour of the world.'[60]

But the Lord had not come. And still the fallen world ran its course.

Things Can Only Get Better

There were those who felt relief. Even by the standards of the previous decades, the years preceding the millennium of Christ's Passion had been terrible ones: fit, certainly, to give a foretaste of what Antichrist's coming might actually have meant for the world. Rains had fallen without cease, famine had been universal, rumours of cannibalism too. In the Burgundian town of Tournus, it was said, ready-cooked human flesh had been sold openly in the marketplace. At Cluny, the granaries had stood empty; and Odilo, so as to raise funds for the starving, had been reduced to selling some of the monastery's most famous treasures, including even the jewel-encrusted orb donated to it by the Emperor Henry II. Only wolves and castellans, both of them preying on the ruined poor, had profited from the horrors of the times. Yet miraculously, with the coming of 1033, everything seemed to improve. Rudolf Glaber, as assiduous as ever in tracing the touch of God's finger upon the world, marked from his monastery how the violent rainstorms had abruptly ceased. Instead, 'the happy face of the sky shone and blew with gentle breezes, and with serenity proclaimed the magnanimity of the Creator. The whole surface of the earth began to flourish. The harvests promised to be splendid. Want itself was ended.'[61]

Or so Glaber enthused. In truth, his sudden mood of optimism was no less unbalanced, perhaps, than had been his earlier obsession with terrifying portents of doom. The skies might well have cleared – but on earth there was still violence and lawlessness and oppression. To those who had imagined that the convulsions of the age might spell the imminence of the end days, and who had laboured mightily in the expectation of their coming, the failure of the New Jerusalem to descend could hardly be regarded as a cause for unconfined rejoicing. Profound and desperate emotions had been stirred. The penitents journeying to the Holy Land, the crowds flocking to the peace councils, the heretics retiring to the woods: all had dared to hope that they might see Christ descend in His glory, and set the world to rights. Now that hope was gone. Among the poor, no doubt, whose yearning for a reign of saints the Church had sought to orchestrate as well as to temper, the sense of disappointment was especially devastating. Even Glaber could not help noting how, for all the sunny weather, the menace of knightly violence had, if anything, only darkened. 'Like dogs returning to their vomit or pigs to wallowing in their mire',[62] the castellans had not forsaken their taste for robbery, no matter the pious oaths they might have sworn. The Millennium had passed, and the earthly order, by which the strong were set above the weak, had not dissolved. Still, on its rocky outcrop, the castle continued to lower.

Yet if it was the poor who had most cause to feel despair, then they were not alone. Bishops and monks too had yearned to believe in the possibilities of an authentic peace of God: a peace, not of iron, but of love. Now, even if they could not readily admit to it, many found themselves oppressed by a sense of loss. The passage of the years, which previously had struck them as pregnant with mystery and meaning, appeared abruptly leached of both. Time had lost its edge. To a degree unprecedented in the history of the West, the Christian people felt themselves poised on the brink of a new beginning: a sensation that many found disturbing rather than any cause for exhilaration. The past, which had always been valued by them as the surest guide to

their future, had suddenly come to appear, in the wake of time's failure to end, a place remote and alien. In truth, the gulf which separated
the new millennium from the wreckage of the old had not opened up
overnight. Years, decades, centuries of transformation had served to
create a landscape in the West that Charlemagne, let alone
Constantine, would have found unrecognisable. Yet the consciousness
of this, the consciousness of change, was indeed something new. 'Such
is the dispensation of the Almighty – that many things which once
existed be cast aside by those who come in their wake.'[63]

So reflected Arnold of Regensburg: the same monk who, a few years
earlier, had seen the great dragon swooping above the plains of
Hungary. Evidently a man with a taste for the sensational, Arnold
openly disdained the past as a wilderness, one fit to be tamed and
cleared, just as the dark forests, with their idol-haunted, corpse-hung
groves, had been hacked down by Christian axes to make way for
churches and spreading fields. His was a startling perspective, certainly – and yet less exceptional than it might have been only a few
decades before. 'The new should change the old – and the old, if it has
no contribution to make to the order of things, should be utterly jet-
tisoned.'[64] There were many, during the feverish and expectant years
of the millennium of Christ's life, who had come to share in this opinion. Nor had the spirit of reform died in 1033. If anything, indeed, the
opposite: for the failure of Christ to establish His kingdom on earth
had left many reformers all the more determined to do it for Him.

And this, at its most radical, was a dream of liberty. The example of
Cluny, which owed a duty of obedience to no lord save St Peter, continued to serve reformers as the most luminous one of all. There was
nothing that more dazzlingly proclaimed the supernatural purity of
the monastery than its freedom from the bullying of officious outsiders. And yet, in reality, Cluny was not wholly exempt from mortal
supervision. Although St Peter was a mighty patron, his protection
could only ever be as effective as that provided by his earthly vicar, the
Pope. A not altogether comforting reflection, it might have been
thought – for Rome was many miles from Cluny, and the papacy

invariably racked by scandal. Nevertheless, over the decades, a succession of popes had proved themselves unexpectedly muscular guardians of Odilo and his monastery. Letters dispatched from the Lateran, warning the local bishops and princes to keep their hands off Cluny and to respect its independence, had proved surprisingly effective. Rather to its own surprise, the papacy had found itself able to snap its fingers and watch the great men of Burgundy jump. Tentatively at first, and then with an increasing peremptoriness, it had sought to take advantage of this hitherto unsuspected power. As a result, the papal defence of Cluny had begun to seem to many an increasingly suggestive one. If the Bishop of Rome could poke his nose into the affairs of Burgundy, then why not those of everywhere else? To be sure, a pope such as Benedict IX, who had bribed his way to the papal throne in 1032 at the scandalously youthful age of eighteen, was generally far too busy indulging his insatiable sexual appetites to explore the full implications of this question; but there were those prepared to do it for him. The papacy might be sunk in depravity, yet there were many in the ranks of the reformers prepared to view it, nevertheless, as the best hope for a tainted and tottering world. Only a pope, the heir of St Peter, could possibly hope to secure for the entire Church what had already been secured for Cluny. Only a pope could properly serve as the champion of its liberty.

Which in turn made the restoration of the papacy to a fitting state of grace a matter of the utmost – indeed cosmic – urgency. No longer could it be permitted to serve as the plaything of vicious Roman dynasts. Yet as the rumours that swirled around Pope Benedict grew steadily more scandalous, fetid with tales of sorcery, bestiality and murder, so the notion that the papacy might ever reform itself appeared grotesquely far fetched. How fortunate it was, then, for the spiritual health of the Christian people, that the Holy Father was not their only potential leader. 'It is in the king and emperor that we possess the supreme defender on earth of our liberty,'[65] the princes of Germany and Italy had solemnly declared, in praise of Conrad II. The conceit of Otto III, who had believed it his God-given duty to redeem the world, still flourished mightily at the court of his successors. Vicar of St Peter a pope might be, but an emperor, at his coronation, would be hailed as something even more spectacular: the representative of Christ Himself. What monarch could possibly doubt, then, having listened to such an awesome salute, that he had an absolute duty to intrude upon the dimensions of the spiritual and offer his leadership to the Church? Impregnated as he had been by the fearful power of the chrism, he was no longer merely a king but 'a sharer in the priestly ministry'.[66]

Certainly, within the limits of the *Reich* itself, no emperor had ever hesitated to treat even the grandest bishops as his subordinates. All were subject to him; all had depended for their original election upon his say-so. As both symbol and demonstration of this, it was the emperor himself who would preside over a bishop's investiture, handing the nominated candidate a staff shaped like a shepherd's crook, and obliging him to swear a ferocious oath of loyalty. If such a ritual struck many as not wholly dissimilar to the submission of a vassal to his lord, then perhaps this was only fitting. In the *Reich*, far more than in any other Christian realm, bishops had a formal duty to uphold the royal order. Indeed, there were many of them who ruled in the place of dukes or counts over immense swaths of imperial territory. They served the emperor as his counsellors; they provided men for his armies; they administered his estates. Take away the bishops, and the empire would barely have a government at all.

Yet if the emperor had no compunction about putting the Church to work for him, then the Church, in turn, naturally expected the emperor to serve it as its protector. Such a duty, in the early years of the new millennium, had come to appear an ever more pressing one. As in France, so in Germany: a concern to secure bridgeheads of the supernatural upon a sin-infected earth had become a veritable obsession of anxious Christians. Perhaps this was hardly surprising: for Cluny lay no great distance beyond the *Reich*'s western border. Yet if Odilo was as much the favourite of emperors as he was of popes and kings, then he was far from being the only one. In the monasteries of the Low Countries and the Rhineland especially, the roots of reform reached back many decades, and owed little to the example of Cluny. Above all, over the course of the decades on either side of the Millennium, they had served to foster a novel and unsettling obsession: one with which Adémar, at any rate, might have empathised. What in Aquitaine, however, was confined to visions and feverish dreams could be found displayed for all to see in the naves of prominent churches in the Rhineland.

As early as 970, a crucifix had been erected in the cathedral of Cologne that portrayed something truly shocking: an image of the Saviour Himself, His eyes closed, His head lolling in death, His feet and hands nailed to the instrument of his execution. Half a century on, and the notion of 'fastening to Christ's Cross the picture of a dying man'[67] remained a horrifying one to many Christians – and yet already the custom had spread as far as England. God Himself was being rendered human. Indeed, a model of imitation: for fascination with the grisly details of Christ's sufferings invariably shaded, among the leaders of the imperial reform movement, into a yearning to emulate them. One celebrated abbot from the Low Countries, Poppo of Stablo, was especially admired for beating himself on the chest with a jagged stone whenever he had a spare moment, and for never smiling. Monks who found themselves subjected to Poppo's disciplines perhaps not surprisingly tended to loathe him – but a succession of emperors stood in awe of his austerities. So it was, for instance, that when he announced himself appalled by a craze among the daredevils of the court for covering themselves in honey and then allowing a ravenous bear to lick them clean, Henry II promptly and contritely banned it. So it was too that Conrad II, despite being so given to worldly pleasures that he was widely rumoured to have sold his soul to the Devil, treated the fearsomely humourless abbot with the most wide-eyed respect, and entrusted many of his favourite monasteries to Poppo's flinty zeal. Such a relationship appeared to optimists a shining model for the future of Christendom: Caesar and saintly churchman united in the heroic task of reform.

In 1039, with the death of Conrad, this task was inherited by his son, a young man uniquely well qualified to shoulder it. Henry III, in contrast with his father, was a king of rare piety and conscientiousness. Like Poppo, and for an identical reason, it was his earnest ambition never to laugh. In 1043, when he married Agnes, the daughter of the Duke of Aquitaine, jesters were solemnly banned from the nuptials. It was true that Poppo himself, suspicious of the reputation of the Aquitainians for frivolity and luxurious fashions, had greeted the coming of a Frenchwoman to the imperial court with alarmed disapproval – but he need not have worried. Agnes, a descendant of the founder of Cluny, was in truth a bride ideally suited to her husband: together, whenever they were able, the royal couple sought to attend Mass at least five times every day.

Yet Henry, though sensitive and melancholic, yielded to none of his predecessors in the imperious character of his rule. His displays of humility, heartfelt though they were, did nothing to diminish his firm conviction that the sway of the Christian people had been granted him directly by God. In 1043, when Henry graciously announced from the pulpit of Constance cathedral that he forgave all his enemies, he did so as the head of a peace conference: one that had been summoned, not by his bishops, but by himself. A year later, when he appeared before his soldiers as a public penitent, it was as a victor on a corpse-strewn battlefield, amid the broken banners of rebels shattered on his sword. As a worthy offering to St Peter, he could think of no more suitable gift than 'a golden spear'[68] – a trophy wrested from a rival warlord. Such a king, eager for the legitimisation that only an anointing in Rome could bring, was hardly the man to feel overly inhibited in his dealings with even the most troublesome of pontiffs. Which was just as well: for by the autumn of 1046, when Henry finally felt secure enough in his authority over the *Reich* to lead an expedition southwards into Italy, he found not one pope waiting for him there, but three.

This truly monstrous state of affairs provided a fitting climax to the scandal-stained career of Benedict IX. Two years previously, with even the normally unshockable Romans starting to weary of his crimes, the

Crescentians, heirs of the would-be pope-maker who had been beheaded by Otto III, had launched a sudden attempt to seize back the papacy for themselves. Taking the Holy Father by surprise, they had succeeded in driving him temporarily from Rome, and installing as his replacement their own local bishop, an anonymous patsy quite unworthy of his new title Sylvester III. Two years on, and Benedict was back, installed on his old throne, and defiantly eyeballing the Crescentians: wretched testimony to the abiding relish among Roman dynasts for cat-fights in the Lateran. Yet already the mastery of the papacy was starting to evade them: for no longer was it merely the local nobility who aspired to secure the election of a pope. Prominent reformers, appalled by the descent of Rome yet further into the mire, had wearied of merely wringing their hands. Accordingly, in the spring of 1045, they had thrown their weight behind the election of a third pope, the son of a converted Jew, as rich as he was pious, who had taken the name Gregory VI, and stirringly proclaimed himself the patron of reform. Here, for the young and idealistic, had been a moment of hope that they would never forget.

Typical of those inspired by Gregory's election was a former pupil of his, a brilliant and pugnacious monk by the name of Hildebrand, whose humble origins as the son of a Tuscan carpenter had served only to emphasise all the more decisively his status as a high-flyer.[69] Educated first in a monastery opposite the Palatine that had always served as Odilo's favourite rest-stop in Rome, and then in the Lateran itself, he had come to burn with a passionate conviction that the ordering of the fallen world was the papacy's alone to achieve. In Gregory VI, Hildebrand believed, the Church had at last found a worthy champion. He duly offered the new Pope his tigerish devotion. Gregory, in turn, appointed Hildebrand his chaplain. The bond between the two men would never fail. And yet by 1046, barely a year into his papacy, Gregory's credibility was already coming under fire, even from those who had originally supported him, as the full, mortifying details of his election began to dribble out.

For Gregory, it emerged, had dirtier hands than had ever been supposed. Benedict IX was his godson; and the wealthy Gregory, in an attempt to persuade his incorrigibly avaricious rival to stand down, had slipped him a hefty bribe. That this might have been regarded as a problem appeared never to have crossed Gregory's mind: for it was precisely the kind of manoeuvre that the Roman elite had always taken for granted. Times, however, had changed. Among prominent reformers, all of whom were pledged to the purification of the Church, the notion that a priestly office, let alone the papacy, might be bought and sold for profit was utterly horrifying. Indeed, so they pointed out, it was one that had haunted the ministry of the very apostles themselves: for St Peter, in the earliest years of his preaching, had been approached by a wizard named Simon, and offered gold in exchange for his ability to work miracles. 'I see that you are in the gall of bitterness,' the Prince of Apostles had replied dismissively, 'and in the bond of iniquity';[70] and ever since the sin of trading in supernatural powers and offices had been known as 'simony'. True, Gregory's perplexity at finding himself branded guilty of such an offence was, perhaps, understandable – 'for so widespread had the custom become that hardly anyone even knew it to be a sin'.[71] Those who held the shining example of Cluny before them, however, and who argued for a clergy liberated from the reins of the rich and powerful, had no doubt that it was indeed a sin – and a pestiferous one at that. And among their number – fatefully for Gregory – was Henry III.

Who was, after all, a would-be emperor – and impatient to be anointed. Sublimely confident in his own right to order the Church, Henry duly prepared himself to cut the Gordian knot. Shortly before Christmas, he summoned the three rival popes to Sutri, a small town just north of Rome. Gregory – the only one to appear – was formally deposed by a hastily convened synod; so too Sylvester. Three days later, in Rome itself, Benedict was also given the push. Henry, taking a leaf out of Otto III's book, then nominated one of his own countrymen to serve as pope, who, obediently moving into the Lateran, took the name Clement II. A few days later, on Christmas Day itself, the German king was formally anointed as the heir to Charlemagne.

263

Few among the ranks of the reformers thought to raise a protest against his high-handedness. Indeed, joining in the salutes to him as God's representative on earth was none other than the by now fabulously venerable Odilo: potent testimony to the widespread enthusiasm for the labour of surgery that Henry had performed upon the papacy. True, there were some who still clung to their former loyalties: Hildebrand, for instance, stubborn in all things, flatly refused to abandon Gregory, even when the wretched abdicatee was exiled to the Rhineland. Yet he could not dispute the calibre of the men appointed by the new emperor to the Lateran; nor the earnestness of his attempts to wrest control of it once and all from criminality. When Clement II, less than a year into his papacy, died of lead poisoning, and the incorrigible Benedict, borne upon a great surge of bribery and intimidation, swept back into the Lateran for an unprecedented third time, Henry showed not the slightest hesitation in having him kicked off his throne yet again. A second German pope was dispatched to Rome; and then, when he also promptly expired, a third.

By now it was the winter of 1048 – and Gregory VI as well was dead. Hildebrand, ever passionate in his loyalties, was free at last to give them to someone else. All he needed was a worthy recipient. That December, in a mark of the favour with which he had already come to be regarded in imperial circles, the young priest was summoned to a council held in the ancient city of Worms. There, with the blaze of the king's presence illumining the winter nights, and spilling reflections across the black and icy waters of the Rhine, he met Henry's nominee for St Peter's throne. 'A new light was seen to rise upon the world.'[72] Certainly, it did not take Hildebrand long to know himself in the presence of a leader truly worthy of his devotion.

And so, of course, he pledged it.

Sailing from Byzantium

Hildebrand's enthusiasm was hardly surprising. Bruno of Toul was the very model of a prince of the Church: tall, good-looking and a distant cousin of the emperor himself. Proficient in all the skills required of an imperial bishop, he had served variously as a judge, a general and a diplomat. Yet Bruno's talents were not merely those required of an earthly lordship. At his birth, it was said, 'the whole of his little body had been found marked with tiny crosses'[73] in a certain portent of a saintly future. And so it had proved. Much given as he was to spectacular displays of charity, and even to washing the feet of the poor, Bruno appeared to his admirers that most splendid of paradoxes, the ideal Christian leader: 'for he combined the wisdom of a serpent with the innocence of a dove'.[74] Hildebrand certainly thought so. All the hopes for the reform of the Church that he had previously pinned on Gregory he now transferred to Bruno. That same December, he signed up to accompany his new hero on the road back to Rome.

A journey that in itself gave a potent foretaste of the pontificate that was to come. Braving the snows and floods of winter, Bruno made his way southwards unaccompanied by any of Henry's soldiers, and dressed only in the robes of a humble pilgrim. Angels, it was said, spoke to him on the way, and when at last he entered Rome he did so barefoot. Even then, it was only once the locals had publicly implored him to become their bishop that he deigned to take his place on the throne of St Peter, and adopted the name Leo IX. These gestures were shrewdly calculated to win him the support of his ever-fractious Roman flock; but aimed as well at the entirety of the Christian people. Leo may have been an imperial nominee, yet it was crucial to both his and Henry's purposes that they demonstrate as publicly as possible that no money had passed between them. Such was the scale of the task that they faced, in labouring to secure for the Church a new beginning, purged once and for all of the pollution of worldliness, that neither man could afford to be branded a simonist. Tellingly, in a vision granted him shortly before becoming Pope, Leo had been shown a hideous old woman dressed in filthy rags, who had importuned him and tugged at his robes; 'and when the man of the Lord was driven by her unmannerly conduct to mark her face with the sign of the cross, the hag fell to the ground like a dead woman but rose up again, her appearance now one of wonderful beauty'.[75] That power, to draw a sign of the Cross upon the body of the Church, and to watch it restored to its former loveliness, was one that Leo had no wish to compromise. Too much depended on him. Too much was at stake.

Energy and determination, ambition and emollience: such were the qualities that Leo's long career as an imperial bishop had served to hone. Now he had the chance to test them on the grandest stage of all. Only weeks into his papacy, and already he was holding a council in Rome: by its terms, the laws against simony were thunderously reaffirmed, and several simonist bishops deposed, while the Bishop of Sutri, who had falsely protested his innocence, was struck down by a stroke. Satisfying developments all – and yet only a beginning. Leo, possessed by a literally cosmic sense of mission, was hardly the man to rest content within the limits of Rome. No sooner had the council in the Lateran been concluded than he was off again, retracing his steps. By June he was back in his native Rhineland, and by early October he had crossed into the kingdom of France – the first pope to visit it in 171 years. As in Rome, so along the route of his northern travels, his calls for the clergy to reform itself tended to be greeted by the local bishops with a mixture of perplexity and outrage. Most of them, far from agreeing with Leo that simony was indeed a mortal threat to the health of Christendom, persisted in regarding it as a perfectly sensible and unexceptional practice, and one that had served to keep the Church on its feet for centuries. Not surprisingly, when Leo summoned the bishops of France to a council in Reims, a majority kept well away. All were promptly excommunicated. But even those few who did attend were given cause to regret it.

For as the bishops entered the church where the council was to be held, and bowed before the altar, they found themselves confronted by an awful and intimidating sight. There, brooding over the entire scene, was a casket containing the bones of Reims' patron saint. Summoned to stand and swear on the relics that they had not paid for their positions, most of the bishops opted to remain in their seats and squirm in mortified silence. When one archbishop did rise and try to defend a colleague, he found himself struck miraculously dumb by the power of the outraged saint. His client fled in disgrace that same night; and, from that moment on, a succession of simonist bishops were obliged to stammer out their confessions and grovel for mercy. Indeed only one man emerged from the proceedings with his reputation truly burnisshed. Odilo, after more than half a century as the head of Christendom's most celebrated monastery, had finally died at the beginning of the year; and all eyes were duly fixed upon his successor. How fortunate it was, then, that not so much as a hint of impropriety had attached itself to the election of Hugh of Semur. Making his public confession before the Pope, the new abbot of Cluny forthrightly denied any wrongdoing. 'The flesh was willing,' he explained, 'but mind and reason revolted.'[76] A statement that was, in its perfect fusion of worldliness and simplicity, almost worthy of Leo himself.

Yet if Abbot Hugh's backing for the cause of reform was welcome, it hardly came as a great surprise. What did astound the papal party, astound and delight it, was the seething, raucous mass of supporters who had flocked to Reims from miles around, immense crowds of the faithful who kept themselves and the Holy Father awake all night by singing and shouting his name, and then, in the morning, by jeering the unfortunate simonists as they slunk through the streets to confession. The millennium of the Passion had passed, and the New Jerusalem had not arrived; but still, among the poor and the trampled, there remained an undimmed yearning for a peace of God. Christ might have been delayed, but there before them was the Pope, the Vicar of St Peter himself, no longer a vague abstraction but a man of flesh and blood – and demanding changes of the priesthood that the oppressed were only too desperate to see. A Church no longer in hock

267

to grasping earthly lords – what would this provide the wretched if not a true sanctuary? No wonder, then, that Leo's tour of the lands of the North, 'unprecedented in our time', should have served to generate 'such jubilation and applause'.[77] It went without saying that Leo himself, the cousin of Caesar, had not the slightest intention of placing himself at the head of a band of peasants. Although events at Reims certainly were exhilarating, they also served as a warning to the Pope and his advisers that excitement might easily get out of hand. More than once the crowds had indulged themselves with a riot. Psalms and screams had intermingled in the streets. Nevertheless, the discovery that they had the full force of popular opinion behind them was one that the reformers would never forget. It lent them reassurance, and confidence, and even greater ambition.

Certainly, as Leo trailed his triumphant way back to Italy, it was evident to his exultant supporters that a pope might indeed serve to make the weather far beyond the limits of Rome. Some, however, drew conclusions that were even more soaring. 'The royal priesthood of the holy Roman see constitutes an empire both heavenly and earthly.'[78] This vaunting claim was made by a man renowned, not for excitability but rather for his emotionless, indeed chilly, powers of reasoning. Humbert of Moyenmoutier was a monk from the same region of Lorraine in which Leo had served as a bishop, and the two men had long been confidants. Summoned to accompany the Pope to the Lateran, the haughty and brilliant Humbert had soon emerged as his effective number two. Boldly, he set about pushing Leo's claims to leadership of the Church to ever more potent extremes. Stitching together musty precedents with a lawyerly dexterity, the Donation of Constantine not least, Humbert found himself able to demonstrate with great conviction a most momentous conclusion: that the papacy had an ancient entitlement to the rule of the entire Christian world. Yet even that was not the limit of where his logic led him. 'For such is the reverence among Christians for the holder of the apostolic office of Rome,' Humbert coolly insisted, 'that they prefer to receive the holy commandments and the traditions of their faith from the mouth of the head of the Church rather than from the holy Scriptures or the writings of the Fathers.'[79] Here was justification, in effect, not merely for papal weight-throwing, but for permanent revolution.

Quite what this might mean in practical terms was a different matter. There was a hint, however, to be glimpsed in Humbert's promotion, in 1050, to a new post: that of cardinal bishop. While this title was venerable, dating back almost to the time of Constantine, the cardinalate itself had always played an essentially ceremonial role in the life of the Roman Church: serving the Pope as little more than a gilded dumping ground for superannuated aristocrats. Now, however, under the radical new management style introduced to the Lateran by Leo, all that began to change. Indeed, remarkably, within the space of only a few hectic years, he would succeed in transforming the college of cardinals into a veritable powerhouse of administrative talent manned, not by decrepit locals, but by prominent reformers drawn from far beyond the limits of Rome. Leo, as practical as he was visionary, had never been so naïve as to imagine that his ambitions for the Christian people could be achieved merely at the prompting of his own exhortations. Accordingly, then, he looked to his ministers to provide him with what he himself, as an imperial bishop, had once provided Henry III: government. Humbert and his colleagues duly set to work, sweeping away cobwebs from the creaking administrative machinery of the Lateran, dusting down ancient books of law that might serve the papal purpose and posting legates with imperious missives across the length and breadth of Christendom. The duties that might be paid, in short, less to a bishop than to a Caesar.

Except, of course, that there were limits to what even a servant as wily and efficient as Humbert could achieve. Startling although the sudden starburst of papal prestige appeared to dazzled Christians, it remained, to a large degree, a thing of smoke and mirrors. Above all, Leo lacked what, in a fallen world, even the humblest castellan depended upon for survival: an iron fist. This, as it had done for centuries, still threatened the papacy with danger. Rome remained a city on the front line of the Latin world. In Sicily, of which Humbert had

The Italy of Leo IX and his successors

rather optimistically been made the archbishop, Islam was putting down roots more deeply than ever, with Christians a fast-shrinking minority penned into the island's north-east corner, and Palermo, its staggeringly wealthy capital, become almost completely Muslim. In Apulia, along the Adriatic coast, Constantinople maintained her grip upon the region's major ports, and nurtured her inveterate ambition to secure the whole of southern Italy for the *Basileus*. Yet these two foes, the Saracens and the Byzantines, formidable powers though they might be, offered at least the reassurance of familiarity. Far more alarming was a menace that appeared to have sprung up from nowhere, and almost overnight. In 1050, following up his northern tour, the ever itchy-footed Leo headed southwards. What he found there stunned and appalled him. It appeared that nothing had changed since the days of Otto II. Everywhere there stretched blackened fields, ruined vineyards and half-burned churches. In villages ashen and abandoned, or along empty, silence-haunted roads, it was not unusual to find twisted corpses, veiled beneath white dust and fed upon by flies. And often, on the brow of a distant hill, there might be glimpsed a sinister presence: the silhouettes of horsemen. These were not Saracens, however – nor Byzantines. Instead, shockingly, they were Latin Christians, the compatriots of five bishops who just the previous year had been delegates at the Pope's own synod of Reims, immigrants to Italy only recently descended from the margins of the North: warriors, men of iron, sprung from 'that most restless of nations – the Normans'.[80]

And that they were savage, even by the standards of murderous brutality that had for so long prevailed in the South, was an article of faith among all who had ever had the misfortune to confront them – whether native, or Byzantine, or Arab. Indeed, an aptitude for inspiring terror was what had originally been the Normans' primary selling point. In the war-torn badlands of Apulia, hired swords had always been at a premium; and anyone with a horse and armour was in a seller's market. In 1018, a band of Norman travellers had been recruited to take part in a revolt against the Byzantines;

four years later, they were garrisoning a Byzantine fort against an invasion by Henry II. This provided a stirring precedent for any cash-strapped knight with a taste for adventure and violence. All that was needed to make it in southern Italy, it appeared, was a ready sword and a facility for treachery. Soon enough, like the scent of spilled blood borne to wolves, news of the pickings to be had in southern Italy had begun to sweep Normandy. Adventurers from the duchy, and from neighbouring counties too, had hurried to join the gold rush. The trickle of freebooters had rapidly swelled into a flood. Not, however, that their leaders had been content to stay mercenaries for long. 'For the Normans are avid for rapine,' as one Italian put it bluntly, 'and possess an insatiable enthusiasm for seizing what belongs to others.'[81] Above all, just like any castellan back in France, they wanted land.

A consideration that the natives had been fatally slow to take into account. Already by 1030, in a spectacularly short-sighted gesture, the ruler of Naples had granted a Norman freebooter his own fortress some ten miles north of the city, and awarded him the rank of count. In 1042, on the opposite side of the peninsula, a second Norman warlord, William of Hauteville, had been elected by his followers the Count of Apulia. Such a title was without the faintest shred of legal authority, of course; but William, who had not won his nickname of 'Ironarm' for nothing, had made every effort to give it some heft. The same tactics of terrorism and intimidation that had left entire regions of France studded with makeshift castles had been deployed to no less devastating effect against the hapless communities of Apulia. Nothing had served to throw the predators off course. Even the death of William himself in 1046 had led only to his replacement as count by Drogo, his brother. Indeed, the Hautevilles, like the Normans themselves, appeared veritably hydra-headed.

One year later, a third sibling, Robert, had arrived in Italy – and immediately set about giving a masterclass in how to raise an enduring lordship from nothing. Mistrusted by Drogo – and not without justification – for his alarming combination of talent and ambition, he had been briskly dispatched to Scribla, an out-of-the-way fortress in Calabria, the toe of Italy, where it had been intended by his brother that he should sit and rot. Robert, however, despite finding himself surrounded by swamps, the droning of mosquitoes and little else, was hardly the man to moulder. Resolutely, he had set about bettering his fortunes. Despite his initial lack of either men or gold, a genius for brigandage had soon served to win him both. One particular trademark was to set fire to crops, and then demand payment for putting out the flames; another was to ambush the local bigwigs by dragging them down from their horses.

Yet Robert did not depend solely upon gangsterism to get his way. Brutal he might be – but he was also renowned for his generosity. Even at his very poorest, he made sure to scatter largesse. Foot-soldiers who signed up to follow him could do so confident – such were Robert's talents as a horse thief – that they would soon be mounted knights. His reputation was an enviable one: a lord who made it a point of honour always to do well by his followers. A lord, furthermore, who was evidently going places. By 1050, a mere three years after his first arrival in Calabria, Robert 'had gorged himself on land'.[82] Not only had he left the swamps of Scribla far behind him, but he had won himself a well-connected wife, the loyalty of over two hundred knights and a new nickname: '*Guiscard*', 'the cunning one'.

Men such as Robert could not afford to pause for a moment in the pursuit of their ambitions. Conscious of themselves as a tiny minority in a hostile and resentful land, and nervously aware of just how precarious their situation was, the Norman captains and their knights knew that they had little recourse but to persist with their strategy of terror. Certainly, they were in no mood to listen to demands that they 'cease their cruelties and abandon their oppression of their poor'[83] – not even when the demands came from a pope. A few weeks into his tour of southern Italy, then, and already Leo had concluded that the Normans were a challenge even more pressing than simony.

Which meant that it was his duty, as the shepherd of the Christian people, to confront and muzzle them. But how? That April, a sudden

273

diversion from the Pope's customary business of holding synods and lecturing bishops served to offer a clue. Leaving the lowlands of Apulia behind him, Leo took a road that wound upwards over crags and through deep beech forests to the summit of a mist-haunted mountain named Gargano. Here, back in 493, the archangel Michael had materialised suddenly before a startled cowherd, and announced that a nearby cave was to serve him as a shrine; more than half a millennium on, a great radiance of candles and golden fittings illumined the chapels that had been furnished within the cavernous and dripping depths. 'Flourishing in joy and bliss',[84] the sanctuary was as numinous with a sense of mystery as any in Christendom: for what Gargano offered pilgrims was nothing less than an intersection with the glory and terror that was to come at the end of time. 'General of the hosts of heaven',[85] St Michael had been titled: fittingly enough, for he it was, before the Day of Judgement, who was destined to slay Antichrist on the Mount of Olives, and to overthrow the dragon, 'that ancient serpent, who is called the Devil'.[86] No wonder, then, that the fame of his shrine had come to spread far beyond the limits of Apulia – and to strike a particular resonance with those mighty warriors of God, the kings of Saxony. Both Henry the Fowler and Otto the Great had ordered the image of St Michael inscribed upon their battle standards; Otto II and Theophanu had travelled as pilgrims to Gargano itself; and Otto III, as penance for the atrocities that marked his time in Rome, had toiled barefoot up the mountain to the shrine. Even in the wake of Henry II's death, with the *Reich* ruled by a dynasty that was no longer Saxon, reverence for the warrior archangel had remained as passionate as ever in imperial circles. Leo certainly shared in it. After all, as Bruno of Toul, he had not shrunk from emulating St Michael, and leading soldiers into battle – although naturally, as befitted a priest, he had refrained from drawing a sword himself.

And to be sure, Leo was far too alert to all the various shades of opinion in Christendom not to appreciate that there were many who regarded the martial spirit of his own native Church with the profoundest suspicion. Nevertheless, as he prayed within the candle-washed depths of Mount Gargano, and gazed up at icons of St Michael fitted out in the radiant weaponry of heaven, he was surely asking himself a number of fateful questions. What, for instance, if exhortation and diplomacy could not serve to rein in the ravening of the Normans? And what if Henry III, the anointed Caesar, preoccupied as he was with the breaking of the princes of the *Reich* to his will, refused to embark upon a second Italian adventure? What, in such circumstances, would Leo's responsibility be? The answer appeared as unavoidable as it was inconceivable. Surely the Pope himself would then have to raise an army, ride to war and crush the enemies of the Christian people, amid all the shock and carnage of battle. For what alternative would there be?

An excruciating dilemma. Small wonder that Leo should have found himself squirming painfully on its horns – and ever more so as the crisis deepened. In the summer of 1051, Drogo de Hauteville was assassinated in his private chapel, prompting his outraged compatriots to tighten the screws yet further on the wretched natives. Simultaneously, smooth-talking ambassadors from Constantinople had suddenly become a fixture in the Lateran: for the *Basileus*, waking up to the appalling prospect that the very existence of a Byzantine Italy might be at stake, had decided, for want of any better alternative, to seek out an alliance with Rome. In the summer of 1053, with no assistance received from the *Reich* beyond a contingent of seven hundred Swabian swordsmen, Leo had finally had enough. A momentous step was taken. For the first time, a pope formally blessed a standard of battle. Princes from across southern Italy were summoned to follow it against the Norman devils. Absolution from the stain of bloodshed – 'an impunity for their crimes'[87] – was promised to all who answered the call. Here was no mere raising of local levies, such as popes had often done before, but rather a startling and fateful innovation: the launching of nothing less than a papally sanctioned holy war.

And it was the pontiff himself who led his army. Even though Leo, during the course of the synod at Reims, had solemnly reaffirmed the age-old prohibition against a priest bearing arms, his presence out on campaign was certainly sufficient to swell the numbers at his command. Loathing of the Normans did the rest. As the grey outline of Mount Gargano began to loom on the eastern horizon, and a rendezvous with his new Byzantine allies drew ever nearer, Leo could feel well content. Even when the enemy, frantically mustering their scattered forces, and riding hell for leather northwards, unexpectedly interposed themselves between the papal forces and those of Constantinople, he was not unduly alarmed. The Normans, despite their success in keeping their opponents apart, were exhausted, hungry and comprehensively outnumbered. Against all the teeming hordes kicking up dust behind the Pope, they could set barely three thousand. Unsurprisingly, they sought a truce. Equally unsurprisingly, the Pope refused to grant one. Having laboured so hard to get the Normans where he wanted them, he was now resolved to crush them once and for all. Except that the Normans did not wait to be crushed. Instead, without warning, and even as their ambassadors were keeping Leo distracted still with negotiations, their horsemen threw themselves upon the papal ranks, with all the ferocity of starving wolves assailing a flock of sheep. The Italians turned tail and fled. Only the Swabians, hulking, long-haired giants armed with massive, two-handed swords, stood firm amid the rout. Not until the end of the day were they finally overwhelmed. Pre-eminent among the captains who finally succeeded in trampling them down, 'slicing off their heads from their shoulders, and splitting open their guts',[88] was Robert Guiscard.

Pope Leo IX, standing on the battlements of the nearby town of Civitate, watched it all. As the moans of the wounded and dying were borne to him on the evening breezes, so the consequences of the ruin that had overtaken his policy were already closing in on him. The citizens of Civitate, approaching him in mortified defiance, announced that they were no longer prepared to offer him shelter. The Vicar of St Peter was duly delivered up into the hands of the Normans. Both sides appeared equally embarrassed by the circumstances of their meeting.

The victors, falling to their knees, wept and begged Leo for forgiveness. Then, with a fulsome show of respect, they escorted the unhappy pontiff inland to Benevento, a city that lay directly on the northernmost border of their sphere of influence. Indeed, formally, it owed allegiance to the papacy itself: a fig leaf which barely served to conceal the grim reality of Leo's captive status. Nine months he was kept a prisoner there. Only once he had finally accepted the right of the Normans to their conquests, it seems, was he released. As he left for Rome, he cut a pathetically broken figure, unable even to climb into his saddle. To many, the spectacle of the celebrated wayfarer lying in his litter was a salutary one. Even some of Leo's closest allies had been appalled by his recourse to the sword. The Pope had sought to sanctify a policy of warfare – and the policy had been found terribly wanting. Surely, then, his critics asserted, it was God Himself who had pronounced the judgement.

Yet Leo, though sick and weary, had not abandoned his conviction that the attempt to cleanse southern Italy of the Normans had been a righteous one. No less desperately than Christian souls required purging of their sins, and the Church of simony, the sword-gashed world needed healing. So it was, in yet another startling innovation, that Leo pronounced the Swabians who had fallen at Civitate to have been martyrs; and so it was too, even in Benevento, that he had persisted in secret negotiations aimed at renewing an anti-Norman alliance. With Henry III, the Emperor of the West, distracted by unrest in Bavaria, there had been only one other Caesar to call upon. Accordingly, in the late winter of 1054, Leo had ordered an embassy to embark for Constantinople. The fullest measure of how seriously its mission was taken lay in the identity of its leader: none other than Cardinal Humbert.

By early April, even as the Lateran began to buzz with rumours that the Holy Father was near death, his ambassadors were nearing their destination. From afar, blazing like dots of fire, they began to make out a gleaming of golden roofs, until at length, as their ship passed into the narrow strait of the Bosporus, there rose stretched out before them on

the northern shore a panorama of incomparable beauty and magnificence. Cardinal Humbert, that loyal servant of the Bishop of Rome,
could now gaze out for the first time at an authentic capital of a
Roman empire. Constantinople remained what she had been for
seven hundred years: the Queen of Cities and the bulwark of
Christendom. On her ancient and massive walls, twelve miles long in
all, men still stood guard just as their ancestors had done, when they
had served to withstand the fearsome lust for conquest of the
Saracens. In her forum, proclamations issued by a Caesar were still
read out to a Roman people. Along her streets, and through the massive space of her hippodrome, her armies had only a few years
previously marched in a splendid triumphal procession: 'a reminder to
the Romans that ardour breathes new life into the dead'.[89] Above all,
dominating the cityscape, and putting even the promontory-clinging
sprawl of the imperial palace in the shade, there rose the stupendous
cupola of the largest cathedral in the world, the Church of Holy
Wisdom, Hagia Sophia: a monument that had been hailed in triumph
by its builder as surpassing the very Temple of Solomon.

All of which, no doubt, in a Christian bishop, should have inspired
a sense of wonder and reverence – and yet Cardinal Humbert, if he felt
any such emotions, did not care to betray them. An ambassador he
might be – but he certainly had no wish to appear a supplicant.
Treading the streets of the New Rome, he found himself all the more
bristlingly conscious of the dignity of the Old. As well he might have
done: for the pretensions of Constantinople were calculated to infu-
riate the tight-lipped scholar who had demonstrated to his own
perfect satisfaction that his master ruled as the head of the universal
Church. Not even through gritted teeth could Humbert bring himself
to agree with his hosts that their Patriarch might rank as the peer of
the Pope. Naturally, had he only been able to confine himself to the
business of diplomacy, this would hardly have mattered. Both sides,
after all, were desperate to secure a military alliance against their
common foe; and the *Basileus*, Constantine IX, was a man celebrated
for his affability and taste for the low brow. Listening to people with

entertaining speech defects was his surest source of diversion – not debating theology.

Altogether sterner in his tastes, however, was the Patriarch himself, Michael Cerularius, a man of whom it was tactfully observed by one associate that 'he had a taste for speaking his mind'.[90] Prickly, irascible and intransigent, he was in every way a fitting opponent of the cardinal. Already, even before Humbert's arrival in Constantinople, the two men had been firing off abusive letters to each other. When they were brought face to face, their insults grew progressively more vicious. Soon enough, to Constantine's frustration and embarrassment, he found all his attempts to negotiate a coalition with Rome against the Normans drowned out by their din. The rival prelates, not content with arguing over the rights and wrongs of the claims of the Pope to pre-eminence, made a point of dredging up every point of disagreement that had ever existed between their churches: a strategy which gave them both plenty to row about.

It did not take long for relations between the two men to pass the point of no return. As Humbert began labelling his opponents pimps and disciples of Mohammed, Cerularius withdrew to his palace in an ostentatious sulk. By summer, with the Patriarch still maintaining his icy silence, the streets filling with angry mobs and any hope of forging a common policy against the Normans in ruins, what little remained of Humbert's patience spectacularly snapped. On 16 July, dressed in the full splendid regalia of a prince of the Roman Church, he marched into the Cathedral of Hagia Sophia, accompanied by his fellow legates. Ignoring the massed ranks of the clergy who were gathered there to celebrate Mass, the cardinal strode with an awful solemnity beneath the flickering of a thousand candles, past a multitude of coloured columns, and up to the gilded altar. There, paying no attention to the rising hubbub of indignation from behind him, he slapped down a bull of excommunication against the Patriarch, before turning briskly on his heels. Two days later, as the streets of Constantinople seethed with fury, he departed for Rome. Cerularius himself, meanwhile, never a man to duck a fight, made sure to anathematise Humbert in turn. He consigned the fateful bull to a public bonfire. Any remaining partisans of an alliance with the papacy were arrested.

That the negotiations might have gone better was self-evident enough. Nevertheless, many remained unclear as to how serious the bust-up had actually been. Had it been a spat or a permanent schism? No one was sure at first. Rows between the twin capitals of Christendom were certainly nothing new. Relations had been rocky for centuries, and popes and patriarchs had indulged in mutual excommunications before. In fact, as Cerularius and his cheerleaders gleefully pointed out, the bull of excommunication delivered against them had been legally invalid: for Leo IX, who had originally sent the embassy, had died back in the spring, leaving his legates without formal authority to anathematise anyone. Indeed, even some of those who had accompanied Humbert into Hagia Sophia on that momentous July day of 1054 still clung to the hope that the breach between the two churches might yet be healed. Three years later, when one of them was elected Pope, and took the name Stephen IX, he immediately dispatched a mission of his own to Constantinople in a desperate attempt to repair the damage – but it was aborted by his almost immediate death. No further missions were sent. Already, in the space of a few years, the mood in Rome had decisively shifted. What was at stake, many reformers had begun to accept, was nothing less than a fundamental point of principle. Cardinal Humbert had sounded out a trumpet blast on a truly decisive field of battle. The message that it sent to the rest of Christendom could hardly have been more ringing: no one, not even the Patriarch of the New Rome, could be permitted to defy the authority of the Pope.

Schism with the Eastern Church was not the only cost that had to be borne by the papacy. Any prospect of a renewed coalition with the Byzantines in southern Italy now stood in ruins. The Normans appeared ineradicable: 'as deadly to their softer neighbours as the bitter wind to young flowers'.[91] Rome herself had begun to look exposed. Then unexpectedly, in the autumn of 1056, that greatest and most formidable patron of reform, the Caesar of the West, Henry III, fell sick. His death on 5 October, coming virtually out of the blue and at a relatively youthful age, only added to the general mood of twitchiness in the Lateran. The new king was Henry's son and namesake: a boy of only five years. The new regent was the queen: the pious and unworldly Agnes. So a child and a woman were charged with serving the papacy, at a fateful moment in its fortunes, as its earthly protectors.

And yet in danger lay opportunity. Henry III had certainly served to reform the see of Rome; but he had also placed it in his shadow. There were those within papal circles – men such as Humbert and Hildebrand – who had begun to resent this: for the order of which they dreamed was one in which it was the Pope who put the emperor in the shade. Now, with the Caesar of Constantinople condemned as a heretic, and the western Caesar merely a child, a tantalising prospect had opened up. Clearly, if the world were to be brought to its proper order, then the reins of authority would need to be entrusted to someon. And who better, who more fitting, than the heir of St Peter, the Bishop of Rome?

A question on which a very great deal would hang indeed.

6

1066 AND ALL THAT

The Making of a Bastard

Cardinal Humbert's mission to Constantinople might have been ill-fated, but it had been part of a swelling trend. Travellers from the West were an increasingly common sight in the ancient capital of the East. Few of them went, as the cardinal had done, for reasons of diplomacy. Most were on their way to Jerusalem. Even though the massive surge of pilgrims that had marked the one-thousandth anniversary of Christ's Resurrection had gradually ebbed away in the wake of His failure to descend from heaven, a steady stream continued to trickle through the Queen of Cities, gawping at the relics, taking in the sights, then catching a ferry onwards across the Bosphorus. Indeed, for anyone with a guilty conscience, a taste for adventure and a travel bag full of loot, a really gruelling pilgrimage still ranked as a must-do experience. Perhaps it was no surprise, then, that the most enthusiastic pilgrims of all tended to be Normans. Even dukes had been known to share in the mania. Back in 1026, one of them, Richard III, had sponsored the largest single party of pilgrims that Christendom had then seen: seven hundred in all. Nine years later, and the new duke, Richard's brother, Robert, had gone one better: he had headed off for Jerusalem himself.

Even in 1035, at a time when many of the duke's countrymen were still serving the *Basileus* in Italy as mercenaries, the Byzantine high command had grown sufficiently familiar with the Normans to know that it did not greatly care for them. Nevertheless, the swagger of Robert's entry into Constantinople would long be remembered. Restless, impulsive and buccaneering, the Norman duke had cut a dash sufficient to impress even the spectacle-sated Byzantines, and to win for himself the sobriquet of 'the Magnificent'. Tribute to his gilded inheritance: for his father had been Duke Richard II, that same shrewd and calculating operator who had succeeded in transforming his duchy into such an oasis of prosperity that even King Ethelred of the English had sought asylum at his court. Robert's progress to the Holy Land had duly dazzled like the arc of a meteor. His very mules had been shod with gold, it was said, and his camp-fires – in a climactic extravagance – fuelled with pistachio nuts. Even that most celebrated and seasoned of all pilgrims, Fulk Nerra, when he met up with Robert in Constantinople, had found himself put in the shade. The final seal on this image of flamboyant piety, however, had been set, not in the Holy Land, but on the journey homewards. Taken sick just south of the Bosphorus, Robert had retired to bed in the fabled city of Nicaea, a place redolent of antiquity and holiness – for it was there, back in the time of Constantine, that the creed of the Christian faith, the pro-fession of belief still spoken across the whole wide expanse of Christendom, had originally been settled upon. There he had breathed his last. Perhaps, as one monk theorised, God Himself had taken the duke, 'because he was too good for this world'.[1]

Or perhaps not. Despite the exemplary manner of Robert's death, the truth was that he made for an improbable paragon. Notorious for his bullying of bishops, and an inveterate rebel in the years before his own accession, he had never entirely escaped suspicion of a crime that would well have merited a penitential trek to Jerusalem: involvement in his brother's early death. Whether justified or not, the rumours that Robert might have poisoned Richard III spoke volumes about the car-nivorous reputation that still shadowed Normandy. Even the disproportionate number of pilgrims from the duchy, far from dispelling the vague aura of menace that clung to the Normans, tended only to add to it. A pilgrimage was an expensive business and one that might readily lend itself to a spot of cheery freebooting on the side. It had certainly not been forgotten in Apulia, for instance, that the very first mercenaries from Normandy to be employed in the region had originally been recruited on Mount Gargano, within the shrine of St Michael itself.[2] Hardly surprising, then, over the succeeding decades, that the reception given in Italy to Norman pilgrims should have grown increasingly hostile. Violence had bred violence in turn. The likelier Norman visitors to Mount Gargano were to find themselves being clubbed to death by irate locals, the likelier they were to travel for safety in large and well-armed bands. It had not taken long for the distinction between pilgrim and brigand to grow an exceedingly blurred one indeed.

No wonder, then, that the wanderlust of the Normans appeared, when viewed from Italy or Constantinople, a characteristic no less alarming than their brutality or their daring, their ferocity or their greed. Just as the Franks, back in the age of Rollo, had imagined the lands of the Northmen as a womb splitting apart with an excess of axe-wielding progeny, so similarly, in the decades that followed the Millennium, did the objects of Norman aggression take for granted that they were the victims of a population explosion back in Normandy. As evidence for this thesis, they needed only to cite those most alarming of all Norman captains: Robert Guiscard and his brothers. Tancred, the patriarch of the Hauteville clan, had fathered twelve sons in all, five with one wife, and seven with her successor, not to mention a clutch of daughters – but his expectations, despite an aptitude for slaughtering boars that had served to win him the admiration of Duke Richard II himself, had never quite kept pace with his fecundity. So it was that most of his sons, rather than scrap over the few mean fields that were the limit of their inheritance, had opted instead to travel abroad, and attempt to carve out their fortunes in the sun. Such a resolve in itself would hardly have served to distinguish them – for other princedoms too were teeming with able warriors on the make. What did strike con-temporaries as exceptional, however, was the sheer scale of the Hautevilles' designs: a craving for wealth and dominance that those who stood in its way soon came to identify as characteristically Norman. 'For this is a people who set out and leave behind small fortunes in the expectation of acquiring a greater. And they do not follow the custom of the majority who pass through this world, who are content with prospering as the servants of others – for it is their aim instead to have everyone else subject to them, and acknowledging their lordship.'[3]

And so it had ever been. A century and more had passed now since Rollo and his followers, fanning out from their dragon-ships, had set about despoiling the natives of what would one day become Normandy – and yet a taste for extravagant property grabs continued to define their descendants. Lethally, joyously even, though the Normans had adapted themselves to the Frankish way of war, there remained, in the way they rode to battle, something of the instincts of the Viking war band still. A leader who could not provide his follow-ers with plunder and opportunity was a leader in deep trouble – and of no one was this truer than the Duke of Normandy himself. 'For men had to be fired with a longing to serve him: with spoils and gifts if young and untested, and with a wealth of flourishing estates if already great by birth.'[4] Such an obligation, however, in an age when Normandy was hemmed in all around by the mushrooming donjons of neighbouring princedoms, was not as simple to fulfil as it had once been. The same duchy which under the cunning and piratical rule of Richard II had been famed as a haven of order was starting to appear, during the reigns of his two sons, an altogether less stable proposition. The ambitions of the Norman warrior class, as vaunting and ruthless as they had ever been, were turning in on themselves. Not everyone was willing to take the road to Italy. Many preferred to satisfy their land lust at the expense of their own neighbours in Normandy. Once, under Richard II, uppity lords would have found themselves com-pelled to wear saddles on their backs and crawl before the duke for mercy – but Robert, unlike his father, had lacked the will to rein them in. The pressure on him always to fight, to expand and to succeed had grown a wearisome one; so that by the time he finally opted to shrug it aside altogether, and depart for Jerusalem, his duchy appeared on the verge of disintegration, stained as it was with bloodletting, and riven by gangsterism.

And then he died – and Normandy was left in a more perilous condition still. So perilous, indeed, that there were some who suspected poison, and a plot to destabilise the duchy for good. With good reason, perhaps – for there was certainly a most plausible mastermind to hand. Track record, motive and opportunity: Fulk Nerra, Robert's companion out on the eastern pilgrimage trail, combined them all.[5] The Count of Anjou, whose princedom was separated from Normandy only by a single hoof-gashed buffer, the unfortunate county of Maine, had long been angling to roll back Norman power. Now, with Robert dead, such a goal appeared eminently achievable. Normandy had effectively been decapitated.

The new duke was a boy of only eight years old, a bastard of Robert's by the name of William. In Anjou, predictably enough, much was made of his parentage. William's mother, his enemies alleged, was the daughter of a man whose loathsome duty it had been to prepare corpses for burial: a wretch irredeemably polluted by filth and rottenness and death.[6] The charge was certainly a damaging one – for it served directly to cast aspersions upon the new duke's fitness to rule. The science of heredity was a serious matter, after all. As the ancients had long since proved, both sperm and menstrual blood were suffused with the essence of an individual's soul – and since, as everyone knew, it was their commingling that served to form an embryo, it implied that baseness as well as nobility might be implanted within a womb, there to flow within a foetus's veins. Robert, by slaking his lusts upon a corpse-handler's daughter, had most likely bred a monster. The vileness of the grandfather, so William's enemies charged, could hardly help but manifest itself within the grandson. The young duke, if only permitted to grow to adulthood, appeared fated to serve as the shroud-winder, not of the dead, but of very kingdoms.

Or would have been, perhaps, had the slanders been remotely true. In fact, far from practising a low-bred and abhorrent trade, William's grandfather had been an official in the ducal court.[7] Not a warrior, to be sure – but then bastardy, among the Normans, had never been reckoned a fatal taint. Indeed, often they had seemed positively to approve of it: 'for it has always been their custom, for as long as they have been settled in France, to take as their princes the offspring of concubines'.[8] The resigned shrugs with which outsiders tended to note this was hardly surprising, perhaps. Things might well have been worse. The marital habits of the Northmen had long been a matter of scandal. In Sweden, for instance, a barbarous land so remote that it lay even beyond the limits of the North Way, it was reported that men might have up to three or four wives at a time – 'and princes an unlimited number'.[9] But then the Swedes were unregenerate pagans. In lands where the Northmen had become Christians, princes were generally content to satisfy themselves with two. So it was, for instance, that even the ostentatiously pious Canute, when he married Emma, Ethelred's Norman widow, and restored her to her former status as Queen of the English, had opted not to dwell on the awkward fact that he was already married. Aelfgifu, an Englishwoman who had been with him since the very earliest days of his arrival in England, had already given him two sons: a reserve of heirs that Canute had not the slightest intention of squandering. Indeed, in 1030, he packed one of them off, along with Aelfgifu herself, to govern the Norwegians, who had recently been brought to submit to his rule. Although his own bishops might fulminate sternly against bigamy, the practice brought Canute too many advantages for him to contemplate abandoning it. In Normandy too, it had often proved a godsend. One wife from the Frankish world, and one from the Norman: such had long been the preference of the dukes. In the marriage bed as elsewhere, they liked to face both ways.

Except that even in Normandy the times were gradually changing. For there too, as the decades of the new millennium slipped by, the fathering of children on numerous wives was coming to seem an increasingly unacceptable habit, the practice of sinister peoples 'igno-rant of divine law and chaste morals':[10] the Saracens, for instance, or – most barbarous of all – the Bretons. Such an attitude shift reflected, in part, the sheer smouldering weight of the Church's disapproval: its insistence that marriage was properly an exclusive partnership of equals. Perhaps even more significant, however, was the nobility's own vague but dawning realisation that it was not plunder which repre-sented the surest guarantee of establishing a family's greatness, but the transmission, Capetian-style, of an undivided patrimony. That being so, the right of a lord's heir to succeed to his father's lands had to be established beyond all possible doubt. William might have been ille-gitimate – and yet it was significant that he was also an only son. Duke Robert had very consciously refrained from taking a wife. Only once he had summoned the lords of Normandy to his court, and formally presented William to them as his successor, had he ventured to leave for the Holy Land. No one had been left in any doubt as to who his heir was to be.

Not that, in a society as loot-hungry as that of the Normans, an oath of loyalty to an eight-year-old could be taken for granted – nor was it. The years of William's minority would long be remembered in Normandy as a time of violence and cruelty exceptional even by the standards of what had gone before. Rival warlords, with no one to leash them in, found themselves free to indulge all their most razor-clawed instincts. Nothing more brutally illustrated what might be at stake than the fashion, one bred of increasingly savage and incessant feuding, for abducting rivals, even from wedding feasts, and subjecting them to horrific mutilations. Blindings were particularly popular; cas-trations too. As well they might have been: for those who aimed to found a flourishing dynasty naturally had to look to neuter the com-petition. Meanwhile, 'forgetful of their loyalties, many Normans set about piling up mounds of earth, and then constructing fortified strongholds on them for themselves'.

As it had done in the southern princedoms, so now in Normandy, a sudden rash of castles served as the surest symptom of a spreading anarchy. 'Plots began to be hatched, and rebellions, and all the duchy was ablaze with fire.'[11] As for William himself, he was soon inured to the spectacle of slaughter: two of his guardians were hacked down in quick succession; his tutor as well; and a steward, on one particularly alarming occasion, murdered in the very room in which the young duke lay asleep. Yet even as blood from the victim's slit throat spilled across the flagstones, William could feel relief as well as horror: for he at least had been spared. The feuding that resulted in the assassination of so many appointed to his household never had him as its object. Violence-shadowed the years of his childhood certainly were; but throughout them all he retained his hold on the title that had been bequeathed to him, and him alone, by his father: the Duke of Normandy.

To see how much more perilous things might have been for him had Robert fathered a brood of heirs with different women, and left behind a tangled succession, William had only to look across the Channel. There, with a determination that marked her out as a true member of the Norman ducal clan, Queen Emma was engaged in a frantic power struggle of her own. Like Normandy, England had recently been thrown into a state of crisis: for in the autumn of 1035, at around the same time that the news had reached Emma of her nephew's death in Nicaea, the man who had previously guaranteed her rank for her, her second husband, the great Canute, was being laid within his own coffin. Solemnly, before their marriage, he had sworn an oath that he would 'never set up the son of any other woman to rule after him';[12] but no sooner had he breathed his last than Harold, Aelfgifu's younger son, was moving in on the English throne. Not for nothing, it seemed, was the young prince nicknamed 'Harefoot' – and Emma, certainly, had found herself left behind in the dust. Her own son by Canute, Harthacanute, was absent in Scandinavia; nor, despite her increasingly frantic summons, was he willing to abandon his inheritance there, for the Norwegians were in revolt, and with such success that their new king, Magnus, had begun to menace Denmark itself.

By 1036, Harefoot's grip on England was tightening. Emma, having first barricaded herself inside Winchester in an effort to keep Wessex at least secure for her son, then tried spreading rumours that the usurper was not Canute's son at all, but a bastard who had been smuggled into the hated Aelfgifu's bed. Next, after that tactic had failed to draw blood, she dispatched an urgent appeal for assistance to Edward and Alfred, her two sons by Ethelred – which was, if anything, an even more shameless throw. Emma had seen neither of them for twenty years. Throughout the whole of Canute's reign, they had been living as exiles in Normandy – quite forgotten and unlamented, so it had always seemed, by their hard-nosed mother, the queen.

And not by her alone. Edward might have been crown prince of the House of Cerdic – but there was little enthusiasm among the kingdom's power brokers for the restoration of its native dynasty to the throne. Much had changed since the time of Ethelred. Canute had made sure to promote a new breed of earl to the rule of England. Such men owed nothing to the *Cerdicingas*. Indeed, the highest flying of them all, an English lord of previously obscure family by the name of Godwin, had good reasons for bearing a personal grudge against Ethelred's line: for back in the darkest days of the Viking assaults on England, he had witnessed his father unjustly accused of treason by the old king, and driven into exile. A salutary demonstration, no doubt, of the need always to keep on the right side of the powerful – and Godwin himself, in his own relations with royalty, certainly always made sure to swim with the tide. Smooth, prudent and opportunistic, he had duly succeeded in keeping afloat even amid the tempest-rack of the Danish subjugation of England – and to such effect that he had ended up with an earldom, and Canute's own sister-in-law, Gytha, as a wife. By the time Emma dispatched her summons to Normandy, begging her two sons to come and join her, Godwin held the rank of the Earl of Wessex, no less. Many of the lands that had once belonged to Ethelred were now his. The ships that patrolled the Channel, the troops that guarded the south coast – most were his as well. And Emma's two sons, landing in England, duly ran straight into Godwin's men.

Who gave them a thoroughly bruising reception. Edward, greeted in his ancestral homeland as though he were nothing more blue-blooded than a common pirate, was soon scarpering back to Normandy, his tail between his legs. Alfred, crossing southern England in a frantic attempt to reach his mother, was intercepted by Godwin's men, handed over to Harefoot in chains, and blinded. So brutal were the mutilations inflicted on him that the wretched prince died soon afterwards of the wounds. The following year, having finally been driven out of Winchester by Harefoot's agents, Emma escaped to Flanders, there to endure a bleak and wintry exile. Implacable still in the pursuit of her vendettas, she had no sooner arrived than she was putting about a story that it was Harefoot who had sent the fateful letter to her sons, and that her own seal on it had been a forgery. Edward, at any rate, was less than convinced. In 1038, when Emma summoned him to join her in Bruges, he refused. Even the perils of life in Normandy, it appeared, were preferable to his mother.

A grim and sordid episode – and to the young Duke William, whose reluctant guest Edward remained, a most instructive one. Certainly, it would have confirmed for him the stern lesson that his ancestors had always taught their young: that to be a prince was nothing, if not also a conqueror. William, unlike his father, did not shrink from the harsh destiny to which this bound him, but rather embraced it. He had been well instructed in what it took to be a leader of the Norman people. His ambition, one that everyone with a care for his education had worked tirelessly to inculcate, was to fashion himself anew, to become a being forged out of steel. Such, indeed, was the labour of transformation that all those Normans who aspired to greatness were obliged to take upon themselves. Even girls, as they played in a castle's stables or ran around its courtyard, were being raised within a world of sweat and iron – and childhood, for their brothers, was all a preparation for war. 'Arms and horses and the exercises of hunting and hawking: such are the delights of a Norman.'[13] The delights, perhaps – but also, far more crucially, the means of putting him to ceaseless test.

291

For only if a young man were prepared to risk death in the pursuit of some savage forest beast, or to practise with his sword all the hours of a day, or to perform prodigies of horsemanship, might he hope to win for himself that sweetest of felicities: the approbation of his fellows. Rank could be reckoned nothing without this. True of every lord, it was especially true of the duke. From his earliest days, William had been surrounded by his kinsmen. Amid all the shocks and convulsions of his childhood, they had been perhaps the only constant. 'Nurri', they were termed: young men 'nourished' by William's side, his brothers-in-arms, and more than brothers. Sharers in his upbringing, they too were being raised as carnivores through gruelling training.

No longer were the arts of killing the simple matter they had once been, back in the days of Rollo's war bands. To handle a lance properly while in the saddle, whether throwing it or couching it below the arm, in the most up-to-date and lethal manner, with all a horseman's weight behind it: here was a skill that might take years to perfect. Other martial disciplines, even more essential, even more cutting-edge, were an even greater challenge to master. It was a telling tribute, then, to the education received by William and his companions, that one of them, his closest friend, William fitz Osbern, would emerge as the acknowledged master of castle-building. Fulk Nerra, poisoner of Duke Robert though he might have been, had his heirs in Normandy as well as in Anjou. The strategy that he had pioneered, of using castles as instruments of aggression, was one that might almost have been designed to appeal to the eager wolf pack growing up around the Norman duke. Attack, spoliation, conquest: fitting pursuits for warrior lords.

And yet, for William himself, not the only ones. If war was his primary duty, then he did not forget that he had a duty as well to give his people peace. Naturally, he saw no contradiction between these twin vocations: for it would only ever be as a warlord that he could hope to stamp his will on his turbulent people. Master of a race of predators, he had no choice save to establish himself as the most lethal predator of all. 'For discipline the Normans with justice and firmness, and they will prove themselves men of great valour, who press invincibly to the fore in arduous undertakings and, proving their strength, fight resolutely to overcome all enemies. But without such rule they tear each other to pieces and destroy themselves – for they hanker after rebellion, cherish sedition, and are ready for any treachery.'[14]

William could have no doubt, then, even as he devoted himself to the practice of war, that he was performing God's work. No doubt either that Providence, fulfilling its mysterious designs through seeming accidents and twists of fate, might serve to demonstrate that God in turn was working for him. Indeed, as an illustration of how heaven's blessings might fall unexpectedly upon the head of a deserving prince, he had only to track the fortunes of a long-term guest at his own court. If the fiasco of Edward's first return to England had confirmed for William the priceless value of a metalled fist, then its conclusion would serve to teach some very different lessons. That the wicked might be overthrown. That the favoured of God might be granted a sudden opportunity to raise themselves up on to a throne. That a man might travel from Normandy to England and become a king.

Four years had passed since the fatal blinding of Edward's brother. Then abruptly, in March 1040, Harold Harefoot, the man chiefly responsible for the atrocity, died. Three months later, Harthacanute, Canute's remaining son, landed in Kent, accompanied by sixty ships and Emma, his gloating mother. True, he hardly came trailing clouds of glory: for back in Denmark, he had been obliged to abandon Norway for good and agree, as the price for securing a peace treaty, that should he die without an heir, then the Norwegian king Magnus would succeed to his various kingdoms. Nevertheless, despite Harthacanute's less than triumphant record, there was no one in England to oppose him; and the new King of England, just to rub this in, immediately ordered his half-brother's corpse dug up, dragged through a sewer and then dumped into the Thames. The following year, he invited his other half-brother, Edward, to return from Normandy. Clearly, it could only have been the hand of God which had prompted Harthacanute to take this unexpected step: for in June 1042, as he drank at a wedding feast, 'he suddenly fell to the earth with an awful convulsion; and those who were close by took hold of him, and he spoke no word afterwards, but passed away'.[15]

The way now stood open, rather to the surprise of everyone, for the restoration to the English throne of its ancient royal line. Prominent in the ranks of enthusiasts for Edward's claim was none other than that seasoned weathervane, Earl Godwin. Coolly abandoning his loyalty to the house of Canute, and smoothing over his involvement in the death of the wretched Alfred, the Earl of Wessex moved quickly to build bridges. The other earls of England were soon brought to agree with him. Certainly, there was no one who thought to make any mention of the claim of Magnus of Norway. On Easter Day 1043, Edward was duly crowned and anointed king. Two years later, on 23 January 1045, at the age of forty, he was married for the first time. His youthful queen, Edith, was beautiful, skilled at embroidery, fluent in five languages – and the daughter of Earl Godwin.

A moving demonstration of reconciliation, undertaken for the good of the English people, and well befitting a Christian king? Certainly, in years to come, Edward would indeed come to be hailed as a model of saintly piety: as 'the Confessor'. Yet the truth was that he did not lack for vindictiveness. Upon his own mother, for instance, he inflicted a thoroughly public disgrace: the confiscation of all her treasure, and temporary banishment from the court. But then Emma – despite rumours that had her conspiring with King Magnus – had already been de-fanged for good. Nothing remained for her, following her son's accession, save to wither in obscurity and wait for death. The contrast with Earl Godwin could hardly have been more striking. He retained, even after Edward's coronation, the status that he had held before it: that of king-maker. And perhaps, in due course, in the wake of his daughter's brilliant marriage, that of grandfather to a king.

To any ambitious prince, then, the startling turnaround in Edward's fortunes offered warning as well as inspiration. Across the Channel, Emma's great-nephew would have marked with interest the lesson of her fall, and of the wedding of King Edward to the Lady Edith. As well he might have done – for William was coming of age. The resolution implanted and fostered within him, never to live in anyone's shadow, never to tolerate a rival, always to conquer, 'shone brilliantly and clearly in him'[16] – and was ready at last to be tested upon the stage of the duchy itself. In 1047, confronted by a rebellion led by his own cousin, the young duke rode out to battle for the first time, and emerged from the resulting mêlée bloodily and heroically triumphant. Then, returning from the campaign, he set about ramming home his victory by dismantling a number of illegally raised castles. That same year, in an even more pointed measure, he presided over a council at Caen, and proclaimed the Peace of God. Not that there had been any role in it for uppity peasants – nor even for uppity bishops. In Normandy, no one was to be permitted to rival, still less challenge, the authority of William himself. 'For who can possibly argue that a good prince should tolerate rebellious brigands?'[17] In time, bringing order where there had been anarchy, the Peace of God would indeed be imposed across the duchy – to the greater glory, however, not of the Church, nor even of the saints, but of the duke alone. The Truce would hold – except when William was minded to break it. The Normans would lay down their weapons – except when wielding them in William's cause. Peace would be brought to Normandy – and war to William's neighbours.

But which neighbours, and at what cost to them? Here were questions that still remained to be answered.

Land-Waster

January 1045: the month of the marriage between King Edward and the Lady Edith – and of a second royal wedding. A strange symmetry: for the two grooms had long shared numerous correspondences. Like Edward, Harald Sigardurson belonged to a dynasty that had been toppled by Canute; like Edward, he had fled into exile; and like Edward, he

SWEDEN

SWEDEN

Gulf of Finland

Baltic Sea

Novgorod

THE

R. Volga

PRUSSIANS

POLAND

R U S

GREAT

Kiev

R. Dnieper

PECHENEGS

Caspian
Sea

Black Sea

Constantinople

N

| 0 | 300 miles |
| 0 | 500 km |

The eastern frontier of Christendom

had spent many decades preparing for the moment when he could at last reclaim his patrimony. Both men, in due course, would find their destinies fatefully intertwined – as would the family of Godwin too.

Yet the marriage of the second prince was being held not in England, nor anywhere near it, but far towards the rising of the sun, on the margin of interminably spreading forests, amid wastes so impossibly distant that the learned had once reckoned them the prison of Gog and Magog. It was a mark of the times, indeed, that an ancient Christian people such as the English could find themselves embroiled in the affairs of anywhere so remote. Even among the Northmen the vastness of the landmass that stretched eastwards of the Baltic was capable of inspiring a shudder. 'Sweden the Great', they termed it – or 'Sweden the Cold'. Giants lived there, it was reported, and dwarfs, and men with mouths between their nipples who never spoke but only barked, 'and also beasts and dragons of enormous size'.[18] Yet the Northmen, a people incorrigibly adventurous, had never been ones to shrink from the rumour of terrors. Already, as early as 650, a Swedish explorer of the Baltic had won for himself the sonorous title of 'Far-Reacher'; and there were many, over the succeeding centuries, who had followed in his wake. Beating their way up the rivers that flowed into the Gulf of Finland, gliding across icy lakes, straining as they bore their vessels overland past churning rapids, they had ventured ever further southwards, until at length, borne along widening currents, the Northmen had found themselves debouching into the warm waters of the South, the Black Sea and the Caspian, with easy passage onwards to fabulous cities rich in silks and gold. The seeming wilderness of Sweden the Great had proved itself in truth the very opposite: a land of opportunity. No less than the surging waters of the Atlantic, mighty rivers such as the Dnieper and the Volga had served the Northmen as highways to adventure and betterment. 'Like men they journeyed for distant treasure.'[19] Onwards, swelling the gold rush, the crews of their ships had pressed. Tirelessly, their oars had dipped and flashed. No wonder that the natives, watching them from the banks, had referred to them simply as 'rowers' – as the '*Rus*'.[20]

Such a name, redolent as it was of energy and effort, had fitted the newcomers well. It might be lucrative to transport furs and slaves to feed the appetites of the great cities of the South, yet the journey was a gruelling one: 'full of hardship and danger, agony and fear'.[21] Whether it was pulling on their oars, or manning the raw wooden palisades of their trading stations, or slaughtering anyone who sought to muscle in on their cartel, the Rus had found themselves with little choice but to operate as a team. Although they were tiny in number, intruders within a vast and hostile land, the very knowledge of how perilous were their circumstances had served to instil in them a ferocious sense of discipline. They had fought and traded together as '*Varangians*': men bound together by a common pledge, a '*vár*'. The dangers and the profits: the Rus had shared them both.

And steadily, over the decades, their swords had reddened, and their coffers overflowed. Transit posts had evolved into forts; forts into booming towns. The most imposing of all these went by the name of Kiev: a stronghold raised on a ravine-scored hill beside the Dnieper, ideally placed to control the flow of traffic along the river. Ideally placed as well to cow the natives, and to extort tribute from them, and to recruit them to serve in ever-swelling war bands. Inexorably, in the decades that preceded the Millennium, the Rus had succeeded in establishing themselves as something more than merely merchants – as princes. In 980, when one of them, the bastard son of a Kievan warlord by the name of Vladimir, had succeeded in returning from exile in Scandinavia and seizing power in his native city with the backing of Varangians from Sweden, he had laid claim as well to an immense and shadowy protection racket: one that extended from the Black Sea to the Baltic.

This startling achievement put the lordships won by Northmen elsewhere into a somewhat sobering perspective. Everything in the lands of the Rus – 'Russia' – existed on a vaster and more fabulous scale. In 1015, on Vladimir's death, his sons had fought a great and terrible war that had seemed, by the reports of it that echoed dimly from the frozen battlefields, the shadow play less of mortal princes than of fantastical heroes sprung from the tall tales of pagans. For months, the armies of rival brothers had faced one another across the raging torrents of the Dnieper. The younger, Yaroslav, was nicknamed 'the Lame'; and his enemies, screaming abuse from the far bank above the howling of the steppeland gales, had jeered at him as a cripple. But then, with the coming of winter, the river had begun to freeze over, and Yaroslav, lame or not, had succeeded in leading his forces across the thickening floes. Trapping his enemies, he had driven them backwards on to thin ice, and their doom.

Still the war had raged. Three times Yaroslav had confronted the armies of his brother – and three times he had dyed the snows red with their blood. His victory, in the end, had been total. His brother, pursued in his imaginings by invisible huntsmen, had fled to Poland and died there a madman, stabbing at empty air with his sword. Other brothers too, over the decades, had been eliminated. Yaroslav himself, meanwhile, laying claim to the rule of Kiev, had set about the task of fashioning his rickety mafia state into a realm such as any king in Christendom might admire – and with such success that he would end up remembered, not as 'the Lame', but as 'the Wise'.

It was in Scandinavia, however, that his fame shimmered most glamorously of all: for to the Northmen he appeared the cynosure of princes, renowned as far as Iceland for his cunning, his opulence and the seductiveness of his daughters. Even though Yaroslav himself, with his Slavonic name, his Slavonic habits and his Slavonic tongue, was no more a Viking than was his distant cousin, the Duke of Normandy, he had not forgotten his roots. As a young man, he had been sent by his father to rule a stronghold only a few days' journey from the northern seas: the celebrated 'New Castle', or Novgorod. Raised on the site of a fabulously ancient shrine, with a black-watered lake on one side and limitless forests on the other, and fashioned so entirely out of wood that even its documents were made of birch bark, the town was still, more than a century after its foundation, brash with frontier spirit. As such, it had long been a magnet for adventurers from across the North. Olaf Trygvasson, for instance, was said to have travelled there as a boy after having been ransomed from slavery, and to have met with his original captor in the town's market place, where he killed him on the spot with an axe. Then, in 1028, another celebrated Norwegian exile had made for Novgorod. Olaf Haraldsson, 'the Stout', as he was known, had been a Christian king very much in the tradition of Trygvasson. Brutal and domineering, and 'with eyes as hard as a serpent's',[22] he had passed a rumbustious decade browbeating his various rivals and committing spectacular atrocities, all in the name of Christ – until at length, wearying of his bullying, the Norwegian lords had invited in Canute.

Two years later, impatient to be revenged on his enemies, Olaf the Stout had returned across the Baltic. This was a doomed throw – for not even the installation as regent of Canute's English wife Aelfgifu had been sufficient to provoke the Norwegians into resuming their support for their exiled king. While still in Novgorod, it was said, Trygvasson had appeared to Olaf in a dream, and reassured him that 'it is a glorious thing to die in battle'[23] – which was just as well, for in the summer of 1030, at a village named Stiklestad, his ragtag gang of clansmen and desperadoes had been cut to pieces. Olaf himself, crippled by an axe blow just above his knee, and skewered through with a spear, had been finished off by having his neck hacked open to the vertebrae. And meanwhile, above the battlefield, it was claimed, the sky itself had begun to bleed.

Yet though the scene of slaughter had been monstrous, not everyone in Olaf's retinue had fallen. Enough of them had survived to spirit their lord's corpse away, and to help the more prominent among the wounded to escape. Among the fugitives had been the king's halfbrother: Harald Sigardurson. Only fifteen years old at the time, he had a lust for glory and a taste for violence that had already served to mark him out as an authentic chip off the old block. Just as Olaf had done two years previously, so now, after Stiklestad, the princely refugee had skulked his way over mountains and through dripping forests; and just like Olaf, he had ended up in Novgorod. There, treading the planks laid down across oozing mud that constituted the city's high street, he had made his way to the palace – the 'kremlin', as it was termed by the Rus – and begged for asylum. Yaroslav, evidently a dab hand at spotting potential, had promptly recruited the exile to serve him as a Varangian.

For three years, the increasingly hulking Harald had applied himself to becoming 'the king of warriors':[24] smiting the sledded Polacks and winning golden opinions of his patron. Not quite golden enough, however: for in 1035, when Harald asked for the hand of Elizabeth, one of Yaroslav's daughters, the father had turned him down flat. It was a measure of how dazzlingly the prestige of the Rus had come to blaze that their princesses were by now reserved only for the very cream of European royalty – and Harald, as a Varangian captain, had hardly measured up. Only the prospect that he might achieve things worthy of Elizabeth – and secure sufficient gold to impress her notoriously grasping father – had served to leave him with cause for hope. And so it was, resolved to make a name for himself before his intended could be handed over to some more prestigious suitor, that Harald had headed south. Leaving Yaroslav's court, he had known that he had only a narrow window of opportunity: for Elizabeth, by 1035, was already ten years old.

All the more fortunate for Harald, then, that his destination had effectively chosen itself. Even though the Vikings in Russia had long been regular visitors to 'Serkland', where the dark-skinned Tartars and Saracens lived, and even though they had brought back treasures garnered from the very limits of the horizon, whether silver *dirhams* from Baghdad, or golden tableware from Egypt, or idols of a peculiar god named the Buddha from strange realms unheard of, all along they had never doubted where the surest wellspring of riches lay. To the Northmen, Constantinople was, quite simply, the capital of the world: 'the Great City', '*Miklagard*'. For almost two hundred years it had glittered in their dreams, 'tall-towered Byzantium',[25] a repository of everything that was most beautiful and wondrous on Middle Earth. Indeed, imagining how Odin's stronghold in the heavens might appear, the Northmen could do no better than to picture it as a city

301

much like Caesar's golden capital, roofed with precious metals, gleaming with splendid palaces, and encircled by a giant wall.

Of Constantinople's own impregnability, they had few doubts: for at regular intervals the Rus had set themselves to capturing it, and been repeatedly rebuffed, their longboats either sunk in mysterious storms whipped up by the prayers of the defenders, or else incinerated by sinister weapons of fire sprayed from Byzantine warships. Even Yaroslav, in 1043, would have a crack at capturing the Great City – and end up losing his entire fleet for his pains. Yet though these eruptions from the Dnieper were periodic, and thoroughly alarming to the Byzantines themselves, who would invariably be taken by surprise by the sudden appearance of barbarians in the Bosphorus, the truth was that they were little more than the spasming of a cultural cringe. The Rus might have been Swedish in origin, and Slavonic by adoption – and yet deep in their heart of hearts, where inferiority complexes invariably lurk, they yearned to be Byzantine.

Which was why, as the princes of Kiev set about the task of fashioning an empire of their own, imitation had increasingly superseded intimidation. Back in 941, during one of their abortive assaults on the Great City, the Rus had amused themselves by using monks for target practice and hammering nails into the foreheads of priests; forty-odd years later, and Prince Vladimir had agreed to be baptised. Cannily, however, before taking the plunge, he had made sure to evaluate the opposition. Embassies had duly been dispatched to investigate the mosques of the Saracens and the cathedrals of the Germans. 'But we saw no glory there.' Then they had visited Miklagard; and been led into the city's churches. 'And we knew not whether we were on heaven or on earth. For on earth there is no such splendour or such beauty. We only know that God dwells there among men.' Such had been the awestruck verdict delivered back to Kiev. 'We cannot forget that beauty.'[26]

This, even by the standards of the great game that Byzantine diplomats had been playing with such proficiency for centuries, had ranked as a signal coup. So much so, indeed, that the *Basileus*, swallowing his instinctive distaste for marriage alliances with barbarians, had sent Vladimir his own sister: the very ultimate in Christian queens. A grim fate for any princess brought up in Constantinople – and yet the new '*tsarita*', even as she settled into her new quarters beside the Dnieper, had at least been able to console herself that her sacrifice was not in vain. No matter that the Rus had remained prone to the occasional lurch into lunatic aggression: at least they were no longer pagan, nor in league with the Saracens, nor beholden to the Germans. Harald, making his way southwards to Miklagard, would have found in Kiev many a tribute raised to the abiding allure of the Queen of Cities. Palaces and domed churches, gateways and mighty walls: here, set upon a landscape that barely a century before had been mere featureless savagery, were the unmistakable stamps of the New Rome.

Not that the trade was all one way. Merchants arriving from the Dnieper, loaded down with any number of exotic treasures, whether walrus ivory, or amber, or fish glue, or wax, continued to flock to the lantern-lit markets of the Great City. Even with all the various indignities imposed on them by the imperial bureaucracy, all the quotas, and registration forms, and quality-control inspections, the skimmings to be had in Miklagard remained the stuff of avaricious report across the North. Furs, in particular, still garnered fabulous profits. Hardly fabulous enough for Harald, however. Not for him the option of becoming a 'skin', as merchants were dismissively known. He was, after all, a warrior, and the brother of a king. Toweringly as he loomed, and with a self-regard to match, only one profession had been worthy of his talents. 'Fierce, proud warriors standing up to ten feet in height'[27] were the kind of mercenaries that the Byzantines had always prized. As a consequence, Varangians were even more in demand in Constantinople than in Kiev or Novgorod. Only tame a Northman, a succession of emperors had found, and all the qualities that rendered him so alarming as an adversary – his animal savagery, his proficiency with an axe, his ferocious beard – could serve to make of him a truly pedigree bodyguard. Like house-broken attack dogs, Varangians were famed for their loyalty. Seventy of them, it was said, in their mortification at having failed to prevent the murder of Nicephorus Phocas, had opted to fight to the death rather than make an accommodation with his assassins. No wonder, then, at the most awesome moment in any emperor's life, when he stood beneath the flickering gold of the dome of Hagia Sophia to be crowned God's viceroy, and to take up for the first time the attributes of his new majesty, the sceptre and the purple cloak, the sword and the scarlet boots, that there, massed all around him, their axes slung over their shoulders, their outfits chillingly barbarous, would be serried a posse of Varangians. To guard a Caesar was a truly awesome charge. Indeed, a responsibility that might be worthy of a prince.

Admittedly, enthusiasm for the Varangians among imperial circles was not universal. 'Wine-bags', they were nicknamed in the palace: testimony to a taste for late-night revelling that weary courtiers had learned to dread. Never, however, had there been a Varangian who generated quite the noise that Harald did. Brags about his exploits in the imperial service would end up echoing as far afield as Iceland. 'Harald,' as one overexcited flatterer put it, 'you forced all the lands of the Mediterranean to submit to the Emperor!'[28] A claim that would certainly have been news to the *Basileus* himself, let alone the Saracens – but tribute, nevertheless, to the unprecedented strut and clamour that Harald had brought to the business of being a Varangian. In Sicily, it was claimed, he had captured no fewer than eighty towns. In the Holy Land, he had bathed in the River Jordan, and conquered Jerusalem – 'an easy task for Harald'.[29] In Constantinople, he had been thrown into prison by a lovelorn empress, helped to blind an emperor and fought with a dragon. The plausible and the utterly fantastical, in the rumours of Harald's deeds, were promiscuously mixed. And to sensational effect – for in the North he was soon a living legend. Even Yaroslav had ended up impressed. As well he might have done – for he had been sent the hard proof of his would-be son-in-law's achievements. Piled up for safe keeping in an island compound outside Novgorod was a great

304

heap of treasure, 'a hoard of wealth so immense that no one had ever seen its like before':[30] Harald's winnings.

Finally, by 1044, with Constantinople growing increasingly too hot for him, and the still single Princess Elizabeth turned nineteen, the conquering hero had felt that the time was ripe to head back north to claim his by now nubile prize. Loading up his coffers with yet more gold, and making a spectacular getaway in a stolen galley, he had duly returned up the Dnieper to Yaroslav. And so at last, with the New Year, it had come about: the consummation of all his hopes. 'The warlike king of Norway won the match of his desire.' So one poet celebrated the occasion. 'He gained a princess – not to mention a hoard of treasure.'[31]

Yet for all the dash that Harald had no doubt cut on his arrival in Novgorod, with 'his clothes of silk, given him by the King of Miklagard',[32] mere glamour on its own, no matter how spiced up with gold, would hardly have been sufficient to win him Yaroslav's daughter. During the decade and more of his absence from Scandinavia, however, his prospects had spectacularly improved: for he had become the brother of a saint, no less. Olaf the Stout, whose attempt to reclaim Norway had ended amid such bloody ruin, had been splendidly compensated for the loss of his earthly throne with one in heaven. A most improbable elevation, it might have been thought – and yet a succession of miracles had served to prove Olaf's sanctity beyond all doubt. For even with the carnage of Stiklestad reeking in the nostrils, it was said, his blood had served the wounded as a curative; and a whole year after his death, when his corpse was dug up from a sandbank, it had been found miraculously intact, with hair and nails still growing. Transferred to a church altar in the port of Trondheim, a foundation of Olaf Trygvasson, the relics had continued to heal the sick and injured at a prodigious rate. By the time of Harald's return to the North, his brother's death had been transfigured into a martyr's 'passion'.[33] Across the whole span of the Viking world, from Novgorod to Dublin, a brutal warlord had begun to be venerated as a 'holy king'.[34] This startling turnaround was vivid testimony to the yearning among the Northmen, even as they turned their backs on their ancient gods, for a saint whom they could hail as their own.

Good news for Harald, certainly, as he set off for home, 'freighted with hard won honour and gleaming gold'.[35] But he was not the only beneficiary of his dynasty's new-found association with the heavenly: for Magnus, the young king who had expelled the Danes from Norway, was St Olaf's son. In 1045, he stood at the summit of his power: King of Denmark as well as of Norway, thanks to the treaty he had signed back in 1039 with Harthacanute, and with a claim to the rule of England too. These were just the kind of pickings to whet the appetite of a predator such as Harald; and sure enough, no sooner had he set foot on his native soil than he was throwing his weight around, and demanding a share of his nephew's lands. Magnus, who was hardly the man to be intimidated by anyone, not even a celebrated hero such as his uncle, refused to give way; and for the next two years, amid a bewildering welter of compacts signed and broken, the two of them circled each other, sniffing for advantage. Then in 1046, Magnus died unexpectedly while out on campaign; and Harald succeeded uncontested to the rule of the lands he had fled sixteen years before. 'Who knows,' he had reassured himself then, while on the run from the killing fields of Stiklestad, 'my name may yet become renowned far and wide in the end.'[36] And so it had proved.

Nor, having won his throne, did he intend ever to be forced into exile again. Harald's record as king over the two decades of his reign would be a ruthless one. '*Hardrada*', his subjects came to call him: 'Hard-Ruler'. Funded by his plentiful stock of treasure, he threw himself with his customary swagger into all the traditional activities of a Viking king: slapping down his rivals among the local chiefs, waging pointless wars against his neighbours, incinerating their towns, and menacing their coastlines with showy dragon-ships. Even as the cult of St Olaf went from strength to strength, and Trondheim began to swell with pilgrims drawn from across the Christian world, Harald remained wedded to the old ways, in which Christendom existed primarily as a resource to be plundered. Inevitably, then, as his reservoirs of Miklagard gold finally began to run out in the mid-1060s, he did as generations of Viking warlords had done before him: look around for a foreign milch-cow. Specifically, he looked to England.

As well he might have done – for the English by now were as rich as they had ever been. Although Edward had proved to be a doggedly unsensational king, pallid even, his reign had nevertheless served to provide his subjects with something truly precious: a respite from upheaval. Prosperity had returned to the kingdom: its trade had swelled, its wealth had grown, its towns had boomed. To be sure, there had been the odd alarm. In 1045, for instance, nervous of Magnus's intentions, Edward had assembled a massive fleet to patrol the coast-line of Kent. Then, early in the 1050s, a rupture between the king and the Earl Godwin had appeared to threaten civil war. But men on both sides, rather than storming headlong over the abyss, had opted instead to pause and draw back. 'For they reflected that it would be a great piece of folly if they joined battle, for in the two hosts there was most of what was noblest in the kingdom, and they considered that they would be opening a way for their enemies to enter the country and to cause much ruin.'[37] Relations between Edward and Godwin, however uneasily, had been patched up. Even though the earl himself had died soon afterwards, concord between his heirs and the king had been pre-served. Edward, devoting himself to the pleasures of the hunt and to the occasional miraculous cure of the sick, had increasingly been con-tent to leave the running of the kingdom to Godwin's sons. And to two of them, in particular. One, Tostig, had been appointed to the rule of Northumbria; his elder, Harold, had inherited the earldom of Wessex. 'Two great brothers of a cloud-born land, the kingdom's sacred oaks,' they were hailed by one enthusiast. 'With joined strength and like agreement they guard the bounds of England.'[38]

All in all, then, for Harald Hardrada, it might have been thought, this was a most unpromising state of affairs. But was it? Firmly rooted though both the Godwinsons might appear, the truth was that one of them, after a decade in power, was coming to be battered by increas-ingly stormy crosswinds. Northumbria, Tostig's earldom, remained what it had always been: a realm much given to violence. In the savagery of the landscape, and in its remoteness from the kingdom's West Saxon heartlands, there was held up a fitting mirror to the inveterate factionalism of the locals. Even the women, on occasion, would think nothing of sticking the heads of captured Scotsmen on poles. Hardly the place, in short, to look with much favour on a southern earl. Tostig, a man renowned for his courage and cunning, but also possessed of an often fiery temper, had tended to respond to hints of restiveness with all the forcefulness he could muster. As a result, he had ended up widely hated. By 1065, the Northumbrian lords had had enough. Raising an army, they marched first on York and then on Wessex itself. Edward, despite initial attempts to stand firm, had found himself powerless to resist their demands: that Tostig be deposed from his earldom and replaced with the Northumbrians' own nomination, a young lord by the name of Morcar. Even Harold, recognising that his brother's cause was doomed, had shrunk from making the kingdom bleed in Tostig's defence. A statesmanlike call, no doubt – but one that had left Tostig himself with a burning, indeed almost frenzied, sense of grievance. That November, as the humiliated earl left England for exile in Flanders, he did so breathing vengeance on his brother.

And casting about for any foreign warlord who might be persuaded to assist him. The time for such treason was ripe. Edward, as Tostig well knew, had recently suffered a number of strokes, and by Christmas he was rumoured to be mortally ill. The moment of its king's death was always a fateful one for any kingdom – but for England, that New Year, it promised to be especially so. For Edward had no son, nor even a daughter, to succeed him. Later ages would attribute this withering of his line to a godly vow of chastity, or else to his hatred of the Godwins – but neither explanation appears a likely one. Edward, in his own way, it seems, had grown close to Edith, and dependent upon her for advice – whether in matters of dress, or interior decoration, or the very gravest affairs of state. Perhaps, then, as many of the English were coming to fear, the otherwise inexplicable barrenness of their king's marriage was a punishment imposed upon them for their sins. Edward, with shallow subtlety, had always exploited his childlessness for his own ends, promising the throne to rival candidates as and whenever he had required their assistance. Now, however, it seemed, with no obvious heir to the throne, there would have to be a reckoning. No wonder, then, as the New Year came and went, and reports from the royal sickbed steadily worsened, that the English looked forward to 1066 with a sense of mounting anxiety.

And all the while, beyond the northern seas, the King of Norway was biding his time. Soon enough fateful tidings were being brought to him from London. Edward was dead; and sat upon his throne, consecrated and crowned with indecent speed, or so it was reported, was no man of royal blood, but Harold Godwinsson. Affront and opportunity: Harald Hardrada took the news as both. Dusting down the claim to England that he had inherited long back from his nephew, he duly began to plan for war. The precise object of his task force, however, he still kept close to his chest; for he intended that his hammer blow, when it fell, should come out of the blue. How gratifying it was, then, that emissaries from Tostig should have arrived at his court in the very midst of his preparations, proposing what he had already settled upon.[39] How gratifying as well that even in the skies all things seemed to be moving in his favour: for in the spring there appeared above the lands of the North a mysterious star with a blazing tail. Well might men in England have been filled with dread at the sight, and reported seeing phantom ships out at sea:[40] for there existed no more infallible portent of a looming crisis than a comet. By the late summer, when Harald's forces were ready at last to embark, the omens had grown even more pointed. One warrior, a member of the king's own bodyguard, dreamed that he saw an ogress holding a knife and a trough of blood; another that he saw a hag riding on a wolf, and that the wolf had a corpse in its mouth.

Admittedly, there were some among Harald's followers who read these sanguinary visions as a foreboding, not of their lord's victory, but rather of his doom: for the old carnivore was fifty, and long in the tooth. Not for Harald himself, however, any pessimistic notions that he might be venturing on an adventure too far – still less that the very era of the sea kings might be slipping him by. Naturally, as befitted the brother of a martyr, he had made sure to pray at Olaf's shrine before departing, and to obtain some keepsakes by giving the saintly hair and nails a trim; but his most potent treasure, as he set sail for England, was one that any of his pagan ancestors would have hailed. 'Land-Waster', it was called: 'a banner that was said to bring victory to whomever it preceded into battle'.[41] Canute had owned one very similar, 'woven of the plainest and white silk', but on which a raven, in time of war, would mysteriously materialise, 'opening its beak, flapping its wings, and restive on its feet'.[42] Deep magic and even deeper time: such banners spoke profoundly to the Northmen of both. Liegemen of Christ they might have become, but in the fluttering of Land-Waster there beat for them the reassurance that they were heroes still, just as their pagan ancestors had been.

By early September, Harald and his monstrous fleet of some 300 ships were doing what so many Viking expeditions had done before them, and slipping down the coast of Scotland bound for Northumbria. Only Tostig, who met up with Harald on his way, had been given due warning of his plans: everyone else in England was taken utterly by surprise. Landing just south of York, the invaders discovered to their delight that Harold Godwinsson was far away in Wessex, and that only Earl Morcar and his brother, Edwin, were on hand to confront them. On 20 September, 'the thunderbolt of the North'[43] struck at the Northumbrian forces and shattered them. Morcar and Edwin both survived their defeat; but they were now powerless to prevent Harald from forcing York into surrender, and taking hostages from among the leading citizens. Next, withdrawing some seven miles east of the city, to a convenient road junction by the name of Stamford Bridge, the Norwegian king paused, to await the submission of all Northumbria. With Morcar's levies safely put out of action, and Harald Godwinson presumed still far away to the south, it seemed

N

Stiklestad
Trondheim

NORWAY

SCOTLAND

North Sea

NORTHUMBRIA

DENMARK

York ● ● Stamford Bridge

ENGLAND

WESSEX
Winchester ● London
● ● Hastings
Pevensey

English Channel

FLANDERS

● Rouen

NORMANDY
MAINE

0   400 km

0   200 miles

1066

there was nothing to worry about. Everything was going to plan. Land-Waster, which in the battle against the northern earls had carried all thunderously before it, was once again proving its invincibility.

But then, on 25 September, with an unseasonably warm sun standing high in the sky, Harald and Tostig caught sight of a sudden smudge on the western skyline – and realised that it was approaching them fast. Perhaps, they thought at first, a band of Northumbrians was riding in to submit; but soon, as the earth began to shudder, and the glittering of shields and mail coats emerged through the dust, 'sparkling like a field of broken ice',[44] the appalling truth dawned. Somehow, impossible though it seemed, Harold Godwinsson had arrived at Stamford Bridge. Frantically, Harald ordered his men to withdraw to the far side of the river. Simultaneously, he sent messengers galloping with furious speed to where his ships lay moored twelve miles to the south, along with their store of mail shirts, and a whole third of his men. But it was too late. For a brief while, it was true, the enemy were held up at the bridge – by a single warrior, according to one account, who kept all at bay with the swinging of his axe, until an Englishman, with underhand cunning, 'came up in a boat and through the openings of the planks struck him in the private parts with a spear'.[45] The delay, however precisely it had been achieved, was sufficient for Harald to draw up his men on the flats of the far bank – but not for his reinforcements to join him. Even though the Norwegians fought savagely, they could have no real hope of victory without their armour. Sure enough, the river was soon flowing incarnadine. In the end, the survivors broke and fled for their ships. All the afternoon, the English hunted them down. As the light began to fade and crows wheeled upon the carrion-perfumed breezes of evening, there lay spread out beneath them a scene of quite exceptional slaughter. The English victory had been a work of almost utter annihilation. Of the three hundred and more ships that had arrived in England with Harald Hardrada, it was said, only twenty ever made it back to Norway.

And Harald himself, along with Tostig, lay among the mangled dead. So too, trampled down and stained with filth and gore, did his famous banner. At the end, Land-Waster's magic had failed – and, as it turned out, failed for good.

Conquest

The carnage at Stamford Bridge would long be remembered by the Northmen. As well it might have been – for never again would they cross the seas with the ambition of conquering a Christian land. The consigning of their most celebrated sea king to a foreign grave was a brutal measure of just how fast their horizons were closing in. Shortly before Harald Hardrada made his last stand, it was said, a party of horsemen had ridden out from the English lines and crossed to where the Norwegians stood facing them, lined up in a shield wall. One of the embassy, calling to Tostig, passed on a greeting from his brother, King Harold, and an offer: 'one-third of all the kingdom'. Tostig, shouting back, demanded to know what his ally, King Harald Hardrada, might expect. 'And the rider said, "King Harold has already declared how much of England he is prepared to grant the Norwegian: seven feet of earth, or as much as he needs to be buried, bearing in mind that he is taller than other men."'[46]

These were the last words ever spoken between the two brothers – for the rider had been none other than Harold Godwinsson himself. Wit and a defiant cool were the authentic qualities of a man who all his life had been passing 'with watchful mockery through ambush after ambush'.[47] In Harold's scorning of the invader, however, and the granting to him only of sufficient earth to cover his bones, there had been something more than mere braggart play. The presumption that a land might indeed be sacred to those who trod it was neither an idle nor a novel one. So it was, for instance, that Earl Britnoth, opposing an earlier generation of Vikings at Maldon, had pledged himself ringingly to the defence of *folc and foldan*: 'people and soil'.[48] That the two were synonymous was a presumption widely shared across much of

Christendom. Even in regions where borders and loyalties were infinitely more confused, and confusing, than in England, men had long been in the habit of identifying themselves with a *'natio'* – a nation. 'People joined together by a single descent, custom, language and law,'[49] one abbot, writing in the Rhineland a whole century before the Millennium, had defined the word.

True, there were certain 'nations', the Normans pre-eminent among them, whose beginnings were so recent that their mongrel character could never hope to be smoothed over – but this was a problem only for parvenus. Generally, among the more venerable peoples of Christendom, it was taken for granted that all those who shared a common homeland necessarily shared a common ancestry too; indeed, that they had been united by blood even back in the most primordial of times, when they too, like the pagans who were rumoured still to haunt the steppelands beyond the frontiers of the Rus, had been wanderers, without any roots at all. A convenient notion: for since no one could actually be certain what had happened in such an obscure and distant age, the field had been left free for the learned to rustle up any number of glamorous ancestors for themselves. Frankish genealogists, for instance, had traced the pedigree of their people back to the ancient Trojans; the Saxons, not to be outdone, had claimed to be the offspring of the soldiers of Alexander the Great. Most ingenious of all, perhaps, were the Scots, who bragged, with a formidable disregard for plausibility, that they were originally from Egypt, descendants of the same Pharaoh's daughter who had discovered Moses in the bulrushes – and whose name, so they cheerfully insisted, in a manner designed to clinch their argument, had been Princess Scota.

Far-fetched such stories might have been – and yet they were no less potent for that. Indeed, the myths that peoples told about themselves, and the sense that they had of themselves as distinctive nations, tended to be much more deeply rooted than the monarchies that ruled them. Not that this, for an upstart dynasty, was necessarily a disadvantage. Back in 936, for instance, when Otto I succeeded to his father's throne, he had been able to do so not merely by right of inheritance, but 'as the choice of all the Franks and Saxons'.[50] For Harold Godwinsson, in 1066, the benefits of posing as the people's prince were even more self-evident. Lacking as he did so much as a drop of royal blood, his surest claim to legitimacy lay in the fact that his peers, and perhaps even the dying Edward himself, had all given him the nod.[51] Nor, despite the mildly embarrassing detail that both his name and mother were Danish, could there be any doubt as to why he had been considered worthy to rule as the supreme representative of the English. Harold had been – as even his bitterest enemies acknowledged – 'the most distinguished of Edward's subjects in honour, wealth and power'.[52] No one was better qualified to guard his countrymen against foreign invaders. 'Our king'[53] he was duly hailed in the wake of his slaughter of Hardrada's army. Harold, at Stamford Bridge, had successfully defended both '*folc and foldan*'.

Yet even as he cleaned his sword of Norwegian blood, the circumstances that had brought him to the throne continued to menace his prospects. Back in 1063, in the wake of a hard-won victory over the Welsh, Harold had been presented with the head of his murdered enemy: a baneful and portentous trophy. Three years on, and his ability to claim the scalps of his adversaries had come to rank as the only certain measure of his fitness to rule. Not even with Hardrada safely fertilising the soil of Northumbria could he afford to relax. Other predators, other invaders, still cast their shadows. All that summer of 1066, Harold had been standing guard on the Channel – and now, with his warriors force-marched up the length of England, he was grimly aware that he had left his southern flank unprotected. Wearily, then, with the crows still flocking and clamouring above the fields of Stamford Bridge, he set about retracing his steps. He could have no doubts as to the urgency of his mission. Long before becoming king, Harold had made it a point 'to study the character, policy and strength of the princes of France'[54] – and of one in particular. Grant so much as the sniff of an opening, he had to reckon, and the Duke of Normandy would take it.

For certainly, by 1066, there could be no doubting that William ranked as a truly deadly foe. His apprenticeship was long since over. Seasoned in all the arts of war and lordship, and with a reputation fit to intimidate even the princes of Flanders and Anjou, even the King of France himself, his prime had turned out a fearsome one. So too had that of his duchy. Quite as greedy for land and spoils as any Viking sea king, the great lords of Normandy, men who had grown up by their duke's side and shared all his ambitions, had emerged as an elite of warriors superior, in both their discipline and training, to any in Christendom. For a decade and a half William and his lieutenants had been probing southwards, engaging in a uniquely lethal and innovative style of combat, pitting themselves against those most proficient castle-builders, the castellans of Anjou. The buffer zone of Maine, which back in the early 1050s had passed almost entirely into Angevin hands, had been systematically broken to William's will. Patience had been blended with daring; attrition with escapades; months spent ravaging vineyards with sudden midnight surgical strikes. 'Terror had been sown across the land.'[55] Nor, even with Maine securely in his grasp, had William been content to rest in his saddle. Campaigning had become a way of life for him, and for all those who followed his standard. Horses still had to be exercised, castles built, estates and towns and riches won. No surprise, then, that England, where the great men still fought on foot, and defended their wooden halls with little more than ditches, and were not organised for ceaseless warfare, should have served to beckon the restless and hungry duke. To most Englishmen, accustomed as they were to look for danger from across the northern seas, the notion that the upstart Normans might represent a genuine menace to their ancient and wealthy kingdom had appeared a fanciful one – but not to Harold. He, at any rate, had taken pains to analyse William at close quarters. He had made sure to observe in the field how the duke's castles were built, and the aggressive use to which they could be put, and the ominous potential of the Norman cavalry. Indeed, he had even ridden with William on a raid into Brittany – and performed so heroically during the course of the expedition that he had been rewarded for his feats with a gift of armour from the duke himself.

This startling feat of espionage had been achieved only a couple of years before the fateful testing time of 1066. Quite what it was that had brought Harold to Normandy in the first place would later be much debated. The Normans would insist that he had been sent by Edward to promise William the succession; the English that he had travelled there of his own volition in order to negotiate a marriage alliance or perhaps the release of a hostage. It is not impossible that both claims were true. Altogether more certain, however, is that Harold, after a calamitous initial journey to Normandy – one that had featured both a shipwreck and a spell in the dungeon of a local princeling – had ended up as William's guest. Though this might have been awkward for him, Harold was not his father's son for nothing: and so it was, smoothly and with a fine show of Godwin opportunism, that he had set himself to a close study of the man whom he would long since have fingered as his likeliest rival for the English throne. Carefully veiling his own ambitions, he had encouraged William to spill out everything. Sure enough, the duke had openly acknowledged to his charming and attentive guest how he did indeed intend to press his right to England, by virtue of his relationship to his long-dead great-aunt, the Lady Emma, and by sundry blessings that he claimed to have received from King Edward. Harold, more than content to play his rival for a fool, had duly sworn to support and advance William's cause. His reward had been yet further gifts, and a ship back home to England. 'Watchful mockery' indeed.

No wonder, then, in the early weeks of 1066, that William should have responded to the news of Harold's accession with icy and bitter rage: he felt the fury of a man who had been cheated as well as robbed. Particularly shocking to him was the memory of how his guest, pledging his support, had done so with a gesture of awful and public solemnity, his hand laid on a relic box, a deed of fateful boldness: for what was an oath if not a challenge flung directly at God?

'But alas' – as those who knew the new king had long appreciated – 'he was a man always too quick to give his word'.[56] It was all very well for Harold to claim that his oath of loyalty to William had been extorted from him under duress, and that he had been crowned entirely by right, according to the wishes and customs of the English people. Such details did not serve to absolve him, for there existed laws more awesome and binding than those of any mortal kingdom. William, at any rate, understood this well enough. Indeed, he had always capitalised powerfully upon it. He was a man, after all, who had turned the Peace of God so thoroughly to his own advantage, and imposed it with such an iron fist, that other princedoms, in comparison with Normandy, could appear to the Normans themselves mere bear pits, 'rife with unbridled wickedness'.[57] No surprise, then, that the duke, in his determination to secure his right to England, should have moved quickly to explore what else God might be able to do for him. He was acutely sensitive, in a way his wily but light-hearted rival was not, to the changing spirit of the times – a spirit that set a premium on the universal over the local. Certainly, he had no doubts that the laws of England could be made to seem as nothing when compared with the awful majesty of the one supreme law: that of God Almighty Himself. William, whose stern religiosity had always been combined with a talent for spotting trends, was a ruler surpassingly well fitted to appreciate the new enthusiasms that were animating the highest reaches of the Church – and what they might mean for himself. One of his bishops had sat alongside Leo IX at the Council of Reims. One of his abbots had been a school friend of Alexander II, the reigning Pope. The mighty tide of reform, which far from subsiding with Leo's death had continued to swell and surge and advance, could hardly help, then, in the great crisis of 1066, but be a matter of surpassing interest to William.

Nor, in turn, could William fail to arouse a matching enthusiasm among reforming circles in Rome. In the summer of 1066, even as Harald Hardrada was preparing to unfurl Land-Waster, a very different banner was being readied for the Duke of Normandy. 'The standard of

St Peter the Apostle'[58] bore no moving ravens on it, nor any other hint of magic, and yet there could be no doubting its awesome and supernatural potency – for it had been blessed in person by none other than the Holy Father himself. A remarkable development. Barely a decade had passed since Leo IX, provoking a storm of shock and outrage, had ordered a papal banner to be carried for the first time into battle; nor, in the interim, had the controversy subsided. Although William's ambassador had been received sympathetically in Rome, the suggestion that the Pope grant official backing to the invasion of England – a Christian kingdom! – had provoked furious opposition from his advisers. Not, however, from his most influential aide of all: the man who, even more than Alexander himself, was the true designer of papal policy. Hildebrand, by 1066, had risen far. His official rank, that of archdeacon, barely hinted at the degree to which he had become the pre-eminent, indeed the indispensable, power behind St Peter's throne.

'If you would thrive at Rome, say this at the top of your voice, "More than the Pope, I obey the lord of the Pope!"'[59] Such was the homage, half mocking, half admiring, paid to Hildebrand. To the steely resolve that he had always possessed, and his abiding passion for the cause of reform, he brought what were by now years of experience garnered in the very cockpit of the Lateran. Though his own personal sense of sanctity was passionate and exalted, it had not prevented him from honing the often ruthless instincts of a natural politician. Certainly, Hildebrand had no doubts that a reformed England was a prize well worth fighting for. A veritable bog of simony, even by the standards of the rest of Christendom, it urgently needed draining. If William, who had always shown himself a model partner of the Church, could achieve that, then he would have served the cause not only of the reformers but of the sin-steeped English themselves. True, as Hildebrand freely acknowledged, 'there are many among my brothers who revile me for this judgement, and charge me with labouring to bring about a terrible sacrifice of human lives'[60] – but his own conscience was clear. The end would surely justify the means. An assault on England could worthily be ranked a holy war. And so it was that Hildebrand had leaned on the Pope, and the Norman duke had received his banner.

Naturally, even had Alexander II rebuffed William, the Normans would hardly have set about sheathing their swords. Already, at a series of councils held throughout the spring, the great lords of the duchy had committed themselves to the perilous enterprise of invasion: for they had been bred to hunger after land. Yet still they had their qualms. Some of these were practical; but others were more profoundly rooted. Greed and a joy in violence were not always easy to square with a devotion to the teachings of the Prince of Peace. Dread of the King whose sway embraced the universe, and whose conquest had been over death itself, was deep dyed within many Normans: they could not, as their pagan ancestors had done, gorge themselves on the riches of a Christian nation, and be content to do so as pirates, as adventurers, and nothing more. And of no one was this truer than William himself: for it was his ambition to kill an anointed king, and to encompass his crown, and then to be touched in his turn by the terrifying mystery of the chrism.

Doubtless, then, that summer of 1066, as the same winds that were sweeping the Norwegian war fleet towards England kept the Norman ships stranded impotently in harbour, the presence of St Peter's banner by William's side would have served to reassure him that the Almighty had not, after all, abandoned his cause. Doubtless too, on the evening of 27 September, when the winds finally fell, and the fateful order was given to set sail, he would have reflected on the curious workings of Providence, that had kept him delayed for so long, and amid so many frustrations, only to grant him the perfect moment to make his crossing. For the Channel lay open. William, tucking into a hearty supper on board his flagship, could look forward to a thoroughly uneventful voyage. Meanwhile, his destination, where Harold had been stationed all summer on the expectation of his coming, was waiting ungarrisoned. No wonder, then, as the sun rose the following morning, and revealed to William a great forest of masts, his ships, and ahead of them the empty coastline of England, 'he glorified God's mercy from the very depths of his heart'.[61]

And felt himself perfectly justified, as his men began to wade through the shallows on to the beach, or else to coax their horses down unsteady gangplanks, in readying them for the great labour of conquest that lay ahead. William's first move was a wholly predictable one: to throw up a couple of makeshift castles. One was raised within the mouldering remains of a Roman fort named Pevensey; the other on the far side of a bleak expanse of lagoons and salt flats, beside the fishing port of Hastings. From here, running along a ridge so fringed on either side by creeks that it ranked effectively as a peninsula, a single road led onwards to London. Harold, brought the devastating news of William's landing while he was still far to the north, naturally expected the invaders to take it. He knew better than anyone in England, after all, what to dread from their way of war. Horsemen fanning out unopposed across the heartlands of Wessex. Granaries being plundered, towns and villages being torched. Rough and ready castles dotting the trace lines of devastation. Only if Harold could keep William bottled up could he hope to spare his '*folc and foldan*' such a fate. The knowledge of this, combined with his instinctive taste for taking his enemies by surprise, spurred him on ever southwards, without thought of pausing. No time to wait for reinforcements – still less to give his already battle-weary men any rest. Speed was of the essence.

Except that William, in reality, was heading nowhere. Shortly after setting up his headquarters in Hastings, he and his most trusted henchman, William fitz Osbern, had ventured out in person to reconnoitre the local terrain. The isolated nature of their base camp, the single road connecting them to the mainland, the marshes on either side of it: all these 'they had boldly explored'.[62] Stay where they were, they had quickly realised, and they were liable to end up trapped. If Harold did come against them, then they would have no choice but to meet him in open combat. And most seasoned commanders would have done anything to avoid that perilous business. Yet the very risks contingent on opting for battle, the desperate quality of the gamble, the chance that the whole course of the war, and indeed of William's entire career, might be decided by a single moment were considerations positively to be embraced.

So it was, as the days passed, that the Normans did the very opposite of what had been expected of them: they hunkered down. Days passed, then a week. Occasionally, from across the creeks that bordered Hastings, black smoke would plume into the sky, the signature of one of William's raiding parties – but otherwise the invaders did not stir. A second week passed. Still, their nerves taut, the duke and his chieftains and his warriors waited. Then, on the evening of Friday 13 October, scouts came galloping into the Norman camp, slipping down from their saddles with their urgency of their news. White dust had been glimpsed in the distance. The English army was closing in. The usurper was almost at the gates.

Almost – but not quite. Frantically, William recalled his foragers, then gave them and all his army a hurried command to prepare for battle. Dusk saw the Norman camp swept by clamour and confusion. Indeed, such was William's own haste that he put his mail shirt on back to front. Yet naturally, despite the general mood of alarm, he remained the Duke of Normandy still, a man of iron: he did not surrender to panic. On the contrary – having almost been ambushed by Harold, he was now resolved to ambush Harold in turn. 'There is no other way of escape.'[63] With that brutal home truth ringing in their ears, William ordered his men to take the road from Hastings, to advance along the ridge that would bring them face to face with their approaching foes. There were still several hours to dawn when the Normans left camp. On they marched, three, four, five miles. Steadily, to their right, beyond dense woods, the sky was lightening. Still, though, no sign of the enemy. The sun began to rise. Then, at around eight o'clock, breasting a hill some six miles out of Hastings, the Normans saw a valley ahead of them, and the slope of a second hill, and there, emerging on to its crest, brilliant with gilded banners, the English vanguard. Did William, at such a sight, permit himself the very thinnest of smiles? No doubt – for it was all as he had hoped. Harold's men were still assembling – rendezvousing for an intended final march on Hastings. Their ranks were unformed. 'The woods all around glittered full of their spears.'[64] The surprisers had been surprised.[65]

Yet still, in the Norman ranks, the awful inevitability of what now faced them would have caught at many a stomach. Pitched battle, though rare, ranked as the ultimate index of a man. Scarcely less to be dreaded than death or injury were shame and disgrace. It was not unknown for warriors, confronted by an enemy, to start vomiting – or else 'to fake being sick'.[66] William and his fellow war leaders, whose entire lives had been preparation for such a moment, were hardly the men to turn tail now; even so, gazing at the brow of the hill ahead of them, at the solid wall of shields that was blocking their way, at the bejewelled battle standard emblazoned with a warrior that marked the presence of Harold, they would have known better than to scorn their foe. No matter that the English way of war – 'disdaining the solace of horses and trusting in their strength to stand fast on foot'[67] – appeared to anyone raised in France quite hilariously primitive: the truth was that Harold had in his ranks fighters no less trained or deadly than the most seasoned Norman horseman. He too, like the lords of Constantinople and Kiev, commanded a bodyguard of Varangians: axe-wielding professionals, skilled in all the arts of evisceration, known by the English as 'housecarls'.[68] These ranked as perhaps the most formidable foot-soldiers in all Christendom, and they would have to be cut down if the invasion was not to fail – for only with Harold dead would any victory count as decisive. As the first Norman arrow showers rattled down upon the round shields of the English, and William's infantry began climbing the hill ahead of them, to test the swing of the housecarls' axes, he knew that his fate was no longer his own to control. It had passed into the hands of God.

Not that anyone would have expected the divine judgement to be delayed for long. Rare was the battle that lasted for more than an hour or so. The moment of crisis, when all would be decided upon a rumour or a sudden flight, was bound to sweep the field soon. And so it almost proved. Most shields were still unriven, most helmets without dents, most blades barely notched, when all of a sudden word began to pass through the Norman ranks that William had fallen. His men were thrown into panic. As they turned and started stumbling and slipping back down the hill, it seemed as though the retreat was on the verge of becoming a rout: for pockets of the English were leaving the shield wall to pursue them. All hung in the balance.

But William, though his horse had been brought down and he himself flung on to the ground, was not dead. Raising both his helmet and his voice, rallying his dispirited men, reminding them that they were warriors still, he succeeded in steeling his buckling line. And now it was the turn of the English to face a seeming breaking point. Those who had been pursuing their retreating adversaries down the hill found themselves suddenly turned upon. Surrounded, they proved easy meat. Hoofs and trampling feet pulped their bodies into the mud. The slope of the hill turned slippery, a shambles of viscera and broken limbs. For a second time, it seemed as though the battle was decided. But just as the Normans had been rallied, so now did the English refuse to flee. Harold's great banner still fluttered defiantly in the breeze. The shield wall, though sorely depleted, held. The day remained unresolved.

And even as the hours continued to pass, and the sun slowly to set, and the shadows to lengthen over the increasingly corpse-strewn slope of the battlefield, the confusion did not cease. 'It was', as one Norman would express it later in stupefied terms, 'an unheard-of kind of combat, with one side launching ceaseless attacks and manoeuvres, the other standing firmly as though rooted to the ground.'[69] Not all the exhaustion of men weighed down by the great weight of their shields and helmets and coats of iron could serve to diminish the desperate savagery of the battle. An hour before sunset, and still William's men were hurling themselves against the English, their spears splintered, as William's own was, their swords no less 'dyed with brains and blood'[70] than their duke's. Yet still the housecarls stood firm, swinging with their double-headed axes, bludgeoning their assailants, hacking through metal and flesh and bone. Certainly, planted as they were upon their hill, they could not hope to win – but then again, merely to hold their position, to win through to the night, to force a draw, would rank almost as a victory. William, isolated as he was in a hostile county, and with the sea at his back, could not afford a stalemate. Only succeed in standing firm until the coming of dusk, then, and Harold would most likely win the war.

But he did not last the hour. Many stories would later be told about his end; one, the most repeated, had him being hit in the eye by an arrow.[71] Whether true or not, it is certain that Norman horsemen, trampling Harold down, left him as just one among a heap of corpses piled around the toppled royal banner, just one among the fallen on a day of slaughter fit to put even Stamford Bridge into the shade. As darkness fell, and what was left of the English turned at last and fled into the gathering darkness, to be hunted throughout the night by William's exultant cavalry, it was the reek of blood and emptied bowels, together with the moans and sobs of the wounded, that bore prime witness to the butchery. Come the morning, however, and daylight unveiled a spectacle of carnage so appalling that even the victors were moved to pity. 'Far and wide the earth was covered with the flower of the English nobility and youth, drenched in gore.'[72] So hacked about was Harold's own body, and so disfigured the face, that it could barely be recognised.

Fit image of the mutilation with which the kingdom itself had been served. True, not all the lords of England had fallen at Hastings; nor had their fight been brought wholly to an end by the slaughter. Yet with Harold dead, and his brothers fallen beside him, and his most loyal followers too, there was no one left to coordinate the resistance. The Normans, with their predators' nostrils ever sensitive to the scents of weakness and despair, were hardly the people to let a wounded foe slip free. By Christmas Day, William was sitting in the same abbey where Harold had been crowned at the beginning of the year, to receive a crown of his own. Within the church itself, the moment of his coronation was greeted, as was the English custom, with a great cry of acclamation, a thunderous acknowledgement that the Norman duke now ruled as the anointed heir to Alfred and Edgar and Edward; but outside, in the streets, William's guards mistook the shouting for a riot, and set about assaulting the locals and torching their houses. It was a brute reminder to the conquered English of the true source of their new king's legitimacy.

To foreign observers as well, William appeared merely one more in a long line of northern predators, and his winning of a crown a feat of robbery such as any Viking chieftain might have revelled in. 'The Duke crossed the cold channel,' as one Dane put it, 'and reddened the bright swords.'[73] Yet that was not how William himself saw his great exploit. At the most awe-inspiring moment of his life, as he was crowned on the very anniversary of the birth of Christ, the new king had begun to tremble uncontrollably, betraying for the first and only time in his life, perhaps, a sense of fear and self-doubt. Hearing screams rise from outside the abbey, even as he could feel the chrism impregnating him with its sacral charge, William would surely have dreaded with a sudden certitude that his offences were rank, that God had not blessed him with His favour at all, and that the blood through which he had waded, the filth and horror and stench of it, was charged eternally to his soul. The moment had passed – and William had been left William still. Yet he did not forget the experience. Years later, when a jester saw the king sitting 'resplendent in gold and jewels', and shouted out, 'Behold, I see God! behold, I see God!',[74] he had been whipped for his joke. It was not the blasphemy that had caused such grievous offence, but rather the implied mockery of William's most profoundly held conceit: that he had been raised to the throne of England by the hand of Providence.

If the Normans, who knew that in truth it was their own sword arms which had won their bastard duke the crown, sometimes found this hard to take, then so did the English. William's coronation oath, that he would uphold the laws and customs of his new subjects, had been sworn with all due solemnity – and sure enough, for the first few years of his reign, he did indeed attempt to include them as partners within his new regime. But the English earls could never quite forgo a taste for revolt – with the result that, soon enough, an infuriated William was brought to abandon the whole experiment. In its place, he instituted a far more primal and brutal policy. Just as his ancestors had cleansed what would become Normandy of its Frankish aristocracy, so now did William set about the systematic elimination from England of its entire ruling class. The lands of the kingdom – its '*folc and foldan*' – were henceforward to be in the charge of Normans, and no one else. This, however, as a feat of dispossession, owed less to the example of Rollo than to William's well-honed mastery of the cutting edge. No longer was England to remain isolated from the revolution that had so transformed the princedoms of France. Pevensey and Hastings were destined to prove only the first of the castles raised by the conquerors. The proficiency of William fitz Osbern, in particular, was noted by the English as a grim and fearsome thing: 'for he built castles far and wide throughout this country, and distressed the wretched folk, and always after that it grew much worse'.[75] Which was putting it mildly: for the task of the Norman lords, set as they were amid a sullen and fractious people, was no different in kind to that of the most upstart castellan in France.

In England, however, it was not just scattered hamlets and villages that needed to be broken, but a whole kingdom. In the winter of 1069, when the inveterately rebellious Northumbrians sought to throw off their new king's rule, William's response was to harry the entire earldom. Methods of devastation familiar to the peasantry of France were unleashed across the north of England: granaries were burned, oxen slaughtered, ploughs destroyed. Rotting corpses were left to litter the road. The scattered survivors were reduced to selling themselves into slavery, or else, if reports are to be believed, to cannibalism. Even enthusiasts for William's rule confessed themselves appalled. 'On many occasions,' wrote one of them, 'I have been able to extol him according to his merits, but this – this I dare not praise.'[76]

And yet, as William might legitimately have pointed out, the practice of ravaging was an ancient one in England. Edgar had done the same – and he was remembered as 'the Peaceable'. Hard and ruthless 'the Conqueror' might be, but for all that, he was no Harold, given to breaking his promises lightly. The oath he had sworn at his coronation, to uphold the laws of England, was one that he would labour all his life to keep. In his determination to keep together his new realm, its unity, its public order and its peerless administration, William was indeed a king in the most formidable tradition of the *Cerdicingas*. Duke of Normandy too, and favourite of the reformers in the Lateran; he was a ruler of many parts. No statesman of his age was less the prisoner of the past – or more adept at turning it to his own ends. Tradition and innovation: would both continue to be exploited by William with a trail-blazing facility. That his reign was destined to prove one perpetual experiment, an attempt to weave a tapestry from a multiplicity of different strands, whether drawn from England, or Normandy, or Rome, would ultimately serve to render his achievements only the more lasting. He might have been the bastard descendant of pirates – but he would end up master of the most formidable instrument of royal power in the whole of Christendom. He had dared – and he had won.

True, doubts as to the price paid for this victory were never altogether dispelled. 'For what has a man profited,' as Abbot Hugh of Cluny wrote pointedly to William, 'if he shall gain the whole world, but lose his own soul?'[77] Even Hildebrand himself, the very man who had pushed for the Conqueror to be granted a papal banner, appears to have felt a slight measure of queasiness at the sheer scale of the bloodletting that he had helped to sponsor. In 1070, only a few months after the harrying of Northumbria, a papal legate imposed a public penance on all who had fought at Hastings. Shortly afterwards, in a further show of expiation, the foundations of a new abbey began to be dug on the very site of the fateful battle. The altar, so William had decreed, was to stand precisely where Harold had fallen: a command that required the entire top of the hill to be levelled. Religiosity, arrogance, and a quite awe-inspiring monumentalism: the new monastery combined them all. If it was intended to express contrition, then so too was it designed to overawe. 'Even a Greek or Saracen', claimed one Norman, describing the Conqueror's prodigious sponsorship of churches, 'might find himself impressed.'[78] As well he might. The great buildings that William could afford to build, unprecedented engineering experiments raised in stone, were indeed on a scale to compare with anything to be found in Constantinople or Córdoba. So too was the state that he ruled. No matter that he had founded it, like Battle Abbey, upon a field of blood – its foundations were destined to last.

7

AN INCONVENIENT TRUTH

Just Say No

It took a conqueror to seize a kingdom. Kings, however, if they were weak, and especially if they were children, might be captured with altogether greater ease. Even the very highest ranking of them – even future emperors. Eighty years had passed since the abduction of the infant Otto III in 984 – and now, once again, the *Reich* was ruled by a child. Henry IV, son and namesake of the great emperor who had done so much to implant the cause of reform in Rome, had been crowned king back in 1056, when he was only five years old. Self-reliant and sharp-witted he may have been – but not even the most precocious boy could hope to stamp his authority at such a tender age. Just as Duke William, throughout his minority, had found himself powerless to prevent the steady collapse of order within Normandy, so was the infant Henry, for all his talents, bound to remain the toy of those who had the keeping of him. Control the king and take control of the kingdom: so it seemed to the more unscrupulous among the great lords of the *Reich*. Henry, for as long as he remained under age, at any rate, could hardly help but rank as a likely candidate for a kidnapping.

So it was, in the spring of 1062, when the Archbishop of Cologne came gliding down the Rhine in a particularly handsome galley and

Henry IV's *Reich*

docked at the island palace of Kaiserswerth, where the court had been celebrating Easter, the king's guardians should have been fully on their guard. But they were not. A serious lapse: for Henry himself – impulsive, mercurial and twelve years old – was just the boy to jump at the chance of exploring a state-of-the-art showboat. No sooner had he stepped on board, however, than all the oars began to beat, 'and he was immediately propelled out into the middle of the river with a quite remarkable speed'.[1] The young king, despite not being able to swim, boldly jumped overboard: an attempt at escape that would have left him drowned had one of the archbishop's accomplices not dived in after him, and hauled him back to safety. To captivity as well. Rowed upriver to Cologne, where he discovered that even the Holy Lance, that most awesome of all his possessions, had been filched, Henry found himself the impotent cipher of his abductors: a whole swaggering gang of dukes and prelates. Hardly the experience, in short, to bolster his faith much in either princes or bishops.

Yet though the scandal of his abduction had been traumatic for the young king himself, it was even more so for his mother. Agnes of Aquitaine, pious and conscientious, had been ruling on Henry's behalf ever since her husband's death: a challenging responsibility for a woman, certainly, but not wholly without precedent, even so. If Theophanu, that formidable and glamorous guardian of the infant Otto III, continued to serve as the most celebrated model of a queenly regent, then she was far from the only one. Great lords, with their predilection for hunting, feuding and fighting, were much given to dying before their heirs had come of age. Grandmothers, widows and aunts: any or all might be called upon to step into the breach. Indeed, at one point, back in 985, there had been so many women in Christendom ruling on behalf of under-age wards that they had all met up at a special summit, to swap dynastic gossip and formulate marriage plans for their charges. Such displays of female influence might have lacked the honest masculine impact of a sword blow or a lance punch, but they could be just as effective. Agnes herself, in the course of her regency, had provided a particularly striking demonstration of how a woman could succeed where even a mighty warrior had failed: for one of the great things that she had achieved for her son was to secure for him the stalwart backing of a prince who, only a few years previously, had been an inveterate rebel against her husband.

Duke Godfrey, 'the Bearded', as he was known, had presented a double menace to Henry III: both in his own right, as a great landowner in Lorraine, along the western frontier of the *Reich*, and by virtue of a brilliant marriage that had brought him an even more impressive swath of land in northern Italy. Godfrey was the second husband of the raven-haired and beauteous Lady Beatrice: her first, a notably ruthless warlord by the name of Boniface, had hacked out a lordship that included much of Tuscany and extended all the way northwards to the foothills of the Alps. This formidable dowry was rendered all the more alarming, in Henry III's considered opinion, by the fact that Beatrice was his own cousin, and a descendant of Henry the Fowler, no less. Rather than grant Godfrey the continued posses-sion of such a catch, the emperor had opted instead to invade Tuscany, seize Beatrice and Matilda, her one surviving child by Boniface, and cart both mother and daughter back to a gilded confinement in the Rhineland. Yet Agnes, in the wake of her husband's death, had sought a different approach. Duke Godfrey himself had been 'restored to the king's grace, and to peace'.[2] His right to Tuscany had been officially acknowledged. Beatrice and the eleven-year-old Matilda had been released. From that moment on, presiding over his Tuscan lordship from his principal stronghold, an ancient, dilapidated, but increasingly vibrant town named Florence, Godfrey had provided Agnes's regime with its most loyal bulwark. Fitting, then, perhaps, that the dynasty itself should have taken its title, not from Florence, nor from any other lowland town filled with antique ruins and sleek merchants, but rather from an altogether more bristling and impregnable fortress, Count Boniface's original base, a castle perched high on a remote and moun-tainous rock: Canossa.

Yet not all the empress's gambles had paid off to similar effect.

Nearer to home, her policy of building up the power of ambitious princes had tended to result in an ominous fragmenting of the royal power base. Sponsorship did not always result in gratitude. Come the great crisis of Agnes's regency, and even a prominent kinsman of the infant king, the formidably blue-blooded Duke Rudolf of Swabia, had shown himself perfectly content to turn his back upon the empress – despite the fact that it was she who had originally raised him to the eminence of his dukedom.[3] Other favourites had behaved even more shabbily. Prominent among the lords directly responsible for Henry's abduction, for instance, had been a second prince who owed a dukedom to the empress: a count from Northeim, in lower Saxony, by the name of Otto, appointed only six months previously to the rule of Bavaria. Justifying their treachery, Duke Otto and his fellow conspirators had shown a particularly fine line in hypocrisy. Agnes, they charged, despite every appearance to the contrary, was in truth a giddy creature of whim and sensuality – so much so that all her rule of the kingdom had been governed by nothing more elevated than 'her private passions'.[4] A particularly vicious libel: for it had served to cast all the empress's attempts at diplomacy as the merest feminine teasing and seduction. Such was the kind of mud that any powerful lady might expect to have flung at her – but for the devout Agnes, it was a particular agony. In the wake of her son's kidnapping, and the signal failure of the great lords of the *Reich* to rally to her support, the empress had been left to wring her hands over the ruin of more than merely her political authority. Something infinitely precious had been dragged through the mire too: her reputation for pious living. A terrible blow – so terrible, indeed, that the despairing Agnes judged that it could only have been a punishment delivered upon her for her sins by the Almighty.

For the next three years, an irresolute and anguished figure, the empress would haunt the scenes of her humiliation, torn between anxiety for her son and 'a yearning to renounce the world'.[5] For as long as Henry remained legally her charge, she could not bring herself to abandon the court altogether – but then, shortly after Easter in

1065, at a splendid ceremony in Worms, a sword was belted around the young king's waist, and at last he ranked as a man. Almost his first action after coming of age, a pointed demonstration of muscle flexing, was to dismiss as his principal adviser the same man whose ship had borne him away three years previously: the Archbishop of Cologne. It was gratifying in the extreme for Agnes to witness the disgrace of the man who had brought about her own downfall – but proof as well that Henry no longer had any need of her. So it was, obeying the promptings of her own hag-ridden conscience, that she finally took to the road. 'The knowledge of my sins terrifies me,' she had confessed three years earlier, 'more than any ghost, more than any vision.'[6] That autumn, one among the great multitude of pilgrims seeking to cast aside their old lives, to ready themselves for the hour of judgement, to secure a new beginning, she entered Rome. Humbly, as befitted a penitent, she approached the tombs of the apostles on a broken-down nag, dressed in clothes of the roughest grey sack-cloth, and 'clutching not a sceptre but a psalter'.[7] Yet in one respect, at least, the empress remained an empress still. Seeking spiritual comfort, she did not bother to scout around for it. Instead, imperious in her very humility, Agnes went directly to St Peter's and summoned a cardinal.

And not just any cardinal. In 1065, with the formidable Humbert having died four years earlier, the man chosen by the empress to serve as her confessor ranked as perhaps the most intellectually dazzling of all the leaders of the Roman Church. Originally raised to the cardinalate back in the winter of 1057, at the prompting of the inevitable Hildebrand, Peter Damian had brought qualities to the papal cause that were very much his own. Less steely than the archdeacon, less awesomely focused and competent, he was also far bolder in the flights of his imagination, more creative, more brilliant. Indeed, rare was the innovation so radical that he could not take it to some provocative new extreme. Well, then, might Hildebrand have pushed for his promotion: for Peter, with his genius for thinking the unthinkable, was ideally qualified to serve as the outrider of reform. Sure enough, with papal ministers struggling to convince other churches that the Bishop of Rome did indeed possess a universal lordship over them, the new cardinal had gone straight for the jugular: anyone who denied it, he had declared flatly, was a heretic.[8] A most portentous doctrine: for it had promised to the Pope an authority such as not even a Caesar had presumed to claim. To his ministers too, of course – and they, at any rate, had already shown themselves perfectly happy to muscle in on imperial prerogatives. In 1059, moving to usurp a power that Henry III had always jealously maintained as his own, the cardinals had laid claim to a truly momentous dignity: the right to choose a pope. Peter, letting joyous rip, had responded to this decree with an exuberant immodesty. He and his fellow cardinals, he proclaimed, were nothing less than 'the spiritual senators of the universal Church'. Here was a stirring allusion: for once, back in ancient times, it was a Senate formed of the wisest and noblest of the Roman people that had guided its city to the mastery of the world. Now, Peter argued, it was the duty of the cardinals to aim at a yet greater feat of conquest. 'For this is the endeavour to which they should devote all their talents: the subjugation of the entire human race to the laws of the one true emperor – Christ.'[9]

It was just the kind of clarion call that Hildebrand had surely been hoping that Peter would sound. Yet the author himself, for all his outward show of self-confidence, was inwardly racked by anguish and self-doubt. Meeting with Agnes in the candle-washed shadows of St Peter's, hearing her confession, encouraging her in her resolve to retire to a convent, he could see in the troubled empress only a reflection of his own inner turmoil. The cardinal too, though a prince of the Church, knew what it was to fear greatness. All the opportunities that high rank had brought him, all the glory, the power, the fame, appeared to him in truth only the most devilish temptations. Upon Hildebrand, indeed, he had bestowed the nickname – not altogether a jesting one – of 'my holy Satan'.[10] Peter could hardly neglect his duties as a cardinal, nor scorn his responsibilities to the Christian people; and yet he dreaded, all the same, what the fruits of such a lordship might be. Deep within his heart, no less devoutly than any heretic, he believed that it was in wild places without churches and hectoring archdeacons, out in forests, in swamps, in caves, that the surest hope of redemption lay. Arrayed in all the splendid robes of his office, Peter yearned only to be wearing filthy rags. Surrounded by the swirl and clamour of the Roman crowds, he longed for solitude. Pacing palaces, he dreamed of the rocky and unadorned cave in which, before becoming a cardinal, it had been his calling for many years to live. 'You purify the hidden places of the soul,' Peter had fondly saluted his cell. 'You wash away the squalor of sin. You cause men's souls to shine with the brightness of an angel.'[11]

And once, kneeling on the bare rock of his cave, lost in an ecstasy of tears and prayer, Peter had been granted a glimpse of Christ Himself. Like Adémar, he had witnessed his Saviour 'pierced through with nails, and hanging from a cross'.[12] Unlike Adémar, however, he had been so close to the terrifying spectacle that he had been able to crane his neck upwards and raise his parted lips to the wounds. To drink the blood of God! There was nothing in all the universe that could possibly taste sweeter. What, in comparison, could the entire fallen world appear except a realm of dust and distraction and shadow? No wonder, then, that Peter, in his yearning to free himself from the bonds of the earthly, should have fretted that all his obligations as a leader of the Christian people, oppressive as they were, might be serving to keep him an exile from the City of God. For he knew, none better, what it was to be an outcast, and deprived of the hope of love.

Born in Ravenna in 1007, the last of a large and impoverished clutch of siblings, all his childhood had been one wretched sequence of rejections. His mother, slumping into post-natal depression, had refused to feed him; then she and her husband both, while Peter was still a baby, had abruptly died; brought up by one of his brothers, the young orphan had been starved, and beaten, and at length sent out to work as a swineherd. One day, guarding the pigs, he had come across a gold coin glinting in the mud – and for a brief moment, visions of everything that he could buy with it had served to dazzle the famished and shivering boy. But then, setting his thoughts against such ephemeral pleasures, Peter had steeled himself to answer a profounder need:

going to a priest, he had handed over his precious coin, and paid for a Mass to be said for the soul of his father. More than food and more than clothes, what Peter had been missing were the parents he could never have. No wonder, then, all his life, that he should have longed with such desperation to behold the face of God: his Father in heaven. No wonder either that he should always have taken it for granted that, to do so, he would have to suffer.

In which, of course, he was not alone. Growing up in Ravenna, Peter would sometimes have glimpsed, out in the swamps that stretched beyond the city, the disciples of St Romuald, stooped dots set amid a mosquito haze. The memory never left him. Redeemed from servitude by a second brother, given an education, and emerging from it as the most brilliant teacher of his day, Peter had nevertheless flinched from taking the road that might have led to further advancement – and so it was, during or shortly after the fateful year 1033, that he had opted instead to follow the path of Romuald. From that moment on, never quite able to shake off a leaden sense that the end days remained imminent, he had imagined God sitting over him in unblinking judgement. Not a pleasure, but the experiencing of it would be a torment. Even finding himself the object of others' generosity was sufficient to induce dizzy spells, and a feeling that hungry worms were seething in his guts. 'In all conscience,' he cried out, after having had a vase forced on him by an admirer, 'I would have preferred to be struck down with leprosy than bear the wound inflicted by this gift!'[13]

Yet by a sombre irony, it was the very eloquence with which Peter expressed his yearning to be free of all earthly distractions that doomed him to his celebrity. Whatever other pleasures he felt able to give up, he could never quite abandon his addiction to firing off letters, to offering commentary, to self-promotion. Certainly, as Peter well knew, there were other hermits whose austerities were far worthier of fame than his own. One of them, a neighbour from his days as a hermit, was a particular hero. Dominic – 'Metal Corset Man',[14] as he was known to his admirers – had bound his limbs as well as his stomach with bands of iron; stood upright all day while reciting psalm after psalm after psalm; and flogged himself until his whole emaciated body was left 'as bruised as barley in a mortar'. That heaven approved of these feats appeared indisputable, for every so often a previously unheard-of miracle had been known to stamp itself upon Dominic's brow, and hands, and feet: 'the stigmata of Jesus Christ'.[15] Nevertheless, there were many, even among the ranks of the reformers, who confessed themselves revolted by such extremes of self-mortification – and who found in Peter himself a model far worthier of emulation. What served to prick their consciences were not the regular floggings that he was forever urging upon them but his very public struggle against appetites with which all could identify.

And hunger, perhaps, especially. Indeed, to Peter, who could remember full well what it was to starve, fasting was, if anything, an even greater ordeal than a scourging, and food the object of all his intensest hostility and desire. Not for him the gracious tolerance of lordly overeating that had been shown by Abbot Odilo. Mercilessly, Peter excoriated the rich for their grossness: for the pendulous folds of their paunches, for the violent flush of their crimson cheeks, for the embarrassing manner in which they were given 'to belching and breaking wind'.[16] Hildebrand himself, noted ascetic though he was, had duly been shamed into giving up leeks and onions. Great lords were not so readily embarrassed – but even among their ranks, a growing enthusiasm for reform had begun to menace the old easy-going admiration for a spreading belly. Obesity was passing out of fashion. It was a sign of the times, for instance, that Duke Rudolf's brother, the Bishop of Worms, a man who had long been celebrated for his prodigious bulk, should have found himself regarded, 'not with wonder, but with revulsion'.[17]

Yet gluttony, though it might increasingly provoke ridicule, hardly threatened bishops with revolution. There were other appetites, however, to which flesh was also heir – and which, over recent decades, had come to strike many as a corrosive menace to the proper ordering of the very world. Already, this same startling conviction had set whole cities to totter. In 1057, for instance, priests had found themselves being boycotted, openly assaulted and even threatened with death, all in the streets of Milan. A development fit to send shock waves throughout Christendom: for not only was the city perhaps the largest in the whole of the Latin West, a rare example of an ancient settlement that had actually burst its Roman walls, complete with hospitals, public baths and even pavements, but its archbishop was so fantastically grand that it was all he could do not to look down his nose at the Pope.

What on earth, then, could possibly have provoked such a crisis in so venerable and self-satisfied a church? It was a measure of the seriousness with which this question was taken in Rome that one of the two legates sent to investigate it had been none other than the high-flying bishop who, three years later, would move into the Lateran as Pope Alexander II. The other had been Peter Damian. Arriving in Milan, the two legates had found the city convulsed by running street battles. On one side were henchmen of the archbishop, an old crony of Henry III by the name of Guy; on the other, insurrectionists from the countryside and the poorer quarters of town. 'Patarenes', their enemies called them: a deliberate sneer, derived from the name of the local rag market. Yet though class tensions in the city undoubtedly were violent, it was not issues of poverty that obsessed the Patarenes. Rather, what had originally set them at the throats of Guy and his clergy was a custom so hallowed by tradition that for centuries no one in Milan had thought so much as to raise an eyebrow at it. A custom that had permitted priests to marry, to live openly with their wives – and to have sex.

This was a red rag to Peter, of course. Perhaps, even had the Patarenes not been rampaging around the troubled city, forcing priests at knife point to swear oaths of chastity, he would still have looked favourably on their demands; for the taking down of the Archbishop of Milan a peg or two had long been an ambition of papal strategists. Nevertheless, the notion that a priest – a *priest*! – might feel himself justified in pawing at a concubine's flesh, in stimulating 'the pleasure that scratches the itch within',[18] and then in handling at a holy Mass the body and blood of Christ Himself, was naturally fit to throw Peter into apoplexies. To be sure, he had never had any intention of condoning the Patarenes' thuggery. Violence filled him with horror: he had always regarded Leo IX's war-making as an abomination, and in Milan it had been his aim to rebuild 'with great discretion whatever he found there in a state of ruin'.[19] But when it came to expressing the disgust he felt at the very notion of a married priest, discretion was hardly an option – for if a vase or a leek or an onion were a hellish temptation, then how much more so was a woman. Unlike a pot or vegetable, after all, she might take an active interest in being handled by a man. 'Titbits of the devil, refuse of paradise, slime that fouls minds, blade that slays souls, wolfsbane of drinkers, poison of table companions, the stuff of sin, the occasion of death.' Such vehemence was hardly surprising. To Peter, in terror of exile from God's presence as he was, it made no more sense for a priest to lie with a woman than for a fasting hermit to move into a kitchen. The seductions of a concubine, the perfumes of a pie: both, as a matter of the utmost urgency, had to be kept at bay. No wonder, then, in addressing the wives of priests, that Peter should have been roused to what even for him were spectacular heights of excoriation. 'Yes, it is you I address, you harem of the ancient enemy, hoopoes, screech-owls, night owls, she-wolves, horse leeches.' And so on, and so on, and so on. 'Whores, harlots, kissing-mouths, sloughs for fat pigs, couches for unclean spirits, nymphs, sirens, blood-sucking witches.'[20] Brutal language indeed. Yet in the sheer violence of Peter's revulsion was the measure of his ultimate dread – which was not of women, nor even of sex, but of the coming of the hour of judgement.

And in expressing it, he spoke for multitudes. From the rag-pickers of Milan, with their riots against married priests, to great aristocrats such as Duke Godfrey and the Lady Beatrice, both of whom had piously sworn to forgo a marital bed, it was evident that chastity had become a pressing – indeed a consuming – issue for whole swaths of the Christian people. 'Now, at the end of the ages, when men are multiplied beyond number, is the time of continence.'[21] Maybe – and yet the sense of urgency with which this view had come to be sanctioned by reformers such as Peter, often in the face of furious opposition from their fellow priests, was something startling, nevertheless. A papal legate, had he come across campaigners such as the Patarenes only twenty years previously, would surely have sawn off his leg rather than look sympathetically on their cause. Back in the first decades of the new millennium, any obsession with chastity on the part of the poor, even more than vegetarianism or a taste for living in forests, had been regarded by the Church with the blackest suspicion. 'They affect a profound distaste for sex,' Adémar said of the heretics in Aquitaine. True, he had gone on to insist, in a manner meant to be reassuring, that in private they indulged 'in every kind of orgy' – but this had been only another example of his being economical with the truth.[22] For Adémar to have acknowledged the appalling reality, that heretics were indeed capable of keeping themselves chaste, even as priests were cheerfully rutting with their wives, would have been, quite simply, insupportable. For what then would have served to distinguish the priesthood from the great mass of Christian people? What then would have served to mark the Church out as the ultimate bastion on earth of the celestial? What, indeed, people would surely have begun to ask, was the point of it at all?

It was all the more fortunate, then, that once again – as with every other gauntlet flung down by heresy – there had been dauntless warriors of God on hand to meet the challenge. Monks, unlike priests, had always been expected to live as virgins. Chastity, no less than poverty, was one of the defining marks of their separation from the fallen world. Even so, during the approach to the Millennium, it had begun to serve an even profounder purpose. Just as in the woods and trackless wilds where heretics were prone to roam, so in famous monasteries such as Cluny, virginity had become the mark of men who dared compare themselves to the hosts of heaven. Never to have sex, never even 'to eject semen by rubbing the penis, just as snot is blown out of the nose',[23] was a sacrifice that fitted a monk to rank with a martyr. So, at any rate, it had boldly been declared at Cluny – where, for a decade, scribes had set themselves to producing a whole dossier of documents designed to push the argument. And when had they begun this task? *Anno Domini* 999. A telling date, no doubt. Certainly, there would have been no one at Cluny unaware of the role that virgins were destined to play at the end of time, before the throne of Christ, the Lamb. For it was their songs which St John, in the book of his revelation, had foretold were to sound from heaven. 'It is these who have not defiled themselves with women, for they are chaste; it is these who follow the Lamb wherever He goes; these have been redeemed from mankind as first fruits for God and the Lamb, and in their mouth no lie was found, for they are spotless.'[24] So St John had written.

The passage of the decades, and the failure of the Lamb to materialise, had not in any way served to diminish the potency of Cluny's spotless state. Just the opposite, in fact. The chastity of its monks remained easily the most awesome marker of the monastery's holiness. Of its independence from the outside world as well. Not for the warrior virgins of Cluny the tangle of earthly commitments that offspring would have brought. No place for mewling bastards within their sacred walls. A relief to the monks themselves, no doubt – and to their neighbours, certainly, a mighty comfort. To great lords, those hard-nosed and calculating men, it offered a specific reassurance: that donations to the monastery, and especially donations of land, would not end up being turned against them by ambitious monks out to father dynasties of their own. To others, men and women fretful at the prospect of Christ's return, and who might once have been tempted to embrace chastity themselves, and the path of heresy, in an attempt to prepare for the hour of judgement, it offered a profounder consolation: that they were justified, after all, in putting their faith in men of God. Yet if the monks of Cluny were correct, and a virgin was indeed worthy to rank beside a martyr, then so too was the converse: that a priest who slept with a woman was barely a priest at all.

And what then of that supreme mystery, the awful power entrusted to him to mediate between heaven and earth, by transforming, at a holy Mass, bread and wine into the body and blood of Christ? 'Dog shit',[25] according to the Patarenes, was all that the touch of a married priest was worth. Such language was a bit strong, perhaps, even for Peter – but he could sympathise with the sentiment, nevertheless.[26] Just as simony always tended to be defined by reformers as a kind of leprosy or pestilence or rottenness, so the marriage bed of a priest was invariably represented as a stew of filth. On occasion, indeed, angels had been known to materialise and make the point literally. Peter, writing to Hildebrand shortly before leaving on his mission to Milan, had described one particularly spectacular miracle: the public shaming of a priest whose reputation had always been irreproachable until that moment. Even as he was celebrating Mass, it was reported, an angel had appeared before the full view of the church and set to scrubbing him down, before finishing by emptying the bucket of by now grimy black water over his head. The priest, spluttering and sobbing, had thereupon confessed to the stunned congregation that he had slept with a servant girl only the night before. One slip, one single surrender to his lusts – and all had been ruined.

No wonder that many priests, bewildered by the sudden sea change in public opinion, one that sought to condemn their wives as whores and their own physical needs as a menace to the cosmos, found the new demands being placed upon them insupportable. 'In every struggle with titillating pleasure,' was Peter's own tip, 'try to meditate on the grave'[27] – either that or hurry off to Mass. Advice kindly offered, no doubt – but not entirely adequate, even so, to the frailties of every priest. There were many, it seemed, who needed to be hectored, even menaced, rather than simply encouraged. This was why, even as reformers sought to combine their great campaign against simony with a no less ambitious insistence that priests live as chastely as monks, there were some who looked to harness their supporters among the Christian people to a policy of active intimidation. Peter, that committed pacifist, was not one of them, of course; but there

were others who argued with no less passionate a sense of righteousness that desperate circumstances might indeed require desperate
measures. The stakes were cosmically high. Could there be anything
more important, in the final count, than the readying of God's
Church for the coming of the end days?

One episode, in particular, served to illustrate the kind of value
judgement that its leaders were increasingly opting to make. In 1065,
a knight from Milan by the name of Erlembald, a pious man much
given to charitable works and pilgrimages, arrived in Rome and paid a
call on Hildebrand. He was troubled and in need of spiritual guidance.
Should he join a monastery, he asked the archdeacon, as he had originally been planning to do – or should he accept a very different
calling, a summons just recently received from the Patarenes, to fashion them into an authentic fighting force and lead them as their
generalissimo? Hildebrand's answer was not long in coming. It took
the form – a whole year before the granting of a similar standard to
Duke William of Normandy – of a papal banner. Returning to the
Patarenes beneath the fluttering of this 'battle flag of St Peter's',[28]
Erlembald duly threw himself into the brutal business of scouring
simony and priestly unchastity from Milan for good: the first-ever
knight to have received a formal papal blessing. Whether as a consequence of this or not, victory marked all his efforts. 'He subdued the
city by the sword and also by gold, and by many and diverse oaths;
none of the nobles could withstand him.'[29] Indeed, by 1071, such was
the scale of Erlembald's success that the wretched Archbishop Guy,
holed up in his cathedral, and in increasingly poor health, had
resolved on a clandestine resignation.

Spies in Milan, however, keeping track of his intentions, were soon
bringing news of all his plans to Rome; and Hildebrand moved quickly
to capitalise. Sending both funds and instructions to the Patarene captain, he ordered his protégé to prepare a coup. By August, when the
sick and weary archbishop finally breathed his last, Erlembald was
primed. The Patarenes, backed by the presence of a papal legate,
pushed for the election of a successor, a young clerk by the name of

Atto; and on 6 January 1072, he was duly chosen. Erlembald, escorting the new archbishop to his palace amid a fearsome clattering of hoofs and glimmering of mail, sat him down there to celebrate his elevation with a sumptuous banquet. Yet the Patarenes, for all the speed and ruthlessness of their actions, had overstepped a fateful bound. Momentous forces – more momentous than even Hildebrand could imagine – were being set in train. The attempt to enthrone Atto, far from healing the fissures in Milan, was doomed only to widen them – and indeed to precipitate a crisis so devastating, so unexpected and so wholly without precedent that it would end up racking the whole span of Christendom and transforming it for all time.

That a Patarene nominee as archbishop was a direct threat to the Church establishment in Milan went without saying – but it was also, and far more ominously, a slap in the face for Henry IV. The young king had not forgotten that it was his father, almost three decades previously, who had invested Guy with his staff and ring of office. Indeed, shortly before his death, the failing archbishop had returned them both to the imperial court, together with a proposal that the emissary to whom they had been entrusted, a deacon by the name of Godfrey, be invested with them in turn. King Henry, who was by now in his early twenties, and positively itching to throw his weight around in Italy, had needed no second encouragement. Godfrey had duly been graced with Guy's staff and ring – and packed off back to Milan. An abortive mission, it might have been thought: for no sooner had he arrived in town to claim his throne than he was being hunted down by Erlembald's heavies, chased into a lonely fortress, and put under siege.

Even amid all Godfrey's humiliations, however, there was one thing at least left to bring a smile to his lips: that though he might be mired in impotence, so too was his rival, Atto. Erlembald's grip on Milan had proved less secure than he had trusted: for on the very day of his nominee's election, indeed even as he sat down at the formal banquet to celebrate it, he and his Patarene bodyguards had suddenly found themselves being ambushed. A mob whipped up by the local clergy had burst into the archbishop's palace, chased Atto into his bedroom, and beaten him black and blue. Even the papal legate had suffered the mortification of being stripped of all his clothes. Although Erlembald had quickly succeeded in restoring order, it had not been soon enough to prevent Atto from swearing to his captors that he would 'never again intervene in the bishopric'.[30] Such an oath could not readily be dismissed. Milan, as a result, had found herself stuck with two archbishops – neither one of whom was able to take up his office.

A shocking state of affairs, to be sure – and yet barely hinting at the full scale of the crisis yet to come. In the summer of 1072, Pope Alexander II, at a formal synod of the Roman Church, pronounced that Atto was not bound by the oath he had given his assailants – and was therefore the rightful Archbishop of Milan. A few months later, in early 1073, Henry IV leaned on the bishops of Lombardy to stand as Godfrey's patrons at his consecration. Alexander's response was to excommunicate not only Godfrey himself, not only the Lombard bishops, but, just for good measure, some of Henry's own closest advisers. Only once they had all been dismissed, the Pope declared, would he re-establish contact with the king: until that moment, he was to be regarded as 'outside the communion of the Church'.[31] Almost without anyone quite understanding how it had happened, papacy and empire, those twin pillars of Christendom, were at open loggerheads.

Less than three decades had passed since Henry III, descending upon the shrine of the apostles, had dismissed three popes at a stroke, and set about laying the foundations for the great project of reform. In that time, though much had been attempted and achieved by the reformers, it had never been any part of their intention to humiliate the youthful Caesar. Just the opposite, in fact: Henry had always been the focus of their very highest hopes. Born of two exemplary parents, he had also been entrusted at his christening to the care of Abbot Hugh of Cluny, who had raised him dripping from the font, and been named his 'spiritual father'[32] – so that the youthful king was triply a child of reform. Even once Henry had come of age, a vague feeling of responsibility, even of condescension, continued to characterise how reformers such as Hildebrand regarded him. On several occasions, indeed, ordering the Empress Agnes out of her cloistered retirement, they had dispatched her on the gruelling journey back across the Alps, so determined had they been to keep a watchful eye on her son.

Other missions, those considered too embarrassing or awkward for a woman to handle, they had entrusted to Peter Damian. Although Peter was old by now, and reluctant to leave his hermitage, he had undertaken them willingly enough: for he had always disapproved of sending Agnes, his spiritual ward, back to the scenes of her earthly greatness. In 1069, for instance, he had made the trek to the imperial court on a particularly delicate matter. Henry, bored of his new wife, the Lady Bertha, and complaining of her lack of sex appeal, had abruptly announced that he wished to divorce her. Peter, summoning all his considerable reserves of authority, had alternately menaced and wooed the young Caesar into backing down: the first time that a papal reformer had ever succeeded in imposing his will upon a king. 'If you are really determined in this matter,' Henry sighed, with a crashing lack of graciousness, 'then I suppose I must brace myself to shoulder as best I can a burden that I cannot shed.'[33] Yet Peter himself, despite the undoubted scale of his triumph, had very deliberately refrained from making a song and dance about it. Bridges had not been burned. Lines of communication had been left open. Proof had been offered that the king and the papacy, even when tensions were running high, were not necessarily doomed to conflict.

But this was already, amid the gathering mood of crisis, a lesson well on the way to being lost. Peter, the leader among the reformers who had always been best qualified to teach it, was fading fast. He died in 1072, just a few months before the Empress Agnes, despairing of persuading her son to listen to her, gave pious backing to the excommunication of his advisers. A few weeks later, in April 1073, Alexander too was dead. The people of Rome, rather than wait for the cardinals to nominate a successor, were soon taking the law into their own hands. They knew precisely whom they wanted as their new pope:

'Hildebrand for bishop!'[34] Even as Alexander was being laid to rest in the Lateran, the cry went up across the whole city.

'Like the raging of the east wind, which buffets with violent blasts,'[35] Peter Damian had once described the inimitable archdeacon. Now, swept up from Alexander's funeral amid the unanimous cheering of the Roman people, carried out of the basilica despite all his own modest protests, universally hailed by the name of Gregory, Hildebrand was borne from the Lateran past open fields, past blossom-heavy orchards, past crumbling ruins, down into the very heart of the Holy City itself, where, in an ancient church filled with relics of St Peter, he was formally installed upon the throne of the Prince of the Apostles.

The far-distant King Henry might not have given his nod – but the people certainly had.

At a fateful moment for Christendom, Hildebrand had been installed as Pope.

So Fearful a Weight

'See, I have set you this day over nations and over kingdoms, to pluck up and to break down, to destroy and to overthrow, to build and to plant.'[36] So the voice of God, it was recorded in Holy Scripture, had once addressed a Jewish priest by the name of Jeremiah. The verse was a particular favourite of the new pope's – as well it might have been. Though the ancient prophet, rather like Gregory VII himself, had lived at a time of wrenching and alarming change, not even the most appalling calamities had been able to shake his conviction that it was the Almighty Himself who had summoned him to his mission: to confound the wicked, and to admonish kings, and to shepherd a confused and wandering people. In short, to be right.

What better model could there be for a man such as Gregory? True, his protests as he was hauled from the Lateran to his enthronement had been more than merely the display of false modesty that was expected of any candidate for a bishopric: 'We are a sinner and unequal to the bearing of so fearful a weight.' A heartfelt confession, certainly. Yet rather than betraying any great crisis of confidence, it had in truth trumpeted the very opposite: an invincible sense of purpose, of calling, of destiny. Gregory VII was Hildebrand still. If indeed he did sometimes feel that his shoulders might buckle beneath the burden that he could feel, Atlas-like, laid upon them, then who could wonder at that? To the new pope, and to all the supporters of reform, it appeared self-evident that the forces of good were everywhere being menaced by those of evil, in the great cosmic struggle that was destined to climax with the hour of judgement, and the final coming of God's kingdom. There could be no doubting, then, either the urgency or the gravity of Gregory's task. 'For to our small self, the care and oversight of all the churches have been committed.'[37]

Small, perhaps – but formidably well qualified. Not since the age of Constantine had there been a man enthroned in Rome who could boast a more detailed knowledge of the various lands and limits of the world. Indeed, as Gregory pointed out with relish, 'the law of the Roman pontiffs has governed more princedoms than ever that of the Caesars did'[38] – so that a legate, bringing letters and reports to the Lateran, might be as likely to come galloping from Hungary, or Poland, or the distant kingdoms of the Northmen, as from anywhere within the ancient heartlands of Christendom. Although the new pope was thoroughly Roman in everything except his birth, his habit of thinking was nevertheless a global one. Whether it was the King of England, or the Abbot of Cluny, or the generalissimo of the Patarenes, Gregory had long been in the habit of regarding even the most celebrated men of the age as his agents. Of humble birth he might have been, and impeccably austere in all his personal habits – and yet an imperial cast of mind came to him no less naturally for that. Processing past the haughty monuments of an ancient and vanished empire, he showed no compunction in displaying himself to the Roman people arrayed in the traditional crown and robes of a Caesar: the first pope ever to flaunt such insignia in public. In private, seeking

The baptism of Vladimir, the prince of Kiev, was a momentous marker of the influence of Constantinople on the Rus warlords of the Wild East. Stupefied by the wealth and beauty of '*Miklagard*', 'the Great City', many found themselves torn between the desire to emulate its sophistication and an ambition to loot it. (Bridgeman Art Library)

Olaf Haraldsson: brutal, domineering – and the patron saint of the Northmen.
(Werner Forman Archive)

Harold Godwinsson publicly pledges loyalty to his rival for the throne of England, Duke William of Normandy. Although the swearing of oaths was regarded by good Christians as a fearsome thing, Harold had a reputation for taking the matter less seriously, perhaps, than he might have done. (akg-images/Erich Lessing)

It was the death of Harold that doomed the English cause in the wake of Hastings – for it left William effectively unopposed as king. Exactly how Harold died is unclear. The famous image in the Bayeux Tapestry, which appears to show him with an arrow in the eye, was almost certainly re-stitched at some point in the eighteenth century. The original, to judge from an engraving of the Tapestry published in 1733, showed not an arrow, but a spear. (akg-images/Erich Lessing)

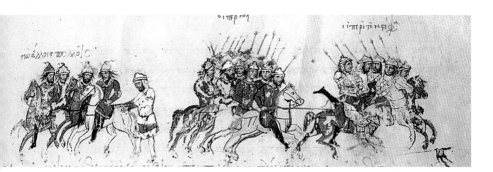

e years after Hastings, a no less decisive battle was fought at the opposite end of Christendom. The
eat of a Byzantine emperor and his army at Manzikert left the Asian heartlands of the empire open to
scything incursions of Turkish cavalry. Towns that had been Roman for more than a thousand years
re soon being lost to Constantinople for good. (Werner Forman Archive)

Henric⁹ quartus

Henry IV, King of the German *Reich* and – from
1084 – Emperor of the West. 'Such were the
turns of his fortune,' as one admirer put it,
'that it would be impossible for me to describe
them, and for you to read about them, without
tears.' (akg-images)

In the great struggle between Emperor and Pope, Henry IV might pose as a Caesar – but Gregory VII reigned as the heir of a saint. Not just any saint, either: for Rome's first bishop had been none other than Saint Peter, the 'rock' on which the Church had been built. 'I will give you the keys of the kingdom of heaven,' Christ had told him 'and whatever you bind on earth shall be bound in heaven, and whatever you loose on earth shall be loosed in heaven.' Here was a fearsome authority – and one that Gregory had not the slightest hesitation in claiming as his own. (Werner Forman Archive)

A papal throne in the Lateran. It is said that when Gregory pronounced his sentence of excommunication against Henry, his throne miraculously cracked in two. (Vatican Museum)

iew of the Rhine and the town of Tribur, as seen from the hill of Oppenheim. Back in the autumn of 6, the great river constituted the dividing line between Henry and a menacing assembly of German ices, summoned to Tribur to debate their king's possible deposition. It was Henry's determination to p hold of his crown, even at the cost of accepting mortifying peace terms, which set in motion the nts that would lead him to Canossa. (Author photo)

A contrite Henry IV begs his godfather, Abbot Hugh of Cluny, and his second-cousin, the Countess Matilda, to intercede on his behalf with Gregory VII at Canossa. The illustration is from a biography of Matilda. Had it been from a biography of Henry, the scene would no doubt have been given a somewhat different spin. (Biblioteca Apostolica Vaticana)

Canossa. The ruined state of the castle only compounds the sense of bleakness and isolation. Even in September, when this photograph was taken, the winds can be violent and icy. (Author photo)

Alexius Comnenus, who succeeded to the throne of Constantinople in 1081, at a time when the Byzantine Empire appeared on the verge of utter collapse. His deft deployment of bribes to Henry IV, and a facility for stirring up revolts against his Norman enemies, enabled Alexius to haul his empire back from the very brink. (AKG London)

The seeming ruin of all Gregory's ambitions. In the top panel, Henry IV is shown sitting in triumph, following his coronation as emperor by the anti-pope Clement III, while on the right Gregory is being expelled from Rome. In the bottom panel, the exiled pontiff is shown lying on his deathbed.

On the same day that Gregory VII died, the Muslim city of Toledo opened its gates to the Christian king of Leon, Alfonso VI. 'We rejoice with a most joyful heart,' as Gregory's successor, Urban II, would put it, 'and we give great thanks to God, as is worthy, because in our time He has deigned to give such a victory to the Christian people.' (Corbis)

bruno. eodem die ipso mona/
terio uibente papa tria uittib'
pmif cancellis facrarunt alta
ria. Tunc papa ntr fac'do niif
fafq; agendo. p alia falutis ho
taniia. cozl epif g cardinalibuf
multozq; pfonif. huicemodi
[......]an habuit ad p[....],

tutelanq; commendauit. nifi
deo et beato Petro eiufq; uica
rus.romanif fcilicet pontificb'
quoz numero uel ordini duuna
me dignatio licet indignum af
fociauit. me olim monachum
priozemq; monafteru huuif fub
domno ac uenerabili hugone

Urban II consecrates the high altar of the colossal new church at Cluny. The Pope stands on the left and Abbot Hugh, with his monks, on the right. (Art Archive)

Temple Mount in Jerusalem. Here, amid the darkness that would precede the light of the Second Comin[g] Antichrist was fated to manifest himself, enthroned in sanguinary glory. In 1099, when Jerusalem fell to the warriors of the First Crusade, the bloodshed on the Temple Mount was especially terrible. (Corbis)

to order his thoughts about the destiny that God had entrusted to him, Gregory dared to go even further. To an unpublished memorandum, he confided a series of awesome convictions: 'that the Roman pontiff alone is by right called "universal"'; 'that all princes kiss the feet of the pope alone'; 'that he is permitted to depose emperors'.[39] Assertions so vaunting that even the author shrank from stating them aloud.

And yet in truth, for all the unhesitating sternness with which Gregory was prepared to upbraid the pretensions of uppity princes, his concern was not with the ordering of their kingdoms, still less with any madcap attempt to refound the Roman Empire, but rather with a project that he saw as incalculably more important. Just as the monks of Cluny had laboured to make of their monastery a bulwark of the celestial set amid the woods and fields of Burgundy, so it was the gigantic ambition of Gregory to see the universal Church transfigured in an identical manner, in every princedom, in every town, in every village. For only then, once it had been freed for good from the cankered touch of grasping kings, and brought to shimmer with a radiant and unspotted purity, would it properly be able to serve the Christian people as a vision on earth of the City of God. Despite his crown and robes, it was no worldly power to which Gregory laid claim, but one infinitely greater. No wonder, then, that his admirers were agog. 'You are endeavouring things more awesome than our weakness can imagine,' wrote one abbot in a letter of congratulation to the new pope. 'Like an eagle you soar above all lower things, and your eyes are fixed upon the brightness of the sun itself.'[40]

Not that Gregory could afford to turn his gaze entirely from earthly matters. That he had inherited a crisis in the papacy's relations with Henry IV went without saying – as too did the pressing need to resolve it. Indeed, for so long as the king refused to dismiss his excommunicated advisers, the new pope felt himself unable even to write to the imperial court, and inform it of his election. Nevertheless, supremely conscious as he was of his global responsibilities, Gregory could not permit the breach with Henry IV to monopolise all his attention. The *Reich* was not the sum of Christendom. To the east, there lay another Christian empire – and in 1073, even as Gregory was being enthroned as the Bishop of Rome, he feared that a literally fiendish danger was menacing the Second Rome. 'For everything has been laid waste, almost to the very walls of Constantinople.'[41] News so shocking as to seem barely believable – and yet every traveller returning from overseas had confirmed it. What could be stirring there, then, in the East, if not the armies of very hell? The Devil, so Gregory himself suspected, was openly showing his hand – and with the goal, a chillingly genocidal one, of putting the Christian people to slaughter 'like cattle'.[42]

Certainly, the portents that had heralded the original brewing of the crisis in Byzantium, many decades previously, had indeed seemed infernal. In the winter of 1016, dragons had swooped in over Armenia, on the easternmost limit of the empire, 'vomiting fire upon Christ's faithful', and volumes of the Holy Scriptures had begun to tremble. Yet the simultaneous appearance there of Muslim horsemen 'armed with bows and wearing their hair long like women'[43] – 'Turks', as they called themselves – had initially provoked no undue alarm among the Byzantines. Barbarians had been testing their empire for centuries, after all, and yet still it triumphantly endured, as was clearly the will of God. Nevertheless, as the decades went by, and the Turks did not drift away, but instead seemed only to swell in numbers and power, an increasingly larcenous presence on the eastern frontier, so there were those in Constantinople who had at last deigned to feel some anxiety. In 1068, one of them had been crowned *Basileus*. Three years later, reversing the traditional Byzantine policy of avoiding pitched combat at all costs, he had gathered together all the reserves he could muster, marched with them directly into the badlands of the East, and set about hunting down the barbarians. In August 1071, on a plain overlooked by a fortress named Manzikert, the imperial task force had at last caught up with its quarry, forced a battle – and been annihilated. The *Basileus* himself, taken captive, had ended up on his face before a Turkish warlord, as a leather slipper pressed down upon his neck.

Meanwhile, with 'the sinews of the Roman Empire',[44] its armed forces, ripped and shredded beyond all hope of repair, the victors had immediately begun fanning out from the killing fields of Manzikert to claim their spoils. Roads which for a thousand years and more had served the cause of Roman greatness now stretched open and defence-less all the way westwards to the sea. As rival factions in Constantinople, with a near-criminal irresponsibility, devoted them-selves to scrapping over what remained of the stricken empire, so the Turks had been left to range across its Asian heartlands virtually as they pleased. 'I am the destroyer of towers and churches,'[45] the invaders liked to boast. Not that they confined themselves to merely wanton destruction. Even as they trampled down ancient cities, and stabled their horses in famous monasteries, they made sure to enslave all the Christians they could, and drive the remainder into headlong flight. Refugees, flooding into Constantinople, only added to the mounting sense there of a cataclysm without precedent. 'Illustrious personages, nobles, chiefs, women of position, all wandered in begging their bread.'[46] No wonder, then, that the sense of confusion, and of a whole world turned upside down, should have served to feed rumours of an imminent cosmic doom — and to sow panic as far afield as the Lateran.

And even if the turmoil in the East did not portend the coming of Antichrist, what then? Would the threat to Christendom be rendered any less real? Here were questions which Gregory, with his unrivalled array of international contacts, was uniquely well placed to ponder. Not for him the limited horizons of a mere king. In the summer of 1073, even as he was struggling to make sense of the appalling reports from Byzantium, telling news was brought to him of the sufferings of Christians in another one-time stronghold of the faith. North Africa, where St Augustine had written his great book on the City of God, had been under Saracen rule for many centuries; and now the local emir had imprisoned the leader of the church there, and beaten him, 'as though he were a criminal'.[47] Gregory, writing to the unhappy arch-bishop, sought to console him by floating the cheery prospect that

God might soon 'condescend to look upon the African church, which has been toiling for such a long while, buffeted by the waves of various troubles'.[48] A pious hope – but little more than that. In truth, as Gregory well knew, the African church was dying on its feet. Of the two hundred bishoprics and more that it had once boasted, a mere five remained. Food for thought indeed. After all, if the Africans, the very countrymen of St Augustine, could end up lost so utterly to Christendom that barely a Christian remained among them, then who was to say that the same terrible fate might not one day befall the people whom Gregory freely described as 'our brothers – those who hold the empire beyond the sea in Constantinople'?

Indeed, in his bleakest moments, he would confess to a dread that the Church, far from being brought by his leadership to a triumphant and universal purity, might instead 'perish altogether in our times'.[49] To wallow in despair, however, was hardly Gregory's style. Even as he marked how many of Christendom's frontiers were bleeding, so also could he point to others that bore certain witness to God's continuing favour and protection. Barely twenty years had passed since Leo IX's promotion of Humbert to the archbishopric of Sicily: an appointment that at the time had appeared less a statement of intent than the expression of a pipedream. Certainly, not even the most militant optimist in Leo's train, not even Hildebrand himself, would have dared to imagine back in 1050 that he might live to see the restoration of the Great Mosque of Palermo, where for more than two centuries the Saracens had been performing their unspeakable rites, to its original function as a cathedral.

Yet in 1072, only the year before Hildebrand's elevation to the papacy, that was precisely what had happened. Grown men had sobbed, invisible choirs of angels had sung and a mysterious beam of light had illumined the altar. It was a fittingly miraculous way to mark a seeming miracle: the restoration to Christendom of a metropolis so stupefyingly vast that it could boast a quarter of a million inhabitants, 500 mosques and no fewer than 150 butchers. Nor was it only the Cross that now rose above Palermo. For the new and fretful pope, there was an additional cause for satisfaction. Planted on the battlements, token of the city's subjection to the Roman Church as well as to Christ, there billowed a flag with the familiar insignia of St Peter: a papal banner.

It went without saying, of course, that such a victory could only ever have been won at the point of a sword. The corsairs of Sicily had always been brutal, yet even they had found themselves unable to compete for sheer ruthlessness with the new warlords on the Italian scene. Palermo's fall had effectively set the seal on a second Norman conquest. Indeed, the invasion of wealthy islands was becoming quite a speciality of Christendom's 'shock troops'.[50] Even erstwhile enemies might be brought to a grudging respect for what the Normans them-selves, with a becoming lack of modesty, liked to vaunt as their own exceptional 'boldness and prowess'.[51] Back in 1059, for instance, it had been former associates of Leo IX, the Pope defeated at Civitate, who had first dangled the prize of Sicily before a man they had always pre-viously execrated.

Robert Guiscard, the most notorious of the Norman freebooters as he was also the most powerful, had long since crossed the shadowy divide that marked out banditry from lordship. Desperate as the reformers were for some authentic muscle, and with Guiscard himself not averse to being graced with a touch of respectability, the way had duly been opened for a spectacular *rapprochement*. The Normans of southern Italy, amid much papal nose-holding, had been welcomed in from the cold. Their chief, in exchange for acknowledging himself a vassal of the Holy Father, had been formally invested with the duke-dom of the lands he had already filched – 'and in future, with the help of God and St Peter, of Sicily too'.[52]

Not that the new duke of Apulia had ever needed a licence to go on the attack against anyone. Even without the stamp of papal approval, Guiscard would doubtless still have cast a greedy eye on the island – and the conquest of Sicily, when it duly came, had hardly been a ven-ture such as Peter Damian, let alone Adalbert or Alcuin, would have thought to bless. Indeed, on occasion, it had been literally written in blood: for in 1068, after one particular victory, Norman scribes had broadcast their triumph by dipping their pens into the viscera of the slaughtered Saracens, and then dispatching the resulting accounts to Palermo via captured messenger pigeons. Yet if shows of calculated savagery such as this had undoubtedly played a key role in undermining Saracen morale, then the Normans themselves never doubted that all their victories derived ultimately from a power even mightier than themselves. In Sicily, at any rate, they could reckon themselves on the side of the angels. Guiscard, camped outside Palermo, had ringingly condemned the city as a lair of demons: 'an enemy to God'.[53]

His brother, Roger, the very youngest of the Hauteville clan, and the Norman leader who had committed himself most wholeheartedly to the winning of Sicily, was even more forthright in describing as his only motivation 'a desire to exalt the Holy Faith'.[54] That this had been no hypocritical affectation, but rather a pious statement of the truth, had been evident in the indisputable proofs of divine favour that had accompanied all his exploits: great cities captured against the odds, battles won with the assistance of saints mounted on blinding white horses, the fluttering above Roger's own head of an unearthly standard adorned with the Cross. To be sure, the rewards he ended up reaping had hardly been confined to the dimension of the spiritual: for his progress, from penniless youngest son to Count of Sicily, had been only marginally less spectacular than that of Guiscard himself.

Yet still, amid all his triumphs, Roger never forgot what he owed to his celestial patrons, and to St Peter in particular. A cut of the loot was regularly forwarded to Rome. In 1063, Alexander II had even taken a delivery of camels, plundered from a Saracen baggage train. In exchange, as well as the inevitable banner, the Holy Father had granted Roger and his men something even more precious: 'absolution for their sins'.[55] A momentous innovation: for never before had a pope thought to bestow such a personal benediction upon warriors who had spilled the blood of heathens. Tentatively, but no less portentously for that, the papacy was groping its way towards a notion that the defeated Saracens, ironically, would have recognised well enough: that wars, if conducted to win back territory lost to infidels, might not only be justified, but even, perhaps, be regarded as a positive duty, one owed by the faithful to God.

A philosophy for which Gregory himself, it might have been thought, would have had a peculiar sympathy. And so, to a degree, he did. Nevertheless, as he listened anxiously to travellers' reports from the eastern front, and pondered his response, there was one thing he knew for certain: that he had no intention of entrusting the redemption of a tottering Byzantium to Guiscard and his crew. The Pope, unlike his predecessor, had persisted in regarding the Norman adventurers in Italy as bandits and terrorists. It was not enough that the Duke of Apulia, far from rallying to the support of his Christian brothers of Constantinople, had coolly taken advantage of the buildup to the Manzikert campaign to grab their last remaining outposts in Italy for himself. Even worse, Gregory darkly suspected him of plotting a push northwards – into papal territory. Initial attempts to smooth things over between the Pope and the Norman captain quickly petered out when Guiscard flatly refused to trust an offer of safe conduct. By the early months of 1074, Gregory had so lost patience with his menacing vassals that he had begun to rank them alongside the Turks as enemies of Christendom. In March, the breakdown in relations between Pope and duke was sealed by the latter's excommunication. Yet while this drastic step had undoubtedly been prompted by Gregory's determination not to be taken for a ride by Guiscard, so also did it reflect something far profounder: a fearsome struggle within himself.

The English and the Milanese, perhaps, would have laughed hollowly at the notion – but Gregory himself never doubted that he was above all a man of peace. His wide-eyed relish for battle standards had always tended to outrun the dictates of his private conscience. No matter how justified he might feel in making blood-curdling appeals to the judgement of the sword, the grim realities of warfare never ceased at the same time to haunt and trouble him. The same hardnosed politician who had urged Erlembald not to abandon the profession of arms also sternly affirmed that to be a knight was by its very nature to exist in a state of sin. The same seasoned strategist who had recognised more clearly than anyone that a threat to Constantinople was a threat to the whole of Christendom, and indeed had begun actively planning a military expedition to meet the peril, flinched from facing up to what such a mission might actually require. Gregory's true wish was not for brutal and battle-hardened warriors such as Guiscard's Normans, but for would-be martyrs. 'For as Christ laid down His life for us, so should we lay down our own lives for our brothers.'[56] An injunction that came from the heart: for Gregory, whose courage was no less steely than his will, had every intention of riding at the head of his projected task force in person. Nor did Constantinople represent the limit of his ambitions, by any means. His ultimate hope, after repulsing the Turks, was to lead the armies of Christendom onwards, until at last they had reached that most fateful of all destinations: 'the sepulchre of the Lord'.[57]

And if there sounded something oddly familiar about this plan, then perhaps that was no coincidence. Jerusalem, after a lull of several decades, had begun to glimmer tantalisingly again on the horizon of many people's dreamings. So too a dread – or anticipation – of the end of the world. In 1054, for instance, some three thousand pilgrims had set off for the Holy Land, prompted by the sudden and fearsome blazing of a mysterious star;[58] ten years later, and an even larger expedition, twelve thousand in all, it was claimed, had repeated the journey, crosses sewn on to their cloaks, 'deceived by a certain vulgar opinion that the day of Judgement was at hand'.[59] Vulgar, perhaps; but not only the poor and credulous had made the journey: bishops, and archbishops, and great princes had gone along too. Indeed, prophecies of the end time had lately been circulating around the very summit of the Christian world. In Italy especially, among opponents of reform, great play had begun to be made once again of that hoary figure of fantasy, the last Roman emperor – and naturally enough, it was Henry IV whom they looked to cast in the role.

Times, however, had changed; and the heir of the Caesars was no longer alone in claiming the rule of Christendom. '*Dux et pontifex*', 'general' as well as 'pontiff,'[60] was what Gregory aspired to be. And something more besides? Certainly, amid all the troubles of the age, the Pope's plan to lead an army to the Holy Sepulchre could hardly help but appear a pointed trampling on imperial toes. What earthly kings, and Henry IV especially, would make of Gregory's ambitions, only time would tell. Gregory himself, however, as he prepared for the great challenges that lay ahead of him, could afford to feel sternly unconcerned. He was, after all, the heir of St Peter. The Almighty was on his side.

'It does not escape us,' he wrote a year after his accession, 'how diverse are men's opinions and judgements concerning us – for some, pointing to identical cases and actions, will think us cruel, others unduly mild. To all of them, however, we can give no truer or more appropriate answer than that of the Apostle: "But with me it is a very small thing that I should be judged by you or by any human court."'[61]

All the world, so Gregory believed, had been given into his hands. To him been entrusted the fateful task of reordering it – nor, in the final reckoning, was there anyone entitled to stand in his path.

The Road to Canossa

'That he is permitted to depose emperors.' Perhaps it was just as well that Gregory chose to keep this particular proposition from the youthful Caesar. Henry IV, as befitted the heir of Constantine and Charlemagne, was hardly the man to accept that he could be deposed by anyone. King of the various princedoms of Germany, he also laid claim to the rule of Italy – Rome included. Yet it is doubtful that Henry, even had he been alerted to the new pope's pretensions, would have been able to do much about them. Not straight away, at any rate. There was way too much already on the royal plate. Far from being in any position to contemplate a campaign in Italy, Henry was locked into a desperate struggle to maintain his authority within Germany itself. War, having already plunged the empire of Constantinople into chaos, had come as well, in the summer of 1073, to the empire of the West.

It was no race of pagans that had brought about this sudden calamity, however, no breed of savage invaders from beyond the frontiers of Christendom, but rather a people who ever since the time of Otto the Great had appeared the very wellspring of imperial greatness: none other than the Saxons. Yet Otto's own dynasty had long since passed away; and its replacement in 1024 by a line of Rhineland kings, sprung from the opposite end of the *Reich*, had led many in Saxony to feel increasingly exploited and oppressed. Even during the triumphant reign of Henry III, the local princes had been growing fractious; and some of them, during the troubled years of his son's minority, had actively plotted to do away with the infant king. Mistrust had bred mistrust in turn; and the adult Henry, with that same blend of suspiciousness and obstinacy that marked so many of his dealings, had disdained to mollify the restless Saxons. Instead, taking a leaf out of the Norman book, he had set himself to securing his hold on the dukedom in the most up-to-date manner possible: by raising castles. A threat to the local nobility, of course – but also to the entire Saxon people. As in France, as in England, so in Saxony, the battlements suddenly sprouting up on 'high hills and wild places'[62] appeared to the locals an inversion of all that they held most precious: forbidding and sinister threats to their ancient liberties.

Henry's greatest castle, a stronghold raised at the foot of the Harz mountains, where Christendom's most lucrative gold mines were to be found, was regarded with particular hatred: for its walls and towers appeared all too grimly suited to the fell situation in which they had been raised. Indeed, at the very onset of the insurrection, when the Saxon rebels sought to trap Henry there, they found it an impossible task, so dense was the forest surrounding the Harzburg. 'No matter all the efforts of the besiegers, they could not prevent the comings and goings of those who were shut in.'[63] Henry, fleeing the castle without supplies, and relying on a huntsman to guide him through the trackless wilds, reached safety at last only after having travelled through bogs and briars for three whole days.

It was a common fantasy, no doubt, among the oppressed

everywhere to see a castle-builder forced into humiliating flight. That the Harzburg and every other royal stronghold be levelled, that the onward march of military innovation be reversed, and that the 'tyranny' which it facilitated be kept at bay: such were the demands of the Saxon rebels. Yet, for all the indignant talk of fortifications spreading across 'every hill and mountain, so as to threaten Saxony with ruin',[64] an excess of castle-building on its own could hardly serve to sanction treason against an anointed king. Other justifications too were urgently needed. So it was that the insurgents, dredging up memories of Henry's scandalous attempt to secure a divorce, fell to accusing him of a whole host of sinister practices: incest, groping abbesses, and hints of even worse. Such charges, in an age which had witnessed even the saintly Agnes accused of nymphomania, might easily have been dismissed as the common currency of political abuse – except that Henry, like his mother before him, was finding himself acutely vulnerable to muck-raking.

For just as under the empress, so now under the king, the most venomous gossip of all was being whispered by princes. The movers and shakers of the *Reich*, having developed a taste for insubordination during Henry's minority, were finding it hard to kick the habit. It was no coincidence, perhaps, that the leader of the rebellious Saxons should have been Otto of Northeim: the same duke who, back in the days of Agnes's regency, had featured so prominently in the kidnapping at Kaiserswerth. True, Otto was a Saxon himself; but even among the princes of the Rhineland there was no lack of would-be jackals. Far from backing their lord against the rebels, the southern dukes were widely suspected of plotting his deposition. The greatest of them all, Rudolf of Swabia, was an object of particular royal suspicion. Already, in 1072, both Agnes and Henry's godfather, Abbot Hugh of Cluny, had been called upon to patch up relations between the king and his most powerful vassal. Then, at Christmas-time in 1073, trouble had flared up again. A court insider, tipping off Rudolf that Henry was plotting his assassination, had insisted on proving his claim by undergoing trial by combat. Only the unexpected abduction of the accuser 'by a terrible demon', just a few days before the duel was due to be fought, had served to exonerate the king.[65] Or had it? There were many who remained unconvinced. The charges against Henry – that he was a tyrant, a murderer, an enthusiast for every kind of vice – continued to swirl.

Self-evidently, then, with the Saxons still up in arms against him, and the southern princes manoeuvring to stab him in the back, it was hardly the time to be picking a fight with the Pope. There would be opportunity enough to do that, Henry judged, and to slap the uppity Gregory down for good, once the *Reich* had been successfully pacified. So it was that, rather than risk the slightest papal sanction being granted to his enemies' slurs, he brought himself to grovel – even going so far as to acknowledge that he might possibly have backed the wrong horse in Milan. 'Full of pleasantness and obedience,'[66] a delighted Gregory described the royal tone to Erlembald. The likelier alternative, that the king might be stringing him along and playing for time, appeared not to have crossed the papal mind.

And time, sure enough, was what Henry had won for himself. In February 1074, amid the snow and ice of winter, he signed up to what appeared a humiliating peace, agreeing by its terms to demolish all his castles, and to restore Otto of Northeim to the full warmth of the royal favour. In truth, however, the king had gained far more than he had lost. Any prospect of a coalition between the ever-slippery Otto and the southern princes had now been successfully stymied. Even more promisingly, a wedge had been driven between the duke and the frustrated mass of the Saxon peasantry. In March, taking the law into their own hands, a great army of the '*vulgus*' – 'the common people' – stormed the Harzburg, then began tearing it to pieces block by block. Even the royal chapel was burned to the ground. Finally, in a climactic desecration, the grave of Henry's stillborn eldest son was dug up, and his tiny bones slung out amid the cinders and rubble. News of this outrage, not surprisingly, inspired widespread horror among the great. The southern dukes might mistrust the king powerfully, but they detested rioting peasants even more. The flattening of the Harzburg, ironically enough, spelled disaster for the Saxon cause. In the summer of 1075, Rudolf and a host of other lords at last submitted to joining Henry in a full-scale expedition against the rebels. On 9 June, amid the nightmarish swirling of a dust-storm, the Saxons were routed, and the wretched '*vulgus*' put satisfyingly to the sword. By the autumn, Henry's mastery of Saxony was sufficiently complete for him to order his castles there to be rebuilt. Even the most fractious of the princes appeared ready to bow their necks to the royal yoke. So it was, for instance, that the royal lieutenant installed in the Harzburg, and compelled to supervise its wholesale restoration, was none other than the captain who had led the initial assault on the castle: that inveterate turncoat and survivor, Duke Otto of Northeim.

Finally, after all the many setbacks and frustrations that had previously served to hobble him so grievously, it seemed that the young king was on the verge of securing what he had always regarded as his birthright: the chance to rule as his great father had done. Even as stone-masons and workmen returned to the Harzburg, and the great lords of the *Reich* hurried obediently to celebrate Christmas at the royal table, Henry was looking to set the seal on his victory. Some work still remained to be done, of course. Not everyone who had thought to challenge the royal authority over the years had yet been put sufficiently in his place. Indeed, dukes such as Rudolf and Otto might be overweening, but they were neither of them half so officious, nor half so condescending, as the jumped-up Tuscan monk who sat in the Lateran. To Henry, the son of a Caesar who had forced three papal abdications in the space of a week, the notion that any bishop, even a bishop of Rome, might pose as the leader of Christendom was grotesque and insufferable. He had affected to listen politely to Gregory's fantastical scheme for an expedition to Constantinople, but it was with no little satisfaction that he tracked its ultimate abortion. Gregory himself, far from leading the warriors of Christendom to the Holy Sepulchre, had been left with nothing to show for all his plans except a lingering taint of failure and scandal. A salutary demonstration, Henry could reflect contentedly, that the duties of a Caesar were not easily usurped by anyone – the heir of St Peter included.

A point only emphasised by the peculiarly glaring contrast between the papal debacle and his own spectacular triumph. It was back in June 1074, exactly a year before Henry himself would lead the flower of the *Reich* to victory over the rebel Saxons, that Gregory had embarked on his expedition. First stop: a rendezvous with its somewhat improbable chief supporter. 'My most beloved and loving daughter,'[67] Gregory was in the habit of addressing the Lady Matilda of Tuscany. For the Pope, there was no embarrassment in acknowledging his obligations to a woman who was not yet thirty. Though Matilda's stepfather, Duke Godfrey the Bearded, had died back in 1069, her mother, the Countess Beatrice, had succeeded admirably in keeping all the broad dominions of the House of Canossa to herself – and in grooming her only child to inherit their rule. Spirited, beautiful and blonde, Matilda was hardly a typical lieutenant of reform – and yet already she had proved herself a most invaluable one. Raised by her chaste and devout mother to believe passionately in everything that the new pope stood for, she had not hesitated to offer him an army of thirty thousand knights, nor to commit to accompanying his proposed expedition herself. Gregory, far from trying to dissuade her, had been so enthused by her 'sisterly aid'[68] that he had set about recruiting the venerable Empress Agnes to the venture as well. Soon enough, the Countess Beatrice had signed up too. Gregory's opponents, however, rather than quaking in their boots at this impressive show of female backing, had responded with hilarity. Guiscard's Normans, in particular, had been loud in their derision. Perhaps, had Gregory succeeded in crushing them before embarking for Constantinople, as had been his intention, the mockery would have been silenced – but he had not. Only a fortnight into the campaign, news had reached Beatrice and Matilda of an insurrection back in Tuscany. With their forced withdrawal, Gregory had found himself with little choice but to abandon the whole expedition. Then, once back in Rome, he had fallen ill. The Holy Sepulchre had been left to seem a very long way off indeed.

Nor, a year and more on from the fiasco, had the damage been wholly repaired. Taunts that the rule of the Church had been handed over to a gaggle of women were widespread. Lurid allegations too of 'a most appalling scandal'. To many bishops in particular, fed up as they were with hectoring demands from Rome that they impose a monkish lifestyle upon their priests, Gregory's warm relationship with Matilda appeared the rankest hypocrisy. What was it, they charged, if not 'intimacy and cohabitation with a strange woman'?[69] Palpably unfair – but then again, as Henry himself knew all too well, innuendo hardly had to be true for it to be damaging. In the *Reich* especially, where bishops tended to be even haughtier than elsewhere in Christendom, and even more toweringly conscious of their own dignity, there were plenty who had developed an active stake in thinking the worst of the new pope. 'The man is a menace!' sniffed one archbishop. 'He presumes to boss us around as though we were his bailiffs!'[70] Others, recoiling from Gregory's brusque demands that priests be obliged to abandon their wives, demanded to know whether he planned to staff the Church with angels. Such a show of sarcasm had absolutely zero effect on Gregory himself. Indeed, by 1075, his prescriptions against married priests, and simony too, were attaining a whole new level of peremptoriness. In February, four bishops were suspended for disobedience. Then, in July, one of them, a particularly inveterate simonist, was deposed. Finally, as the year drew to its close, Gregory unleashed against the sullen and recalcitrant imperial Church the reformers' most devastating weapon of all. 'We have heard', he wrote in an open letter to King Henry's subjects, 'that certain of the bishops who dwell in your parts either condone, or fail to take notice of, the keeping of women by priests.' Such men, rebels against the authority of St Peter, he now summoned to the court of popular opinion. 'We charge you', Gregory instructed the peoples of the *Reich*, 'in no way to obey these bishops.'[71]

This papal gambit appeared dangerous and perverse, irresponsible and criminal to the outraged bishops themselves. To Henry IV as well – for naturally, at a time when he had only just succeeded in stamping out the bushfires of rebellion in Saxony, the last thing he wanted to see imported north of the Alps was anything resembling the Patarenes. It was the role and the duty of his bishops, after all, to serve him as his principal ministers: only destabilise them, and the entire *Reich* risked being set to totter. Even that, however, was not the deadliest threat posed by Gregory's determination to bring the imperial Church to heel: for always, rumbling beneath the royal feet as it had done ever since the crisis first erupted in Milan, there waited a potentially even more explosive danger. For all Henry's show of temporary contrition, the row over who had the right to invest the city's archbishop – whether king or Pope – had still not been resolved; and in February, growing impatient, Gregory had sought to force the issue, and impose his candidate for good, by taking a fatal step. By the decree of a formal synod of the Roman Church, 'the King's right to confer bishoprics from that moment on was openly prohibited':[72] a measure targeted at Milan, to be sure, but with potentially devastating implications for royal authority across the whole span of the *Reich*. After all, without the right to invest bishops, how would Henry nominate his ministers, impose his authority, administer the kingdom? What future for the empire then? Gregory might not have intended it, but his attempt to win a battle threatened him with out-and-out war.

It was a far-reaching miscalculation. Lulled into a false sense of security by the young king's seeming tractability, Gregory had fatally misjudged the royal temper. In truth, Henry's policy of appeasement towards the papacy had only ever been a temporary expedient. His invariable instinct, whenever forced into a corner, was to come out fighting. By the autumn, with the Saxons defeated at last, Henry had successfully punched his way out of one – and could devote all his energies to escaping the other. Fortunately for him, much had changed to his advantage over the previous few months. Firstly, back in late March, the cathedral in Milan had been swept by a terrible fire: a disaster interpreted by most Milanese as a judgement on the Patarenes. A few weeks later, and any lingering doubts that God had turned decisively against Erlembald were dispelled when the papal captain was ambushed and cut down, his supporters among the clergy mutilated, and his remaining supporters driven into exile. By early autumn, with the Saxons crushed and Milan swept clear of Gregory's supporters, Henry felt ready to move at last. Ignoring the rival claims of Atto and Godfrey to the bishopric, he coolly nominated a third candidate: a deacon who had travelled in his train to the Saxon wars, by the name of Tedald. Nor was that the limit, by any means, of Henry's provocations. For almost three years, he had found himself being pressed by Gregory to dismiss the advisers excommunicated by Alexander II – and had prevaricated. Now, in a pointed rubbing of salt into the papal wounds, he opted to dispatch one of them to Milan, to serve Tedald as his enforcer. A bullish and defiant assertion of royal authority, to be sure – but it was also, in the context of the gathering crisis, yet one further miscalculation. Though the Pope had badly underestimated the king, it would soon become clear that the king had underestimated the Pope even more.

On New Year's Day 1076, as Henry sat in royal splendour surrounded by the great princes of the *Reich*, seemingly the master of all he surveyed, three cloaked and breathless envoys were ushered into his presence. Barely three weeks it had taken them to ride the winter roads from Rome to Saxony: a telling measure of how urgent their mission was. Along with a letter from Gregory, written in a tone more of sorrow than of anger, they bore a verbal message for the king: one sterner, more prescriptive, altogether more threatening. Either Henry was to acknowledge all his offences, the Pope had decreed, and do penance for them – or else 'not only would he be excommunicated until he had made due restitution, but he would also be deprived of his entire dignity as king without hope of recovery'.[73] Such an ultimatum spoke loudly of Gregory's courage, his sense of conviction, and his invincible self-confidence: for by now he had a far better understanding of his adversary's character. Throwing down the gauntlet as he had done, he would have anticipated the likely response. A response that, sure enough, was not slow in coming.

A mere thirty years had passed since Henry III, at the Synod of Sutri, had laid on a masterclass in the art of removing troublesome popes.

Now, determined to show himself a chip off the old block, his son
aimed to reprise the coup. Three weeks into the new year, a full two-
thirds of the *Reich's* bishops assembled in splendid conference at
Worms. Their mission was one about which Henry made absolutely no
bones: to ensure the disposal of the Pope. The bishops' solution? To
insist that Gregory's elevation had been merely as the favourite of the
Roman mob, rather than as the choice of Henry and the cardinals –
and that as a result he was no pope at all. A neat manoeuvre – and one
with which Henry was naturally delighted. Just to spice things up a bit,
however, he made sure that some additional allegations were thrown
in for good measure: that Gregory had repeatedly perjured himself;
that he had treated the imperial bishops like slaves; that he had been
carrying on with the Lady Matilda. All was then set down, and dispatched by envoy to the man now referred to dismissively by the
imperial bishops as 'Hildebrand'. Henry himself was even ruder. 'Let
another sit upon St Peter's throne,' he proclaimed ringingly, 'one who
will not cloak violence with a pretence of religion, but will teach the
pure doctrine of St Peter. I, Henry, by God's grace king, with all our
bishops say to you: come down, come down!'[74]

But Gregory did not come down. Instead, no sooner had he
received Henry's invitation to abdicate than he prepared to order the
gates of hell unbarred and swung open wide, ready to receive the
obdurate king. In the very church in which he had first been hailed as
Pope, before a full assembly of the Roman Church, and in the presence
of the relics of St Peter, he ordered the letter from Worms to be read
out – and the howls of horror which it provoked were terrible to hear.
One week later, when Gregory formally confirmed the awful sentence
of excommunication against the king, the throne of St Peter, it is said,
split suddenly in two. A wonder fit to chill the blood: for one half of
Christendom was indeed now sundered from the other. The terms of
Gregory's anathema were dreadful and unparalleled. 'I take from King
Henry, son of the Emperor Henry, who has risen against the Church
with unheard-of pride, the government of the entire kingdom of the
Germans and of the Italians. And I absolve the Christian people from

any oath that they have taken, or shall take, to him. And I forbid anyone to serve him as king.'[75] A deposition that, once pronounced, echoed terrifyingly across Christendom. Indeed, nervousness as to what they might have brought down upon themselves and upon the *Reich* immediately began to afflict Henry's bishops with serious second thoughts. At Easter, when the king summoned them to denounce 'Hildebrand' to the Christian people, only one, William of Utrecht, was bold enough to do so – and his cathedral was promptly struck by lightning. One week later, and he was afflicted with excruciating stomach cramps. One month later, and he was dead. William's fellow bishops, rather than persist in their support for a king who was so clearly accursed, now increasingly began to fall away. Many of them, anxious for their own souls, hurried to make their peace with Gregory – who, for his part, was diplomatically quick to welcome them back into the fold. Henry, having been cheered on all the way in the declaration of war that he had made at Worms, now found himself being abandoned on the very field of battle.

Nor was it only the bishops who were proving fair-weather friends. The great lords of the *Reich*, who back at Christmas had seemed so cowed, so dutiful, so loyal, had in truth merely been biding their time. Like their brother princes of the Church, they had tracked 'the great disasters that plagued the commonwealth'[76] with much show of pious consternation but also with not a little smacking of their lips, for upheaval spelled opportunity for them. Sure enough, by the summer, the embers of Saxon resentment were blazing back into open flames. In August – in infallible proof that the wind had changed – Otto of Northeim opted to jump ship yet again. Even more ominously, as Henry struggled and failed to contain the renewed rebellion, the southern princes were also preparing themselves to show their hand. In September, Duke Rudolf and a host of formidable allies sent out a summons to the nobility of the entire *Reich*, inviting them to the town of Tribur, on the east bank of the Rhine, there to attempt, as they put it, 'to bring a close to the various misfortunes that for many years had disturbed the peace of the Church'.[77] Or, to put it more plainly: to discuss the possible deposition of the king. Every lord who travelled to Tribur understood the potential stakes. So too did the king himself. Weakened as he was by the sequence of calamities that had overwhelmed him since Easter, he knew full well that he had no hope of preventing the assembly by force. Instead, mustering what few supporters he could still count upon, he limped his way to the town of Oppenheim, directly opposite the great gathering of princes, on the far bank of the Rhine – and there, like a wounded lion, kept a beady but impotent watch upon those who might think to attempt to dispatch him.

And certainly, the peril was very great. On 16 October, a letter from Gregory was read out by his legate to the assembled princes, in which the Pope for the first time broached the possibility of electing a new king, should Henry continue unregenerate. The Saxon leaders, however, and not a few of the southern dukes, were already set upon his deposition; and for a whole week they sought to force their case upon their peers. To a majority of the princes, though, such a step was simply too drastic to countenance – and Henry, sensing a chance to save his skin, even at a ferocious cost, duly signalled his willingness to bow his neck before the man he now referred to, once again, as 'the lord Pope Gregory'.[78] For ten days, envoys from the rival camps were ferried back and forth across the Rhine – until in due course a shaky compromise had been hammered out. The details of it, for Henry, were mortifying. He was required to swear an oath of obedience to Gregory; to revoke the sentence of Worms; to banish his excommunicated advisers once and for all. One term, however, more than any other, appeared particularly ominous: for the Pope, Henry's enemies had insisted, was to be invited to an assembly at Augsburg, there to sit in judgement on the king, to consider whether to grant him absolution, and to listen to the Saxons and the southern dukes press for his deposition. A Damocles' sword indeed. And yet, despite it all, Henry had secured his primary objective, and foiled that of his foes. For the while, at any rate, he remained the king.

Nor, even though the assembly at Augsburg had been set for

February, the anniversary of his excommunication, and a date that by now was only three months away, had he been left altogether without freedom of manoeuvre. First, Henry dispatched an urgent letter to Gregory, pleading to be allowed to come to Rome for his absolution, where it could be granted to him in cloistered privacy. Next, when this request was bluntly refused, he settled upon a desperate expedient. Knowing that Gregory, if he were to make Augsburg for February, would have to travel throughout the winter, Henry resolved to do the same. His plan: to head southwards, cross the Alps, and look to meet the Pope, not in Augsburg, but in Italy. 'For as the anniversary of the King's excommunication drew steadily nearer, so he knew that he had no choice but to be absolved before that date. Otherwise, by the sentence of the princes who would sit together in judgement on him, his cause would be fatally doomed, and his kingdom lost for ever.'[79]

So it was, shortly after Christmas, in the very dead of winter, that Henry began his ascent of the Alps. Ahead of him, icy and deep buried in snow, there wound the road that would lead him, in due course, to Italy, and the gates of Canossa.

Everything Turned Upside Down

Early in the summer of 1076, as the full horror of the crisis afflicting Christendom was starting to dawn on people, the Abbot of Cluny had been confronted by a terrifying apparition. William of Utrecht, the same bishop who only one month previously had dared to condemn Gregory as a false pope from the very pulpit of his cathedral, had materialised suddenly before Hugh, licked all about by fire. 'I am dead,' the bishop had cried out in agony, 'dead, and deep buried in hell!,'[80] before vanishing as mysteriously as he had appeared. Sure enough, a few days later, grim confirmation of the vision's tidings had been brought to Cluny. The Bishop of Utrecht was indeed no more.

Prompted by this alarming experience, Abbot Hugh had dutifully set himself to the task of redeeming his godson from the prospect of a similarly infernal fate. In early November, crossing into the *Reich*, he had selflessly put his own prospects of salvation into jeopardy by meeting with the excommunicated king, and urging him to hold true to his chosen course of penitence. Then, heading on southwards, Hugh had journeyed to Rome, where he had sought absolution for his dealings with Henry from the Pope himself. Gregory had granted it readily enough. Relations between the two men had long been close. 'We walk by the same way,' as Gregory would later express it, 'by the same mind, and by the same spirit.'[81] Indeed, aside from his much-loved spiritual daughter, the Countess Matilda, Hugh was the only person to whom the sternly self-disciplined pontiff ever thought to confess his private anxieties. It was telling, no doubt that what he most admired in the abbot were precisely those qualities of compassion and emollience that he so often felt obliged, by virtue of all his responsibilities as the shepherd of the Christian people, to guard against in himself. Hugh's attempts at peacemaking, though initially brushed aside, were certainly not begrudged. Leaving Rome that icy December on his fateful attempt to reach Augsburg, and his rendezvous with the German princes, the Pope made sure to keep the Abbot of Cluny by his side. Soon afterwards, crossing into Tuscany, he was joined by the Lady Matilda. So it was, in the new year, as the startling news was brought to the papal party of Henry's crossing of the Alps, that Gregory, amid all the panic of his hurried doubling back to Canossa, found himself bolstered by the companionship of the two people upon whose support he had always most depended. Their advice, at this supreme crisis-point of his life, was unhesitating. Both, before Henry's arrival at the gates of Matilda's stronghold, had met with the king and promised to plead his cause. Both duly kept their word. Both, as Gregory sat by his window and stared out at the royal suppliant shivering in the snow below him, vigorously urged the course of mercy.

As well they might have done. For Matilda, though she remained unstintingly loyal to the Holy Father, the benefits of securing the friendship of Henry, her overlord and second-cousin, were obvious – not least because, with the death of her mother the previous year, she now ruled alone as the protectress of her lands. Hugh, meanwhile, in his concern to see his godson redeemed from the yawning jaws of hell, felt little call to consider what impact Henry's absolution might have upon Gregory's plans and hopes for the reordering of the fallen world. The monks of Cluny, after all, were already as close to an angelic state as it was possible for flesh and blood to be. Far from labouring to bring the remainder of humanity to share in their own miraculous condition, their instinct had always been instead to man the ramparts of their abbey. Whereas Gregory did not hesitate to charge seasoned warriors such as Erlembald to fight for the cause of reform from their saddles, Hugh would invariably urge the opposite course upon them, and encourage any penitent knight to swap his mail coat for a cowl. Indeed, the glamour and mystique of Cluny's name being what it was, even dukes, on occasion, had been known to abandon their princedoms for the abbey's cloisters. 'The shepherds flee, as do the dogs who are the protectors of their flocks,' Gregory, in naked frustration, had once raged at Hugh. 'Only take or receive a duke into the quiet of Cluny, and you will be leaving a hundred thousand Christians without a guardian!'[82] Even though the Pope knew both himself and the abbot to be allies in a common struggle, there were times, desolating times, when he feared that they might be pulling in opposite directions. At such moments, the knowledge of how alone he was with all his responsibilities would bear down on him in a peculiarly crushing manner. 'For we bear a huge weight not only of spiritual but also of temporal concerns; and we daily fear our falling under the impending burden, for in this world we can in no way find means of help and support.'[83] Such was the bleak confession that Gregory had made to Hugh back in 1074, during the very first year of his papacy. He might well have repeated it, and with even more justice, at Canossa.

Certainly, his delay in calling Henry in from the cold was not, as his critics would subsequently allege, the expression of a stiff-necked arrogance, but rather of irresolution, perplexity and self-doubt. Gregory, that man of iron certitude, did not know what to do. The king's manoeuvre had comprehensively outflanked him. As a result, he found himself confronted by an agonising dilemma. Absolve Henry, Gregory knew, and all the confidence that the German princes had placed in him would inevitably be betrayed. Refuse to show the humbled king mercy, however, and he would be betraying the duty that he owed to the Almighty Himself: to serve Him as the channel of His forgiveness and grace. Such a consideration, in the end, had to be reckoned paramount. So it was, on the third day of Henry's penitence, that the Holy Father duly gave the guards on the gates the nod. The king was admitted into the castle at last, blessed with a kiss, and invited to Mass. Yet all along, in the back of Gregory's mind, the dread would have lurked that he was being fooled, that he had been outsmarted, that his adversary had triumphed.

An anxiety, it seems, that was gnawing at Henry too. Entering his cousin's stronghold, his stomach was knotted up. When he and Gregory sat down together to mark their reconciliation with a meal, the occasion was not a success. No blame for this could possibly have been attached to the standard of fare on offer: for the Lady Matilda was heir to a long line of gourmands, and the balsamic vinegar of Canossa, in particular, was internationally renowned. Both Pope and king, however, showed precious little appetite. Gregory, as ascetic as ever, contented himself with the odd nibble at a herb or two; while Henry as well, despite his three days of penance, ate barely a mouthful. His discomfort, perhaps, was only to be expected. Feasts, which should properly have been rituals for bringing home to his subjects the full scale of his royal dignity and power, had all too often ended up emphasising the very opposite. Back when he was young, his guests had regularly amused themselves by having punch-ups over the seating arrangements. On one notorious occasion, indeed, two bishops had brought in rival gangs of heavies to help decide which of them should have the precedence. On another, a group of monks, indignant at Henry's gifting of their monastery to the Archbishop of Cologne, had gatecrashed the royal hall and vandalised the dinner table, in full view of all the court. Unsurprisingly, then, any hint of awkwardness at a meal tended not to bring out the best in the king. Now that he had secured what he wanted from Gregory, he certainly had no wish to linger any longer than he had to at the scene of his humiliation. After one further summit with the Pope, held near by at a second of Matilda's strongholds, Henry was off. By April, after a hurried tour of northern Italy, he was back in the *Reich*.

Where, already, Gregory's dark forebodings about how the German princes might respond to his absolution of the king were proving themselves all too justified. Henry's enemies, brought the news of Canossa, had reacted to it with astonishment and consternation. Barely a month after receiving Gregory's half-defiant, half-apologetic justification of his decision, the rebel princes had met in grim-faced assembly in Franconia, in the town of Forcheim. There, rather than wait for Gregory himself to arrive in Germany, as had previously been their intention, they had briskly set about delivering a judgement of their own. On 13 March, they had formally agreed that Henry, no matter what might have been decided on the topic at Canossa, should remain well and truly deposed.[84] Then, two days later, and in the wake of a patently predetermined vote, the election had been announced of a new king: Duke Rudolf of Swabia. A fateful step: for although, over the course of the centuries, there had often been anti-popes, never before had there been an anointed anti-Caesar. The insurgency within Henry's kingdom was fast becoming something intractable. What had previously been spasmodic rumblings were by now coming to shake the very fabric of the *Reich*. The threat was not merely of dynastic feuding, such as had perennially afflicted it, but of a far more total form of conflict: civil war of a remorselessness such as no Christian realm had ever endured before.

Not that this was immediately apparent to Henry. Reinvigorated by the success of his gambit at Canossa, he came strutting back across the Alps aglow with self-confidence, and spitting disdain for his upstart challenger. Most of the southern princes, shrinking from the course of open treason, reluctantly shuffled in behind him; Swabia, Rudolf's own dukedom, was invaded and laid waste; Rudolf himself, abandoning his attempt to tour the *Reich* in a serene and stately manner, as befitted a king, was sent scampering for Saxony. Once arrived in that hotbed of rebellion, however, he and his supporters succeeded in hunkering down so impregnably that Henry, despite repeated efforts, found it impossible to shift them. The result was a stalemate – and an increasingly bloody one too. Battle after battle was fought – and every one indecisive. Armies composed primarily not of mail-clad horsemen but rather of conscripted foot-soldiers, merchants and billhook-carrying peasants, provided both kings with sufficient spear-fodder to keep returning to the killing-fields. Warfare on such a scale appeared to the Germans themselves something unprecedented and terrifying; and so, inevitably – for the habit of anticipating apocalypse was by now deeply ingrained in the Christian people – there were many who saw in it a foretaste of the end days. The Saxons, even as they fought in the name of a cause dusted down from books of pagan history – what had been termed by the ancients '*libertas*', or 'liberty'– simultaneously never doubted that they ranked as the sword-arms of heaven. Henry, in their fervent opinion, had been deposed both justly and irrevocably, as 'an open enemy of the Church'. To die in the cause of their nation's freedom was therefore to die as martyrs for Christ as well. Gregory's own legates to Saxony, riding in Rudolf's train and offering his warriors their blessing, had repeatedly confirmed as much. Henry, one of them had stated baldly, was 'a limb of Antichrist'.[85]

A pronouncement for which Rudolf was, of course, most grateful. Nevertheless, as he struggled desperately to extend his writ beyond the limits of Saxony, he could have done with a little more cheerleading from the Holy Father himself. Not that he was alone in feeling disappointment on that particular score. Henry too, in the wake of Canossa, regarded papal backing as his right: fit reward for his penance. Both kings, taking it for granted that the Almighty was on their side, duly pressed for a papal condemnation of the other; but Gregory, tempering his natural decisiveness for once, sought to maintain a severe neutrality. He certainly was anguished by the slaughter in Germany, and desperate to see it brought to an end, yet his principal concern remained, as it had ever been, the securing of the freedom of the

Church. If Henry was clearly less to be trusted on that score than Rudolf, then so also did he seem the likelier to prevail as the ultimate victor: a consideration fit to inspire even Gregory to a course of wait and see.

And yet the conclusion that most men would have drawn from this – that there were inevitable limitations set upon what any pope might hope to achieve in a world swayed by the sword – was one that he still disdained to draw. Combustible, scorching, volcanic: Gregory remained what he had ever been. Even as a baby, it was said, unearthly sparks had flickered across his swaddling clothes; and as an adult too, not only had a miraculous halo of flames been known on occasion to illumine his head, but before ever being raised to the throne of St Peter, he had been granted a vision of his future, one spectacularly lit by fire. For he had dreamed a famous dream: 'a prophecy of papal excellence and power, that flames came out of his mouth and set the whole world ablaze'. To Gregory's enemies, impious as they were, this had appeared a clear portent of the destruction that he was fated to unleash upon the Christian people; but his supporters had known better. 'For doubtless,' as one of them put it, 'the fire had been that same fire cast upon the earth by the Lord Jesus Christ: a kindling eagerly to be desired.'[86]

Nor, even as Germany burned, did Gregory himself ever pause to doubt this. Unremittingly, with a persistence and an energy that appeared even to his bitterest opponents something prodigious, he stuck to the task of re-forging the entire Christian world upon the anvil of his will. Not a region of Christendom but its customs, if they appeared to Gregory to flout those of the Roman Church, might provoke a lordly scolding. Informed, for instance, that there was a fashion on Sardinia for priests to sport luxuriant beards, he did not hesitate to lecture the local authorities in the most peremptory manner: 'we charge you', he wrote sternly, 'that you should make and compel all the clergy under your power to shave'.[87] Such a close attention to details of personal grooming might, perhaps, have been thought to lie beneath the papal dignity – but Gregory knew otherwise. What else was his mission, after all, if not to restore wholeness to a fractured world, from the top to the very bottom? No possible effort, then, in the pursuit of such an awesome goal, could properly be spared him. Nothing for it, in the final reckoning, but to impose a uniform obedience upon the Church wherever it was found, and at every level. For only then could it be rendered truly universal.

And the best way of securing this desirable end? To Gregory, a man with a proven taste for thinking big, the solution had seemed self-evident enough. Surely, he had mused, heaven's purpose would best be served if all the various realms of Christendom were to become the personal property of St Peter, and his earthly vicar – himself. Never a man to duck a challenge, he had duly dusted down the Donation of Constantine, and written to various princes, floating the startling suggestion that they might like to sign over their kingdoms 'to the holy Roman church'.[88] Yet even Gregory, never a man to sell his own expectations short, seems to have appreciated that the idea, by and large, was a non-starter. A few months after Canossa, for instance, addressing the various kings of Spain, he had no sooner asserted that the entire peninsula belonged to St Peter than he was hurriedly acknowledging that, 'to be sure, both the misfortunes of past times and a certain negligence of our predecessors have hitherto obscured this'.[89] Which was putting it mildly. Indeed, in sober truth, rulers needed to be either very pious, like the Countess Matilda, or else very hungry for legitimacy, like Robert Guiscard, to become vassals of St Peter. Even Gregory himself, though he remained indomitably convinced of the papacy's entitlements, was not wholly oblivious to this. He may have been unbending in his aspirations – but in his methods often much less so. After all, as the Norman battle line had so potently demonstrated at Hastings, there was no shame in a tactical withdrawal, so long as it served the cause of an ultimate victory. When the Conqueror himself, for instance, invited by a pushy legate to become a vassal of St Peter, responded with a diplomatic snort, Gregory opted not to force the issue. William was, compared with Henry, a model partner of the Roman Church; why, then, risk the alienation of a king who was capable of serving 'as a standard of righteousness and a pattern of obedience to all the princes of the earth'?[90]

For Gregory, then, as for any general engaged in a war on multiple fronts, strategy was not merely a matter of clinging on to positions, no matter what, but also of judging which lines could legitimately be abandoned, in the cause of securing a lesser advantage. Certainly, as the bruising events leading up to Canossa had demonstrated, he was hardly afraid to go head to head with kings; and yet Gregory was sensitive as well to the advantages that might be gained from conciliation. In Spain, for instance, as in England, he ended up opting not to push his luck: for the King of León, no less than William the Conqueror, was a man who combined great devotion to the Roman Church with an imperious and iron-forged temper. Indeed, such was the fearsome reputation of Alfonso VI that he was darkly rumoured to have been guilty of fratricide, no less: for in 1072, ascending the throne, it had been in succession to his brother, murdered in a crime that – officially, at any rate – had never been solved. With a second brother incarcerated for life, and one of his cousins falling mysteriously off a cliff, such a king was clearly a man whose interests it might be perilous to cross – nor did Gregory choose to. Indeed, aside from a brief spat provoked by Alfonso's choice of an unsuitable wife, relations between Pope and king grew so cordial that in 1079, only two years after the rebuff of his attempt to lay claim to Spain for St Peter, Gregory could hail his correspondent for his 'exalted humility and faithful obedience'.[91] Slightly over the top, it might have been thought – except that, from the perspective of Rome, it did not appear so at all. Alfonso might not have acknowledged himself a vassal of the papacy – but as a patron of reform, at any rate, he was fit to rank alongside any prince in Christendom. No matter that the Spaniards, harking back to the glory days when Toledo had been the holy city of the Visigoths rather than a Saracen capital, still clung to outmoded and heretical rituals – Alfonso had cheerfully abolished them all. In 1080, by swingeing royal decree, the Roman form of Mass was imposed upon his entire kingdom. Alfonso himself, in a dramatic gesture, drop-kicked a Visigothic service-book into a bonfire. This was precisely the kind of robust leadership that Gregory had always valued in a king.

For, although he was a man of God, the Holy Father was hardly unseasoned in the ways of the world. As a leader himself with a whole lifetime of diplomatic manoeuvrings to his credit, Gregory had few illusions as to the character of the warlords with whom he was obliged, as Pope, to deal. Nevertheless, this did not mean, of course, that the inevitable compromises which were forced upon him as a result necessarily sat easily with his conscience. That the universal Church remained dependent on the support of often murderous princes never ceased to frustrate and pain him. Several years into his papacy, indeed, and sometimes, in his darker moods, Gregory would find himself brought to question the very basis of worldly power. 'For who does not know', he raged bitterly on one occasion, 'that kings and dukes derive their origin from men ignorant of God, murderers who raised themselves above their former equals by means of pride, plunder and treachery, urged on all the while by the Devil, who is the prince of this world?'[92]

A startling question – and one that only a man of humble origins, perhaps, would ever have thought to ask. To Gregory himself, a man who had toiled all his life to secure the Church as a bulwark against the legions of 'the ancient enemy',[93] suspicion of the Devil's cunning was only natural: a spur to ever more urgent labours. Yet even as he could reflect with satisfaction on the sheer global reach of all his efforts, and on how an immense sway of the earth's scattered peoples, from the Swedes to the Irish, had been successfully urged to a common obedience, Gregory was increasingly conscious of a satanic and gathering darkness. It was all well and good for him to summon princes on the world's edge to acknowledge the universal authority of 'St Peter and his vicars, among whom divine providence has appointed that our lot should be numbered'[94] – and yet what if, even as he did so, the most hellish menace of all were lurking within Christendom's heartlands? What, indeed, if the advance guard of Antichrist were already massing to assail the throne of St Peter itself? This, by the seventh year of his papacy, was the monstrous possibility by which

Gregory found himself increasingly shadowed. 'And truly,' he reflected, 'it can be held no wonder – for the nearer the time of Antichrist approaches, so the more violently does he strive to destroy the Christian religion.'[95]

Back in late 1077, as Henry's pious and venerable mother lay dying, what had most consoled her was the conviction that her son and her spiritual father, the two men to whom she had devoted so much of her life, were reconciled at last, and that Christendom's great breach was repaired for good. Perhaps, then, it was just as well that the Empress Agnes had passed away when she did. Despite the kiss of forgiveness that Gregory had bestowed upon Henry at Canossa, and for all the spirit of compromise that had characterised their mutual dealings in its immediate wake, both had remained wedded to positions that neither man could possibly concede: positions that were, in the ultimate reckoning, irreconcilable. Henry, alert at last to the full revolutionary implications of Gregory's policies, was resolved never to surrender his right of investiture; just as Gregory, thunderously convinced of his divine vocation, remained no less committed to stripping it away for good. Small wonder, then, that the tensions which had seemed so dramatically eased at Canossa had soon begun to escalate again. In the autumn of 1078, Gregory, making all too clear what had hitherto been left diplomatically opaque, had issued a fateful decree: 'that no priest may receive investiture of a bishopric, abbey, or church from the hand of an emperor or king'.[96] Henry's response was to invest two archbishops that very same Christmas. A year and more on, and still there had been no royal climbdown. Why, indeed, should there have been? Henry had every reason to feel confident. In Saxony, Rudolf's support was showing signs of splintering at last. Certainly, there was not the remotest prospect now of the anti-king making a breakout from his increasingly beleaguered power base. Henry could consider himself as secure upon his throne as he had been since the body-blow of his excommunication. No wonder, then, called upon formally for the first time to abandon his right of investiture, that he had opted to call Gregory's bluff.

And no wonder either, Gregory being Gregory, that the Pope had likewise refused to budge. The challenge, it seemed to the outraged pontiff, was only incidentally to himself: for Henry was trampling on the very purposes of God. Early in 1080, shortly before a synod was due to be held in Rome, the Virgin Mary had duly appeared to Gregory in a vision, and reassured him of heaven's backing for the dreadful steps that it was now his clear and pressing duty, as the leader of the universal Church, to take. Sure enough, on 7 March, the Pope greeted the assembled delegates to his council with a mighty groan, and then, his words tumbling out from him in an anguished torrent, pronounced that Henry was once again 'justly cast down from the dignity of the kingship because of his pride, disobedience and falsehood'.[97] The show of neutrality that Gregory had maintained with such rigorous forbearance since Forcheim was abandoned at last. All the weight of his authority, and all the invisible legions of God that he had no reason to doubt were his to command, he now committed to the support of Rudolf. Everything that he had ever laboured to achieve, in short, was being gambled on a single proposition: that it lay within his power to destroy Henry for good. That same Easter, in the awful setting of St Peter's, Gregory did not hesitate to make explicit the full, terrifying scale of what was now at stake between him and his adversary. 'For let it be known to all of you,' he pronounced, 'that if he does not recover his senses by the feast of St Peter, he will die or be deposed. If this fails to happen, I ought no more to be believed.'[98]

Gregory, though, was unwilling to trust his fortunes entirely to the protection of the apostle. That summer, looking to secure an earthly shield for himself in addition to his celestial one, he took a deep breath, swallowed his scruples, and agreed to meet with Robert Guiscard. The Duke of Apulia, who had responded to his excommunication back in 1074 by seizing Amalfi and menacing Benevento, was now formally absolved, and reconfirmed as a papal vassal. A humiliating climbdown for Gregory, to be sure – but an unavoidable one as well. Sure enough, late that June, right in the midst of his negotiations with the Norman duke, ominous news arrived from Germany. Henry, it was reported, repeating his tactics of four years earlier, had responded to Gregory's deposition of him by summoning a council of his bishops, and leaning on them to depose Gregory in turn. A whole array of crimes had been laid at the door of 'Hildebrand': warmongering, of course, and the inevitable simony, but also, and more originally, a taste for pornographic floor shows.

Nor was that the worst. Henry had also taken a further and still more threatening step. A new pope had been nominated: the Archbishop of Ravenna, a distant relative of the Countess Matilda by the name of Guibert. Not surprisingly, then, on the feast day of St Peter, 29 June, Gregory's supporters waited with bated breath for this impostor to be struck down along with Henry; but nothing happened. Not only did the two men remain resolutely alive and flourishing, but it seemed to many, as summer turned to autumn, that the Almighty had adopted a policy of actively backing the anathematised king. On 15 October, for instance, as the Lady Matilda set out along the road to Ravenna in an attempt to kidnap her upstart relative, she and her army of knights were ambushed and so severely mauled that they had no choice but to retreat ignominiously to a nearby bolt hole.

Simultaneously, in Saxony, by the side of a swollen river south of Merseburg, an even worse calamity was befalling Gregory's cause. Rudolf of Swabia, meeting Henry in yet another savage but indecisive battle, had his sword-hand hacked clean off, and within a matter of hours had bled to death. A maiming as just as it was awful, it appeared to his foes: for the fatal blow had been delivered to the hand with which the anti-king had once sworn to be Henry's vassal. Gregory's prophecy, 'that in this year the false king would die',[99] now appeared all too grimly ironic. God had indeed delivered a judgement, it seemed – but it was not Henry who had been found wanting.

And even Gregory himself, who naturally scorned to share in this analysis, had been left by Rudolf's death feeling perhaps just a measure of perplexity at the mysterious workings of the Almighty, and looking anxiously to the north. No matter that the Saxons remained as obdurately unpacified as they had ever been: they had also been left exhausted and leaderless, and Henry could afford to ignore them at last. The road to Rome lay open so, come the spring, he took it. By May, he and his army were camped out before the city's gates. There, however, much to Henry's frustration, they found themselves obliged to halt. No matter that the would-be emperor had made sure to bring Guibert with him, in anticipation of a coronation in St Peter's: what he had neglected to bring were sufficient troops to intimidate the Romans, who had no desire for a swap of bishops. 'Instead of candles, they met the king with spears; instead of singing clergy, with armed warriors; instead of anthems of praise, with reproaches; instead of applause, with sobs.'[100] Gregory, gazing out at his enemy's camp from the battlements of the Castel Sant'Angelo, a brooding stronghold just across from St Peter's, could afford to breathe a huge sigh of relief. By June, as the Roman marshlands shimmered pestilentially in the heat, the royal army had begun packing up its bags.

But for how long would Henry be gone? And if he did return in the new year, and in sufficient force to cow the Romans – what then? Although Gregory was buoyed by the solid backing of his flock, he could hardly help but reflect on the disappointing lack of support he had received from those better qualified, perhaps, to draw their swords in his defence. True, the Countess Matilda, ever loyal, ever valiant, had refused to submit to her royal cousin; but the effective limit of her resistance had been to hunker down in her Apennine strongholds, while being systematically despoiled of all her lowland possessions. Indeed, there was only one captain in Italy truly qualified to blunt the threat posed by Henry: that very same prince whose backing it had cost Gregory so much nose-holding to secure only the previous year. Robert Guiscard, however, despite all the increasingly frantic appeals sent to him from the Lateran, had shown a marked disinclination to rally to his overlord's cause: for his concern, as it had ever been, was ultimately with no one's prospects save his own. The Duke of Apulia had always been a man to follow his dreams – and these, by the summer of 1081, had attained a truly grandiose dimension. Rather than marching to combat Henry, Guiscard had instead been preoccupied with his most glamorous and spectacular stunt yet: nothing less than an invasion of the Byzantine Empire.

An ambitious project, certainly – but not a wholly vainglorious one, even so. Seven years had passed since the failure of Gregory's planned expedition to Constantinople, and still the fortunes of the New Rome remained firmly locked in a downward spiral: 'the Empire was almost at its last gasp'.[101] Even as the Turks continued with their dismemberment of its Asian provinces, so a fresh wave of invaders, the inveterately savage Pechenegs, had arrived to darken the northern frontiers, while in the capital itself the treasury and barracks alike were almost bare. Indeed, to the demoralised Byzantines, it appeared 'that no other state in living memory had plumbed such depths of misery'.[102] Their ruin appeared almost total.

Yet Guiscard, even as his nostrils were flaring hungrily at the scent of blood borne to him from across the Adriatic, had fretted as well that the opportunity might be slipping him by to make a kill.

In Constantinople, after a wearying turnover of emperors in which no fewer than seven pretenders had laid claim to the throne in barely twenty years, a young general had recently come to power in the wake of yet another coup. Alexius Comnenus, however, unlike his predecessors, was a man of formidable political and military talents: an emperor who, given half a chance, might even succeed in setting the empire back on its feet. Guiscard, resolved not to give Alexius any chance at all, had duly struck as hard and fast as he could. In June, having crossed the Adriatic, he placed the Albanian coastal stronghold of Durazzo under siege. In October, attacked by a Byzantine relief force led by the *Basileus* himself, and including in its ranks a sizeable contingent of English Varangians, all of them naturally eager for vengeance on the compatriots of their conqueror, he won a crushing victory. The English, having taken sanctuary in a church, were reduced efficiently and satisfyingly to ashes after Robert had their refuge set on fire. Shortly afterwards, Durazzo itself was betrayed into his hands. It appeared that the Normans were on the brink of yet another conquest.

But Alexius was not finished yet. Reverting to time-honoured

Byzantine strategy, he frantically dredged up what few reserves of treasure were still left to him – and dispatched them to Henry. 'And so it was that he incited the German king to enmity against Robert.'[103] Simultaneously, he set about fostering a revolt in Apulia – and to such effect that Guiscard, faced with the prospect of losing his power base, had little alternative but to abandon all his dreams of winning Constantinople and hurry back to Italy. For the next two years, pre-occupied as he was with stamping out the flames of insurrection in his own dukedom, he would have no reserves spare to send to Gregory – and this despite the fact that Henry, subsidised by Byzantine gold, was by now a permanent presence in Italy, a standing menace to the Normans as well as to the Pope. It was true that Rome herself, pro-tected by her ancient walls, continued to defy all his attempts to take her, blockades and assaults alike; but by 1083, after three years of inter-mittent siege, the pressure was starting to tell. Then abruptly, on 3 June, a calamity. A breach was made in the fortifications that encircled the Vatican, across the Tiber from the rest of the city; Henry's forces flooded through the gap; St Peter's cathedral was captured. Gregory, standing on the battlements of Sant'Angelo, had to watch in impotent horror as his great enemy took possession of the holiest shrine in Christendom: the last resting place of the Prince of the Apostles.

This was a seemingly decisive moment: for there appeared nothing now to stop Henry from being crowned emperor. Yet the king, despite his capture of St Peter's, and despite having Guibert on hand to do the imperial honours, still hesitated. No matter the vitupera-tions of his pet bishops, it was Gregory, in the opinion of the vast mass of the Christian people, and of the Romans above all, who remained the one true Pope. Accordingly, rather than force through a corona-tion that his enemies would be able to dismiss as illegitimate, and in the hope of taking full possession of a still defiant Rome, Henry sought compromise.

As before, the man entrusted with attempting to negotiate this was that instinctive peacemaker, the Abbot of Cluny: for Hugh, amid all the convulsions and calamities that had followed Canossa, had somehow succeeded in keeping a foot still in both camps.[104] Indeed, ever since 1080, when Gregory had written to him to ask if there was anyone he could recommend for the cardinalate, there had been a permanent touch of Cluny at the papal court: for the nominated candidate, a Frenchman by the name of Odo, had been the abbey's number two, its 'major prior'. But in 1083, as opposed to 1077, Hugh's attempts at conciliation were doomed to failure: Gregory sent him packing. Only a few months on, however, as Henry's noose around Rome continued to tighten, and a succession of well-directed bribes began to sap the city's resistance at last, even Gregory had begun to suspect that the writing might be on the wall. By the autumn, it was the Pope who was hoping to open negotiations. Yet still the two sides remained as far apart as ever. That November, when Odo was sent by Gregory to explore terms, Henry was so enraged by what he saw as the continuing inflexibility of the papal bottom line that he briefly had the cardinal flung into prison.

Soon enough, however, and the royal blood pressure had begun to drop; and come the new year, Henry could afford positively to relax. What had previously been a trickle of defections from the ranks of Gregory's supporters was fast becoming a flood. Deacons, papal officials, even the odd cardinal: all were crossing over to Henry's side. Even more significantly, a majority of the Roman people were finally prepared to abandon their bishop as well. On 21 March 1084, a group of them unbolted the gates of their city – and Henry, after four years of waiting, rode into his ancient capital at last. Nor was he alone in laying claim to a much-anticipated inheritance. After all, with Gregory still bottled up in the Castel Sant'Angelo, the Lateran had been left standing vacant: the ideal opportunity, then, for a new tenant to move in. So it was, a bare three days after Henry's entry into Rome, that Guibert adopted the name Clement III and was formally enthroned as Pope. Shortly afterwards, over Easter, it was Henry's turn to be graced with the very grandest of promotions. Flanked by the Holy Lance, that ancient relic of awful power, he was first anointed by Clement, and then, the following day, crowned emperor: the heir of Charlemagne, of Otto the Great, of his own father. Rome, after a wait of many decades, could hail a consecrated Caesar once again.

But not for long. Even as Henry, resolved to finish off Gregory once and for all, was settling down to the siege of the Castel Sant'Angelo, disturbing news was brought to him from the south. Robert Guiscard and his brother, Count Roger of Sicily, were on the march at long last. The new emperor, having obtained the coronation that he had come to Rome to secure, opted not to hang around. His escape, and the Anti-pope's too, proved to have been just in the nick of time. A bare three days after their hurried exit from the capital, and Norman out-riders were clattering up to the city walls. The Romans, gazing out in horror at the immense army descending upon them, one that included not only a great shock force of knights but even Saracens levied from Sicily, kept their gates firmly barred, and writhed in inde-cision. Abandoned by their emperor, and all too conscious of the Hautevilles' fearsome reputation, they feared the worst – as well they might have done. For Guiscard was already growing impatient. After three days of waiting, he duly led a night-time assault, and smashed his way into the city. Gregory, sprung from the Castel Sant'Angelo, was led in triumph to the Lateran – but even as he celebrated his release with a sumptuous Mass of thanksgiving, his Norman liberators were already fleecing his flock down to the very bones. Finally, after three terrible days, the despairing Romans attempted a fightback – only to end up being slaughtered as well as robbed. Gregory, gazing out from the Lateran, had to endure the sight of his entire beloved city up in flames. Never before had the capital of Christendom endured so brutal, so destructive, and so complete a sack. The most terrible atroc-ities of all, it was reported, were committed by Count Roger's Saracens.

Such was the fate that Gregory, the heir of St Peter, had brought down upon the last resting place of the apostle: to be ransacked by infi-dels. As the smoke began to drift away at last, and the blood on the streets to dry, it was perfectly evident, even to the Pope himself, that his position in the ruined city had been rendered untenable: for the curses and clenched fists of the people who had once been his firmest supporters would make it impossible for him to continue in Rome without the protection of the Hautevilles. Accordingly, when Guiscard left at the end of July, he had little choice but to set out with him. No less than Pope Leo after Civitate, Gregory was now effectively a prisoner of the Normans. Indeed, if anything, his failure appeared even more total than Leo's had been. Everything that he had ever fought for seemed in a state of ruin. His great adversary, crowned in triumph emperor, still sat on the throne of the *Reich*. Back in Rome, no sooner had Gregory left the city than the weasel Clement was slipping back into the Lateran. Gregory himself, set up by Guiscard in quarters just south of Amalfi, knew in his heart of hearts that he had been left much diminished and humiliated. Grimly, in a letter addressed simply 'To the faithful', he sought to make sense of it all. 'Ever since by God's providence mother church set me upon the apostolic throne,' he assured the Christian people, 'deeply unworthy and, as God is my witness, unwilling though I was, my greatest concern has been that holy church, the bride of Christ, our lady and mother, should return to her true glory, and stand free, chaste and catholic. But because this entirely displeased the ancient enemy, he has armed his members against us, in order to turn everything upside down.'[105] Certainly, that same winter, falling suddenly and mortally sick, Gregory had no doubt that the world did indeed lie in the shadow of Antichrist. No other explanation for the calamities that had befallen him and his great cause appeared possible. 'I have loved righteousness,' he declared on 25 May, 'and I have hated iniquity, therefore I die in exile.'[106] They were the last words that he would ever speak.

However, the shadow of Antichrist was not nearly so spreading as Gregory, lying on his deathbed, had darkly thought. Time would show that his pontificate, far from having led to the ruin of the Church's *libertas*, its freedom, had served instead to entrench it, and much else, beyond all prospect of reversal. The great mass of the Christian people, despite – or perhaps because of – the unprecedented upheavals of the previous decade, remained no less committed to the cause of reform than they had ever been; as did many of the foremost leaders of the Church, whether cardinals, bishops or abbots; and still, in the courts of great princes across Christendom, Gregory's inimitable blend of lecturing and encouragement continued to reverberate. Even in the *Reich* itself, where Henry's triumph appeared complete, the reality was somewhat different. The cause of reform in Germany, as Cardinal Odo had discovered when he arrived there late in 1084 as Gregory's legate, had put down deep roots indeed. 'What else is talked about even in the women's spinning-rooms and the artisans' workshops?'[107] one monk, hostile to Gregory, had exclaimed back in 1075. A decade on, and the talk had grown even louder.

So the calamities which had marked the end of the most momentous pontificate for many centuries had not served to herald the coming of Antichrist. On the contrary, much that Gregory had laboured so titanically and tumultuously to secure would more than survive his passing. As a reassurance of this, had he only been brought the news of it by some supernatural vision or angelic messenger, the dying Pope could have pointed to a signal triumph: proof that the Almighty was indeed still smiling upon Christendom. For on 25 May 1085, the very day of Gregory's death, Christian arms had secured a glorious and much yearned-for conquest. Gates closed to them for many centuries had been opened at last. A holy city had been restored to the universal Church. Once again, as it had done long before, a cross stood planted in triumph upon the rocky battlements of Toledo.

Deus Vult

On 18 October 1095, as dawn broke over the halls and towers of Cluny, a sense of bustle, of excitement even, was already palpable across the great monastery. A guest was shortly expected – and not just any guest. Indeed, such was the abbey's aura of holiness, and such its pedigree too, that it took a truly exceptional class of visitor to put those who trod its carpeted flagstones in the shade. The angelic monks of Cluny, who numbered dukes and penitent bishops among their ranks, were rarely outshone. Not that they would have felt, as they tracked the preparations of the abbey servants, and stole an occasional glance towards the road on the eastern horizon, that there was any infringement of their dignity in the offing. Just the opposite, in fact. The man the brethren were waiting to greet was no stranger to their cloisters. Once, indeed, he had been their 'major prior'. Now, more than any Cluniac before him, he offered living proof of the heights that might be attained by an old boy of the abbey.

Fifteen years had passed since Odo's departure for Rome. In that time, he had proved himself the ablest, the shrewdest and the most committed of Gregory's followers. For all his devotion to the memory of the great pope who had raised him to the cardinalate, however, Odo was a man of very different talents to his patron – and just as well. The time for blood and thunder had passed. With an anti-pope installed in the Lateran, and much of Christendom, in the wake of Gregory's death, content to acknowledge Clement as the authentic heir of St Peter, a touch of Cluniac cool was precisely what the beleaguered reformers had most needed. Like Abbot Hugh, whom Gregory, in rueful and half-envious admiration, had nicknamed 'the smooth-talking tyrant',[108] Odo was a formidable conciliator: a born showman who combined exceptional persuasiveness with a steely measure of calculation, and who invariably came out a winner. So it was, back in 1085, after only five years as a cardinal, that he had been one of two heavyweight candidates to succeed Gregory, and continue the fight against Clement; and so it was too, after the election of his rival, that he had made sure to get on the new pope's side, and be nominated as his successor. He had not had long to wait. Two years into the new pontificate, and the throne of St Peter had been left vacant again. Odo had duly been elected to fill it. Taking the name Urban II, he had set himself to the great task of completing what Gregory had left undone – and, as a particular priority, to crushing the authority of Clement, the Anti-pope, once and for all.

Eight years down the road, and he was well on his way to success. A subtle reader of men's ambitions, and a master of the well-directed concession, Urban had a taste for tactics that blended rigour with discretion. By sternly ring-fencing the fundamentals of reform, and by giving way on everything else, his accomplishment had been to consolidate Gregory's achievements far more effectively than Gregory himself would ever have done. '*Pedisequus*',[109] his opponents sneeringly labelled him: a mere lackey, a body servant, scurrying along dutifully in the footsteps of his predecessor. This, however, was to confuse Urban's show of equanimity with a lack of initiative or assertiveness. In reality, no less than Gregory had been, the new pope was of a lordly disposition. Indeed, if anything, the habits of lordliness came more naturally to him than they ever had to the humbly born Hildebrand: for Odo's parents had been noble, and he had grown up informed by the restless attitudes and aspirations of the warrior class of France. Certainly, as befitted someone who had spent his earliest years in a castle, his familiarity with the cutting edge was far from confined to the business of the Church. More than any pope before him, Urban II had the measure of the new breed of knightly captain.

Indeed, perhaps, shared something of its ruthlessness himself. Just as the natural instinct of any castellan was to add to his own lands by hacking away at those of his rivals, so similarly, on the immeasurably vaster stage of Christendom, had Urban aimed to extend his authority by boxing in Henry and Clement as restrictively as he could. Remorselessly, he had worked to exploit every imperial humiliation, every imperial defeat – and there had recently been plenty of both. Rebellion in Bavaria, the continuing and implacable opposition of the Countess Matilda, and treachery from within the royal family itself: all, since the palmy days of Henry's coronation, had served to cripple the emperor's interests. Indeed, by 1095, so tightly were his enemies pressing in on him that the heir of Constantine and Charlemagne had ended up trapped in a tiny corner of western Lombardy, unable even to cross the Alps back into his homeland.

Urban, looking to rub this in, had duly summoned a council under

Henry's very nose, just south of Milan, in a field outside Piacenza: a city that, officially at any rate, lay within the Anti-pope's home diocese of Ravenna. A steady succession of Clement's former adherents, summoned from across Christendom, had publicly submitted themselves there to Urban's authority. Henry's second wife, a Kievan princess by the name of Eupraxia, and as unhappily married as Bertha had been, had also appeared at the council, following her abduction from imperial custody by agents of the Countess Matilda: sensationally, and to the delegates' delighted horror, she had publicly accused her husband of hosting gang-rapes on her.[110] Then, in a climactic triumph, Urban had met with Henry's eldest son, Conrad, a long-term rebel against his father and widely rumoured to have been Eupraxia's lover – and promised to crown him emperor. The young prince, in exchange, had signed up unreservedly to the reformers' cause. Indeed, in an ostentatious display of submission to Urban's purposes, Conrad had even served the pontiff as a groom, walking by the side of the papal mount and holding its bridle. Who, Urban might well have reflected, was the *pedisequus* now?

No wonder, then, following such a cavalcade of successes, that he had felt sufficiently confident of his grip on Italy to risk travelling onwards into southern France. Indeed, as his partisans delighted in pointing out, the fact that he had the freedom of much of Christendom, while the emperor remained humiliatingly penned up in Lombardy, was in itself yet another stunning boost to the Pope's prestige. More were to follow almost daily over the course of Urban's tour of France: for he had found himself being greeted there with an enthusiasm, a rapture even, that far exceeded even his own expectations. In part, no doubt, this reflected the fact that he was himself a Frenchman; and in part as well the meticulousness with which the visit had been planned. Yet something more was afoot. Not since Leo IX's brief trip to Reims had a pope been seen north of the Alps – and during that half-century the affairs of Christendom had been convulsed from top to bottom. Now, with a Vicar of St Peter actually treading French soil once again, the people of the various princedoms of the south, from Burgundy to Aquitaine, had been able to deliver their judgement on the developments of the past fifty years – and they were doing so with relish. Not only princes and abbots, either. Men and women who once, back in the shadow of the Millennium, might have flocked to see the relics of saints in fields, or else taken to the woods, there to attempt to live as the apostles had done, now gathered to glimpse the Pope. No wonder, over the half-century and more since 1033, that the peace movement had faded away, and heresy too: for both, in effect, had served their turn. The cause of those who had dreamed of a reordering of the fallen world, and demanded a cleansing of everything in human affairs that was most spotted and polluted, was now the cause of the Roman Church.

And Urban, taking the road that led to Cluny, and looking about him that October morning of 1095, would doubtless have marked in what he saw a blessed and mighty reassurance: that his life's great mission, to tame what had been most savage, and to consecrate what had been most damnable, was one shared by the great mass of the Christian people. Indeed, unmistakable proofs of their efforts would have been observable to him along the entire course of his travels: for everywhere, in recent times, 'places which were once the haunt of wild beasts and the lairs of robbers had come to resound to the name of God, and the veneration of the saints'.[111] It was around Cluny, however, above all other places in France perhaps, that this great work of reclamation was most gloriously evident: for there the felling of woods, and the draining of marshes, and the settling of wastelands had been continuous for more than a century, so that to those who travelled past them the very fields appeared reformed. Yet they in turn could merely hint at the true wonder which still awaited the pilgrim; and even Urban himself, familiar as he was with the approach to his old abbey, would surely have reined in his horse as he breasted the eastern hill above Cluny and paused in stupefaction. For there below him was a sight unlike anything he had ever seen: a building better suited to serve as a symbol of his labours than any other in Christendom.

Abbot Hugh had ordered work begun on it some two decades previously. The need had been pressing: for while in heaven there was no limit to the number of angelic voices that might practicably be raised in praise of God, at Cluny, unfortunately, there had been. No longer was the church that had played host to the devotions of the abbey's brethren back in the heroic decades before the Millennium remotely fit for purpose. Fifty monks, over the course of a century, had become two hundred and fifty – and still their ranks were swelling. Accordingly, rather than bow to the constraints set upon him, and settle for compromise or insufficiency or retreat, Abbot Hugh had boldly set himself to meet the challenge head on. A new church, its outline vaster than any church previously built, its half-completed roofs already towering over the old, and the ribs of its massive vault seeming to heave and reach for heaven, had begun to rise up from the valley.

True, the project still had a long way to go – but already, even as it stood, the great edifice was one fit to take the breath away. And Urban's breath, perhaps, especially. For fifteen years previously, as he had set out from Cluny for Rome, there had been nothing but half-dug foundations to see where massive domes and towers now rose; and Urban too, during those fifteen years, had been engaged upon his own great labour of reconstruction. Between the universal Church that it was his duty, as the heir of St Peter, to rebuild and improve and extend, and the church being raised at Cluny which was designed to serve as the 'maior ecclesia', or 'principal church', of Christendom, there was a difference, perhaps, only of degree. How telling it was that the Prince of the Apostles, that same celestial guardian to whom the Pope, as his earthly vicar, most naturally looked for assistance and protection, had been spotted performing the occasional maintenance check on the building works at Cluny. Urban and Abbot Hugh were men with a conjoined ambition. Their goal as architects was 'a dwelling-place for mortals that would please the inhabitants of heaven'.[112]

To the Pope, then, entering the massive space that the builders

395

had already completed, the experience could hardly help but be an inspiring one. An immense and exquisitely carved altar stood before him, radiant, overpowering even, with a sense of holiness. Above it there hung a metal dove, and inside the dove, placed within a golden dish, was kept the very body of Christ Himself: that same consecrated bread which, the scale of the new seating arrangements being what it was, could now be presented to the angelic monks in a single go. The setting too, lit by the wash of seven immense candles, was one of unprecedented beauty and magnificence: for whether it was the stonework of a second great altar situated beyond the first, or the delicate leafage which adorned the mighty capitals, or the ruby glimmer of the wax-painted frescoes on the distant walls, everything was designed to evoke for an awed sinner a sense of paradise. The shadow of the Last Judgement, which had haunted the imaginings of Cluny for the near two centuries of its existence, still appeared to its virgin brethren to lie dark across the world; and so it was, just as Odo and Odilo had done, that Hugh aimed to provide a haven from the gathering storm waves of that terrible day. 'For we, who are placed upon the seas of this world, should always strive to avoid the currents of this life.'[113]

Yet in truth, as the very splendour of the *maior ecclesia* served to trumpet, the circumstances of the Christian people had changed immeasurably since the founding of the abbey. After all, back in the days when there had been nothing to see at Cluny but a ducal hunting lodge, it had seemed to many that Christendom itself was on the verge of being submerged utterly, lost for good beneath the flood tides of blood and fire which for so long, and with such ferocity, had been breaking against it. Indeed, as late as 972, one of the monastery's own abbots, Odilo's predecessor, had been kidnapped and held to ransom by Saracen bandits. A century on, however, and the heartlands of Christendom appeared secure once and for all against heathen appetites. Former breeding grounds of paganism had long since been won for the Cross. Along the fir-darkened tracks of the North Way, where offerings to Odin had lately been hung from the trees, pilgrims now journeyed to bow their heads before the tomb of the martyred St Olaf; beside the Danube, Hungarians who still roamed its banks with tents or reeds for fashioning huts, just as their ancestors had always done, now dreaded to pitch a camp too far from a church, lest they be fined or else cursed by a saint. Indeed, a man might travel a thousand miles from Cluny, a thousand miles and even more, and still not pass the limits of Christendom.

To be sure, he would have needed to set out in the right direction first. Not all the one-time despoilers of the Church had been brought to repent of their depredations. If Cluny were indeed, as Urban pronounced, 'the light of the world',[114] then so too, admittedly, did there remain certain benighted regions where its rays had failed to penetrate. Abbot Hugh himself, writing to a Saracen ruler in Spain, and pushing the argument that Mohammed had been an agent of the Devil, had found his letters being afforded a less than ecstatic reception.[115] His missionaries too. Back in 1074, for instance, after a monk from Cluny had travelled to al-Andalus and offered to walk through fire if his audience would only abandon their heresy, the Saracens had contemptuously ducked the challenge. So the monk, in high dudgeon, 'had shaken the dust from his feet, turned on his heels, and set off back for his monastery'.[116]

At least, though, as he trudged home across the Pyrenees, he had been able to console himself with the reflection that he, at any rate, was unlikely to have a run-in with Saracen bandits. The monks of Cluny might have failed to win them for Christ — but conversion, as the events of the past century had served robustly to demonstrate, was not the only way to counter the menace of the Saracens. The days when an abbot on his travels might be kidnapped by one of their war bands were long since gone. Indeed, to a startling degree, the boot was now on the other foot. In 1087, for instance, a war fleet led by Pisan adventurers had taken belated revenge for the sacking of their city eighty-odd years before by descending on an African port, stripping it bare and carting off the proceeds in triumph to fund a new cathedral. Then, in 1090, a further famous victory: the last outposts of Saracen rule in Sicily had surrendered to Count Roger. One year on, and it had been the turn of the corsairs of Malta to submit to Norman rule, and be comprehensively cleaned out. Along with the gold, hundreds of Christian captives had been set free from the pirates' warehouses. The slave trade to Africa, that centuries-old drain upon the strength of Italy, had been left comprehensively spiked. It was not only Sicily and Malta that had been secured for Christendom, but the waters beyond them. The sea lanes of the Mediterranean were safe at last for Christian shipping – and for Christian merchants, and Christian money-making ventures, above all.

'God it is,' as Urban reflected in wonder, 'in His wisdom and strength, who takes away princedoms, according to His desire, and transforms utterly the spirit of the times.'[117] Christendom, which had once been bled almost to death, was starting to quicken at last. Blessed the poor might be – but riches too, if they could only be held to a proper purpose, were hardly to be scorned as instruments of heaven's favour. The cathedral-builders of Pisa could certainly bear witness to that. So too, and even more gloriously, could Abbot Hugh himself. A church such as he had embarked upon, after all, needed to be paid for somehow. What a blessing it was, then, that the monks of Cluny had recently secured a patron well qualified to make up any shortfall. Indeed, so prodigious had been the sums on offer from him that Abbot Hugh, back in 1090, had travelled all the way to Burgos in far-away Spain to negotiate the handover in person. Alfonso VI, the fearsome King of León, had good cause to be generous to the famous monastery. Back at the darkest moment of his career, with his brother still firmly on the throne, and himself locked up in a dungeon, he had prayed to St Peter for deliverance. That he had been set free almost immediately afterwards, and that his fortunes, from that moment on, had taken a quite spectacular upswing, Alfonso attributed entirely to the intercession with the apostle of the monks of Cluny. And who was Abbot Hugh to argue with that?

Perhaps, had Alfonso's coffers been filled with treasure looted

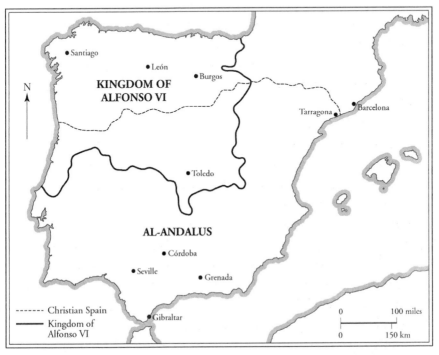

Spain: the *Reconquista* begins

from fellow Christians, he might have hesitated, even so. Fortunately, however, there had been no need for any abbatial qualms. No less than the Hautevilles, the King of León was a man with a great facility for defeating Saracens – and for bleeding them dry. Over the course of only a few decades, the haughty predators of al-Andalus, like those of Sicily, had become, to their natural horror, the prey of their one-time victims. With the Caliphate an ever-fading memory, the great city of Córdoba still pockmarked with rubble and weeds, and the dominion it had once ruled shattered into a mosaic of petty kingdoms, the balance of power in the peninsula, for the first time since the original coming of the Saracens to Spain, had shifted decisively. True, it had taken most Christians a while to have their eyes fully opened to this: for the afterglow of the vanished Caliphate, like light from an exploded star, still illumined the scenes of its former greatness. Alfonso himself, however, had not been dazzled: for to the penetrating gaze of a natural pathologist he had brought an insider's specialist knowledge. Though the courts of al-Andalus might still glitter, there was a weakness festering beneath their surface, which Alfonso, as a young man, had been able to detect and observe in person. Back in 1071, after his release from his brother's dungeon, and before seizing the throne of León for himself, he had fled across the no man's land that marked the limit of Christendom and sought refuge at a court inside al-Andalus. And not just any court but the one which had appeared to stand supreme, in the wake of Córdoba's ruin, as the wealthiest and most luminous in all Spain: Toledo.

The memories of his term of exile there were to stay with Alfonso throughout his life. Devoted son of the Roman Church he might have been – but not all his militant piety could detract from his profound appreciation, and even love, of his enemies' glamour. From clothes to calligraphy to concubines, his private tastes often veered towards the Saracen. Toledo too, learned, elegant and unabashedly luxurious, was destined always to hold a cherished place in his heart – and as something more than just the holy city of his ancestors. Yet Alfonso was no sentimentalist. If he was far from immune to the attractions of al-Andalus, then so too had he made a most profitable and incisive study of those strategies of extortion that had always been the dark side of Saracen greatness. Just as the Muslims, in the first flush of their own victories, had gloried in the number of Christians subjected to their yoke, and shrunk from any thought of converting them to Islam lest the tax base be impaired, so for an identical reason, had Alfonso held off from any grand policy of conquest. Rather than overthrow the various kings of al-Andalus, it had been his policy instead to humiliate and debilitate them by extorting regular payments of tribute. The heirs of the Umayyad Caliphate, proud Muslims one and all, had found themselves being treated, in effect, as the *dhimmis* of a Christian master.

Nor, such was Alfonso's mood of confidence, had he shown the slightest compunction about rubbing Saracen noses in the role reversal. One of his agents, for instance, dropping in on the King of Granada, a city in the far south of al-Andalus, had been brutally upfront about his lord's intentions. 'Now that the Christians are strong and capable,' he had acknowledged cheerily, 'they desire to take back what they have lost by force. This can only be achieved by weakening and encroaching on al-Andalus. In the long run, when it has neither men nor money, we will be able to recover it in its entirety without difficulty.'[118]

As evidence for this the Muslims had only to look at the sobering example of Toledo: for in due course, so anaemic had its regime ended up that its prince had been reduced to the desperate expedient of inviting in the King of León. The juiciest plum in the entire Iberian peninsula had simply dropped into Alfonso's lap; the strategically vital heartlands extending all around it as well. Not a region of al-Andalus, from that moment on, but its flank had lain directly exposed to the iron-shod trampling of Christian horsemen. Well, then, from far afield, might Urban have hailed Toledo's fall as a triumph for all Christendom. 'We rejoice with a most joyful heart, and we give great thanks to God, as is worthy, because in our time He has deigned to give

401

such a victory to the Christian people.'[119] And to the monks of Cluny, perhaps, especially so. Certainly, it was hard not to see in the steady rumbling of treasure carts from Spain to Burgundy a mark of the inexorable and awful character of heaven's judgement. For just as the Great Mosque in Córdoba, the only place of worship in western Europe that could possibly compare in size with the *maior ecclesia*, had been adorned with the loot of Santiago, so now, when Abbot Hugh paid his workmen, did he do so with Saracen gold.

Not that Cluny had profited from the winning of Toledo in terms of plunder alone. In 1086, one of its own brothers, a saintly but astute monk by the name of Bernard, had been appointed archbishop of the captured city. Abbot Hugh, writing to congratulate him, had urged Bernard never to forget that he was now a captain serving directly on Christendom's front line. His responsibilities, therefore, were not merely to the Christian people, but to their enemies as well. 'Do good, live irreproachably, be true to the highest moral standards, and your example will do more to inspire and convert the infidels than any number of sermons.'[120] Here, of course, between Hugh and his more cynical patron, was revealed a telling divide. To Christians far removed from the peculiar multicultural circumstances of Spain, any notion of maintaining pagans in their faith, merely so that their wealth might be extorted from them more legitimately, was a monstrous one. What was their gold when compared with the potential harvest of their souls? Better by far, in Hugh's opinion – and in Urban's – that the flow of treasure from Spain be turned off altogether than that the great cause of cleansing, and purifying, and transforming humanity be compromised. War might be justified – but only if it were in the service of the reform of all the world.

Alarmingly, however, and despite the giddy hopes that had been roused by the capture of Toledo, it was already becoming evident, a mere decade on from that great victory, that the winning of Spain for Christ was not going entirely according to plan. Urban, during his stay at Cluny, would have heard, every morning without fail, the same psalm being chanted by the monks: a request to God for the King of

León to continue victorious in battle. But God, for whatever reason, seemed for the moment to have stopped listening. The fortunes of war had recently turned against Alfonso. The fractious potentates of al-Andalus, desperate to find some way of reining in his ambitions, had found themselves reduced to taking the same desperate step that already, only a few decades previously had proved so fatal to the Caliphate: inviting in the Berbers. Still, as the King of Seville put it, better to run the risk of ending up a camel-herd than looking after pigs. Sure enough, steeled by their reinforcements from Africa, the princelings of al-Andalus had been able to bring Alfonso, at last, to defeat – and then promptly found their kingdoms being swallowed up by their erstwhile allies. For Alfonso himself, the second development had been scarcely less of a setback than the first. The Berbers, as hardy, ascetic and enthusiastic for *jihad* as ever, were altogether more formidable opponents than those with whom he had hitherto happily been toying. Although Toledo remained securely his, and although his centre just about held, the onward advance of Christian arms towards Gibraltar had been brought to a sudden and juddering halt. Unsurprisingly, then, back in Cluny, where there was a massive church still standing half completed, the news had been greeted with some alarm.

In papal circles as well. To Urban, as it had done previously to Gregory, a concern with the frontiers of Christendom, and the lands that lay beyond them, came instinctively. As how, indeed, could it not have done? Papal authority was nothing, after all, unless it were global. Such, at any rate, over the previous decades, was the presumption that Gregory and his supporters had come increasingly to take for granted. Now, in turn, the sheer scale of what they had dared – and of what they had achieved as well – had fortified Urban in a peculiarly vaunting notion: that the whole world might be his to shape. Not even all the energies he had devoted to smashing the authority of emperor and Anti-pope had served to distract him from keeping a lordly eye on broader horizons. So it was, for instance, back in 1089, that Urban had actively sought to promote colonisation within the ruins of Tarragona, a long-abandoned city just inside al-Andalus itself: for it was his hope to see erected there 'a barrier and a bulwark to defend the Christian people'.[121] So it was too, at the Council of Piacenza, that he had taken time out from parading Henry's estranged queen to consult with diplomats from Constantinople. Spain, after all, was not the only front where Christian fortunes were directly menaced. Embattled Alfonso might be, but he was not half so embattled as the *Basileus*.

True, things did not appear quite as terminal for Alexius Comnenus as they had done at the start of his reign. The young emperor, clawing the fortunes of his people back from the very brink, had recovered well from his initial defeat at the hands of Robert Guiscard. Total ruin had been averted. It helped that Guiscard himself had died on campaign back in 1085, a bare two months after Gregory VII; and it had helped that the nomadic Pechenegs, whose talent for spreading mayhem was second to none, had been brought in 1091 to a resounding defeat. Even the Turks, those most menacing adversaries of all, had lately begun to show an encouraging taste for in-fighting. Alexius, tracking developments carefully from beyond the Bosphorus, had been positively itching to capitalise on their squabbling. With Turkish settlers digging in along the length of the Aegean coast, and one warlord even established inside Nicaea, within striking distance of the Queen of Cities herself, he was painfully aware that the opportunity for staging an imperial comeback in the East might soon have passed him by for good. Yet Alexius could not afford to take any risks. The raising of an army large enough to storm Nicaea, let alone attempt the recovery of the lost provinces beyond it, would require the stripping of every last reserve from the rest of the empire. The very survival of Constantinople would then be left hanging in the balance. A second Manzikert, and everything would be lost. And so it was, looking around for reinforcements that might offer him a reasonable prospect of success, while also remaining safely expendable, that Alexius's gaze had turned towards the West.

Where Urban, brooding on the global scale of Christendom's

problems, had his own agenda. To be sure, no less than Alexius, he dreaded that Constantinople might fall: for he shared in the anguished conviction of the *Basileus* that the collapse of the eastern front was a mortal danger to the Christian people everywhere. Simultaneously, however, he would not have forgotten what it was that Gregory, twenty years before, had identified in the self-same crisis: the symptoms of a universal disorder, and the stirrings of Antichrist. Clearly, then, although the great labour of reforming the world had already come far, it still had a long way to go. Whether it was to be seen in the trampling down of a Christian frontier by infidel horse-men, or in the pretensions of an excommunicated Caesar, or in the sweaty fumblings of a priest with his concubine, shadow still persisted everywhere across the fallen world.

Indeed, if anything, in that summer of 1095, it appeared to be thick-ening and threatening a truly cosmic darkness – for the universe itself had been taken sick. Back in the spring, even as delegates from the Council of Piacenza were heading homewards, bright stars, 'all crowded together and dense, like hail or snowflakes', had begun to plummet earthwards. 'A short while later a fiery way appeared in the heavens; and then after another short period half the sky turned the colour of blood.'[122] Meanwhile, in France, along the very roads taken by the Pope, there were marks of famine to be seen everywhere, and reports of strange visions to be heard, and prophecies of fabulous won-ders. 'And this', in the opinion of many, 'was because already, in every nation, the evangelical trumpet was sounding the coming of the Just Judge.'[123]

Where better, then, amid such feverish expectations, for Urban to pause and take stock of things than in the holy abbey of Cluny? On 25 October, one week after his first sighting of Abbot Hugh's stupefy-ing church, the Pope formally dedicated its two great altars to the service of God. Simultaneously, in solemn and ringing tones, he con-firmed the abbey in its status as a bridgehead of the celestial on earth. Not just the abbey either – for the new altars, awesomely charged with the supernatural as they were, appeared to Urban a source of light fit to radiate far beyond the bounds of the church itself. Far beyond the valley in which they stood as well, far beyond Burgundy, far beyond France. Any assemblage of brick and mortar, in short, provided that it took Cluny as its head and model, could be reckoned to share in the fearsome blaze of its purity. So, at any rate, Urban pronounced – as perhaps, with his responsibilities to the whole of Christendom, he was bound to do. For if, as the Holy Father devoutly believed, Cluny offered to those who approached it a reflection of the heavenly Jerusalem, then why should not all the beleaguered Christian people, no matter where they might be, share in at least some of its power?

Yet to cast Cluny in such a role did rather beg a further question: what of the earthly Jerusalem? Abbot Hugh's church might be gloriously qualified to serve as a light to the world, yet not even the altars of the *maior ecclesia* could compare for sheer holiness with the spot where Christ Himself had hung upon a cross and then risen in triumph over death. To Urban, listening to his former brethren as they filled Christendom's most majestic space with the strains of their angelic singing, this reflection could hardly help but appear a troubling one. If it were true that monasteries far and wide derived their sanctity from that of Cluny, then so likewise did the world itself take its character from the holy city that stood at its head; a holy city that for centuries had been positively leprous with the pollution of pagan rule. How, then, to a pope who had devoted his entire life to the heroic labour of setting Christendom upon a proper order, could the knowledge of this not serve as both a torment and a ferocious reproach? Great things had certainly been achieved over the previous decades; but Urban, praying before the altars of the *maior ecclesia*, would have known deep within his soul that the cause of reform could never truly be completed until the Holy Sepulchre had been wrested from Saracen control. 'For if the head is diseased, then there is not a limb but will suffer pain from its ailing.'[124] A great and terrible challenge – but not one, in the final reckoning, that Urban was prepared to duck.

406

And the time was fast approaching for him to demonstrate as much. A month after his dedication of the *maior ecclesia*, and Urban was presiding over his second council of the year: an even larger assembly of reform-minded bishops and abbots than Piacenza had seen. The setting was a potent one: the ancient town of Clermont, in the rugged heart of the Auvergne. Here, as the delegates to the council busied themselves with looking to the future of the Church, reminders of the past were all around them. Looming on the eastern horizon, for instance, there rose a great dome of volcanic rock, where a pagan temple still stood: a sobering memorial to a time when there had been no Christian people at all, but only worshippers of demons. Long and gruelling had been the task of reordering the world, and bringing it under the protection of Christ. In Clermont, as if to bear witness to the process by which Christendom had been fashioned, almost every church contained within its walls antique stonework, or columns, or sarcophagi.[125] Nor was the labour of constructing a truly Christian order completed yet. Much still remained to be done – and Clermont could testify to this. Back in 958, the town had hosted the first assembly to be directed specifically against the predations of bullying lords; and although, since the millennial anniversary of Christ's Resurrection, the Peace of God had faded as a mass movement, it had certainly not been forgotten. Violence continued endemic across much of France. Urban, with his background, knew this well enough. Accordingly, during the week of the Council of Clermont, he sought not only to resurrect the Peace, but to extend it throughout Christendom.

To all those without weapons, wherever and whoever they might be – whether women or peasants, merchants or monks – the full and fearsome protection of the Roman Church was now officially extended. Son of a French nobleman that he was, however, Urban made sure to appeal as well to the lords themselves, and the castellans, and their followers. To the old dream of the peace campaigners – that braggart knights might somehow be transfigured into warriors of Christ – he was preparing to add a novel and fateful twist. On 27

November, with the council drawing to a close, the Pope announced that he would do as the leaders of the Peace of God had done decades previously, and address an assembly of the Christian people in an open field. The number of those who gathered there in the mud and cold of the early Auvergnat winter was not large – perhaps no more than three or four hundred – but what they heard was fated to echo far beyond the limits of Clermont. No accurate record of Urban's sermon was made; but as to the core of its message there could be no doubt. Listed as an official decree of the council, here was a startling and wholly electrifying formula for salvation: 'If any man sets out from pure devotion, not for reputation or monetary gain, to liberate the Church of God at Jerusalem, his journey shall be reckoned in place of all penance.'[126]

Only a century before, contemplating how 'infidels had won the ruling of the sacred places', another Frenchman, a native of the Auvergne who had grown up not a hundred miles from Clermont, had despaired of Christian arms ever winning back the Holy Sepulchre. They were, so Gerbert of Aurillac had flatly declared, 'too weak'.[127] Certainly, by any objective standard, the ambition of securing Jerusalem for Christendom appeared no less impractical in 1095 than it had done back in the lifetime of the first French pope. To embark on a mission that would require the average lord to raise perhaps four or five times his annual income;[128] to aim at the defeat of enemies who had already brought the oldest and most powerful state in Christendom to the very brink of ruin; and to attempt it all for the sake of a city that had not the slightest strategic or military value: here were considerations, it might have been thought, fit to weigh on the mind of any adventurer.

Perhaps even Urban himself, well aware as he would have been of how Gregory's attempt to win the Holy Sepulchre had subsided into fiasco, was initially braced for a less than enthusiastic response. Certainly, it seemed never to have crossed his mind that the gauntlet which he had flung down with such gusto at Clermont, a challenge targeted squarely at the men of his own class, might prove irresistible as well to those who did not belong to the ranks of the nobility or the castellans. There were forces in play much greater than the Pope had ever appreciated – and now, despite all his reputation for prudence, it was he who had set them loose. The disciple and heir of Gregory he may have been – and yet still, even for Urban, the full scale of the recent changes in Christendom, and of the revolution in the affairs of the Christian people, appeared almost too great to grasp.

'*Deus vult!*' the crowds had shouted at Clermont: 'God wills it!'[129] The utter conviction of this, spreading like wildfire wherever the Pope's message was reported, spoke partly of excitement – and partly as well of sheer relief. To be cleansed, to be spotless, to be at one with the celestial host of the angels: here was a yearning that any man or woman might share. No longer, if it had ever been, was it confined to the ranks of monks, or of those who had sought, over the course of many decades now, and at the cost of unprecedented convulsions, to secure the reform of the Church. A warrior too, one at the service of his lord, and armed with weapons soon to be sticky with blood, might feel it – and feeling it, shiver with dread, knowing the crossroads before which he stood. 'For which of the two paths was he to follow: that of the Gospels or of the world?'[130]

Such a question, even for those secure in the righteousness of their own cause, even for those fighting beneath a banner of St Peter, had never been a simple one to answer. No matter, for instance, back in 1066, that William's men had been following their duke to war against a usurper, and with the full blessing of the Pope himself: they had still been obliged, in the wake of the slaughter at Hastings, to undertake penance or else to remain filthy with the sin of murder. A great and excruciating tension, then: for it had set the desperation for salvation against the need – and perhaps the longing – to fight. Now, however, with a single sermon, a single ordinance, that tension appeared resolved. No wonder, then, as news of what had been decreed by Urban spread, that there should have been 'a great stirring of heart throughout all the Frankish lands'[131] – and far beyond. A whole new road to the City of God had suddenly opened up before the Christian people. The heroic labour of buttressing the world against Antichrist, and of preparing for the dreadful hour of Judgement, had all of a sudden become one in which the great mass of them could share. Not a pilgrim but he could know, as he set off for the Holy Sepulchre, that he was helping to set the universe to rights.

'Then will appear the sign of the Son of Man in heaven.'[132] Sure enough, five months after the Council of Clermont, and even as the Pope was celebrating Easter in central France, a mysterious cross materialised in the sky. Just as it had done many centuries before, during the fabled reign of the first Christian Caesar, now it struck those who saw it as a certain portent of victory. Yet as thousands upon thousands of pilgrims set to sewing the image of it upon their clothes, or branding it on their flesh, or, as Guiscard's eldest son would do, ripping up their cloaks to fashion crosses out of the shredded fabric, they were preparing for war unprompted by any Constantine. The crusaders, as they would come to be known, followed no emperor.[133] Henry, still an excommunicate, still cooped up haplessly in northern Italy, would hardly have deigned to set himself at the head of anything summoned by Urban – even had he not been impotent to do so. Alexius, informed to his consternation that 'the whole of the West was on the march'[134] and descending directly on Constantinople, worked hard to bribe and browbeat the leaders of the pilgrimage into a nominal obedience to himself – but hardly with the intention of leading them onwards to Jerusalem. Better than anyone else, he knew what such a venture would demand.

True, Alexius was careful not to wallow openly in pessimism. He even went so far as to float the odd rumour, hinting mysteriously that it was his destiny to lay down his crown before the Holy Sepulchre.[135] Conspiratorial whisperings such as this, however, were intended exclusively for Western consumption. In reality, the beleaguered *Basileus* had not the slightest desire to play at being the last emperor. The preservation of Constantinople, not the liberation of Jerusalem, was his true responsibility. Fortunately, once the crusaders had all been transported across the Bosphorus, safely away from the Queen of

Cities, it proved possible, albeit briefly, for the two ambitions to be squared. In June 1097, Nicaea was brought to capitulate, and the banner of the Second Rome fluttered once again over the birthplace of the Christian creed. Then, the following month, in a bloody and desperate struggle, the crusaders broke a formidable Turkish army in open battle. For the remainder of the year, even as they lumbered on their way through increasingly bleak and hostile territory, the Turks shrank from confronting them head on.

The following spring, taking full advantage of his enemies' reverses, Alexius dispatched his brother-in-law to mop up in the crusaders' wake. Then, in the summer, he led out a second army himself. By June, perhaps half of the territories lost to the Turks in the wake of Manzikert had been restored to imperial rule. Meanwhile, of the crusaders themselves, the news was grim in the extreme. Alexius, who had been pondering whether to join forces with them, was reliably informed by a deserter that the entire expedition stood on the verge of utter destruction. Accordingly, rather than risk his gains, the *Basileus* opted to consolidate them. He withdrew to Constantinople, leaving the crusaders to their fate.

A decision that had been, by all objective standards, the only rational one. The reports brought to Alexius that the crusade faced certain ruin were only marginally exaggerated. The odds against the winning of the Holy Sepulchre, always steep, had become, by the summer of 1098, astronomical. The Sultan of Baghdad, resolved to annihilate the invaders once and for all, had dispatched an immense army, 'swarming everywhere from the mountains and along different roads like the sands of the sea'.[136] Against this prodigious task force, the crusaders, who had numbered perhaps one hundred thousand the previous spring as they streamed towards Constantinople, could muster at best a threadbare twenty thousand – non-combatants included.[137] Disease, starvation and casualties in battle; the loss of virtually the entire expedition's supply of horses and mules, so that even dogs had ended up being employed as pack animals; the lack of anything approaching a unified leadership: all these factors, as the crusaders themselves freely acknowledged, should have spelled their doom. 'For certainly, in my opinion,' as one contemporary put it, 'what they went through was an ordeal without precedent. Never before had there been among the princes of the world men who exposed their bodies to such suffering, solely in the expectation of a celestial reward.'[138]

No wonder, then, when the ferociously outnumbered crusaders succeeded in yet again shattering the Turks upon their steel, when they continued to win famous cities long lost to Christendom, and when, on 7 June 1099, they finally arrived in triumph before the walls of Jerusalem, there were few among them who doubted that they had arrived as well at a turning point in the order of heaven and earth. No one could know for certain what wonders might follow their capture of the Holy Sepulchre – but merely to win it would rank as wonder enough. Ambition, greed and ingenuity: all these qualities, honed by the three long and terrible years of the pilgrimage, had served to bring the crusaders to the very brink of a miracle. Yet in the mingled sense of urgency and brutality that they had displayed, and in their conviction that there was nothing in the world that might not be changed and improved by their own labours, there lay the proof of a revolution long pre-dating their taking up of the Cross. For better and for worse, the previous century had seen Christendom, and the Christian people, transformed utterly. The arrival of the crusaders before the walls of the Holy City was merely a single – albeit the most spectacular – manifestation of a process which, since the convulsive period of the Millennium, had made of Europe something restless, and dynamic, and wholly new. Nor would it be the last.

A thousand years had passed now since an angel, parting the veil which conceals from mankind the plans of the Almighty for the future, had given to St John a revelation of the last days. And the saint, writing it down, had recorded how a great battle was destined to be fought; and how the Beast, at its end, would be captured and thrown into a lake of fire. But before that could be brought about, and the world born anew, Christ Himself, 'clad in a robe dipped in blood', was destined to lead out the armies of heaven. 'From his mouth issues a sharp sword with which to smite the nations, and he will rule them with a rod of iron; he will tread the wine press of the fury of the wrath of God the Almighty.'[139]

On 15 July, the crusaders finally broke into Jerusalem and took possession of the object of all their yearnings. The wine press was duly trodden: the streets were made to flow with blood. And at the end of it, when the slaughter was done, and the whole city drenched in gore, the triumphant warriors of Christ, weeping with joy and disbelief, assembled before the Sepulchre of the Saviour and knelt in an ecstasy of worship.

Meanwhile, on the Temple Mount, where it had been foretold that Antichrist would materialise at the end of days enthroned in fearsome and flame-lit glory, all was stillness. The slaughter upon the rock of the Temple had been especially terrible, and not a living thing had been left there to stir. Already, in the summer heat, the corpses were starting to reek.

Antichrist did not appear.

Timeline

All dates are *anno Domini*.

?33   The crucifixion of Jesus.

?64   The execution of St Peter in Rome.

?95   St John writes the Book of Revelation.

?287 The martyrdom of St Maurice and the Theban Legion.

312   Constantine captures Rome, supposedly after a vision of Christ.

330   The founding of Constantinople.

426   St Augustine completes his book on the City of God.

?507 The conversion of Clovis, King of the Franks.

711   The Muslim invasion of Spain.

751   Pepin makes himself king, deposing the dynasty of Clovis.

754   Pope Stephen II, having crossed the Alps, anoints Pepin.

800   Charlemagne is crowned Emperor of the West by Pope Leo III.

843   The Treaty of Verdun: Charlemagne's empire is divided between his three grandsons.

846   Muslim pirates sack St Peter's in Rome.

856   Viking pirates sack Orléans.

899   The Hungarians begin their raids on Christendom.

905   The termination of the Carolingian line of emperors: the imperial throne of the West is left vacant.

910   The founding of the abbey of Cluny.

911   Rollo, a Viking warlord, agrees to convert to Christianity, and is granted the overlordship of what will become Normandy.

919 Henry, the Duke of Saxony, is elected King of East Francia.

929 Abd al-Rahman III, Emir of Al-Andalus, proclaims himself Caliph.

936 Henry, King of East Francia, dies, and is succeeded by his son, Otto.

939 The Battle of Andernach: Otto crushes a revolt led by his brother.

955 The Battle of the Lech: the threat to Christendom from the Hungarians is destroyed for good.

962 Otto is crowned emperor by Pope John XII.

966 The baptism of Miesco, Duke of the Poles.

967 Magdeburg is established as an archbishopric.

969 The assassination in Constantinople of Nicephorus Phocas, and his replacement as emperor by John Tzimiskes.

972 The arrival of Theophanu, John Tzimiskes's niece, in Rome. A council is held at Aurillac, designed to promote the Peace of God.

973 The death of Otto. He is succeeded by his son, Otto II. Edgar, King of the English, stages an imperial coronation at Bath, and establishes a single currency.

975 The death of Edgar.

978 The murder of Edward, Edgar's son, at Corfe. He is succeeded as king by his half-brother, Ethelred.

982 The Battle of Cotrone. Otto II retreats to Rome.

983 The revolt of the Slavs. Otto II dies in Rome. His infant son, Otto III, is crowned king.

986 The settlement of Greenland.

987 Hugh Capet is elected King of France. Fulk Nerra becomes Count of Anjou. Sweyn Forkbeard deposes his father, Harald Bluetooth, to become King of Denmark.

988 Vladimir of Kiev converts to Christianity.

991 The Battle of Maldon. Fire in Rome almost destroys St Peter's.

992 The death of Adso of Montier-en-Der while on pilgrimage to Jerusalem.

994 Odilo becomes Abbot of Cluny. The relics of St Martial are

publicly displayed on a hill above Limoges in a successful attempt to arrest a pestilence.

996   Otto III appoints his cousin as the first German pope, and is crowned as emperor. Robert II 'the Pious' becomes King of France. Al-Hakim becomes the Fatimid Caliph of Egypt.

997   The martyrdom of St Adalbert. The suppression of a peasant insurrection in Normandy. Al-Mansur, the effective ruler of al-Andalus, sacks Santiago.

998   Otto III suppresses an insurrection in Rome.

999   Otto III appoints Gerbert of Aurillac as Pope.

1000   Otto III visits the shrine of St Adalbert in Poland and the tomb of Charlemagne in Aachen. The conversion of Iceland to Christianity. The death of Olaf Trygvasson, following his defeat by Sweyn Forkbeard.

1002   The death of Otto III. He is succeeded by Henry II. The death of al-Mansur. Ethelred orders a pogrom of Danes living in England: the St Brice's Day Massacre.

1003   Henry II enters an alliance with the Wends.

1004   Muslim pirates sack Pisa.

1006   Count Richard II of Normandy lays claim to the title of 'duke'.

1009   The massacre of the Berber residents of Córdoba. The Church of the Holy Sepulchre is demolished on the orders of the Caliph al-Hakim.

1010   Berber forces lay Córdoba under siege. Jews are persecuted – and almost certainly massacred – for the first time in France.

1013   The fall and sack of Córdoba. Sweyn Forkbeard invades England.

1014   The death of Sweyn Forkbeard and the return from exile in Normandy of Ethelred.

1016   The death of Ethelred. Canute establishes himself as King of England. Turkish horsemen attack Armenia.

1018   A band of Norman mercenaries take service with the Byzantines in southern Italy.

1022   Twelve clerics are burned to death for heresy in Orléans.

1024   The death of Henry II marks the extinction of the Liudolfing dynasty. Conrad II is elected as king.

1026   A mass pilgrimage, sponsored by Duke Richard III of Normandy, arrives in Jerusalem.

1027   Canute arrives in Rome for Conrad II's coronation as emperor.

1028   The public frustration of Adémar's attempt to prove that St Martial had been one of Christ's original apostles.

1030   The Battle of Stiklestad and the death of Olaf, King of Norway. Olaf's half-brother, Harald Hardrada, seeks sanctuary with Yaroslav, the King of the Rus.

1031   Olaf's body is exhumed and found to be incorrupt: he starts to be hailed as a st.

1033   Adémar – and a great crowd of other pilgrims – arrive in Jerusalem. Peter Damian becomes a hermit.

1035   The arrival in Jerusalem of Duke Robert of Normandy is followed soon afterwards by his death in Nicaea. He is succeeded as duke by his infant son, William. The death of Canute. Harald Hardrada travels to Constantinople.

1039   Henry III succeeds his father, Conrad II, as king of the *Reich*.

1043   Henry III marries Agnes of Aquitaine. Edward 'the Confessor' is crowned as King of England.

1044   Harald Hardrada flees Constantinople.

1045   Harald Hardrada marries Elizabeth, Yaroslav's daughter.

1046   The Synod of Sutri: Henry III disposes of three rival popes, and replaces them with a German appointee of his own.

1047   The arrival of Robert of Hauteville – soon to be nicknamed 'Guiscard' – in southern Italy. Duke William of Normandy wins his first battle. Harald Hardrada becomes undisputed King of Norway.

1048   Bruno of Toul is crowned in Rome as Pope Leo IX. He tours the Rhineland, and stages a council in Reims. Hugh of Semur becomes Abbot of Cluny in succession to Odilo.

1053   The Battle of Civitate: Leo IX is taken prisoner by the Normans.

1054   Cardinal Humbert's embassy to Constantinople: its ultimate result is schism between the churches of the Old and the New Rome. The death of Leo IX.

1055   Beatrice and Matilda of Tuscany are exiled by Henry III to the Rhineland.

1056   The death of Henry III. He is succeeded as king by his infant son, Henry IV.

1057   Peter Damian becomes a cardinal. Street battles break out in Milan between supporters of the archbishop and insurrectionists known as the 'Patarenes'. Beatrice and Matilda return to Tuscany.

1059   The cardinals lay claim to the right to choose a pope. Peter Damian arrives in Milan in an attempt to make peace between the archbishop and the Patarenes. Robert Guiscard is accepted as a papal vessel, and invested with the dukedom of Apulia.

1061   The Normans invade Sicily.

1062   Henry IV is kidnapped by the Archbishop of Cologne.

1065   Henry IV comes of age. His mother, Agnes, leaves for Rome.

1066   The death of Edward the Confessor. Harold Godwinsson succeeds him as King of England. The Battle of Stamford Bridge: the defeat and death of Harald Hardrada. The Battle of Hastings: the defeat and death of Harold Godwinsson. William of Normandy is crowned as King of England.

1070   A public penance is imposed on all who fought at Hastings.

1071   The Battle of Manzikert.

1072   Rival bishops are appointed in Milan. The death of Peter Damian. Palermo is captured by the Normans. Alfonso VI becomes King of León.

1073   Archdeacon Hildebrand is elected Pope. He takes the name Gregory VII. Rebellion against Henry IV breaks out in Saxony.

1074   The abandonment of Gregory's expedition to Constantinople and Jerusalem.

1075   Henry IV suppresses the revolt in Saxony. Gregory charges the Germans not to obey disobedient bishops. Henry imposes his own candidate on the archbishopric of Milan.

1076   Gregory threatens Henry IV with excommunication. At a conference in Worms, two-thirds of the German bishops renounce their loyalty to Gregory. Gregory excommunicates Henry. Rebellion breaks out again in Saxony, and Henry is threatened with deposition by a gathering of rebellious princes at Tribur.

1077 Henry IV stages a public penance at Canossa, and is absolved from excommunication. An assembly of princes at Forcheim elects Duke Rodulf of Swabia as king. Civil war in the *Reich*. The death of Agnes.

1078 Gregory formally bans the investiture of bishops by emperors and kings.

1080 Gregory excommunicates Henry IV for a second time. Henry nominates an anti-pope. Rudolf of Swabia dies in battle. Alfonso VI imposes the Roman form of the Mass on his kingdom.

1081 Henry IV marches abortively on Rome. Alexius Comnenus becomes emperor in Constantinople. Robert Guiscard crosses the Adriatic.

1082 Robert Guiscard withdraws again to Apulia.

1083 Henry IV captures St Peter's.

1084 Henry IV captures Rome and is anointed as emperor by Clement III, the newly crowned anti-pope. He retreats before the advance of Robert Guiscard, who rescues Gregory from the Castel Sant'Angelo and sacks Rome.

1085 Death of Gregory. Alfonso VI captures Toledo. Death of Robert Guiscard.

1087 Urban II is crowned as Pope.

1090 The last Muslim outpost in Sicily submits to Norman rule.

1095 The Council of Piacenza. Urban II tours France. He consecrates the '*maior ecclesia*' of Cluny. At a council held at Clermont, he calls for an armed expedition to restore Jerusalem to Christendom.

1097 The capture of Nicaea from the Turks.

1099 The capture of Jerusalem.

Notes

Preface

1. Lampert of Hersfeld, p. 285. Lampert's description of Henry's journey across the Alps has often been criticised for its melodramatic tone, but the descent from the Mont Cenis pass is indeed a steep one, and all the sources are agreed that the winter of 1076–7 was exceptionally bitter.
2. Wipo. Quoted by Morris, p. 19.
3. Quoted by Cowdrey (1998), p. 608.
4. Gregory VII, *Register*, 3.10a.
5. *Ibid.*, 4.12.
6. For the likelihood that the future Pope had attended Henry's coronation in 1054, see Cowdrey (1998), pp. 34–5.
7. Tellenbach (1940), p. 1.
8. Otto of Freising, *The Two Cities*, 6.36.
9. Bonizo of Sutri, p. 238. The reference is to Henry's original excommunication.
10. Southern, *Western Society and the Church in the Middle Ages*, p. 34.
11. Quoted by Zimmerman, p. 3.
12. Moore (2000), p. 12.
13. Ironically, the phrase comes from the Bible: Psalm 113. The anecdote is quoted by Leyser (1965), p. 60.
14. Blumenthal, p. 64.
15. The thesis that the decades either side of the Millennium witnessed a unique crisis in the order of Christendom was most brilliantly elucidated by the great French historian Georges Duby. The twin poles of the debate today are represented by two other formidable French scholars: Pierre Bonnassie and Dominique Barthélemy. An excellent though cussedly sceptical survey of the historiography can be found in Crouch (2005).
16. Ferdinand Lot. Quoted by Edmond Pognon (1981), p. 11.
17. *Les Fausses Terreurs de l'An Mil*, by Sylvain Gouguenheim.
18. Carozzi, p. 45.

420

19 An argument that derives principally from Richard Landes, Professor of History at Boston University, and doyen of all those scholars who, over the past couple of decades, have argued for the existence of what he himself has termed 'The *Terribles espoirs* of 1000 and the Tacit Fears of 2000' (Landes, Gow and Van Meter, p. 3).

20 From the second vision of the Visionary of St Vaast. The quotation provides the frontispiece for a seminal essay by the German scholar Johannes Fried, one of the first to argue in convincing detail for the influence of apocalyptic hopes and anxieties upon Christendom at the turn of the first Millennium. Taken from the English translation in Landes, Gow and Van Meter, p. 17.

21 Fulton, p. 72.
22 Glaber, 4.1.
23 Rees, p. 186.
24 Lovelock, p. 189.
25 *Ibid.*, p. 7.
26 Odo of Cluny, col. 585.

1 The Return of the King

1 Matthew 4.9.
2 Daniel 7.19.
3 Matthew 5.9.
4 Matthew 26.52.
5 1 Peter 5.13. The first independent allusion to Peter's presence in Rome does not date until AD 96.
6 Revelation 17.4–6.
7 *Ibid.*, 20.2.
8 Romans 13.1.
9 2 Thessalonians 2.6.
10 Mark 13.32.
11 Revelation 21.2.
12 Christians were expelled from the army some time around 300, just before the great persecution launched by the Emperor Diocletian in 303. This has raised considerable doubts about the veracity of the story of St Maurice, since he and his legion are supposed to have been martyred for refusing to take part in this self-same persecution. For a convincing explanation of the legend's origin, see Woods.
13 Eucherius of Lyon, 9.
14 Lactantius, 44.5.
15 Augustine, *City of God*, 5.25.
16 Eusebius, *Life of Constantine*, 3.31.
17 *Ibid.*, *In Praise of the Emperor Constantine*, 1.
18 'Examples of prayers for the Empire and the Emperor' (c), Folz (1969), p. 176.

19 Revelation 18.19.

20 *Ibid.*, 20.8.

21 Pseudo-Methodius, quoted in Alexander (1985), p. 40.

22 *Ibid.*, p. 50.

23 Avitus of Vienne, p. 75.

24 Augustine, *City of God*, 4.15.

25 *Ibid.*, 19.17.

26 Revelation 20.1–3.

27 Augustine, *City of God*, 20.7.

28 Gregory I, *Moralium Libri*, col. 1011.

29 *Ibid.*, *Regulae Pastoralis Liber*, col. 14.

30 The bishop was Pope Gregory I, 'the Great': *Homiliarum in Evangelia*, col. 1213.

31 Augustine, *On Order*, 2.1.2.

32 The etymology was originally St Jerome's. Scholars nowadays hold it to be inaccurate.

33 Michael Psellus, p. 177.

34 Pre-eminently by Justinian.

35 This was a very ancient tradition, dating back at least to the early third century, and maybe earlier.

36 Not until the reign of Gregory VII, however, did this become an official prescription.

37 A letter of Pope Gregory II. Quoted by Ullman (1969), p. 47.

38 *Lex Salica*, pp. 6–8.

39 1 Peter 2.9. Pope Paul I, in 757, quoted the verse in a letter to Pepin. See Barbero, p. 16.

40 *Donation of Constantine*, p. 326.

41 *Ibid.*, p. 328.

42 Aethicus Ister, *Cosmographia*. Quoted by Brown, p. 413.

43 2 Samuel 5.20.

44 Alcuin, Letter 9. Ironically, the comment was made in the context of the first Viking raid on Northumbria.

45 Charlemagne, 2.138.

46 Angilbertus, line 504.

47 Einhard, 28.

48 For the calculations that enabled this to be adduced, see Landes (1988) – a brilliant, though controversial, piece of scholarly detective work. See also Fried, p. 27.

49 Alcuin, Letter 43.

50 Futolf of Michelsberg. Quoted by Goetz, p. 154.

51 'Poeta Saxo', p. 70.

52 Regino of Prüm, p. 129.

53 From the protocols of an imperial synod at Trosly, 909. Quoted by Bloch (1989), vol. 1, p. 3.

54 Otto of Freising, p. 66.
55 'A Letter on the Hungarians'. Cited by Huygens, p. 232.
56 *Ibid.*
57 *Ibid.* The phrase is a quotation from Gregory the Great.
58 Cited by Fried, p. 31.
59 Abbo of Fleury, col. 471 A.
60 *Ibid.*
61 *Heliand*, pp. 119–20.
62 Adso of Montier-en-Der, p. 90.
63 *Ibid.*
64 *Ibid.*

2 The Old Order Changeth . . .

1 Thietmar, 6.23.
2 Or rather not strictly speaking a capital, but what in Latin was termed a
   '*civitas*': an untranslatable word. It was so described by Otto I, in his diploma
   of 937.
3 Widukind, 1.36.
4 Thietmar, 6.23.
5 Alcuin, Letter 113.
6 Widukind, 1.15.
7 Liudprand, *History of Otto*, 2.20.
8 Widukind, 1.41.
9 Liudprand, *Antapodosis*, 4.25.
10 Widukind, 2.1.
11 *Ibid.*, 2.36.
12 *Ruodlieb*, fragment 3.
13 *Heliand*, chapter 58, lines 4865–900. The poem almost certainly dates from the
   reign of Charlemagne's son, Louis I. The lines quoted echo Matthew 26.53.
14 Widukind, 3.46.
15 *Ibid.*, 3.49.
16 Otto I, p. 503.
17 Thietmar, 2.17.
18 *Ibid.*, 7.16.
19 *Ibid.*, 2.17.
20 Widukind, 3.75.
21 Leo the Deacon, 1.1. The apocalyptic tone of Byzantine writers of the late
   tenth century is all the more striking for the fact that Constantinople had
   not adopted the *anno Domini* dating system.
22 See Mango, p. 211.
23 Leo the Deacon, 2.8.
24 See Paul Magdalino, 'The Year 1000 in Byzantium', in Magdalino (2003), p. 244.

25 By the admittedly venomous and resentful Liudprand of Cremona. *The Mission to Constantinople*, 3.
26 John Skylitzes, p. 271.
27 Thietmar, 4.10.
28 Albert of Metz, p. 698.
29 Liudprand, *Antapodosis*, 1.3.
30 Liudprand, *The Mission to Constantinople*, 10.
31 Matthew 24.11.
32 The originator of the phrase was St John of Damascus, in his book *On the Heretics* – although, as Sahas points out, he applied it to 'the religion of the Ishmaelities', rather than to Mohammed himself (footnote 7, p. 69).
33 The number of military expeditions in which Mohammed took part is set by an early Muslim historian, Ibn Ishaq, at twenty-seven; he is supposed to have fought personally in nine of these. For the execution of seven hundred prisoners of war in the market place of Medina, see Armstrong, p. 207. The most celebrated opponent of Mohammed to be assassinated on the Prophet's orders was Ka'b ibn al-Ashraf, a poet overly given to writing erotic verses about Muslim women.
34 From a Greek polemic, probably written around 640. Quoted by Crone and Cook, pp. 3–4.
35 An opinion expressed in the unlikely context of a military treatise, written in the sixth century by a Byzantine combat engineer. Quoted by Dennis (1985), p. 21.
36 Qur'an 9.29.
37 Leo VI, *Tactics*, 18.24.
38 *Ibid.*, 2.45.
39 Thietmar, 3.20.
40 *Ibid.*, 3.23.
41 *Ibid.*, 3.21.
42 The phrases come from a verse epitaph inscribed on the tomb of Basil II (reigned 976–1025), aptly nicknamed the 'Bulgar-slayer'.
43 Quoted in Bonner (2004), p. xxi.
44 Ibn Hawqal, *The Face of the Earth*. Quoted in Whittow, p. 328.
45 John VIII. Quoted in McCormick (2001), p. 736.
46 Bernard the Monk, *Itinera Hierosolymitana*, pp. 310–11.
47 Erchempert, 17.
48 Qur'an 7.4.
49 *Ibid.*, 8.1.
50 *Ibid.*, 8.41.
51 Umar, who ruled as the second Caliph. Quoted by Brague, p. 35.
52 Qur'an 9.29.
53 John of St Arnoul, 136.
54 *Ibid.*, 132.

55 *Ibid.*, 133.
56 Hrotsvit of Gandersheim, line 12. The phrase is all the more suggestive for coming, not from a Muslim source, but from a poem written by a Saxon nun. The phrase refers specifically to the city of Córdoba, and it is widely accepted that Hrotsvit may have obtained her information from a member of John's embassy to the Caliph.
57 See Bulliet, pp. 38–51.
58 Ibn Hawqal, *The Face of the Earth*. Quoted in Fierro, p. 16.
59 The words date from the thirteenth century, but the sentiment was timeless. Ibn Idhari. Quoted by Kennedy, p. 22.
60 Liudprand, *Antapodosis*, 6.6.
61 Quoted in Karsh, p. 63.
62 A celebrated hadith, narrated by Al-Bayhaqi.
63 Gibbon, vol. 3, p. 348. All the figures relating to the caliphal library at Córdoba are exaggerations.
64 Widukind, 3.56.
65 Richer, 3.55.
66 *Ibid.*, 3.52.
67 Thietmar, 3.18.
68 Gerbert, Letter 23.
69 *Ibid.*, Letter 51.
70 Thietmar, 4.10.
71 Or perhaps the autumn. See Althoff, p. 52.
72 Gerbert, *Acta Concilii Remensis ad Sanctum Basolum*, p. 676 *MGH SS*, 3.676.
73 'A Song for SS. Peter and Paul's Day', *Primer of Medieval Latin*, p. 340.
74 John Canaparius, 21.
75 Arnold of Regensburg, 2.34.
76 Paulinus of Aquileia, 5.7. In sober point of historical fact, there is no firm evidence that Christians were ever martyred in the Colosseum.
77 Arnold of Regensburg, 2.34.
78 *Annales Quedlinburgenses*, p. 73.
79 *Ex Miraculis Sancti* Alexii, p. 620.
80 Thietmar, 4.48.
81 John Canaparius, 23.
82 Bruno of Querfort, *Passio Sancti Adalberti*, 23.
83 'Deus Teutonicus'. See Jones and Pennick, p. 170.
84 The chronology of this is generally accepted, but not universally. See, e.g., *The Letters of Gerbert*, p. 285.
85 Gerbert, Letter 221.
86 *Ibid.*, Letter 230.
87 *Ibid.*, Letter 232.
88 *Ibid.*, Letter 231.
89 *Annales Hildesheimenses*, 3, Preface.

90 Leo of Synada, p. 20.

91 *Annales Quedlinburgenses*, p. 74.

92 John the Deacon, p. 31.

93 *Vita Sancti Nili*, p. 617.

94 From the 'Graphia Aureae Urbis Romae', a guidebook to the wonders of Rome written in the twelfth century, but drawing on descriptions written around the Millennium. Quoted in Schramm 2 (1929), p. 76.

95 One source (the *Gesta Episcoporum Cameracensium*) describes Otto's palace as being built on the Aventine Hill, opposite the Palatine: a mistranscription that has resulted in much confusion. For a good analysis of the controversy, and a definitive resolution, see Augenti, pp. 74–5.

96 Leo of Vercelli, verse 8. Baghdad is titled 'Babylon'.

97 *Ibid.*, verse 10.

98 Gallus Anonymus, p. 37.

99 *Chronicon Novaliciense*, 106.

100 Revelation 19.14.

101 Thietmar, 4.47.

102 Adam of Bremen, 2.40.

103 Thietmar, 4.48.

104 Thangmar, p. 770.

105 Peter Damian, *Vita Romualdi*, pp. 45–6.

106 Peter Damian, *Letters*, vol. 1, p. 199. The Gospel verse cited is Matthew 24.27.

107 Bruno of Querfort, *Vita Quinque Fratrum*, 7.

108 *Ibid.* The Latin word is *'honore'*: literally, the 'badge' or 'attribute' of royalty.

109 *Ibid.*

110 Adémar, 3.31.

111 Quoted by Fried, p. 39.

112 *Rhythmus de Obitu Ottonis III*. Quoted by Gregorovius, p. 496.

113 Bruno of Querfort, *Vita Quinque Fratrum*, 7.

3 . . . *Yielding Place to New*

1   Adso of Montier-en-Der, p. 96. The last phrase is from 2 Thessalonians 2.8.

2   Flodoard, p. 138.

3   From a twelfth-century chronicler of Laon. Quoted by Poly, p. 292.

4   Flodoard, p. 101.

5   *Chronicon Mosomense*, 1.7.

6   Fulbert of Chartres, Letter 47.

7   Glaber, 2.8.

8   Byrhtferth, pp. 132–3.

9   Andrew of Fleury, *Vie de Gauzlin, Abbé de Fleury*, 68a.

10 Abbo of Fleury, col. 472 C.

11 Matthew 24.7–8. The verses were echoed in the letter of Gauzlin, Abbot of

Fleury, to King Robert (Andrew of Fleury, *Vie de Gauzlin*, 68b).

12 Adémar, 205.
13 Louis IV, 1, 4.
14 Dudo, p. 81.
15 *Gesta Consulum Andegavorum*, 47.
16 Glaber, 2.4.
17 *Gesta Consulum Andegavorum*, 45–6.
18 *Archives d'Anjou*, vol. 1, p. 60.
19 *Cartulaire du Ronceray*, no. 4.
20 From a letter Fulk wrote to the local archbishop. Quoted by Bachrach (1985), p. 245.
21 Glaber, 2.7.
22 *Documents pour l'Histoire de l'Église de Saint-Hilaire de Poitiers*, p. 74.
23 Bachrach (1985), p. 252.
24 In Latin, '*fidelissimus*'. Quoted by Guillot, p. 16.
25 *Liber Miraculorum Sancte Fidis*, 1.33.
26 Matthew 24.12.
27 Richer, 4.37.
28 Adalbero of Laon, line 37.
29 Glaber, 4.12.
30 *Ibid.*, 2.17.
31 Aelfric, 19–20. The writer was English, but the horrors of an early start can be reckoned universal.
32 Hariulf, 4.21.
33 *Vita et Miracula Sancti Leonardi*, 3.
34 Sigehard, 2.
35 Glaber, 2.10–12.
36 Odo of Cluny, col. 562. Odo was citing – or believed that he was citing – St Jerome.
37 From an oath imposed on knights at Beauvais in 1023. Reproduced in Head and Landes, pp. 332–3.
38 Quoted by Iogna-Prat (2002), p. 37.
39 Andrew of Fleury, *Vie de Gauzlin*, 44a.
40 Matthew 25.35–6.
41 John of Salerno, *Life of St Odo*, 2.4.
42 Revelation 21.2.
43 John of Salerno, *Life of St Gerald of Aurillac*, 2.8.
44 The Rule of St Benedict, 'Of Humility' (chapter 7).
45 Peter the Venerable, 1.12.
46 Glaber, 5.13.
47 *Liber Tramitis Aevi Odilonis Abbatis*, p. 4.
48 Quoted by Constable (2000), p. 415. The phrase comes from the confirmation of Cluny's privileges issued in 931 by the Pope.

49 Odo of Cluny, col. 585.

50 John of Salerno, *Life of St Gerald of Aurillac*, 1.8.

51 *Ibid.*, 2.17

52 Glaber, 4.14.

53 Letaldus of Micy, *Delatio Corporis Sancti Juniani ad Synodem Karoffensem*. Reproduced in Head and Landes, p. 328.

54 Glaber, 4.16.

55 *Liber Miraculorum Sancte Fidis*, 2.4.

56 *Ibid.*, 1.13.

57 Glaber, 4.16.

58 From an anathema pronounced against the murderers of an archbishop of Reims in 900. See Fichtenau, p. 396.

59 Fulbert of Chartres, 'The Joy of Peace', in *Letters and Poems*, p. 263.

60 The council has also variously been dated to 1018, 1019 or 1021.

61 Odo of Cluny, col. 581.

62 Revelation 14.3–4. The monk was Aldebald of St Germain d'Auxerre.

63 Adalbero of Laon, line 156.

64 *Ibid.*, lines 295–6.

4 Go West

1 Henry II, p. 424.

2 *Ibid.*, p. 170.

3 Wulfstan, *Lectio Sancti Evangelii Secundum Matheum 2*.

4 Adam of Bremen, 4.26.

5 Thietmar, 8.2

6 Geoffrey of Malaterra, 1.1.

7 Jordanes, 4.

8 Adam of Bremen, 4.26.

9 Snorri Sturluson, *King Harald's Saga*, p. 67.

10 Dudo, p. 15.

11 *Egil's Saga*, Page, p. 70.

12 *Ibid.*

13 *The Raven's Tale*, Page, p. 107.

14 *The Lay of Helgi, Killer of Hunding*, Page, p. 130.

15 *Cartulaire de l'Abbaye de Saint-Aubin d'Angers*, no. 21.

16 *Hávamál*, Page, p. 141.

17 The narrative given here depends upon sources that are either fragmentary or late. Nevertheless, it is broadly accepted. For the best account, see Crouch (2002), pp. 2–8.

18 Adémar, 140.

19 Dudo, p. 149.

20 *Ibid.*, p. 29.

21 *Inventio et Miracula Sancti Vulfranni*, 7.

22 Dudo, p. 150.

23 *Plaintsong* of William Longsword, in Van Houts, p. 41.

24 Dudo, p. 8.

25 Warner of Rouen, 40–1.

26 It is possible, of course, that there were older charters that used the title but have not survived. Some historians have argued that it was applied to Richard I during the last years of reign.

27 Richer, 1.156.

28 *Blickling Homilies*, p. 76.

29 The author himself makes an allusion to the date within the text of his homily – a level of precision that is unusual, and surely suggestive.

30 *Blickling Homilies*, p. 82.

31 In truth, the descent of the House of Wessex from Cerdic may not have been quite as unbroken as its propagandists liked to claim – but it was almost universally accepted, nevertheless.

32 *History of the Ancient Northumbrians*. Quoted by Wood (1981), p. 184.

33 The site of the battle, 'Brunanburh', remains unknown. For a typically stirring account of the attempt to solve the mystery, see 'Tinsley Wood' in Wood (1999).

34 *The Annals of Ulster*, entry for 939.6.

35 See Loomis (1950) for a fascinating piece of historical detective work, tracing how a 'holy spear' might indeed have passed from Charlemagne, via Duke Hugh, into the care of Athelstan.

36 Or given secret burial in a commoner's house, or even, according to one account, burned. If the latter, then the body venerated as Edward's could not, of course, have been his.

37 *The Anglo-Saxon Chronicle* (Peterborough Manuscript), entry for 979.

38 *Ibid.* (Abingdon Manuscript).

39 *Blickling Homilies*, p. 64.

40 Campbell (2000), p. 173.

41 Warner of Rouen, 75–7.

42 Wulfstan, *The Sermon of the Wolf to the English*.

43 *Aelfric's Catholic Homilies*, p. 37.

44 William of Malmesbury, 2.2.

45 Adam of Bremen, 2.40.

46 *Ibid.*, 2.57. For the hirsute character of women in the furthest reaches of Scandinavia, see 4.32.

47 That Trygvasson led the Viking army at Maldon is something more than inference, something less than a certainty. To maintain it, as the leading authority on the battle has put it, is 'to give oneself the benefit of the doubt, but such leaps are the stuff of Anglo-Saxon history' (Scragg, p. 90).

48 *Battle of Maldon*, p. 294.

49 Although our earliest source for the epithet is posthumous, it seems probable that it originated during Ethelred's lifetime.

50 *The Anglo-Saxon Chronicle*, entry for 1002.

51 Matthew 13.37–40.

52 Renewal by King Ethelred for the monastery of St Frideswide, Oxford: *EHD*, document 127.

53 Quoted by Wulfstan, *Lectio Sancti Evangelii Secundum Matheum*.

54 *Blickling Homilies*, p. 145.

55 Adam of Bremen, p. 229.

56 *Hávamál*, Page, p. 142.

57 Adam of Bremen, 4.39.

58 Ari Thorgilsson, p. 66.

59 Snorri Sturluson, *Heimskringla. King Olaf Trygvasson's Saga*, 37.

60 Forkbeard's presence at Maldon, like that of Trygvasson, has to be inferred. See the essay by Niels Lund, 'The Danish Perspective', in Scragg (pp. 137–8).

61 Saxo Grammaticus, 10.8.4.

62 Thietmar, 7.36.

63 Snorri Sturluson, *Heimskringla. King Olaf Trygvasson's Saga*, 121.

64 *The Anglo-Saxon Chronicle*, entry for 1014.

65 Ottar the Black, p. 308.

66 *Encomium Emmae Reginae*, 2.4.

67 Wulfstan, *The Sermon of the Wolf to the English*.

68 *Völuspá*, Page, p. 209.

69 For the argument that *Völuspá* was inspired by Wulfstan, see Joseph Harris, p. 94.

70 *Völuspá*, Page, p. 210.

71 *EHD*, p. 424.

72 *Ibid.*, pp. 416–18.

5 Apocalypse Postponed

1 2 Thessalonians 2.4.

2 *City of God*, 20.19.

3 *Encomium Emmae*, 2.21.

4 Glaber, 3.13.

5 Matthew 24.2.

6 Glaber, 21.3.

7 'What we should like most of all to know', as the great historian of medieval Spain, Richard Fletcher, put it, 'is why the bishop was convinced that the relics discovered were those of St James' (Fletcher 1984, p. 59). One legend claims that he was led to the plain where the body lay buried by a mysterious star; but this is a late tradition, and reflects a heroic attempt to derive the shrine's name of Santiago de la Compostella from the Latin

phrase '*campus stellae*', or 'plain of the star'. In fact, most scholars now agree that the word 'compostella' derives from a diminutive of '*compostum*', or 'burial place'.

8 The words of Gottschalk, Bishop of Le Puy in the Auvergne, who travelled to Santiago in 951, the first pilgrim to do so that we know of by name.

9 Such, at any rate, was the standard fate of Christian captives brought to Córdoba. See Fierro, p. 107.

10 Qur'an 8.12.

11 Abd Allah b. Buluggin al-Ziri al-Sanhaji, p. 44.

12 Al-Nuwayri. Quoted by Scales, p. 65.

13 Qur'an 2.191. 'Tumult and oppression' is the translation of the notoriously untranslatable word '*fitna*', which can mean chastisement, faction fighting, schism or civil war – and at its most extreme the period of total anarchy that will precede the end of days. The word was used by Muslim historians to describe the fall of the Caliphate of Córdoba, and its aftermath.

14 Ibn Hazm, chapter 23.

15 *Ibid.*, chapter 26.

16 *Ibid.*, chapter 23.

17 From the hadiths collected by Ibn Maja, 2.4086.

18 From the hadiths collected by Abu Dawud, 2.421.

19 Muqaddasi. Quoted by Peters, p. 237.

20 *Ibid.*

21 The testimony of a Muslim, Ibn al-Athr. Quoted by Canard, p. 18.

22 Matthew 12.40.

23 Or possibly early 1008: the dating depends on the evidence of a Muslim historian, Ibn al-Qalanisi.

24 Adémar, 3.47. The description derived from the eyewitness account of the Bishop of Périgueux, who had been in Jerusalem at the time, and subsequently related what he had seen to Adémar.

25 Again, on the evidence of Ibn al-Qalanisi. See Assad, p. 107.

26 Adémar, 3.46.

27 *Ibid.*, 3.35.

28 *Ibid.*, 3.46.

29 *Ibid.*, 3.47.

30 For a definitive statement, see Moore (1987), p. 89.

31 For a powerful statement of this argument, see Landes (1996).

32 Quoted by Landes (1995), p. 41.

33 Glaber, 3.24.

34 The testimony of a Persian traveller, Nasir-i-Khusrau, who visited the church in 1047. Biddle (p. 79) quotes it as evidence that the restoration project must have been begun long before the traditional date of 1048, which derives from the much later chronicle of William of Tyre. As Biddle also points out (p. 81), the speed with which the church was rebuilt offers

the likeliest explanation for the silence of Western writers about the destruction of 1009 in the decades that preceded the First Crusade. 'The event of 1009 was not mentioned, not because it had passed out of memory, nor because men did not care, but rather because architectural history was not relevant.'

35 Quoted by Landes (1995), p. 45. For a brilliant explication of how and why Adémar sought to obscure the apocalyptic tenor of his times, see *ibid.*, pp. 144–53 and 287–308. Anyone who writes on Adémar must be for ever in Landes's debt.

36 Glaber, 2.22.

37 The precise date of Vilgard's heresy is unknown.

38 Adémar, 3.143.

39 Andrew of Fleury, *Miraculi Sancti Benedicti*, p. 248.

40 The degree to which mass heresy existed, or was a nightmare conjured up by its chroniclers, is intensely controversial. For the view that it was a reflection of faction battles among a clerical elite, see Moore's essay (2000). For a strongly stated – and, in my opinion, thoroughly convincing – counter-view, see Landes (1995), pp. 37–40.

41 It is true that one heretic, a theologian by the name of Priscillian, had been executed back in 383 – but even then on an official charge of sorcery. One intriguing theory holds that it was his tomb which subsequently came to be venerated at Santiago. See Fletcher (1984), p. 59.

42 Adémar, 3.138.

43 From a letter by a monk named Heribert. Quoted by Lobrichon (1992), p. 85.

44 Adémar, 3.138.

45 Wazo of Liège, p. 228.

46 Landulf Senior, p. 65.

47 Adam of Bremen, 4.8.

48 John of Salerno, *Life of Odo*, 2.3.

49 Wazo of Liège, p. 228.

50 From 'The Miracles that Happened at Fécamp': van Houts, p. 78.

51 *Liber Miraculorum Sancte Fidis*, 2.12.

52 Glaber, 3.19.

53 Quoted by Landes (1995), p. 177. See also Landes (1991).

54 For the full extraordinary story of Adémar's forgeries, see *ibid.*

55 Glaber, 4.1

56 *Ibid.*, 4.21.

57 *Ibid.*, 4.18.

58 Arnold of Regensburg, p. 563.

59 Glaber, 4.18.

60 Quoted by Landes (1995), p. 322.

61 Glaber, 4.14.

62 *Ibid.*, 4.17.

63 Arnold of Regensburg, p. 547.

64 *Ibid.*

65 Wipo, p. 40.

66 Wido of Osnabrück, p. 467.

67 From the anathema against the Eastern Church delivered by Cardinal Humbert. Ironically, he appears to have regarded the practice of depicting Christ dead upon the Cross as a peculiarly Greek one.

68 Arnulf of Milan, 3.4.

69 Hildebrand's precise origins are controversial. The claims that are repeated here – that they were humble – were so widespread as to seem to me irrefutable; but some scholars have argued that Hildebrand was in fact Gregory VI's nephew, either by marriage or by blood. If the latter, then the foremost steward of the Catholic Church in the eleventh century was the grandson of a Jew. The biographies of Cowdrey (pp. 27–8) and Morghen (pp. 10–11) represent the opposite poles of opinion on this. That Hildebrand became a monk while still a boy is, again, the expression of a consensus rather than a certainty.

70 Acts of the Apostles 8.23.

71 Peter Damian, *Vita Romualdi*, p. 33.

72 Desiderius of Monte Cassino, p. 1143.

73 *Life of Pope Leo IX*, 1.2.

74 *Ibid.*, 1.15.

75 *Ibid.*, 2.3.

76 Hildebert, col. 865.

77 John of Fécamp, col. 797.

78 From the notorious letter written by Humbert to the Patriarch of Constantinople, and published under Leo's name: *PL* 143, col. 752.

79 Humbert, *De Sancta Romana Ecclesia*. Quoted by Schramm 2 (1929), p. 128.

80 Otto of Freising, *The Two Cities*, 6.33.

81 Desiderius of Monte Cassino, 1.2.

82 Amatus of Monte Cassino, 3.7.

83 *Ibid.*, 3.16.

84 *Blickling Homilies*, p. 137.

85 Liudprand, *The Mission to Constantinople*, 3.34.

86 Revelation 12.9. The prophecy that Michael would kill the Antichrist dates back to the late fourth century.

87 Hermann of Reichenau, p. 132.

88 William of Apulia, 2.240–1.

89 Michael Psellus, p. 116.

90 *Ibid.*, p. 269.

91 Orderic Vitalis, 5.27.

6 1066 and All That

1 *Miracula S. Wulframni*. Quoted by Haskins, p. 259.
2 According to the tradition preserved by William of Apulia, at any rate. Amatus of Monte Cassino tells a different story, but in his account too, the first Normans recruited as mercenaries in southern Italy are described as originally having been pilgrims.
3 Amatus of Monte Cassino, 1.2.
4 Dudo, 269. He is referring to Richard I.
5 The theory is Bachrach's. See *Fulk Nerra*, pp. 228–9.
6 Not, as is conventionally alleged, a tanner. See Van Houts (1986).
7 See Searle (1986).
8 Glaber, 4.22.
9 Adam of Bremen, 4.21.
10 William of Poitiers, 1.44.
11 William of Jumièges, vol. 2, p. 92.
12 *Encomium Emmae Reginae*, 2.16.
13 Geoffrey of Malaterra, 1.3.
14 Orderic Vitalis, 4.82.
15 *The Anglo-Saxon Chronicle* (Abingdon Manuscript), entry for 1042.
16 William of Poitiers, 1.7.
17 *Ibid.*, 1.48.
18 Snorri Sturluson, *The Ynglinga Saga*, 1.
19 From an epitaph inscribed on a rune stone, memorialising adventurers who had travelled to 'Serkland'. Quoted by Page, p. 89.
20 The derivation of the name is widely, but not universally, accepted. The so-called 'Normanist controversy' – the question of whether the Rus were predominantly Scandinavian or Slavic – has been a point of issue between Western and Russian scholars for two hundred years. See Franklin and Shepherd, pp. 28 *passim*, for a concise overview.
21 Constantine VII Porphyrogenitos, p. 94.
22 Snorri Sturluson, *Heimskringla. The Saga of Olaf Haraldsson*, chapter 238.
23 *Ibid.*, chapter 199.
24 Snorri Sturluson, *King Harald's Saga*, chapter 2.
25 *Ibid.*
26 *Russian Primary Chronicle*, p. 111.
27 Michael Psellus, p. 33.
28 Snorri Sturluson, *King Harald's Saga*, chapter 5.
29 *Ibid.*, chapter 12. One plausible suggestion is that Harald's undoubted presence in Jerusalem related to the restoration of the Church of the Holy Sepulchre. See Ellis Davidson, p. 219.
30 Snorri Sturluson, *King Harald's Saga*, chapter 16.
31 *Ibid.*, chapter 17.
32 *Laxdaela Saga*, chapter 77. The description of the hero's return from service

with 'the King of Miklagard' would surely have served for Harald's as well.

33 Adam of Bremen, 2.61.
34 From a Mass for St Olaf found in an English missal, dated to 1061. See Iversen, p. 405.
35 Snorri Sturluson, *King Harald's Saga*, chapter 17.
36 *Ibid.*, chapter 1.
37 *The Anglo-Saxon Chronicle* (Worcester Manuscript), entry for 1051.
38 *Life of King Edward who Rests at Westminster*, pp. 58–9.
39 Although, according to Orderic Vitalis, it was Tostig himself who arrived in Norway to make the proposal.
40 Such, at any rate, is what appears to be implied by the scene that appears below the illustration of Halley's Comet in the Bayeux Tapestry.
41 Snorri Sturluson, *King Harald's Saga*, chapter 22.
42 *Encomium Emmae Reginae*, 2.9.
43 Adam of Bremen, 3.17.
44 Snorri Sturluson, *King Harald's Saga*, chapter 87.
45 Henry of Huntingdon, 2.27. The story was also interpolated into a version of *The Anglo-Saxon Chronicle*, and may conceivably be authentic, for it is evident that the English were indeed briefly held up at the bridge. I include the story as a tribute to my first history teacher, Major Morris, whose blackboard drawing of the Viking being skewered through his privates first served to awaken me to the joys of medieval history.
46 Snorri Sturluson, *King Harald's Saga*, chapter 91.
47 *Life of King Edward who Rests at Westminster*, p. 53.
48 *Battle of Maldon*, p. 294.
49 Regino of Prüm, p. xx.
50 Widukind of Corvey, 2.1.
51 *The Life of King Edward*, the Bayeux Tapestry, and even William of Poitiers, a gung-ho Norman, all imply that Harold had been nominated by the dying Edward.
52 William of Poitiers, 1.41.
53 *The Anglo-Saxon Chronicle* (Worcester manuscript), entry for 1066.
54 *Life of King Edward who Rests at Westminster*, p. 51.
55 William of Poitiers, 1.38.
56 *Life of King Edward who Rests at Westminster*, p. 81.
57 William of Poitiers, 1.48.
58 Orderic Vitalis, vol. 2, p. 143.
59 Peter Damian. Quoted by Cowdrey (1998), p. 42.
60 Gregory VII, *Register*, 7.23.
61 William of Poitiers, 2.7.
62 *Ibid.*, 2.9.
63 *Ibid.*, 2.15.
64 *Carmen de Hastingae Proelio*, p. 46.

65 This seems to me the likeliest interpretation of Harold's tactics, but it is not the only one. It is possible, of course, that he had always intended to fight a defensive battle – or indeed to blockade William inside Hastings, and not fight a battle at all. For an eclectic range of opinions, see Morillo. For a scythingly sceptical analysis of how little we know about the precise details of the battle, see Lawson (2007).

66 *The Anglo-Saxon Chronicle*, entry for 1003.

67 *Carmen de Hastingae Proelio*, p. 46.

68 Though no source specifically names them as being present at Hastings, the description of them in contemporary accounts of the battle leaves little room for doubt.

69 William of Poitiers, 2.21.

70 *Carmen de Hastingae Proelio*, p. 49.

71 That Harold was struck in the eye by an arrow is one of the most celebrated details of English history – but its fame derives principally from the Bayeux Tapestry, a hugely problematic piece of evidence. Other sources, however, some of them near contemporary, do lend credence to the tradition. See Lawson (2007), pp. 226–33.

72 William of Poitiers, 2.25.

73 Thorkill Skallasson. Quoted by Van Houts (1995), p. 836.

74 Milo Crispin, 13.33.

75 *The Anglo-Saxon Chronicle* (Worcester manuscript), entry for 1066.

76 Orderic Vitalis, 2.232.

77 Hugh of Cluny, p. 143.

78 William of Poitiers, 2.42.

7 An Inconvenient Truth

1 Lampert of Hersfeld, p. 80.

2 Sigebert of Gembloux, p. 360.

3 Rudolf's kinship to Henry is probable but not absolutely certain. See Hlawitschka.

4 Lampert of Hersfeld, p. 92.

5 *Ibid.*, p. 81.

6 Cited in Struve (1984), p. 424.

7 Peter Damian, *Letters*, vol. 4, p. 151.

8 *Ibid.*, vol. 3, p. 27.

9 *Ibid.*, p. 80.

10 *Ibid.*, vol. 2, p. 371.

11 *Ibid.*, vol. 1, p. 283.

12 *Ibid.*, vol. 3, p. 130.

13 *Ibid.*, p. 165.

14 Literally '*Loricatus*': a man armed with a breastplate.

15 Peter Damian, *Vita Dominici Loricati*, col. 1024. This is the first known record of the phenomenon.
16 Peter Damian, *Letters*, vol. 4, p. 61.
17 Lampert of Hersfeld, p. 100.
18 Rather of Verona, 2.3.
19 Bonizo of Sutri, p. 203.
20 Peter Damian, *Letters*, vol. 4, pp. 276–7.
21 Bishop Otto of Bamberg, writing at the start of the twelfth century: testimony to the enduring presumption that the world was about to end. Cited by Morris, p. 37.
22 Adémar, 3.138.
23 Odo of Cluny, col. 570.
24 Revelation 14.5. The virgins are the same as the 144,000 harpists whom a scholar at Auxerre had independently identified with the monks of Cluny.
25 Arnulf of Milan, 3.9.
26 The question of whether an unworthy priest invalidated the miracle of the Mass was an ancient one, and orthodoxy – originally articulated, inevitably, by St Augustine – argued that it did not. Peter Damian, in his public pronouncements, at any rate, went along with this. For a convincing argument that he may have had private doubts, however, see Elliott.
27 Peter Damian, *Letters*, vol. 2, p. 319.
28 Arnulf of Milan, 3.15.
29 Landulf Senior, 3.29.
30 Bonizo of Sutri, p. 216.
31 Gregory VII, *Register*, 1.85.
32 From the only surviving letter written by Henry III to Abbot Hugh: *PL* 159, 932.
33 Lampert of Hersfeld, p. 120.
34 Bonizo of Sutri, p. 220.
35 Peter Damian, *Letters*, vol. 3, p. 107.
36 Jeremiah 1.10.
37 Gregory VII, *Register*, 9.35.
38 *Ibid.*, 2.75.
39 *Ibid.*, 2.55a. From the so-called '*Dictatus Papae*', 'Dictation of the Pope'.
40 Abbot Walo of Metz. Quoted by Cowdrey (1998), p. 92.
41 Gregory VII, *Register*, 1.49.
42 *Ibid.*, 2.37.
43 Matthew of Edessa. Quoted by Vryonis, p. 81.
44 Michael Psellus, p. 98.
45 Specifically, it was a boast of Danishmend Ghazi, a celebrated warlord who in the wake of Manzikert hacked out a princedom in the north-east of what is now Turkey. See Vryonis, p. 195.
46 Matthew of Edessa. Quoted by Vryonis, p. 170.

47 Gregory VII, *Register*, 1.22.

48 *Ibid.*, 1.23.

49 *Ibid.*, 2.31.

50 Geoffrey of Malaterra, 1.9.

51 Amatus of Monte Cassino, 2.8.

52 Guiscard's oath is reproduced in full in Loud, pp. 188–9.

53 William of Apulia, p. 178.

54 *Ibid.*, p. 174.

55 Geoffrey of Malaterra, 2.33. Even though Malaterra was writing after the First Crusade, and so may have been influenced by the ethos that surrounded it, historians generally accept that there was a strong religious dimension to how the Normans – and the papacy – viewed the conquest of Sicily. For a dissenting view, see Lopez.

56 Gregory VII, *Register*, 1.49.

57 *Ibid.*, 2.31.

58 In fact, a supernova.

59 *Vita Altmanni Episcopi Pataviensis*, p. 230. The 'vulgar opinion' was prompted by the fact that in 1065 the anniversaries of Christ's conception, the Annunciation, and his death, Good Friday, coincided. The same thing happened in only one other year in the eleventh century: 1076, the same year that Gregory was hoping to arrive in Jerusalem.

60 Gregory VII, *Register*, 2.31.

61 *Ibid.*, 1.77. The 'Apostle' is St Paul: 1 Corinthians 4.3.

62 Bruno of Merseburg, 16.

63 Lampert of Hersfeld, p. 156.

64 *Ibid.*, p. 150.

65 *Ibid.*, p. 174.

66 Gregory VII, *Register*, 1.25.

67 Gregory VII, *Epistolae Vagantes*, 5.

68 *Ibid.*

69 From the fateful letter sent by the imperial bishops to Gregory from Worms: *Quellen zur Geschichte Kaiser Heinrich IV*, p. 474.

70 Quoted by Cowdrey (1998), p. 117.

71 Gregory VII, *Epistolae Vagantes*, 11.

72 Arnulf of Milan, 4.7.

73 Gregory VII, *Epistolae Vagantes*, 14.

74 Henry IV, 12. From a longer version of the letter originally sent to Gregory, and disseminated for propaganda purposes.

75 Gregory VII, *Register*, 3.10a.

76 Lampert, p. 257.

77 *Ibid.*, p. 53.

78 Henry IV, 14.

79 Lampert, p. 285.

80 Bruno of Merseburg, 74.

81 Gregory VII, *Register*, 8.3.

82 *Ibid.*, 6.17.

83 *Ibid.*, 1.62.

84 Gregory would later claim that he had not restored Henry to the kingship at Canossa, but at the time he seems to have left the matter ambiguous. Henry himself certainly believed his deposition to have been reversed.

85 Cited by Robinson (1999), p. 172.

86 Paul of Bernried, 5.

87 Gregory VII, *Register*, 8.10.

88 *Ibid.*, 2.13. From a letter to the King of Hungary.

89 *Ibid.*, 4.28.

90 *Ibid.*, 7.23.

91 *Ibid.*, 7.6.

92 *Ibid.*, 8.21.

93 Gregory VII, *Epistolae Vagantes*, 54.

94 *Ibid.*, 57. The letter was sent to Toirdhealbhach Ó Briain, 'the illustrious king of Ireland'.

95 Gregory VII, *Register*, 8.21.

96 *Ibid.*, 6.5b.

97 Paul of Bernried, 107.

98 Bonizo of Sutri, p. 255.

99 Sigebert of Gembloux, p. 364.

100 Bonizo of Sutri, pp. 248–9.

101 Anna Comnena, p. 124.

102 *Ibid.*, p. 125.

103 *Ibid.*, p. 126.

104 That Henry carefully withdrew from Rome before Hugh's arrival suggests that it was he, rather than Gregory, who lay behind the abbot's diplomatic mission. For a counter-view, see Cowdrey (1970), pp. 161–2.

105 Gregory VII, *Epistolae Vagantes*, 54.

106 Gregory VII, *Register*, Appendix 3.

107 Sigebert of Gembloux, *An Apology against Those who Challenge the Masses of Married Priests*. Quoted by Leyser (1965), p. 42.

108 Gilo, 1.7.

109 Beno, 2.2.

110 With what truth it is impossible to say.

111 Guibert de Nogent, *A Monk's Confession*, 1.11.

112 *Miraculi Sancti Hugonis*. Quoted by Iogna-Prat (2002), p. 217.

113 From a Cluniac charter of the late eleventh century. Quoted by Cowdrey (1970), p. 130.

114 Urban II, col. 486. The bull was issued in 1097.

115 The evidence that Hugh sent such letters is circumstantial, but convincing.

See Cutler (1963).

116 *Vita Sancti Anastasii*, 5.
117 Urban II, cols. 370–1.
118 The agent's words were recorded by the King of Granada himself: unsurprisingly they appear to have made quite an impression. They are quoted by O'Callaghan, p. 30.
119 Urban II, col. 288.
120 Hugh of Cluny, p. 147.
121 Urban II, cols. 302–3.
122 Ekkehard of Aura. Quoted by Riley-Smith, p. 33. Riley-Smith's astronomical investigations have confirmed that the celestial phenomena reported by contemporaries were authentic.
123 'Historia peregrinorum euntium Jerusolymam': *ibid.*
124 Fulcher of Chartres, p. 56. The allusion is specifically to the papacy but in the context applies no less forcefully to Jerusalem.
125 See Delort, p. 64.
126 Quoted by Cowdrey (*History* 55), p. 188.
127 Gerbert of Aurillac, Letter 36.
128 For this estimate, see Bull (1993), p. 4.
129 Robert the Monk, p. 729.
130 Ralph of Caen, p. 22.
131 *Gesta Francorum*, p. 1.
132 Matthew 24.30.
133 The Latin word '*crusata*' did not come into use until the thirteenth century.
134 Anna Comnena, pp. 308–9.
135 For Alexius's self-presentation as the last emperor, see Charanis and Shepard (1997).
136 Albert of Aachen, 4.13.
137 Estimates as to the precise numbers on the Crusade are inevitably hedged about by uncertainty. See Phillips, p. 6.
138 Guibert de Nogent, *The Deeds of God through the Franks*, p. 225.
139 Revelation 19.13–15.

Bibliography

Primary sources

Sources for medieval history tend to be much less freely availaible than their equivalents from the classical period. Not only do a majority remain untranslated, but many are accessible only in intimidating volumes of nineteenth-century scholarship. Two resources are particularly indispensable. One is the *Patrologia Latina*, an immense compendium of sermons, saints' lives and other writings on ecclesiastical themes, gathered together in no fewer than 221 volumes by a single French priest, Jacques-Paul Migne. The other is the *Monumenta Germaniae Historica*, an even more titanic anthology of sources for the study of medieval history, begun in 1826 and ongoing to this day. Its title notwithstanding, the range of texts it embraces is far from confined to Germany. It is, however, authentically monumental.

The following abbreviations were unavoidable:

AASS: Acta Sanctorum Quotquot Orbe Colunter, ed. Société des Bollandistes (Antwerp, Brussels and Paris, 1643–1940)

EHD: English Historical Documents 1, c. 500–1042, ed. Dorothy Whitelock (London, 1979)

MGH: Monumenta Germaniae Historica
    AA: Auctores Antiquissimi
    Libelli: Libelli de lite imperatorum et pontificum
    SRG: Scriptores Rerum Germanicarum in usum scholarum separati editii
    SS: Scriptores
PG: Patrologia Graeca
PL: Patrologia Latina

All quotations from the Bible are from the Revised Standard Version. All quotations from the Qur'an are from the translation by Abdullah Yusuf Ali (Indianapolis, 1992).

Abbo of Fleury: *Apologeticus ad Hugonem et Rodbertum Reges Francorum*, in *PL* 139
Abd Allah b. Buluggin al-Ziri al-Sanhaji: *Al-Tibyan*, tr. A. T. Tibi (Leiden, 1986)

Adalbero of Laon: *Poème au roi Robert*, ed. C. Carozzi (Paris, 1979)

Adam of Bremen: *History of the Archbishops of Hamburg-Bremen*, tr. Francis J. Tschan (New York, 2002)

Adémar of Chabannes: *Ademari Cabannensis Chronica*, ed. Pascale Bourgain (Turnhout, 1999)

Adso of Montier-en-Der: 'Letter on the Origin and Time of the Antichrist', in *Apocalyptic Spirituality: Treatises and Letters of Lactantius, Adso of Montier-en-Der, Joachim of Fiore, The Franciscan Spirituals, Savonarola*, tr. Bernard McGinn (New York, 1979)

Aelfric: *Colloquy*, ed. G. N. Garmonsway (London, 1947)

Aelfric: *Aelfric's Catholic Homilies*, ed. Malcolm Godden (London, 1979)

Albert of Aachen: *Historia Ierosolimitana*, ed. Susan B. Edgington (Oxford, 2007)

Albert of Metz: *Fragmentum ed Deoderico primo episcopo Mettensi*, in *MGH SS* 4 (Hanover, 1854)

Alcuin: *Letters*, in *Alcuin of York, c. A.D. 732 to 804: His Life and Letters*, by Stephen Allott (York, 1974)

Amatus of Monte Cassino: *The History of the Normans*, tr. Prescott N. Dunbar (Woodbridge, 2004)

Andrew of Fleury: *Miraculi Sancti Benedicti*, ed. Eugene de Certain (Paris, 1858)

Andrew of Fleury: *Vie de Gauzlin, Abbé de Fleury*, ed. Robert-Henri Bautier (Paris, 1969)

Angilbertus: *Karolus Magnus et Leo Papa*, in *MGH Poetae Latini aevi Karolini* 1 (Berlin, 1881)

Anna Comnena: *The Alexiad*, tr. E. R. A. Sewter (London, 2003)

Annales Hildesheimenses, in *MGH SRG* 8 (Hanover, 1878)

Annales Quedlinburgenses, in *MGH SS* 3 (Hanover, 1839)

Annals of Ulster, tr. Seán Mac Airt and Gearóid Mac Niocail (Dublin, 1983)

Archives d'Anjou, ed. Paul Marchegay, 3 vols. (Angers, 1843–56)

Ari Thorgilsson: *Book of the Icelanders*, ed. Halldór Hermannsson (Ithaca, 1930)

Arnold of Regensburg: *Vita S. Emmerami*, in *MGH SS* 4 (Hanover, 1841)

Arnulf of Milan: *Liber Gestorum Recentium*, in *MGH SRG* 67 (Hanover, 1994)

Augustine: *City of God*, tr. Henry Bettenson (London, 2003)

Augustine: *On Order*, tr. Silvano Borruso (South Bend, 2006)

Avitus of Vienne: *Epistulae*, in *MGH AA* 6.2 (Berlin, 1888)

Battle of Maldon, in *EHD*

Beno: *Benonis et Aliorum Cardinalium Schismaticorum Contra Gregorium VII. et Urbanum II. Scripta*, in *MGH Libelli* 2 (Hanover, 1892)

Bibliotheca Cluniacensis, ed. Martinus Marrier and Andreas Quercetanus (Mâcon, 1915)

Blickling Homilies, tr. Richard J. Kelly (London, 2003)

Bonizo of Sutri: *To a Friend*, in *The Papal Reform of the Eleventh Century*, tr. and ed. I. S. Robinson (Manchester, 2004)

Bruno of Merseburg: *Saxonicum Bellum*, in *MGH Deutsches Mittelalter* 2 (Leipzig, 1937)

Bruno of Querfort: *Passio Sancti Adalberti*, in *MGH SS* 4 (Hanover, 1841)

Bruno of Querfort: *Vita Quinque Fratrum*, in *MGH SS* 15 (Hanover, 1887)

Byrhtferth: *Byrhtferth's Manual*, tr. and ed. S. J. Crawford (London, 1929)

Carmen de Hastingae Proelio, in Morillo, pp. 46–52

Bibliography

Cartulaire de l'Abbaye de Saint-Aubin d'Angers, ed. B. de Broussillon, 2 vols. (Paris, 1903)

Cartulaire du Ronceray, ed. Paul Marchegay (Angers, 1856)

Charlemagne: *Epistolae*, in *MGH Epistolae Karolini Aevi* (Berlin, 1892–1925)

Chronicon Mosomense: Chronique ou Livre de Fondation du Monastère de Mouzon, tr. and ed. Michel Bur (Paris, 1989)

Chronicon Novaliciense, in *MGH SS 7* (Hanover, 1846)

Collectanea Byzantina II, ed. S. G. Mercati (Bari, 1970)

Constantine VII Porphyrogenitos: *De Administrando Imperio*, tr. R. J. H. Jenkins (Dumbarton Oaks, 1967)

Corpus Scriptorum Muzarabicorum, ed. J. Gil, 2 vols. (Madrid, 1973)

Desiderius of Monte Cassino: *Dialogi de Miraculis Sancti Benedicti*, in *MGH SS 30/2* (Leipzig, 1934)

Documents pour l'Histoire de l'Église de Saint-Hilaire de Poitiers (768–1300), ed. L. Rédet (Poitiers, 1847)

Donation of Constantine, ed. Ernest F. Henderson, in *Select Historical Documents of the Middle Ages* (London, 1910), pp. 319–29

Dudo of Saint-Quentin: *History of the Normans*, tr. Eric Christiansen (Woodbridge, 1998)

Egil's Saga, tr. C. Fell and J. Lucas (London, 1975)

Einhard: *The Life of Charlemagne*, in *Two Lives of Charlemagne*, tr. Lewis Thorpe (London, 1969)

Encomium Emmae Reginae, tr. Alistair Campbell (Cambridge, 1998)

Erchempert: *Historia Langabardorum Beneventarnorum* (http://www.thelatinlibrary.com/erchempert.html)

Eucherius of Lyon: *The Passion of the Martyrs* (Van Berchem, pp. 55–9)

Eusebius: *Eusebius' Life of Constantine*, tr. Averil Cameron and Stuart G. Hall (Oxford, 1999)

Eusebius: *In Praise of the Emperor Constantine* (http://www.ucalgary.ca/~vandersp/Courses/texts/eusebius/euseprai.html)

Ex Miraculis Sancit Alexii, in *MGH SS 4* (Hanover, 1841)

Flodoard: *Annales*, ed. Philippe Lauer (Paris, 1905)

Fontes ad Topographiam Veteris Urbis Romae Pertinentes, VIII, Regio Urbis X, Mons Palatinus, ed. G. Lugli (Rome, 1960)

Fulbert of Chartres: *The Letters & Poems of Fulbert of Chartres*, ed. F. Behrends (Oxford, 1976)

Fulcher of Chartres: *The First Crusade: The Chronicle of Fulcher of Chartres and Other Sources*, ed. Edward Peters (Philadelphia, 1998)

Gallus Anonymus: *The Deeds of the Princes of the Poles*, tr. Paul W. Knoll and Frank Shaer (Budapest, 2003)

Geoffrey of Malaterra: *De Rebus Gestis Rogerii Calabriae et Siciliae Comitis et Roberti Guiscardi Fratris Eius*, ed. E. Pontieri (Bologna, 1927)

Gerbert of Aurillac: *Acta Concilii Remensis ad Sanctum Basolum*, in *MGH SS 3* (Hanover, 1838)

Gerbert of Aurillac: *The Letters of Gerbert with his Papal Privileges as Sylvester II*, tr. Harriet Pratt Lattin (New York, 1961)

Gesta Consulum Andegavorum: Chroniques des Comtes d'Anjou et des Seigneurs d'Amboise, ed. L. Halphen and R. Poupardin (Paris, 1913)

Gilo: *Vita Sancti Hugonis Abbatis*, ed. H. E. J. Cowdrey, in *Studi Gregoriani* 11, 1978

Glaber, Rodulfus: *Opera*, ed. John France, Neithard Bulst and Paul Reynolds (Oxford, 1989)

Gregory I: *Homiliarum in Evengelia*, in *PL* 76

Gregory I: *Moralium Libri*, in *PL* 75

Gregory I: *Regulae Pastoralis Liber*, in *PL* 77

Gregory VII: *The 'Epistolae Vagantes' of Pope Gregory VII*, tr. H. E. J. Cowdrey (Oxford, 1972)

Gregory VII: *The Register of Pope Gregory VII 1073–1085*, tr. H. E. J. Cowdrey (Oxford, 2002)

Guibert de Nogent: *A Monk's Confession: The Memoirs of Guibert of Nogent*, tr. Paul J. Archambault (Philadelphia, 1995)

Guibert de Nogent: *The Deeds of God through the Franks: A Translation of Guibert de Nogent's Gesta Dei per Francos*, tr. R. Levine (Woodbridge, 1996)

Hariulf: *Gesta Ecclesiae Centulensis*, in *Chronique de l'Abbaye de Saint-Riquier*, ed. F. Lot (Paris, 1894)

Heliand: The Heliand: The Saxon Gospel, tr. G. Ronald Murphy (Oxford, 1992)

Henry II, in *MGH Diplomata Regum et Imperatorum Germaniae* 3, ed. H. Bresslau, H. Bloch and R. Holtzmann (Hanover, 1900–3)

Henry IV: *Die Briefe Heinrichs IV*, in *MGH Deutsches Mittlealter* 1 (Leipzig, 1937)

Henry of Huntingdon: *The History of the English People 1000–1154*, tr. Diana Greenway (Oxford, 1996)

Hermann of Reichenau: *Chronicon de Sex Aetatibus Mundi*, in *MGH SS* 5 (Hanover, 1844)

Hildebert: *Vita Sancti Hugonis*, in *PL* 159, cols. 857–94

Hrotsvit of Gandersheim: *Pelagia*, in *Opera Omnia*, ed. Walter Berschin (Munich, 2001)

Hugh of Cluny: *Two Studies in Cluniac History 1049–1126*, ed. H. E. J. Cowdrey (Rome, 1978)

Ibn Hazm: *The Ring of the Dove: A Treatise on the Art and Practice of Arab Love*, tr. A. J. Arberry (London, 1997)

Inventio et Miracula Sancti Vulfranni, ed. Dom J. Laporte (Rouen, 1938)

Itinera Hierosolymitana et Descriptiones Terrae Sanctae, ed. T. Tobler and A. Molinier (Osnabrück, 1966)

John Canaparius: *Vita Sancti Adalberti*, in *MGH SS* 4 (Hanover, 1841)

John the Deacon: *Chronicon Venetum*, ed. G. Monticolo (Rome, 1890)

John of Fécamp: *Epistola ad Leonem IX*, in *PL* 143, cols. 797–800

John of St Arnoul: *La Vie de Jean, Abbé de Gorze*, ed. Michel Parisse (Paris, 1999)

John of Salerno: *St Odo of Cluny: Being the Life of St Odo of Cluny by John of Salerno and the Life of St Gerald of Aurillac by St Odo*, tr. G. Sitwell (London, 1958)

John Skylitzes: *Synopsis Historiarum*, ed. I. Thurn (Berlin, 1973)

Jordanes: *The Gothic History of Jordanes*, tr. Charles C. Mierow (Princeton, 1915)

Bibliography

Lactantius: *De Mortibus Persecutorum*, ed. J. L. Creed (Oxford, 1984)

Lampert of Hersfeld: *Annales*, in *MGH SRG* 38 (Hanover, 1894)

Landulf Senior: *Historia Mediolanensis*, in *MGH SS* 8 (Hanover, 1848)

Laxdaela Saga, tr. Magnus Magnusson and Hermann Palsson (London, 1969)

Leo VI: *Tactica*, in *PG* 107, cols. 419–1094

Leo of Synada: *The Correspondence of Leo, Metropolitan of Synada & Syncellus*, ed. M. P. Vinson (Washington, DC, 1985)

Leo the Deacon: *The History of Leo the Deacon: Byzantine Military Expansion in the Tenth Century*, tr. Alice-Mary Talbot and Dennis F. Sullivan (Washington, DC, 2005)

Lex Salica, in *MGH Leges Nationum Germanicarum* 4/2 (Hanover, 1969)

Liber Miraculorum Sancte Fidis, ed. A. Bouillet (Paris, 1897)

Liber Tramitis Aevi Odilonis Abbatis, ed. P. Dinter (Siegburg, 1980)

Life of King Edward who Rests at Westminster, tr. F. Barlow (Oxford, 1992)

Life of Pope Leo IX, in *The Papal Reform of the Eleventh Century*, tr. and ed. I. S. Robinson (Manchester, 2004)

Liudprand of Cremona: *Antapodosis* and *History of Otto*, in *The Works of Liudprand of Cremona*, tr. F. A. Wright (London, 1930)

Liudprand of Cremona: *Relatio de Legatione Constantinopolitana (The Mission to Constantinople)*, ed. Brian Scott (Bristol, 1993)

Leo of Vercelli: 'Panegyric on Otto III', in *Kaiser, Rom und Renovatio*, by P. E. Schramm, pp. 62–4

Louis IV: *Recueil des Actes de Louis IV, Roi de France (936–954)*, ed. P. Lauer (Paris, 1914)

Michael Psellus: *Fourteen Byzantine Rulers*, tr. E. R. A. Sewter (London, 1966)

Milo Crispin: *Vita Beati Lanfranci Cantuariensium Archiepiscopi*, in *PL* 150, cols. 53–4

Odo of Cluny: *Collationes*, in *PL* 133

Orderic Vitalis: *The Ecclesiastical History of Orderic Vitalis*, tr. Marjorie Chibnall, 6 vols. (Oxford, 1968–80)

Ottar the Black: *Knútsdrápa*, in *EHD*, pp. 335–6

Otto I: *Diplomata*, in *MGH Diplomata Regum et Imperatorum Germaniae* 1 (Hanover, 1879–84)

Otto of Freising: *The Two Cities*, tr. C. C. Mierow (New York, 1928)

Paul of Bernried: *The Life of Pope Gregory VII*, in *The Papal Reform of the Eleventh Century*, tr. and ed. I. S. Robinson (Manchester, 2004)

Paulinus of Aquileia: *Carmina*, in *MGH Poetae 1* (Berlin, 1881)

Peter Damian: *Vita Dominici Loricati*, in *PL* 144, cols. 1009–24

Peter Damian: *Vita Romualdi*, ed. G. Tabacco (Rome, 1957)

Peter Damian: *The Letters of Peter Damian, 1–120*, tr. Owen J. Blum, 4 vols. (Washington, DC, 1989–98)

Peter the Venerable: *De Miraculis*, in *PL* 189, cols. 851–954

'Poeta Saxo': *Annalium de gestis Caroli Magni imperatoris libri quinque*, in *MGH Poetae Latini Aevi Carolini* 4 (Berlin, 1899)

Primer of Medieval Latin: An Anthology of Prose and Poetry, ed. Charles H. Beeson (Washington, DC, 1986)

Quellen zur Geschichte Kaiser Heinrich IV, ed. F.-J. Schmale and I. Schmale-Ott (Darmstadt, 1961)

Ralph of Caen: *The Gesta Tancredi of Ralph of Caen: A History of the Normans on the First Crusade*, tr. Bernard S. Bachrach and David S. Bachrach (Aldershot, 2005)

Rather of Verona: *The Complete Works of Ratherius of Verona*, ed. P. L. Reid (Michigan, 1991)

Regino of Prüm: *Chronicon cum Continuatione Treverensi*, in *MGH SRG* 10 (Hanover, 1890)

Richer: *Histoire de France (888–995)*, tr. R. Latouche (Paris, 1930)

Robert the Monk: *Historia Iherosolimitana*, in *Recueil des Historiens des Croisades: Historiens Occidentaux* 3 (Paris, 1866)

Ruodlieb, tr. Gordon B. Ford (Leiden, 1965)

Russian Primary Chronicle, tr. S. H. Cross and O. P. Sherbowitz-Wetzor (Cambridge, Mass., 1953)

Saxo Grammaticus: *History of the Danes*, tr. Peter Fisher and Hilda Ellis Davidson (Cambridge, 1979)

Sigebert of Gembloux: *Chronica*, in *MGH SS* 6 (Hanover, 1884)

Sigehard: *Miracula S. Maximini*, in *Acta Sanctorum Quotquot Toto Orbe Coluntur*, ed. Iohannes Bollandus *et al.* (Antwerp, 1688)

Snorri Sturluson: *Heimskringla: A History of the Norse Kings*, tr. Samuel Laing (London, 1844)

Snorri Sturluson: *King Harald's Saga*, tr. Magnus Magnusson and Hermann Palsson (St Ives, 1966)

Snorri Sturluson: *The Ynglinga Saga* (http://omacl.org/Heimskringla/ynglinga.html)

Thangmar: *Vita Sancti Bernwardi Episcopi Hildesheimensis*, in *MGH SS* 4 (Hanover, 1841)

Thietmar of Merseburg: *Ottonian Germany: The Chronicon of Thietmar of Merseburg*, tr. David A. Warner (Manchester, 2001)

Urban II: *Epistolae et Privilegia*, in *PL* 151

Vita Altmanni Episcopi Pataviensis, in *MGH SS* 12 (Hanover, 1856)

Vita et Miracula Sancti Leonardi, ed. A. Poncelet, in *AASS*, November 3

Vita Sancti Athanasii, in *PL* 149

Vita Sancti Nili Abbatis Cryptae Ferratae, in *MGH SS* 4 (Hanover, 1841)

Warner of Rouen: *Moriuht*, ed. Christopher J. McDonough (Toronto, 1995)

Wazo of Liège: *Gesta Episcoporum Leodiensium*, in *MGH SS* 7 (Hanover, 1846)

Wido of Osnabrück: *Liber de Controversia inter Hildebrandum et Heinricum Imperatorem*, in *MGH Libelli I* (Hanover, 1891)

Widukind of Corvey: *Res Gestae Saxonicae*, in *MGH SS* 3 (Hanover, 1838)

William of Apulia: *La Geste de Robert Guiscard*, ed. M. Mathieu (Palermo, 1961)

William of Jumièges: *The Gesta Normannorum Ducum of William of Jumièges, Orderic Vitalis and Robert of Torigni*, tr. E. M. C. van Houts, 2 vols. (Oxford, 1992–5)

William of Malmesbury: *Vita Wulfstani*, ed. Reginald R. Darlington (London, 1928)

William of Poitiers: *The Gesta Guillelmi of William of Poitiers*, tr. R. H. C. Davis and M. Chibnall (Oxford, 1998)

Wipo: *Gesta Chuonradi II Imperatoris*, in *MGH SRG* 61 (Hanover, 1915)

Bibliography

Wulfstan: *Lectio Sancti Evangelii Secundum Matheum* (http://webpages.ursinus.edu/ jlionarons/wulfstan/II.html)

Wulfstan: *The Sermon of the Wolf to the English* (http://english3.fsu.edu/~wulfstan)

Secondary sources

Adelson, Howard L.: 'The Holy Lance and the Hereditary German Monarchy', *The Art Bulletin* 48/2, 1966

Airlie, Stuart: 'After Empire – Recent Work on the Emergence of Post-Carolingian Kingdoms', *Early Medieval Europe* 2/2, 1993

Alexander, Paul J.: 'Byzantium and the Migration of Literary Works and Motifs: The Legend of the Last Roman Emperor', *Medievala et Humanistica* 2, 1971

Alexander, Paul J.: 'The Medieval Legend of the Last Roman Emperor and its Messianic Origin', *Journal of the Warburg and Courtauld Institutes* 41, 1978

Alexander, Paul J.: *The Byzantine Apocalyptic Tradition* (Berkeley and Los Angeles, 1985)

Ali, Shaukat: *Millenarian and Messianic Tendencies in Islamic History* (Lahore, 1993)

Allen, Roland: 'Gerbert, Pope Silvester II', *English Historical Review* 28, 1892

Allen Brown, R.: *The Normans and the Norman Conquest* (London, 1969)

Althoff, Gerd: *Otto III*, tr. Phyllis G. Jestice (Pennsylvania, 1996)

Armstrong, Karen: *Muhammed: A Western Attempt to Understand Islam* (London, 1992)

Arnold, Benjamin: *Medieval Germany 500–1300: A Political Interpretation* (London, 1997)

Ashbridge, Thomas: *The First Crusade: A New History* (London, 2004)

Assaad, Sadik A.: *The Reign of Al-Hakim bi Amr Allah (386/996-411/1021): A Political Study* (Beirut, 1974)

Atkinson, Leigh: 'When the Pope was a Mathematician', *College Mathematics Journal* 11, 2005

Augenti, Andrea: *Il Palatino nel Medioevo: Archeologia e Topografia (Secoli VI–XIII)* (Rome, 1996)

Bachrach, Bernard S.: *Early Medieval Jewish Policy* (Minneapolis, 1977)

Bachrach, Bernard S.: 'Pope Sergius IV and the Foundation of the Monastery at Beaulieu-lès-Loches', *Revue Bénédictine* 95, 1985

Bachrach, Bernard S.: *Fulk Nerra: the Neo-Roman Consul, 98– 1040* (Berkeley and Los Angeles, 1993)

Barbero, Alessandro: *Charlemagne: Father of a Continent*, tr. Allan Cameron (Berkeley and Los Angeles, 2004)

Barlow, Frank: *Edward the Confessor* (London, 1970)

Barlow, Frank: *The Norman Conquest and Beyond* (London, 1983)

Barlow, Frank: *The Godwins: The Rise and Fall of a Noble Dynasty* (Harlow, 2002)

Barraclough, Geoffrey: *The Crucible of Europe: The Ninth and Tenth Centuries in European History* (London, 1976)

Barstow, Anne Llewellyn: *Married Priests and the Reforming Papacy* (New York, 1982)

Barthélemy, D.: 'Encore le Débat sur l'An Mil!', *Revue Historique de Droit Français et Étranger* 73, 1975

Barthélemy, D.: 'La Mutation Féodale a-t-elle eu Lieu? Note Critique', *Annales E. S. C.* 47, 1992

Barthélemy, D.: 'Debate: The Feudal Revolution', *Past and Present* 152, 1996

Barthélemy, D.: 'La Paix de Dieu dans son Contexte (989–1041)', *Cahiers de Civilisation Médiévale* 40, 1997

Barthélemy, D.: *L'An Mil et la Paix de Dieu: La France Chrétienne et Féodale (980–1060)* (Paris, 1999)

Bartlett, Robert: *The Making of Europe: Conquest, Colonization and Cultural Change, 950–1350* (London, 1993)

Bashear, Suliman: 'Early Muslim Apocalyptic Materials', in Bonner (Burlington, 2004)

Bates, David: *Normandy before 1066* (London, 1982)

Bäuml, Franz H.: *Medieval Civilization in Germany, 800–1273* (London, 1969)

Baylé, Maylis: 'Le Décor Sculpté de Saint-Georges-de-Boscherville: Quelques Questions de Style et d'Iconographie', in *Anglo-Norman Studies* 8, ed. R. Allen Brown (Woodbridge, 1986)

Berman, Constance Hoffman (ed.): *Medieval Religion: New Approaches* (New York, 2005)

Berman, Harold J.: *Law and Revolution: The Formation of the Western Legal Tradition* (Cambridge, Mass., 1983)

Bernhardt, John W.: *Itinerant Kingship and Royal Monasteries in Early Medieval Germany, c. 936–1075* (Cambridge, 1993)

Beumann, Helmut: *Die Ottonen* (Stuttgart, 1991)

Biddle, Martin: *The Tomb of Christ* (Stroud, 1999)

Bisson, T. N.: 'The "Feudal Revolution"', *Past and Present* 142, 1994

Bisson, T. N.: 'Medieval Lordship', *Speculum* 70, 1995

Bitel, Lisa M.: *Women in Early Medieval Europe, 400–1100* (Cambridge, 2002)

Blanks, David R.: 'Islam and the West in the Age of the Pilgrim', in Frassetto (New York, 2002)

Bloch, Marc: *Les Rois Thaumaturges* (Paris, 1924)

Bloch, Marc: *Feudal Society*, Vols. 1 and 2, tr. L. A. Manyon (London, 1989)

Blum, Owen J.: *St Peter Damian: His Teaching on the Spiritual Life* (Washington, DC, 1947)

Blumenthal, Uta-Renate: *The Investiture Controversy: Church and Monarchy from the Ninth to the Twelfth Century* (Philadelphia, 1995)

Bois, Guy: *The Transformation of the Year One Thousand: The Village of Lournand from Antiquity to Feudalism*, tr. Jean Birrell (Manchester, 1992)

Bonnassie, Pierre: *From Slavery to Feudalism in South-Western Europe*, tr. Jean Birrell (Cambridge, 1991)

Bonnassie, Pierre: *Les Sociétés de l'An Mil: Un Monde Entre Deux Ages* (Brussels, 2001)

Bonner, Michael (ed.): *Arab–Byzantine Relations in Early Islamic Times* (Burlington, 2004)

Bonner, Michael: *Jihad in Islamic History: Doctrines and Practice* (Princeton, 2006)

Bouchard, Constance Brittain: 'The Origins of the French Nobility: A Reassessment', *American Historial Review* 86, 1981

Bouchard, Constance Brittain: *Sword, Miter, and Cloister: Nobility and the Church in Burgundy, 980–1198* (Ithaca, 1987)

Boussard, Jacques: 'L'Origine des Familles Seigneuriales dans la Région de la Loire Moyenne', *Cahiers de Civilisation Médiévale* 5, 1962

Boutruche, Robert: *Seigneurie et Féodalité*, 2 vols. (Paris, 1968–70)

Bowlus, Charles R.: *The Battle of Lechfeld and its Aftermath, August 955: The End of the Age of Migrations in the Latin West* (Aldershot, 2006)

Brackmann, Albert: 'Die Politische Bedeutung der Mauritius-Verehrung im Frühen Mittelalter', *Sitzungsberichte* 30, 1937

Brague, Rémi: *The Law of God: The Philosophical History of an Idea*, tr. Lydia G. Cochrane (Chicago, 2007)

Brandes, W.: 'Liudprand von Cremona (*Legatio* Cap. 39–410) und eine Bisher Unbeachtete West-östliche Korrespondz über die Bedeutung des Jahres 1000 A.D.', *Byzantinische Zeitschrift* 93, 2000

Branner, Robert (ed.): *Chartres Cathedral* (New York, 1969)

Brett, Michael: *The Rise of the Fatimids: The World of the Mediterranean and the Middle East in the Fourth Century of the Hijra, Tenth Century CE* (Brill, 2001)

Brisbane, Mark, and Gaimster, David: *Novgorod: The Archaeology of a Russian Medieval City and its Hinterland* (London, 2001)

Brooke, Christopher: *Medieval Church and Society: Collected Essays* (London, 1971)

Brooke, Christopher: *Europe in the Central Middle Ages 962–1154* (London, 2000)

Brown, Gordon S.: *The Norman Conquest of Southern Italy and Sicily* (Jefferson, 2003)

Brown, Peter: 'Society and the Supernatural: A Medieval Change' (*Daedalus*, 1975)

Brown, Peter: *The Rise of Western Christendom: Triumph and Diversity, A.D. 200–1000* (Oxford, 1996)

Brühl, Carlrichard: 'Die Kaiserpfalz bei St. Peter und die Pfalz Ottos III. auf dem Palatin', *Quellen und Forschungen aus italienischen Archiven und Bibliotheken* 34, 1954

Brühl, Carlrichard: *Deutschland–Frankreich: Die Geburt zweier Völker* (Cologne, 1990)

Bull, Marcus: *Knightly Piety and the Lay Response to the First Crusade: The Limousin and Gascony, c. 970–c. 1130* (Oxford, 1993)

Bull, Marcus (ed.): *France in the Central Middle Ages 900–1200* (Oxford, 2002)

Bulliet, R.: *Conversion to Islam in the Medieval Period: An Essay in Quantitive History* (Cambridge, Mass., 1979)

Büttner, H.: 'Der Weg Ottos des Grossen zum Kaisertum', *Archiv für Mittelrheinische Kirchengeschichte* 14, 1962

Bynum, Caroline Walker: *Holy Feast and Holy Fast: The Religious Significance of Food to Medieval Women* (Berkeley and Los Angeles, 1987)

Callahan, Daniel: 'Adémar of Chabannes, Apocalypticism and the Peace Council of Limoges of 1031', *Revue Bénédictine* 101, 1991

Callahan, Daniel: 'The Problem of the "Filioque" and the Letter from the Pilgrim Monks of the Mount of Olives to Pope Leo III and Charlemagne. Is the Letter Another Forgery by Adémar of Chabannes?', *Revue Bénédictine* 102, 1992

Callahan, Daniel: 'Adémar of Chabannes, Millennial Fears and the Development of Western Anti-Judaism', *Journal of Ecclesiastical History* 46, 1995

Cambridge Medieval History III, c. 900–c. 1024, ed. Timothy Reuter (Cambridge, 1999)

Cambridge Medieval History IV, c. 1024–c. 1198, ed. David Luscombe and Jonathan Riley-Smith, 2 vols. (Cambridge, 2004)

Campbell, James (ed.): *The Anglo-Saxons* (London, 1982)

Campbell, James: *Essays in Anglo-Saxon History* (London, 1986)

Campbell, James: *The Anglo-Saxon State* (London, 2000)

Canard, Marius: 'La Destruction de l'Église de la Résurrection par le Calife Hakim et l'Histoire de la Descente du Feu Sacré', *Byzantion* 35, 1965

Cantor, Norman F.: 'The Crisis of Western Monasticism, 1050–113', *The American Historical Review* 66/1, 1960

Cantor, Norman F.: *Medieval History: The Life and Death of a Civilization* (New York, 1968)

Carozzi, Claude: *La Fin des Temps: Terreurs et Prophéties au Moyen Âge* (Paris, 1999)

Chapelot, Jean, and Fossier, Robert: *The Village and House in the Middle Ages*, tr. Henry Cleere (London, 1985)

Charanis, Peter: 'Byzantium, the West and the Origins of the First Crusade', *Byzantion* 19, 1947

Chibnell, Marjorie: *The Debate on the Norman Conquest* (Manchester, 1999)

Chibnell, Marjorie: *The Normans* (Oxford, 2000)

Christiansen, Eric: *The Norsemen in the Viking Age* (Oxford, 2002)

Clark, Victoria: *The Far-Farers: A Journey from Viking Iceland to Crusader Jerusalem* (London, 2003)

Cohen, Jeremy (ed.): *From Witness to Witchcraft: Jews and Judaism in Medieval Christian Thought* (Wiesbaden, 1996)

Conant, Kenneth John: 'The Apse at Cluny', *Speculum* 7/1, 1932

Conant, Kenneth John: 'Mediaeval Academy Excavations at Cluny, X', *Speculum* 45/1, 1970

Constable, Giles: *Three Studies in Medieval Religious and Social Thought* (Cambridge, 1995)

Constable, Giles: *Cluny from the Tenth to the Twelfth Centuries* (Aldershot, 2000)

Contamine, Philippe: *War in the Middle Ages*, tr. Michael Jones (Oxford, 1984)

Cook, David: *Studies in Muslim Apocalyptic* (Princeton, 2002)

Corbet, Patrick: *Les Saints Ottoniens: Sainteté Dynastique, Sainteté Royale et Sainteté Féminine Autour de l'An Mil* (Sigmaringen, 1986)

Cowdrey, H. E. J.: 'Unions and Confraternity with Cluny', *Journal of Ecclesiastical History* 16, 1965

Cowdrey, H. E. J.: 'Pope Urban II's Preaching of the First Crusade', *History* 55, 1970

Cowdrey, H. E. J.: *The Cluniacs and the Gregorian Reform* (Oxford, 1970)

Cowdrey, H. E. J.: 'The Peace and the Truce of God in the Eleventh Century', *Past and Present* 46, 1970

Cowdrey, H. E. J.: *Popes, Monks and Crusaders* (London, 1984)

Cowdrey, H. E. J.: 'The Gregorian Papacy, Byzantium, and the First Crusade', in Howard-Johnston (Amsterdam, 1988)

Cowdrey, H. E. J.: *Pope Gregory VII 1073–1085* (Oxford, 1998)

Cowdrey, H. E. J.: *Popes and Church Reform in the 11th Century* (Aldershot, 2000)

Crone, Patricia, and Cook, Michael: *Hagarism: The Making of the Islamic World* (Cambridge, 1977)

Crouch, David: *The Normans: The History of a Dynasty* (London, 2002)

Crouch, David: *The Birth of Nobility: Constructing Aristocracy in England and France, 900–1300* (Harlow, 2005)

Cushing, Kathleen G.: *Reform and Papacy in the Eleventh Century: Spirituality and Social Change* (Manchester, 2005)

Cutler, Anthony: 'Who Was the "Monk of France" and When Did He Write?', *al-Andalus* 28, 1963

Cutler, Anthony: 'Gifts and Gift Exchange as Aspects of the Byzantine, Arab, and Related Economies', *Dumbarton Oaks Papers* 55, 2001

Daniel, Norman: *The Arabs and Mediaeval Europe* (London, 1975)

Davids, Adelbert: *The Empress Theophano: Byzantium and the West at the Turn of the First Millennium* (Cambridge, 1995)

Davis, R. H. C.: *The Normans and Their Myth* (London, 1976)

Debord, André: 'Motte Castrale et Habitat Chevaleresque', in *Mélanges d'Histoire et d'Archeologie Médiévale en l'Honneur du Doyen M. de Böuard* (Paris, 1982)

Delort, Robert (ed.): *La France de l'An Mil* (Paris, 1990)

Dennis, George T.: *Three Byzantine Military Treatises* (Washington, DC, 1985)

Dennis, George T.: 'Defenders of the Christian People: Holy War in Byzantium', in Laiou and Mottahedeh (Washington, DC, 2000)

De Vries, Kelly: *The Norwegian Invasion of England in 1066* (Woodbridge, 1999)

Dhondt, J.: *Étude sur la Naissance des Principautés Territoriales en France (Ixe–Xe Siècles)* (Bruges, 1948)

Dolley, R. H. M. (ed.): *Anglo-Saxon Coins* (London, 1961)

Douglas, David C.: *William the Conqueror* (London, 1964)

Douglas, David C.: *The Norman Achievement* (London, 1969)

Duby, Georges: *La Société aux Xie et XIIe Siècles dans la Région Mâconnaise* (Paris, 1953)

Duby, Georges: *L'An Mil* (Paris, 1980)

Duby, Georges: *The Three Orders: Feudal Society Imagined*, tr. Arthur Goldhammer (Chicago, 1980)

Duckett, Eleanor: *Death and Life in the Tenth Century* (Ann Arbor, 1967)

Dunbabin, Jean: *France in the Making, 843–1180* (Oxford, 2000)

Dunn, Maryjane, and Davidson, Linda Kay: *The Pilgrimage to Compostela in the Middle Ages: A Book of Essays* (New York, 1996)

El Cheikh, Nadia Maria: *Byzantium Viewed by the Arabs* (Cambridge, Mass., 2004)

Elliott, Dyan: *Fallen Bodies: Pollution, Sexuality, and Demonology in the Middle Ages* (Philadelphia, 1999)

Ellis, Hilda Roderick: *The Road to Hel: A Study of the Conception of the Dead in Old Norse Literature* (Cambridge, 1943)

Ellis Davidson, H.R: *The Viking Road to Byzantium* (London, 1976)

Emmerson, Richard Kenneth: *Antichrist in the Middle Ages: A Study of Medieval*

Apocalypticism, Art, and Literature (Manchester, 1981)

Emmerson, Richard K., and McGinn, Bernard: *The Apocalypse in the Middle Ages* (Ithaca, 1992)

Enright, Michael J.: *Iona, Tara and Soissons: The Origin of the Royal Anointing Ritual* (Berlin, 1985)

Erdmann, Carl: 'Endkaiserglaube und Kreuzzugsgedanke im 11. Jahrhundert', *Zeitschrift für Kirchengeschichte* 11, 1932

Erdmann, Carl: *Ottonische Studien*, ed. Helmut Beumann (Darmstadt, 1968)

Erdmann, Carl: *The Origin of the Idea of Crusade*, tr. Marshall W. Baldwin and Walter Goffart (Princeton, 1977)

Evans, J.: *Monastic Life at Cluny, 910–1157* (Oxford, 1931)

Fichtenau, Heinrich: *Living in the Tenth Century: Mentalities and Social Orders*, tr. Patrick J. Geary (Chicago, 1991)

Fierro, Maribel: *Abd al-Rahman III: The First Cordoban Caliph* (Oxford, 2005)

Fleckstein, Josef: *Early Medieval Germany*, tr. Bernard S. Smith (Amsterdam, 1978)

Fletcher, Richard: *Saint James's Catapult: The Life and Times of Diego Gelmírez of Santiago de Compostela* (Oxford, 1984)

Fletcher, Richard: 'Reconquest and Crusade in Spain, c. 1050–1150', *Transactions of the Royal Historical Society* 37, 1987

Fletcher, Richard: *Moorish Spain* (Berkeley, 1992)

Fletcher, Richard: *The Conversion of Europe: From Paganism to Christianity 371–1386 AD* (London, 1997)

Fletcher, Richard: *Bloodfeud: Murder and Revenge in Anglo-Saxon England* (London, 2002)

Flori, Jean: *La Guerre Sainte: La Formation de l'Idée de Croisade dans l'Occident Chrétien* (Paris, 2001)

Flori, Jean: *L'Islam et la Fin des Temps: L'Interprétation Prophétique des Invasions Musulmanes dans la Chrétienté Médiévale* (Paris, 2002)

Folz, Robert: *Le Souvenir et la Légende de Charlemagne dans l'Empire Germanique Médiéval* (Paris, 1950)

Folz, Robert: *The Concept of Empire in Western Europe: From the Fifth to the Fourteenth Century*, tr. Sheila Ann Ogilvie (London, 1969)

Foot, Sarah: 'The Historiography of the Anglo-Saxon "Nation-State"', in *Power and the Nation in European History*, ed. Len Scales and Oliver Zimmer (Cambridge, 2005)

Forte, Angelo, Oram, Richard, and Pedersen, Frederik: *Viking Empires* (Cambridge, 2005)

Fossier, Robert: *Enfance de l'Europe*, 2 vols. (Paris, 1982)

Fossier, Robert: *Peasant Life in the Medieval West*, tr. J. Vale (Oxford, 1988)

Fossier, Robert (ed.): *The Cambridge Illustrated History of the Middle Ages: Volume II: 950–1250*, tr. Stuart Airlie and Robyn Marsack (Cambridge, 1997)

France, John: 'The Destruction of Jerusalem and the First Crusade', *Journal of Ecclesiastical History* 47, 1996

France, John: *Western Warfare in the Age of the Crusades, 1000–1300* (Ithaca, 1999)

Franklin, Simon, and Shepard, Jonathan: *The Emergence of Rus, 750–1200* (London, 1996)

Frassetto, Michael (ed.): *Medieval Purity and Piety: Essays on Medieval Clerical Celibacy and Religious Reform* (New York, 1998)

Frassetto, Michael (ed.): *The Year 1000: Religious and Social Response to the Turning of the First Millennium* (New York, 2002)

Freedman, Paul: *Images of the Medieval Peasant* (Stanford, 1999)

Fried, Johannes: 'Awaiting the End of Time', tr. Scott Denlinger and Edward Peters, in Landes, Gow and Van Meter (Oxford, 2003)

Fuhrmann, Horst: *Germany in the High Middle Ages: c. 1050–1200*, tr. Timothy Reuter (Cambridge, 1986)

Fulton, Rachel: *From Judgment to Passion: Devotion to Christ & the Virgin Mary, 800–1200* (New York, 2002)

Gabriele, Matthew: 'Otto III, Charlemagne, and Pentecost A.D. 1000: A Reconsideration Using Diplomatic Evidence', in Frassetto (New York, 2002)

Gasc, Hélène: 'Gerbert et la Pédagogie des Arts Libéraux à la Fin du Dixième Siècle', *Journal of Medieval History* 12/2, 1986

Gay, Jules: *L'Italie Méridionale et l'Empire Byzantine depuis l'Avènement de Basile I jusqu'à la Prise de Bari par les Normands (867–1071)*, 2 vols. (New York, 1960)

Geary, Patrick: 'Humiliation of Saints', in *Saints and Their Cults: Studies in Religious Sociology, Folklore and History*, ed. Stephen Wilson (Cambridge, 1983)

Geary, Patrick: *Phantoms of Remembrance: Memory and Oblivion at the End of the First Millennium* (Princeton, 1994)

Gibbon, Edward: *The History of the Decline and Fall of the Roman Empire*, 3 vols. (London, 1994)

Gil, Moshe: *A History of Palestine, 634–1099*, tr. Ethel Broido (Cambridge, 1992)

Glenn, Jason: *Politics and History in the Tenth Century: The Work and World of Richer of Reims* (Cambridge, 2004)

Glick, Thomas F.: *From Muslim Fortress to Christian Castle: Social and Cultural Change in Medieval Spain* (Manchester, 1995)

Glick, Thomas F.: *Islamic and Christian Spain in the Early Middle Ages* (Brill, 2005)

Goez, Werner: 'Zur Persönlichkeit Gregors VII', *Römische Quartalschrift* 73, 1978

Goez, Werner: 'The Concept of Time in the Historiography of the Eleventh and Twelfth Centuries', in *Medieval Concepts of the Past*, ed. Gerd Althoff, Johannes Fried and Patrick J. Geary (Cambridge, 2002)

Görich, Knut: *Otto III Romanus, Saxonicus et Italicus: Kaiserliche Rompolitik und sächsische Historiographie* (Sigmaringen, 1994)

Gougenheim, S.: *Les Fausses Terreurs de l'An Mil: Attente de la Fin des Temps ou Approfondissement de la Foi?* (Paris, 1999)

Green, Dennis H., and Siegmund, Frank: *The Continental Saxons from the Migration Period to the Tenth Century: An Ethnographic Perspective* (San Marino, 2003)

Gregorovius, Ferdinand: *History of the City of Rome in the Middle Ages: Volume 3: 800–1002 A.D.*, tr. Annie Hamilton (London, 1903)

Griffith, Paddy: *The Viking Art of War* (London, 1995)

Guillot, Olivier: *Le Comte d'Anjou et son Entourage au Xie Siècle* (Paris, 1972)

Hadley, D. M.: *Masculinity in Medieval Europe* (London, 1999)

Hallam, Elizabeth M.: *Capetian France (987–1328)* (London, 1980)

Hamilton, Bernard: *Monastic Reform, Catharism and the Crusades, 900–1300* (London, 1979)

Harris, Jonathan: *Byzantium and the Crusades* (London, 2003)

Harris, Joseph: 'Eddic Poetry', in *Old Norse-Icelandic Literature: A Critical Guide*, ed. Carol J. Clover and John Lindow (Ithaca, 1985)

Haskins, Charles H.: 'The Materials for the Reign of Robert I of Normandy', *English Historical Review* 31, 1916

Head, Thomas: *Hagiography and the Cult of Saints: The Diocese of Orléans, 800–1200* (Cambridge, 1990)

Head, Thomas, and Landes, Richard (eds.): *The Peace of God: Social Violence and Religious Response in France around the Year 1000* (Ithaca, 1992)

Heath, Ian: *Byzantine Armies, 886–1118* (Oxford, 1979)

Herrin, Judith: *The Formation of Christendom* (Princeton, 1997)

Herrin, Judith: *Women in Purple: Rulers of Medieval Byzantium* (London, 2001)

Higham, N. J.: *The Death of Anglo-Saxon England* (Stroud, 1997)

Hill, Boyd H.: *The Rise of the First Reich: Germany in the Tenth Century* (New York, 1969)

Hill, Boyd H.: *Medieval Monarchy in Action: The German Empire from Henry I to Henry IV* (London, 1972)

Hill, David (ed.): *Ethelred the Unready: Papers from the Millenary Conference* (Oxford, 1978)

Hill, Paul: *The Road to Hastings: The Politics of Power in Anglo-Saxon England* (Stroud, 2005)

Hlawitschka, E.: 'Zur Herkunft und zu den Seitenverwandten des Gegenkönigs Rudolf von Rheinfelden', in *Die Salier und das Reich*, ed. S. Weinfurter (Sigmaringen, 1991)

Hodges, Richard: *The Anglo-Saxon Achievement* (London, 1989)

Hofmeister, Adolf: *Die Heilige Lanze ein Abzeichen des Alten Reichs* (Breslau, 1908)

Holtzmann, Walther: 'Studien zur Orientpolitik des Papsttums und zur Entstehung des ersten Kreuzzuges', *Historische Vierteljahrschrift* 22, 1924

Howard-Johnston, J. D.: *Byzantium and the West c.850–c.1200* (Amsterdam, 1988)

Hubert, Étienne: *Espace Urbain et Habitat à Rome du Xe Siècle à la fin du XIIIe Siècle* (Rome, 1990)

Hunt, Noreen: *Cluny under Saint Hugh 1049–1109* (London, 1967)

Huygens, R. B. C.: 'Un Témoin de la Crainte de l'An 1000: La Lettre sur les Hongrois', *L'Atomus* 15, 1957

Iogna-Prat, Dominique: 'Continence et Virginité dans la Conception Clunisienne de l'Order du Monde autour de l'An Mil', *Comptes Rendus de l'Académie des Inscriptions et Belles-lettres*, 1985

Iogna-Prat, Dominique: *Order & Exclusion: Cluny and Christendom Face Heresy, Judaism, and Islam (1000–1150)*, tr. Graham Robert Edwards (Ithaca, 2002)

Isawi, C.: 'The Area and Population of the Arab Empire: an Essay in Speculation', in *The Islamic Middle East, 700–1900: Studies in Economic and Social History*, ed. A. L. Udovitch (Princeton, 1981)

Iversen, Gunilla: 'Transforming a Viking into a Saint: The Divine Office of St Olav', in *The Divine Office in the Latin Medieval Ages*, ed. Margot E. Fassler and Rebecca A. Baltzer (Oxford, 2000)

Jeep, John M. (ed.): *Medieval Germany: An Encyclopedia* (New York, 2001)

Jenkins, Romilly: *Byzantium: The Imperial Centuries, AD 610–1071* (London, 1966)

Jones, Gwyn: *A History of the Vikings* (Oxford, 2001)

Jones, Prudence, and Pennick, Nigel: *A History of Pagan Europe* (London, 1995)

Joranson, Einar: 'The Great German Pilgrimage of 1064–1065', in *The Crusades and Other Historical Essays Presented to Dana C. Munro by His Former Students*, ed. Louis J. Paetow (New York, 1928)

Kantorowicz, Ernst: *The King's Two Bodies: A Study in Medieval Political Theology* (Princeton, 1957)

Karras, Ruth Mazo: *Sexuality in Medieval Europe* (New York, 2005)

Karsh, Efraim: *Islamic Imperialism: A History* (New Haven, 2006)

Kedar, Benjamin Z.: *Crusade and Mission: European Attitudes toward the Muslims* (Princeton, 1984)

Kelly, J. N. D.: *The Oxford Dictionary of Popes* (Oxford, 1986)

Kennedy, Hugh: *Muslim Spain and Portugal: A Political History of al-Andalus* (Harlow, 1996)

Kennedy, Hugh: 'From Antiquity to Islam in the Cities of al-Andalus and al-Mashriq', in *Genèse de la Ville Islamique en al-Andalus et au Maghreb Occidental*, ed. P. Cressier and M. García-Arenal (Madrid, 1998)

Keynes, Simon: *The Diplomas of King Aethelred 'the Unready' 978–1016: A Study in Their Use as Historical Evidence* (Cambridge, 1980)

Körner, Sten: *The Battle of Hastings, England, and Europe 1035–1066* (Lund, 1964)

Kovacs, Judith, and Rowland, Christopher: *Revelation* (Oxford, 2004)

Koziol, Geoffrey: *Begging Pardon and Favor: Ritual and Political Order in Early Medieval France* (Ithaca, 1992)

Krautheimer, R.: *Rome: Profile of a City, 312–1308* (Princeton, 1980)

Kreutz, Barbara M.: *Before the Normans: Southern Italy in the Ninth and Tenth Centuries* (Philadelphia, 1991)

Lacey, Robert, and Danziger, Danny: *The Year 1000: What Life was Like at the Turn of the First Millennium* (London, 1999)

Ladner, Gerhart B.: *L'Immagine dell'Imperatore Ottone III* (Rome, 1988)

Laiou, Angeliki E., and Mottahedeh, Roy Parviz (eds.): *The Crusades from the Perspective of Byzantium and the Muslim World* (Washington, DC, 2000)

Landes, Richard: 'Lest the Millennium be Fulfilled: Apocalyptic Expectations and the Pattern of Western Chronography, 100–800 CE', in *The Use and Abuse of Eschatology in the Middle Ages*, ed. W. Verbeke, D. Verhelst and A. Welkenhuysen (Leuven, 1988)

Landes, Richard: 'La Vie Apostolique en Aquitaine au Tournant du Millennium: Paix de Dieu, Culte de Reliques et Communautés "Hérétiques"', *Annales* 46, 1991

Landes, Richard: 'Sur les Traces du Millennium: La "Via Negativa"', *Le Moyen Âge* 99, 1993

Landes, Richard: *Relics, Apocalypse, and the Deceits of History* (Cambridge, Mass., 1995)

Landes, Richard: 'On Owls, Roosters, and Apocalyptic Time: A Historical Method for Reading a Refractory Documentation', *Union Seminary Quarterly Review* 49, 1996

Landes, Richard: 'The Massacres of 1010: On the Origins of Popular Anti-Jewish Violence in Western Europe', in Cohen (Wiesbaden, 1996)

Landes, Richard (ed.): *Encyclopedia of Millennialism and Millennial Movements* (New York, 2000)

Landes, Richard: 'The Fear of an Apocalyptic Year 1000: Augustinian Historiography, Medieval and Modern', *Speculum* 75, 2000

Landes, Richard: 'The Fruitful Error: Reconsidering Millennial Enthusiasm', *Journal of Interdisciplinary History* 32/1, 2001

Landes, Richard: 'Giants with Feet of Clay: On the Historiography of the Year 1000' (www.bu.edu/mille/scholarship/1000/AHR9.html)

Landes, Richard, Gow, Andrew, and van Meter, David C.: *The Apocalyptic Year 1000: Religious Expectation and Social Change, 950–1050* (Oxford, 2003)

Lavelle, Ryan: *Aethelred II: King of the English 978–1016* (Stroud, 2002)

Lawson, M. K.: *Cnut: England's Viking King* (Stroud, 2004)

Lawson, M. K.: *The Battle of Hastings 1066* (Stroud, 2007)

Le Goff, Jacques: *Time, Work, and Culture in the Middle Ages*, tr. Arthur Goldhammer (Chicago, 1980)

Leclercq, Jean: *Saint Pierre Damien: Ermite et Homme d'Église* (Rome, 1960)

Leithart, Peter J.: 'The Gospel, Gregory VII and Modern Theology', *Modern Theology* 19/1, 2003

Lemerle, Paul: 'Byzance et la Croisade', in *Relazioni del X Congresso Internazionale di Scienze Storiche* (Florence, 1955)

Lévi-Provençal, Évariste: *Histoire de l'Espagne Musulmane*, 3 vols. (Paris, 1950)

Lewis, Andrew W.: *Royal Succession in Capetian France: Studies on Familial Order and the State* (Cambridge, Mass., 1981)

Leyser, K. J.: 'The Polemics of the Papal Revolution', in *Trends in Medieval Political Thought*, ed. Beryl Smalley (Oxford, 1965)

Leyser, K. J.: *Rule and Conflict in an Early Medieval Society: Ottonian Saxony* (Oxford, 1979)

Leyser, K. J.: *Medieval Germany and its Neighbours, 900–1250* (London, 1982)

Leyser, K. J.: *Communications and Power in Medieval Europe: The Carolingian and Ottonian Centuries*, ed. Timothy Reuter (London, 1994)

Leyser, K. J.: *Communications and Power in Medieval Europe: The Gregorian Revolution and beyond*, ed. Timothy Reuter (London, 1994)

Lieu, Samuel: 'From History to Legend and Legend to History: The Medieval and Byzantine Transformation of Constantine's *Vita*', in *Constantine: History, Historiography and Legend*, ed. Samuel Lieu and Dominic Montserrat (London, 1998)

Linehan, Peter: 'At the Spanish Frontier', in Linehan and Nelson (London, 2001)

Linehan, Peter, and Nelson, Janet L. (eds.): *The Medieval World* (London, 2001)

Little, Lester K.: 'The Personal Development of Peter Damian', in *Order and Innovation in the Middle Ages: Essays in Honor of Joseph R. Strayer*, ed. William C. Jordan, Bruce McNab and Teofilo F. Ruiz (Princeton, 1976)

Little, Lester K., and Rosenwein, Barbara H. (eds.): *Debating the Middle Ages: Issues and Readings* (Oxford, 1998)

Lobrichon, Guy: 'The Chiaroscuro of Heresy: Early Eleventh-Century Aquitaine as Seen from Auxerre', in Head and Landes (Ithaca, 1992)

Lobrichon, Guy: 'Jugement dernier et Apocalypse', in *De l'Art Comme Mystagogie: Iconographie du Jugement Dernier et des Fins Dernières à l'Époque Gothique* (Poitiers, 1996)

Logan, F. Donald: *The Vikings in History* (London, 2005)

Loomis, Laura Hibbard: 'The Holy Relics of Charlemagne and King Athelstan: The Lances of Longinus and St Mauricius', *Speculum* 25, 1950

Loomis, Laura Hibbard: 'The Passion Lance Relic and the War Cry Monjoie in the *Chanson de Roland* and Related Texts', in *Adventures in the Middle Ages: A Memorial Collection of Essays and Studies*, ed. Helene Bullock (New York, 1962)

Lopez, R.: 'The Norman Conquest of Sicily', in *A History of the Crusades: The First Hundred Years*, ed. M. W. Baldwin (Philadelphia, 1969)

Loud, G. A.: *The Age of Robert Guiscard: Southern Italy and the Norman Conquest* (Harlow, 2000)

Lovelock, James: *The Revenge of Gaia* (London, 2007)

Lynch, Joseph H.: 'Hugh I of Cluny's Sponsorship of Henry IV: Its Context and Consequences', *Speculum* 60/4, 1985

MacKinney, Loren C.: 'The People and Public Opinion in the Eleventh-Century Peace Movement', *Speculum* 5, 1930

MacLean, Simon: 'Apocalypse and Revolution: Europe around the Year 1000', *Early Medieval Europe* 15/1, 2007

Magdalino, Paul (ed.): 'The History of the Future and its Uses: Prophecy, Policy and Propaganda', in *The Making of Byzantine History: Studies Dedicated to Domald M. Nicol*, ed. R. Beaton and C. Roueché (Aldershot, 1993)

Magdalino, Paul: 'The Byzantine Background to the First Crusade', *Canadian Institute of Balkan Studies*, 1996

Magdalino, Paul: *Byzantium in the Year 1000* (Brill, 2003)

Magnou-Nortier, Elisabeth: *Pouvoirs et Libertés au Temps des Premiers Capétians* (Maulévrier, 1992)

Mango, Cyril: *Byzantium: The Empire of New Rome* (London, 1980)

Marín-Guzmán, Roberto: 'Some Reflections on the Institutions of Muslim Spain: Unity in Politics and Administration', *American Journal of Islamic Social Sciences* 21, 2004

McCormick, Michael: *Eternal Victory: Triumphal Rulership in Late Antiquity, Byzantium, and the Early Medieval West* (Cambridge, 1986)

McCormick, Michael: *Origins of the European Economy: Communications and Commerce, A.D. 300–900* (Cambridge, 2001)

McGinn, Bernard: *Visions of the End: Apocalyptic Traditions in the Middle Ages* (New York, 1979)

McGinn, Bernard: *Antichrist: Two Thousand Years of the Human Fascination with Evil* (New York, 1994)

McKitterick, Rosamund: 'Continuity and Innovation in Tenth-Century Ottonian Culture', in *Intellectual Life in the Middle Ages: Essays Presented to Margaret Gibson*, ed. Lesley Smith and Benedicta Ward (London, 1992)

McKitterick, Rosamund: 'Ottonian Intellectual Culture in the Tenth Century and the Role of Theophanu', *Early Medieval Europe* 2/1, 1993

McKitterick, Rosamund: *History and Memory in the Carolingian World* (Cambridge, 2004)

McKitterick, Rosamund (ed.): *The Early Middle Ages: Europe 400–1000* (Oxford, 2001)

Menocal, María Rosa: *The Ornament of the World: How Muslims, Jews, and Christians Created a Culture of Tolerance in Medieval Spain* (New York, 2002)

Milis, Ludo J. R.: *Angelic Monks and Earthly Men* (Woodbridge, 1992)

Miller, Timothy S., and Nesbitt, John: *Peace and War in Byzantium: Essays in Honor of George T. Dennis, S.J.* (Washington, DC, 1995)

Moore, R. I.: *The Birth of Popular Heresy* (London, 1975)

Moore, R. I.: *The Origins of European Dissent* (London, 1977)

Moore, R. I.: *The Formation of a Persecuting Society: Power and Deviance in Western Europe, 950–1250* (Oxford, 1990)

Moore, R. I.: 'Heresy, Repression and Social Change in the Age of Gregorian Reform', in *Christendom and its Discontents: Exclusion, Persecution, and Rebellion, 1000–1500*, ed. Scott L. Waugh and Peter D. Diehl (Cambridge, 1996)

Moore, R. I.: 'The Birth of Heresy: A Millennial Phenomenon', *Journal of Religious History* 24/1, 2000

Moore, R. I.: *The First European Revolution, c. 970–1215* (Oxford, 2000)

Morghen, Raffaello: *Gregorio VII e la Riforma della Chiesa nel Secolo XI* (Palermo, 1974)

Morillo, Stephen (ed.): *The Battle of Hastings* (Woodbridge, 1996)

Morris, Colin: *The Papal Monarchy: The Western Church from 1050 to 1250* (Oxford, 1989)

Morrison, Karl F.: 'The Gregorian Reform', in *Christian Spirituality: Origins to the Twelfth Century*, ed. Bernard McGinn and John Meyendorff (London, 1986)

Moulin, Léo: *La Vie Quotidienne des Religieux au Moyen Âge (Xe–XVe Siècle)* (Paris, 1978)

Mütherich, F.: 'The Library of Otto III', in *The Role of the Book in Medieval Culture*, ed. Peter Ganz (Turnhout, 1986)

Navari, Joseph: 'The Leitmotiv in the Mathematical Thought of Gerbert of Aurillac', *Journal of Medieval History* 1, 1975

Nelson, Janet L.: *Politics and Ritual in Early Medieval Europe* (London, 1986)

Nelson, Janet L.: *The Frankish World, 750–900* (London, 1996)

Nelson, Janet L.: *Rulers and Ruling Families in Early Medieval Europe* (Aldershot, 1999)

Niles, John D., and Amodio, Mark: *Anglo-Scandinavian England: Norse–English Relations in the Period before the Conquest* (Lanham, 1989)

Noble, T. F. X.: *The Republic of St Peter: The Birth of the Papal State, 680–825* (Philadelphia, 1984)

Norwich, John Julius: *The Normans in the South, 1016–1130* (London, 1967)

Ortigues, E., and Iogna-Prat, D.: 'Raoul Glaber et l'Historiographie Clunisienne', *Studi Medievali* 26/2, 1985

O'Callaghan, Joseph F.: *Reconquest and Crusade in Medieval Spain* (Philadelphia, 2003)

Bibliography

O'Leary, De Lacy: *A Short History of the Fatimid Khalifate* (London, 1923)

O'Shea, Stephen: *Sea of Faith: Islam and Christianity in the Medieval Mediterranean World* (London, 2006)

Page, R. I.: *Chronicles of the Vikings: Records, Memorials and Myths* (Bath, 2002)

Partner, Nancy (ed.): *Writing Medieval History* (London, 2005)

Paxton, Frederick S.: *Christianizing Death: The Creation of a Ritual Process in Early Medieval Europe* (Ithaca, 1990)

Pelteret, David A. E.: *Slavery in Early Mediaeval England: From the Reign of Alfred until the Twelfth Century* (Woodbridge, 1995)

Pérez de Urbel, Justo: 'El Culto de Santiago in el Siglo X', *Compostellanum* 16, 1971

Peters, F. E.: *Jerusalem: The Holy City in the Eyes of Chroniclers, Visitors, Pilgrims, and Prophets from the Days of Abraham to the Beginnings of Modern Times* (Princeton, 1985)

Phillips, Jonathan (ed.): *The First Crusade: Origins and Impact* (Manchester, 1997)

Pognon, Edmond: *La Vie Quotidienne en l'An Mille* (Paris, 1981)

Pognon, Edmond: *Hugues Capet et la France Féodale* (Paris, 1989)

Poly, Jean-Pierre: 'Le Capétien Thaumaturge: Genèse Populaire d'un Miracle Royal', in Delort (Paris, 1990)

Poly, Jean-Pierre, and Bournazel, Eric: *The Feudal Transformation, 900–1200*, tr. Caroline Higgitt (New York, 1991)

Rees, Martin: *Our Final Century: Will Civilisation Survive the Twenty-First Century?* (London, 2003)

Reilly, B. F.: *The Contest of Christian and Muslim Spain, 1031–1157* (London, 1992)

Reston, James: *The Last Apocalypse: Europe at the Year 1000 A.D.* (New York, 1998)

Reuter, Timothy: 'The End of Carolingian Military Expansion', in *Charlemagne's Heir*, ed. P. Godman and R. Collins (Oxford, 1990)

Reuter, Timothy: *Germany in the Early Middle Ages, c. 800–1056* (London, 1991)

Reuter, Timothy: 'Debate: The Feudal Revolution', *Past and Present* 155, 1997

Reuter, Timothy (ed.): *The Medieval Nobility: Studies on the Ruling Classes of France and Germany from the Sixth to the Twelfth Century* (Amsterdam, 1979)

Reynolds, Susan: 'Medieval *Origines Gentium* and the Community of the Realm', *History* 68, 1983

Reynolds, Susan: *Kingdoms and Communities in Western Europe 900–1300* (Oxford, 1997)

Riché, Pierre: 'Le Mythe des Terreurs de l'An Mille', in *Les Terreurs de l'An 2000* (Paris, 1976)

Riché, Pierre: 'Les Conditions de la Production Littéraire: Maîtres et Écoles', in *Lateinische Kultur im X. Jahrhundert*, ed. Walter Berschin (Stuttgart, 1991)

Riley-Smith, Jonathan: *The First Crusade and the Idea of Crusading* (London, 1986)

Riley-Smith, Jonathan: *The First Crusaders, 1095–1131* (Cambridge, 1997)

Robinson, I. S.: 'Gregory VII and the Soldiers of Christ', *History* 58, 1973

Robinson, I. S.: *The Papacy 1073–1198: Continuity and Innovation* (Cambridge, 1990)

Robinson, I. S.: *Henry IV of Germany, 1056–1106* (Cambridge, 1999)

Roesdahl, Else: *Viking Age Denmark*, tr. Susan Margeson and Kirsten Williams (London, 1982)

Roesdahl, Else: *The Vikings*, tr. Susan Margeson and Kirsten Williams (London, 1987)

Rösener, W.: *Peasants in the Middle Ages*, tr. Alexander Stützer (Chicago, 1992)

Rosenstock-Huessy, Eugen: *Out of Revolution: Autobiography of Western Man* (New York, 1938)

Rosenstock-Huessy, Eugen: *Driving Power of Western Civilization: The Christian Revolution of the Middle Ages* (Boston, 1949)

Rosenwein, Barbara H.: *Rhinoceros Bound: Cluny in the Tenth Century* (Philadelphia, 1982)

Rosenwein, Barbara H.: *To Be the Neighbor of Saint Peter: The Social Meaning of Cluny's Property, 909–1049* (Ithaca, 1989)

Russell, James C.: *The Germanization of Early Medieval Christianity: A Sociohistorical Approach to Religious Transformation* (Oxford, 1994)

Sahas, Daniel J.: *John of Damascus on Islam: The 'Heresy of the Ishmaelites'* (Leiden, 1972)

Sansterre, Jean-Marie: 'Otton III et les Saints Ascètes', *Rivista di Storia della Chiesa in Italia* 43/2, 1989

Sassier, Yves: *Hugues Capet: Naissance d'une Dynastie* (Paris, 1987)

Sawyer, Birgit, Sawyer, Peter, and Wood, Ian (eds.): *The Christianization of Scandinavia* (Alingsas, 1987)

Sawyer, P. H.: 'The Wealth of England in the Eleventh Century', *Transactions of the Royal Historical Society* 15, 1965

Sawyer, P. H.: *Kings and Vikings: Scandinavia and Europe, AD 700–1100* (London, 1982)

Scales, Peter C.: *The Fall of the Caliphate of Córdoba* (Leiden, 1994)

Schiavone, Aldo: *The End of the Past: Ancient Rome and the Modern West*, tr. Margery J. Schneider (Cambridge, Mass., 2000)

Schimmelpfennig, Bernhard: *The Papacy*, tr. James Sievert (New York, 1992)

Schillebeeckx, Edward: *The Church with a Human Face* (New York, 1985)

Schramm, Percy E.: *Kaiser, Rom und Renovatio: Studien und Texte zur Geschichte des römischen Erneuerungsgedankens vom Ende des karolingischen Reiches bis zum Investiturstreit*, 2 vols. (Leipzig and Berlin, 1929)

Schramm, Percy E.: *Herrschaftszeichen und Staatssymbolik*, 3 vols. (Stuttgart, 1954–6)

Scragg, Donald (ed.): *The Battle of Maldon AD 991* (Oxford, 1991)

Searle, Eleanor: 'Possible History', *Speculum* 61, 1986

Searle, Eleanor: *Predatory Kinship and the Creation of Norman Power, 840–1066* (Berkeley and Los Angeles, 1988)

Seitter, Walter: *Katechonten: Den Untergang Aufhalten* (Berlin, 2001)

Settipani, Christian: 'Les Comtes d'Anjou et Leurs Alliances aux Xe et Xie Siècles', in *Family Trees and the Roots of Politics: The Prosopography of Britain and France from the Tenth to the Twelfth Century*, ed. K. S. B. Keats-Rohan (Woodbridge, 1997)

Sevcenko, Ihor: 'Unpublished Texts on the End of the World about the Year 1000 AD', in *Mélanges Gilbert Dagron* (Paris, 2002)

Shahar, S.: *Childhood in the Middle Ages* (London, 1990)

Shepard, Jonathan: 'The Uses of the Franks in Eleventh-Century Byzantium', *Anglo-Norman Studies* 15, 1993

Shepard, Jonathan: 'Cross-purposes: Alexius Comnenus and the First Crusade', in

Phillips (Manchester, 1997)

Shepard, Jonathan: 'Courts in East and West', in Linehan and Nelson (London, 2001)

Slupecki, Leszek Pawel: *Slavonic Pagan Sanctuaries* (Warsaw, 1994)

Smith, Julia M. H.: *Europe after Rome: A New Cultural History 500–1000* (Oxford, 2005)

Smith, Julia M. H. (ed.): *Early Medieval Rome and the Christian West* (Leiden, 2000)

Southern, R. W.: *The Making of the Middle Ages* (London, 1953)

Southern, R. W.: *Medieval Humanism and Other Studies* (Oxford, 1970)

Southern, R. W.: *Western Society and the Church in the Middle Ages* (London, 1970)

Stafford, Pauline: *Unification and Conquest: A Political and Social History of England in the Tenth and Eleventh Centuries* (London, 1989)

Stafford, Pauline: *Queen Emma and Queen Edith: Queenship and Women's Power in Eleventh-Century England* (Oxford, 1997)

Stafford, Pauline: 'Powerful Women in the Early Middle Ages: Queens and Abbesses', in Linehan and Nelson (London, 2001)

Stenton, Frank: *Anglo-Saxon England* (Oxford, 1971)

Struve, Tilman: 'Zwei Briefe der Kaiserin Agnes', *Historisches Jahrbuch* 104, 1984

Struve, Tilman: 'Die Romreise der Kaiserin Agnes', *Historisches Jahrbuch* 105, 1985

Sumption, Jonathan: *Pilgrimage: An Image of Mediaeval Religion* (London, 1975)

Taylor, Catherine: 'The Year 1000 and Those Who Laboured', in Frassatto (New York, 2002)

Tellenbach, Gerd: *Church, State and Christian Society at the Time of the Investiture Contest*, tr. R. F. Bennett (Oxford, 1940)

Tellenbach, Gerd: *The Church in Western Europe from the Tenth to the Early Twelfth Century*, tr. Timothy Reuter (Cambridge, 1993)

Thompson, Damian: *The End of Time: Faith and Fear in the Shadow of the Millennium* (London, 1996)

Ullman, Walter: *The Growth of Papal Government in the Middle Ages: A Study in the Ideological Relation of Clerical to Lay Power* (London, 1955)

Ullman, Walter: *Principles of Government and Politics in the Middle Ages* (London, 1961)

Ullman, Walter: *The Carolingian Renaissance and the Idea of Kingship* (London, 1969)

Ullman, Walter: *A Short History of the Papacy in the Middle Ages* (London, 1972)

Vallvé Bermejo, J.: *El Califato de Córdoba* (Madrid, 1992)

Vatikiotis, P. J.: 'Al-Hakim Bi-Amrillah: The God-King Idea Realised', *Islamic Culture* 29/1, 1955

Vatikiotis, P. J.: *The Fatimid Theory of State* (Lahore, 1957)

Van Berchem, Denis: *Le Martyre de la Légion Thébaine: Essai sur la Formation d'une Légende* (Basel, 1956)

Van Houts, Elisabeth: 'The Origins of Herleva, Mother of William the Conqueror', *English Historical Review* 101, 1986

Van Houts, Elisabeth: 'The Norman Conquest through European Eyes', *English Historical Review* 110, 1995

Van Houts, Elisabeth: *The Normans in Europe* (Manchester, 2000)

Verhelst, D.: 'Les Conceptions d'Adson Concernant l'Antichrist', *Recherches de Théologie Ancienne et Médiévale* 40, 1973

Vogel, Jörgen: *Gregor VII. und Heinrich IV. nach Canossa* (Berlin, 1983)

Vryonis, Speros: *The Decline of Medieval Hellenism in Asia Minor and the Process of Islamization from the Eleventh through the Fifteenth Century* (Berkeley and Los Angeles, 1971)

Wach, Joachim: *Sociology of Religion* (Chicago, 1944)

Walker, Ian W.: *Harold: The Last Anglo-Saxon King* (Stroud, 1997)

Wallace-Hadrill, J. M.: *The Barbarian West, 400–1000* (London, 1964)

Wallace-Hadrill, J. M.: *Early Medieval History* (Oxford, 1975)

Warner, David A.: 'Henry II at Magdeburg: Kingship, Ritual and the Cult of Saints', *Early Medieval Europe* 3/2, 1994

Wasserstein, David J.: *The Rise and Fall of the Party-Kings: Politics and Society in Islamic Spain 1002–1086* (Princeton, 1985)

Wasserstein, David J.: *The Caliphate in the West: An Islamic Political Institution in the Iberian Peninsula* (Oxford, 1993)

Watkins, Basil: *The Book of Saints: A Comprehensive Biographical Dictionary* (London, 2002)

Watson, Andrew M.: *Agricultural Innovation in the Early Islamic World: The Diffusion of Crops and Farming Techniques, 700–1100* (Cambridge, 1983)

Whittow, Mark: *The Making of Orthodox Byzantium, 600–1025* (Basingstoke, 1996)

Wickham, Chris: 'Italy and the Early Middle Ages', in *The Birth of Europe: Archaeological and Social Development in the First Millennium A.D.*, ed. Klaus Randsborg (Rome, 1989)

Wickham, Chris: *Land and Power* (London, 1994)

Wickham, Chris: 'Debate: The Feudal Revolution', *Past and Present* 155, 1997

Wickham, Chris: *Framing the Early Middle Ages: Europe and the Mediterranean, 400–800* (Oxford, 2005)

Wilkinson, John: *Jerusalem Pilgrims before the Crusades* (Warminster, 1977)

Williams, John: 'Cluny and Spain', *Gesta* 27, 1988

Williams, Schafer (ed.): *The Gregorian Epoch: Reformation, Revolution, Reaction?* (Lexington, 1964)

Wolf, Kenneth Baxter: *Making History: The Normans and Their Historians in 11th Century Italy* (Philadelphia, 1995)

Wolff, Philippe: *The Awakening of Europe*, tr. Anne Carter (London, 1968)

Wood, Michael: *In Search of the Dark Ages* (London, 1981)

Wood, Michael: *In Search of England: Journeys into the English Past* (London, 1999)

Woods, David: 'The Origin of the Legend of Maurice and the Theban Legion', *Journal of Ecclesiastical History* 45, 1994

Wormald, Patrick: '*Engla lond*: The Making of an Allegiance', *Journal of Historical Sociology* 7, 1994

Zimmerman, Harald: *Der Canossagang von 1077: Wirkungen und Wirklichkeit* (Mainz, 1975)

Zotz, Thomas: 'Carolingian Tradition and Ottonian-Salian Innovation: Comparative Observations on Palatine Policy in the Empire', in *Kings and Kingship in Medieval Europe*, ed. Anne J. Duggan (London, 1993)

Index